HOLLYWOOD PLAYERS: THE THIRTIES

BY JAMES ROBERT PARISH

As author
THE FOX GIRLS*
THE PARAMOUNT PRETTIES*
THE SLAPSTICK QUEENS
GOOD DAMES
HOLLYWOOD'S GREAT LOVE TEAMS*
ELVIS!
THE GREAT MOVIE HEROES
GREAT CHILD STARS
FILM DIRECTORS GUIDE: WESTERN EUROPE
GREAT WESTERN STARS
THE JEANETTE MacDONALD STORY
THE TOUGH GUYS*

As co-author
THE EMMY AWARDS: A PICTORIAL HISTORY
THE CINEMA OF EDWARD G. ROBINSON
THE MGM STOCK COMPANY: THE GOLDEN ERA*
THE GREAT SPY PICTURES
THE GEORGE RAFT FILE
THE GLAMOUR GIRLS*
VINCENT PRICE UNMASKED
LIZA!
THE DEBONAIRS*
THE SWASHBUCKLERS*
THE GREAT GANGSTER PICTURES
THE GREAT WESTERN PICTURES
FILM DIRECTORS GUIDE: THE U.S.
HOLLYWOOD PLAYERS: THE FORTIES*
THE ALL-AMERICANS*

As editor
THE GREAT MOVIE SERIES
ACTORS TELEVISION CREDITS: 1950-72 & SUPPLEMENT

As associate editor
THE AMERICAN MOVIES REFERENCE BOOK: THE SOUND ERA
TV MOVIES

BY WILLIAM T. LEONARD

As co-author
HOLLYWOOD PLAYERS: THE FORTIES*
FILM DIRECTORS GUIDE: THE U.S.

*Published by Arlington House

HOLLYWOOD PLAYERS

THE THIRTIES

**James Robert Parish
and William T. Leonard**

Editor:

T. Allan Taylor

Research Associates:

John Robert Cocchi   Don E. Stanke   Florence Solomon

Introduction:

DeWitt Bodeen

ARLINGTON HOUSE
PUBLISHERS
NEW ROCHELLE, NEW YORK

Manufactured in the United States of America

Parish, James Robert.
   Hollywood Players, the Thirties.

   Includes index.
   1. Moving-picture actors and actress—United States—Biography. I. Leonard, William T., joint author. II. Title.
PN1998.A2P3919   791.43′028′0922 [B]   76-17647
ISBN 0-87000-365-8

Dedicated to

MARIE DRESSLER

The Grande Dame of the Cinema
(1869 – 1934)

KEY TO THE FILM STUDIOS

AA	Allied Artists Picture Corporation
AIP	American International Pictures
AVCO EMB	Avco Embassy Pictures Corporation
BV	Buena Vista Distributions Co., Inc.,
CIN	Cinerama, Inc.
COL	Columbia Pictures Industries, Inc.
EL	Eagle Lion Films, Inc.
EMB	Embassy Pictures Corporation
FBO	Film Booking Offices
FN	First National Pictures, Inc. (later part of Warner Bros.)
FOX	Fox Film Corporation (later part of Twentieth Century-Fox)
LIP	Lippert Pictures, Inc.
MGM	Metro-Goldwyn-Mayer, Inc.
MON	Monogram Pictures Corporation
PAR	Paramount Pictures Corporation
PRC	Producers Releasing Corporation
RKO	RKO Radio Pictures, Inc.
REP	Republic Pictures Corporation
20th	Twentieth Century-Fox Film Corporation
UA	United Artists Corporation
UNIV	Universal Pictures, Inc.
WB	Warner Bros., Inc.

ACKNOWLEDGMENTS

RESEARCH MATERIAL CONSULTANT:
DOUG McCLELLAND

RESEARCH VERIFIER:
EARL ANDERSON

RICHARD BRAFF
ALAN BROCK
MRS. LORAINE BURDICK
KINGSLEY CANHAM
HOWARD DAVIS
MRS. ELAINE EBO
MORRIS EVERETT, JR.
Filmfacts (ERNEST PARMENTIER)
Film Fan Monthly
Film Favorites (CHARLES SMITH)
Films and Filming
Films in Review
Focus on Film
LEATRICE JOY GILBERT
PIERRE GUINLE
MRS. R. F. HASTINGS
Hollywood Revue of Movie Memorabilia
RICHARD HUDSON
KEN D. JONES

LOIS KIBBEE
MILES KREUGER
ANGELA LANSBURY
ERIC LINDEN
DAVID McGILLIVRAY
ALBERT B. MANSKI
ALVIN H. MARILL
MRS. EARL MEISINGER
JIM MEYER
PETER MIGLIERINI
Movie Poster Service (BOB SMITH)
Movie Star News (PAULA KLAW)
RICHARD PICCHIARINI
MICHAEL R. PITTS
DR. HENRY ROSS
TOM RYDER
Screen Facts (ALAN G. BARBOUR)
MRS. PETER SMITH
ROZ STARR SERVICE
CHARLES K. STUMPF

And special thanks to Paul Myers, curator of the Theatre Collection at the Lincoln Center Library for the Performing Arts (New York City) and his staff: Monty Arnold, David Bartholomew, Rod Bladel, Donald Fowle, Maxwell Silverman, Dorothy Swerdlove, Betty Wharton, and Don Madison of Photo Services.

TABLE OF CONTENTS

1. Eddie Albert.............................. 18
2. Hardie Albright 26
3. Robert Armstrong................... 34
4. Lynn Bari 42
5. Binnie Barnes 50
6. John Beal 58
7. Louise Beavers......................... 66
8. Ralph Bellamy 76
9. Charles Bickford...................... 86
10. John Boles 94
11. Mary Brian 102
12. Bruce Cabot 110
13. Helen Chandler 118
14. Mae Clarke 126
15. Donald Cook 132
16. Larry "Buster" Crabbe.............138
17. Richard Cromwell 146
18. Constance Cummings 154
19. Frances Dee.............................162
20. Brian Donlevy 170
21. James Dunn.............................178
22. Ann Dvorak..............................186
23. Sally Eilers 194
24. Frances Farmer.......................202
25. Glenda Farrell 210
26. Stepin Fetchit 220
27. Preston Foster..........................226
28. Richard "Skeets" Gallagher......234
29. William Gargan 240
30. Wynne Gibson..........................248
31. Bonita Granville 254
32. Mitzi Green 260
33. Richard Greene 266
34. Phillips Holmes........................274
35. Ian Hunter..............................282
36. Josephine Hutchinson..............288

37. Kay Johnson............................294
38. Allan Jones 302
39. Victor Jory...............................310
40. Arline Judge............................318
41. Paul Kelly 326
42. Elissa Landi.............................336
43. Francis Lederer.......................344
44. Eric Linden 352
45. Margaret Lindsay.....................358
46. Anita Louise............................364
47. Paul Lukas 372
48. David Manners.........................380
49. Burgess Meredith.....................386
50. Douglass Montgomery.............394
51. Dickie Moore 402
52. Chester Morris.........................408
53. Wayne Morris...........................416
54. Lloyd Nolan.............................424
55. Jack Oakie 432
56. Gail Patrick 438
57. Roger Pryor.............................446
58. Gene Raymond.........................452
59. Gilbert Roland.........................460
60. Cesar Romero..........................466
61. Simone Simon..........................474
62. Penny Singleton.......................482
63. Anna Sten 488
64. Gloria Stuart............................496
65. Genevieve Tobin 502
66. Lee Tracy.................................508
67. Helen Twelvetrees....................516
68. Jane Withers............................524
69. Anna May Wong........................532
70. Fay Wray.................................540
71. Jane Wyatt...............................548
Index......................................559

INTRODUCTION

by DeWitt Bodeen

In considering the movie players of the Thirties, it's necessary, first, to consider the Thirties themselves.

When the stock market crashed in the fall of 1929, putting an abrupt end to the madness of the mad Twenties, there was a brief hiatus while Wall Street brokers jumped out of skyscraper windows and everybody lamented the folly of having bought stocks on margin. Was this what making money meant? Nothing?

Then, very soon, all too soon, the Thirties began.

And we were broke. Dead flat, on our asses, broke. This was what being without money meant. Men and women who had been buying and selling hundreds of thousands of dollars of stocks and bonds every day were now selling apples on street corners.

That the motion picture industry survived this catastrophe is a testament to its own enduring importance. This is the first century that has been completely recorded pictorially, and the whole terror, confusion, and reaching up from nothing at all of those depression years is documented on film if anybody has the heart and courage to look at it. Going to the movies at least once a week had been a part of the American way of life, like eating, sleeping, going to church on Sunday, and falling in love. Moviegoing continued, but on a different scale: admission prices dropped; double bills, giveaway nights and Bingo came in. You might win if you went to the movies.

Until 1933 people were living by their wits and a shred of faith, wondering if this would be the last of American life as they knew it. On election night, when the countdown began and Americans waited to see who would be our next president—Franklin Delano Roosevelt or Herbert Hoover—there were tired, moneyless, and angry citizens camped on the outskirts of the White House, waiting for the verdict. It was the most desperate hour in American history. People all over the country also waited.

Franklin Delano Roosevelt was elected president, and there arose a new era of hope. Americans believed in him, and they believed anew in their country.

This is all on film, which you can look at, if you like. Better still, you can look at the feature films Hollywood made during this decade, because they reflect better than anything else the temper of the times.

What was happening in Hollywood was equally desperate and revolutionary. In the autumn of 1927, Warner Bros. had premiered Al Jolson in *The Jazz Singer,* a part-talkie, with not only dialogue but sound effects and songs. It was soon obvious that a new era in film-making was beginning. By 1929 every studio was reconciled to the fact that sound was in for good—it was no passing fancy—and the studios would have to convert

11

to it, no matter what or whom they might have to jettison, no matter what they might have to invest in new equipment. So the talking film began. This meant sound, music, and . . . talk. How the films chattered. They spoke snarled, conversed, and yapped.

I sometimes think that otherwise memorable films that had been originally silently shot and then forced into an amalgam of part-talkie or only sound and music were lost in this sudden, frantic change-over. Mary Pickford has said that it was all a topsy-turvy world: talkies should have come first, and then silents, because they were the greater art. Lillian Gish and others in the profession agreed, but they, like America's Sweetheart, adapted to the change, and, indeed, Miss Pickford won the second Academy Award for her performance in her first talking film, *Coquette.*

In the period of those first two years, everything was tried in making movies with sound. Most of what once had been was either improved upon or ruthlessly discarded. If it didn't work, there was always a new way. When Vitaphone developed problems, Movietone saved the day. Forgotten for the moment were the wonderful creative advances that had been made, especially the camera that moved around. For a horrible time the camera was locked in one box, and film became static and nearly perished of loquaciousness.

In spite of this, most of the old stars managed to survive. Pickford, Fairbanks, Lillian Gish, Garbo, Bebe Daniels, Richard Dix, Harold Loyd, Will Rogers, Ramon Novarro, Betty Compson, Joan Crawford, and finally, even Chaplin—the last hold-out—all these stars of the silents, with training in the living theatre, adapted themselves to the new medium, and became greater stars than ever before.

There were also the stars of the silents who had had no stage experience; they studied with coaches, and learned how to speak, even sing; they adapted themselves to the talking medium and became superstars, like Gloria Swanson, Norma Shearer, Bessie Love, Constance Bennett.

There were the fallen stars, too—the great ones who were toppled from or abandoned their high places, like Norma and Constance Talmadge, Corinne Griffith, Colleen Moore, and, most tragically, John Gilbert, the highest-paid star at MGM. First National, with most of its stars down the drain, must have been relieved to amalgamate with Warner Bros.

Then there were the greats from the theatre who came in to displace those who were dethroned: Ann Harding, Irene Dunne, Spencer Tracy, Helen Hayes, Ina Claire, George Arliss, Edward G. Robinson, Katharine Hepburn. The Barrymores returned to Hollywood to realize their best years in film; and even the great Alfred Lunt and Lynn Fontanne displayed in one incomparable movie, *The Guardsman,* how comedy should be performed.

Paramount provides a perfect example of what happened in this change-over period. Before talkies, its biggest stars were Clara Bow, Bebe Daniels, Richard Dix, William Powell, Clive Brook, Emil Jannings, Pola Negri, Gary Cooper, Florence Vidor, Esther Ralston, and Adolphe Menjou.

Clara Bow was finally allowed to make her talking debut, and it was okay; her voice matched her image. But Miss Bow had personal problems: an inability to make up her mind, scandal and lawsuits in her private life, and chronic lateness on the set. (Much the same thing happened decades later with Marilyn Monroe.) The studio finally settled its contract with Miss Bow. Later she made two more talking features for Fox, but neither was very good. That "damned charm," the "It!" that had made Clara Bow a star of the silents did not transfer well to talking films. She was like *Sunset Boulevard!* Norma Desmond, glaring in anger at that confounded mike which had messed up her paradise.

For Bebe Daniels it was different. When she realized that Paramount was not going to give her a real break in talkies, she bought up her contract, and signed with William Le Baron, who had become head of production at the new RKO/Radio. *Rio Rita* was filmed as quietly as any picture could be on the primitive sound stages of the time; at least there wasn't much pre-production ballyhoo. Nobody knew Bebe Daniels could sing. Hollywood was therefore thrown on its ear when *Rio Rita* opened at the Carthay Circle, and Bebe Daniels proved that not only could she handle lines like a trouper but she could also sing like a prima donna. She was on the threshold of the best part of her career.

Much the same thing happened with Richard Dix. He made a few nondescript talking features for Paramount, then signed with his old friend, Le Baron, at RKO/Radio. After a few introductory programmers, he made *Cimarron,* won an Academy Award nomination, and had a whole new career lasting though the Thirties and into the Forties.

William Powell had a featured lead in Paramount's first all-talking feature, *Interference,* as did Clive Brook. They both proved that they knew what they were doing with a mike overhead; they hadn't been stars on the stage for nothing. They were given new contracts, and lasted on a higher level than they had enjoyed in the silents.

Emil Jannings and Pola Negri were allowed to finish out their contracts in silent features, but they had accents (horrible word then), and they both returned to Germany, where their careers as talking stars blossomed anew. Jannings became a great UFA star in the films of Nazi Germany. Negri, however, escaped from Germany, although Hitler cried that she was his favorite, and begged her to return. Instead, she had outstanding successes in France and England. She also made several talkies in Hollywood, but retired and lives today in Texas.

Gary Cooper became a real star for Paramount; they showed wisdom in putting him in action films like *The Virginian* and *The Spoilers,* for which he was perfectly cast, and his minimal dialogue and his mastery of reaction were exactly right for his visual image.

Florence Vidor apparently never made a talking film; in the only talking feature she made—*Chinatown Nights*—she, in fact, was badly dubbed. There was nothing wrong with her voice, but she didn't want to continue in films. She fled East instead, and became the wife of Jascha Heifetz.

Paramount lost interest in Esther Ralston (some say it was because her husband was too interfering) although she had a background of theatre and was her loveliest just at the time the studio did not pick up its option. She continued to star and then went to supporting roles, notably at MGM, but eventually she retired from films, entered television where she made a big hit as a soap opera star. Today she is an actor's agent in New York.

With Adolphe Menjou, Paramount was obviously confused. They sent him to New York, where he made features in French with Claudette Colbert, and then he went to the Paramount Studios in Paris to make more French films. When he finally returned to the U.S.A, no longer a Paramount star, he was ready for the best years of his life as a free-lancer in supporting roles.

At least Paramount was smart about one of its contract players. They gave roles to Jean Arthur that paved her way to stardom. Miss Arthur played on the stage at the Pasadena Playhouse, then went to Broadway, and played in several productions, including one for the Theatre Guild. When she returned to Hollywood, she was an undisputed star. On the other hand, Paramount wrote off Louise Brooks when she could have become one of their brightest players. She was unique, and nobody ever replaced her particular charisma. Grudgingly, the studio kept Richard Arlen and Buddy Rogers; the latter was much-loved by audiences as well as by Mary Pickford, who married him. Arlen is one of those under-rated players who became important when he had an important role, but always was in there plugging.

13

The powers-that-were at Paramount, admitting that the talking picture was in, were determined to make it come of age as fast as possible. The easiest way was to dump their silent stars and take on a whole new contract list of players who had their roots in the theatre. Every studio did this in the Thirties. There was no question about the new players knowing how to talk or sing or dance; they had demonstrated their abilities on stage. Accordingly, Paramount made supporting players and then, in some instances, stars, of Ruth Chatterton, Claudette Colbert, Nancy Carroll, Sylvia Sidney, Kay Francis, Miriam Hopkins, Tallulah Bankhead, Jeanne Eagels, Fredric March, Walter Huston, Henry Fonda (all from the Broadway theatre). They fostered the career of Carole Lombard, prettiest of the last assemblage of the Sennett Bathing Beauties, and groomed her for stardom. Evelyn Brent had been a film player since 1914, and had proved how glittering she could be in her talking debut, *Interference,* and the studio promoted her to more important roles. Gary Cooper and Joel McCrea, who had never had stage experience, nevertheless were at ease before the microphone and camera, and they stayed on as players who became stars.

With a show of bravado, Paramount decided that accents weren't so bad after all, and brought Maurice Chevalier from Paris to make musicals for them. Chevalier became France's gift to Hollywood, and his films at this time made nothing but money.

Barbara Stanwyck and Margaret Sullivan gave some of their most attractive performances at Paramount during the Thirties. Cary Grant came to stardom there, and Mae West, Broadway's Diamond Lil, even saved the studio from the receivers with one film, *She Done Him Wrong.*

And, thanks to Josef von Sternberg, Marlene Dietrich came to Paramount. She was their glamour bonanza, even when the studio separated her from a temperamental von Sternberg and put her under the tutelage of Lubitsch, Borzage, and Mamoulian.

Much the same thing happened at all the studios. Only MGM, with the exception of John Gilbert, made greater stars of its silent stellar list in talkies: Garbo, Shearer, Crawford, Dressler, Beery, and Gable. Then there came Jeanette MacDonald, Nelson Eddy, Robert Montgomery, Rosalind Russell, Myrna Loy, and Jean Harlow—and there were more stars at MGM than there were in the heavens.

What happened to featured players in Hollywood was just as interesting. Some of them were so good, like Madge Evans, Hardie Albright, Chester Morris, and Russell Hardie, that they came awfully close to being named stars. Almost all of them came from the theatre and had no problem adapting to talkies; they knew what they were doing, so they worked constantly. Others, like Johnny Weissmuller and Buster Crabbe, came from the world of athletics; they swam and swung from trees, and learned how to be movie actors out of the water and beyond the forest.

The old guard remained, like Pauline Frederick, Marjorie Rambeau, John Halliday, Alison Skipworth, Mary Astor, Polly Moran, Beulah Bondi, Victor Moore, Lilyan Tashman, Lois Wilson, Conrad Nagel, ZaSu Pitts, and Thelma Todd. As the Thirties progressed, new players from Broadway came to swell the supporting lists, contributing some of filmdom's best performances. Who can forget Alice Brady, Gladys George, Verree Teasdale, Zita Johann, Una Merkel, or Billie Burke? And there were those who quickly became stars, like Bob Hope, Bing Crosby, Dorothy Lamour, or Ray Milland and Fred MacMurray.

New players were contracted—not only the promising young ones who had attracted attention on Broadway, but also those who came from the regional theatres all over the nation. Especially from the Pasadena Playhouse, which was not more than twenty-five miles from Hollywood, came a galaxy of new players—Dana Andrews, Robert Young, Eve Arden, Robert Taylor, Frances Dee, Victor Jory, Samuel S. Hinds, Onslow Stevens,

14

Robert Preston, William Henry, Thomas Browne Henry, Morris Ankrum, Moroni Olsen, Wayne Morris, Michael Whalen, Tyrone Power, William Holden, Lloyd Nolan, Douglass Montgomery, Gig Young, and Gloria Stuart.

In the Thirties, the way to get a stock contract at a studio was to get a part in a play and let a talent scout discover you. They covered every production thoroughly and systematically. The word was out: be noteworthy in some other medium and we will find you and offer a contract if we can use you.

From Broadway came James Cagney, Joan Blondell, and the entire Warner Bros. stock company that dominated the screen. The films Warner Bros. made in this decade may well be the most lasting of them all; they wear well, at least, nearly half a century later. And consider Allen Jenkins, Hugh Herbert, Frank McHugh, Glenda Farrell, Aline MacMahon, Mae Clarke, Louise Fazenda, Ruth Donnelly, Eddie Albert, and Guy Kibbee —the whole crew of ladies and gents who never were dull for one moment, who always got a hand when they appeared.

Warner Bros. was also wonderful for taking rejects from other studios and creating top stars of them: they gave Bette Davis, who hadn't been especially memorable in her first appearances, a chance to show what she could really do. Miss Davis became queen of the Warner Bros. lot; in fact, queen of Hollywood, after her loan-out to RKO for *Of Human Bondage.* Ann Sheridan didn't get very far at Paramount, but she became a real star at Warner Bros. as the mistress of the *double entendre,* the hard-boiled lady with the heart of gold. Humphrey Bogart, who had gotten nowhere as a leading man at other studios, came to Warner Bros. by request of Leslie Howard to re-create his stage role as Duke Mantee, the gangster on the run, in *The Petrified Forest.* He stayed to become the studio's most popular male star. Even Paul Muni had made some films that didn't do much for him at Fox, but at Warner's he became a great star.

During the last years of the Twenties, the new talking screen added singing and dancing to its attractions. The musical film enjoyed a brief popularity, and then died for a couple of years. *42nd Street* brought the film musical back, and it's never left since. Busby Berkeley was the genius of the Thirties musical. At RKO/Radio, the team of Fred Astaire and Ginger Rogers made the most carefree and beautiful of all song and dance films, and Paramount let Mamoulian and Lubitsch make unforgettable music with Chevalier and Jeanette MacDonald. At the end of the decade the great MGM musicals were drawing them in, and Judy Garland was captivating the world on her way to see the wonderful Wizard of Oz.

In assessing the films and actors of this decade, one must never lose sight of the period. It was a time of change. Everything people had held dear had been proved worthless. From the end of World War I, people thought that money was the be-all, the end-all of life, just as World War II had convinced people that power was the thing that counted most. The movies of the Thirties reflect the disillusionment of those who valued money highest, just as those of the Sixties began to dramatize the folly of power.

Until 1933, gangsters ruled the front pages and, God knows, there were plenty of features, some of them superb, dramatizing gangsterdom. Most of all, the Thirties proved that man at his lowest reaches for the highest. Escape from the humdrum world was the goal. Some of the really great and lasting moments of beauty flashed on the screens of the Thirties: Garbo in *Camille,* Garbo in anything; magic re-created from the world's great literature in *David Copperfield, Wuthering Heights, Romeo and Juliet, A Tale of Two Cities.*

There were social documents like *I Am a Fugitive from a Chain Gang, You Only Live Once, Fury,* and *They Won't Forget.* There was a merry-go-round of mad, zany, wacky comedies, the likes of which have never been duplicated, because the times needed them then. They effectively combined the merry with the romantic—social comedies like Frank Capra's *Mr. Deeds Goes to Town*, *Mr. Smith Goes to Washington*, and *You Can't Take It With You*; and the gay, romantic ones like *Bringing Up Baby*, *Holiday*, *My Man Godfrey*, *Twentieth Century*, *Easy Living*, *The Awful Truth*, and *Theodora Goes Wild*.

At the very end of the decade there arrived the ultimate escapist romance, a film that still draws packed houses every time it is re-issued—David O. Selznick's production of Margaret Mitchell's *Gone With the Wind*.

Consider the players whose careers are discussed in the following pages. Their screen careers began during the Thirties, but they lasted beyond that time. The performances they gave were every bit as important as those contributed by the stars. Some became stars themselves; some have retired; some have died; some are still acting. They came from Broadway, vaudeville, and radio, from the foreign stage, from the regional theatres, from the extra ranks. Some even started at the top with no acting experience at all. They all managed, however, because they were of their time, the Thirties, a time for survival.

Reality might have been drab and worrisome, but you left it all behind when the lady in the box-office punched your ticket and you entered Never-Never Land. There, up on that huge screen, the Players of Hollywood gave you the escape, the adventure, the fantasy, and the romance that somehow today is much more real than what went on outside the movie house.

HOLLYWOOD PLAYERS:
THE THIRTIES

1

Eddie Albert

The changeover in actor types from the Thirties and Forties did not occur overnight. Rather it was a gradual repolarization of "typical" standards and styles, as Hollywood reflected the shift from Depression ideals to pre World War II orientation and tastes. One of those performers who bridged the decades—and remained in the limelight—was Edward Albert.

Edward Albert Heimberger was born on Wednesday, April 22, 1908, in Rock Island, Illinois, to realtor Frank Daniel and Julia (Jones) Heimberger. When the family moved to Minneapolis, Minnesota, Edward attended St. Stephen's Parochial School and Central High School. He entered the University of Minnesota for two years, paying his school expenses by singing at amateur nights. Then he joined a performing trio known as "The Threesome" which was frequently heard on radio.

He left the University when The Threesome found radio work in St. Louis, Cincinnati, and Chicago. Eventually the trio played small clubs in Manhattan. When The Threesome disbanded, Eddie formed an act with Grace Bradt, performing on NBC radio as "The Honeymooners—Grace and Eddie" in 1935. However, his eyes were focused on Broadway and in December, 1935, he started rehearsals as Ben Martin in *O, Evening Star.* Jobyna Howland and Ezra Stone were also in this play which opened on January 8, 1936, but lasted only five performances.

It was George Abbott who produced and directed Fred Finklehoff and John Monk's riotous comedy of the misadventures of a clutch of cadets at Virginia Military Institute. In *Brother Rat* Edward was cast as the prize baseball pitcher Bing Edwards who married against the school's rules, and, just before "the big game," learns his wife is pregnant. *Brother Rat* was a great success on Broadway after its December 16, 1936, opening and continued for 577 performances. Later when Mr. Abbott resurrected a fallen flop called *Room Service,* which he rewrote and directed, Albert was given the role of the hapless playwright. The fanciful comedy enjoyed a 500-performance run.

Warner Bros. acquired the screen rights to *Brother Rat* and hired Eddie to repeat his stage role. If anything, Albert was funnier in the film than he had been on the stage. The picture, briskly directed by William Keighley, was a great success. Warners signed Eddie to a term contract after the release of the film in 1938. However, Albert returned to Broadway to display another phase of his talent in a musical comedy.

George Abbott adapted Shakespeare's *The Comedy of Errors* into a delightful farce, rechristened *The Boys from Syracuse,* for which Rodgers and Hart composed a lovely

With Jane Wyman and Ronald Reagan in *Brother Rat* (WB '38).

score. Directed by Abbott, with dances by George Balanchine, the play opened on Broadway on November 13, 1938, with Albert as Antipholus of Syracuse and short Jimmy Savo as his Dromio. Displaying his vocalizing talent, Eddie sang "This Can't Be Love" and "You Have Cast Your Shadow." After *The Boys from Syracuse* had romped for 235 performances, Eddie returned to Warner Bros. There he played in the screen version of Rodgers and Hart's *On Your Toes* (1939), appearing uneasy in the Ray Bolger stage role. The film version was not very successful on any account. He ended 1939 by giving a solid performance as Dr. Clinton Forrest, Jr., married to Rosemary Lane, in Warner Bros.' sequel to *Four Daughters* (1938) called *Four Wives* (1939). Eddie and Rosemary Lane would repeat their roles for the final film in the series, *Four Mothers* (1941).

Warners failed to recapture the success of *Brother Rat* in their follow-up *Brother Rat and a Baby* (1940) with Albert again as Bing Edwards and two-year-old Peter Benson Good playing his son, "Commencement." *An Angel from Texas* (1940), the studio's updated remake of *The Butter and Egg Man*, a Twenties' stage and film success, cast Eddie in it, and for their fourth remake it remained a bright farce. By now a staple part of the studio stock company, Albert next appeared in a lightweight comedy, *My Love Come Back* (1940), trading romantic quips with Olivia de Havilland. He then switched to a more serious role as Max Wagner, co-starring with Edward G. Robinson, in *A Dispatch from Reuter's* (1940).

The Burbank studio's habit of remaking past successes led them to adapt *Kid Galahad* (1937) to a circus background which they dubbed *The Wagons Roll at Night* (1941).

19

Humphrey Bogart and Sylvia Sidney had the leads, with Eddie playing lion tamer Matt Varney. The *New York Times* observed, "Except for the lions and Mr. Albert *The Wagons Roll at Night* is honky-tonk."

At Warner Bros., Wayne Morris, Ronald Reagan, and Jeffrey Lynn were given the bulk of the wholesome screen lead roles, and Eddie was usually given the picked-over remains. He was dropped into two program films, and wandered through the Anatole Litvak-directed *Out of the Fog* (1941), an arty version of Irwin Shaw's play *The Gentle People.* Bette Davis and Olivia de Havilland were not the only ones who could be choosey; Eddie turned down an assignment in a dull musical Warners was preparing, *Navy Blues* (1941), and sailed off for Mexico on his boat. While Herbert Anderson was playing his scheduled role, Eddie had the crew return to a California port and he went off prospecting in the desert, claiming he wanted "to shake off the shackles of civilization." In June, 1941, E. D. Barrow of the New York Yankees baseball team endorsed Eddie for the role of Lou Gehrig in the proposed film *The Pride of the Yankees* (1942), but the plum part went to Gary Cooper. In the gossip columns Albert was being linked romantically with Loretta Young's sister, Georgiana (who would eventually wed Ricardo Montalban).

After his rebellion against the studio, Eddie decided to free-lance, playing two roles at Universal in 1942 and then moving over to RKO for a trio of films. At the time he was being mentioned as a romantic item in the life of RKO's Anne Shirley, then divorced from John Payne and more recently dating Victor Mature (who had decided that Rita Hayworth was more his type). With Miss Shirley, Eddie appeared in *Lady Bodyguard* (1943) and *Bombardier* (1943). Following these roles, he was rather bland in *Ladies' Day* (1943), a Lupe Velez comedy focusing on the game of baseball.

Six feet tall, with light brown hair and blue eyes, Eddie was maintaining his reputation as a resourceful, dependable supporting lead when he joined the Navy as a lieutenant. He was assigned to the Pacific. In 1974 he would recall that the most frightening moment of his life was spent crouched in a shell hole with Japanese machine gun bullets whizzing above his head. This was during the Allied invasion of Tarawa in the Gilbert Islands. His companion in the shell hole said, "I've seen a lot of action, but this is the worst. I've never seen anything like this!" After the firing had ceased and they had run for cover, Albert asked someone who his shell hole companion was. "Oh, that's Colonel Evans Carlson—of Carlson's Raiders" was the reply. Albert thought, "If that was the worst action he'd ever seen, what the hell was I doing there?"

The actor returned to Hollywood in 1945, and on December 5 of that year he married a lovely actress-songstress-dancer, Marie Marguerita Guadelupe Bolando y Castilla, known professionally as Margo. (She had been wed for three years to actor Francis Lederer, divorcing him in 1940.) Eddie returned to the screen for several of his earnest, good-natured buoyant-type roles, having retained his youthful demeanor. He was in a pleasant comedy, *Rendezvous with Annie* (1946), at Republic with Gail Patrick, and then was Loretta Young's old flame ready to fill in for absent spouse David Niven in *The Perfect Marriage* (1946). Albert proved his dramatic mettle by appearing to good advantage in Susan Hayward's forceful drama, *Smash-up — The Story of a Woman* (1947). The next year he turned to comedy, underplaying his role opposite Gale Storm, Binnie Barnes, and Gilbert Roland in the Nevada-set *The Dude Goes West* (1948). After playing a second banana in *You Gotta Stay Happy* (1948), an overanxious screwball comedy with Jimmy Stewart and Joan Fontaine, Albert returned to the stage.

Any Irving Berlin musical was always anticipated with great hope. In 1949 the great songster collaborated with playwright Robert E. Sherwood on a new show, *Miss Liberty,* directed by Moss Hart and produced by all three. Oliver Smith mounted the show

20

With Vera Zorina in *On Your Toes* (WB '39).

beautifully, with costumes by Motley and dances by Jerome Robbins. But the story was banal and the score was less than top-drawer Berlin. Eddie was first-billed in an excellent cast, highlighted by veteran actress Ethel Griffies as the Countess. With Mary McCarty, Eddie sang "A Little Fish in a Big Pond" and with Allyn McLerie he warbled "Let's Take an Old-Fashioned Walk." The show did manage to have a respectable run of 308 performances.

When Eddie returned to Hollywood, television had already frightened the industry and decent roles were hard to find. He was Lucille Ball's comic foil in *The Fuller Brush Girl* (1950) and supported Gary Cooper in an underrated service comedy, *You're in the Navy Now* (1951). He remained at Twentieth Century-Fox to play with Betty Grable in her *Meet Me After the Show* (1951), but Macdonald Carey and Rory Calhoun were the two primary male leads.

On December 10, 1951, seasoned Albert tried television on the "Somerset Maugham Theatre's" Smith series, and in 1952 was a regular on the series "Leave It to Lester." Meanwhile he continued with film-making, co-starring in the Ben Hecht produced-directed-written *Actors and Sin* (1952). Eddie was in the second part of this episodic piece, a wild spoof of Hollywood that got out of hand. For William Wyler's (Sister) *Carrie* (1952), Albert offered a fine breezy performance as a talkative salesman who seduces Jennifer Jones.

Albert's first Oscar nomination for Best Supporting Actor (a category to which he seemed consigned after World War II) was for his expert playing of the news photographer Irving Radovich in *Roman Holiday* (1953). However, he lost out to Frank Sinatra of *From Here to Eternity*.

The year 1954 found Albert busy on various TV shows, including being m.c. on NBC's "Saturday Night Revue." That year he and Margo adopted a Spanish orphan in Madrid, Maria del Carmen. Eddie returned to Rodgers and Hart for the television special *A Connecticut Yankee*, with Janet Blair and Boris Karloff. Later in 1955, on June 4, he played and sang the role of Bumerli with Rise Stevens and Akim Tamiroff in the video version of *The Chocolate Soldier*. It was a busy year for the Alberts who developed a nightclub act that met with huge success across the country. They made recordings together and continued to delight audiences with their singing, guitar playing, and polished professionalism.

On the big screen in 1955, Eddie played in the less than exciting *The Girl Rush* with Rosalind Russell, but gave an admirable character study of the Persian peddler Ali Hakim in *Oklahoma!* (1955). Later, he ended the screen year by salvaging Lillian Roth (Susan Hayward) in *I'll Cry Tomorrow*. Turning to the theatre, on October 10, 1955, he opened in Boston in the tryout of a new play, *Reuben, Reuben,* only to close in that city shortly thereafter.

Albert *should* have been Oscar-nominated for his role of the despicable, hysterical, cowardly captain in *Attack!* (1956) but was not. He remained in uniform for the secondary role of Captain McLean in *The Teahouse of the August Moon* (1956). In addition, he was among those trapped in the unfortunate screen version of Ernest Hemingway's *The Sun Also Rises* (1957), but he had a better opportunity to shine as the hanger-on in *The Joker Is Wild* (1957), Frank Sinatra's snappy rendition of the life of Joe E. Lewis. Albert also continued to give sporadic appearances on television.

In 1958, Eddie Albert left Hollywood for French Equatorial Africa. The locale was selected by director John Huston to film *The Roots of Heaven* (1958). The heat was so intense that shooting began at dawn and ended at noon. Eddie's performance of the American news photographer Abe Fields was one of the few things in the Errol Flynn-

Trevor Howard film that critics complimented. In England, Albert made *Orders to Kill* (1958), an unsuccessful enemy agent film featuring Lillian Gish.

When he returned to the States, Eddie replaced David Wayne in the Broadway musical *Say, Darling*. He then reappeared in Hollywood to join a miscast Gregory Peck in the F. Scott Fitzgerald "biography," *Beloved Infidel* (1959). Much better was the television version of *The Silver Whistle* on "Playhouse 90," which featured Albert in the role played on Broadway by Jose Ferrer.

Unwilling to slow down his professional pace, Albert replaced Robert Preston in the spring of 1960 in the Broadway hit *The Music Man*. He was on hand for the show's 1,000th performance. On film he was in *The Young Doctors* (1961) and then joined Jane Wyatt in a fanciful *The Two Little Bears* (1961), which had the screen couple's two sons turned into bears. For television's "Theatre 62" Eddie played an offbeat role (for him) as the quiet killer in *The Spiral Staircase*, with Elizabeth Montgomery, Lillian Gish, and Gig Young.

After his role as Colonel Norval Algate Bliss in *Captain Newman, M. D.* (1963), Albert assumed his appointment as special World Envoy for "Meals for Millions," a philanthropic project that provided nutritious meals at low cost to underprivileged people throughout the world. (After World War II Eddie, with a former Navy buddy, Lieutenant Jack Fletcher, had produced two educational films, *Human Growth* and *Human Beginnings*. Both efforts gained considerable professional acclaim. At the same time, Eddie had become active in the Environmental Defense Fund Project, and had worked for UNICEF and the National Wildlife Society.)

It was in September, 1965, that Eddie really came into his own, professionally. As Oliver Wendall Douglas, a New York attorney who moves his glamorous city-bred wife (Eva Gabor) to a farm in Hooterville Valley, he was the star of the teleseries "Green Acres," which lasted for six lucrative seasons, until 1970. It was an easygoing role that earned him financial security and a tremendous video following. (It helped to pay for his $350,000 Pacific Palisades house.)

After his lengthy situation comedy stand, Eddie played in two telefilm dramas, *See the Man Run* (1971) and *Fireball Forward* (1972). Then he accepted the comparatively small but highly charged role of Mr. Corcoran in Elaine May's *The Heartbreak Kid* (1972). His performance as the money-oriented father gave the film stature and he was Oscar-nominated. However, the Best Supporting Actor Award was won that year by Joel Grey of *Cabaret*. It was also in this year that Eddie and Margo's son Edward (born: February 20, 1951) rose to stardom in the film version of *Butterflies Are Free*.

On April 8, 1973, Albert returned to Broadway in a comedy of a middle-aged marriage, *No Hard Feelings*. Nanette Fabray was his co-star in this vehicle, which opened and closed the same night. (It had, however, twenty-one previews.) The next year, he was to be seen as the sadistic prison warden with Burt Reynolds in *The Longest Yard* (1974) and was a tough police chief in John Wayne's *McQ* (1974) and Billy Dee Williams' *The Take* (1974). He even popped up in a segment of TV's "Here's Lucy," suspecting the redheaded comedienne to be a weirdo fan.

Eddie appeared with his son, Edward, for the first time professionally in the third season premiere episode of "Kung Fu." In late November, 1974, constantly busy Albert appeared as the first of five television Benjamin Franklins as the 72-year-old Ambassador to France. Albert was superb, and many critics thought his interpretation of Franklin far better than those of the other performers in this series: Melvyn Douglas, Richard Widmark, and two Bridges, Lloyd and Beau. While the Franklin episode was being televised, Eddie was in Rome for the U.S. Department of Agriculture serving as a special consultant to the World Hunger Action Coalition during the World Food Conference in Rome.

With roles in Walt Disney's *Escape to Witch Mountain* (1975), Burt Reynolds' *Hustle* (1975), and Elliott Gould's *Whiffs* (1975). Albert's career shows no signs of abating. In the fall of 1975, he debuted on a new CBS-TV series, "Switch," in which he is an ex-cop and Robert Wagner is an ex-con man. The show is not a runaway hit but it has gathered a steady following. Reviewing the program for *TV Guide,* Cleveland Amory reported, Albert is "so good at being not too bright that we wonder if it doesn't worry him sometimes."

Besides personal commitments (his wife Margo claims Eddie is "the world's easiest touch" for any con artist with a quick-buck proposition), television, and motion pictures, he also does profitable video commercials at $100,000 per product. (On the other hand he does volunteer video ads, such as the spot ads for Unity Church.)

Albert's philosophy of life can be summed up in his own words: "to walk through the day smiling is a glorious contribution."

EDDIE ALBERT

Brother Rat *(WB 1938)*
On Your Toes *(WB 1939)*
Four Wives *(WB 1939)*
Brother Rat and a Baby *(WB 1940)*
An Angel from Texas *(WB 1940)*
My Love Came Back *(WB 1940)*
A Dispatch from Reuter's *(WB 1940)*
Four Mothers *(WB 1941)*
The Wagons Roll at Night *(WB 1941)*
Thieves Fall Out *(WB 1941)*
Out of the Fog *(WB 1941)*
The Great Mr. Nobody *(WB 1941)*
Treat 'Em Rough *(Univ 1942)*
Eagle Squadron *(Univ 1942)*
Ladies' Day *(RKO 1943)*
Lady Bodyguard *(RKO 1943)*
Bombardier *(RKO 1943)*
Strange Voyage *(Mon 1945)*
Rendezvous with Annie *(Rep 1946)*
The Perfect Marriage *(Par 1946)*
Smash-Up—The Story of a Woman *(Univ 1947)*
Time out of Mind *(Univ 1947)*
Hit Parade of 1947 *(Rep 1947)*
The Dude Goes West *(AA 1948)*
You Gotta Stay Happy *(Univ 1948)*
The Fuller Brush Girl *(Col 1950)*
You're in the Navy Now *(20th 1951)*
Meet Me after the Show *(20th 1951)*
Actors and Sin *(UA 1952)*
Carrie *(Par 1952)*
Roman Holiday *(Par 1953)*

The Girl Rush *(Par 1955)*
Oklahoma! *(Magna 1955)*
I'll Cry Tomorrow *(MGM 1955)*
Attack! *(UA 1956)*
The Teahouse of the August Moon *(MGM 1956)*
The Sun Also Rises *(20th 1957)*
The Joker Is Wild *(Par 1957)*
The Gun Runners *(UA 1958)*
The Roots of Heaven *(20th 1958)*
Orders to Kill *(United Motion Pictures Organization 1958)*
Beloved Infidel *(20th 1959)*
The Young Doctors *(UA 1961)*
The Two Little Bears *(20th 1961)*
Madison Avenue *(20th 1962)*
The Longest Day *(20th 1962)*
Who's Got The Action? *(Par 1962)*
Miracle of the White Stallions *(BV 1963)*
Captain Newman, M.D. *(Univ 1963)*
Seven Women *(MGM 1965)*
The Party's Over *(AA 1968)*
The Heartbreak Kid *(20th 1972)*
The Take *(Col 1974)*
McQ *(WB 1974)*
The Longest Yard *(Col 1974)*
Escape to Witch Mountain *(BV 1975)*
The Devil's Rain *(Bryanston 1975)*
Hustle *(Par 1975)*
Birch Interval *(Gamma III 1976)*
Whiffs *(20th 1976)*

2

Hardie Albright

During the mid-Thirties there was an inexplicable canard traveling through Broadway's theatrical set that reflected the manic Hollywood casting system. Whenever a highly successful stage show was purchased by the studios, especially if the leading role required an actor of considerable talent and depth, out went the cry "Hardie Albright will play it." It all started when Albright, six feet tall with blond hair and intelligent blue eyes, arrived in Hollywood to start shooting his first motion picture. It was Fox's screen version of Elmer Harris' play *Young Sinners* (1931). On Broadway blond Gene Raymond had starred as Gene Gibson in the story of the jazz-age gin generation, a part that Albright inherited in the road company of the show.

Hardie Albright was born in Charleroi, Pennsylvania, on Wednesday, December 16, 1903. His mother, whose maiden name was MacHardie, was Scottish and his father, Albrecht, was Jewish. Hardie made his first stage appearance at the age of six, toured as a child, returned for his education in the small town outside Pittsburgh, and later entered Carnegie Institute of Technology. While there he majored in drama, played a successful *Hamlet,* and graduated in 1923 with a Bachelor of Arts degree. Thereafter Hardie spent a year studying art at the Art Institute of Chicago, but decided his prime interest was the theatre.

After apprenticeship with several stock companies, he joined Eva Le Gallienne's Civic Repertory Theatre, making his Broadway debut with that group as Nunu in *Saturday Night* (October 25, 1926). He next played Alexy Karkovitch Fedotik for thirty-nine performances with the Civic troupe from November 8, 1926, in *The Three Sisters.* On tour with the Le Gallienne ensemble, he was seen as Sebastian in *Twelfth Night,* Erhardt Borkman in *John Gabriel Borkman,* and Antonio in *The Cradle Song.* On January 16, 1928, he joined Withrop Ames' production of *The Merchant of Venice,* starring George Arliss as Shylock and Peggy Wood as Portia. Albright played the role of Salanio for sixty-four performances on Broadway and continued the role on an extensive road tour with the venerable Mr. Arliss, of whom he became a close friend.

Hardie's debut feature film, *Young Sinners,* emerged a rather tedious affair hardly duplicating the stage success. Fox next cast him as millionaire Stuart Elliott in *Hush Money* (1931) with Joan Bennett, Myrna Loy, and, in a bit role, George Raft. In his fledgling film performances, Albright did not dazzle the critics, but his interpretations were always better than his roles and there was the promise of better things to come.

26

Publicity pose c. '32.

For his third Fox picture he was perfectly cast as ambitious John Breen in *Skyline* (1931), enthusiastically playing a young idealist who escapes the drudgery of a river barge life by swimming ashore in Manhattan. Once on dry land he finds a sympathetic sponsor in skyscraper builder Thomas Meighan. The latter turns out to be his father. Following the release of *Skyline,* co-player Myrna Loy, who portrayed Meighan's mistress in the film, won a long-term contract from MGM. Albright won critical recognition for his performance and, from his old friend George Arliss, a letter of heartfelt congratulations. Arliss wished him continued success in motion pictures and concluded his note with, "My boy, my boy! I knew you could do it!"

His final Fox picture, *Heartbreak* (1931), brought him excellent notices for his role as dashing air pilot Count Carl Walden in a World War I Austrian-background drama. He is the one who is shot down, mistakenly, by his twin sister's (Madge Evans) lover, Charles Farrell. Albright's splendid acting was more noticeable undoubtedly due to the unfortunate miscasting of Farrell. Albright was not pleased with his Fox assignments and made arrangements to buy back his contract in order to free-lance.

He was announced to replace Charles "Buddy" Rogers in Paramount's *Dancers in the Dark* (1932), but William Collier, Jr. played the role. Instead, Hardie went to Warner Bros. which, in 1932, had lent their David Manners to United Artists for the screen version of *The Greeks Had a Word for It.* Ironically it was Manners who got to play Dey Emery on screen in the part that had won Hardie a Fox film contract.

At Warners, Albright's career was scarcely better than his brief tenure at Fox. Most of his assignments were secondary or supporting roles. Warner Bros. remade Edna Ferber's *So Big* in 1932 with Barbara Stanwyck as the self-sacrificing farmer woman, Selina, who dreams of her son's success as an architect. Albright played the grown son, and rising young actress Bette Davis was Dallas, the young artist with whom he falls in love. While at Warners, Hardie joined with George Arliss in two films. He played the juvenile lead in Arliss' *A Successful Calamity* (1932) and was the great English actor's snobbish nephew Benjamin in the comedy *The Working Man* (1933). In the latter film, his romantic interest was Bette Davis. (The two also played together in *Cabin in the Cotton* [1932], in which he was subordinate to star Richard Barthelmess in the Michael Curtiz-directed study of cotton fields, sharecroppers, and fury in the deep South.)

The Purchase Price (1932) seemed little more than a celluloid exercise in masterful miscasting from Barbara Stanwyck to George Brent to Hardie. In *Jewel Robbery* (1932), a synthetic frou-frou, Albright was overwhelmed by the sophisticated banter of William Powell and Kay Francis in this burglar-and-the-lady yarn. Ruth Chatterton, George Brent, and Hardie wallowed through a depressing chronicle hardly needed for the Depression years called *The Crash* (1932). He played a supporting role in Warren William's well-acted absorbing biographical drama of Swedish Ivar Kreuger, *The Match King* (1932).

Two of Hardie's brightest screen appearances were for Paramount. As Walter von Prell in Rouben Mamoulian's stylish *Song of Songs* (1933), he had several effective scenes with Marlene Dietrich. Albright proved his gift for lighter acting in the studio's wacky comedy, *Three-Cornered Moon* (1933), in which he had the romantic lead opposite effervescent Claudette Colbert. As the self-styled "genius" Ronald, Albright gave a fine interpretation of the man who cannot bear to confront the idea of steady employment. For a change, a film was equal to or better than its stage original, and Hardie's performance should have won him finer film assignments. Instead, he languished in an above average war-in-the-sky story, *Crimson Romance* (1934), and was the homicidal college professor who finally commits suicide in *The Ninth Guest,* a modest Columbia thriller.

With Boots Mallory and Conway Tearle in *Sing Sing Nights* (Mon '34).

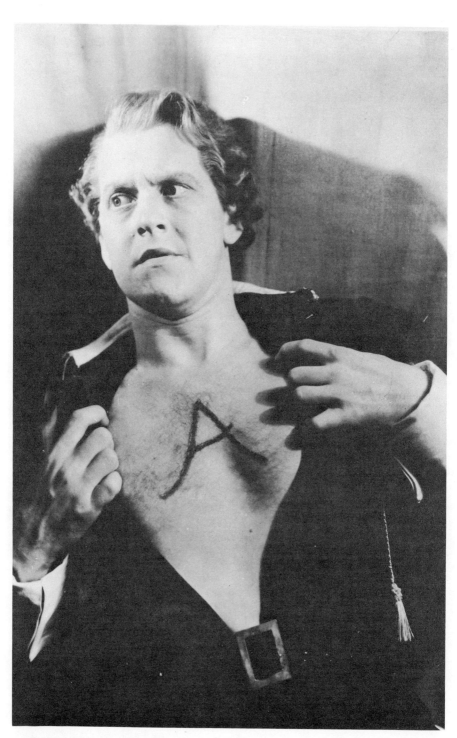

In *The Scarlet Letter* (Majestic '34).

Back in 1926, MGM had filmed a fine version of Nathaniel Hawthorne's *The Scarlet Letter* with Lillian Gish, Lars Hansen, and Henry B. Walthall. Eight years later, Majestic Pictures turned out a new, skimpy production starring Colleen Moore, an unfortunate piece of miscasting. Nevertheless, Albright gave a stirring performance as the Reverend Arthur Dimmesdale, gaining stature and sympathy as this self-branded hypocrite. Walthall repeated his role of Roger Prynne. (This picture would have a mild art house revival in the 1960s.)

After *The Scarlet Letter*, Albright's career diminished to that of lesser roles. Meanwhile, on April 7, 1934, in Riverside, California, he married Martha Sleeper. She was a bright young actress who had started out in two-reel comedies, proved her ability on the New York stage, and later would enjoy some success in pictures. (Six years to the month of their marriage, she would divorce Albright to marry Harry Dresser Deutchbein. Eventually she would retire to San Juan, Puerto Rico, where she would own and operate a chic shop on the Via Fortaleza.) Since at the time Hardie married Miss Sleeper, he was rehearsing a show, their honeymoon was spent in San Francisco, the site of his week-later opening as Richard Kurt in S.N. Behrman's comedy *Biography*, starring Alice Brady.

Although Albright continued making pictures, Samuel Goldwyn's *Nana* (1934) showcased him in a decidedly minor role. On radio, he was heard on various programs, including the "National Drama Broadcast" series *The Merchant of Venice*, with Peggy Wood, Bramwell Fletcher, and Sir Guy Bates Post.

On October 30, 1935, he returned to the New York stage in a trifle, *Play, Genius, Play!*, which lasted only five performances. As Hardie's play was closing on Broadway, his wife's vehicle was opening. She was in *Good Men and True* at the Biltmore Theatre. Meanwhile, Hardie rushed into rehearsals of a new comedy by John Murray and Allen Boetz. He played the lead, and was supported by Jack Albertson, John Litel, Ezra Stone, and Philip Loeb. The play opened to poor notices in Philadelphia and closed at a loss of $25,000 to producer Sam H. Harris. Two years later, the property was revived by George Abbott, who reduced the pedestrian script to a one-set comedy, and, with the original authors, rewrote the play. It opened on Broadway to become a bright hit, but only Philip Loeb of the original cast was retained. The show was *Room Service*.

The last effective and showy role Hardie had on the screen was in the Barbara Stanwyck-Robert Young *Red Salute* (1935). He earned good notices for playing the season's most despicable villain, an intense radical student leader. Thereafter his screen appearances were almost entirely in supporting parts. With his wife he appeared in a West Coast edition of *Russet Mantle* (1936), which she had done on Broadway. He returned to New York the next year to join Dorothy Hall in *Behind Red Lights*. Despite being a dull, cheap, and overly verbose melodrama, it lasted for 177 performances.

Dr. Victor R. Small's controversial book *I Knew 3,000 Lunatics* was adapted into a three-act drama by Hardie, and produced by Cheryl Crawford, the play opened at the Fulton Theatre in New York on March 24, 1938. Sanford Meisner was the onstage doctor who perfects a medical formula, believing it will arrest mental defectives. The Albright play ran fifty-three performances and in 1939 Hardie turned to directing summer theatre. Among his projects was *Stage Door*, starring Louise Platt. The following year he returned to Hollywood for a spate of easily forgettable films. In 1946, he made his final screen appearance to date, as "Smiley" (almost a summation of his picture career) in the Paul Muni fantasy *Angel on My Shoulder*, with Claude Rains in the title role.

Sadly, Hardie was one of the performers in the mid-Forties who appeared in a Hygenic Production for director William Beaudine. It was one of the first sexploitation films, and why Hardie Albright would appear in such trash is open to conjecture. The disaster was contested in and out of the courts for over a decade. In 1957, it was finally released by Hallmark as *Mom and Dad*. Luridly advertised with such catch-lines as "See the Birth of a Baby!" it was terribly out-of-date. At the New York showing of the picture, fast-talking hawkers would speed up and down the theatre aisles between screenings selling booklets on "sexual enlightment." The whole dreary affair resembled a second-rate burlesque show.

In more recent years, Hardie, who wed Arnita Wallace, by whom he had a daughter, taught drama at UCLA (in 1962) and wrote several books, including *Acting: The Creative Force* and *Stage Direction in Transition*. Occasionally he would appear on a TV show, such as "Gunsmoke" or "Twilight Zone."

On Sunday, December 7, 1975 he died at Mission Community Hospital in Mission Viejo, California. The seventy-one-year-old performer died of congestive heart failure and pneumonia.

Today Hardie is remembered as one of the many bright-eyed talented youths corraled into the Hollywood talkie round-up who played well within their narrow range. Praise from such stalwarts as Le Gallienne, Arliss, and Otis Skinner unfortunately led to nothing else than a lackluster cinema adventure. He was a misdirected performer whose talent was not sufficiently supported nor enhanced by the studios.

HARDIE ALBRIGHT

Young Sinners *(Fox 1931)*
Hush Money *(Fox 1931)*
Heartbreak *(Fox 1931)*
Skyline *(Fox 1931)*
A Successful Calamity *(WB 1932)*
So Big *(WB 1932)*
The Purchase Price *(WB 1932)*
Jewel Robbery *(WB 1932)*
The Crash *(FN 1932)*
Three on a Match *(FN 1932)*
Cabin in the Cotton *(FN 1932)*
This Sporting Age *(Col 1932)*
The Match King *(FN 1932)*
The Working Man *(WB 1933)*
Song of Songs *(Par 1933)*
Three-Cornered Moon *(Par 1933)*
The House on 56th Street *(WB 1933)*
Nana *(UA 1934)*
Crimson Romance *(Mascot 1934)*
The Ninth Guest *(Col 1934)*
White Heat *(Pinnacle 1934)*
Beggar's Holiday *(Tower 1934)*
The Scarlet Letter *(Majestic 1934)*
Two Heads on a Pillow *(Liberty 1934)*

The Silver Streak *(RKO 1934)*
Sing Sing Nights *(Mon 1934)*
Women Must Dress *(Mon 1935)*
Ladies Love Danger *(Fox 1935)*
Calm Yourself *(MGM 1935)*
Champagne for Breakfast *(Col 1935)*
Red Salute *(UA 1935)*
Granny Get Your Gun *(WB 1940)*
Ski Patrol *(Univ 1940)*
Carolina Moon *(Rep 1940)*
Flight from Destiny *(WB 1941)*
Men of the Timberland *(Univ 1941)*
Bachelor Daddy *(Univ 1941)*
Marry the Boss' Daughter *(20th 1941)*
The Loves of Edgar Allan Poe *(20th 1941)*
Lady in a Jam *(Univ 1942)*
The Pride of the Yankees *(RKO 1942)*
Army Wives *(Mon 1944)*
Captain Tugboat Annie *(Rep 1945)*
The Jade Mask *(Mon 1945)*
Sunset in Eldorado *(Rep 1945)*
Angel on My Shoulder *(UA 1946)*
Mom and Dad *(Hallmark 1957)*

3

Robert Armstrong

The ever popular *King Kong* (1933) is so highly praised for its trick photography that it is remembered largely as the famous cinema study of Beauty (Fay Wray) and the Beast. No filmgoer who has seen Kong losing a battle with airplanes while astride the top of the Empire State Building can forget the visual effects.

But also responsible for the film's success were directors Merian C. Cooper and Ernest Schoedsack, as well as the story's hero, Bruce Cabot, and the picture's straight man, Robert Armstrong. Tough, cocky Armstrong was an ideal choice for the role of intrepid movie director Robert Denham in *Kong* and, when RKO made a sequel to *King Kong,* Armstrong was again film-maker Denham, who is saved by Kong's son during an earthquake that sinks the fabulous island.

Robert Armstrong was born on Thursday, November 20, 1890, in Saginaw, Michigan, the son of Mr. and Mrs. William Armstrong, and the nephew of playwright Paul Armstrong (*Alias Jimmy Valentine, The Deep Purple,* and *Romance of the Underworld,* among others). Mr. Armstrong moved his family to Seattle, Washington, where Robert graduated from high school and went on to the University of Michigan, studying Homer and the ukulele with equal fervor. He joined the campus glee club and organized a student dramatic club. When he completed his law course, Robert wrote, produced, and directed a sketch, "A Campus Rehearsal," and, with two college alumni, toured the Sullivan-Considine vaudeville circuit, eventually playing in New York City.

When his uncle Paul wrote a vaudeville sketch called "Woman Proposes," he hired nephew Robert as stage manager and director. Both uncle and nephew agreed their present leading man was terrible. Uncle Paul persuaded Robert to take over the lead. When the stage bookings ended, Robert secured a part in a play, *The Bank's Half Million,* but World War I erupted and he enlisted ·in the infantry as a private. He emerged from the Great War as a first lieutenant. He returned to Broadway at the Belmont Theatre on October 13, 1919, as Tom Miner in *Boys Will Be Boys,* and on May 3, 1920, he opened at Cohan and Harris' Theatre in *Honey Girl,* a musical version of the highly successful play *Checkers.* The following two years he spent doing stock in Asheville, North Carolina, and then joined the national company of *The Man Who Came Back.*

Armstrong's big professional break arrived with the role of a dimwitted, lightweight boxing champ, Eddie "Chick" Cowan, in *Is Zat So?* The play had been rejected for production by George M. Cohan, so playwrights James Gleason and Richard Taber produced it themselves in Milwaukee with financial aid from Fannie Brice and others. The Shuberts then brought the popular show into New York, and Armstrong's strong, fancifully played boxer was loudly applauded. Later he directed a road company of the show as well as the London production in which he and James Gleason opened in February 15, 1926, playing their original roles. London's *Play Pictorial* for September 1, 1926, devoted its entire issue to *Is Zat So?*, and Gleason and Armstrong were featured on the cover. The following year Fox filmed the play with George O'Brien and Edmund Lowe in the Armstrong and Gleason roles, respectively.

On October 20, 1926, Robert was back on Broadway in *Sure Fire* with Gene Lockhart, Norman Foster, and Hugh O'Connell. However, the play survived only thirty-seven performances. Yet Robert was signed for a new musical, *Judy.* He starred with Patti Harrold, and the play opened in Chicago. By the time the show arrived on the main stem, Charles Purcell and Queenie Smith had replaced Armstrong and Harrold. But Robert's expert playing in *Is Zat So?* had not gone unnoticed on the West Coast, and he was subsequently signed to a term contract by Pathé, making his film debut in a DeMille Picture production, *The Main Event* (1927), in which he played another prizefighter.

After playing the role of Chris in Pathé's *The Leopard Lady* (1928), he was loaned to Fox for Howard Hawks' *A Girl in Every Port* (1928), teamed with Victor McLaglen as one of two sailors on the loose. He remained with Fox for the lead in their *Square Crooks* (1928) and then went over to Metro for the part of Gene in their *The Baby Cyclone* (1928).

Pathé's list of contract players was meagre but the studio had several good performers. Next, Robert played a gangster with William (later *Hopalong Cassidy*) Boyd in *Celebrity* (1928). Unfortunately, Robert was typecast as yet another boxer. At least in *Show Folks* (1928) he was a stage manager of a musical revue, performing with Carole Lombard, Eddie Quillan, and Lina Basquette—almost half of the Pathé roster. In 1929 the studio kept him busy clearing Phyllis Haver of a murder charge in *Shady Lady*. He gave a salty performance as rum-runner Babe Callahan in *Ned McCobb's Daughter*. In *The Leatherneck* he was killed off, and he was a reporter again in *Big News*, again with Lombard. For Tay Garnett's *Oh, Yeah!* Armstrong was rematched with James Gleason (who also doubled as dialogue director for the film), and he played the lead role in *The Racketeer*, again with Miss Lombard. It was his seventh Pathé lead that year.

Armstrong seemed destined to play almost nothing but prizefighters on the screen, or a rehash of his *Is Zat So?* image. But he was indeed funny as a would-be champion boxer with a poor track record in Fannie Brice's *Be Yourself* (1930). It was in this almost-forgotten film that Miss Brice sings "Cooking Breakfast for the One I Love" while cheerfully preparing Armstrong's ham and eggs. He was a prizefighter again in *Dumbbells in Ermine* (1930) and was rather effective as the criminal-murderer opposite Joan Crawford in MGM's *Paid* (1930). In addition he signed a new contract with RKO, which had taken over control of Pathé.

The change in management had little effect on Armstrong's roles and, before long, he was murdering the King's English if not his opponents as pugilist Kayo McClure in *The Tip-Off* (1931), also starring Ginger Rogers. Ginger was the lone female in RKO's *Suicide Fleet* (1931) with Bill Boyd, James Gleason, and Armstrong as Dutch. Universal's boxing film *Iron Man* (1931) had Lew Ayres donning the boxing shorts, with Armstrong as his manager, both battling sexpot Jean Harlow. Again Robert dominated the proceedings with his expert performing.

As Martin Trowbridge, Armstrong was hunted with bow and arrow by madman Leslie Banks in *The Most Dangerous Game* (1932), in which Fay Wray was the heroine. He switched to playing a villain exposed by Edna May Oliver in *The Penguin Pool Murder* (1932). Robert gave a realistic performance as an ex-con learning legal, if crooked, business methods while a masseur for Wall Street brokers in *The Billion Dollar Scandal* (1932). There were many critics who thought Armstrong's screen type to be a slightly more refined and handsomer adaptation of the parts so typically played by Wallace Beery or George Bancroft. Armstrong was lost in a London fog with the rest of the cast in *Blind Adventure* (1933), and then led his film company to the island home of *King Kong*. His convincing portrayals were evident in his versatility as a boozing braggart newsreel cameraman in *Above the Clouds* (1933) and in his walking away with John Gilbert's picture *Fast Workers* (1933) at MGM.

Bob was again paired with James Gleason in Paramount's *Search for Beauty* (1934), his first release after *The Son of Kong* (1933) sequel, in which Helen Mack was the new heroine. Armstrong went through much of the Thirties playing gangsters, none-too-bright guys, and, of course, prizefighters. But he played these potentially one-dimensional roles to the hilt and could steal a scene or the picture, unless his fellow professionals were up to his timing. He could perform comedy with a flair and make a despicable villain believable, or play a straight supporting role, such as in James Cagney's *G-Men* (1935). He even showed to advantage in such a sophisticated whodunit as *The Ex-Mrs. Bradford* (1936), with sleuths William Powell and Jean Arthur.

With Mae Clarke in *Fast Workers* (MGM '33).

In *Without Orders* (RKO '36).

With Douglas "Wrong Way" Corrigan and Eddie Quillan in *The Flying Irishman* (RKO '39).

Ex-wives ran rampant throughout Armstrong's personal life. He had been married and divorced from Peggy Allenby and Jeanne Kent, and, finally, he married Louise de Bois, who would eventually survive him. During these marital adventures Armstrong continued film-making, in a long list of B films, but occasionally landing in a classier A production.

By the Forties, fifty-year-old Armstrong was content to play in a serial for Universal. In *Sky Raiders* (1941) he played Lieutenant Ed Carey for twelve episodes, with partner Donald Woods, both of them protecting a secret fast-pursuit plane they designed for the U.S. Army. In 1942 he popped up in a couple of A films, including *My Favorite Spy* with Bob Hope and the elegant Madeleine Carroll. Then in 1942 he was back at Universal making another chapterplay, *Gang Busters*. For thirteen episodes he portrayed Detective Tim Nolan bringing a gang of big-city thugs to justice. The next year he switched his allegiance in the serial field by playing a villain posing as The Hangman who kills off his partners after discovering rich helium deposits in Africa in *Adventures of the Flying Cadets*.

It was on August 31, 1944, that Armstrong, too old for military duty in the war effort, returned to the stage. He played a crooked promoter in the short-lived (only seven performances) *Sleep No More*. Reviewing the play, *Billboard* magazine reported, "Robert Armstrong comes back to the stem to play the promoter. Armstrong knows his farce onions as anyone who remembers *Is Zat So?* will testify. He puts everything he's got into his job, it's a losing game!"

Armstrong returned to Hollywood where he was cast in James Cagney's *Blood on the Sun* (1945), in which he played Colonel Tojo. It was a part that should not have created too much turmoil for the makeup department, as Robert's almond-shaped, squinting

38

eyes normally had an Oriental cast about them. Following a set of filler films, he returned to Universal for another go-round at the serial game, this time in *The Royal Mounted Rides Again* (1945). He was the heavy, Price, owner of the Yukon Palace and leader of an outlaw gang, who is finally captured, naturally, in the thirteenth and last episode.

In the post-War years, Robert's features were geared to double-feature entries, but in 1947 he made an impressive character of the sergeant of police in John Ford's beautifully atmospheric drama *The Fugitive*, with Henry Fonda and the exquisite Dolores Del Rio. By 1949 Robert was still a supporting player, this time in a limp United Artist entry, *The Lucky Stiff*.

Long before the Michael Douglas-Karl Malden teleseries, Republic filmed its *The Streets of San Francisco* (1949) with Robert as a police lieutenant and Mae Clarke as his wife. Together they adopt the son of a gangster. He also returned to RKO that year for another fling at fantasy produced by John Ford and Merian C. Cooper (who also wrote the story), directed by Ernest B. Schoedsack, with special effects again by Willis O'Brien. Everyone hoped it would be another *King Kong* at the box-office. This one they named *Mighty Joe Young* (1949). Again the oversized ape was the hero, but he could not match the grandeur of *Kong* and the picture veered between satire and unfulfilled drama that was more diverting than breathtaking. Armstrong played Mac O'Hara, but all the human players supporting Joe came off second best.

Considering the cutback in film production in Hollywood in the Fifties, it was amazing that Robert got any screen work. In 1950 he did two quickies, and in 1952 he was back at RKO for *The Pace that Kills*. He entered television in the middle of the decade. He appeared with Brian Keith in *Pals to the End* and joined with fellow fugitive Dane Clark in forcing cab driver Eddie Albert to chauffeur them to freedom on a "G.E. Theatre" episode. Armstrong was also to be seen on several installments of the "Perry Mason" series. He made about one picture a year until 1957, when at age sixty-seven, he chose to retire. He did return briefly to the screen for a teenage trifle, *For Those Who Think Young* (1964), which featured James Darren, Paul Lynde, and Nancy Sinatra. Along with Allen Jenkins, Jack La Rue, and George Raft, Armstrong had one of the guest bit roles.

In his five decades of picture-making, Armstrong's best remembered oncamera line was, of course, from *King Kong*. In the graphic story, after the mighty Kong has been shot down from the top of the Empire State Building, Robert says, " 'Twas beauty that killed the beast."

After a brief illness burly Robert Armstrong died at the age of eighty-two at the Santa Monica, California, hospital on April 20, 1973. Ironically, the following day, the mentor, producer, and imaginative man who had made *King Kong*, Merian C. Cooper, died of cancer.

ROBERT ARMSTRONG

The Main Event *(Pathé 1927)*
The Leopard Lady *(Pathé 1928)*
A Girl in Every Port *(Fox 1928)*
Square Crooks *(Fox 1928)*
The Baby Cyclone *(MGM 1928)*
The Cop *(Pathé 1928)*
Celebrity *(Pathé 1928)*
Show Folks *(Pathé 1928)*
Shady Lady *(Pathé 1929)*
Ned McCobb's Daughter *(Pathé 1929)*
The Leatherneck *(Pathé 1929)*
The Woman from Hell *(Fox 1929)*
Big News *(Pathé 1929)*
Oh Yeah! *(Pathé 1929)*
The Racketeer *(Pathé 1929)*
Be Yourself *(UA 1930)*
Dumbbells in Ermine *(WB 1930)*
Big Money *(Pathé 1930)*
Danger Lights *(RKO 1930)*
Paid *(MGM 1930)*
Easy Money *(RKO 1931)*
The Tip-Off *(RKO 1931)*
Suicide Fleet *(RKO 1931)*
Iron Man *(Univ 1931)*
Ex-Bad Boy *(Univ 1931)*
Panama Flo *(RKO 1932)*
Is My Face Red? *(RKO 1932)*
The Lost Squadron *(RKO 1932)*
Hold 'Em Jail *(RKO 1932)*
The Most Dangerous Game *(RKO 1932)*
Radio Patrol *(Univ 1932)*
The Penguin Pool Murder *(RKO 1932)*
The Billion Dollar Scandal *(Par 1933)*
Blind Adventure *(RKO 1933)*
King Kong *(RKO 1933)*
I Love that Man *(RKO 1933)*
Above the Clouds *(Col 1933)*
Fast Workers *(MGM 1933)*
The Son of Kong *(RKO 1933)*
Search for Beauty *(Par 1934)*
Palooka *(UA 1934)*
She Made Her Bed *(Par 1934)*
The Hell Cat *(Col 1934)*
Manhattan Love Song *(Mon 1934)*
Kansas City Princess *(WB 1934)*
Flirting with Danger *(Mon 1934)*
The Mystery Man *(Mon 1935)*
Sweet Music *(WB 1935)*
G-Men *(WB 1935)*
Gigolette *(RKO 1935)*
Little Big Shot *(WB 1935)*
Remember Last Night? *(Univ 1935)*
Dangerous Waters *(Univ 1936)*
The Ex-Mrs. Bradford *(RKO 1936)*
Public Enemy's Wife *(WB 1936)*
All American Chump *(MGM 1936)*

Without Orders *(RKO 1936)*
The Three Legionnaires *(General 1937)*
It Can't Last Forever *(Col 1937)*
Nobody's Baby *(MGM 1937)*
The Girl Said No *(Grand National 1937)*
She Loved a Fireman *(WB 1938)*
There Goes My Heart *(UA 1938)*
The Night Hawk *(Rep 1938)*
The Flying Irishman *(RKO 1939)*
Man of Conquest *(Rep 1939)*
Unmarried *(Par 1939)*
Winter Carnival *(UA 1939)*
Flight at Midnight *(Rep 1939)*
Call a Messenger *(Univ 1939)*
Framed *(Univ 1940)*
Forgotten Girls *(Rep 1940)*
Enemy Agent *(Univ 1940)*
Behind the News *(Rep 1940)*
San Francisco Docks *(Univ 1940)*
Mr. Dynamite *(Univ 1941)*
The Bride Wore Crutches *(20th 1941)*
Citadel of Crime *(Rep 1941)*
Dive Bomber *(WB 1941)*
Sky Raiders *(Univ serial 1941)*
My Favorite Spy *(RKO 1942)*
Baby Face Morgan *(PRC 1942)*
Let's Get Tough *(Mon 1942)*
It Happened in Flatbush *(20th 1942)*
Gang Busters *(Univ serial 1942)*
Around the World *(RKO 1943)*
The Kansan *(UA 1943)*
Adventures of the Flying Cadets *(Univ serial 1943)*
The Mad Ghoul *(Univ 1943)*
The Navy Way *(Par 1944)*
Action in Arabia *(RKO 1944)*
Goodnight, Sweetheart *(Rep 1944)*
Mr. Winkle Goes to War *(Col 1944)*
Belle of the Yukon *(RKO 1944)*
Gangs of the Waterfront *(Rep 1945)*
Blood on the Sun *(UA 1945)*
The Falcon in San Francisco *(RKO 1945)*
Arson Squad *(PRC 1945)*
The Royal Mounted Rides Again *(Univ serial 1945)*
Gay Blades *(Rep 1946)*
Blonde Alibi *(Univ 1946)*
Criminal Court *(RKO 1946)*
G. I. War Brides *(Rep 1946)*
Decoy *(Mon 1946)*
The Fall Guy *(Mon 1947)*
Exposed *(Rep 1947)*
The Fugitive *(RKO 1947)*
The Sea of Grass *(MGM 1947)*
Return of the Bad Men *(RKO 1948)*
Paleface *(Par 1948)*

The Lucky Stiff *(UA 1949)*
The Streets of San Francisco *(Rep 1949)*
The Crime Doctor's Diary *(Col 1949)*
Mighty Joe Young *(RKO 1949)*
Captain China *(Par 1949)*
Sons of New Mexico *(Col 1950)*

Destination Big House *(Rep 1950)*
The Pace that Thrills *(RKO 1952)*
Las Vegas Shakedown *(AA 1955)*
The Peacemaker *(UA 1956)*
The Crooked Circle *(Rep 1957)*
For Those Who Think Young *(UA 1964)*

4

Lynn Bari

Should the Academy of Motion Picture Arts and Sciences one day devise a special award for "Queen of the B's," there would be several contenders, pretenders, and nominees. But the Oscar for this dubious honor would probably go to Lynn Bari. She began her Hollywood years in the early Thirties and for three decades performed in a long list of program films with only an infrequent major production in her line-up. In 1942 Lynn told the press, "So far I've been the good girl in B's and the menace in A's. I don't know why it is, but whenever they decide to give me a part in a big picture, they make me a meanie."

Lynn Bari (also known as Marjorie Bitzer) was born Marjorie Schuyler Fisher in Roanoke, Virginia, on Thursday, December 18, 1913. While she was just entering her 'teens,' the family moved to Hollywood, California, where her father took a position at the Institute of Religious Sciences. She was sent to a dramatic school to reduce her self-consciousness and awkwardness. However, when she learned Metro-Goldwyn-Mayer was hiring dancers, she applied and was accepted not for her dancing ability but for her lovely, exotic high-cheekboned face and beautiful figure. Her debut film was Joan Crawford-Clark Gable's *Dancing Lady* (1933).

In 1934 Lynn signed a long-term contract with Fox. Initially she played bit parts and walk-ons, and supplied a pulchritudinous background for many films throughout the decade. By 1938 she was being cast in a string of quickies, although she played Klari with William Powell and Annabella in the high-class *The Baroness and the Butler* (1938). But it was in the low-budget films that Lynn excelled, such as *Mr. Moto's Gamble* (1938). The latter was originally intended as a Warner Oland-Charlie Chan entry, but the star died and it was converted into one more entry in the Peter Lorre-Oriental sleuth series. Every once in a while Miss Bari would be "lifted" to a major feature, such as Barbara Stanwyck's *Always Goodbye* (1938), in which Lynn portrayed a golddigger.

By the Thirties, series pictures had attained a steady box-office following, and there was always hope that a cheaply made B film would make the grade for a continuing series. Keeping this thought in mind, the studio cast Lynn as Terry Wilson, with June Lang, in *Meet the Girls* (1938). But the hoped-for series never materialized..Then she was Dianne Woodward helping daredevil newsreel cameraman Brian Donlevy in Twentieth's *Sharpshooters* (1938), which the studio hoped would become another profitable continuation venture. But like *Meet the Girls, Sharpshooters* was a single entry.

With Michael Whalen and Marvin Stephens in *Speed to Burn* (20th '38).

With Ian Hunter, Binnie Barnes, Johnny Russell, and Barbara Stanwyck in *Always Goodbye* (20th '38).

With Paul McVey, June Lang, Emmett Loran, and Harlan Briggs in *Meet the Girls* (20th '38).

Bari occasionally was given the romantic interest in a film, such as Ann Carver with Warner Baxter in *Return of the Cisco Kid* (1939) and the leads opposite Preston Foster in *Chasing Danger* (1939) and *News Is Made at Night* (1939), the latter two being both well-paced B's. Also in 1939 she wed agent Walter Kane. As she later explained, "I always wanted to be with somebody that I loved, but it was a tempestuous marriage and lasted only a few years. I was working very hard in pictures; at that time we worked six days a week. I'd get up at 4:30 in the morning, and sometimes I worked till seven at night and sometimes till midnight. With the full work load I had and the exhaustion I felt, the marriage was just too much for me to absorb."

While trying to cope with her marriage, Lynn continued at Fox with the Ritz Brothers in their zany *Pack up Your Troubles* (1939). She then was Barbara Hunter shooting John Halliday in *Elsa Maxwell's Hotel for Women* (1939) and played with Sidney Toler, the new Oriental sleuth, in *Charlie Chan in City of Darkness* (1939). In 1940 she was excellent in the supporting role as Edna McCauley in Twentieth's lavish *Lillian Russell,* starring Alice Faye. But then Miss Bari was back to a sixty-seven minute quickie as a murderess in *Earthbound* (1940). There seemed to be no justice for the experienced performer.

As the cocky waitress-owner of a waterfront cafe in *Pier 13* (1940), with Lloyd Nolan, *Photoplay* noted, "Lynn Bari is in a role which gives her a real chance to show she's good." She played the romantic distraction of frontiersman Jon Hall in *Kit Carson* (1940) at United Artists and was back with Lloyd Nolan (and George Montgomery) in a better-than-average low-budget entry, *Charter Pilot* (1940).

Although she had made seven features in 1940, there were only six assignments for her the next year. In Twentieth's bright remake of *Blood and Sand* (1941) with Tyrone Power, Rita Hayworth, and Linda Darnell, Bari played the small role of Encarnation. One of the great delights of Sonja Henie's *Sun Valley Serenade* (1941) was Glenn

With Robert Young in *Josette* (20th '38).

Miller's band. Lynn appeared as the band's vocalist Vivian Dawn singing "I Know Why" (her voice was dubbed by Lorraine Elliot), and, again, *Photoplay* was star-gazing: "Lynn Bari is a coming star if ever we saw one." After Lynn's playing in *The Perfect Snob* (1941), *Photoplay* bemoaned, "Why Lynn Bari was tossed into this pot stew we'll never know."

In 1942, Lynn maintained her steady pace by playing in the espionage thriller *Secret Agent of Japan,* taking the lead in *The Night before the Divorce,* going over to RKO to join George Sanders in *The Falcon Takes Over,* and then landing the female lead in Henry Fonda's *The Magnificent Dope* at Fox. *Photoplay* gushed about her obvious talents in this entry. For "Lux Radio Theatre" in September, 1942, Lynn repeated her role from *The Magnificent Dope,* accompanied by Henry Fonda and Don Ameche.

Lynn was stunning as the vocalist with Glenn Miller's band in Twentieth's *Orchestra Wives* (1942) and, with her singing now dubbed by Pat Friday, she sang "Serenade in Blue" and dueted "At Last" with Ray Eberle. In January, 1943, she left for the East Coast to co-represent the studio (with Roddy McDowall) at President Roosevelt's annual Birthday Ball and for the local premiere of the studio's *China Girl* (1942), in which she played Captain Fifi, a Japanese secret agent. She told the press: "In *China Girl,* I'm the lowest kind of a louse—a Japanese spy. Do I mind? Of course I mind! I'm dreaming of the day when I'll be the nice, sweet girl in A pictures—but, of course, as long as they really keep me busy I'm not actually complaining." Prior to her Eastern trek she had started divorce proceedings against Walter Kane. On March 22, 1942, she was heard on "Lux Radio Theatre" in *Each Dawn I Die* with George Raft and Franchot Tone.

Lynn met Sid Luft at a dinner party at the home of Bill Goodwin. They were immediately attracted to one another. The tall Luft with his big grin, dark brown eyes, and wavy brown hair charmed Lynn. He had been an aircraft instructor for the Royal Canadian Air Force at Edmonton, Alberta, Canada, and was presently a test pilot for Douglas Aircraft. During Lynn's trip East, Luft crashed while testing a plane, and Lynn spent a small fortune calling the Santa Monica Hospital until she returned to the Coast three weeks later, only to leave the following day for a 21-day bond-selling tour with Ronald Colman.

When Lynn's final decree from Kane was legal on November 26, 1943, she married Luft on Sunday, November 28, 1943, at the home of producer William Perlberg. Prior to her Eastern tour and the Luft wedding, she had purchased George Montgomery's home, lock, stock, and barrel, which included a steadily growing family of rabbits. Lynn described her new home as, "It's the first house I've ever owned, and it's so charming that I'll hardly have to make any changes—maybe just add a few feminine touches. The rabbits actually were a gift. Every time I go out into the backyard there are more of them!"

For the Benedict Bogeaus remake of *The Bridge of San Luis Rey* (1944) Lynn was loaned by her studio to play the pivotal role of Micaela, the "Perichole," with Francis Lederer unsatisfactorily playing the dual roles of Manuel and Esteban in a cast that included Nazimova, Louis Calhern, and Akim Tamiroff. Lynn was not up to the role and in no way matched the performance of Lili Damita in MGM's 1929 edition. But Miss Bari offered a good performance as Edward G. Robinson's wife suspected of espionage in *Tampico* (1944). Then she was another band singer, this time with Benny Goodman's group, in *Sweet and Lowdown* (1944) and later played Mrs. Eddie Rickenbacker adequately (Fred MacMurray was the famous flyer) in *Captain Eddie* (1945).

Then she was shuttled back to the B's, as the nurse of killer-psychiatrist Vincent Price in *Shock* (1946), school librarian Miss Palmer competing with Jeanne Crain for Glenn Langan's affections in *Margie* (1946)—a major film—and then appeared in a haywire whodunit as actress Frances Ransom, with George Raft, in RKO's *Nocturne* (1946). She made two filler pictures in 1948 and one in 1949 before branching into what was for her a new phase of show business—the stage.

Lynn joined a road company of Moss Hart's *Light up the Sky*, in which she starred with Sam Levene, Margie Hart, and Glenn Anders. This long tour was followed by another impressive run in the Chicago production of *Goodbye, My Fancy*. If her career was taking a more compelling course, her marriage (that had produced a son John) was under siege, with confirmed rumors that husband Sid Luft was dating Judy Garland openly. She filed for divorce from Michael Sidney Luft and received her decree on December 26, 1950.

Son John was given into Lynn's custody, and Luft, who had been a secretary for Eleanor Powell and a producer of B pictures, now became Judy's constant impresario. Luft and Garland were married in June, 1952, and daughter Lorna arrived that November. A son, Joseph, was born in March, 1955.

Lynn had entered television in 1950 via the ABC series "Detective's Wife." After several guest-starring appearances, she was given the lead of G. F. Allen in the teleseries "Boss Lady" that ran from July, 1951, through 1952. Lynn made three forgettable features in 1951. By 1954 she was playing fourth fiddle to Donald O'Connor, a talking mule, and zany ZaSu Pitts in *Francis Joins the WACs*. After a supporting role in an Abbott and Costello screen comedy in 1955, she wed a psychiatrist, Dr. Nathan Rickles. In 1956 she returned to Twentieth Century-Fox for *The Women of Pitcairn Island* and continued with TV guest spots.

For the debut of the series "Overland Trail" Lynn appeared in the first episode in 1960. For "The Plainsman" teleseries she was on hand for *The Matriarch* segment. Meanwhile her personal life underwent turmoil and trial when Sid Luft re-entered her life, seeking custody of their son John, suing for custody on the grounds that Lynn did not want the responsibility for him because she was sending him to the Chadwick School. "Chadwick was one of the finest schools in the country," Lynn explained. "I sent Johnny there because he couldn't cut it at the Beverly Hills school; he did beautifully at Chadwick. He was happy there and well adjusted. Sid and Judy had agreed it was a great place for him to go because he would be with Liza Minnelli [Judy's daughter by Vicente Minnelli]; they'd be like brother and sister growing up together there—and they were.

"Suddenly Sid claimed it was all wrong for me to send Johnny there," Lynn continued. "If there was something wrong with the school why would he and Judy have sent Liza there? It didn't do her any harm, did it?" A misguided judge agreed the Lufts could provide a "well-organized" home and gave them custody of Johnny. Unfortunately the Lufts' home had little or no resemblance to organization and the presiding judge had never inquired about Dr. and Mrs. Nathan Rickles' home. Two months later another, more astute judge returned Johnny to his mother and stepfather, and Rickles' daughter, by the doctor's first marriage, made a happy family group.

Lynn continued accepting television assignments. She starred in Arthur Laurents' tragic *A Clearing in the Woods* in San Francisco and later was seen on stage in the musical *Plain and Fancy*, as well as in *All the Way Home* and *Ballad of the City*. She also played in one of the national touring companies of *Barefoot in the Park*. In 1964 she filmed *Trauma* and was seen on television in a "Perry Mason" series segment. In the summer of 1964 she played the straw-hat stages with Alan Mowbray in *Enter Laughing*. In 1967 Lynn was seen on telecast episodes of "The Girl from U.N.C.L.E." and "The F.B.I." series.

By 1972 her marriage to Dr. Rickles was faltering. Lynn summed it up with: "The marriage just didn't work out. Don't get me wrong. There must have been something wonderful about this man or I wouldn't have married him. But I hadn't realized how difficult the life of a psychiatrist can be. I acted as his secretary and his nurse; I was also taking care of the six-bedroom house in which we lived and of Johnny and of Nathan's young daughter by a previous marriage trying to give her love and a feeling of emotional security. I stood it as long as I could; then to preserve what was left of my sanity, I decided I'd better get a divorce." The divorce occurred on July 26, 1972.

Then, Lynn returned to the stage. For six months she toured as the alcoholic heroine of Neil Simon's *The Gingerbread Lady.* When the show played in Dallas, Texas, the city's newspaper, the *Herald,* reported, "She is a terrific actress. No one could question that after having seen Miss Bari so dominate the stage, giving so much power, poignancy and biting comic emphasis to the role." She flew from Dallas back to California to get her divorce and returned the same night to Dallas for her role in *The Gingerbread Lady.* In the late summer of 1973, Lynn joined an all-star cast for the summer circuit production of *Follies,* starring with Vivian Blaine, Robert Alda, Hildegarde, and Selma Diamond. Lynn played ex-Follies girl Carlotta Campion, a role that had been played on Broadway by Yvonne De Carlo. Lynn was fine in the show and sang the number "I'm Still Here" with great charm. She had aged perceptively and was very thin, but the exotic loveliness of Miss Bari shone through.

The future holds no retirement plans for Lynn. She claims: "I'll be doing another stage play soon and if anything interesting comes up in the way of a TV show or a movie, I'll take it. I would never marry again. I think that after you've been married three times, you're out. Each time I felt I was marrying for a good reason but I was wrong."

LYNN BARI

Dancing Lady *(MGM 1933)*
Meet the Baron *(MGM 1933)*
Coming out Party *(Fox 1934)*
Stand Up and Cheer *(Fox 1934)*
Search for Beauty *(Par 1934)*
Caravan *(Fox 1934)*
George White's 1935 Scandals *(Fox 1935)*
Show Them No Mercy *(Fox 1935)*
Spring Tonic *(Fox 1935)*
The Man Who Broke the Bank at Monte
    Carlo *(Fox 1935)*
Redheads on Parade *(Fox 1935)*
Thanks a Million *(Fox 1935)*
Music Is Magic *(Fox 1935)*
My Marriage *(20th 1935)*
Everybody's Old Man *(20th 1936)*
The Song and Dance Man *(20th 1936)*
Ladies in Love *(20th 1936)*
Crack-Up *(20th 1936)*
Pigskin Prade *(20th 1936)*
Sing, Baby, Sing *(20th 1936)*
36 Hours to Kill *(20th 1936)*
Wee Willie Winkie *(20th 1937)*
Sing and Be Happy *(20th 1937)*
This Is My Affair *(20th 1937)*
Lancer Spy *(20th 1937)*
Love Is News *(20th 1937)*
Wife, Doctor and Nurse *(20th 1937)*
On the Avenue *(20th 1937)*
I'll Give a Million *(20th 1938)*
Josette *(20th 1938)*
Rebecca of Sunnybrook Farm *(20th 1938)*
Speed to Burn *(20th 1938)*
The Baroness and the Butler *(20th 1938)*
Walking Down Broadway *(20th 1938)*
Mr. Moto's Gamble *(20th 1938)*
Battle of Broadway *(20th 1938)*
Always Goodbye *(20th 1938)*
Meet the Girls *(20th 1938)*
Sharpshooters *(20th 1938)*
Return of the Cisco Kid *(20th 1939)*
Chasing Danger *(20th 1939)*
News Is Made at Night *(20th 1939)*
Pack up Your Troubles *(20th 1939)*
Elsa Maxwell's Hotel for Women *(20th 1939)*
Charlie Chan in City of Darkness *(20th 1939)*

Hollywood Cavalcade *(20th 1939)*
Pardon Our Nerve *(20th 1939)*
Free, Blonde and 21 *(20th 1940)*
City of Chance *(20th 1940)*
Lillian Russell *(20th 1940)*
Earthbound *(20th 1940)*
Pier 13 *(20th 1940)*
Kit Carson *(UA 1940)*
Charter Pilot *(20th 1940)*
Blood and Sand *(20th 1941)*
Sleepers West *(20th 1941)*
We Go Fast *(20th 1941)*
Moon over Her Shoulder *(20th 1941)*
Sun Valley Serenade *(20th 1941)*
The Perfect Snob *(20th 1941)*
Secret Agent of Japan *(20th 1942)*
The Night before the Divorce *(20th 1942)*
The Falcon Takes Over *(RKO 1942)*
The Magnificent Dope *(20th 1942)*
Orchestra Wives *(20th 1942)*
China Girl *(20th 1942)*
Hello Frisco, Hello *(20th 1943)*
The Bridge of San Luis Rey *(UA 1944)*
Tampico *(20th 1944)*
Sweet and Lowdown *(20th 1944)*
Captain Eddie *(20th 1945)*
Shock *(20th 1946)*
Home Sweet Homicide *(20th 1946)*
Margie *(20th 1946)*
Nocturne *(RKO 1946)*
The Man from Texas *(EL 1948)*
The Spiritualist *(EL 1948)*
The Kid from Cleveland *(Rep 1949)*
I'd Climb the Highest Mountain *(20th 1951)*
On the Loose *(RKO 1951)*
Sunny Side of the Street *(Col 1951)*
Has Anybody Seen My Gal? *(Univ 1952)*
I Dream of Jeanie *(Rep 1952)*
Francis Joins the WACs *(Univ 1954)*
Abbott and Costello Meet the Keystone Cops
    (Univ 1955)
The Women of Pitcairn Island *(20th 1956)*
Damn Citizen *(Univ 1958)*
Trauma *(Parade 1964)*
The Young Runaways *(MGM 1968)*

5

Binnie Barnes

Ever since America was a British colony, England has been shipping sundry exports across the Atlantic. One of the most delightful to reach the U.S. in the Thirties was Binnie Barnes, a beautiful sparkling performer who seemed incapable of giving a bad performance, no matter how odious the picture in which she was stuck. While she never rose to the heights of stardom as such countrywomen as Vivien Leigh and Deborah Kerr, Miss Barnes added a great deal to the Hollywood of the Thirties and thereafter. When she chose to subordinate her career to that of her fledgling producer husband, Mike Frankovich, she became one of the colony's most effervescent hostesses. Society's gain was the filmgoers' loss.

Gitelle Enoyce Barnes was born in Caledonia Market, London, England, on Saturday, March 25, 1905, to an Italian mother, who worked as a seamstress, and to a father who was a London Bobby. When she was fourteen years old her beloved dad died, leaving Gitelle and her mother a small farm in Kent called Seven Oaks Green. There the young girl arose at four A.M., milked cows, and drove on an established round delivering the milk. For her chores on this milk route, she was paid approximately fifty cents a week. She made a few extra ''bob'' by combing, brushing, and feeding dogs on the neighboring aristocratic estates. Later she found employment testing electric light bulbs and, in the same factory, learned the trade of soldering.

Reflecting on the early years, ever-candid Binne said, ''Work was good for me. And it was fun having a go at one thing and another. I got to know all kinds of people. Lord, the different ones that poked their heads out of doors when I was delivering milk! That was the time, early in the morning, to see them as they really were without any frills. I'll never forget one old crone who wore diamond earrings—probably slept in them—and a second-hand lady with the airs of a duchess!''

She returned to London for a clutch of jobs in shops to ''shilling hops'' at the Palais de Danse until she landed a hitch as hostess for the Cosmo Club. She met an American, ''Tex'' McLeod, who then was devising a vaudeville act to tour South Africa. McLeod taught a willing Binnie to speak with an American Southwest States drawl, to twirl a rope Will Rogers-style, to yell ''yippee,'' and to sing a few ditties. She was billed as ''Texas Binnie Barnes.'' Years later, Binnie credited Tex for her introduction. to show business. Returning to London she found bookings in variety programs and in cabaret, and made a bid for the stage.

Publicity pose for *Diamond Jim* (Univ '35).

Andre Charlot, the successful London producer of revues, asked Binnie to audition and, pleased with the results, gave her a job in *Charlot, 1928,* which opened at the Vaudeville Theatre on August 29, 1928. She had a solo—a torch song, "Deja," that became popular in England and on the Continent. The Charlot engagement led to her first straight show at the Apollo Theatre (October, 1929) in *The Silver Tassie,* with Charles Laughton. She then played the role of Rosa in *Little Tommy Tucker,* with Melville Cooper, in London. She found screen work with Ida Lupino's father, Stanley, in two-reel comedies, in which she eventually received the classic pie-in-the-face treatment and earned the nickname of "Pie-Face." She made her feature motion picture bow with Heather Angel and Hugh Williams in *A Night in Montmartre* (1931), a formula blackmail story. Meanwhile, back in the theater, Noël Coward remembered her *The Silver Tassie* performance and wrote for her the role of Fanny Bridges, a music hall singer, in his chronicle *Cavalcade* (October, 1931).

During the happy run of *Cavalcade* Binnie made over a dozen features and married a quiet, studious, charming man who owned an antique shop. She had met Samuel Joseph eight years before in 1924.

Her array of screen portrayals established her as a coming actress in British films, along with Merle Oberon, Wendy Barrie, *et al.* The film that brought her to the attention of America and Hollywood was the extraordinarily successful *The Private Life of Henry VIII* (1933), in which she played the doomed Catherine Howard. The next year she was deliciously wicked and provocative as the bawdy inn wench Rosita in Douglas Fairbanks, Sr.'s *The Private Life of Don Juan* (1934).

Like many other Britishers, she found the temptation of a Hollywood contract too delicious to refuse. She arrived in America and reported to Universal Studios for her first Hollywood film. She played a role that would almost personify Hollywood's image of her: that of the other woman in *There's Always Tomorrow* (1934). Her performance as Frank Morgan's mistress was well defined, serious, and well played, particularly at the point when she gallantly returns the philandering Morgan to his wife (Lois Wilson) and their children.

At this time Binnie also received her first taste of publicity, California-style. "I opened the door and at the curb was a truck of equipment that was being unloaded. The crew marched into my home with all their lights, a cameraman with two assistants, and two representatives of the publicity department. In a few moments my living room looked like a movie set. All day long they 'shot' me while the publicity men plied me with ceaseless questions about my milk-maid days and my try as a student nurse at London's Great Northern Hospital."

Binnie next made a cameo appearance in Universal's *Gift of Gab* (1934), returned to England for more picture-making, and then came back to Universal for their exceptionally well done *Diamond Jim* (1935). Binnie could not help but wonder why an English actress had been chosen to play an American beauty. "You can't be more surprised than I was. It knocked me right off my pins. You see, they cabled me to come over and play Miss Russell's chum, Edna McCauley, the fashionable dressmaker. But when I got here they were in a jam and grabbed me to get them out of it. They'd tested about a thousand girls for the Lillian Russell part, but, although they got beauty galore, they couldn't get just what they were after." Universal could not have made a better choice; Binnie's Russell complemented perfectly Edward Arnold's flamboyant performance in the title part.

Binnie was again teamed with Edward Arnold in *Sutter's Gold* (1936), a very elaborate production (especially by Universal standards) that pleased neither critics nor the public. Universal loaned her to MGM for two supporting roles that she made notewor-

With Randolph Scott in *The Last of the Mohicans* **(UA '36).**

thy, although the films were not: *Rendezvous* (1935) and *Small Town Girl* (1936). For United Artists' flavorful remake of *The Last of the Mohicans* (1936), she turned in a fine interpretation of Alice Munro and later returned to Universal to play a gold digger with her eyes set on Victor McLaglen in *The Magnificent Brute* (1936). She joined her *Henry VIII* co-star Wendy Barrie in *Breezing Home* (1937) and ended her long-distance marriage to Samuel Joseph with a finalized divorce that she had filed September 22, 1936.

Deanna Durbin made a marked impression with her *Three Smart Girls* (1937) and Universal was fortunate to have Binnie in the cast as the scheming dame out to get sweet daddy Charles Winninger. By now Binnie was romantically linked with Don Alvarado and others, but remained on extremely friendly terms with her ex-spouse. Casting directors were well aware of Binnie's flair for playing the worldly, wicked, predatory "other woman" and cast her as such in *The First Hundred Years* (1938). She moved from this contemporary story to a tale of the Middle Ages, *The Adventures of Marco Polo* (1938), in which she played Alan Hale's nagging wife. Binnie traded quips and looks with Katharine Hepburn in *Holiday* (1938) and bolstered the quickie *Gateway* (1938) at Twentieth Century-Fox with her impersonation of a nimble-witted divorcée.

While playing Ralph Richardson's inconstant wife in *The Divorce of Lady X* (1938),[1] filmed in color in England, she was busily denying rumors of marriage to both Moss Hart and Jean Negulesco. She then astounded the film colony by entertaining her ex-husband, Samuel Joseph, when he visited Hollywood. Binnie was always an astute business woman, owning four dress shops in London and making a neat profit of some $60,000 by selling a Beverly Hills apartment house she had wisely purchased several years before. She received daily reports from her London businesses, profits and progress, and did most of the wholesale buying for the shops herself. Tall and slender, Binnie was a disciple of the sun, excelled in playing golf and tennis, and enjoyed horseback riding. Her philosophy was simple and direct: "Do the best you know how, be honest with everyone—but particularly with yourself."

[1]The property had been filmed before by Korda in 1933 under its original title, *Counsel's Opinion.* In the 1933 version Binnie played the leading feminine role which went this time to Korda's new interest, Merle Oberon.

With Barbara Read, Charles Winninger, Nan Grey, and Deanna Durbin in *Three Smart Girls* (Univ '37).

Wife, Husband and Friend (1939) would have been a dreary picture had it not been for Binnie's playing of an operatic artiste. She again displayed her versatility by playing Milady de Winter in the Ritz Brothers' zany *The Three Musketeers* (1939). Her catty, trouble-making divorcée, Blanche, in *Daytime Wife* (1939) proved she could take an unsympathetic part and play it to the hilt. For Warners, Binnie turned in a rapidly paced interpretation of a bogus French countess out to ensnare Pat O'Brien in *'Til We Meet Again* (1940). As in *Lady X*, Merle Oberon was again the top-billed female star. One critic noted of Miss Barnes' interpretation, "Her voluptuous lips, gliding walk and the gleam in her eye do not establish her as a candidate to be entrusted with another girl's husband or boyfriend. As long as there must be 'other women' in the movies, Miss Barnes feels that she might just as well play them." No one portrayed them better.

In October, 1940, Louella Parsons was back on the vaudeville circuit. Binnie and her husband of four weeks, former sports announcer and UCLA football star Mike Frankovich, joined the gossip columnist's stage show that played film-vaudeville houses across the country. The troupe included Sabu, William Orr, Robert Stack, Brenda Joyce, and Illona Massey. The irrepressible Binnie stopped every show with her bit. Wearing a tightly fitted blouse and baggy white pantaloons, she sang a satire from the English Music Halls, "Why Am I Always a Bridesmaid and Never a Blushing Bride?" The Parsons' show finale was a wild spoof of the conga with Louella and the entire troupe shaking maracas and themselves.

Prior to her marriage to Frankovich, Binnie had joined in an all-star revival of Noël Coward's *Tonight at 8:30,* with all proceeds going to the British War Relief Association of Southern California for direct transmission to the British Red Cross in London. All directors (there were eight) and players, including Edna Best, Herbert Marshall, Freddie Bartholomew, Edmund Gwenn, *et al.,* donated their services. Binnie was in the segment *Red Peppers,* with Reginald Gardiner as her partner, and Bartholomew, Claude Allister, Ernest Cossart, and Blanche Yurka in the one-act delight.

In 1973 Binnie would say of her nearly thirty-five-year marriage: "I had to do it to please or shock Louella Parsons. Louella used to say to Mike, 'Why did you marry that dreadful woman? A nice Jewish boy like you, marrying that dreadful English Catholic.' She had it backward and never did get it straight." One of Binnie's anniversary gifts to Mike was converting from Judaism to Catholicism. "He told me that was the loveliest present he ever got."

About her long, successful marriage and her intrepid raising of three children, Michael, Michelle, and Peter, Binnie is still ecstatic. "He's a dreamboat, a dynamic man, very intelligent. He was All-American, and a Phi Beta Kappa. When I married him I was supposed to be a star and people said, 'How can you marry a football player?' They forgot he was a quarterback. He calls all the plays." But he never called her Binnie, but "Dear" and one year gave her a diamond pin spelling out "Dear" which she wears as proudly as Arlene Francis wears her own diamond-encrusted heart. She and Mike were long-standing friends of Columbia Pictures mogul Harry Cohn. They were favorite bridge partners with the head of the studio, despite the fact that Binnie sued Columbia for being forced to wear a black bra and black panties for her role in Rosalind Russell's *This Thing Called Love* (1941). (She had been told the scene would be shot in silhouette.)

After her marriage, Binnie countinued her career, but never let it take precedence over her marriage. In fact, for a time, she supported her husband while he got started in the film-producing field. She was a delight in Claudette Colbert's *Skylark* (1941) and was the saving grace of the weak Jeanette MacDonald-Nelson Eddy musical, *I Married an Angel* (1942). She gave the picture a greatly needed boost with her lyrical advice on catching a man by singing the song "A Twinkle in Your Eye."

Her roles continued along the previous Hollywood-molded formula of the wisecracking dame or home-wrecker or ambitious hustler. Occasionally she had a chance at outlandish comedy, as in *Up in Mabel's Room* (1944) and *Getting Gertie's Garter* (1945). In *It's in the Bag* (1945) she played the highly brassy wife of Fred Allen. In 1945 Binnie became a panel member of radio's "Leave It to the Girls," along with Dorothy Kilgallen, Eloise McElhone, and others.

Since Christmas Eve, 1950, Gloria Swanson and Jose Ferrer had starred in a highly successful revival of Hecht and MacArthur's comedy *Twentieth Century* and on June 4, 1951, they were replaced by Robert Preston as the flamboyant producer and Binnie stepped into Miss Swanson's shoes as the tempestuous star Lily Garland. Her first crack at Broadway was less than notable, *Billboard* writing, "Miss Barnes' co-starring chore is not equally successful (as Preston's). Screenwise, she may be fine, but it must be faced that on a Broadway stage she is no Gloria Swanson. Her obvious lack of timing may again be set down to opening night nervousness, a matter which will likely correct itself via continued playing. But there is no excuse for her frequent awkwardness and arrant over-playing. What the Swanson can do with a shrug takes all of Barnes' arms and legs. If she can bring herself to forget that she's Binnie Barnes—and there seems no good reason why she can't—and get down to playing Lily Garland, she could be an excellent choice for the part. Even now she has moments that are top drawer." Paradoxically, for Binnie (she must have recalled *"The Twentieth Century Blues"* Noël Coward had written for her in *Cavalcade),* she never returned to the Broadway stage.

On July 1, 1951, she made her video debut on the premiere episode of "G.E. Guest House." On the initial telecast, hosted by Oscar Levant, she appeared with guest Cornelia Otis Skinner and drama critic Whitney Bolton. The same year she appeared on the screen in her husband's production of *Fugitive Lady* (1951) as the heavy, killed in a car crash over a cliff.

In 1953 Binnie returned to the screen in another Frankovich production, *Decameron Nights.* Joan Fontaine and Louis Jourdan headed the cast of this four-episode romantic pastiche. To bolster the production values of her husband's *Fire Over Africa* (1954), with Maureen O'Hara, Binnie made another guest appearance. Twelve years later she returned to the screen again, at Columbia for *The Trouble with Angels* (1966), directed by Ida Lupino, the daughter of her one-time pie-thrower. In 1968 when Columbia decided to make a sequel to this Rosalind Russell vehicle, Binnie was asked to repeat her role in *Where Angels Go—Trouble Follows.* In these years her video output was confined to two "Donna Reed Shows," the first in January, 1963, the last in March, 1966.

In 1973, the still bubbly Binnie agreed to participate in *Forty Carats,* produced by Frankovich for Columbia with Liv Ullmann and Edward Albert in the leads. In 1974 Binnie popped up as a "Mystery Guest" on the long-running TV quiz show "What's My Line," looking her usual lovely and sparkling self. "I'm in good shape," she admitted. "I enjoy gardening, planting flowers, avocado trees; of course, I don't mow the lawn. I swim every day. I do calisthenics. I walk a lot. We live on a hill in Beverly Hills. I park the car at the bottom of the street and walk down Sunset and back again. When you don't exercise, you go slack. I have an enormous amount of energy. I don't know why. I look at the health addicts who take all those vitamins, nine or more a day, and they don't look any better than I do. I just wash my face, put on lipstick and mascara, and that's it."

Binnie is not concerned with age. "It doesn't matter how old you are, it's how you feel. I'm frequently asked if I've had a face-lift. I haven't. I think I'll wait until I'm 80. I'll need it then. Every woman has a right to have her face fixed if it makes her feel good.

You have a right to look as well as you can. When I'm ready for it, I'll say to Mike, 'Goodbye, dear. I'm going to do it.' But Mike will probably bellow 'DEAR' and that will settle that nonsense.''

BINNIE BARNES

Night in Montmarte *(Gaumont 1931)*
Love Lies *(British International 1931)*
Dr. Josser, K.C. *(British International 1931)*
Out of the Blue *(British International 1931)*
Down Our Street *(Par British 1931)*
Murder at Covent Garden *(Woolf and Feedman Film Service 1931)*
Strip, Strip, Hooray *(British International 1931)*
Partners Please *(Producers Distributing Corp. 1931)*
The Last Coupon *(British International 1932)*
Old Spanish Customers *(British International 1932)*
Why Saps Leave Home *(British International 1932)*
Innocents In Chicago *(British International 1932)*
Council's Opinion *(London Films 1933)*
The Charming Deceiver [Heads We Go] *(British International 1933)*
Their Nights Out *(Wardour 1933)*
Taxi to Paradise *(Fox British 1933)*
The Private Life of Henry VIII *(UA British 1933)*
The Silver Spoon *(Gaumont 1934)*
Nine Forty-Five *(British International 1934)*
Forbidden Territory *(Progress Pictures 1934)*
The Lady Is Willing *(Col 1934)*
Gift of Gab *(Univ 1934)*
The Private Life of Don Juan *(UA 1934)*
There's Always Tomorrow *(Univ 1934)*
One Exciting Adventure *(Univ 1934)*
No Escape *(WB British 1934)*
Diamond Jim *(Univ 1935)*
Rendezvous *(MGM 1935)*
Sutter's Gold *(Univ 1936)*
Small Town Girl *(MGM 1936)*
The Last of the Mohicans *(UA 1936)*
The Magnificent Brute *(Univ 1936)*
Three Smart Girls *(Univ 1937)*
Breezing Home *(Univ 1937)*
Broadway Melody of 1938 *(MGM 1937)*
The First Hundred Years *(MGM 1938)*

The Adventures of Marco Polo *(UA 1938)*
Holiday *(Col 1938)*
Always Goodbye *(20th 1938)*
Gateway *(20th 1938)*
Tropic Holiday *(Par 1938)*
Three Blind Mice *(20th 1938)*
Thanks for Everything *(20th 1938)*
The Divorce of Lady X *(UA 1939)*
Wife, Husband and Friend *(20th 1939)*
The Three Musketeers *(20th 1939)*
Man about Town *(Par 1939)*
Frontier Marshal *(20th 1939)*
Daytime Wife *(20th 1939)*
'Til We Meet Again *(WB 1940)*
New Wine *(UA 1941)*
This Thing Called Love *(Col 1941)*
Angels with Broken Wings *(Rep 1941)*
Tight Shoes *(Univ 1941)*
Skylark *(Par 1941)*
Three Girls about Town *(Col 1941)*
Call out the Marines *(RKO 1942)*
I Married an Angel *(MGM 1942)*
In Old California *(Rep 1942)*
The Man from Down Under *(MGM 1943)*
Up in Mabel's Room *(UA 1944)*
Barbary Coast Gent *(MGM 1944)*
The Hour before the Dawn *(Par 1944)*
It's in the Bag *(UA 1945)*
The Spanish Main *(RKO 1945)*
Getting Gertie's Garter *(UA 1945)*
The Time of Their Lives *(Univ 1946)*
If Winter Comes *(MGM 1947)*
The Dude Goes West *(AA 1948)*
My Own True Love *(Par 1948)*
The Pirates of Capri *(Film Classics 1949)*
Fugitive Lady *(Rep 1951)*
Decameron Nights *(RKO 1953)*
Fire over Africa *(Col 1954)*
Shadow of the Eagle *(UA 1955)*
The Trouble with Angels *(Col 1966)*
Where Angels Go—Trouble Follows *(Col 1968)*
Forty Carats *(Col 1973)*

⑥

John Beal

Sometimes a performer, despite his talent and reasonably good looks, was not able to provide the necessary charisma to transform his leading man status into stardom. Such was the case of RKO's John Beal.

He was born in Joplin, Missouri, on Friday, August 13, 1909, to former concert pianist Agnes Harragan Bliedung and her husband Edmund A., owner of a large department store. Before graduating from Joplin High School in 1926, young James Alexander played the leading role in the senior class play. An aptitude for drawing took a detour when he entered the Wharton School of Finance at the University of Pennsylvania in 1927. But his talent for performing won him a place in the famed Mask and Wig Club, and he appeared in their 39th annual production in 1927 as Margaret Stuart in *Hoot Mon!* (or *Clans across the Seas*) singing "Just Let Me Live Like a Gypsy." For the Mask and Wig's 1929 fling he was a bond salesman in *This Way Out!* and in his final year at Penn he played the lead in *John Faust, PhD.,* singing "How Can a Devil Be Good" and "Hunter of Happiness." The director of this show was a brilliant actor and director named Jasper Newton Deeter who had founded one of the nation's best repertory companies at Rose Valley, Pennsylvania.

Deeter invited Beal to join his Hedgerow Theatre Repertory Company, so in May, 1930, John made his first appearance there in *The Inheritors.* He studied acting under Deeter and appeared in Hedgerow's productions of *Liliom* and *Mr. Pim Passes By.*

In September, 1930, Beal[2] made it to Broadway as an understudy in Frank Craven's *That's Gratitude,* followed in March, 1931, by a two-line bit in *Give Me Yesterday,* for which John also doubled as assistant stage manager. Prior to the latter play, he had returned to Philadelphia's Lyric Theatre in Jasper Deeter's production of *Ten Nights in a Bar Room.* The show's stage manager was Helen Craig whom, three years later, John would wed on Friday the thirteenth, July, 1934, in New York. (Daughters Theodora Emily and Tandy Johanna were born in November, 1942, and March, 1948, respectively.) The Beals are still married. (In August, 1975, their daughter Tita wed United Nations economist Eric Kruger.)

While seeking a foothold in New York's theatre, John enrolled at the Art Students League in Manhattan to increase his talent for drawing and painting. (He would later continue his studies at Los Angeles Chouinard Art School, and also study privately with

---

[2]There is some dispute as to whether John obtained his stage name from a casting director or by adopting the name of a University of Pennsylvania classmate, John Joseph Beal, who later became the actor's secretary.

With Katharine Hepburn in *The Little Minister* (RKO '34).

several famed artists.) Critics began noticing young Beal when he played in *No More Frontiers* at the Provincetown Playhouse in October, 1931, and he attracted attention with his acting-singing in *Wild Waves* in February, 1932. *Another Language,* which had tried out in the summer of 1931, opened on Broadway on April 25, 1932, and was a smash hit, running for 344 performances. John repeated his role as the idealistic nephew, in a cast that included Margaret Wycherly, Margaret Hamilton, Glenn Anders, and Dorothy Stickney. Beal's honest, splendid playing of the ambitious Jerry led him to Hollywood.

Metro-Goldwyn-Mayer filmed *Another Language* in 1933 and John repeated his well-shaded performance in a cast that included Helen Hayes and Robert Montgomery. (John would repeat his role yet again on "Lux Radio Theatre" in May, 1937, with Bette Davis, Fred MacMurray, and May Robson, and on another broadcast, in 1939, with Lillian Gish.) On the strength of his work in *Another Language,* critics hailed him as one of Hollywood's most promising discoveries, and the studios made him flattering film offers.

Beal still looked toward Broadway. "When I was in college plays," he told the press, "I received several screen offers. I declined them because I felt I was not equipped to make the best advantage of the opportunity. I feel the same way now. As a matter of fact, I do not think I am a very definite screen type. I would not be satisfied to be 'just another juvenile' breaking into pictures. I want to be able to play individual characterizations and I know that, without the benefit of greater achievements in the theatre, I will not be in a position to secure them in pictures."

So on November 20, 1933, John returned to Broadway in *She Loves Me Not,* with Burgess Meredith and Florence Rice. Beal learned to play the piano by ear and rote, and managed to finger some Arthur Schwartz songs in *She Loves Me Not.* His fascination with art continued (he sketched several of the cast members), and he studied singing, declaring that it was a great help for the regular speaking voice. After his 248 performances as Paul Lawton, he signed a contract with RKO.

John Barrymore had been cast in *Hat, Coat and Glove* (1934) as a lawyer defending his wife's lover (John Beal) against a murder charge. But Barrymore, already on the physical decline, had to be replaced by Ricardo Cortez. The picture was mildly successful and Beal performed well in the juvenile lead. On April 14, 1934, John participated in a one-hour broadcast from Hollywood headlining George Arliss, Loretta Young, Constance Bennett, Ronald Colman, Spencer Tracy, and Russ Columbo. Beal and Florence Rice did a scene from *She Loves Me Not* as part of the radio program.

John was fortunate in his next assignment: the plum role of Gavin Dishart, *The Little Minister* (1934), opposite RKO's new reigning Queen, Katharine Hepburn. As the young pastor of Auld Lich Kirk, John was splendid in a mild-mannered, straightforward way, but the film did little to advance Miss Hepburn's already stagnating screen career.

On loan to United Artists, John was properly idealistic as Marius in *Les Miserables* (1935), in which Fredric March and Charles Laughton were the stars. RKO's remake of *Laddie* (1935) was a charming little film with John in love with the outclassed daughter (Gloria Stuart) of uppercrust Englishman Donald Crisp. John was again assigned opposite Katharine Hepburn in what RKO hoped would be a rekindling of the magic flame Hepburn and John Barrymore created in *A Bill of Divorcement* (1933). Kate was to play an aspiring composer in love with alcoholic musical conductor Barrymore. But The Great Profile's actual alcoholic deterioration forced RKO to substitute Francis Lederer in the part. However, Mr. Lederer could not work with Miss Hepburn and Charles Boyer finally played the lush orchestra leader while Beal was believable as the young millionaire rejected by Hepburn in favor of her rehabilitating Boyer from the drunken depths. It was all-unabashed soap opera, but played for all its worth by the cast. On October 7, 1935, John was heard with Helen Chandler on a radio broadcast of *The Wren*.

In Hollywood John had renewed his friendship with former theatre friends, among whom was playwright Lynn Riggs. Riggs felt Beal was right for his new play, and John, whose RKO contract permitted him stage work, opened on Broadway on January 16, 1936, in *Russet Mantle*. Beal's wife Helen was in the cast, as was Harry Bellaver, another former Hedgerow player. Beal enthused to the press, "I hope some day, if I keep on acting, that I will be a good actor. And the stage is the only place to learn to be a good actor." *Russet Mantle* lasted for 117 performances.

For RKO's upcoming screen version of Maxwell Anderson's *Winterset* (1936), John was announced for the part of the Shadow, with Lionel Barrymore as the Judge and Anne Shirley as the female lead. By the time the feature went through the cameras, RKO had imported Burgess Meredith and Margo to repeat their original stage roles, and Edward Ellis had become the Judge and Stanley Ridges the Shadow. Beal and Miss Shirley were shuttled instead into another remake of Bret Harte's *M'Liss* (1936), in which both were unfortunately miscast. John was then announced as the juvenile lead-singer of RKO's proposed musical *Convention in Cuba*, to feature Betty Grable and Helen Broderick. Instead of making that film, John was assigned to a heavily laden melodrama, *We Who Are About to Die* (1936), based on David Lamson's book written while in prison on death row. Beal played with great intensity the role of a framed convict getting a last minute reprieve from death row, with proof of his innocence supplied by Ann Dvorak and Preston Foster.

John's RKO career was reduced to B's and sub-B's in such trifles as *The Man Who Found Himself* (1937), with Joan Fontaine, and *Border Cafe* (1937), with Harry Carey,

With Ann Dvorak in *We Who Are About to Die* (RKO '36).

which concluded Beal's studio contract. He signed with MGM for which he made *Double Wedding* (1937). William Powell and Myrna Loy were the stars of the film, while John's screen partner was his *She Loves Me Not* co-player, Florence Rice. Gladys George was the lead in Metro's second talkie version of *Madame X* (1937), with John cast as her lawyer son. Then he was matched with Florence Rice again, this time in *Beg, Borrow or Steal* (1937), a minor film starring Frank Morgan. Beal ended his second studio tenure with *Port of Seven Seas* (1938), an unlikely rendition of Marcel Pagnol's play *Fanny*. John replaced James Stewart in the small role of Marius.

Through the sharp performances of Edward G. Robinson, Wendy Barrie, and John, Columbia's *I Am the Law* managed to elevate itself into an upper class B film. At Paramount John played the romantic lead opposite Jean Parker in *The Arkansas Traveler* (1938), with Bob Burns and Fay Bainter. The quartet repeated their performances on "Lux Radio Theatre" in January, 1939. Meanwhile, in early October, 1938, John and his wife opened in *Soliloquy* in Santa Barbara. The show was further tried out in Los Angeles and San Francisco, and then moved on to Broadway where it folded after two performances. John remained in New York for what proved to be another quick-closing show, *Miss Swan Expects*.

The summer found John on the straw-hat circuit in *The Petrified Forest* and *Goodbye Again*. The fall of 1939 saw John in the short-lived *I Know What I Like*. Meanwhile he returned to Hollywood for a featured role in the Bob Hope-Paulette Goddard remake of *The Cat and the Canary* (1939). He made one more film, *The Great Commandment* (1939), at Twentieth Century-Fox and then left Hollywood for two years. He toured the summer circuit in *No Time for Comedy* with Arlene Francis, and, while his wife Helen was having great success on Broadway in *Johnny Belinda*, Beal signed with the Theatre Guild for *Liberty Jones*. Despite the directing of John Houseman, the writing of Philip Barry, and the casting of Nancy Coleman, Tom Ewell, Norman Lloyd, Joseph Anthony, Constance Dowling, Craig Mitchell, and John, the show shut down in February, 1941, after only 22 performances.

Until he enlisted in the Army Air Forces Transport Command in 1942, becoming a staff sergeant, John turned out a set of bottom-of-the-bill film entries. A rare exception was Warner Bros.' *Edge of Darkness* (1943), which depicted Norwegian war courage. In this Errol Flynn-Ann Sheridan melodrama, John did well as the traitorous Johann. Later, during his military service, he would transfer to the motion picture unit of the air force, appearing in and directing some fifteen films.

When his war service concluded, John replaced Elliott Nugent in the long-running *The Voice of the Turtle* in January, 1946. *Carrot and Cub* with John and Bert Lytell tried out in New Haven and Philadelphia, but never made it to Broadway for the spring, 1947, season.

Beal returned to Hollywood for minor roles in similar pictures through 1949, finding time between studio work to appear in West Coast stage productions of *Eurydice* with Viveca Lindfors, and Anouilh's *Antigone* with his wife and Colin Keith-Johnson. John also founded the Actors' Hobby Market.

It was another replacement assignment that brought John back to Broadway. He filled the role vacated by William Eythe in the musical revue *Lend an Ear* as of November 14, 1949. After the New York run, he toured with the show.

At the Brattle Theatre in Cambridge, Massachusetts, in January, 1952, he played the lead in *Ivanov* and then returned to the Coast for a stand-out role of Doc, an experimental prison psychologist in Stanley Kramer's *My Six Convicts* (1952). During the summer of 1952 he was the genie in the Civic Light Opera's production of *Jollyanna*, starring Bobby Clark and Mitzi Gaynor.

With Bob Burns in *The Arkansas Traveler* (Par '38).

Like many another former youthful leading man, John found steady employment on television. He was in the musical *Hit the Deck* on the small screen in 1950 and popped up on a wide variety of video anthology shows. Along with Franchot Tone, Edward Arnold, Robert Cummings, and others, John helped to make "Studio One's" telecast of *12 Angry Men* quite memorable. Beal headed a comedy-audience participation series for CBS-TV in 1953 called "Freedom Rings" and that summer was in the stage tryout of *The Trip to Bountiful* that made it to Broadway at the end of the year (briefly) without John. During 1954 he toured the U.S. and Canada with *The Fourposter* and then took over (in May, 1955) the part of Captain Fisby in the long-running Broadway hit *Teahouse of the August Moon*.

While in New York, John filmed *Brave Tomorrow,* playing a TV writer whose marriage is on the skids until he suffers a heart attack while boarding a train at Grand Central Station. His illness reunites him with his wife (Augusta Dabney). It was to be released by RKO, but instead was first shown on "Robert Montgomery Presents" as *The Long Way Home* and was later released in 1957 by Universal as *That Night! The Vampire* (1957) was another movie variation of *Dr. Jekyll and Mr. Hyde* and featured John as a doctor taking transformation capsules. Between TV assignments in 1958, John filled out the year by playing *Mister Roberts* in Canada, *Everyman Today* at Wooster, Massachusetts, and, in January, 1959, was seen in *The Chase* in Milwaukee.

For New Haven's WHNC, John hosted, interviewed, and commented on "Hollywood's Best" during a season when he was seen on nearly every major TV show. For Twentieth Century-Fox he played the dreary, alcoholic brother of Margaret Leighton in a platitudinous version of William Faulkner's *The Sound and the Fury* (1959). The next year he was on ABC-TV's "Road to Reality," a series about group therapy. His final

Hollywood film was Walt Disney's *Ten Who Dared* (1960), in which he was the one-armed Major exploring the Colorado River.

Beal's versatility and talent, if largely ignored by Hollywood, found steady outlets on the stage and television. Throughout the Sixties he was frequently employed on TV. In the summer of 1966 he played the straw-hat theatres in *A Man for All Seasons* and joined with Sylvia Sidney in *The Little Foxes*. He was at the Cherry Lane Theatre in Greenwich Village in the fall of 1966 with three one-act Thornton Wilder plays.

Beal's belief that the stage was the catalyst for becoming a good actor never ceased. He constantly worked, seeking the challenges that Hollywood never offered him. He was among the group who joined the 1969 Broadway revival of *Our Town,* was in the short-lived musical version of *Billy (Budd)* that opened and closed March 22, 1969, and in June of that year opened in the Lincoln Center Repertory production of *In the Matter of J. Robert Oppenheimer. The Candyapple* in which he appeared was a fall, 1970, Broadway disaster, and the next summer he replaced Robert Ryan as James Tyrone in the NYC revival of *Long Day's Journey into Night.* As the Seventies roll on, so does Mr. Beal, and he is seen in small roles on television as, for example, a recent featured role on "Kojak."

Beal's screen career remains another example of the deplorable waste of talent in which Hollywood indulged with such gusto throughout the Thirties.

JOHN BEAL

Another Language *(MGM, 1933)*
Hat, Coat and Glove *(RKO 1934)*
The Little Minister *(RKO 1934)*
Les Miserables *(UA 1935)*
Laddie *(RKO 1935)*
Break of Hearts *(RKO 1935)*
M'Liss *(RKO 1936)*
We Who Are About to Die *(RKO 1936)*
The Man Who Found Himself *(RKO 1937)*
Border Cafe *(RKO 1937)*
Danger Patrol *(RKO 1937)*
Double Wedding *(MGM 1937)*
Madame X *(MGM 1937)*
Beg, Borrow or Steal *(MGM 1937)*
Port of Seven Seas *(MGM 1938)*
I Am the Law *(Col 1938)*
The Arkansas Traveler *(Par 1938)*
The Cat and the Canary *(Par 1939)*
The Great Commandment *(20th 1939)*
Ellery Queen and the Perfect Crime *(Col 1941)*

Doctors Don't Tell *(Rep 1941)*
Atlantic Convoy *(Col 1942)*
Stand by All Networks *(Col 1942)*
One Thrilling Night *(Mon 1942)*
Edge of Darkness *(WB 1943)*
Let's Have Fun *(Col 1943)*
Key Witness *(Col 1947)*
So Dear to My Heart *(RKO 1948)*
Alimony *(EL 1949)*
Song of Surrender *(Par 1949)*
Chicago Deadline *(Par 1949)*
Messenger of Peace *(Astor 1950)*
My Six Convicts *(Col 1952)*
Remains to Be Seen *(MGM 1953)*
The Country Parson *(Astor 1954)*
The Vampire *(UA 1957)*
That Night! *(Univ 1957)*
The Sound and the Fury *(20th 1959)*
Ten Who Dared *(BV 1960)*

7

Louise Beavers

In his book *The Negro in Films* (1952) Peter Noble says of Louise Beavers' film career that it is "a striking example of wasted talent." Like her professional contemporary in movies, Stepin Fetchit, Louise was usually forced into playing a stereotyped portrayal of the "typical" black, and was never allowed by film-makers to give full range to her array of acting talents. And it was not even Miss Beavers' fortune to win recognition as *the* best portrayer of cinema mammies—a role with which she was often stuck. That distinction went to Hattie McDaniel, who won a Best Supporting Actress Award for her performance in *Gone with the Wind* (1939). But one needs only witness a few of Louise's celluloid appearances to realize how capable a performer she was, whether as the beloved friend of Claudette Colbert in *Imitation of Life* (1934) or later, as the energetic housekeeper of Cary Grant and Myrna Loy in *Mr. Blandings Builds His Dream House* (1948).

She was born in Cincinnati, Ohio, on Saturday, March 8, 1902, and when she was eleven years old the family moved to California, where she graduated from Pasadena High School and sang in the church choir. Her mother, a voice teacher, started Louise's voice training at an early age and, after high school, instead of going into concert work as her mother had planned, Louise joined an all-female minstrel show. Occasionally she took a turn in vaudeville. She spent a brief time studying nursing because she liked the white uniforms, but the profession depressed her. Also, she spent some time as an attendant in the dressing room of a famous photographer and later applied for a job as maid to one of Paramount's brightest stars, Leatrice Joy. Miss Joy recently reflected, "I think I engaged Louise because of her beautiful expression and her lovely smile. She was lovely to look upon really, and she understood me. I was very grateful." Between her duties as Miss Joy's personal maid, Louise did walk-ons, crowd scenes, and brief bits in silent pictures, beginning in 1924.

Louise would play the role of Maum Maria in Cecil B. DeMille's *Reap the Wild Wind* (1942), but her first experience with the colorful director was twenty years earlier. Details Leatrice Joy: "Louise was the only one in that entire studio who was never afraid of Mr. DeMille. One of my clearest memories of DeMille's demand for realism was one day when he was standing tensely just out of camera range during the shooting of a scene in which I was the glamorous queen of a Bacchanalian feast in the film called

With Will Rogers and Marion Nixon in *Too Busy to Work* (1932).

Manslaughter. Strapped to his side Mr. DeMille had two large pearl-handle revolvers. Part of the decor immediately flanking the side of my throne were two large Bengal Tigers—live. By the end of the day, with the lights going on and off, plus the confusion of hundreds of extras, these poor beasts were becoming restless. I could feel their hot breath against my legs. Mr. DeMille's desire for realism was sometimes alarming.

"The wardrobe women arrived at this point to attach a 19-yard, gold-encrusted velvet train I was supposed to wear for the final shooting of the scene. They started to sew the heavy train to my shoulder straps. My beloved Louise stood there and did not like the idea, brushed the wardrobe women aside, ripped out all the stitches they had sewn and clipped the train to my shoulder straps with small safety pins. Then she addressed everyone on the set, including Mr. DeMille, 'When these two cats has had enough and they start running and Mr. DeMille starts shootin' them guns, I don't want this child bothered with no 19 yards of train.' " Leatrice admitted it could have been very danger-ous and, had the tigers become too restless, Mr. DeMille would have been forced to do something about it. The actress has always remained deeply grateful to Louise for her foresight and protection.

Miss Joy recalls another earlier occasion when Louise came to the rescue. In 1921 Leatrice had just signed a contract with Paramount and was assigned to their resident genius director, Cecil B. DeMille, for a film called *Saturday Night,* with Conrad Nagel. She was frightfully nervous and filled with a starlet's fear, overly anxious to prove herself. Then word came that the queen of the lot, Gloria Swanson, was visiting the DeMille set. Leatrice panicked, pacing her dressing room listing reasons why she could not act in front of Paramount's star of stars. Louise remained silent and let Leatrice's pacing run down, then took her hand and, with her famous smile and a chuckle in her voice, said: "Honey, you know what you're going to do? You're not going to be staying here in this dressing room of yours, a scared star. You're going right out of here and bid the time of day to Miss Swanson, and, if you care to, you can always—over your shoulder, like—say, 'Miss Swanson, draw up a chair, honey, and learn off me!' " Louise was ever most considerate and extremely loyal, and *knew* she worked for the only star on the Paramount lot, or on any other lot in Hollywood. Everyday studio gossip was beneath her. She preferred spreading happiness rather than discontent. Miss Joy adds, "I always considered Louise my severest critic, and my best friend has never been properly placed according to her value in our beautiful world of picture people."

Louise's first screen role of any definition was as a cook in Universal's *Uncle Tom's Cabin* (1927). After Mary Pickford selected her for the role of Mammy Julia in *Coquette* (1929), Louise was never at a loss for movie assignments. In Miss Pickford's autobiogra-phy, *Sunshine and Shadows* (1955), she chose a still from *Coquette* (for which she won an Oscar) in which she is being comforted by Louise Beavers. Louise went to Warner Bros. to play Hannah and sing "Some of These Days" in Dolores Costello's *The Glad Rag Doll* (1929), and remained on that lot to play Lilyan Tashman's maid in *Gold Diggers of Broadway* (1929). The chic Miss Tashman asked Louise to be her personal maid, and an agreement was reached where her duties with Tashman would not conflict with movie parts. The arrangement was soon disbanded and Louise stayed with the more profitable and less frustrating movie business.

Most of Louise's celluloid roles were of the same cut and pattern, but her jovial, smiling face was becoming known to the world's movie audiences. One of her choicest maid parts was in Fox's *Good Sport* (1931) where, as the domestic named September, she outlines just what keeps a kept woman to naive, wide-eyed Linda Watkins. Louise could be seen in over a dozen pictures yearly and, when given something other than the usual generalization of a family maid, she performed beautifully.

One of Louise's more colorful film assignments was due to Mae West's genius for casting the right performer in the right role. When she was preparing to film her play *Diamond Lil* she chose Louise for the role of her maid Pearl. *She Done Him Wrong* (1933) was shot in eighteen days after beginning November 21, 1932, and was the acknowledged money-earner that saved Paramount from selling out to Metro-Goldwyn-Mayer. The film was highly censorable for the day and age, but the dialogue sparkled with wit "a la West." Louise's scenes with Mae were priceless, and well timed, such as when she mentioned onscreen she wouldn't want no policeman to catch her with no petticoats on and Mae cracked, "No policeman? How about a nice fireman?" And when Louise's Pearl reminds Mae she was never poor by saying, "But you ain't been in the circumstances where da wolf was at your door," Mae replied, "The wolf at my door? Why, I remember when he came into my room and had pups." The two actresses played well together.

Louise continued appearing in picture after picture and was excellent as Jean Harlow's ever loyal companion-maid in *Bombshell* (1933) at Metro. Louise's personal life was quiet, and she lived with her mother. When pressed about her love life, she claimed, "A husband is just one more mouth to feed" (in the late Fifties she would marry Le Roy Moore). When asked about her career, Louise laughed, "They tell me I get better as I get older. So I guess I'll be going to the studio in a wheel chair before I'm through, but I'll be going as long as there's a part for me." The great part for her arrived in 1934 when Universal filmed Fannie Hurst's *Imitation of Life*.

Imitation of Life was the first important Hollywood feature to humanize the Negro servant and to include a subplot of the black servant's daughter trying to pass as white. It was controversial, attacked by both the white and black press and championed by others. And Louise, as Delilah, was superb. *Motion Picture Herald* wrote, "Miss Bea-

With Claudette Colbert in *Imitation of Life* (Univ. '34).

With Betty Roadman and Evelyn Venable in *The Headleys at Home* (Standard '38).

vers, the extremely capable Negro actress, comes very near to being the star of the picture partially because her problem as the Negro mother is the more poignant of the picture's dual theme." *Photoplay* enthused in selecting the film and Louise's performance as one of the month's best, "You'll weep gallons but you'll love this warm, human story of the fine friendship between two mothers of different races allied in the common cause of their children. Bea Pullman (Claudette Colbert) sells maple syrup for a living when along comes shining black Aunt Delilah (Louise Beavers—and what a performance!) with her little girl Peola. Result: Aunt Delilah's Pancake Flour eventually makes a fortune for the two women."

The widespread criticism among the black community following the release of *Imitation of Life* was countered by Fannie Hurst who felt her Negro characters were serious, and so afforded wider scope for Negro actors and actresses. The prime objections of the black community were Aunt Delilah's refusal to share in the financial rewards of the successful business (preferring "the biggest funeral Harlem ever did see, complete with white horse pulling a white hearse") and her telling her daughter Peola to "Bow your head. You got to learn to take it. Your pappy kept beating his fists against life all his days until it eat him through."

Louise disliked cooking, and the picture featured her flipping pancakes, which she particularly detested. Yet she forced herself to gain weight to complete Aunt Delilah's screen image and learned to speak with a southern drawl that was foreign to her. In Donald Bogle's *Toms, Coons, Mulattoes, Mammies and Bucks* (1973) the first illustration in the book is of Louise as a "jolly, but submissive, cook, forever on the verge of

Publicity pose, c. '39.

heartfelt tears as she whips up a batch of pancakes." Bogle also notes that "Louise Beavers had the first opportunity in talkies to create a wholly elevated Christian Negro with her doctrine of black Christian stoicism."

With help from the NAACP Louise succeeded in having the word "nigger" deleted from the script, but her victory was weakened when she was called to the front office on several occasions and made to pronounce the word "Negro" repeatedly. Her performance deserved a nomination for an Academy Award as one of the best performances of the year by an actress. But because of the prevailing climate of racism, the occasion never arose. Columnist Jimmy Fidler a Southerner by birth, was outraged by such neglect and took the industry to task as being racially prejudiced.

With the critical acclaim she received after the national release of *Imitation of Life,* Louise arrived in New York City on February 13, 1935, to open an "in person" tour to commence two days later at the Roxy Theatre. She was billed as "Hollywood's foremost character actress" and did a scene from *Imitation of Life,* sang several songs, and managed a creditable dance. She was one hundred percent pro.

When she returned to Hollywood, however, it was back to playing the stereotype faithful servant. But every once in a while she would garner an exceptional role such as that of the former slave Toinette, raising and loving a white orphaned boy in *Rainbow on the River* (1936), with Bobby Breen. Her performance was a joy to behold. In 1939 she was Carole Lombard's cook, Lily, in *Made for Each Other,* and in 1942 was the housekeeper in Paramount's *Holiday Inn* (her favorite role), in which she sang a duet, "Abraham," with Bing Crosby. In *Jack London* (1943) her scenes with fiery Michael O'Shea clearly showed that, given the opportunity, Louise could be an interesting dramatic actress. But the roles of servitude continued.

As Cary Grant's maid Gussie, she supplied her ad executive-employer with the winning slogan for baked ham: "Not ham! Wham! If you ain't eating WHAM, you ain't eating Ham." All of which helped to make the film *Mr. Blandings Builds His Dream House* more delightful. In 1950 she gave a tender, touching performance as Jackie Robinson's mother in *The Jackie Robinson Story* and then in 1952 made three minor pictures.

"Somebody bawl for Beulah?" came from a shining black face belonging to a jovial woman of large proportions for her five-feet, four-inch structure that contained considerable charm and energy. Ethel Waters had been the original *Beulah* on television in 1950, followed by Hattie McDaniel, who had played the character on radio. But on April 29, 1952, the role of the housekeeper, companion, and counsellor of TV's Henderson family was placed in the tender hands of Louise Beavers. As "Beulah" she solved the family problems while trying to land a reluctant husband, conceding, "I'm a gal whose love life isn't cookin' cuz most of the single men are tookin'." Louise's constant warm nature could bring reality to such lines as "If love is sweepin' the country I must be using the wrong type of broom."

On July 22, 1952, Hattie McDaniel, Louise's very close friend, returned to pinch hit as "Beulah" for six weeks while Miss Beavers took a vacation.

On March 9, 1956, Louise was seen in the role of Effie on TV's "Star Stage" telecast of *Cleopatra Collins,* starring Betty Grable. On February 24, 1957, she made her legitimate stage debut. Huntington Hartford's pretentiously produced *Praise House* opened at San Francisco's Alcazar Theatre. Louise starred as a psalm-singing Mammy, but could not do much with the poorly conceived role and play. The show faded quickly and Louise returned to television for the March 27, 1957, episode of "Playhouse 90" entitled *The Hostess with the Mostess,* in which Shirley Booth was Perle Mesta. In 1958 Louise was once again a cook in *The Goddess,* with Kim Stanley, and in 1960 she played Rose in

All the Fine Young Cannibals, in which Pearl Bailey took what little acting honors there were in the dreary movie. Louise's final screen appearance was as Bob Hope and Ruth Hussey's maid in United Artists' *The Facts of Life* (1960).

On October 25, 1962, Louise entered a Hollywood hospital after years of struggling with diabetes. She died on October 26, 1962, after spending over three decades in motion pictures. On February 17, 1976, Louise, Joseph Baker, and Canada Lee were posthumously inducted into the Black Filmmakers Hall of Fame at ceremonies held at the Paramount Theatre in Oakland, California. Leatrice Joy, who had remained friendly with Louise across the years, now writes: "Somehow it is rather difficult to realize that Louise is dead. No. I say no because how can anyone bury in the ground the qualities of sincerity, loyalty, tenderness? All these were my Louise. And, I'm sure wherever she is she is still spreading those God-given qualities and is busy as a bumble bee, making everyone happy."

LOUISE BEAVERS

Uncle Tom's Cabin *(Univ 1927)*
Coquette *(UA 1929)*
The Glad Rag Doll *(WB 1929)*
Barnum Was Right *(Univ 1929)*
Gold Diggers of Broadway *(WB 1929)*
Nix on Dames *(Fox 1929)*
Wall Street *(Col 1929)*
Second Choice *(WB 1930)*
She Couldn't Say No *(WB 1930)*
Recaptured Love *(WB 1930)*
Wide Open *(WB 1930)*
Back Pay *(WB 1930)*
Safety in Numbers *(Par 1930)*
Millie *(RKO 1931)*
Heaven on Earth *(Univ 1931)*
Party Husbands *(WB 1931)*
Annabelle's Affairs *(Fox 1931)*
Up for Murder *(Univ 1931)*
Don't Bet on Women *(Fox 1931)*
Girls about Town *(Par 1931)*
Sundown Trail *(RKO 1931)*
Good Sport *(Fox 1931)*
Six Cylinder Love *(Fox 1931)*
Ladies of the Big House *(Par 1931)*
The Expert *(WB 1932)*
Freaks *(MGM 1932)*
Night World *(Univ 1932)*
It's Tough to Be Famous *(WB 1932)*
Young America *(Fox 1932)*
Midnight Lady *(Chesterfield 1932)*
Street of Women *(WB 1932)*
What Price Hollywood? *(RKO 1932)*
Unashamed *(MGM 1932)*
Divorce in the Family *(MGM 1932)*
The Strange Love of Molly Louvain *(FN 1932)*
Wild Girl *(Fox 1932)*
Hell's Highway *(Univ 1932)*
Too Busy to Work *(Fox 1932)*
Pick Up *(Par 1933)*
She Done Him Wrong *(Par 1933)*
42nd Street *(WB 1933)*
Girl Missing *(WB 1933)*
What Price Innocence *(Col 1933)*
A Shriek in the Night *(Allied 1933)*
Hold Your Man *(MGM 1933)*
Her Bodyguard *(Par 1933)*
The Big Cage *(Univ 1933)*
Notorious But Nice *(Chesterfield 1933)*
Bombshell *(MGM 1933)*
Her Splendid Folly *(Progressive 1933)*
In the Money *(Chesterfield 1933)*
Bedside *(WB 1934)*
I've Got Your Number *(WB 1934)*
Cheaters *(Liberty 1934)*
Glamour *(Univ 1934)*
Hat, Coat and Glove *(RKO 1934)*

The Merry Frinks *(Univ 1934)*
Imitation of Life *(Univ 1934)*
West of the Pecos *(RKO 1934)*
I Believed in You *(Fox 1934)*
Merry Wives of Reno *(WB 1934)*
A Modern Hero *(WB 1934)*
Registered Nurse *(WB 1934)*
Annapolis Farewell *(Par 1935)*
Bullets or Ballots *(WB 1936)*
Wives Never Know *(Par 1936)*
General Spanky *(MGM 1936)*
Rainbow on the River *(RKO 1936)*
Make Way for Tomorrow *(Par 1937)*
Wings over Honolulu *(Univ 1937)*
Love in a Bungalow *(Univ 1937)*
The Last Gangster *(MGM 1937)*
Scandal Street *(Par 1938)*
Life Goes On *(Million Dollar Productions 1938)*
Brother Rat *(WB 1938)*
Reckless Living *(Univ 1938)*
The Headleys at Home *(Standard 1938)*
Peck's Bad Boy with the Circus *(RKO 1938)*
Made for Each Other *(UA 1939)*
The Lady's from Kentucky *(Par 1939)*
Reform School *(Million Dollar Productions 1939)*
Women without Names *(Par 1940)*
Parole Fixer *(Par 1940)*
No Time for Comedy *(WB 1940)*
I Want a Divorce *(Par 1940)*
Virginia *(Par 1941)*
Belle Starr *(20th 1941)*
Sign of the Wolf *(Mon 1941)*
Kisses for Breakfast *(WB 1941)*
Shadow of the Thin Man *(MGM 1941)*
The Vanishing Virginian *(MGM 1941)*
Reap the Wild Wind *(Par 1942)*
Young America *(20th 1942)*
Holiday Inn *(Par 1942)*
The Big Street *(RKO 1942)*
Tennessee Johnson *(MGM 1942)*
Seven Sweethearts *(MGM 1942)*
Good Morning, Judge! *(Univ 1943)*
Du Barry Was a Lady *(MGM 1943)*
Top Man *(Univ 1943)*
All by Myself *(Univ 1943)*
Jack London *(UA 1943)*
There's Something about a Soldier *(Col 1943)*
Follow the Boys *(Univ 1944)*
South of Dixie *(Univ 1944)*
Dixie Jamboree *(PRC 1944)*
Barbary Coast Gent *(MGM 1944)*
Delightfully Dangerous *(UA 1945)*
Lover Come Back *(Univ 1946)*
Banjo *(RKO 1947)*

Good Sam *(RKO 1948)*
Mr. Blandings Builds His Dream House *(RKO 1948)*
For the Love of Mary *(Univ 1948)*
Tell It to the Judge *(Col 1949)*
Girl's School *(Col 1950)*
The Jackie Robinson Story *(EL 1950)*
Colorado Sundown *(Rep 1952)*
I Dream of Jeanie *(Rep 1952)*

Never Wave at a WAC *(RKO 1952)*
Goodbye, My Lady *(WB 1956)*
You Can't Run Away from It *(Col 1956)*
Teenage Rebel *(20th 1956)*
Tammy and the Bachelor *(Univ 1957)*
The Goddess *(Col 1958)*
All the Fine Young Cannibals *(MGM 1960)*
The Facts of Life *(UA 1960)*

8

Ralph Bellamy

Among the players of the Thirties was a six-foot, one-inch, blue-eyed actor whom Hollywood took too much for granted. The film capital soon decided that casting him in any film would assure at least one good performance and thus created a niche for this fine actor. The industry categorized him as a character who was "dull and charming." That Ralph Bellamy survived such professional malpractice is a credit to his quiet, unassuming pursuit of his career. Only later in life would he find rewarding acting assignments, and those were generally in mediums other than motion pictures.

Ralph Rexford Bellamy was born on Friday, June 17, 1904, in Chicago, Illinois, to advertising executive Charles Rexford Bellamy and his wife Illa Louise (Smith) Bellamy. At the New Trier High School young Ralph headed the dramatic club, graduating in 1922, after forming his own North Shore players. He used the play *Suppressed Desires* for their opening performance.

His artistic fervor was definitely oriented towards the theatre. He was related to GeorgeAnne Bellamy who once played Juliet to David Garrick's Romeo in the eighteenth century. He was also related to Edward Bellamy, author of *Looking Backward,* a book that enjoyed phenomenal success. A cousin, Eben Rexford, gained immortality by writing the song "Silver Threads among the Gold."

Ralph made his stage debut under the tutelage of elderly Shakespearean actor William Owen. Owen offered him the difficult leading role in *The Servant in the House* as well as the roles of Old Matt and Wash Gibbs in *The Shepherd of the Hills.* Later Ralph made a midwest tour on the Chautauqua circuit. He played in several stock companies in the midwest (Madison, Wisconsin, and Evansville, Indiana), and in 1922 he married Alice Delbridge. Ever since telling his parents in 1920, "I've just made a decision. I'm going to be an actor," Bellamy remained steadfast and never sought any other job. He would play any role assigned to him, regardless of the character's age. By 1924 he was appearing in repertory with The Beach and Jones Tent Show Troupe and, a year later, in a company managed by actor Charles Winninger.

The Ralph Bellamy Players were organized in 1925 at the Princess Theatre in Des Moines, Iowa, and for two seasons played the midwest with Ralph as *Rip Van Winkle* and the Reverend Davidson in *Rain.* The Bellamy troupe traveled from Des Moines to Rochester, Providence to Nashville. During one of their engagements Ralph met actress Catherine Willard who would later score a Broadway hit in *The Great Gatsby.* After

With Ruth Chatterton in a pose for *The Magnificent Lie* **(Par '31).**

Alice Delbridge divorced Bellamy in Detroit, Michigan, in 1931, he would marry Miss Willard on July 6, 1931, in Reno, Nevada. They would become the parents of two children, Lynn and Willard.

After the Bellamy Players were disbanded, Ralph came to New York where he made the rounds of all the casting offices. He was finally given the role of Ben Davis in *Town Boy*. In this play he made his Broadway debut at the Belmont Theatre on October 4, 1929. Unfortunately the show closed the next day.

Ralph toured with Hope Williams in *Holiday* and later with Helen Hayes in *Coquette*. He returned to Broadway in the role of Texas in Lynn Riggs' *Roadside*. Brooks Atkinson wrote in the *New York Times* "In this bravado part Ralph Bellamy spoke with the authority of a strapping adventurer." Percy Hammond commented that he played the role with sweep and gusto and commended him for his "pipe-organ voice." *Roadside,* which opened on September 26, 1930, only lasted eleven performances. But it did bring Ralph offers of motion picture contracts.

He signed with Joseph Schenck at $650 a week, but he had to borrow funds from his New York pals to get to the West Coast. Schenck immediately loaned Bellamy to MGM and he made his picture debut as gangster-killer Johnny Franks in George Hill's *The Secret Six* (1931), supporting Wallace Beery, Clark Gable, and Jean Harlow. A fellow producer confided to Schenck at the time that although Bellamy was a good actor he was not right for the screen. Schenck released him from his contract after loaning him to Paramount to play the blind World War I soldier who falls in love with New Orleans cafe singer Ruth Chatterton in *The Magnificent Lie* (1931). He gave a good performance in the picture, and the results brought him offers from other studios.

Fox cast him as a ruthless German captain in charge of a World War I prison camp in *Surrender* (1931). This led the actor to signing a short term pact with that studio. Fox loaned him to Columbia for a badly written newspaperman role in Frank Capra's sudsy *Forbidden* (1931), starring Barbara Stanwyck. Back at Fox Ralph was an incorruptible police chief with Spencer Tracy in *Disorderly Conduct* (1932). *Young America* (1932), again starring Tracy, was directed by Frank Borzage and had Ralph as a sympathetic judge of a juvenile court. By contrast he was Elissa Landi's villainous ex-husband in *The Woman in Room 13* (1932). His celluloid performances continued with an unusual standard of excellence but the public chose not to accept him as a screen matinee idol.

Raoul Walsh transported company and crew to Sequoia National Park to film *Wild Girl* (1932), a remake of the old tale of *Salomy Jane*. Ralph was gambler John Marbury in a West where men were men and girls (in this case Joan Bennett) were too shy to be kissed. Then, Ralph was an airport superintendent battling with stunt flier Pat O'Brien in Universal's *Air Mail* (1932). After playing Boss Carter Cavendish having an affair with Sally Eilers in *Second Hand Wife* (1933), Bellamy left Fox for fresher fields.

In *Parole Girl* (1933) he gave an appealing performance, and in Tay Garnett's *Destination Unknown* (1933) he was outstanding in the Christ-like symbolic role of "The Stowaway" saving a sinking ship. For the 1932–1933 screen season, Bellamy was announced for *Havoc*, with Spencer Tracy and Peggy Shannon; *The Red Dancer,* with Elissa Landi; and was supposed to take the lead role in Noël Coward's unproduced play *The Last Trick,* to be retitled *Forgotten Kisses*. He appeared in none of these ventures.

Accepting free-lance jobs, Ralph did a job of fine proportions as the dipsomaniac city editor for James Cagney in *Picture Snatcher* (1933) and gave a well-paced performance as a surly deep sea diver in *Below the Sea* (1933). He excelled at playing heavies, such as Speed Hardy, an air circus owner whose two-timing wife (Arline Judge) inspires him to kill her lover (Eric Lindon), only to end up by inadvertently killing his brother (Bruce Cabot) in *Flying Devils* (1933). Sometimes Ralph would land film leads such as that opposite Katharine Hepburn in the unconvincing *Spitfire* (1934) or as the weak, bewildered man having trouble with wives one (Irene Dunne) and two (Constance Cummings) in *This Man Is Mine* (1934). At Columbia Ralph gave a good performance as Detective Trent in the whodunit *One Is Guilty* (1934) and later returned to Fox to take a role Spencer Tracy had refused, that of J. F. Van Avery in an unexciting ghost town tale, *Helldorado* (1935). A strange bit of casting was having Ralph appear as a dull-witted Polish bridegroom with Anna Sten in her unsuccessful *The Wedding Night* (1935).

Through the mid-Thirties, Ralph's screen roles were in the same casting rut, despite the fact he gave professional performances in most of them; and only occasionally did he get a showy role, such as that of the wealthy cripple in Carole Lombard's *Hands Across the Table* (1936). Likewise, his talent was readily apparent in his playing of the dual roles of eminent physician James Blake and criminal "Slick" Rawley in Columbia's quickie *The Man Who Lived Twice* (1937).

Then he was assigned the part of the big, bashful Oklahoma playboy, Daniel Leeson, in Columbia's hilarious *The Awful Truth* (1937). His expert playing in this Irene Dunne-Cary Grant madcap comedy earned him a Best Supporting Actor Oscar nomination, but he lost to Joseph Schildkraut of *The Life of Emile Zola*. For Warner Bros. in 1938 Bellamy played the good-natured Philip Chester in *Fools for Scandal* (1938), a lesser Carole Lombard vehicle. Then as film producer Elliott Friday, Ralph was frequently amusing in the runaway comedy of James Cagney and Pat O'Brien in Warner Bros.' *Boy Meets Girl* (1938).

Bellamy probably lost more heroines to heroes than any other player on the screen. For example, in RKO's *Carefree* (1938) he was Ginger Rogers' discarded romance. For

With Gloria Shea and Fred Kohler in *Dangerous Intrigue* (Col '36).

With Walter Kingsford in *Smashing the Spy Ring* (Col '39).

Tay Garnett's *Trade Winds* (1938) Bellamy played a comedy character role of a detective pursuing Joan Bennett. Critics carped that he was still playing his role in *The Awful Truth* throughout all this, and that it was becoming tiresome. In 1939 his screen roles were colorless except for an exceptionally fine portrayal of a psychiatrist in *Blind Alley*. In *His Girl Friday* (1940), the droll remake of *The Front Page*, Ralph was set dressing as Rosalind Russell's umbrella-carrying intended bridegroom.

In the mid-Thirties Ralph and Charles Farrell were out riding on horseback one day in Palm Springs, California, when they discovered a parcel of property for sale. Together they started the famed Palm Springs Racquet Club. While Bellamy's interest in the Club would fade, Farrell would run the resort spot successfully for many years. Ralph was more interested in the study of archaeology and the intricacies of the Mayan culture. His undemanding screen work helped to pay for his hobbies.

Throughout the early Forties he kept busy on screen. He was a flight superintendent in Warner Bros.' *Flight Angels* (1940), was another hick, Western character in Edward G. Robinson's *Brother Orchid* (1940), and then was excellent as a G-man in *Queen of the Mob* (1940), with Blanche Yurka as a Ma Barker-type figure. Critics heralded "the authentic performances of Ralph Bellamy and Maria Ouspenskaya" in *Dance, Girl, Dance* (1940).

It was in 1940 that Ralph became a silver screen sleuth when cast in *Ellery Queen, Master Detective*. It was the first of four low-budget mysteries he would make for Columbia with Margaret Lindsay as free-lance mystery writer-secretary Nikki Porter and Charlie Grapewin as the elder Inspector Queen. Between the Columbia detective entries, Bellamy was seen as a dentist involved in murder with Errol Flynn in *Footsteps in the Dark* (1941), and he again lost the girl (this time Merle Oberon) in *Affectionately Yours* (1941). Ralph gave excellent support in *Dive Bomber* (1941), an Errol Flynn service thriller. After relinquishing his Ellery Queen role to William Gargan, Bellamy went to Universal for two of their horror specialties.

Ralph underplayed and made unobtrusive Colonel Montford in Universal's excellent *The Wolf Man* (1941) and was the romantic lead with Evelyn Ankers in *The Ghost of Frankenstein* (1942), in which Lon Chaney, Jr. was the monster and Sir Cedric Hardwicke was the son of Dr. Frankenstein. In Gregory La Cava's less-than-funny comedy *Lady in a Jam* (1942), Bellamy capered as Irene Dunne's ex-flame. In *The Great Impersonation* (1942) Ralph played another dual role (and very well) as Sir Edward Dominey and Baron von Ragenstern in a look-alike double spy affair. During 1942 Ralph was frequently heard on "Lux Radio Theatre"—in April in *The Fighting 69th* with Pat O'Brien, and in November in *Sullivan's Travels* with Veronica Lake. After a cameo appearance in *Stage Door Canteen* (1943) he decided the time had come to shake off the dusty image Hollywood had created for him.

Back on Broadway he was in *Tomorrow the World* which opened on April 4, 1943, and ran for five hundred performances. In this anti-Nazi drama, Shirley Booth was featured, and Ralph played troubled college professor Michael Frame. Bellamy considered *Tomorrow the World* a deeply penetrating experience that renewed his faith in his acting prowess. During the run of that show, he produced and directed the play *Pretty Little Parlor,* a Broadway show (with Sidney Blackmer, Stella Adler, and Ed Begley) that only lasted eight performances. During his stage run, Ralph appeared on some dozen radio programs.

Nevertheless, Ralph did return to Hollywood, this time to play a magazine illustrator unnerved by neurotic, bitchy Anne Baxter in *Guest in the House* (1944). In the slow-paced murdery mystery *The Lady on a Train* (1945) he was cast opposite Deanna Durbin. That same year, on August 6, Catherine Willard Bellamy won a divorce from

Ralph on charges of mental cruelty. Later that year Ralph wed organist Ethel Smith. And he won one of the best roles in his career: presidential hopeful Grant Matthews in *State of the Union.*

The Howard Lindsay and Russel Crouse play was vastly acclaimed after its November 14, 1945, opening and would run for a total of 765 performances. Bellamy remained in the leading role throughout the run but Kay Johnson was succeeded by Margalo Gilmore in the role of the dominating newspaper publisher. As Bellamy's onstage wife, Kay Francis replaced Ruth Hussey, in 1946 and she was spelled by Edith Atwater before returning to the cast in June, 1947.

During this mid-Forties period Ralph made two recordings for RCA Victor, "The Rubaiyat of Omar Khayyam" and Walt Whitman's "Leaves of Grass," plus narrating radio's *10th Man* program for the National Mental Health Foundation. In March, 1948, Ralph was heard on radio's "Cavalcade of America" show with Joan Caulfield in *Roses in the Rain* and narrated NBC's American Legion telecast *If Fight We Must.* In November, 1949, Ralph, who had already divorced Ethel Smith, renewed his acquaintanceship with marriage. His new bride was actor's agent Alice Murphy, and they settled into a West 57th Street apartment and bought a five-acre home in Clinton, New Jersey.

It was television that brought Bellamy a new burst of popularity. In September, 1949, his detective series, "Man against Crime," debuted and was highly successful. Of this *live* series, Bellamy commented, "Everybody concerned with the show spends half his life in taxi-cabs, darting from one unit to another. No wonder it costs so much to put on the show. What we must have is centralization of activities. The cost will drop and we'll get better shows." The 1952 *TV Digest* winner for favorite mystery drama was "Man against Crime." Ralph acknowledged the award, which was a solid token for his superb portrayal of private eye Mike Barnett. "From the stage hands on through the producer, there is an *esprit de crops* that eventually comes through the screen. Without it no show can be a success."

Content with his television success and his latest marriage, Ralph delved into oil painting and was amazed when his first canvas was sold.

During the rigors of the teleseries, he returned to the stage in another prize role. Sidney Kingsley's *Detective Story* was produced by authors Howard Lindsay and Russel Crouse and, for his role of Detective McLeod, Ralph spent over a month in various New York City police precincts studying their operations and problems. Starring with Meg Mundy, Ralph opened in *Detective Story* at the Hudson Theatre on March 23, 1949. The drama was a huge hit and Bellamy received accolades from the press for his superior performance. He gave a tough, honest and impressive portrayal, without any theatrical gimmickry, of the vindictive police enforcer virtually obsessed with incarcerating criminals. *Detective Story* ran for 581 performances.

In both *State of the Union* and *Detective Story* Bellamy had invested his own money and he realized a substantial profit on both shows. He also suffered the fate of most Broadway stars who see their plum roles given to others in the movie versions of the hit shows: in Ralph's case it was Spencer Tracy in MGM's *State of the Union* and Kirk Douglas in Paramount's *Detective Story.*

With his *Detective Story* co-star, Meg Mundy, Ralph appeared on television's "U.S. Steel Hour" in *Fearful Decision.* This June, 1954, performance won him an Emmy nomination. Back in 1949 Bellamy had served as vice president of the Actor's Equity Association and, in 1952, he became that organization's president, succeeding actor Clarence Derwent. Bellamy was diligent and efficient in the non-salaried post, helping to raise actors' base pay twenty percent and attending all Tuesday council meetings of AEA. Howard Lindsay commented on Bellamy's ability, "He's one of the best actors we have around. He's really a better actor than he seems and he's also one of the nicest people in the world. In his capacity as President of Equity, he's a good balance wheel to the entire profession."

For "Hallmark Hall of Fame" in November, 1955, Ralph appeared as Pastor Anderson in a television production of *The Devil's Disciple*. Sometimes Ralph's television appearances overlapped as when on April 26, 1956, he was on both "Ford Theatre" in *Alibi* and "Climax" in *Sit Down with Death*. Rarely did Bellamy return to films, but in 1955 he was back onscreen in Otto Preminger's uneven *The Court-Martial of Billy Mitchell*, with Gary Cooper starred and Ralph as Congressman Frank Reid.

To portray Franklin Delano Roosevelt in the stage edition of *Sunrise at Campobello*, Ralph spent daily workouts at a New York gym, dropping some thirteen pounds from his over-six-foot frame. Through his good friend Edward R. Murrow, he met Alice Hermes, with whom he studied diction in order to acquire the Groton speech pattern typical of FDR. When the play opened on Broadway on January 30, 1958, the critics lauded Bellamy's superb interpretation. *Time* magazine claimed, "Undoubtedly Ralph Bellamy's finest hour in the theatre was his perceptive and demandingly difficult role of a 39-year-old one-time Assistant Secretary of the Navy enjoying a summer holiday in 1921 at his home at Campobello: Franklin Delano Roosevelt. Bellamy brought to fore the indomitable, determined spirit and inner reality of the man who contracted polio after a chill from a swim and lost the use of his legs."

Scripter Dore Schary had approached Eleanor Roosevelt during the writing of the play and, fortunately, she co-operated with the author, to the extent of inviting the cast to her Hyde Park home, where Bellamy was able to piece together bits of his role and polish his performance by a question-and-answer session with Mrs. Roosevelt. Bellamy later claimed that the highest compliment came after the opening night of the play when Eleanor Roosevelt came backstage and told the star, "That was just the way Franklin sounded!"

Although playing the wheelchair-bound FDR was a strenuous assignment, it was worth the effort. Bellamy won the year's Tony Award as Best Actor of the Year. When the show closed on Broadway, Ralph went on a national tour of the show, which lasted until the end of 1959. Warner Bros., in 1960, filmed *Sunrise at Campobello*, with Ralph still portraying FDR, Greer Garson as his wife Eleanor and Hume Cronyn as his able counselor Louis Howe. Bellamy was not even nominated for his superior performance.

Ralph returned to television for his livelihood thereafter and the Bellamys moved to California where they lived in a Beverly Hills home once owned by composer Jerome Kern. Frequently Ralph went hunting between video assignments, and his companion, Andy Anderson of Challis, Idaho, said, "Ralph's a crack shot, a fine woodsman and wonderful company. One of the finest sportsmen I ever had with me." Meanwhile TV critic Jack O'Brien was writing, "He is a dependable pillar of strength in many shows and his walloping, dedicated theatrical intelligence has lifted many a role beyond its seeming script problems."

In May, 1964, Bellamy replaced ailing Wendell Corey as psychiatrist Dr. Theodore Basser on MGM-TV's "Eleventh Hour" series. In 1966 he returned to the screen to join with Burt Lancaster and Lee Marvin in *The Professionals*. On February 13, 1968, Ralph and Jane Wyatt were *My Father and My Mother* of Gene Hackman who cannot understand why his son is institutionalized as retarded and seeks answers from his parents. Bellamy joined the Paramount production of the shocker *Rosemary's Baby* (1968) and in September 1969, he became involved in one of television's more spectacular failures, the series called "The Survivors." He played Baylor Carlyle, father of Lana Turner and George Hamilton. He was more fortunately cast in the telefilm pilot for a proposed series, "The Immortal." For Columbia Pictures he appeared in *Doctors' Wives* (1971), his last feature to date, playing the millionaire father of murdered Dyan Cannon.

In the beginning of 1972 Ralph was back in the satanic cult in CBS-TV's *Something Evil,* with Sandy Dennis and Darren McGavin. In 1973 he played a retired legal wizard returning to the courts only to lose a case to "Owen Marshall." He was in *The Log of the Black Pearl,* a 1974 telefeature, and the next year played one of the world's richest men in Irwin Allen's TV-movie *Adventures of a Queen,* and astutely portrayed U.S. Ambassador Adlai Stevenson in the compelling telefeature *The Missiles of October.* Always the professional, Ralph has consistently been an asset to the acting community. It is a shame that Hollywood seldom assessed his true worth and rarely gave him the vehicles which his talent demanded.

RALPH BELLAMY

The Secret Six *(MGM 1931)*
The Magnificent Lie *(Par 1931)*
Surrender *(Fox 1931)*
Forbidden *(Col 1932)*
West of Broadway *(MGM 1932)*
Disorderly Conduct *(Fox 1932)*
Young America *(Fox 1932)*
Rebecca of Sunnybrook Farm *(Fox 1932)*
The Woman in Room 13 *(Fox 1932)*
Wild Girl *(Fox 1932)*
Air Mail *(Univ 1932)*
Almost Married *(Fox 1932)*
Second Hand Wife *(Fox 1933)*
Parole Girl *(Col 1933)*
Destination Unknown *(Univ 1933)*
Picture Snatcher *(WB 1933)*
Narrow Corner *(WB 1933)*
Below the Sea *(Col 1933)*
Headline Shooters *(RKO 1933)*
Flying Devils *(RKO 1933)*
Blind Adventure *(RKO 1933)*
Ace of Aces *(RKO 1933)*
Ever in My Heart *(WB 1933)*
Spitfire *(RKO 1934)*
This Man Is Mine *(RKO 1934)*
Once to Every Woman *(Col 1934)*
One Is Guilty *(Col 1934)*
Before Midnight *(Col 1934)*
The Crime of Helen Stanley *(Col 1934)*
Girl in Danger *(Col 1934)*
Woman in the Dark *(RKO 1934)*
Helldorado *(Fox 1935)*
The Wedding Night *(UA 1935)*
Rendezvous at Midnight *(Univ 1935)*
Air Hawks *(Col 1935)*
Eight Bells *(Col 1935)*
The Healer *(Mon 35)*
Gigolette *(RKO 1935)*
Navy Wife [Beauty's Daughter] *(Fox 1935)*
Hands across the Table *(Par 1935)*
Dangerous Intrigue *(Col 1936)*
The Final Hour *(Col 1936)*
Roaming Lady *(Col 1936)*
Straight from the Shoulder *(Par 1936)*
Wild Brian Kent *(RKO 1936)*

Counterfeit Lady *(Col 1937)*
The Man Who Lived Twice *(Col 1937)*
The Awful Truth *(Col 1937)*
Let's Get Married *(Col 1937)*
The Crime of Dr. Hallet *(Univ 1938)*
Fools for Scandal *(WB 1938)*
Boy Meets Girl *(WB 1938)*
Carefree *(RKO 1938)*
Girl's School *(Col 1938)*
Trade Winds *(UA 1938)*
Let Us Live *(Col 1939)*
Blind Alley *(Col 1939)*
Smashing the Spy Ring *(Col 1939)*
Coast Guard *(Col 1939)*
His Girl Friday *(Col 1940)*
Flight Angels *(WB 1940)*
Brother Orchid *(WB 1940)*
Queen of the Mob *(Par 1940)*
Dance, Girl, Dance *(RKO 1940)*
Public Deb No. 1 *(20th 1940)*
Ellery Queen, Master Detective *(Col 1940)*
Meet the Wildcat *(Univ 1940)*
Ellery Queen's Penthouse Mystery *(Col 1941)*
Footsteps in the Dark *(WB 1941)*
Affectionately Yours *(WB 1941)*
Ellery Queen and the Perfect Crime *(Col 1941)*
Dive Bomber *(WB 1941)*
Ellery Queen and the Murder Ring *(Col 1941)*
The Wolf Man *(Univ 1941)*
The Ghost of Frankenstein *(Univ 1942)*
Lady in a Jam *(Univ 1942)*
Men of Texas *(Univ 1942)*
The Great Impersonation *(Univ 1942)*
Stage Door Canteen *(UA 1943)*
Guest in the House *(UA 1944)*
Delightfully Dangerous *(UA 1945)*
Lady on a Train *(Univ 1945)*
The Court-Martial of Billy Mitchell *(WB 1955)*
Sunrise at Campobello *(WB 1960)*
The Professionals *(Col 1966)*
Rosemary's Baby *(Par 1968)*
Doctors' Wives *(Col 1971)*

𝔾

Charles Bickford

When 6′ 1¹/₂″ Charles Bickford crashed into the movies in 1929, MGM projected stardom for the redheaded Irish charmer. But he soon proved that he was the lot's foremost rebel. Outspoken, uncooperative, and defiant, he soon became the prime Thirties' example of what happens when an intelligent, realistic iconoclast tries to buck the system. Professionally he was whipped and forced to accept a far lesser spot in the hierarchy than his talent warranted. But as an individual he remained dignified and self-determined, and displayed commendable courage.

Charles Ambrose Bickford was born on Tuesday, January 1, 1889, during a blizzard in Cambridge, Massachestts. The youngest boy in a family of seven children, he was the spittin' image of his maternal grandfather, skipper of a two-masted schooner. Charles' study of engineering at the Boston and Massachusetts Technical Institute qualified him for the Engineering Corps of the U.S. Army during World War I.

He made his stage debut in a second-rate burlesque company in Oakland, California, at twenty-five dollars a week. When the show folded in Brooklyn, after a thirty-week, cross-country tour, Bickford headed for Boston. There he was fortunate in joining the prestigious Castle Square Theatre stock company, which included William Powell, Donald Meek, and Alfred Lunt as former alumni. Within a year, Charles was playing Tybalt in *Romeo and Juliet,* Laertes in *Hamlet,* and Cessio in *Othello.* Although he was anxious to try Broadway, he instead found himself leading man for a small repertory company playing New Brunswick and Nova Scotia. Then he toured for twenty weeks as leading man with a Chicago-based repertory group and spent sixteen weeks as the star of an Ohio River Showboat.

After this stint he headed for Broadway and made his debut there on April 22, 1919, in *Dark Rosaleen,* directed by David Belasco at his theatre, with Thomas Mitchell and Beryl Mercer in the cast. That production lasted eighty-seven performances. His career hit a snag after that and he was forced to haunt booking offices. One of his better offers came in 1922 when he was chosen to replace George Abbott in *Zander the Great* in Detroit. He played the show for twelve weeks in Chicago and received a rave notice from Ashton Stevens, the dean of the city's critics. Following a successful tour of the show, Bickford signed with the star of that show, Alice Brady, for a season of vaudeville. For twenty-four weeks they played in a condensed version of her hit show *Drifting.* During the tour, carefree Bickford became the sparring partner for prizefighter Jim Corbett until Alice Brady called a halt to the boxing.

With Elizabeth Young in *East of Java* (Univ '35).

He returned to Broadway on February 17, 1925, for *Houses of Sand,* which only survived thirty-one performances. His big break came with an offer to play the leading role in Maxwell Anderson's *Outside Looking In,* based on Jim Tully's book about his boyhood adventures among hoboes. Bickford was cast as Oklahoma Red, a vital, well-written role. Appearing as Tully was another talented redhaired Irishman—James Cagney. When the show opened on September 7, 1925, Bickford was proclaimed a star. Film producer-director Herbert Brenon offered Charles a co-starring role with Ronald Colman in the pending Paramount production of *Beau Geste* (1926). But Bickford was not interested. Years later Cecil B. DeMille would say of Bickford "When they carry Charles Bickford to his grave he'd still be kicking and yelling 'The Theatre's better.' "

It was another Maxwell Anderson play (written with Harold Hickerson) that brought Charles to the movies. The drama was *Gods of Lightning* and it was a strong message play dealing with the injustice within the famous trial of Sacco and Vanzetti. The show opened on October 24, 1928, with Charles, Sylvia Sidney, and Barton MacLane in the cast. Although it would only last twenty-nine performances, it received high critical praise. As the strong, bold, outspoken, acrid anarchist Macready, Bickford rose to his dramatic heights in the courtroom scene.

Cecil B. DeMille was then casting for a new leading man for his first talking picture, *Dynamite* (1929), to be made at MGM. He felt Bickford would be qualified for the role and wanted to import him from Broadway. Charles agreed, but would not sign a long-term agreement with Metro. The first day on the set all Hollywood learned a rebel was in their midst. Reacting to DeMille's enthusiasm for the script of *Dynamite,* Bickford said: "Understand me, Mr. DeMille, I am not criticizing the construction of this story. I don't know enough about screen writing for that. But I've been writing and acting in stage plays for many more years than you've been producing motion pictures. And this dialogue stinks!" (Bickford had written three Broadway-bound plays: *Brown Cow, The Cyclone Lover,* and *The Sandy Hooker,* the latter two being comedies prepared with the assistance of Fred Ballard. None were ever New York successes.)

A few days later on the *Dynamite* set, Bickford was baffled to find that DeMille had musicians on the set to play mood music. He informed the Master that anytime he needed that type of stimulus to make him act, he would go back to swinging a pick for a living. *Dynamite* continued on an even keel, although one skirmish over Kay Johnson's fluffing lines, topped with DeMille's sarcastic suggestions regarding her acting, enflamed Bickford. "Why do you take it?" he asked Miss Johnson. "Tell the son-of-a-bitch to go to hell." Miss Johnson followed Charles' suggestion, the scene worked, and the unpredictable DeMille rewarded his stars with twenty dollar gold pieces each for what he considered magnificent performances.

The two C.B.'s developed a mutual admiration for one another and DeMille would use Charles again in his third and final Metro film, a weary version of his first Hollywood-made feature, *The Squaw Man* (1931). Later in the decade, Charles would be the racketeer boss in DeMille's strangely constructed *This Day and Age* (1933) and the villainous gun-runner in DeMille's *The Plainsman* (1936).

But Bickford's reconciled friendship with DeMille was not reflected in fights with MGM head Louis B. Mayer. Mayer had his own way of dealing with rebellious subordinates, and he retaliated by lending Bickford to Fox for Lenore Ulric's *South Sea Rose* (1929) and to Universal for William Wyler's *Hell's Heroes* (1929). The picture was shot in the Mojave Desert and the Panamint Valley, edging on Death Valley, and was the studio's first all-talking outdoor epic. The actor and Wyler feuded during the location-based film; twenty-eight years later on another Western epic, *The Big Country,* the director and Bickford were still at it. A double did Charles' horseback riding (he could not get on or off a horse).

Bickford's great screen opportunity came with his brilliant playing of seaman Matt in Metro's *Anna Christie* (1930), which was Greta Garbo's first talking picture. The film was heralded less for the O'Neill drama than for "GARBO TALKS!" But Bickford's joy and pleasure in filming *Anna Christie* was short-lived, for Metro did not attempt to build him into a major star. Instead he was cast in a dreary love story triangle with Kay Francis and Kay Johnson called *Passion Flower* (1930). He told the press that the William de Mille-directed venture was "Baloney with a Capital 'B' and to make matters worse, I'm the 'Passion.' " He further told the press: "Hollywood people are a little bit ridiculous. They take themselves too seriously. All they can see is Hollywood and the rest of the world doesn't exist for them. Individually, there are swell people in Hollywood, but, collectively, they're absurd. If they'd get a few good directors and a supervisor with a little more brain than a cootie, they might make a good picture or two!" By this point Mayer was referring to Bickford as "That god-damned redheaded Bolshevik!"

Charles was packed off to Mazatlan, Mexico, to play escaped convict Reverend Sims in a great disaster called *The Sea Bat* (1930), which director Wesley Ruggles subtitled "Garbage." After eight weeks the studio brass decided to reshoot the picture in the studio, replacing Ruggles with Lionel Barrymore. Mayer insisted on completing the fiasco at night but Bickford's temper precluded his working in the evenings. As could be expected, Bickford and Mayer ended up in further shouting sessions. Bickford yelled, "I'm redheaded all right, and I may be a son-of-a-bitch, but I'm outraged to be called one by a venomous little junk peddler like you. To hell with you—you posturing little ignoramus!"

Shaking with fury, Mayer told Bickford, "One day you'll come crawling on your knees to apologize for that!" Metro declined to loan Bickford to RKO for *Cimarron* (1931), refused to cast him in their sensational prison picture, *The Big House* (1930), and denied Darryl F. Zanuck's request to borrow Bickford's services for Warners' *The Maltese Falcon* (1931).

But Bickford continued to work in Hollywood, even if it meant second-string features or nonshowy roles. For Universal's *East of Java* (1935) he insisted on entering a cage with a lion for a close-up that nearly resulted in his death when the lion sank his fangs into Bickford's throat. He recovered but lost out on the lead in Fox's Shirley Temple starrer *The Littlest Rebel* (1935). However, at Fox he did play the villain in *The Farmer Takes a Wife* (1935), in which he and debutant Henry Fonda have a battle royal for the affections of heroine Janet Gaynor. There was talk that he would star in and direct a feature at Universal in 1935, but that never materialized. On February 19, 1938, Bickford returned to Broadway for twenty-five performances of Robert Ardrey's play *Casey Jones,* garnering fine personal notices for his playing of the blinded train engineer. When the play closed, he returned to Hollywood where his roles started to improve. He gave excellent performances as prison chaplain Father Joe in *Mutiny in the Big House* (1939) and Slim in the screen version of *Of Mice and Men* (1939). For Universal, he appeared as a notorious bad man robbing miners during the gold rush days in a fifteen-episode serial, *Riders of Death Valley* (1941). The next year he returned to DeMille as the mate of the Tyfib in the superepic *Reap the Wild Wind.* Then George Seaton recommended the seasoned Bickford to Zanuck for the prize role of Peyremaie, Dean of Lourdes, in *The Song of Bernadette* (1943). He was Oscar-nominated for Best Supporting Actor of the Year but lost to Charles Coburn of *The More the Merrier.* Now in his early fifties and on the screen for fourteen years, Bickford was, at least, recognized for his exceptional talent. And his roles, if still of a supporting character, improved in quality and stature.

During his ups and downs in show business, Bickford remained a shrewd Yankee. He invested in a whaling ship enterprise, a parking garage, a hog farm, several fishing

With Ann Dvorak in *Gangs of New York* (Rep '38).

schooners, and, with New York fashion designer Joan Storm, started The House of Bickstorm. And he shielded his personal life and his family with the same acumen he displayed in his profitable enterprises. In 1919 he had married Beatrice Loring, a Philadelphia girl. In 1920 their daughter Doris was born and five years later, son Rex. For thirty-six years the Bickfords would reside in a Spanish style home on top of the Playa del Rey palisades, which provided them with a superior view of the Pacific Ocean.

Berthed at Twentieth Century-Fox in the mid-Forties, Charles was effective as Captain Waddell in *Wing and a Prayer* (1944), as the father of Eddie Rickenbacker (Fred MacMurray) in *Captain Eddie,* and offered a strong performance as the murdering ex-New York detective in *Fallen Angel* (1945). In a topflight cast of David O. Selznick's sweeping, massive Western, *Duel in the Sun* (1946), he managed to excel as Sam, the ranch foreman who fancies sexy Jennifer Jones. In 1946 Bickford was again Oscar-nominated for Best Supporting Actor of the Year for his sly performance as the butler in *The Farmer's Daughter.* Charles lost this year to delightful Edmund Gwenn of *Miracle on 34th Street.* (Charles would repeat his role of Clancy on "Theatre '62's" telecast of *The Farmer's Daughter,* starring Lee Remick and Peter Lawford.)

His dependable trouping carried such neurotic parts as the blinded husband in the melodramatic *The Woman on the Beach* (1947), the brutally realistic Gallagher in the prison thriller *Brute Force* (1947), and the unrelenting lawman in *Four Faces West* to greater heights than they deserved. He was again a priest in the dismal William Bendix *The Babe Ruth Story* (1948). That was the same year that he, along with fellow player Claire Trevor, seriously took up oil painting in which he had merely dabbled for several years. He became quite a good painter.

But 1948 was memorable for Bickford's intense and true playing of the father of deaf mute Jane Wyman in *Johnny Belinda.* Charles was again Oscar-nominated, but lost

90

once again, this time to Walter Huston who won the Best Supporting Actor Award for *The Treasure of the Sierra Madre.*

There would be no further Oscar nominations for Bickford but his performances seldom, if ever, faltered, whether playing an outspoken newspaper correspondent in *Command Decision* (made at MGM, 1948) or sensitively playing Joseph, Cardinal Mindszenty, the Hungarian primate sentenced to life imprisonment, in a less than satisfactory account entitled *Guilty of Treason* (1949).

Although by the Fifties, Charles was white-haired, weather-beaten, and slightly stooped, his performances before the cameras did not suffer. He vigorously played the warm-hearted studio boss in Judy Garland's marathon *A Star Is Born* (1954), was the rugged Dr. Runklemann who dies of a heart attack in *Not As a Stranger* (1955), and played General Guthrie in Otto Preminger's wallowing *The Court-Martial of Billy Mitchell* (1955). Occasionally he was even seen on television. On October 2, 1958, he appeared in the telecast of "Playhouse 90's" *The Days of Wine and Roses,* and in 1962 he repeated his role in Warner Bros. well-made film version, for which Jack Lemmon and Lee Remick both received Oscar nominations.

By 1960, Bickford's career turned to television and he was seen on most of the major dramatic programs. He was especially effective in "Hallmark Hall of Fame's" *Winterset,* with Don Murray and Piper Laurie. For the same program's *The Cradle Song* he was the doctor among such nuns as Helen Hayes, Judith Anderson, and Siobhan McKenna. Bickford's last theatrical feature was *A Big Hand for the Little Lady* (1966). When Lee J. Cobb left the teleseries "The Virginian," Bickford replaced him as of September 14, 1966, as the head of Shiloh Ranch.

With Claire Trevor in *Valley of the Giants* (WB '38).

Charles Bickford wrote his autobiography in 1964. Entitled *Bulls, Balls, Bicycles and Actors,* it was published in 1965. At the end of the frank reminiscences, he gives a parting piece of advice to would-be performers: "Protect yourself in the clinches."

Over his thirty-seven years of film-making, Bickford's fondest memory and greatest pleasure came in 1960 when he journeyed to Durango, Mexico, to join the power-packed cast of *The Unforgiven.* He lost his heart to star Audrey Hepburn, delighted in the entire cast (from Burt Lancaster to Lillian Gish), and took a shine to a kindred, rebellious spirit, director John Huston.

In July, 1967, Bickford was hospitalized at the University of California Los Angeles Medical Center for emphysema. On November 9, 1967, he died after his illness became complicated by pneumonia and blood infection. Actor John McIntire replaced Bickford on "The Virginian" teleseries.

Rebel, artist, actor, father, enemy of the Hollywood establishment, exposer of sham and sycophancy, cantankerous Charles Bickford was an original. His presence is hard to replace.

CHARLES BICKFORD

Dynamite *(MGM 1929)*
South Sea Rose *(Fox 1929)*
Hell's Heroes *(Univ 1929)*
Anna Christie *(MGM 1930)*
Passion Flower *(MGM 1930)*
The Sea Bat *(MGM 1930)*
River's End *(WB 1930)*
The Squaw Man *(MGM 1931)*
East of Borneo *(Univ 1931)*
Pagan Lady *(Col 1931)*
The Men in Her Life *(Col 1931)*
Panama Flo *(RKO 1932)*
Thunder Below *(Par 1932)*
Scandal for Sale *(Univ 1932)*
The Last Man *(Col 1932)*
Vanity Street *(Col 1932)*
No Other Woman *(RKO 1933)*
Song of the Eagle *(Par 1933)*
This Day and Age *(Par 1933)*
White Woman *(Par 1933)*
Little Miss Marker *(Par 1934)*
A Wicked Woman *(MGM 1934)*
A Notorious Gentleman *(Univ 1935)*
Under Pressure *(Fox 1935)*
The Farmer Takes a Wife *(Fox 1935)*
East of Java *(Univ 1935)*
Rose of the Rancho *(Par 1936)*
Pride of the Marines *(Col 1936)*
The Plainsman *(Par 1936)*
Red Wagon *(Alliance-First Division 1936)*
Night Club Scandal *(Par 1937)*
Thunder Trail *(Par 1937)*
Daughter of Shanghai *(Par 1937)*
High, Wide and Handsome *(Par 1937)*
Gangs of New York *(Rep 1938)*
Valley of the Giants *(WB 1938)*
The Storm *(Univ 1938)*
Stand Up and Fight *(MGM 1938)*
Street of Missing Men *(Rep 1939)*
Romance of the Redwoods *(Col 1939)*
Our Leading Citizen *(Par 1939)*
One Hour to Live *(Univ 1939)*
Mutiny in the Big House *(Mon 1939)*

Of Mice and Men *(UA 1939)*
Thou Shall Not Kill *(Rep 1939)*
Girl from God's Country *(Rep 1940)*
Queen of the Yukon *(Mon 1940)*
South to Karanga *(Univ 1940)*
Riders of Death Valley *(Univ serial 1941)*
Burma Convoy *(Univ 1941)*
Reap the Wild Wind *(Par 1942)*
Tarzan's New York Adventure *(MGM 1942)*
Mr. Lucky *(RKO 1943)*
The Song of Bernadette *(20th 1943)*
Wing and a Prayer *(20th 1944)*
Captain Eddie *(20th 1945)*
Fallen Angel *(20th 1945)*
Duel in the Sun *(Selznick 1946)*
The Farmer's Daughter *(RKO 1947)*
The Woman on the Beach *(RKO 1947)*
Brute Force *(Univ 1947)*
Four Faces West *(UA 1948)*
The Babe Ruth Story *(AA 1948)*
Johnny Belinda *(WB 1948)*
Command Decision *(MGM 1948)*
Roseanna McCoy *(RKO 1949)*
Whirlpool *(20th 1949)*
Guilty of Treason *(EL 1949)*
Branded *(Par 1950)*
Riding High *(Par 1950)*
Jim Thorpe—All American *(WB 1951)*
The Raging Tide *(Univ 1951)*
Elopement *(20th 1951)*
The Last Posse *(Col 1953)*
A Star Is Born *(WB 1954)*
Prince of Players *(20th 1955)*
Not As a Stranger *(UA 1955)*
The Court-Martial of Billy Mitchell
  (WB 1955)
You Can't Run Away From It *(Col 1956)*
Mister Cory *(Univ 1957)*
The Big Country *(UA 1958)*
The Unforgiven *(UA 1960)*
Days of Wine and Roses *(WB 1962)*
A Big Hand for the Little Lady *(WB 1966)*

10

John Boles

Fluctuating between musicals, revues, and dramas, John Boles held a unique place among the players of the Thirties. His genial, cavalier manner, coupled with an excellent singing voice, eventually commanded a large audience following here and abroad. (In a 1934 British poll, he was voted sixth most popular American star.) His adaptability to light comedy, screen operettas, and melodramas was a talent shared by few other male performers of the early sound era.

Critics did find his stalwart performing rather bland, stilted, and immobile. But his six feet of handsome, quiet charm, combined with an inbred southern gentility and a well-modulated voice, made him very acceptable to movie-goers. Females accepted him as an illusion of the romantic dream-lover, while his chauvinistic masculine aura found acceptance with the male audience contingent.

John Boles was born on Monday, October 28, 1895, in Greenville, Texas. Intent on becoming a surgeon or joining the family banking business, he graduated from the University of Texas at Austin in June, 1917. Two days later he married his college sweetheart, Marceline Dobbs. The marriage would last fifty-two years. Soon after his marriage he was assigned to the Criminal Investigation Department of the A.E.F., where his proficiency in French and German proved advantageous on many missions on the continent. (After World War I, he attended the peace conference headed by President Woodrow Wilson, General Pershing, and France's Poincaré.)

Returning to Greenville after the war, Boles was heard singing by vocal coach Oscar Seagle. Seagle persuaded John to study with him in New York. Once in Manhattan, the young Texan taught French to earn money for his singing lessons and to support his wife. Seagle then urged him to study in Paris, so John organized a band of musical students. By acting as their business manager, John paid his passage to France. With his wife and daughter, Marcelita, he studied for two years with the famous operatic tenor Jean de Reszke.

Returning to New York City, Boles sought roles in operettas. After auditioning for Lawrence Friedlander, he replaced Jay Velie in the musical hit *Little Jesse James,* featuring Allen Kearns and Miriam Hopkins. John was assigned the show's hit song, "I Love You," and he had a duet with Louise Allen called "Little Jack Horner."

Following the closing of *Little Jesse James,* Boles made his screen debut in Metro-

With Loretta Young in *The White Parade* (Fox '34).

Goldwyn's *So This Is Marriage?* (1924), starring the lovely Eleanor Boardman and Conrad Nagel. Several scenes in this entry were in primitive Technicolor. Then he appeared with Norma Shearer and Conrad Nagel in Metro's *Excuse Me* (1925). On April 13, 1925, John was back on Broadway for thirty-two performances of *Mercenary Mary.* Thereafter he was signed as leading man opposite Geraldine Farrar in her operetta debut, Franz Lehar's *Romany Love*. The Lehar piece was rehearsed for five weeks and then, retitled *The Love Spell,* it opened for the Thanksgiving attraction in Hartford, Connecticut. The show closed there, with Miss Farrar returning to road tours. Years later Boles would say that his association with Farrar was the opportunity of a lifetime. "She was a great woman if ever there was one. Strangely compelling but, withal, humble and well-loved by those who knew her best. She was, possibly, the grandest personality I shall ever encounter!"

Otto Harbach wrote a libretto based on the play *Little Miss Brown*. With music and lyrics by Con Conrad and Gus Kahn, it was produced as *Kitty's Kisses* on May 6, 1926, on Broadway. Directed by John Cromwell, Boles was featured, with Ruth Warren and Nick Long, Jr. in supporting roles. The show ran for forty-six performances and during one of them Gloria Swanson singled out Boles for her leading man in her initial United Artists epic. The film, *The Love of Sunya* (1927), became a showcase for Miss Swanson's emotion, with John playing the role of the man she eventually marries. The New York-filmed feature launched Boles on his screen career.

Universal signed John to a contract and the Boles family headed West. The studio first used John in a dramatic war story called *We Americans* (1928). Lacking further assignments for him, they began loaning his services to other studios. For Pathé, he was in *The*

Bride of the Colorado (1928) and then at Fox, supported Charles Farrell and Greta Nissen in *Fazil* (1928). In Paramount's *The Water Hole* (1928), with Jack Holt and Nancy Carroll, John's character goes berserk in the desert. He was an aviator with Olive Borden in Columbia's *Virgin Lips* (1928), and then played Leatrice Joy's husband in the Cecil B. DeMille-produced *Man-Made Woman* (1928). He ended the year 1928 by playing the lead opposite Mary Astor in Fox's *Romance of the Underworld*.

Universal announced that Boles would star in *Moonlight Madness* and *The Song of Passion,* both to be released in late 1929. He made neither one, but, instead, did two features with Laura La Plante, *The Last Warning* (1929) and *Scandal* (1929). On October 8, 1928, he reported to Warner Bros. to begin shooting on the screen's first sound operetta, *The Desert Song* (1929), in which he played Pierre Birbeau masquerading as "The Red Shadow." With Sigmund Romberg's beautiful score, several scenes in Technicolor, and the team of Boles and newcomer Carlotta King, *The Desert Song* was a huge hit. Now considered a plus factor for any screen operetta, RKO borrowed John for their *Rio Rita* (1929), starring Bebe Daniels and the antic comedy of Wheeler and Woolsey.

Rainbow, dealing with California in the 1840s, was not a notable Broadway success, but Warner Bros. bought the musical, retained two Vincent Youmans songs, and retitled the project *Song of the West* (1930). Vivienne Segal made her motion picture debut in this Technicolor film, with John cast as the hero. On November 14 and 15, 1929, John recorded several of the movie's new songs for Victor records.

Universal recalled their singing star for a musical of their own, to be titled *La Marseillaise.* Director Paul Fejos started the project, but John Stuart Robertson completed the film. It was released as *Captain of the Guard* (1930), with John singing assorted love songs to Laura La Plante in a Louis XVI French setting. He recorded two of the picture's songs ("For You," and "You, You, Alone") for Victor records. The studio followed their French musical romp with a Technicolor revue, *The King of Jazz* (1930), featuring Paul Whiteman and His Orchestra, Bing Crosby and The Rhythm Boys, a long list of vaudeville artists, and, again, Laura La Plante and John. Boles sang the picture's most enduring song hit, "It Happened in Monterey," and joined a chorus for "The Song of the Dawn," recording both songs for RCA Victor. Universal then loaned its prize property to United Artists where John played opposite the exquisite English actress Evelyn Laye in her American film debut, *One Heavenly Night* (1930).

By the end of 1930 the public had tired of musicals, revues, operettas, and so forth. Boles found his singing talent was no longer in demand. Fortunately, he was established on the screen and Universal starred him in a remake of Leo Tolstoy's massive tale *Resurrection* (1931), directed by Edwin Carewe, who had also directed the much better 1927 silent version with Dolores Del Rio. Both Boles and Lupe Velez were beyond their depths as the tragic Russians. Universal announced Boles for the lead in Preston Sturges' *Strictly Dishonorable* (1931), but they borrowed Paul Lukas for that part and assigned Boles to *Seed* (1931).

The John Stahl-directed *Seed* opened a new career for Boles, that of a typical American husband caught in the marriage trap. This entry led to similar films considered mature and risque for the Thirties. As a change of pace he played the stalwart friend of Dr. Frankenstein (Colin Clive) in Universal's prime horror picture *Frankenstein* (1931), and then shifted over to Fox for two features.

Fannie Hurst's *Back Street* was a classic soap opera that demanded a topflight production. Carl Laemmle, Jr. borrowed Irene Dunne from RKO to portray the self-sacrificing heroine who remains faithful to her love of a well-born banker-married man. For the role of Walter Saxel, the affluent, effete socialite with a mistress on the side, Laemmle decided on John Boles. Actually his portrayal lacked sufficient sensual attraction to make believable the basic premise that any warm-blooded woman might spend a lifetime of hope on the pitiful subsistence of emotional crumbs he tosses to her. However, Stahl's direction and the general outline of this genre piece was sufficiently maintained to make the feature a huge success. Then Boles did a dance-hall Cinderella tale, Columbia's *Child of Manhattan* (1933), with Nancy Carroll, and played a romantically minded king in Fox's *My Lips Betray* (1933), with Lilian Harvey. After both Claudette Colbert and Irene Dunne had rejected John Stahl's offer, Margaret Sullavan was lured from Broadway to play the heroine in Universal's *Only Yesterday* (1934). As her lover, Boles was back in harness in another *Back Street* complex. Miss Sullavan's innate charm and splendid acting lifted *Only Yesterday* into the hit class.

Fox again borrowed Boles for a preposterous film intended to launch a new star, Rosemary Ames, which failed miserably. The picture was *I Believed in You* (1934). Fox also chose to reunite Boles with Gloria Swanson in her comeback film, *Music in the Air* (1934). It was an overblown rendition of Jerome Kern's delightful stage hit. Boles was enthusiastic about the film and told the press: "She's really lovely in this. It was a great pleasure to work with her again. And her voice is delightful." The critics shared neither Boles' enthusiasm for the picture nor for Miss Swanson.

Back at Universal John was an elegant, sensitive Viennese baron in a cavalcade of romance and melody with Gloria Stuart as his *Beloved* (1934). Spencer Tracy spiced Fox's musical *Bottoms Up* (1934) and Boles appeared as an alcoholic leading man singing "Waiting at the Gate for Katie." He appeared as himself in the Fox film revue *Stand Up and Cheer* (1934) with Miss Shirley Temple. Fox's miniature gold mine took an instant liking to Boles and was overjoyed in making *Curly Top* (1935) and *The Littlest*

With Claire Trevor in *Wild Gold* (Fox '34).

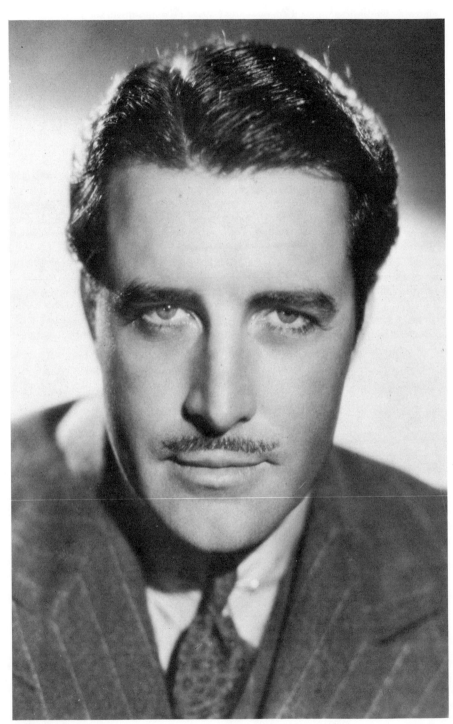

Publicity pose in '35.

Rebel (1935) with him. Boles told the press, "I'd rather work with Shirley than anyone I know. . . ."

Back in the tearjerker vein, he was the cause of Ann Harding's weeping in RKO's *The Life of Vergie Winters* (1934) and then was reteamed with Irene Dunne in the stylish, but dull, account of 1870s' New York society, *The Age of Innocence* (1934). During this period he was a frequent guest on radio programs, enacting scenes from hit movies and plays.

Paramount reportedly paid Boles $50,000 to play the role of disguised federal agent Jim Kearney in their musical version of *Rose of the Rancho* (1936), with Metropolitan Opera prima donna Gladys Swarthout. Boles' enthusiasm for returning to musicals was reflected in his press interviews. *"The Love of Sunya* landed me a contract with Universal. I was no great shakes as an actor and my parts were poor. *The Desert Song* was my first break. But singers soon went out of vogue. I was left high and dry once more at the edge of the bridge, until suddenly came an offer to play a dramatic part in *Seed* with Lois Wilson. Then *Back Street* with Irene Dunne and *The Life of Vergie Winters* with Ann Harding. And now musicals have begun to come back and I've had a chance to do some first class singing in *Rose of the Rancho.*" The Swarthout-Boles combination excited the Paramount hierarchy and there were unfulfilled plans to star the singers in *Madame Butterfly.*

Meanwhile, he was miscast in Twentieth Century-Fox's *A Message to Garcia* (1936) and had the opportunity to play the harassed husband in *Craig's Wife* (1936). With Dorothy Arzner directing, Rosalind Russell went through her paces as the shrew who bedevils Boles. Even kindly moviegoers thought Boles' performance was "dismal." He was more fortunate in being cast as Stephen Dallas in the remake of *Stella Dallas* (1937), in which Barbara Stanwyck and Anne Shirley as mother and daughter, respectively, shone. The three stars repeated their roles for Cecil B. DeMille's "Lux Radio Theatre" on October 11, 1937.

Throughout 1938 Boles made four pictures that could never qualify for even reasonably favorable reviews, including a Paramount opus with Miss Swarthout called *Romance in the Dark* (1938). Many thought that, in this weak film, Boles vied with John Barrymore for overacting honors, trying to pull laughs from a laughless script.

In the summer of 1939, John began a series of "in person" appearances at presentation houses singing "Rio Rita," "One Alone," and "I See Your Face Before Me." These personal appearance jaunts frequently broke house records and gave the actor work for the next three years. His singing voice was rich, requiring no electronic help to amplify his tones.

In the summer of 1940 he made a memorable appearance in Los Angeles and San Francisco as Gaylord Ravenal in *Show Boat.* Norma Terris recreated her original role of Magnolia, Paul Robeson was Joe, Guy Kibbee was Cap'n Andy, and in Los Angeles Helen Morgan was Julie.

It was in 1942 that Boles returned to the screen in a hackneyed Monogram picture. He walked through a role in Universal's *Between Us Girls* (1942), which featured still-beautiful Kay Francis, and showed to better advantage in MGM's musical *Thousands Cheer* (1943).

When this ceaseless worker returned to the East Coast he returned to the legitimate stage to star with Mary Martin and Kenny Baker in *One Touch of Venus* (October, 1943), directed by Elia Kazan. When the show closed in Februrary, 1944, John and Miss Martin took the musical hit on the road for a year. Boles sang Kurt Weill's haunting "West Wind" and other numbers in the show, and was an excellent choice for the production. The year 1948 found him in England appearing in a London Palladium revue, *Sky High;* thereafter he made a concert tour of the major cities of the British Isles.

In September, 1950, he was back on the legitimate stage on the West Coast in *Gentleman Prefer Blondes,* starring Gertrude Niesen. For a low-budget United Artists release, *Babes in Bagdad* (1952), John returned to the screen as Hassan. It was an unbelievably bad harem satire featuring two aging beauties: Paulette Goddard and Gypsy Rose Lee. *Babes in Bagdad* was made in Spain and should have remained there.

In the mid-Fifties, John retired from the screen and show business and went into a Texas habitat, the oil business. "When my career started to slow down, I didn't want to sit around. So when the opportunity came to get into the oil business, I jumped at it. All the fun appears to have gone out of making movies. In the old days, we used to enjoy ourselves!"

On February 27, 1969, John died of a heart attack in San Angelo, Texas, where he lived since 1956. He was survived by his wife Marceline and by his daughters Frances Marcelita and Janet, now Mrs. Daniel Queen and Mrs. Robert Fullerton.

Boles' attitude toward his career was summed up years before when he told an interviewer: "Why attempt to kid the pubic? When a screen actor tells you his art, business, profession, or whatever he chooses to call it, is a serious, dignified pursuit, he is either spouting 'poppycock' or just taking himself too seriously." Boles' easy-mannered approach certainly reflected that attitude. But he also stated, "To me, it is the most fascinating career on earth. I enjoy every phase of it, including such routine details as irregular hours, wardrobe fittings, personal appearances and 'front office' idiosyncrasies."

JOHN BOLES

So This Is Marriage? *(MG 1924)*
Excuse Me *(MGM 1925)*
The Love of Sunya *(UA 1927)*
The Shepherd of the Hills *(FN 1928)*
We Americans *(Univ 1928)*
The Bride of the Colorado *(Pathé 1928)*
Fazil *(Fox 1928)*
The Water Hole *(Par 1928)*
Virgin Lips *(Col 1928)*
Man-Made Woman *(Pathé 1928)*
Romance of the Underworld *(Fox 1928)*
The Last Warning *(Univ 1929)*
The Desert Song *(WB 1929)*
Scandal *(Univ 1929)*
Rio Rita *(RKO 1929)*
Song of the West *(WB 1930)*
Captain of the Guard *(Univ 1930)*
The King of Jazz *(Univ 1930)*
One Heavenly Night *(UA 1930)*
Resurrection *(Univ 1931)*
Seed *(Univ 1931)*
Frankenstein *(Univ 1931)*
Good Sport *(Fox 1931)*
Careless Lady *(Fox 1932)*
Back Street *(Univ 1932)*
Six Hours to Live *(Fox 1932)*
Child of Manhattan *(Col 1933)*
My Lips Betray *(Fox 1933)*

Only Yesterday *(Univ 1933)*
I Believed in You *(Fox 1934)*
Music in the Air *(Fox 1934)*
Beloved *(Univ 1934)*
Bottoms Up *(Fox 1934)*
Stand up and Cheer *(Fox 1934)*
The Life of Vergie Winters *(RKO 1934)*
Wild Gold *(Fox 1934)*
The Age of Innocence *(RKO 1934)*
The White Parade *(Fox 1934)*
Orchids to You *(Fox 1935)*
Curly Top *(Fox 1935)*
Redheads on Parade *(Fox 1935)*
The Littlest Rebel *(Fox 1935)*
Rose of the Rancho *(Par 1936)*
A Message to Garcia *(20th 1936)*
Craig's Wife *(Col 1936)*
As Good as Married *(Univ 1937)*
Stella Dallas *(UA 1937)*
Fight for Your Lady *(RKO 1937)*
She Married an Artist *(Col 1938)*
Romance in the Dark *(Par 1938)*
Sinners in Paradise *(Univ 1938)*
The Road to Happiness *(Mon 1942)*
Between Us Girls *(Univ 1942)*
Thousands Cheer *(MGM 1943)*
Babes in Bagdad *(UA 1952)*

11

Mary Brian

Hollywood's mania for stereotyping players and creating an individual image to perpetuate their mold was also a large deterrent to allowing natural-born talent to blossom. At an early stage in her career, Mary Brian was classified as "the Sweetest Girl in Pictures" and nothing she did on the screen seemed to erase this gooey classification.

She was born Louise Byrdie Dantzler on Monday, February 17, 1908, in Corsicana, Texas. There was a three-year-old brother named Taurence. When she was a month old her father died. Mrs. Dantzler, a school teacher, and her two children moved to Dallas. After Taurence completed high school, the Dantzlers migrated to Hollywood. The year was 1923.

The 5'2" Miss Dantzler, with dark-brown hair and radiant blue-gray eyes heard of a beauty contest to be judged by stars and directors at Ocean Park, California. She entered the event wearing a two-dollar bathing suit, and won second prize, which included the title "Miss Personality," a hundred-dollar bill, and a week's run in a local revue. She was seen by one of the heads of Paramount, where Sir James Barrie's *Peter Pan* (1924) was being cast with many unknown and new young faces. Mary tested for the part of "Wendy" and when the film was released for the Christmas season, Betty Bronson, who played the title role, was set for stardom. As a result of this success, Mary was signed to a seven-year contract by Paramount.

The studio kept Mary busy during the mid-Twenties. She supplied the celluloid love interest as Isobel in the first (and best) *Beau Geste* (1926), with Ronald Colman. Her status rose higher when she was loaned to MGM for *Brown of Harvard* (1926), a feature starring Jack Pickford, but stolen by William Haines. Other loan-outs followed: to Fox for a "Cappy Ricks" tale, *More Pay-Less Work* (1926), with Charles "Buddy" Rogers; to Producers Distributing Corp. for the role of Victorine Tallefer in a screen version of Balzac's *Pere Goriot* called *Paris at Midnight* (1926), with Lionel Barrymore; and then to First National for the role of Molly Taylor in Johnny Hines' *Stepping Along* (1926) and a minor role in the Ben Lyon-Lois Moran *The Prince of Tempters* (1926).

Mary was becoming a favorite romantic lead, and her home studio reaped the rewards of her roles with other studios. For the home lot, she was with W. C. Fields in *Running Wild* (1927) and was Richard Dix's leading lady in *Knockout Reilly, Man Power,* and *Shanghai Bound,* all 1927 releases. She was loaned to First National again, for a part that was a very natural Mary Brian role, as Lillums Lovewell in *Harold Teen* (1928), with Arthur Lake in the title role.

With Richard Arlen in *Song of the Eagle* (Par '33).

The arrival of sound created no panic for Mary and she registered very well on the early soundtracks. Mary was becoming the screen's favorite ingenue, and in each assignment she gave her best. In Gary Cooper's first talkie, *The Virginian* (1929), she was fine as the school "mar'm" Molly Wood. She came east to Paramount's Astoria, Long Island, studio to appear in such films as *The Marriage Playground* (1929), with Fredric March.

Paramount continued casting her as the sweet, young virgin in the early Thirties. In *Only the Brave* (1930), with Gary Cooper and Phillips Holmes, Mary, as southern belle Barbara Calhoun, was overly sweet. She was an earlier period Jean Parker, though more versatile since she could sing and dance. Mary's hope of breaking out of her sweet ingenue mold came with the juicy part of Gwen Cavendish in *The Royal Family of Broadway* (1930). Her illustrious co-stars were Ina Claire, Frédric March, and Henrietta Crosman.

Mary's eternal romantic image on the screen could not compare with her personal romantic life, *if* one believed the voluminous pap poured out by the movie fan magazines and the gossipers in the press. For all her years on the screen, when the Thirties arrived, Mary was only twenty-two, extremely beautiful, and ready bait for the gushings of Louella Parsons and others.

In 1931, she started to free-lance and turned in a creditable performance as Peggy, Pat O'Brien's harassed bride-to-be, in *The Front Page* (1931). Her next best role was as the object of Lee Tracy's affection in the rapid-firing, amusing *Blessed Event* (1932), which was also Dick Powell's screen debut. Mary and Ken Murray (to whom she was then romantically linked) were playing an Eastern vaudeville tour when they came across Powell, who was then master of ceremony for the stage shows at the Mastbaum Theatre in Philadelphia. Mary found Powell enchanting, and once he was in Hollywood they were an "item" in the gossip columns for nearly two years.

Mary's determination that had propelled her through the Hollywood years was evident in her vaudeville trek. "I was determined I wouldn't just go out on the stage and say, 'I am so glad to be here. I hope you enjoyed my last picture.' I don't think it is fair to cheat the public in that manner. I danced—and probably surprised plenty of people. When I am afraid of something, right then I make up my mind to do that thing. I was scared to death to appear on the stage, and for that reason I knew the vaudeville appearance was absolutely necessary. So I rehearsed dancing. If I had called the whole thing off, I would have been defeated, even in my picture work."

In the meantime, Mary continued to be very popular on the Hollywood social scene. She was courted by Charles "Buddy" Rogers, Russell Gleason, Donald Cook, Jack Oakie, Ken Murray, and, of course, Dick Powell. Mary was quite frank in her public analysis of her beaux, including Powell. "I think Dick likes the ladies—all of 'em. He is young and popular and entertaining and so he, too, is a victim of the 'reported engaged' mania. Personally I don't think Dick has a notion of getting serious with anyone just now, and most certainly not me." In March, 1933, columnists were announcing Mary's engagement to long-time friend Buddy Rogers. When in November, 1936, he became engaged to Mary Pickford, Mary observed philosophically, "I think that Buddy's association with Mary Pickford is right for him, for he needs a more dominating type of woman in his life." Miss Pickford became Mrs. Rogers in June, 1937. (Mary was invited to and attended the Pickford-Rogers wedding.)

Mary's screen career hit a downward trend in the mid-Thirties. Her featured role of James Cagney's gal in *Hard to Handle* (1933) was sandwiched between with forgettable parts in B pictures. And her notices were not always complimentary. Critics lauded her beauty and sometimes deplored her inefficient performing. Universal gave her an op-

With Cary Grant in *The Amazing Quest of Ernest Bliss* (UA-British).

Publicity pose c. '39.

portunity to break the "sweetest girl" mold in the role of Sally in their musical *Moonlight and Pretzels* (1933), in which she displayed her dancing talents and led some reviewers to compare her to Warner Bros.' Ruby Keeler. It was Walter Wanger who provided her with a juicy, bitchy role in *Spendthrift* (1936), starring Henry Fonda. As conniving southern shrew Sally Barnaby, she showed her mettle. Unfortunately the film was far from an engrossing study.

At age twenty-eight, Mary had finally broken the typecasting to a degree. But her metamorphosis was incomplete and too late. She went to England where she made three rather good films, including *Riches and Romance* (1936) with Cary Grant, with whom her name was linked, and *Week-end Millionaire* (1937) with old pal Buddy Rogers.

When she returned to the States, she tested for the lead in *A Star Is Born* (1937) that wisely went to Janet Gaynor who was superb in the role. Mary's acceptance of losing such parts was rationalized as, "The contour of my face precludes the possibility of the spiritual quality being made so apparent on the screen, as in Janet's case. The Janet Gaynor type of appeal will never lose its popularity, no matter whether the vogue is Hepburn, Hayes, West or Garbo, but my face is too round for that elfin type."

With no picture offers forthcoming, Mary returned to vaudeville in presentation houses in 1938. That summer, determined to improve her status as an actress, she signed on for the season at the Cape Playhouse at Dennis, Massachusetts. She was starred in the lead of *Honey*, with Margaret Wycherly and June Walker, and continued with supporting roles throughout the season in such plays as *Idiot's Delight* (with Phil Baker), *Pygmalion* (with Sylvia Sidney), *Susan and God* (starring Karen Morley), *Lightnin'* (with Fred Stone), *Stage Door* (starring Madge Evans), and closed the season with *French without Tears* (with Jean Muir).

Obviously, the determined Miss Brian was sharpening her talent. In the autumn of 1938 she returned to the presentation house-vaudeville with a tap dancing act, backed by Buddy Rogers' Orchestra (in which he played, briefly, most of the instruments). During the summer of 1939, Mary was back on the straw-hat stages in *Yes, My Darling Daughter* with Esther Ralston (who had played her mother on screen in *Peter Pan*).

That fall, Mary signed for her first Broadway-bound show. The musical was based on a tale of three sisters pooling their resources to land a millionaire. The Hoagy Carmichael-Johnny Mercer musical was called *Three after Three,* and starred Simone Simon, Mitzi Green, and Mary, with Twentieth Century-Fox's favorite old plantation retainer, Stepin Fetchit. Mary's notices were good, and her singing and dancing were rated very professional. Indeed, her vigorous training was clearly evident. Despite all, the show never seemed to pick up audience interest; it folded in Chicago where it was withdrawn and recast without Misses Simon or Brian.

Mary had another go at Broadway in 1940 with John Shubert's production of *Off the Record* starring Bruce Cabot, Betty Furness, Hugh O'Connell, and Mary. She played Barbara Wilkins, a daughter of the ol' South. The show tried-out in Princeton, New Jersey, Washington, D.C., and then folded in Philadelphia that December.

Marriage finally caught up with Mary on May 4, 1941, when she married magazine illustrator Jon Whitcomb of Fairfield, Connecticut. She was married in the study of the First Baptist Church of Hollywood by Dr. Harold L. Proppe. June Collyer was her Matron of Honor and a large reception was held at the home of her close friends Stuart and June (Collyer) Erwin. On June 21 of that year, Mary had discovered marriage less than bliss and established residence in Carson City, Nevada. There, on August 8, 1941, she was granted a divorce on the charge of mental cruelty.

She returned to the screen for three low-budgeted, lowercased movies in 1943 and made her last screen appearance in 1947's *Dragnet*. The same year she remarried, becoming Mrs. George Tomasini. Her husband was Alfred Hitchock's film editor for several of his best films. The union lasted twenty years until Tomasini's death in 1967.

Over the intervening years Mary has developed her talent for painting and has done portraits of many of Hollywood's notables, turning a hobby into a profitable business. In 1955, Mary had a brief return to acting. She spent thirty-nine weeks playing the mother on the "Meet Corliss Archer" video series.

These days, Mary lives in a ranch house in Studio City, California, surrounded by her Hungarian Puli sheepdogs and her memories. Looking back on her flagrant and free-flowing publicity as an offscreen femme-very-fatale, Mary laughingly recalls passing Bing Crosby's house during that era. At that time, his sons by Dixie Lee were quite young. She stopped to speak to son Gary who clung to the lovely actress. Bing, putting a protective arm around his small boy, said, "Mary, please don't start on this generation! Remember you're an old-timer. Be a good sport. You've had so many beaux you can afford to be. So, please, let my chee-ild a-lone."

MARY BRIAN

Peter Pan (Par 1924)
The Little French Girl (Par 1925)
The Air Mail (Par 1925)
A Regular Fellow (Par 1925)
The Street of Forgotten Men (Par 1925)
Beau Geste (Par 1926)
The Enchanted Hill (Par 1926)
Behind the Front (Par 1926)
Brown of Harvard (MGM 1926)
More Pay—Less Work (Fox 1926)
Paris at Midnight (PDC 1926)
Stepping Alone (FN 1926)
The Prince of Tempters (FN 1926)
Two Flaming Youths (Par 1927)
Knockout Reilly (Par 1927)
Running Wild (Par 1927)
Man Power (Par 1927)
Her Father Said No (FBO 1927)
Shanghai Bound (Par 1927)
High Hat (FN 1927)
Harold Teen (FN 1928)
The Big Killing (Par 1928)
Under the Tonto Rim (Par 1928)
Forgotten Faces (Par 1928)
Varsity (Par 1928)
Someone to Love (Par 1928)
Partners in Crime (Par 1928)
The Man I Love (Par 1929)
River of Romance (Par 1929)
The Virginian (Par 1929)
The Marriage Playground (Par 1929)
Black Waters (Sono Art-World Wide 1929)
The Kibitzer (Par 1930)
Burning Up (Par 1930)
Only the Brave (Par 1930)
Paramount on Parade (Par 1930)
The Social Lion (Par 1930)
The Light of Western Stars (Par 1930)

Only Saps Work (Par 1930)
The Royal Family of Broadway (Par 1930)
Gun Smoke (Par 1931)
The Front Page (UA 1931)
Captain Applejack (WB 1931)
The Runaround (RKO 1931)
Homicide Squad (Univ 1931)
It's Tough to Be Famous (FN 1932)
The Unwritten Law (Majestic 1932)
Blessed Event (WB 1932)
Manhattan Tower (Remington 1932)
Hard to Handle (WB 1933)
Girl Missing (WB 1933)
The World Gone Mad (Majestic 1933)
Song of the Eagle (Par 1933)
Moonlight and Pretzels (Univ 1933)
One Year Later (Allied 1933)
Shadows of Sing Sing (Col 1934)
College Rhythm (Par 1934)
Fog (Col 1934)
Monte Carlo Nights (Mon 1934)
Ever Since Eve (Fox 1934)
Private Scandal (Par 1934)
Charlie Chan in Paris (Fox 1935)
Man on the Flying Trapeze (Par 1935)
Spendthrift (Par 1936)
Three Married Men (Par 1936)
Killer at Large (Col 1936)
Two's Company (B & D Soskin 1936)
The Amazing Quest of Ernest Bliss [Romance
    and Riches] (Garrett Klement 1936)
Week-end Millionaire (Gaumont 1937)
Navy Blues (Rep 1937)
The Affairs of Cappy Ricks (Rep 1937)
I Escaped from the Gestapo (Mon 1943)
Danger! Women at Work (PRD 1943)
Calaboose (UA 1943)
Dragnet (Screen Guild 1947)

12

Bruce Cabot

He has been described as hulking, loose-jointed (6′ 2″ of hulk), long-lipped (critic Pauline Kael compared his lower lip with Chevalier's), and disconcertingly good looking. He has been hailed as "another Clark Gable"; a square-jawed American hero (and heavy) of many of the Thirties' screen adventures; hobnobbing buddy of John Wayne, King Farouk of Egypt, and Errol Flynn (although in later years he would sue the adventurous Errol); and a man's man, a ladies' man. His name on the screen was ever opened to the question whether he would romance and win the girl, or murder her. His personal life could have been written by a studio publicity department. But there was about the blue-eyed actor a charisma that made him appear a free spirit, a heritage he claimed from his one-sixteenth Cherokee blood.

Etienne Pelissier Jacques de Bujac was born in Carlsbad, New Mexico, on Wednesday, April 20, 1904. His father, Major de Bojac, hoped for a West Point career for his son. However, the independent-spirited boy ran away from a military school at the age of fourteen to work as a helper on a bone wagon, scavenging cattle remains on the prairie to be sold for bone meal. From this funereal occupation he joined a second-rate boxing camp, learned the prizefighting game (and its singular jargon), but then made the strategic error of knocking out his employer. He then headed for Texas where, from Houston, he worked his way to France aboard a freighter. From Le Havre he set out for Paris to see his uncle, Herman Harjas, a partner of J. Pierpont Morgan and the firm of Morgan and Harjas. Uncle Herman introduced him to fashionable Paris, and the young man attended the University of Tours for six months. When he returned to America, he enrolled for a brief time at Swanee Military Academy in Tennessee but left to work in the western oil fields. Among his subsequent jobs were selling paper, golf supplies, and automobiles. When he met a beautiful young society girl, he fell in love with her, followed her home to Chicago, and married her. The marriage was short-lived and the impetuous de Bujac headed west for Hollywood where he became a nightclub bouncer. His ease and poise in meeting new people led to his becoming manager and host of the Embassy Roof Club, where he made friends with Marion Davies and Dolores Del Rio, among others. It was Miss Del Rio who was indirectly responsible for his becoming an actor.

The actress introduced young Etienne to some film executives, which netted him a bit at Paramount in *Confessions of a Co-ed* (1931). Miss Del Rio arranged for him to meet

With Barbara Pepper in *The Big Game* (RKO '36).

producer David O. Selznick, then head of RKO studio. As the future Bruce Cabot would later recall: "We talked and I told him I had had stage experience. Of course, it wasn't true, as he must have found out when he gave me my first screen test. It was terrible. But Mr. Selznick had hopes for me. My second test wasn't too awful and the third was pretty good." Etienne did a scene from the play *Chicago* for the tests, and about his screen name said, "My real name is Jacques de Bujac, which, of course, wouldn't do. Mr. Selznick suggested John Bruce or Charles Cabot. And I said: 'Why can't it be Bruce Cabot?' So we settled on that and I've been Bruce Cabot ever since—but not legally. I'm still Jacques de Bujac."

Bruce wired his father the day he signed his RKO contract but the Major never received the telegram. That day he had accidentally killed himself during a hunting trip. Bruce would remain superstitious about the month of April all his life. "I was born on April 20," he once said. "That doesn't kill the fact that the month is tabu for me. My father died on April 12 and I lost all the money I had in the world in the month of April in 1929 and 1930. I fell in love with a girl [Loretta Young] in Hollywood and it came to no good end and hurt me like the devil. It was during the month of April too that I knocked out the boss of that boxing camp. It was during the month of April, every single time, that things happened at the universities to send me hiking."

Cabot's first films at RKO were pedestrian in execution, although *Lucky Devils* (1933) with William Boyd and William Gargan dealt with the offbeat subject of Hollywood stunt men. It was Bruce's fourth RKO picture that won him a bit of immortality. He was assigned the role of intrepid hero Driscoll, rescuing Fay Wray from the love and clutches of *King Kong* (1933). From the long shooting schedule of *Kong*, Cabot was loaned to Paramount to be killed by Helen Twelvetrees' father in *Disgraced!* (1933), in which he played a millionaire having a casual affair with a fashion model (Twelvetrees).

Back at RKO Bruce played an air-circus flyer nobly sacrificing his life to save his younger brother (Eric Linden) and then was given a role in a more prestigious, if only slightly more successful, picture, based on Sinclair Lewis' episodic *Ann Vickers* (1933). Bruce played well the role of dashing Captain Resnick whose World War I seduction of Irene Dunne (and the loss of the child at birth) starts the heroine on a passionate pursuit of social reformation. When the feature was released in September, 1933, Bruce was more involved in his private life than with RKO.

Ruth McClure, daughter of a Fort Worth, Texas, gas station operator, wed at sixteen and a year later produced a daughter. At age eighteen Ruth won her first divorce. The lovely young girl migrated to Hollywood, picked up small bits in pictures, was a stand-in for Pola Negri in *Hotel Imperial* (1927), and, as Adrienne Truex, was seen briefly in Marilyn Miller's *Sally* (1929). Adrienne met and wed millionaire-broker Stephen Ames who established her in a Beverly Hills mansion and who accepted their good friend Bruce Cabot as her escort while he was frequently out of town. On September 15, 1933, Adrienne left for Reno, Nevada, to divorce Ames and there announced her intention to wed Bruce. Her final divorce decree from Ames became official on October 30, 1933, and the following day she was married to Bruce in his mother's Carlsbad, New Mexico, home. Cabot adopted her eleven-year-old daughter by her first marriage to Truex. The marriage was alternately described as blissful and stormy; in three years they separated.

Cabot's fast-living did not contribute to a happy home and eventually Adrienne left for New York. Bruce flew to Manhattan, after finishing location shooting for one of his many film entries, to try to salvage their marriage. He told the press: "We've decided not to see each other for a while. She's a marvelous girl. I'm sorry for all the headaches and heartaches I have caused her. And she'll let me know before the divorce becomes final whether she's to call it off. Meanwhile, I'm hoping." Cabot's promise of reformation persuaded Adrienne to turn down her final decree in July, 1936, but on March 4, 1937, she returned to the courts a second time for her release as Mrs. Jacques de Bujac, accusing Bruce of being unbearable and breaking furniture in their home during his drunken sprees. The second time around was final. Adrienne got the divorce, alimony of $125 a week, and twenty percent of any salary he might make. On October 27, 1939, she would garnish his salary for back alimony payments.

Cabot's career at RKO had become a series of B film leads. When his RKO pact expired he played killer-mobster Joe Keefer in United Artists' *Let 'em Have It* (1935) and gave a surprisingly gripping performance as Killer Patch in Twentieth Century-Fox's *Show Them No Mercy* (1935). Bruce signed a contract with MGM and played in their saga of Mexican outlaw Joaquin Murietta (Warner Baxter) in *Robin Hood of Eldorado* (1936). Bruce had another good assignment in Fritz Lang's first American-made movie *Fury* (1936), in which he played the town bully and rabble rouser in a searing study of mob rule.

For United Artists he offered a fiery performance as the shaven-headed treacherous Indian, Magua, in *The Last of the Mohicans* (1936). However, most of his roles were in minor pictures, alternating between hero and heavy. He was impressive as villainous Jeff Barrett in his friend Errol Flynn's *Dodge City* (1939). That same year he made a vaudeville tour, including playing Atlantic City's famous Steel Pier, then went to England to play a role in *Traitor Spy* (1939). During 1940 he played a set of uninspired roles, including being one of the dynamic cast in Joan Crawford's *Susan and God*. At best, he was colorfully handsome in Hal Roach's *Captain Caution*, featuring Victor Mature. And that year he made his stage debut.

On November 30, 1940, the only son of J. J. Shubert, John, made his producing bow

With Marguerite Churchill in a pose for *Legion of Terror* (Col '36).

113

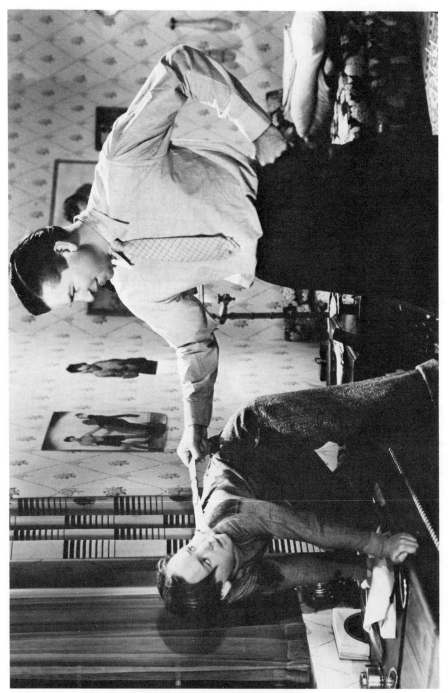

With Tommy Ryan in *Tenth Avenue Kid* (Rep '38).

114

at Princeton, New Jersey, with a comedy called *Off the Record*. The cast included Bruce, Betty Furness, Hugh O'Connell, and Mary Brian. The show moved on to Philadelphia where the political farce collapsed and folded.

Although Bruce did not make it on Broadway, he did win a romantic lead opposite still-glamorous Marlene Dietrich. As seaman Robert Latour he co-starred with her in *The Flame of New Orleans* (1941), the Rene Clair feature that suffered from censor-snipping and an overly coy performance from Fräulein Dietrich. He had a meatier assignment as the commander of an African outpost in *Sundown* (1941), with Gene Tierney and George Sanders. At Warner Bros. he played the lead in a dull, lowercase Western, *Wild Bill Hickok Rides* (1941), with Constance Bennett unlikely cast as a Western saloon singer. Bosley Crowther (*New York Times*) noted of the picture, "It will only be remembered as the one in which a Bennett sister slummed." It was quickly forgotten.

Before Bruce enlisted in the Army on December 5, 1942, at Camp Blanding, Florida, he finished roles in *Silver Queen* (1942) with George Brent, Metro's *Pierre of the Plains* (1942), and the part of Colonel Fontaine in Warner Bros.' remake of *The Desert Song* (1943), with Dennis Morgan and Irene Manning. On December 9 he was sworn into the Air Force for training at Miami, Florida. He saw service in Africa, Sicily, and Italy. After the war he returned to Hollywood to resume his career at Monogram in *Divorce*, a tale of a femme fatale luring a loving husband from home, wife, and children. Bruce played the strayed, stodgy spouse, and the picture starred former top Warner Bros. actress Kay Francis who also co-produced the film with Jeffrey Bernard. He finished 1945 with a minor role in *Fallen Angel* and played the heavy, Doc Baxter, in Alan Ladd's *Salty O'Rourke*. Twentieth Century-Fox's *Smoky* (1946) was distinguished by superlative Technicolor but it was Cabot's performance as renegade Frank that picked the slowly paced picture up after his first scene.

Photoplay magazine, commenting on his performance as Treasury Agent-sleuth Steve Batchellor in *Avalanche* (1946), noted, "Cabot, despite some added poundage after his good war record in Italy, looks fine." He made a Western in 1947 and another oater in 1948 and went to Paramount for their 1949 remake of *Little Miss Marker* (1934), playing bigshot gambler Big Steve Holloway (played in the original Shirley Temple version by Charles Bickford). The Damon Runyon story was retitled *Sorrowful Jones*. When Paramount reteamed Bob Hope and Lucille Ball after their *Sorrowful Jones*, it was for their 1950 remake of *Ruggles of Red Gap* (the fourth screen treatment). Bruce was Lucille's beau, determined she was not to marry Mr. Hope. Mr. Cabot, however, did wed again.

It was a May-November romance when Cabot, forty-seven, married Francesca de Scaffa of Lisbon, Portugal. She was twenty. But the union ended on May 4, 1951, when Francesca left the Cabot residence, later filing for divorce on May 14, charging extreme cruelty and asking for "reasonable" alimony. Bruce's carousing was getting out of hand and on October 5, 1951, he was arrested for drunken driving and fined $100. He later reimbursed Beverly Hills for a tree he uprooted with his car. The judge gave him a ninety-day suspended jail sentence with one year probation and no driving privileges for sixty days, except on business,

During 1951 Bruce managed to make one Western, appearing as Cole Younger in RKO's *Best of the Badmen*, with Robert Ryan and Claire Trevor. In 1952 he made two inconsequential pictures and did two telecasts for "Tales of Tomorrow." (He had made his video debut in 1950 on episodes of "Stars over Hollywood.") Throughout the 1950s Bruce spent most of his time in Europe, participating in Errol Flynn's abortive *William Tell* project. He returned to Hollywood in 1958 to play roles in *Sheriff of Fractured Jaw* and *The Quiet American*. In 1959 he was Gunner Lowrie in *John Paul Jones*, an overblown quasi-biography featuring Robert Stack and, as Catherine the Great, Bette Davis.

He again left for Europe and gravitated to Italy where he made several forgettable pictures, returning in the early Sixties to appear with friend John Wayne in several of the latter's vehicles: as Major Henry in *The Comancheros* (1961), Vaughn in *Hatari!* (1962), Ben Sage in *McLintock!* (1963), and Quartermaster Quoddy in *In Harm's Way* (1965). In 1965 Cabot made two Westerns for A. C. Lyles' budget unit at Paramount. He was last-billed in *The Chase* (1966) and from 1967 to 1970 his screen performances were confined to parts provided by friend Wayne: *The War Wagon* (1967) through *Chisum* (1970). In Paramount's flop *WUSA* (1970) with Paul Newman and Joanne Woodward, Bruce had a featured role as King Wolyoe, and in 1971 he made his last film with Wayne, as Sam Sharpnose in *Big Jake*. His last screen appearance was appearing with Sean Connery, as James Bond, in *Diamonds Are Forever* (1971). Bruce played his part as Saxby while undergoing radiation treatment for lung cancer.

In January, 1972, he was admitted to the Motion Picture Country Home and Hospital in Woodland, California, where he died of lung cancer on May 3.

BRUCE CABOT

Confessions of a Co-ed *(Par 1931)*
Lady with a Past *(RKO 1932)*
Lucky Devils *(RKO 1933)*
The Great Jasper *(RKO 1933)*
King Kong *(RKO 1933)*
Disgraced! *(Par 1933)*
Flying Devils *(RKO 1933)*
Ann Vickers *(RKO 1933)*
Midshipman Jack *(RKO 1933)*
Shadows of Sing Sing *(Col 1934)*
Finishing School *(RKO 1934)*
Murder on the Blackboard *(RKO 1934)*
His Greatest Gamble *(RKO 1934)*
Their Big Moment *(RKO 1934)*
Redhead *(Mon 1934)*
Men of the Night *(Col 1934)*
Night Alarm *(Majestic 1934)*
Without Children *(RKO 1935)*
Let 'em Have It *(UA 1935)*
Show Them No Mercy *(20th 1935)*
The Penthouse Party *(Liberty 1936)*
Don't Gamble with Love *(Col 1936)*
Robin Hood of Eldorado *(MGM 1936)*
Fury *(MGM 1936)*
The Three Wise Guys *(MGM 1936)*
The Last of the Mohicans *(UA 1936)*
Don't Turn 'em Loose *(RKO 1936)*
The Big Game *(RKO 1936)*
Legion of Terror *(Col 1936)*
Sinner Take All *(MGM 1936)*
Bad Guy *(MGM 1937)*
Love Takes Flight *(Grand National 1937)*
Sinners in Paradise *(Univ 1938)*
Bad Man of Brimstone *(MGM 1938)*
Smashing the Rackets *(RKO 1938)*
Tenth Avenue Kid *(Rep 1938)*
Homicide Bureau *(Col 1939)*
Dodge City *(WB 1939)*
Traitor Spy [The Torso Murder Mystery]
 (Pathé British 1939)
Mickey, the Kid *(Rep 1939)*
My Son Is Guilty *(Col 1940)*
Susan and God *(MGM 1940)*
Girls under 21 *(Col 1940)*
Captain Caution *(UA 1940)*

The Flame of New Orleans *(Univ 1941)*
Wild Bill Hickok Rides *(WB 1941)*
Sundown *(UA 1941)*
Silver Queen *(UA 1942)*
Pierre of the Plains *(MGM 1942)*
The Desert Song *(WB 1943)*
Divorce *(Mon 1945)*
Fallen Angel *(20th 1945)*
Salty O'Rourke *(Par 1945)*
Smoky *(20th 1946)*
Avalanche *(PRC 1946)*
The Angel and the Badman *(Rep 1947)*
Gunfighters *(Col 1947)*
The Gallant Legion *(Rep 1948)*
Sorrowful Jones *(Par 1949)*
Fancy Pants *(Par 1950)*
Rock Island Trail *(Rep 1950)*
Best of the Badmen *(RKO 1951)*
Lost in Alaska *(Univ 1952)*
Kid Monk Baroni *(Realart 1952)*
Sheriff of Fractured Jaw *(20th 1958)*
The Quiet American *(UA 1958)*
John Paul Jones *(WB 1959)*
Goliath and the Barbarians *(AIP Italian 1959)*
The Love Specialist *(Italian 1959)*
Rommel's Treasure *(Italian 1959)*
The Comancheros *(20th 1961)*
The Red Cloak *(Sefo Film International 1961)*
Hatari! *(Par 1962)*
McLintock! *(UA 1963)*
Law of the Lawless *(Par 1964)*
In Harm's Way *(Par 1965)*
Black Spurs *(Par 1965)*
Town Tamer *(Par 1965)*
Cat Ballou *(Col 1965)*
The Chase *(Col 1966)*
The War Wagon *(Univ 1967)*
Hellfighters *(Univ 1968)*
The Green Berets *(WB 1968)*
The Undefeated *(20th 1969)*
Chisum *(WB 1970)*
WUSA *(Par 1970)*
Big Jake *(National General 1971)*
Diamonds Are Forever *(UA 1971)*

13

Helen Chandler

Someone once said she had stars where her eyes should have been. If they appeared vacant as she slipped into a private world of deep contemplation, her eyes could also sweep a room with their light-blue darting glances, as she often accurately determined the character of perfect strangers. She appeared small and frail, with her delicate, clear, luminous skin. But that appearance was deceptive, for she had a sturdy constitution and a rebellious nervous system that fluctuated between wild, exuberant gaiety, depths of momentary despair, and sudden enthusiasm of childlike intensity. She was wistful, appealing, highly impressionable on an artistic plane, quickly and briefly embarrassed over trifles, and was, indeed, a very fine actress.

A good deal of her offbeat behavior would seem completely normal today. In the Twenties and Thirties, however, Helen Chandler was considered a bit avant-garde. Once, after reading a book on the life of Gauguin, she rushed out and bought huge supplies of paint tubes, several oversized canvases, and "an inspiring easel plus a bouquet of lovely little brushes." However, oils took too long to dry and this annoying fact destroyed her impressionist period. She had an aversion to banks because they bounced her checks due to her forgetfulness about making deposits. She disliked anything governmental, especially since she was being constantly besieged with income tax "nonsense." She hated opening letters, theorizing, "If you don't open and read something, you can prove you didn't know a thing about it."

Helen was born on Thursday, February 1, 1906, in New York City to Leland S. and Agnes Frances Murray Chandler. While she was still a small child, her parents moved to Jacksonville, Florida, and then to Charleston, South Carolina, where her father bred and raced horses. Her first schooling was in a convent in Charlestown, but the family soon returned to Manhattan when South Carolina passed laws prohibiting racetrack betting. Mr. Chandler became a jeweler, and Helen was enrolled in the Professional Children's School on West 48th Street. During Helen's stay there, her classmates included Lillian Roth, Richard Ross, and Russell Hewitt. Helen first performed at the school, and then, in 1916, with the Union Hill, New Jersey, stock company.

In 1917 Helen accompanied a friend to a rehearsal and Broadway figure Arthur Hopkins, noticing the sparkling blue-eyed child, asked,

With Ralph Forbes in *Christopher Strong* (RKO '33)

A mid-Thirties publicity pose.

HOPKINS: Hello! What's your name?
HELEN: Helen Chandler. What's yours?
HOPKINS: Arthur Hopkins. Have you ever been on the stage?
HELEN: No. Have you?
HOPKINS: In a way. How would you like to be in a play?
HELEN: Very much.

So Helen made her Broadway debut at the Plymouth Theatre on November 5, 1917, as Elizabeth in *Barbara*. Then came roles in *Penrod* (in which she appeared for the first time as Helen Chandler), *Daddy Long Legs,* and *The Light of the World.* In March, 1920, she played one of the princes murdered in the Tower of London by their uncle *Richard III* (John Barrymore). It was the most important production of her childhood years. She was back at the Plymouth Theatre again in December, 1923, as Annabelle in *The Potters.* Featured in the cast was another Professional Children's School pupil, Raymond Guion, later known as Gene Raymond.

The role of Hedvig in Ibsen's *The Wild Duck* has challenged many actresses down the years and it was a tremendous task for sixteen-year-old Helen to play the role in the Actors' Theatre Production starring Blanche Yurka as Gina. Her Hedvig received glowing notices. In addition to the demanding Ibsen role, Helen played Mary in *The Servant in the House* during special matinees of *The Wild Duck* run. She advanced her reputation in the theatre further by playing Ophelia in a modern dress version of *Hamlet* (1925), with Basil Sydney as the Prince and Kay Francis as the Player Queen. There were more stage roles, but by 1926 Helen decided she should be in the movies.

Determined to be discovered for the cinema, Helen went to the Fox Studio, then on New York City's Tenth Avenue, and asked to see Mr. Fox. Mr. Fox was not available, but director Allan Dwan was and he gave her the role of Jenny in his *The Music Master* (1927), a feature with Alec B. Francis and Lois Moran. Impressed with Helen's screen debut, Dwan next assigned her the role of Flora in *The Joy Girl* (1927), which was shot largely in Palm Beach, Florida.

Although she enjoyed the novelty of film-making, she could not resist an opportunity to work for the prestigious Theatre Guild. Thus, in April, 1927, she succeeded Margalo Gillmore as Hester in the Guild's *The Silver Cord.* Later, for The Theatre Guild, Helen would play Margaret in *Faust* (1928). Also in the same cast of the later show were Douglass Montgomery and Eric Linden. On January 7, 1929, Helen played in *The Marriage Bed.* During its six-week run on the West Coast she signed to make a few pictures in Hollywood.

Her initial California film was *Mother's Boy* (1929) at Pathé, she played Morton Downey's sweetheart in the musical. She had similar roles in Fox's *The Sky Hawk* (1929) and as George O'Brien's inspiration in *Salute* (1929). All of the roles were of the ingenue variety, but Helen came across well on the screen. With her next outing before the cameras, she convinced all of Hollywood that an actress had arrived. For Warner Bros.' *Outward Bound* (1930), starring Leslie Howard and a superlative supporting cast, Helen was cast as Ann opposite Douglas Fairbanks, Jr. (Henry). She and Fairbanks, Jr. played the two would-be suicides who find themselves in limbo on a mysterious ship taking a voyage into the unknown. (When William A. Brady revived *Outward Bound* on Broadway in 1938 with Laurette Taylor as Mrs. Midget, Helen repeated her role as Ann.)

Hollywood has always dwelt on comparisons, and Helen's niche was "the new Lillian Gish." In return, Helen said that Miss Lillian was the only screen artist to approach true genius and art on the screen, with Greta Garbo a close second. Then someone discovered there was a remarkable resemblance between Helen and Lotta

121

Crabtree, and she was lured into a publicity stunt duplicating an ancient tintype of Lotta, complete with a vivandiere costume and Helen holding a cigar. The reconstructed pose and resemblance proved uncannily accurate. But Helen had a singular magic of her own that puzzled the film factories. The publicity departments alternately created poses of Helen looking alluringly soignée, coifed and clothed to resemble Garbo, or posed dramatically for a decolletage effect. In actuality, her own naturalness was even more effective.

Her private life was more blissful, for a time. She married British novelist-playwright Cyril Hume on February 3, 1930. However, Mr. Hume soon became disenchanted with Helen's willy-nilly absentmindedness, wondering whether she was more of a child than his five-year-old daughter Barbara by a previous marriage. Although the Humes' agreement was to live within his earnings, his patience was sorely tested when he found Helen had put her entire first-year earnings in Hollywood into a speculative Building and Loan Association she mistook for a bank, losing every cent. In the meantime, Hume labored at MGM writing dialogue for *Trader Horn, The New Moon,* and Helen's delightful *Daybreak* (1931). In that picture, seduced and abandoned by Ramon Novarro, she gave a completely charming and appealing performance as an innocent Viennese piano teacher.

Tod Browning had seen Helen's spirited performance on Broadway in *The Silent House* and subsequently had her signed for the role of Mina Seward in *Dracula* (1931), starring Bela Lugosi. The horror film proved to be Universal's biggest moneymaker of 1931. The picture had many memorable sequences, notably the eerily photographed opening. Helen's immobile, trancelike appearance as the terrified heroine is one of her most memorable screen portrayals.

For Tiffany, Helen did E. B. Sheldon's old chestnut in the title role of *Salvation Nell* (1931), overplaying the role in an outdated, dull script. At RKO she was a delight in her first color picture as Edna May Oliver's daughter in *Fanny Foley Herself* (1931). Two of her most memorable films were *The Last Flight* (1931) and *A House Divided* (1932). The former presented her as the alluring Nikki surrounded by four former aviators (Richard Barthelmess, David Manners, *et al.*) The other was directed by William Wyler and co-starred Walter Huston and Douglass Montgomery. She played the sensitive mail order bride who falls in love with the son (Montgomery) of the man (Huston) she has agreed to wed.

Helen had returned to Broadway in late 1931 for *Springtime for Henry.* After this comedy she came back to Hollywood, only to be relegated to secondary roles. *Vanity Street* (1932) with Charles Bickford was at poverty row's Columbia, and then she made several films for even-lower-regarded Mayfair Pictures. At the bigger studios she was forced to accept smaller parts, as in Warner Bros.' *Goodbye Again* (1933) in the third feminine role after Joan Blondell and Genevieve Tobin. She had the same fate at RKO in *Christopher Strong* (1933), in which an unestablished Katharine Hepburn had the lead, followed by Billie Burke. Making her fate all the more incongruous, Helen continually received a fine reception from the critics.

For the first time since they were together in 1919 on Broadway in *Richard III,* Helen and John Barrymore were cast for the leads in RKO's *Long Lost Father* (1933). Barrymore was still giving brilliant performances. Helen, certainly no singer, sang a song, "It Isn't So Much that I Wouldn't," and romanced onscreen with Donald Cook as a young doctor to whom papa Barrymore conspires to have her wed. While Barrymore went to to film the zany *Twentieth Century* (1934), Helen returned to First National-Warner Bros. to assume a supporting role to Richard Barthelmass in *Midnight Alibi* (1934). She then left for England.

With Natalie Moorhead, G. P. Huntley, Jr., Phyllis Barry, and Alan Mowbray in *Long Lost Father* (RKO '34).

Most likely, she must have reasoned that her career would improve abroad. She told the press that she would like to play Alice in *Alice in Wonderland* and explained her Hollywood problem. "In *Dracula* I played one of those bewildered little girls who go around pale, hollow-eyed and anguished, wondering about things . . . I was! Wondering about when I could get to a hospital and part with a rampant appendix without holding up the picture. I finally had my appendix out between *Dracula* and *Daybreak*." On her screen appearance, "They have problems with me in pictures. With this sharp profile, when they turn me sideways to the camera, I look just like the edge of a Bible." On talkies, "Hang me for heresy if you like but sounding the screen robbed it of glamour. I used to love the silent movies—their beauty, the enchanting lighting, the slow gestures. Just try to open your mouth and look soulful! The voice reveals, ah, it does!"

For Gaumount-British, Helen played the role of a tender pawnshop girl in love with Franz Schubert in *Unfinished Symphony* (1935).

Having divorced Cyril Hume before going abroad, Helen felt free to find a new romance, so, while in London, she renewed her acquaintance with Bramwell Fletcher, who was also there on a filming assignment. They had appeared together on Broadway in a short-lived play, *These Two*, in May, 1934. Then Helen returned to the States, did some radio work, and joined the cast of *It's You I Want*, which opened on Broadway in February, 1935. By this time Fletcher was also on Broadway, appearing in *Within the Gates* with Lillian Gish.

St. Valentine's Day, February 14, 1935, found Helen at the Riverside Church marrying Fletcher. Gladys Swarthout sang "Oh Promise Me" and Helen was an appropriate vision in a silver-gray lace afternoon dress. A large reception for the show business contingent was held in the ballroom of the Hotel Gotham. Helen's show closed on February 16, while Fletcher's five-month run in *Within the Gates* ended on February 23. Mr. and Mr. Bramwell Fletcher spent their honeymoon planning rehearsals for their parts in a new play *The Dominant Sex,* which tried out in Philadelphia in late March, 1935. It lasted for a mere sixteen performances on Broadway in mid-April.

In 1935, the Fletchers returned to England. Helen made two features for Wardour: *It's a Bet* (1935) and *Radio Parade of 1935* (1935), joining with Will Hay in this screen musical. The Fletchers later returned to New York where Helen played Jane, one of Lucile Watson's daughters in a stylish production of *Pride and Prejudice* (1935). She left this successful venture to join the American premiere of *Lady Precious Stream* in the title role, with Bramwell Fletcher cast as the gardener. This "museum piece" hung on for fourteen weeks.

As a decided change of pace, the Fletchers returned to the London stage in the West End edition of *Boy Meets Girl* (1936), that wacky comedy about Hollywood. Crossing the Atlantic once again, Helen was seen on Broadway in *The Holmeses of Baker Street* (1936). Early the next year she and Fletcher headed a touring company of Noël Coward's short-play cycle, *Tonight at 8:30,* which enjoyed a short West Coast run in Santa Barbara before moving on to San Francisco and back down to Los Angeles for successful engagements.

By early 1938 the Fletchers had moved to Chicago for a five-week run of the Coward offering. Helen was later cast in a Michael Todd-produced fiasco called *The Man from Cairo.* By this time, her final film, *Mr. Boggs Steps Out* (1937), made with Stuart Erwin in England, had gone into release.

The last acting assignment the Fletchers accepted together was the revival of *Outward Bound,* in which Bramwell was Mr. Prior. By the time of the national tour of the revival that fall, both husband and wife had left the cast. The gossip columns reported their marital breakup and separation. As fate would have it, Fletcher became involved with Diana Barrymore who had replaced Helen in *Outward Bound.* If Fletcher's union with the often-addled and charmingly vague Miss Chandler, who drank a little, was "unhappy," his life with Diana after their marriage in 1942 (two years after he divorced Helen) was a sheer nightmare.

By the Forties, Helen's health and emotional problems were rampant and she accepted no film offers. She did a few radio broadcasts, but by August, 1940, she was admitted to La Crescenta Sanitarium as a result of a nervous breakdown. By November she had recovered sufficiently to accept an offer to play in a revival of some of the playlets of *Tonight at 8:30.* The production opened at the Curran Theatre in San Francisco on November 25, 1940, all proceeds going to the British War Relief Association.

Helen's last stage appearance was on July 3, 1941, when she played Amy in a revival of George Kelly's *The Show-Off,* starring Joe E. Brown. By this point she had been on the stage and in pictures for twenty-four of her thirty-five years. While she had many fond memories on which to look back, she had not had her life's dream of playing Juliet on the stage materialize, nor satisfied her passion to play Alice in Wonderland.

A few years after her "retirement" she married merchant seaman Walter Piascik and moved to San Francisco. More years passed, and then on November 9, 1950, Helen made headlines when, in the early morning, Sam Cox, the manager of a North Whitley Terrace apartment house, forced his way to a smoke-filled apartment and saved unconscious Helen from certain death. She was rushed to the Hollywood Receiving Hospital with multiple second-degree burns and placed in intensive care. Seaman Piascik had shipped out after establishing Helen in the apartment. Investigators found quantities of sleeping tablets in the room. Helen's return to Hollywood *was* noticed.

Her shattered nerves did not heal as did the second-degree burns. In 1954 she was committed to California's De Witt State Hospital. Five years later she was released as cured and conditioned for home placement. Lillian Roth, whose documentation of her alcoholic problems and tortures, *I'll Cry Tomorrow,* had been followed by a sequel *Beyond My Worth,* was living in Palm Springs, California. Miss Roth invited Helen as a house guest following her release from De Witt. No one could have been more attuned to Chandler's torment nor as sympathetic as Miss Roth, whose mingled admiration for Helen's talent and deep understanding of her problems were actually responsible for Helen's return to reality.

Helen and Walter Piascik were eventually reunited and settled in Venice, California, but Helen made no effort to resume her career. On April 20, 1965, she was admitted to General Hospital in a state of shock and underwent surgery for massive bleeding of an ulcer. On April 30, 1965, she died. At three P.M. on the afternoon of May 3, services were held at Pierce Brothers Funeral Home in Hollywood. There was a very small audience.

HELEN CHANDLER

The Music Master *(Fox 1927)*
The Joy Girl *(Fox 1927)*
Mother's Boy *(Pathé 1929)*
Salute *(Fox 1929)*
The Sky Hawk *(Fox 1929)*
A Rough Romance *(Fox 1930)*
Outward Bound *(WB 1930)*
Mother's Cry *(WB 1930)*
Dracula *(Univ 1931)*
Daybreak *(MGM 1931)*
The Last Flight *(WB 1931)*
Salvation Nell *(Tiffany 1931)*
Fanny Foley Herself *(RKO 1931)*
A House Divided *(Univ 1932)*

Vanity Street *(Col 1932)*
Behind Jury Doors *(Mayfair 1932)*
Christopher Strong *(RKO 1933)*
Alimony Madness *(Mayfair 1933)*
Dance Hall Hostess *(Mayfair 1933)*
Goodbye Again *(FN 1933)*
The Worst Woman in Paris? *(Fox 1933)*
Long Lost Father *(RKO 1934)*
Midnight Alibi *(FN 1934)*
Unfinished Symphony *(Gaumont 1935)*
It's a Bet *(Wardour 1935)*
Radio Parade of 1935 *(Wardour 1935)*
Mr. Boggs Steps Out *(Grand National 1937)*

14

Mae Clarke

Resilient, chipper, flinty—these are some of the adjectives that apply to Mae Clarke, one of the better leading ladies of the early Thirties. One can only wonder what would have happened to her screen career, had she *not* been cast in *The Public Enemy* (1931). In that classic gangster yarn, James Cagney pushed a grapefruit into her face, and gave Mae her own tangy bit of immortality. The notoriety caused by that unique breakfast scene in *The Public Enemy* doubtlessly contributed to her later box-office value, but it is also possible that it may have saddled her with a limited screen image that was too hard to shake.

Walter R. and Violet Klotz lived at 2632 West Seltzer Street in Philadelphia. There on Friday, August 16, 1907, they added a daughter to their family, naming her Violet Mary Klotz. Soon after her birth the family moved to Atlantic City where Mr. Klotz played the organ at a local movie theatre. Daughter Violet attended elementary school there and also studied dancing at Dawson's Dancing School. Between school and dancing lessons, young Violet sold hot dogs on Atlantic City's boardwalk until a friend of her dancing teacher, Earl Lindsay, persuaded her to test her talents in New York City.

She landed a job as a hoofer in a Strand Roof show where another youngster, Ruby Stevens, dancing in the chorus line, took charge of her; they soon became close friends, and later moved to a revue at the Everglades Club. Ruby helped Mae correct her deportment and table manners, and taught her about proper clothing. Dancing jobs continued at the Vanity Club and Anatole Friedland's Cafe, plus chorus jobs in *Sitting Pretty* (1924) and *Gay Paree* (1925). With Walda Mansfield and Ruby, Mae tried out for Willard Mack's new play, *The Noose*. Mae was cast as Georgie, and Ruby Stevens, who later became Barbara Stanwyck, appeared as Dot. Their small roles continued in the play for 197 performances after the October, 1926, opening. Mae toured with the play and married Fannie Brice's brother, Lew, who was seen in several of Broadway's *Passing Shows* and at numerous racetracks.

George White's production of *Manhattan Mary* (promoted as "A New Musical Comedy—Clean from Beginning to End") starred Ed Wynn and featured George White and Ona Munson. Mae Clarke played Viola Fay, joined Harland Dixon in a dance specialty, and other members of the cast in singing "My Blue Bird's Home Again" and "It Won't Be Long Now." The Wynn show was a distinct hit, lasting 265 performances. Later Mae and her husband devised a vaudeville act centered on his first love, horse racing. It was

With Jack Mulhall in *The Fall Guy* (RKO '30).

called "What's the Odds?" in which Mae played a high-class bettor who runs her winnings into a million dollars, but trades the whole bundle for a husband. While on the road with the sketch, Mae was asked to test for Fox Films. She sang, danced, exhibited several emotions, and recited a speech she recalled from *The Noose* (later she discovered Stanwyck had used the same speech for her own screen test). As a result of this test, Mae won a one-year Fox contract.

At twenty-two 5' 2' Mae, with honey-colored hair and penetrating gray eyes, made her first bid for screen fame. She was in *Big Time* (1929), which featured rising Broadway performer Lee Tracy. The story was based on a vaudeville husband-wife team with the distaff side rising to fame in movies. The plot paralleled a little bit too closely Mae's personal life, what with her nearly collapsed marriage to Lew Brice. ("He hated being known as Mr. Mae Clarke, poor guy. But what man wouldn't?") Fox next utilized her musical talents in *Nix on Dames* (1929) which contained a half-dozen easily forgotten songs, with Robert Ames and William Harrigan battling for Mae's favors. Fox lent her to RKO for a role in the film version of George Abbott and James Gleason's Broadway success, *The Fall Guy* (1930). In November 1930, Mae was seen on the screen in the remake of *The Dancers* (1925), in which she accepts marriage to Phillips Holmes after his true love (Lois Moran) has committed suicide. By December she was seen as Helen Gordon in a melange of members of the U.S. Coast Guard, train wrecks, burning ships, and flaming love called *Men on Call*. Fox did not renew her contract.

For Columbia she made a quickie called *The Good Bad Girl* (1931), giving a sincere performance as a girl bent on leaving the rackets who is helped in her efforts by James Hall. For director Lewis Milestone she tested for the ingenue role in *The Front Page* (1931). While Mary Brian got that assignment, Mae persuaded Milestone that she could

With Boris Karloff in *Frankenstein* (Univ '31).

handle the part of the heart-of-gold prostitute Molly Malloy. She played the part to perfection. (Mae would later recall of her oncamera death leap from the newsroom window, "The jump was about six feet and there was a net to catch me. When I hit the net I bounced. And I kept thinking how funny it would be if I should bounce right back into the scene with the cameras grinding.")

The Front Page marked the turning point of her career. Next came Kitty in *The Public Enemy* and *that* much-discussed, -duplicated, and -remembered battle-of-the-sexes scene. A short-term contract with Universal followed. She was assigned to play the prostitute plying her trade on a bridge over the Thames in London, who falls in love with a soldier in *Waterloo Bridge* (1931). She garnered critical acclaim nationally for her emoting. *The Cleveland News* stated, "Mae Clarke earns a class A rating. Chatterton or Garbo could not do this film more capably." Predictions of immediate stardom were proclaimed throughout the press. Mae was reported to be engaged to Universal photographer Harry Freulich, with wedding plans set for the late fall. It was also rumored that she would sign a five-year contract with Universal. However, neither the marriage nor the pact materialized.

While Mae's good friend Barbara Stanwyck had already reached star status, Mae seemed unable to accomplish the jump into the A-film status league. Her acting lacked versatility and emotional depth. However, she was still an important asset to films during the Thirties. She played Dr. Frankenstein's fiancee in *Frankenstein* (1931), the classic grand guignol thriller starring Boris Karloff. The film cost $275,000 to make and Universal would realize over twelve million dollars from its release and rerelease.

Universal loaned Mae to Columbia for two rather good movies. She received fine notices for her playing of a big-city loser who poisons herself in *Three Wise Girls* (1932), which also starred Jean Harlow and Marie Prevost, and she was a tough reporter to editor Pat O'Brien in *Final Edition* (1932). Again, predictions of "instant" stardom filled the press after her fine performance in *Impatient Maiden* (1932), in which she is in love with ambulance driver Lew Ayres. She was again with Ayres when she played a hoofer in Boris Karloff's nightclub in *Night World* (1932). Then came a batch of bottom-of-the-bill entries and Mae's bid for stardom was over.

MGM offered her a showy role in *Made on Broadway* (1933), but she was involved in an automobile accident that resulted in a broken jaw and a long period of hospitalization. Sally Eilers played her role at Metro. On March 25, 1934, she instituted a $21,500 lawsuit against actor Phillips Holmes charging him with negligent driving. Holmes paid her hospital bills, and the matter was "forgotten."

At Metro, Mae turned in a fine performance as Lee Tracy's thrifty wife in *Turn Back the Clock* (1933), and in *Fast Workers* (1933), with John Gilbert and Robert Armstrong, she alone made the film worth seeing. Her dubious fame as the screen's favorite punching bag was accentuated when she returned to Warner Bros. with Cagney in *Lady Killer* (1934). This time around she was dragged out of bed by her hair, pulled across the floor, and pushed a dozen feet down a corridor by James. Her next feature with Cagney would have him behaving on the right side of the law, with Mae as his sweetheart, in Grand National's *Great Guy* (1936).

By 1934, Mae was reduced to playing supporting roles in pictures. Her assignments ranged from Samuel Goldwyn's costly *Nana* (1934) to Warner Bros.' *The Man with Two Faces* (1934), with Edward G. Robinson and Mary Astor. She had a romantic lead with Lew Ayres in *Silk Hat Kid* (1935) and, later, when Ayres tried his hand at directing *Hearts in Bondage* (1936) Mae was James Dunn's leading lady. Announcements were made in 1936 that Mae would marry Dr. Frank G. Nolan, but a year later she became the wife of a China Clipper pilot, Captain Stevens Bancroft.

In 1937, Mae made two double-billers with Jack Holt for Republic and was off the

Modeling an afternoon suit in '34.

screen until 1940, when she returned to join a virtually all-female cast in *Women in War,* including Wendy Barrie, Barbara Pepper, and once great star Elsie Janis. As Nurse Gail Halliday, Mae is killed off in the economy proceedings. Her studio employment became less frequent after her divorce from Bancroft, and she married Captain Herbert Langdon in 1946. Thereafter her career slowed down to one picture a year, and they were mostly Republic program fillers. Then, in 1949, Mae hit cinematic "bottom" by playing the lead of a newspaper photographer, Glenda Thomas, in Republic's twelve-episode serial *King of the Rocket Men.* At age forty-two, Mae was too mature for the derring-do that was required within these chapterplays.

The Fifties brought insignificant small parts in often major films in which she received no onscreen billing. In October, 1953, again single, she was given a suspended twenty-day sentence for failure to report forty-three dollars that she had earned the previous May while drawing unemployment compensation from the State of California. Pleading guilty, she repaid the court thirty-nine dollars, while working as a volunteer telephone answering service for the "Family Theatre" television show.

After her day in court Mae began getting television work on "The Loretta Young Show," "Four Star Theatre," "Public Defender," and "Medic," with a day's work at one of the film studios (as a saleswoman in MGM's *The Catered Affair,* 1956). Throughout the late Fifties and early Sixties she appeared on some three dozen video shows, including a continuing part as Nurse Marge Brown in ABC-TV's "General Hospital" series. Eventually she taught drama for the Parks and Recreation Department at Pico Rivera, California, and continued with small assignments from the studios, such as a bit in *A Big Hand for the Little Lady* (1966).

Mae's most recent splash in the limelight was when she appeared on the televised American Film Institute's Life Achievement Award banquet for James Cagney in March,

130

1974. The handsome, well-coiffed, smartly dressed woman closed her remarks about the star by saying, "We love you, baby!"

Reflecting on her early Thirties' career in Hollywood, it is strange that Mae Clark never attained star status. Barbara Stanwyck expected her to make it. In later years she would comment, "If I'd made a guess as to which of us [referring to Mae, Walda Mansfield, and herself] would make it big, I'd have guessed Mae because she was the better dancer and the most vivacious. I saw her on television a while back and she still looks wonderful."

In the 1970 *Watermelon Man* she played a bit role. The publicists asked her to pose with Godfrey Cambridge as he threatens her with half a grapefruit. Mae laughed and was amused that nearly forty years afterward, the public still recalled her famous *The Public Enemy* bit. "So, what the hell, I went along with the gag," flipped Mae.

MAE CLARKE

Big Time *(Fox 1929)*
Nix on Dames *(Fox 1929)*
The Dancers *(Fox 1930)*
The Fall Guy*(RKO1930)*
Men on Call *(Fox 1930)*
Reckless Living *(Univ 1931)*
The Front Page *(UA 1931)*
The Good Bad Girl *(Col 1931)*
Waterloo Bridge *(Univ 1931)*
The Public Enemy *(WB 1931)*
Frankenstein *(Univ 1931)*
Impatient Maiden *(Univ 1932)*
Three Wise Girls *(Col 1932)*
Final Edition *(Col 1932)*
Night World *(Univ 1932)*
Breach of Promise *(World Wide 1932)*
The Penguin Pool Murder *(RKO 1932)*
As the Devil Commands *(Col 1932)*
Parole Girl *(Col 1933)*
Turn Back the Clock *(MGM 1933)*
Penthouse *(MGM 1933)*
Fast Workers *(MGM 1933)*
Lady Killer *(WB 1934)*
Flaming Gold *(RKO 1934)*
This Side of Heaven *(MGM 1934)*
Let's Talk It Over *(Univ 1934)*
Nana *(UA 1934)*
The Man with Two Faces *(FN 1934)*
The Daring Young Man *(Fox 1935)*
Silk Hat Kid *(Fox 1935)*
Hitch Hike Lady *(Rep 1935)*
The House of 1,000 Candles *(Rep 1936)*
Wild Brian Kent *(RKO 1936)*
Great Guy *(Grand National 1936)*
Hats Off *(Grand National 1936)*
Hearts in Bondage *(Rep 1936)*
Trouble in Morocco *(Col 1937)*
Outlaws of the Orient *(Col 1937)*
Women in War *(Rep 1940)*

Sailors on Leave *(Rep 1941)*
Flying Tigers *(Rep 1942)*
The Lady from Chungking *(PRC 1942)*
And Now Tomorrow *(Par 1944)*
Here Come the Waves *(Par 1944)*
Kitty *(Par 1945)*
Daredevils of the Clouds *(Rep 1948)*
Streets of San Francisco *(Rep 1949)*
Gun Runner *(Mon 1949)*
King of the Rocket Men *(Rep serial 1949)*
Annie Get Your Gun *(MGM 1950)*
The Yellow Cab Man *(MGM 1950)*
The Unknown Man *(MGM 1951)*
The Great Caruso *(MGM 1951)*
Callaway Went Thataway *(MGM 1951)*
3 Guys Named Mike *(MGM 1951)*
Mr. Imperium *(MGM 1951)*
Thunderbirds *(Rep 1952)*
Pat and Mike *(MGM 1952)*
Fearless Fagan *(MGM 1952)*
Singin' in the Rain *(MGM 1952)*
Because of You *(Univ 1952)*
Horizons West *(Univ 1952)*
Confidentially Connie *(MGM 1953)*
Magnificent Obsession *(MGM 1954)*
Women's Prison *(Col 1955)*
Not as a Stranger *(UA 1955)*
I Died a Thousand Times *(WB 1955)*
Wichita *(AA 1955)*
Come Next Spring *(Rep 1956)*
The Catered Affair *(MGM 1956)*
Mohawk *(20th 1956)*
The Desperadoes Are in Town *(20th 1956)*
Ride the High Iron *(Col 1956)*
Voice in the Mirror *(Univ 1958)*
Ask Any Girl *(MGM 1959)*
A Big Hand for the Little Lady *(WB 1966)*
Thoroughly Modern Millie *(Univ 1967)*
Watermelon Man *(Col 1970)*

15

Donald Cook

The need for stalwart, handsome leading men was part of the Thirties' drive to increase the roster of acceptable and talented screen players. Donald Cook filled out this demand in featured niches with frequently fine performances, but an occasional overemoting portrayal. He was never chosen for a studio build-up to star status, but performed his alloted assignments very well indeed. A more gracious actor, on or off screen, would be hard to find.

He was born on Thursday, September 26, 1901, in Portland, Oregon, to Edith Parker and Frank R. Cook. The family banking business was considered to be Donald's future after he graduated from the University of Oregon with a degree in agriculture. But he soon found the banking field a bore and began pursuing the footlights. He teamed with a partner for a fairly amateurish song-and-patter vaudeville routine that did little except get him to Emporia, Kansas.

Later he joined the Kansas City Players, augmenting his new career with bread-and-butter jobs as a bellhop and cattle counter in the Kansas City stockyards. Actress Margaret Anglin, on tour in Kansas City, saw Donald's work with the Community Players and gave him a letter of introduction to New York producer George C. Tyler. Using the name Donn Cook he joined Mrs. Minnie Maddern Fiske's all-star revival of *The Rivals* in 1925. In later years Cook credited Mrs. Fiske's untiring interest in his career with teaching him the fundamentals and nuances of comedy techniques. After the Fiske tour, in which he played Jack Absolute, he joined a stock company in Columbus, Ohio. The following season he ventured into New York City to test his training on Broadway.

He made his Broadway debut as Donn Cook on November 1, 1926, in *Seed of the Brute.* The play featured Robert Ames, Hilda Vaughn, and Doris Rankin, and veered from blackmail to illegitimacy in subject matter. It ran for eighty performances. Thereafter he returned to Columbus for more stock training and was back on Broadway, this time with Pauline Lord, in *Spellbound.* Next came his first real New York success. He was signed for the plum role of Jim Hutton in Philip Barry's hit *Paris Bound,* with Madge Kennedy and Hope Williams. It opened on December 27, 1927, and ran for 197 performances and then enjoyed an extensive road tour.

After a season and a half with the Barry play, Cook was summoned on three days notice to play the novelist in Maxwell Anderson's *Gypsy,* directed by George Cukor. It was a short-lived venture as was the later *Half-Gods.* It was *Rebound,* which opened in February, 1930, that led to bids to him from the West Coast to enter pictures.

With Mae Clarke and Clarence Wilson in *The Penguin Pool Murder* (RKO '32).

For the screen, he changed his name from Donn to Donald. His debut role was as James Cagney's hard-working, upright brother in *Public Enemy* (1931). His performance created a fine balance to Cagney's ruffian. Unfortunately his solid work was not rewarded with more important parts. He supplied the love interest in a dull tale of marriage with Dorothy Mackaill in *Party Husband* (1931) and was Ruth Chatterton's brother in her teary *Unfaithful* (1931). Without much enthusiasm he played the role of Fedor in John Barrymore's *The Mad Genius* (1931).

In Fox's *The Trial of Vivienne Ware* (1932) Cook frequently overacted to his role as a lawyer in love with his client, Joan Bennett. Years later Cook and Miss Bennett would become a regular acting team on the stock circuit, on television, and even on Broadway. *The Man Who Played God* (1932) was George Arliss' remake of an earlier vehicle. The film proved to be the turning point for Bette Davis' career, but for Donald, as the man vying with Arliss for her love, it was just another stock assignment. Most of Cook's screen work consisted of supporting roles, and in 1933 he was back with Ruth Chatterton again in a tear jerker, *Frisco Jenny*, this time as her long-forgotten illegitimate son.

Donald played well opposite Sylvia Sidney in Theodore Dreiser's *Jennie Gerhardt* (1933) and he was Nancy Carroll's lover brushing with death from husband Frank Morgan in *The Kiss before the Mirror* (1933). He was in Barbara Stanwyck's misfire *Baby Face* (1933) and in Carole Lombard's unfelicitous *Brief Moment* (1933). He and Jean Arthur raised Columbia's *Whirlpool* (1934) and *Most Precious Thing in Life* (1934) far beyond the scripts. He performed in a series of celluloid whodunits and then played Steve, married to mulatto Julie (Helen Morgan), in the best film version of *Show Boat* (1936), starring Irene Dunne and Allan Jones.

While his screen roles were run-of-the-reel, he was heard on radio in "Charlie and

With Greta Meyer, Cora Sue Collins, and Sylvia Sidney in *Jennie Gerhardt* (Par '33).

Jessie," with Dianne Bourbon and Florence Lake, "Life Begins," "Martha Webster," and "Mother of Mine," the latter with Agnes Young. Because of his unexciting and unimportant Hollywood assignments Donald returned to the stage. In 1937 he had wed Princess Gioia Tasca di Cuto of Palermo, Sicily, and they both returned to the East Coast where he was subsequently hired by the Theatre Guild.

The Guild's production of S. N. Behrman's new comedy *Wine of Choice* was fraught with problems from its opening in Chicago to further tryouts in Philadelphia. Everyone was unhappy with the play, including Alexander Woollcott, who frequently adlibbed lines he considered superior to anything Behrman had written. In Pittsburgh, Miriam Hopkins left the show and was replaced by Claudia Morgan. The play did reach Broadway but only lasted through the limited Theatre Guild subscriptions. Donald spent the summer of 1938 touring the strawhat circuit, trying out such new plays as *Soubrette*, with Else Argal, and *We, the Willowbys*.

On December 3, 1938, veteran Cook was back on Broadway in Elmer Rice's *American Landscape*, but only for forty-three performances. Fortunately, in the summer of 1939 he was in a hit tryout, Samson Raphaelson's *Skylark*, in which he played opposite Gertrude Lawrence. Their performing together was rich in subtlety, and their precision timing made *Skylark* seem far better than it actually was. The show opened at the Morosco Theatre on October 11, 1939, ran for 256 performances and then toured.

For his next theatre job, he found one of his favorite roles that seemed to go on forever. The role of David Naughton in *Claudia* appeared to be written for him. He was excellent, as were Dorothy McGuire and Frances Starr, and the show was a hit when it debuted in New York on February 12, 1941. When Rose Franken's play closed in

134

March, 1942, Donald had played 453 performances. The extensive tour continued across America and in February, 1943, Phyllis Thaxter replaced Dorothy McGuire. Donald, Frances Starr, and Olga Baclanova continued with *Claudia* through its lengthy tour.

Cook returned to Hollywood with the glowing successes of *Skylark* and *Claudia* preceding him, only to be cast in five programmers for Universal. Then it was back to Broadway to join Tallulah Bankhead in Philip Barry's *Foolish Notion* (1945). The two performers worked well together, but their union of timing was more evident the following season when they played in a revival of *Private Lives* as the battling Elyot and Amanda. Over the next few years he and Miss Bankhead would milk the Noël Coward property for several lengthy engagements.[3] His final Hollywood film was *Our Very Own* for RKO in 1950. He left the film colony for the East where he spent over nine hundred performances as a charming, rakish middle-aged roue in *The Moon is Blue* (1957).

In the late spring of 1954 he starred with Jackie Cooper in Jean Kerr and Eleanor Brooke's hit comedy *The King of Hearts*. The role of Larry Larkin was one of the toughest roles Donald ever attempted. He said, ''The problem is to be likable while at the same time playing a dislikable character.'' No one did *that* better than Cook!

Donald and his wife had settled into a farm home life at Far Hills, New Jersey, but most of his time was spent in the theatre. It was at this point in the mid-Fifties that he became reassociated with Joan Bennett, when he replaced Claude Dauphin in the comedy *Janus*, lasting through the eleven-month tour with Joan.

[3]They toured in the show for 204 weeks, before and after the New York run (October 4, 1948, 248 performances), appearing in every state but Nevada, Maine, and Florida.

With Mary Brian in *Fog* (Col '34).

In her excellent book *The Bennett Playbill* (1970) Joan describes their "first" meeting. "Producer Alfred de Liagre was looking for a leading man, and since I was given cast approval, I suggested the distinguished actor Donald Cook. I'd seen him in his greatest successes, *Skylark, Claudia* and *The Moon Is Blue* and thought him a superb actor. We met during the preparation of *Janus,* and because I felt I knew him, I said 'Hello Donald' to which he replied, formally, 'How do you do, Miss Bennett.' It was the beginning of one of the most important relationships of my life."

Neither Cook nor Joan could remember appearing together in *The Trial of Vivienne Ware.* Over the years Donald believed his leading lady to be Fay Wray, and Miss Bennett felt certain John Boles had been her vis-a-vis in the Fox fiasco. (Commenting on their mutual lapse of memory, Miss Bennett said, "No such memory lapse about Donald Cook would ever occur again, and I consider the four years we worked together among the most charmed of my life. It was a four-year acting lesson. An actor who was the very opposite of the introspective performer, his off-hand charm and ease with a laugh line was incomparable. Endowed with impeccable timing, he knew exactly when to drop the bomb, and his technique was accurately described as 'playing with a steady glib absurdity.' "

Among the summer shows that Cook and Miss Bennett did were *Anniversary Waltz, Bell, Book and Candle,* and *Once More with Feeling.* They starred together briefly on Broadway in a short-lived comedy called *Love Me Little,* directed by Alfred Drake, and for six weeks in 1959, they starred in David Susskind's nighttime TV series, "Too Young to Go Steady." That fall they took to the road in a bus and truck production of *The Pleasure of His Company,* barnstorming as players of another era. The tour lasted nine months although they received a one-month reprieve by replacing Cornelia Otis Skinner and Cyril Ritchard in the road company of the show in Toronto, Canada. The summer of 1960 found Cook and Miss Bennett in *The Gazebo* at Saratoga Springs, New York.

It was in September, 1961, that Donald arrived in New Haven, Connecticut, to play a rich Parisian having an affair with his parlor maid (Julie Harris) in *A Shot in the Dark.* When he failed to appear for a matinee performance, investigation disclosed he had suffered a heart attack. He was found semi-conscious on the floor of his hotel room. He was taken to the Grace-New Haven Hospital where he died on October 1, 1961, at the age of sixty.

To Joan Bennett it was a horrifying blow and she wrote, "I was heartbroken and at a loss myself, not only personally but professionally. Working with Donald, I understood what 'ensemble' playing meant for the first time and felt I never wanted to set foot on a stage again without him." Of course, she did return to the stage.

Over the years in Hollywood, but more especially on the stage, Donald had played to perfection the man of distinction. In so many ways, Donald Cook was just that.

DONALD COOK

Public Enemy *(WB 1931)*
Party Husband *(FN 1931)*
Side Show *(WB 1931)*
Unfaithful *(Par 1931)*
The Mad Genius *(WB 1931)*
Safe in Hell *(FN 1931)*
Taxi! *(WB 1932)*
The Trial of Vivienne Ware *(Fox 1932)*
The Man Who Played God *(WB 1932)*
The Penguin Pool Murder *(RKO 1932)*
The Heart of New York *(WB 1932)*
New Morals for Old *(MGM 1932)*
The Conquerors *(RKO 1932)*
Frisco Jenny *(WB 1933)*
Private Jones *(Univ 1933)*
The Circus Queen Murder *(Col 1933)*
Jennie Gerhardt *(Par 1933)*
The Kiss before the Mirror *(Univ 1933)*
Baby Face *(WB 1933)*
Brief Moment *(Col 1933)*
The World Changes *(WB 1933)*
The Woman I Stole *(Col 1933)*
Fury of the Jungle *(Col 1934)*
Fog *(Col 1934)*
Viva Villa! *(MGM 1934)*
Long Lost Father *(RKO 1934)*
The Ninth Guest *(Col 1934)*
Whirlpool *(Col 1934)*

Most Precious Thing in Life *(Col 1934)*
Jealousy *(Col 1934)*
Fugitive Lady *(Col 1934)*
The Night Is Young *(MGM 1935)*
Behind the Evidence *(Col 1935)*
The Casino Murder Case *(MGM 1935)*
Ladies Love Danger *(Fox 1935)*
Gigolette *(RKO 1935)*
Murder in the Fleet *(MGM 1935)*
Motive for Revenge *(Majestic 1935)*
Here Comes the Band *(MGM 1935)*
Confidential *(Mascot 1935)*
The Spanish Cape Mystery *(Rep 1935)*
Show Boat *(Univ 1936)*
Ring around the Moon *(Chesterfield 1936)*
The Leavenworth Case *(Rep 1936)*
The Calling of Dan Matthews *(Col 1936)*
The Girl from Mandalay *(Rep 1936)*
Can This Be Dixie? *(20th 1936)*
Beware of Ladies *(Rep 1937)*
Circus Girl *(Rep 1937)*
Two Wise Maids *(Rep 1937)*
Bowery to Broadway *(Univ 1944)*
Murder in the Blue Room *(Univ 1944)*
Patrick the Great *(Univ 1945)*
Here Come the Coeds *(Univ 1945)*
Blonde Ransom *(Univ 1945)*
Our Very Own *(RKO 1950)*

16

Larry "Buster" Crabbe

Buster Crabbe returned to the Los Angeles Swim Stadium in June, 1971, for the second annual Senior Sports International Swim Meet. He won two events, anchoring a winning relay team and setting a world record in the 400-meter freestyle swimming event for the over-sixty group. At the time he was sixty-three years old and many decades away from his first victories in the swimming field, where he eventually set sixteen world and American records. He had won thirty-five national championships and, in 1932, when the Olympics were held in Los Angeles, he won the Gold Medal for the U.S. Olympic Swimming Team for the 400-meter freestyle, after placing only third and fourth in the 1928 Olympics at Amsterdam, Holland.

Crabbe's records never threatened the achievements set by Johnny Weissmuller of sixty-seven world records and fifty-two national championships, plus five gold medals, but his screen record far outshone Peter John Weissmuller's, both in the number of pictures made and, above all, in acting ability. The latter-day Mark Spitz has been a more publicized swimming champ than Buster, but Spitz seems to lack the congenial personality and pleasant screen manner that distinguished Crabbe's every appearance.

Buster was born Clarence Linden Crabbe in Oakland, California, on Friday, February 7, 1908. When he was just a few months old the Crabbes[4] moved to Hawaii where his father was a "luna" or overseer on the pineapple plantation of Libby, McNeill, and Libby. His father dubbed his son "Buster," and, as a small child, Clarence Linden became an excellent swimmer, surfer, and horseman. In high school he received sixteen sports letters. After spending one year at the University of Hawaii and just before the 1932 Olympics, he transferred to the University of Southern California.

While a pre-law student at the University of California Buster augmented his allowance by appearing as an extra in films, such as MGM's *Good News* (1930). He was also a stunt man, doubling for Joel McCrea in *The Most Dangerous Game* (1932). As an amateur athlete he could not take money, so his extra movie stunt work dissolved into a solution of "presents." He was an extra in Columbia's sports film *That's My Boy* (1932)

---

[4]He was proud of his ancestry, which included a great, great grandfather, Captain John Meek of Marblehead, Massachusetts, who first visited the Islands around 1820; and another grandfather, George Crabbe, who came from Australia, became chamberlain to a Hawaiian king, and married a native girl.

With Sally Starr, Mary Carlisle, and Charles Starrett in *The Sweetheart of Sigma Chi* (Mon '33).

and, after the 1932 Olympics, was offered a test by MGM for a Tarzan picture, along with many others, including Herman Brix, who later became Bruce Bennett. Also considered for the Tarzan role by Metro were Joel McCrea, Johnny Mack Brown, Tom Tyler, Charles Bickford, and even Clark Gable. Weissmuller was Metro's final choice, and he made six Tarzan epics for them (and six more for RKO). Anxious to compete in the jungle sweepstakes, Paramount was preparing *King of the Jungle* (1933). They tested several candidates for Kaspa the Lion Man and finally selected Buster from among five finalists. Buster would return to the Islands each summer, and on one of his home visits he met Adah Virginia Held on the beach. They were married on April 13, 1933, at Yuma, Arizona.

Paramount was pleased with the results of *King of the Jungle,* and *Time* magazine noted, "From the neck down Crabbe easily equals Weissmuller as an attraction to female audiences; from the neck up he is a vast improvement." On Paramount's radio program, hosted by Stuart Erwin, Buster was heard with Barton MacLane, Randolph Scott, and Fuzzy Knight as an ersatz Western quartet. Paramount gave him a one-line job in Randolph Scott's *Man of the Forest* (1933), a remake of a Zane Grey Western. The studio also picked up his option and loaned him to Principal Pictures for a serial *Tarzan, the Fearless* (1933). The Tarzan picture was filmed in twelve chapters and was also released in an edited 85-minute feature version that opened in August, 1933, at the Roxy Theatre in Manhattan.

While Gary Cooper, George Raft, W. C. Fields, and fast-coming Cary Grant were Paramount's leading male players, Buster began making a mark in the studio's lower-class projects. He was in remakes of two Zane Grey Westerns, *To the Last Man* (1933) and *The Thundering Herd* (1933), both headlining Randolph Scott. The studio also loaned him to Monogram for *The Sweetheart of Sigma Chi* (1933). As Buster recalls, "They made more than my salary back several times over, I was told later, in each film. And I was up to $200 a week by then." He played the lead in Paramount's *Search for Beauty* (1934) opposite Ida Lupino and was the romantic lead in W.C. Fields' *You're Telling Me* (1934).

Instead of building him up on the home lot, the studio continued to loan him out, profitably, to Mayfair for *Badge of Honor* (1934), to RKO for *We're Rich Again* (1934), again to Mayfair for *The Oil Raider* (1934), and to Majestic for *She Had to Choose* (1934). He returned to Paramount to play in *Hold 'em Yale* (1935), a football story, and, in the company's remake of yet another Zane Grey story, *The Wanderer of the Wasteland* (1935), he was Big Ben. In 1935, he finally landed a title role, this time in Paramount's remake of *Nevada* which had originally been played in the studio's 1927 version by Gary Cooper. In two more Zane Grey entries, *Drift Fence* (1936) and *Desert Gold* (1936), he played the leads.

Then Paramount loaned him to Universal for what would become one of his most memorable screen assignments. Alex Raymond's comic strip *Flash Gordon* had been purchased by Universal to be made in thirteen chapters (later released as a feature-length booking, *Rocket Ship*). As the intrepid hero, Buster became part of the industry's serial history. It was later claimed that *Flash Gordon* (1936) was the most popular sound serial ever made. Sets were picked up from Universal's famous horror pictures like *The Mummy* and *The Bride of Frankenstein*. Even with this economy move, the final negative cost of the chapterplay was approaching one million dollars. Nevertheless, *Flash*

With Tom Keene in *Desert Gold* (Par '36).

As serial hero *Flash Gordon* (Univ '36).

Gordon earned more money for Universal the next year than any other film in the studio's inventory. The studio also insisted upon bleaching Buster's hair to a lustrous blond, which greatly disturbed him.

Paramount was pleased with the reaction to *Flash Gordon* and assigned Buster to *Lady, Be Careful* (1936) with Lew Ayres and Mary Carlisle, and promised him better parts on his home lot. He played a football hero in *Rose Bowl* (1936), supporting roles in *Arizona Mahoney* (1936) and *Murder Goes to College* (1937), and turned in a good performance as Eddie in *King of Gamblers* (1937). But these were all B films. He played Jack Holt's silent picture role of Nevada in Paramount's remake of *Forlorn River* (1937), turned in a good performance in *Sophie Lang Goes West* (1937), and was with Anna May Wong and Charles Bickford in the slick, unconventional *Daughter of Shanghai* (1937). At the time he was averaging five to six features a year.

Universal wisely borrowed him again for their *Flash Gordon's Trip to Mars* (1938), a fifteen-chapter serial in which he had to contest with the Clay people and protect heroine Jean Rogers. This chapterplay was also edited as a feature, and released as *Mars Attacks the World*. After a couple more programmers back at Paramount, Buster was again at Universal, this time to play the title role in another serial, *Red Barry* (1938), based on King Features comic strip character. He remained there to appear in *Buck Rogers* (1939), adapted by Norman Hall and Ray Trampe, from Dick Calkins and Phil Nowlan's comic strip, into a twelve-chapter serial and a 69-minute feature called *Planet Outlaws*. Neither *Red Barry* nor *Buck Rogers* attained the success of *Flash Gordon,* but in the year of their release, 1938, Buster truly did; he became the father of Susan Crabbe, who has since made him a grandfather three times.

After playing in *Unmarried* (1939) at Paramount with the screen's champion weeper, Helen Twelvetrees, Buster played Coach Baxter in *Million Dollar Legs* (1939), with Betty Grable. It was to be his final Paramount film. He went to Republic for Gene Autry's *Colorado Sunset* (1939) and was at Universal for their *Call a Messenger* (1939). He then got his swimming gear together and went out to Flushing Meadows, New York, to join Eleanor Holm and Johnny Weissmuller in Billy Rose's *Aquacade* at the New York World's Fair.

When he returned to Hollywood it was to Universal for the final space odyssey serial, *Flash Gordon Conquers the Universe* (1939), in twelve thrilling chapters. He drew a small supporting role in Twentieth Century-Fox's *Sailor's Lady* (1940), which was more notable for Joan Davis' performance, and then had the lead in PRC's *Jungle Man* (1941). For the poverty row Producers Releasing Company, Buster made a series of pictures that turned the Western outlaw Billy the Kid into a hero. Eventually it was decided to change the character's name so as not to elevate so obviously a bad guy. In *Jungle Siren* (1942), also for PRC, he played opposite stripper Ann Corio; and at Paramount he brawled with Richard Arlen in that studio's *Wildcat* (1942). During the war, Buster formed his own water show, similar to, but not as spectacular as, Billy Rose's World Fair splash. He toured the country with this venture and continued heroizing in a stack of B pictures ground out by the low-budget producing companies.

In 1944 Crabbe's son Cullen, nicknamed "Cuffy," was born. Throughout the Forties Buster continued playing Billy Carson (the new name for Billy the Kid). In these innumerable sagebrush tales, his sidekick was former silent comedian Al St. John, playing Fuzzy Jones. One of Buster's favorite roles came along in 1946 in *Swamp Fire* at Paramount. It teamed him with Johnny Weissmuller (in a non-Tarzan role) in a low-budget entry in which Crabbe played a Cajun villain with a French accent and made the aging, somewhat overweight Weissmuller look less than heroic, compared to Buster's trim, sleek torso. Columbia remade James Fenimore Cooper's *The Last of the Mohicans* in 1947, retitling it *The Last of the Redmen.* Buster enjoyed playing the part of the evil Magua, a role that Wallace Beery and Bruce Cabot had played before him. In this year Crabbe's daughter Caren was born.

Even Republic, the champion serial-maker, realized that chapterplays were on the wane in the late 1940s, but they continued to grind out economy versions. Even more poorly produced were the competition from Columbia, where, in 1947, Buster made *The Sea Hound,* a fifteen-chapter entry based on the radio program and comic strip. Buster was more suitable as the villainous clown in Paramount's *Caged Fury* (1948) and two years later was matched with Weissmuller again, this time in *Captive Girl,* one of the ex-Tarzan's *Jungle Jim* series. That same year he also made another Columbia serial, *Pirates of the High Seas,* playing the heroic Jeff Drake. He donned the G-string again for Columbia's fifteen-chapter *King of the Congo* (1952). "Funny how the loincloths got bigger and bigger through the years because of censorship restrictions in the Forties and Fifties, then shrank again in the Sixties to where they didn't even bother with them in the past few years," Buster recalled in 1972. "If I were 21 now, I like to think I'd be 'with it' as much as most young people today. If the role required it, I guess I'd strip. As someone said, 'If you have the body, you do it, I guess.'" [A travesty of Buster's famous *Flash Gordon* series has been playing the pornofields during the early Seventies, only it is now called *Flesh Gordon.* Buster was about forty years too early!]

By the summer of 1955 Buster was not getting many film roles, so he tackled a new phase of show business—the legitimate stage. In July of that year he appeared in Kennebunkport, Maine, in *Dial M for Murder.* Having made his video debut in 1951, hosting "The Buster Crabbe Show" from New York (showings of his earlier Hollywood serials and Westerns), he appeared on "Philco Playhouse" in 1952 in *A Cowboy for Chris.* In this production he played a former movie cowboy trying to make a comeback while living in a cheap Hollywood boarding house.

Then in late 1954 Buster went with his family to Morocco to shoot the video series "Captain Gallant." The producers had signed an English boy for the role of the youth in the series, but Buster succeeded in having Cuffy play the role. Father and son were fine together in the series, which was first aired in February, 1955. It became Crabbe's favorite period of working in front of the camera. Producer Harry Saltzman reinvested his profits from "Captain Gallant" into the later *James Bond* series. Crabbe's "Captain Gallant" was on television for two seasons.

Buster continued making one picture a year. In 1956 he had the lead in United Artists' *Gun Brothers* for Republic and the next year was at Republic for *The Lawless Eighties.* It was in 1957 that Buster's daughter Caren (nicknamed "Sande") died of anorexia, a form of starvation created by an emotional stress that robs one of any desire to eat.

Gunfighters of Abilene (1960) at United Artists was Buster's last film for five years. He spent that summer in his swimming trunks at Flushing Meadows, New York, in another *Aquarama,* featuring Vincent Lopez and his Orchestra. At fifty-two, Buster was still in excellent shape. He came back to pictures in 1965 in two low-budget, nostalgia-bent Westerns, *The Bounty Killer,* with Dan Duryea and Rod Cameron and Audie Murphy's *Arizona Raiders.*

In the later Sixties, Crabbe divided his time between his Camp Menaga for Boys at Saranac Lake in New York; managing a successful swimming pool company; being a representative of the New York Stock Exchange firm of Lieberbaum, Richter and Company; and directing water sports at the Concord Hotel in the Catskills. Crabbe admits: "The Concord's been very good for me because they have me in their ads, you know; they keep the name alive which is important in my business. Actually I think I was kind of an uninteresting person. There was never any glamor for me in the picture business.

There is a certain amount of satisfaction in having people recognize you, but I've never yet had anybody pass me in the lobby—you can hear people talk: some of them are extra loud—say, 'There goes Buster Crabbe, the actor.' Nine times out of ten it's 'There goes Buster Crabbe, the swimmer.' "

In 1971 Buster went back in front of the cameras for *The Comeback Trail,* playing ex-cowboy Duke Montanna returning to pictures. The film was shot in five weeks in New Mexico, and in New York at Studio City. Asked why he would make a comedy Western after all these years, Crabbe replied: "Well, there was comedy in many of my films, but one reason I did it was because I was asked. Comedy is a challenging task for an actor, especially one who doesn't specialize in it. To do this sort of thing in an entirely new way, the extemporaneous way, makes the challenge more formidable. Do a 'real' Western? Naturally, I'd welcome that, too, especially a first-rate one with someone like Wayne or Clint Eastwood, for example. I've been forty years in this business and I still feel I'm learning new things, and I'd like new opportunities to try them out." *The Comeback Trail* has yet to be released.

Crabbe actually should never be concerned about his film career. There will always be generations of youngsters who remember him as *Flash Gordon* and *Buck Rogers.* (He is a favorite guest lecturer at nostalgia conventions.) And, for a swimmer, he really was a better-than-average actor.

LARRY "BUSTER" CRABBE

Good News (MGM 1930)
The Most Dangerous Game (RKO 1932)
That's My Boy (Col 1932)
King of the Jungle (Par 1933)
Man of the Forest (Par 1933)
Tarzan, the Fearless (Principal serial 1933)
To the Last Man (Par 1933)
The Sweetheart of Sigma Chi (Mon 1933)
The Thundering Herd (Par 1933)
Search for Beauty (Par 1934)
You're Telling Me (Par 1934)
Badge of Honor (Mayfair 1934)
We're Rich Again (RKO 1934)
She Had To Choose (Majestic 1934)
The Oil Raider (Mayfair 1934)
Hold 'em Yale (Par 1935)
The Wanderer of the Wasteland (Par 1935)
Nevada (Par 1935)
Drift Fence (Par 1936)
Desert Gold (Par 1936)
Arizona Raiders (Par 1936)
Flash Gordon (Univ serial 1936)
Rose Bowl (Par 1936)
Lady, Be Careful (Par 1936)
Arizona Mahoney (Par 1936)
Murder Goes to College (Par 1937)
King of Gamblers (Par 1937)
Forlorn River (Par 1937)
Sophie Lang Goes West (Par 1937)
Thrill of a Lifetime (Par 1937)
Daughter of Shanghai (Par 1937)
Flash Gordon's Trip to Mars (Univ serial 1938)
Red Barry (Univ serial 1938)
Tip-off Girls (Par 1938)
Hunted Men (Par 1938)
Illegal Traffic (Par 1938)
Buck Rogers (Univ serial 1939)
Unmarried (Par 1939)
Million Dollar Legs (Par 1939)
Colorado Sunset (Rep 1939)
Call a Messenger (Univ 1939)
Flash Gordon Conquers the Universe (Univ serial 1940)
Sailor's Lady (20th 1940)
Jungle Man (PRC 1941)
Billy the Kid Wanted (PRC 1941)
Billy the Kid's Roundup (PRC 1941)
Billy the Kid Trapped (PRC 1942)
Billy the Kid's Smoking Guns (PRC 1942)
Law and Order (PRC 1942)

Jungle Siren (PRC 1942)
Wildcat (Par 1942)
Mysterious Rider (PRC 1942)
Sheriff of Sage Valley (PRC 1942)
Queen of Broadway (PRC 1942)
The Kid Rides Again (PRC 1943)
Fugitive of the Plains (PRC 1943)
The Renegade (PRC 1943)
Western Cyclone (PRC 1943)
Cattle Stampede (PRC 1943)
Blazing Frontier (PRC 1943)
Devil Riders (PRC 1943)
The Drifter (PRC 1943)
Thundering Gunslingers (PRC 1944)
Nabonga (PRC 1944)
Frontier Outlaws (PRC 1944)
Valley of Vengeance (PRC 1944)
The Contender (PRC 1944)
Fuzzy Settles Down (PRC 1944)
Rustler's Hideout (PRC 1944)
Wild Horse Phantom (PRC 1944)
Oath of Vengeance (PRC 1944)
Gangster's Den (PRC 1945)
His Brother's Ghost (PRC 1945)
Shadows of Death (PRC 1945)
Border Badmen (PRC 1945)
Stagecoach Outlaws (PRC 1945)
Fighting Bill Carson (PRC 1945)
Lightning Raiders (PRC 1945)
Prairie Rustlers (PRC 1945)
Gentlemen with Guns (PRC 1946)
Ghost of Hidden Valley (PRC 1946)
Terrors on Horseback (PRC 1946)
Overland Raiders (PRC 1946)
Outlaws of the Plains (PRC 1946)
Swamp Fire (Par 1946)
Prairie Badmen (PRC 1946)
The Last of the Redmen (Col 1947)
The Sea Hound (Col serial 1947)
Caged Fury (Par 1948)
Captive Girl (Col 1950)
Pirates of the High Seas (Col serial 1950)
King of the Congo (Col serial 1952)
Gun Brothers (UA 1956)
The Lawless Eighties (Rep 1957)
Badman's Country (WB 1958)
Gunfighters of Abilene (UA 1960)
The Bounty Killer (Embassy 1965)
Arizona Raiders (Col 1965)
The Comeback Trail (Unreleased 1971)

17

Richard Cromwell

The Thirties produced many future stars, most of them supported by theatre experience or an established name on Broadway. Richard Cromwell was the personification of one of Hollywood's most beloved fantasies—the unknown, inexperienced player whose first appearance becomes an overnight sensation creating a new star in the dream world of filmland. Recently he has been appraised as the Thirties' answer to Richard Chamberlain, whereas he might have been more aptly cast in the title role of television's "The Waltons" series, starring Richard Thomas.

Cecil B. DeMille called him "the ever-appealing Richard Cromwell" and no one would argue that statement with Mr. DeMille. To the screen of the 1930s, Cromwell brought a refreshing vitality that frequently overflowed with forced bravado. On the other hand, his histrionic energy could extend to an imaginative and persuasive recreation, beyond the natural exuberance of the young, of the joy and torments of youth and adolescence. "I became a movie actor so quickly it made my head swim," Cromwell admitted after his first motion picture. "I got a star part by merely wishing, and going to the studio at the crucial moment."

Richard Cromwell was born Roy M. Radabaugh in Long Beach, California, on Saturday, January 8, 1910. His father was extremely creative and invented, among other things, the monoplane still being used in amusement parks. During the influenza epidemic of late 1918, Mr. Radabaugh died. Mrs. Radabaugh was left with five children, from her oldest son, Hudson, to three daughters and eight-year-old Roy. To augment the family funds, the young Roy sold newspapers. His childhood became a daily existence of school and work. After two and a half years at Long Beach High School, Roy went to Los Angeles and enrolled at the Chouinard Art School for another two and a half years, working his way through the school as janitor and maintenance man, while doubling as a soda jerk in a small store at Second and Broadway in Los Angeles.

Actress Anna Q. Nilsson became interested in his art work and engaged Roy to design a book plate for her. This contact led to a series of commissions, from a set of panels in Colleen Moore's home to painting murals depicting scenes in the life of Adam and Eve for the mezzanine walls of the Pantages' Theatre. As time went on, he developed quite a successful career in art, and was able to have his own small art studio-home in Holly-

146

In '31.

wood's English Village. His creation of masks of famous stars brought him commissions from such celebrities as Beatrice Lillie, Ilka Chase, and Joan Crawford. The most famous, photographed, and publicized was his mask of Greta Garbo. Her exotic, if distant, friendship with Cromwell started when they were members of a deep sea fishing trip, and he cherished the elusive Garbo's acquaintance.

Despite his growing prominence in the art world, he told several friends of his suppressed desire to act. He joined several amateur theatre groups to design and paint scenery, but mainly to absorb a good deal of the rehearsal time. At this point, Columbia Pictures had decided to remake Tol'able David (1930), which had been one of D. W. Griffith's silent features, a landmark of 1921, and had starred Richard Barthelmess. Word of the difficulties in casting the title role was known and several of Roy's friends urged him to test for the part.

Casting director Cliff Robertson, with director John G. Blystone, had already tested twenty-two candidates, but it was twenty-year-old Roy who was given the lead. The 5' 10" newcomer was rechristened Richard Cromwell. The studio publicity writers went to work writing glossy releases about a young, starving artist who becomes a star overnight. At last, a Hollywood myth had materialized, but for the "star" part, Cromwell received seventy-five dollars a week, far less than he earned for his art work.

Tol'able David is the narrative of an oppressed, wrongly accused coward who ultimately vindicates his reputation and avenges the crippling of his older brother by savagely battling the bullying, sadistic trio of the Hatburn clan. He also succeeds in bringing in the mail, a position formerly held by his brother until the outlaw Hatburns attacked him. The film opened at New York's Mayfair Theatre on November 14, 1930. It brought excellent reviews from the press. Motion Picture magazine proclaimed the greatest reason for seeing the film was for Cromwell's performance and predicted stardom quickly for him. Photoplay selected the film as one of the month's best, and Richard's performance as one of the best. Motion Picture Herald tagged Cromwell their "Hero of the Week."

Columbia quickly shuttled their new find on tour with the picture. Richard made his first trip East and first appearance on a stage when he arrived for personal appearances with the feature at Manhattan's Mayfair Theatre. He did a radio broadcast about his excitement on being in New York. After seeing the film, President and Mrs. Herbert Hoover invited Cromwell to the White House. Even the dream factories had not imagined such a tremendous reception for the fledgling performer.

Thereafter, Columbia kept him working in quickly made melodramas: with Jack Holt in Fifty Fathoms Deep (1931), the romantic lead opposite Sally Blane amidst a clipper ship mutiny in Shanghaied Love (1931), and as Mae Marsh's football hero son in That's My Boy (1932).

MGM borrowed Richard for what turned out to be one of his best, and favorite, roles that of Ronnie in Emma (1932), with the great Marie Dressler in the title role. Frances Marion concocted the scenario especially for the inestimable talents of Metro's grande dame. Dressler played the devoted housekeeper of Jean Hersholt whose wife dies giving birth to their fourth child, a son named Ronnie. As the grown-up Ronnie, Cromwell was Dressler's favorite. In fact, when Hersholt dies in the story line and the other three children accuse Dressler of having married and murdered him, Cromwell's character comes to her rescue. He is an apprentice aviator who is killed flying home to protect his beloved Emma. Off the soundstages, Cromwell and Miss Dressler became good friends, an association that ended with her death two years later.

From Emma, Richard joined the cast of a dreary chronicle in Warner Bros.' seemingly endless Thirties documentation of fallen women. In The Strange Love of Molly Louvain

With Dorothy Wilson in *The Age of Consent* (RKO '32).

149

With Jean Arthur in *Most Precious Thing in Life* (Col '34).

(1932), Cromwell was wrongly cast as Jimmy, a man having an affair with world-wise and weary Ann Dvorak. Despite Michael Curtiz' astute direction, Richard's overacting was as bad as his part. He was more appropriately cast in RKO's *The Age of Consent* (1932), a story of college life where students have more difficulties with biology off campus than on. Richard, Eric Linden, Arline Judge, and Dorothy Wilson all did well in the co-ed study.

Cromwell's excellent playing in tandem with Tom Brown and Ben Alexander in Universal's *Tom Brown of Culver* (1932) led Cecil B. DeMille to sign him for the role of the high school student leader in *This Day and Age* (1933). He is the one who guides the youths in their capturing and judging of a legally acquitted murderer (Charles Bickford). Although the critics would generally dismiss the feature as a typical DeMille potboiler, this time glorifying the uncontaminated idealism of American youth, it was the highlight of Richard's motion picture career. Certainly of far less import was *Hoopla* (1933), a remake of Kenyon Nicholson's *The Barker*. Richard was cast as the naive youth who is seduced by a midway carnival hula dancer (Clara Bow) as part of a revenge scheme. When the film was released, it was panned on all counts. It became Clara Bow's screen swan song and did not enhance Cromwell's career in any way. Thereafter Richard returned to Columbia for a program entry, *Above the Clouds* (1933), a story of daring flying cameramen, with Robert Armstrong.

Having made over a score of films in three years, he finally bought a home of his own. His original goal of independence for himself was reinstituted and his attitude toward his acting career became negative. "I chose this spot for my house because I can see all over Hollywood," he said. "It gives me a feeling that I have risen above my desires for acting . . . that I can plan afresh. Don't think me ungrateful, but I want none of the glory and the glamor. I got all I wanted from my first picture *Tol'able David*. I proved to myself then that I could get what I wanted. And so I am still after my first ambition, complete independence."

As a stage play *The House of Connelly* was far more effective than when translated to the screen as Janet Gaynor's *Carolina* (1934). Richard joined Lionel Barrymore and Robert Young as co-players in this Fox feature. For Columbia, Dick made *Among the Missing* (1934), in which he played a youth rescued from a life of crime by an aging actress, Henrietta Crosman; and in *Name the Woman* (1934) he was an incompetent newspaper reporter stumbling on a big scoop with Arline Judge's assistance. He and Miss Judge were paired again in Liberty Films' *When Strangers Meet* (1934). Back on the home lot he was cast in an offbeat melodrama, *Most Precious Thing in Life* (1934), which tested the dramatic talents of a young Jean Arthur.

The Lives of a Bengal Lancer (1935) may have been a Gary Cooper outdoors vehicle, but it provided Richard with a very suitable role. He was Sir Guy Standing's son, joining and nearly destroying the 41st Bengal Lancers through his foolish romantic adventures. From Paramount, Richard went over to Fox for Will Rogers' *Life Begins at Forty* (1935), playing Rochelle Hudson's romantic lead. After two quickies at Columbia, Cromwell returned to Paramount as the plebe who supports an aging Commander (Sir Guy Standing) in *Annapolis Farewell* (1935). Remaining at that studio, the actor was teamed with Rochelle Hudson again, this time in W. C. Fields' *Poppy* (1936), a remake of a stage and silent feature property which had starred the irascible comedian.

The summer of 1936 found Richard making his stage debut. The play was *So Proudly We Hail* and it tried out at the Red Barn Summer Theatre in Locust Valley, Long Island. Cast as an embittered nonconformist cadet at a military academy, he is the one who wins the school's medal of honor upon graduation. The play was well received and it opened that September at the 46th Street Theatre in New York. Along with Eddie

Bracken, Charles Walters, and Edwin Phillips, Cromwell received excellent notices. Although the show surprisingly collapsed after fourteen performances, Richard at least had accomplished and fulfilled another dream, proving to himself that he *could* make it on Broadway.

After the stage venture, Richard left for England to work for Herbert Wilcox in *Our Fighting Navy* (1937), released two years later in America as *Torpedoed!* By early January, 1937, Cromwell was in Hollywood at Universal Pictures having his head shaved for the "sequel" to *All Quiet on the Western Front* (1930). The "follow-up" was *The Road Back* (1937), and it detailed the rehabilitation and psychological problems of young German soldiers returning to their defeated Fatherland following World War I. As the humiliated and beaten Ludwig, Cromwell gave an honest performance in this James Whale-directed film. Unfortunately the film was plagued by poor casting in several roles and hacked by sloppy editing. Thereafter Richard labored in Republic's *The Wrong Road* (1937), but the next year was fortuitously cast in Bette Davis' *Jezebel* (1938), playing Henry Fonda's brother, Ted Dillard, who kills George Brent in a duel of honor.

After *Jezebel* his roles dissolved into general run-of-the-studio footage. Occasionally he was reprieved, as in John Ford's *Young Mr. Lincoln* (1939), in which he played Matt Clay who is defended by young Abe Lincoln (Henry Fonda) in a murder trial. While Cromwell's movie career declined, he continued working with his art, becoming more than proficient with ceramics. He enlisted in the Coast Guard in 1942 and served for two years.

After release from the service, Richard Cromwell reverted to being Roy Radabaugh, artist, specializing in his ceramic work. It was at this point that he met the British actress Angela Lansbury, who in 1944 had been Oscar-nominated for Best Supporting Actress in her first film, *Gaslight*. She was then under contract to MGM at five hundred dollars weekly. On September 27, 1945, 35-year-old Richard married 19-year-old Angela in a private ceremony performed by the justice of the peace at Independence, California.

For her third film, *The Picture of Dorian Gray* (1945), Angela was again Oscar-nominated for Best Supporting Actress. If her career was off to a spectacular beginning, her marriage was not. Six months or so after their wedding ceremony, rumors raced around the film colony that the Cromwell household was not very blissful. A few months later the couple separated, and on September 11, 1946, she obtained a divorce on the grounds of mental cruelty.

For unknown reasons Richard chose to return to films briefly in the late 1940s. He was in several reels of nonsense entitled *Bungalow 13* (1948), starring Tom Conway and involving murder, a jade lion, and Margaret Hamilton. In the summer of 1960, press releases announced Richard's screen comeback, but prior to the start of filming of *The Little Shepherd of Kingdom Come* (1961), Richard became ill, and Chill Wills took over the role.

Richard died at the age of fifty of cancer on October 11, 1960. Private funeral services were held at Pierce Brothers Hollywood Mortuary, with only his brother and three sisters attending. Cromwell and Angela Lansbury remained friends throughout his lifetime, and she had spoken with him on the telephone shortly before his death, when she was leaving California to star on Broadway in *A Taste of Honey*. Upon hearing of his death, she recalled he once told her that when he died he would love it to be from asphyxiation from the scent of his favorite flower, gardenia. She sent a pillow of gardenias to Hollywood that arrived on October 13, three days before her 35th birthday, the same age Cromwell had been when they married. When Angela recently related her final tribute to her old friend, she added, "Bless him!"

RICHARD CROMWELL

Tol'able David *(Col 1930)*
Fifty Fathoms Deep *(Col 1931)*
Shanghaied Love *(Col 1931)*
Maker of Men *(Col 1931)*
That's My Boy *(Col 1932)*
Emma *(MGM 1932)*
The Strange Love of Molly Louvain *(FN 1932)*
The Age of Consent *(RKO 1932)*
Tom Brown of Culver *(Univ 1932)*
This Day and Age *(Par 1933)*
Hoopla *(Fox 1933)*
Above the Clouds *(Col 1934)*
Carolina *(Fox 1934)*
Among the Missing *(Col 1934)*
Name the Woman *(Col 1934)*
When Strangers Meet *(Liberty 1934)*
Most Precious Thing in Life *(Col 1934)*
The Lives of a Bengal Lancer *(Par 1935)*
McFadden's Flats *(Par 1935)*
Life Begins at Forty *(Fox 1935)*

Men of the Hour *(Col 1935)*
Unknown Woman *(Col 1935)*
Annapolis Farewell *(Par 1935)*
Poppy *(Par 1936)*
Our Fighting Navy [Torpedoed!] *(Wilcox 1937)*
The Road Back *(Univ 1937)*
The Wrong Road *(Rep 1937)*
Jezebel *(WB 1938)*
Come On, Leathernecks! *(Rep 1938)*
Storm over Bengal *(Rep 1938)*
Young Mr. Lincoln *(20th 1939)*
Enemy Agent *(Univ 1940)*
The Villain Still Pursued Her *(RKO 1940)*
Village Barn Dance *(Rep 1940)*
Parachute Battalion *(RKO 1941)*
Riot Squad *(Mon 1941)*
Baby Face Morgan *(PRC 1942)*
Bungalow 13 *(20th 1948)*

18

Constance Cummings

No other American performer has managed to blaze a trail from a Broadway chorus line to a Hollywood film career of some distinction, and then move on to being leading lady with London's famed National Theatre Company. Constance Cummings' determination to stay in Hollywood after being dismissed from her first picture was admirable. She remained, happily, to contribute several fine performances to the Thirties' cinema.

Kate Logan Cummings had a lovely singing voice and left her southern home to further her voice studies in Manhattan. There she met a young attorney, Dallas Vernon Halverstadt, and after they were wed they migrated to Seattle, Washington. He became a well-known lawyer and, on Sunday, May 15, 1910, their daughter Constance was born. She attended St. Nicholas School in Seattle. When the family moved south to Coronado, near San Diego, she studied at the Cornish School and attended dancing class hoping to emulate her idol, the great ballerina Pavlova.

She also joined the Savoy Stock Company of San Diego in 1926 to appear as Diane in *Seventh Heaven.* She toured in that play in 1927 and also in *Silence.* Mrs. Halverstadt decided her daughter required more training in dance and took her to New York City to study the art with Albertiere, a master in teaching character and interpretative work. When a casting director arrived at Albertiere's studio seeking chorus girls for the road company of *Oh, Kay,* Constance decided to try the legitimate theatre.

After *Oh, Kay,* she found a job as a "Lady of the Ensemble" in George Gershwin's *Treasure Girl,* starring Gertrude Lawrence and Clifton Webb. That show opened on November 8, 1928. The next April, Constance was in the chorus of *The Little Show,* which featured Webb, Fred Allen, and Libby Holman. On one of her rounds of producers' offices, she met author-actor Willard Robertson and told him of her dreams of success. Robertson wrote her into his *This Man's Town,* which opened on March 10, 1930 on Broadway. Pat O'Brien starred and Constance had one line ("Have you a match?"). Despite everyone's efforts, the show burnt out after eight performances.

Then she was engaged to understudy every female part in the already-running *June Moon.* When Linda Watkins was taken ill, Constance substituted as the ingenue. Luckily a few reporters were covering the matinee and gave glowing notices to the intrepid understudy. Five-foot, four-inch, reddish-haired Constance replaced Watkins at the end of the Broadway run and on the lengthy road tour.

At this time Samuel Goldwyn was searching for the female lead in his new Ronald Colman picture, so he had Connie screen-tested in New York. She chose a two-minute

With Frederic Santley, Jack Mulhall, Jameson Thomas, and Betty Bronson in *Lover Come Back* (Col '31).

speech from Shaw's *The Doctor's Dilemma* for her recitation. Goldwyn was satisfied and Mrs. Halverstadt and daughter headed west for Hollywood. The allure of happiness was quickly shattered. Constance recalls, "Mr. Goldwyn told me to dye my hair blond. I refused and we compromised on a wig. Knowing nothing of camera angles or styles, I accepted advice from every one on how to act, what to wear and how to talk until I emerged positively blah!" Both the director, Irving Cummings, and the leading lady, Constance, were summarily dismissed from the picture after several weeks' work.

Colman rallied behind Constance and advised her, "You've fought your way this far. Don't go back—licked! Snap out of it. Be Yourself. Tomorrow is another day!" Colman introduced her to an agent who arranged another screen test for her, and she was subsequently signed by Columbia Pictures. The Colman picture was *The Devil to Pay* (1931), and Loretta Young finally played Constance's part. George Fitzmaurice was credited with the direction, and it turned out to be an amusing picture.

Constance was selected as one of thirteen young actresses for 1931's Wampas Baby Stars of the future, along with Frances Dee, Joan Blondell, Karen Morley, Marion Marsh, Anita Louise, and other less distinguished recipients. On September 23, 1930, Columbia's *The Criminal Code* (1931) started shooting, and Constance gave a routine nice-girl performance in a film that was dominated by superior acting from Walter Huston and Phillips Holmes. With Jack Holt she was in *The Last Parade* (1931), and with Jack Mulhall she attempted *Lover Come Back* (1931); but neither film contrived to advance her career.

She was much better in *The Guilty Generation* (1931), in which she is caught in a vendetta of Italian mobsters Leo Carrillo (her father) and rival Boris Karloff (to whose son, Robert Young, she is secretly wed). Columbia loaned her to RKO for *Traveling Husbands* (1931), and she then returned to the home lot for *Behind the Mask* (1932), with Jack Holt and Boris Karloff. *Photoplay* said of her performance, "They made no mistake when they chose Miss Cummings as a Baby Star."

Constance gained a good deal of attention when Harold Lloyd selected her for his femme lead in *Movie Crazy* (1932) at Paramount. She was showed to good advantage masquerading as a sexy Spanish senorita to test Lloyd's love. (In 1963, segments of the film would be included in *Harold Lloyd's World of Comedy*.) She remained at Paramount to play Miss Healy for whom George Raft ignores Wynne Gibson in *Night after Night* (1932). But for all of Constance's grace and charm, the picture was taken over by a newcomer, Mae West.

Gossip columns were noting that Constance was dating Leslie McFadden, son of the congressman; Mark Busby, a young newspaperman; young actor King Kennedy; and playwright Benn Levy. On the screen she played in *American Madness* (1932), helping banker Walter Huston stem the run on his bank. After two quickies for Columbia, she had a delightful role supporting glib, fast-talking Lee Tracy in *Washington Merry-Go-Round* (1932). At First National she was with Warren William in *The Mind Reader* (1933) and, at Paramount, took part in *Billion Dollar Scandal* (1933), helping Robert Armstrong expose crooked businessmen.

Darryl F. Zanuck paid Walter Winchell $25,000 for a story synopsis that was turned into *Broadway Thru a Keyhole* (1933), produced by his newly formed Twentieth Century Productions. The picture was rife with problems. Peggy Hopkins Joyce was replaced by Lilyan Tashman, who was finally replaced by Blossom Seeley. The cast gave outstanding performances, especially Paul Kelly, as well as Constance, who played a nightclub singer-dancer. One reviewer noted, "Constance Cummings is so charming you forgive her for trying to sing." Four days after the picture's release, November 2, 1933, cast member Texas Guinan died. *Broadway Thru a Keyhole* was her final professional job. At the time Constance was in England getting married.

With George Raft in *Night after Night* (Par '32).

In London she had renewed an acquaintance with Benn V. Levy, whose plays included such hits as *Mrs. Moonlight, Art and Mrs. Bottle, Evergreen, The Devil Passes,* and *Springtime for Henry.* On July 3, 1933, she and Benn Levy were married at the Chelsea Registry Office. The couple honeymooned in Venice. For British International, she appeared in *The Charming Deceiver* (1933), winning good notices for her role of a mannequin masquerading as a movie star. She made her London stage debut in July, 1934, with the Repertory Players in *Sour Grapes,* with Roger Livesey. Onscreen she played in Gaumont-British's *Channel Crossing* (1934). The Levys then returned to Hollywood. Constance was back at Twentieth Century as Spencer Tracy's gal in an exciting tale of telephone repairmen, *Looking for Trouble* (1934).

At Universal for William Wyler's *Glamour* (1934), Constance played a not very bright chorine being moulded into a star by Paul Lukas. Constance was being hailed as "the screen's new emotional star." John Cromwell's well-paced *This Man Is Mine* (1934) gave Constance a showier role than the picture's star, Irene Dunne. Constance played the role of a bitchy vamp to perfection, ending the film with a justifiable black eye from hero Ralph Bellamy. She then returned to a Broadway opening on Christmas day, 1934, in *Accent on Youth,* which played for 204 performances.

Her one 1935 picture aroused more than usual excitement within her, "I was never so thrilled about anything," she said. "Not even my first screen role in *The Criminal Code.* I had devoured the book by Adam Hobhouse in between shows when I was playing *Accent on Youth* on Broadway last winter. I never dreamed that I'd have a chance to place in the picture version, although I must confess that I put myself in that girl's position all the while I was reading with bated breath." The book *The Hangover Murders* became *Remember Last Night?,* directed by James Whale with a topflight cast that included Edward Arnold, Reginald Denny, Robert Armstrong, Robert Young, and Sally Eilers. For the filming, the Levys returned to England on the *Ile de France.*

In the mid-Thirties.

Constance commented on her very happy marriage and rising career on both screen and stage. "It's very nice, dividing our time this way and, of course, it's only possible because of our work in the theatre and pictures. Benn writes. I act. Neither of us encroaches on the other's territory and we're free to go where we please when we like. I don't know whether or not the marriage of an actress and a playwright is one to emulate in every case, but it's a pretty good pattern to follow. People who work in the theatre or movies are engrossed in their work. If a girl marries an 'outsider' she and her husband have no community of interest. They can't talk shop and after the honeymoon are likely to drift apart. An actress and a playwright, however, are in the same sort of work, but don't conflict with one another."

For Gaumont-British, Constance played Edmund Lowe's assistant in the detective thriller *Seven Sinners [The Wrecker]* (1936). For the same studio she appeared with Hugh Sinclair and Noah Beery in *Strangers on a Honeymoon* (1937). Between these two British films she was back on the West End stage in November, 1936, in *Young Madame Conti,* produced by Benn W. Levy from his work, with Herbert Griffith, an adaptation of a German play by Bruno Frank. The London *Bystander* wrote, "The sense of melodramatic tragedy as well, for Constance Cummings puts into the strange, twisted story of a prostitute in love such intense feeling that at times you feel you can hardly bear it." The Levys built a house in the Chelsea district of London and would eventually become near-permanent residents.

Constance was in Margaret Webster's London production of *Three Set Out* in June, 1937. By early autumn of that year arrangements had been made with the Theatre Guild to star Constance in the title role of *Madame Bovary,* Benn Levy's English adaptation of Gaston Baty's dramatization of Flaubert's famous novel. With Levy directing, the show opened in Chicago and moved on to Philadelphia where it received equally enthusiastic reviews. But the presentation did not please the Broadway scribes, and the show collapsed after 39 performances. On January 14, 1938, Constance returned to Broadway, briefly again, in Levy's and Paul Hervey Fox's farce *If I Were You.* The Levys then returned to England once more.

Constance was with Leslie Banks in *Goodbye, Mr. Chips* on the London stage in September, 1938. In 1939 she was in her husband's play *The Jealous God,* with Alexander Knox, and in June opened the Buxton Summer Theatre Festival as *Juliet* to Robert Donat's *Romeo.* She continued on tour with the Old Vic and met George Bernard Shaw, who doubted her ability to portray one of his characters. Constance told the rambunctious playwright, "You can't tell whether I can act by simply talking to me." To which Shaw replied, "Maybe not, but I can tell whether you cannot act." Constance was eventually approved by the Master to play his *St. Joan* in repertory with *The Devil's Disciple,* with Robert Donat in London. During July, Constance appeared with Donat and Stewart Granger in both Shavian plays, plus Shakespeare's *Macbeth* and *Romeo and Juliet.*

Only in England could Constance play the roles of which every actress dreams. In America she was still a talented movie star who could manage a stage play on occasion. With Emlyn Williams and Roddy McDowall, Constance appeared in *This England* (1940), a cavalcade of the history of a landowner versus labor. For MGM-British she was very pleasant with Robert Montgomery in *The Haunted Honeymoon* (1940). Based on a true story of a Welsh foreman salvaging machinery during the war, *Somewhere in France* (1942) was graced by her appearance in it. On stage she was in *Skylark* and in late 1942 opened on the West End in *The Petrified Forest,* with Owen Nares. Near the war's end, Constance was cast as Rex Harrison's wife confronted by the spectre of his former spouse (Kay Hammond) in the celluloid *Blithe Spirit* (1945).

The Levys returned to America early in 1945, and Constance was on Broadway, briefly, in the new play *One Man Show.* She received far better reviews than the play. The couple again left for London, and she toured in the Levy-produced-directed-written comedy *Clutterbuck,* before its debut on August 16, 1946, on the West End stage. It enjoyed a 366-performance run. She completed the Forties by playing in *Happy with Either,* with Wilfred Hyde-White, and *Don't Listen, Ladies!*

In the new decade she continued alternating between films (*Into the Blue,* 1950) and the stage *(Return to Tyassi).* American TV watchers had a fresh opportunity to see Constance perform in the summer of 1952 when she was on ''Video Theatre'' in *Lady from Washington.* That fall she was back in front of British footlights, succeeding Googie Withers in *Winter Journey.* She received splendid notices as the consummate bitch in *The Shrike,* with Sam Wanamaker and Arthur Hill. During the summer of 1953 she appeared on television in the Douglas Fairbanks, Jr., anthology series in the entry *The Scream,* and then was back on the London stage in *Trial and Error.*

John and Julia (1956) returned Constance to film, this time with Peter Sellers. With Richard Basehart and Faith Brook she was in the movie version of *Pay the Piper,* known as *The Intimate Stranger/Finger of Guilt* (1956). On U.S. television she joined George Sanders and Robert Vaughn for a 1956 outing, and the next year was to be seen on ''Schlitz Playhouse of Stars.'' Still continent-jumping, she reappeared in England in March, 1957, to play the title role of *Lysistrata* at the Oxford Playhouse. She polished off the year by performing in her husband's *The Rape of the Belt,* which, three years later, had a short New York run with Constance again in the lead. For Prometheus Films, Constance played an efficiency expert set to be killed, hopefully, by Peter Sellers and Robert Morley in *Battle of the Sexes* (1959).

In the Sixties, aside from two brief film appearances, Constance turned her considerable talents to the stage. One of her notable successes was in May, 1964, when she took over the role of the great she-bitch Martha from Uta Hagen in the London edition of *Who's Afraid of Virginia Woolf?* In 1966 she was in her husband's *Public and Confidential* and later that year in *Justice Is a Woman.* She shared top billing with Joan Greenwood in the April, 1967, revival of Noël Coward's *Hay Fever* (as revised in 1958).

Nicol Williamson's critically acclaimed *Hamlet* opened at the Round House in London in April, 1969. It was imported for Broadway audiences the following month. Constance was fine as Queen Gertrude, but Williamson took the major rewards and accolades.

In the early Seventies, Constance joined the National Theatre Company and for the Old Vic appeared as *Coriolanus'* mother. She was next seen as Leda in *Amphitryon 38.* Her greatest challange was in the extremely demanding role of Mary Tyrone in Eugene O'Neill's *Long Day's Journey into Night,* with Sir Laurence Olivier as her husband James. *Plays and Players* magazine glowed, ''Olivier [is] at his best and Constance Cummings and Denis Quilley have never been better.'' In January, 1973, Sir Laurence and Constance received the *Plays and Players* Award for the best performances of 1972 in *Long Day's Journey.* The couple repeated their O'Neill roles in a three-hour television production in 1973.

Her performance as Lyuba Ranevsky in the National's *The Cherry Orchard* was an anti-climax. Nor did Euripides' *The Bacchae,* with Constance as Agave, fare well with the British critics. On April 8, 1974, she made her first stage appearance since her departure from the National Theatre Company. She received good notices as the Mother in the world premiere of A. R. Gurney, Jr.'s *Children.* For her performance as the alienated wife in *Stripwell* (Royal Court Theatre, October 14, 1975) *Variety* judged her ''excellent.''

In the Queen's New Year's Honors in 1974, Constance was awarded The Order of the British Empire. It was only fitting, since Constance had spent most of her professional career in England. For Constance, it was and is a long way from a Broadway chorine to being such a respected British stage star. Would that her decade of prime film-making, the Thirties, had been more fruitful and challenging.

CONSTANCE CUMMINGS

The Criminal Code *(Col 1931)*
The Last Parade *(Col 1931)*
Lover Come Back *(Col 1931)*
The Guilty Generation *(Col 1931)*
Traveling Husbands *(RKO 1931)*
Behind the Mask *(Col 1932)*
The Big Timer *(Col 1932)*
Movie Crazy *(Par 1932)*
Night after Night *(Par 1932)*
American Madness *(Col 1932)*
The Last Man *(Col 1932)*
Attorney for the Defense *(Col 1932)*
Washington Merry-Go-Round *(Col 1932)*
The Mind Reader *(FN 1933)*
Billion Dollar Scandal *(Par 1933)*
Broadway Thru a Keyhole *(UA 1933)*
The Charming Deceiver [Heads We Go] *(British International 1933)*
Channel Crossing *(Gaumont 1934)*
Looking for Trouble *(UA 1934)*
Glamour *(Univ 1934)*

This Man Is Mine *(RKO 1934)*
Remember Last Night? *(Univ 1935)*
Seven Sinners [The Wrecker] *(Gaumont 1936)*
Strangers on a Honeymoon *(Gaumont 1937)*
This England *(British International 1940)*
The Haunted Honeymoon [Busman's Holiday] *(MGM British 1940)*
The Foreman Went to France [Somewhere in France] *(UA British 1942)*
Blithe Spirit *(Cineguild 1945)*
Into the Blue *(British Lion 1950)*
John and Juliet *(British Lion 1956)*
The Intimate Stranger [Finger of Guilt] *(AA British 1956)*
Battle of the Sexes *(Bryanston 1959)*
A Boy Ten Feet Tall [Sammy Going South] *(Par 1963)*
In the Cool of the Day *(MGM 1963)*
Harold Lloyd's World of Comedy *(UA compilation 1963)*

19

Frances Dee

On a recent Merv Griffin television show that centered on special guest star director William Wellman, a few people with whom Wellman was closely involved, whose careers he had sponsored or encouraged, were also guests. Among those were Mike Connors, Wellman's son-in-law James Franciscus, and Joel McCrea. During the talk show Griffin introduced Mrs. Joel McCrea who was seated in the center of the studio audience. The willowy, trim lady arose from her seat, shyly smiled and nodded at the camera, and then sat down. Still beautiful, slender, and defying the passing years despite gray in her hair, Frances Dee was a joy to behold.

Few more beautiful or talented actresses emerged on the screen of the Thirties than Frances Dee or maintained her excellence of performance. She was one of the few who rose from the ranks of extras to become one of the most promising and delightful players of the decade.

She was born on Tuesday, November 26, 1907, in Pasadena, California. When she was seven, her father, a civil engineer, moved the family to Chicago, where Frances attended Hyde Park High School. She then entered the University of Chicago. During the summer vacation of her freshman year, she returned to California to visit relatives. Learning that Fox Films was hiring college girls as extras for a Lois Moran picture, *Words and Music* (1929), Frances applied. She got a job in the movie at $7.50 a day plus a box lunch. For the young Miss Dee, the acting business seemed more important than the University of Chicago and selling ads for the Chicago *Tribune*. Other days of extra work followed and at Paramount she was an extra in *Monte Carlo* (1930), graduating to a bit part in that studio's *Follow Through* (1930), with Charles "Buddy" Rogers and Nancy Carroll. Fred Datig, Paramount's casting director, had a successful screen test made of Frances, and she was subsequently signed by that studio to a standard player contract.

Maurice Chevalier is credited with "discovering" Frances. "Insisted is just what he did," Frances admits. "The studio wanted a new face to play opposite him and had taken tests of hundred of girls on the lots—stars, leading women and extra girls. When the director saw my test he was favorably inclined, but when he learned that I'd had so little experience, he vetoed my choice. A couple of days later, he was sitting with Chevalier in the studio restaurant when I came in. Chevalier pointed me out and said I

As a Paramount contractee in '30.

was just the girl for the part. The director looked at me and told Chevalier the whole story. But Chevalier insisted that what the part required was an inexperienced girl who had a personality entirely new to the screen." The director was Ludwig Berger and the picture was *Playboy of Paris* (1930), a film distinguished by Chevalier's singing of Richard Whiting's lovely song "My Ideal." The feature was also produced in a French-language version under its original title, *Le Petit Cafe* (1930) with Chevalier's then wife Yvonne Vallee in Frances' role. *Playboy of Paris* proved to be one of Chevalier's lesser successes and the reviews were less than ecstatic. *Photoplay* magazine did note that "Frances Dee, a newcomer, is refreshingly lovely," while the *New York Times* sniffed, "Frances Dee is acceptable in the part of Yvonne."

Frances next played the lead of an impoverished English society girl, Elinor Farrington, opposite Buddy Rogers in *Along Came Youth* (1930). Frances was selected as one of Wampas Baby Stars of 1931 along with Constance Cummings, Joan Blondell, Karen Morley, and Anita Louise, plus Sidney Fox, Rochelle Hudson, and four others (who never really made it). Although she had little to do as Jack Oakie's small-town sweetheart in *June Moon* (1931), Frances performed well. She was rather effective in Paramount's preposterous tale of Calamity Jane (Louise Dresser) being *Caught* (1931) by her own son. For her playing of society girl Sondra Finchley in Josef von Sternberg's *An American Tragedy* (1931), Frances attracted critical notice. At the picture's Los Angeles preview, Paramount star Marlene Dietrich confided to a friend that she had "discovered" Frances. And there was growing, unfounded gossip about the lovely young Miss Dee and von Sternberg who was suddenly the mentor of both Dee and Dietrich. But Frances' inner calm and self-analytical mind told her she was learning from men like von Sternberg. And she did.

Although Sylvia Sidney, Miss Dietrich, Claudette Colbert, and Miriam Hopkins were the reigning female attractions at Paramount, Frances continued to offer sturdy performances, as in *Rich Man's Folly* (1931), an updated version of Charles Dickens' *Dombey and Son*. Frances' romantic interest in the picture was supplied by a fine actor, Robert Ames, who died before the release of this George Bancroft-starring vehicle. Next Frances gave Paul Lukas' slick performance in *Working Girls* (1931) fine support. But then she was wasted in an outmoded, flaming youth fizzle, *This Reckless Age* (1932), with Buddy Rogers and Richard Bennett. Universal borrowed her for *Nice Women* (1932), and co-star Sidney Fox said of her, "I wish I could be like Frances Dee. She never gets excited about anything." But she was learning the motion picture business and admitted, "Frank Tuttle, who directed *This Reckless Age,* taught me tempo and timing. Whatever else his pictures are, they're never slow." And she credited Chevalier, Jack Oakie, and Charles Ruggles for helping her with comedy nuance and timing. At the studio she was developing into one of the better and most promising of the contract players, and enjoyed living with her family in the 100 block of Gower Street, not far from Paramount.

Warner Bros.-First National borrowed Frances to play the wide-eyed ingenue in *Love Is a Racket* (1932), a hodgepodge story of newspaper reporters and gangsters in New York City, co-starring Douglas Fairbanks, Jr., Ann Dvorak, and Lee Tracy. Frances returned to Paramount to play a small role in *Night of June 13th* (1932). She was Wynne Gibson's daughter in *The Strange Case of Clara Deane* (1932), and in the studio's multi-star, episodic film *If I Had a Million* (1932), she was the wife of convicted killer Gene Raymond. Frances supplied the romantic interest in Buster Crabbe's *King of the Jungle* (1933) and in an offbeat mystery, *The Crime of the Century* (1933), she was the daughter of Wynne Gibson and Jean Hersholt. The picture used the gimmick of permitting the viewing audience to solve the case by flashing each character on the screen, and then

164

giving filmgoers a chance to figure out the real culprit. Paramount announced Frances to star with Gene Raymond in Vina Delmar's *A Chance at Heaven* and also for the leading female role in *The West Pointer*, with Cary Grant and Kent Taylor. But Frances knew where she was going, and that was to leave Paramount for fresher fields.

"It was not an exalted idea of my own importance that influenced me to leave Paramount," Frances informed the press. "Neither was it because of any dissatisfaction with the treatment accorded me by the studio. It was simply that I felt the time had come for me to stand or fall on my own merits, rather than to continue working under the advantages and disadvantages of a contract negotiated when I first started in pictures. My roles with Paramount were just those that any contract player might expect. Most of the parts I have played during the past year were good ones—but not good for me." Frances joined RKO.

Sidney Howard's biting indictment of possessive mother love *The Silver Cord* had been a hit on the stage and was transferred to the screen in 1933 by RKO. Laura Hope Crews repeated her role of the strongly willed, domineering mama in John Cromwell's feature, with Irene Dunne, Joel McCrea, Eric Linden, and Frances in focal parts. As Hester, the lovely, love-sick girl confused and bedevilled by Linden's reluctance to leave his conniving mother, Frances excelled, especially as her character rises to the peak of near-suicide when he breaks off their engagement.

If her part in *The Silver Cord* was tragic, reality on the set and off was not. She had fallen in love with one of the country's favorite leading men, Joel McCrea. Following this film she and Joel were cast in RKO's poignant *One Man's Journey* (1933). After completing her role as a newswoman romancing a newsreel man (William Gargan) in *Headline Shooter* (1933), Frances left for New York for a vacation. After a few days McCrea called her, "If I come to New York tomorrow will you marry me?" Frances said yes, and when Joel arrived they took out a marriage license at New York City's Municipal Building and on October 20, 1933, left the Waldorf-Asotria to find a "little, white Country Church," which they discovered at Rye, New York. There they were married in a Methodist Church ceremony by the Reverend George R. Bronson.

When the McCreas returned to Hollywood, Frances was offered the ingenue role in Darryl F. Zanuck's new Twentieth Century Company's production of *Blood Money* (1933). Judith Anderson, in her screen debut, appeared as nightclub owner Ruby. The picture was directed by Rowland Brown and was an inventive underworld drama that must have created considerable chaos in the censorship offices, especially with Frances' role of a psychopathic kleptomaniac who is riddled with masochistic tendencies ("I'd do anything for the man who'd beat me") seeking an artist known for violent rape attacks. Frances gave a convincingly startling performance as the corrupt heiress bedeviling lawbreaker George Bancroft. From the Freudian excess of *Blood Money*, Frances proved her versatility by returning to RKO as the lively Meg in *Little Women* (1933).

For Jesse Lasky's Fox production *Coming Out Party* (1934), Frances was genuinely touching as Joy Stanhope, a society girl in love with a lowly band fiddler (Gene Raymond). Then she was excellent as another society girl, Virginia, in love with poor but industrious interne Bruce Cabot in *Finishing School* (1934). After playing a stock role in *Keep 'Em Rolling* (1934), a picture dominated by Walter Huston, she went into John Cromwell's *Of Human Bondage* (1934). This was the melodrama that made a star of Bette Davis, cast as the waitress-tart Mildred who nearly destroys young interne Philip Carey (Leslie Howard). Within this adaptation of W. Somerset Maugham's novel, it is Frances' Sally Athelny with whom Howard finds peace and contentment. Frances made the brief but significant role of Sally effective and memorable. And she became a mother of a seven-pound son on September 7, 1934. He was named Joel Dee McCrea and

With Philip Trent in *Coming Out Party* **(Fox '34).**

With Leslie Howard and Reginald Owen in *Of Human Bondage* (RKO '34).

nicknamed Jody. By then the McCreas had settled on a ranch Will Rogers had advised Joel to buy in 1933. The one thousand acres later spread to 27,000. After their Hollywood careers were behind them, the McCreas became successful cattle raisers.

Frances was charming as Amelia Sedley in *Becky Sharpe* (1935), the Technicolor feature starring Miriam Hopkins. Then she returned to Fox to star with Francis Lederer in the modern fairy tale *The Gay Deception* (1935). For Twentieth, Frances showed to advantage in an offbeat murder tale, *Half Angel* (1936), in which she was the suspected murderess of Helen Westley. Then Frances retired from the screen to await the birth of her second son, David, who arrived on November 15, 1936. When she returned to the screen it was for Paramount, with Gary Cooper and George Raft in *Souls at Sea* (1937), in which she offered an appealing performance.

Frank Lloyd's *Wells Fargo* (1937) reunited Joel and Frances on screen. Of her performance in this film, *Photoplay* claimed, "No two stars in Hollywood could have done a better job of it than have Joel McCrea and Frances Dee playing the pioneering couple." Their performance brought out a few more superlatives, and they were given *Photoplay's* best performances of the month rating. Frances remained at Paramount to play opposite Ronald Colman's Francois Villon in *If I Were King* (1938), a role she repeated in October, 1939, on "Lux Radio Theatre," with Douglas Fairbanks, Jr., and Sir Cedric Hardwicke. In 1939 she played in Columbia's *Coast Guard* (a minor film), and on April 24, 1939, was heard on "Lux Radio Theatre" in *Broadway Bill* with Robert Taylor and Gail Patrick.

167

Frances' screen career was only sporadically of interest to her, especially after she collapsed on the set of *My Son, My Son* (1940) and had to be replaced by Laraine Day. She did appear in *So Ends Our Night* (1941), which starred Margaret Sullavan, Fredric March, and Glenn Ford, providing an appealing performance as March's wife who is left behind in Nazi Germany. That same year she went to Republic to join with John Wayne in *A Man Betrayed.* Much more advantageous was her performance as the lovely bride of impoverished William Holden in Columbia's *Meet the Stewarts* (1942). She was dignified and charming as the nurse involved with voodoo in Jacques Tourneur's *I Walked with a Zombie* (1943). This imaginative horror film came from Val Lewton's production unit at RKO.

Frances was forever being rediscovered, and when she made *Happy Land* (1943) for Twentieth, *Photoplay* was writing, "The work of Frances Dee as Don Ameche's wife Agnes Marsh causes one to wonder why this lovely and competent actress is permitted to be off the screen for so long a time!" On April 10, 1944, Frances, with Don Ameche and Walter Brennan, repeated their *Happy Land* roles on "Lux Radio Theatre." In 1945 Frances played Lynn Andrews in love with Donald Cook, father of Donald O'Connor, in the amusing Universal comedy *Patrick the Great.* During the summer of 1945, Frances finally fulfilled a long-suppressed desire to make her first stage appearance. She joined with Bramwell Fletcher and Virginia Field in a production of *Berkeley Square* at the Strand Theatre in Stamford, Connecticut.

She returned to Hollywood only to be asked to join the company of a new play, *The Secret Room,* to be directed by Moss Hart. Frances received top billing in her role of Susan Beverley. The play, which opened at the Royale Theatre on November 7, 1945, was not a success and disappeared after only twenty-one performances.

In 1947 Frances reappeared on screen, this time with George Sanders in *Private Affairs of Bel Ami.* The following year she played with Joel McCrea, Charles Bickford, and Joseph Calleia in *Four Faces West.* It was a non-violent sagebrush tale, dependent entirely on characterization; and the four leads were well equipped to portray them. Reviewing the film in *Focus on Film* magazine in 1972, cinema historian Don Miller wrote, "The rounded characterizations in the script are masterfully displayed. Performances are excellent, headed by the husband and wife team of McCrea and Dee and Bickford's and Calleia's dependable trouping."

In 1951 Frances did two "Fireside Theatre" television shows, and for RKO appeared in their case history of a divorce, *Payment on Demand,* with Bette Davis, Jane Cowl, and Barry Sullivan. Frances gave a stand-out performance as Eileen. She then went to Universal for a reversal of divorce—a child wants one from her parents—in *Reunion in Reno* (1951). In 1952 she made *Because of You* with Loretta Young and in 1953 she was delightful as Clifton Webb's patient wife in *Mr. Scoutmaster.* Her final screen appearance to date was in MGM's color picture *Gypsy Colt* (1954), playing wife to Ward Bond and mother to Donna Corcoran. But the star of the picture was the horse playing Gypsy. Frances made another TV appearance that year on "Ford Theatre" in *Unknown Promise* and retired from acting.

In 1955, Frances surprised the film community and her public when she and McCrea became the parents of a third son, named Peter. Through the years there had been rumors of marital discord in the McCrea household. In 1935 the couple had separated, but reconciled. In 1966 it was Joel who filed for divorce, charging his wife with "extreme cruelty." However, the case was dropped, and today the very wealthy couple are still man and wife. Frances resolutely avoids interviews concerning her career. Her chief interest these days is the Moral Re-Armament.

During her unfulfilled film career, 5' 4½" Frances, with brown hair and greenish-gray eyes, was a photographer's delight. In 1946, James Agee, while reviewing *The Best Years of Our Life,* and writing of Teresa Wright, penned: "Like Frances Dee, she has always been one of the very few women in movies who really had a face. Like Miss Dee, she has also always used this translucent face with delicate and exciting talent as an actress, and with something of the novelist's perceptiveness behind the talent. And, like Miss Dee, she has never been around nearly enough."

FRANCES DEE

Words and Music *(Fox 1929)*
Monte Carlo *(Par 1930)*
A Man from Wyoming *(Par 1930)*
Follow Through *(Par 1930)*
Manslaughter *(Par 1930)*
Playboy of Paris *(Par 1930)*
Along Came Youth *(Par 1930)*
True to the Navy *(Par 1930)*
June Moon *(Par 1931)*
An American Tragedy *(Par 1931)*
Caught *(Par 1931)*
Rich Man's Folly *(Par 1931)*
Working Girls *(Par 1931)*
This Reckless Age *(Par 1932)*
Nice Women *(Univ 1932)*
Love Is a Racket *(FN 1932)*
Night of June 13th *(Par 1932)*
The Strange Case of Clara Deane *(Par 1932)*
If I Had a Million *(1932)*
Sky Bride *(Par 1932)*
King of the Jungle *(Par 1933)*
The Crime of the Century *(Par 1933)*
The Silver Cord *(RKO 1933)*
One Man's Journey *RKO 1933*
Headline Shooter *(RKO 1933)*
Blood Money *(UA 1933)*

Little Women *(RKO 1933)*
Coming Out Party *(Fox 1934)*
Finishing School *(RKO 1934)*
Keep 'Em Rolling *(RKO 1934)*
Of Human Bondage *(RKO 1934)*
Becky Sharpe *(RKO 1935)*
The Gay Deception *Fox 1935)*
Half Angel *(20th 1936)*
Souls at Sea *(Par 1937)*
Wells Fargo *(Par 1937)*
If I Were King *(Par 1938)*
Coast Guard *(Col 1939)*
So Ends Our Night *(UA 1941)*
A Man Betrayed *(Rep 1941)*
Meet the Stewarts *(Col 1942)*
I Walked with a Zombie *(RKO 1943)*
Happy Land *(20th 1943)*
Patrick the Great *(Univ 1945)*
Private Affairs of Bel Ami *(UA 1947)*
Four Faces West *(UA 1948)*
Payment on Demand *(RKO 1951)*
Reunion in Reno *(Univ 1951)*
Because of You *(Univ 1952)*
Mr. Scoutmaster *(20th 1953)*
Gypsy Colt *(MGM 1954)*

20

Brian Donlevy

Someone once described Brian Donlevy as a "hard-boiled sentimentalist" with a coarse and tough voice, brusque mien, and a manner that disguised his real character and private life as a soft-spoken, shy, and modest man. He was also native-born Irish, a bugler with General Pershing's American Expeditionary Forces in Mexico, a flyer with World War I's famed Lafayette Escadrille (or so the legend goes), and a midshipman at the United States Naval Academy, as well as an advertising model and a Broadway actor of considerable promise. A persuasive actor who suffered from drinking problems, he was Oscar-nominated and spent forty-eight years in show business.

Waldo Brian Donlevy (christened Grosson Brian Boru Donlevy) was born on Saturday, February 9, 1901, in Portsdown, County Armagh, Ireland. When he was ten months old, his family migrated to Sheboygan Falls, Wisconsin, near where he later attended St. John's Military Academy at Dalefied, Wisconsin. He left that bastion of learning to join General Pershing's war against Pancho Villa in Mexico, serving as a bugler. Lying about his age, he allegedly enlisted in 1917 in the famous Lafayette Escadrille as a sergeant and a pilot. Supposedly, he was wounded twice during the war and returned to America to receive an appointment as a midshipman at the United States Naval Academy at Annapolis. But after discovering that he would be confronted with three years of active sea duty, he resigned from the Academy on March 8, 1922, and headed for New York City.

The handsome young Donlevy was brought to the attention of Frank Lyendecker, illustrator for Arrow Collar and accessory advertisements. Donlevy modeled for Lyendecker as the Arrow Collar man, and began meeting theatrical people; one of the latter, Louis Wolheim, persuaded him to try the legitimate stage. Brian won the role of Corporal Gowdy in *What Price Glory?*, which ran for 435 performances after its September 5, 1924, Broadway bow. During the show's lengthy run, Donlevy shuttled to Brooklyn and Vitagraph Studios to play the part of Ralph in their picture *School for Wives* (1925), featuring Mary Carr and Tyrone Power, Sr. (Brian had made his screen debut in 1923.) It was in Wesley Ruggles' *A Man of Quality* (1926) that Brian played his first screen heavy, the role of a silk smuggler.

Donlevy's brief stay at Annapolis had little to do with his being cast as sailor "Donkey" in Vincent Youmans' musical *Hit the Deck* (April 25, 1927) with Charles King and Louise Groody. After the long run on Broadway and on the road with this

With William Frawley, Jack La Rue, and director Norman Taurog on the set of *Strike Me Pink* (UA '36).

success, Donlevy was back to Broadway in a short-lived show called *Ringside* (August 29, 1928). It was on October 5 of that year that he wed Yvonne Grey, one of Mr. Ziegfeld's glorified American girls, and went into rehearsal for another Youmans show, *Rainbow* (November 21, 1928). In this musical of California in the days of '49, he sang "Virginia" with featured player Louise Brown. The show folded after twenty-nine performances.

Then, Brian found work with Pathé, playing Morton Downey's brother in the screen musical *Mother's Boy* (1929), and opened that November in *Queen Bee* for a short run. He continued alternating between films and Broadway shows, none of which progressed his career very far. Within a six-month period between the end of 1931 and mid-1932, he was in three different shows, in addition to making a Vitaphone two-reeler, *A Modern Cinderella* (1932).

The year 1934 was a good one for Donlevy. He established himself as a performer with a range of versatility in both *No Questions Asked* and *The Perfumed Lady*, and hit his stride as a prizefighter in *The Milky Way*, (May 8, 1934) with nimble-witted Hugh O'Connell as the milkman. After *The Milky Way*, Brian joined *Life Begins at 8:40* (August 27, 1934), a Shuberts-produced musical revue with Bert Lahr, Ray Bolger, Louella Gear, and Frances Williams. The musical played some 237 performances on Broadway before it took to the road.

Brian also took to the road, this time to Hollywood. He started a new movie career as Edward G. Robinson's black-shirted killer in *Barbary Coast* (1935), and continued with thug roles in Sylvia Sidney's *Mary Burns, Fugitive* (1935) and RKO's *Another Face* (1935). It was in February, 1936, that Yvonne Grey divorced Donlevy, winning a $5,000 settlement. Following a supporting part in *Strike Me Pink* (1936) at United Artists, short, stocky Brian signed a term contract with Twentieth Century-Fox.

With Tyrone Power and Alice Faye in *In Old Chicago* (20th '38).

172

Generally he was cast in the studio's B pictures, a procession of entertaining but unmemorable productions. His first year at Fox produced five films (plus a loan-out to Paramount), and he fell in love again. On December 22, 1936, he wed Marjorie Lane, a singer at Hollywood's Trocadero Club. They had a fast ceremony at Tijuana, Mexico, but the bride felt the marriage was too hurried and foreign, and, nine days later, they remarried at the Los Angeles Wilshire Methodist Church.

This Is My Affair (1937), starring Barbara Stanwyck and Robert Taylor, was Donlevy's best film of that year. By 1938 Donlevy's career was definitely progressing. He had a sizeable part as the toughie, Gil Warren, in Henry King's expansive In Old Chicago. Tyrone Power, Alice Faye, Don Ameche, Alice Brady, and the Chicago fire were the picture's stars. In February of 1938 Brian made personal appearances in key cities with the opening of the film and was heard on radio's "Hollywood Hotel" with cast members in brief scenes from the epic film.

Donlevy worked opposite Victor McLaglen in Battle of Broadway (1938), which gave Gypsy Rose Lee another screen role. Then, Brian and McLaglen were teamed again in the British-made We're Going to Be Rich (1938), headlining Gracie Fields and directed by her husband Monty Banks. Playing despicable heavies seemed to be Donlevy's forte, and in his last years at Fox he had some good ones. He had the role of brutal Barshee in Jesse James (1939). On loan-out to Cecil B. DeMille at Paramount, he was another villain, this time as Sid Campeau trying to halt the westward progress of the railroad. He continued his viciousness as trader Callendar in RKO's Allegheny Uprising (1939) and then landed a role that was of award stature.

Beau Geste (1939) had been one of Paramount's big moneymakers in 1926. In 1939 the studio remade this tale of death in the French Foreign Legion with Gary Cooper, Ray Milland, and Robert Preston starred. In the silent version, Noah Beery had been Sergeant Lejaune; in the talkie edition, the surname was changed to Markoff, with Fox's Brian in the key part. While filming the desert tale at Yuma, Arizona, in February, 1939, Donlevy was hospitalized with a stab wound inflicted by a fellow player whose timing was deliberately bad. Brian's reviews for his menacing, sadistic playing of Sergeant Markoff earned him Photoplay's best performance of the month award. In addition, he was nominated for the year's Best Supporting Actor Oscar, but lost to Thomas Mitchell of Stagecoach.

Now typed as a sturdy heavy, Brian offered fine support to Marlene Dietrich and James Stewart in the Western romp Destry Rides Again (1939). Again at Paramount, he had the lead in a studio film that became the sleeper of the year. Preston Sturges' The Great McGinty (1940) was a political satire that showcased Donlevy's talents to a far greater extent than Hollywood or the public had suspected. The New York Times glowed, "Much praise must be bestowed on Brian Donlevy for his masterful comprehension of McGinty, who starts out as a plain dumb palooka and grows into a thoughtful man." (On June 28, 1955, Donlevy would repeat his The Great McGinty on "Lux Video Theatre," and he was as impressive as ever.)

After supporting roles at Universal in When the Daltons Rode (1940) and at Fox in their Brigham Young—Frontiersman (1940), Paramount recalled Brian. He lent stability to their I Wanted Wings (1941), a tale of three Army Air Corps trainees whipped into shape by rough, tough Captain Mercer (Brian). Ray Milland, William Holden, and Wayne Morris were the servicemen trio, while Constance Moore and newcomer Veronica Lake supplied the sultry romance interest. Milland and Donlevy, both experienced pilots, did much of their own flying during the making of the film. Brian stayed at Paramount for supporting roles in Hold Back the Dawn (1941) and Birth of the Blues (1941).

For Metro he appeared as protagonist Jim Sherwood in *Billy the Kid* (1941), in which Robert Taylor was hopelessly miscast in the title role. Sturges used Brian again at Paramount in his *The Great Man's Lady* (1942). Joel McCrea and Barbara Stanwyck were the leads in that one, but Donlevy offered a strong, if brief, performance as Steely Edwards. His best roles seemed to come from Paramount, and he was superb as the ghost of Andrew Jackson in the fantasy of the former President returning to aid a modern bewildered politician (William Holden) in *The Remarkable Andrew* (1942). This was Donlevy's favorite film role.

He was also excellent as Major James P. Devereaux in *Wake Island* (1942) and added stature to his career by playing tough political boss Paul Madvig in Paramount's remake of *The Glass Key* (1942), which featured the new love team of Veronica Lake and Alan Ladd. In one scene Miss Lake was required to punch Donlevy in the jaw. It was an appealing prospect for Veronica, who was convinced (and rightly so) that Donlevy took a dim view of her acting acumen and lack of talent. She swung from the floor, nearly knocking out the stocky Irishman, throwing him into a towering rage. After he asked the blonde ingenue why she had swung and connected with such force, she admitted she did not know how to "pull her punches." She learned before the next take.

From the belting Miss Lake, Brian went to a belter of another class, Miss Diana Barrymore, in something called *Nightmare* (1942) at Universal. Diana and Brian became quick, fast friends, having lunch together in Donlevy's bungalow and arousing the jealousy of Miss Barrymore's husband at the time, Bramwell Fletcher. Diana described Donlevy as "happy, easy-going, devil-may-care—life was a ball to him." But he was rarely anything but professional in his performances, as he demonstrated in MGM's *Stand by for Action* (1942). On February 20, 1943, Brian became the father of a daughter, Judith Ann.

Brian appeared in one of the best anti-Nazi war films, a tale of revenge for the death of Hangman Heydrich, Fritz Lang's *Hangmen Also Die* (1943), playing the murderous Dr. Svoboda. Preston Sturges again utilized his services at Paramount for *The Miracle of Morgan's Creek* (1943), an extravagant spoof of motherhood and politics with Brian again as Governor McGinty. King Vidor's *An American Romance* (1943) again won Brian a plaudit from *Photoplay* for one of the month's best performances, although Vidor's MGM film was not a box-office success.

Since he had been too old for World War II service, Brian continued film-making. In 1945 and 1946 he was with Paramount playing an acceptable Trampas in the studio's remake in Technicolor of *The Virginian* (1946), and then giving a captivating comic performance as bootlegger Tony Minetti in *Our Hearts Were Growing Up* (1946), which continued the adventures of Cornelia Skinner (Gail Russell) and Emily Kimbrough (Diana Lynn). The actor was a restrained Richard Henry Dana, the author, in Paramount's *Two Years Before the Mast* (1946), an Alan Ladd seafaring vehicle. For Metro, Donlevy made a movie based on the testing of the atomic bomb, *The Beginning or the End* (1947), a prophetic reference to his personal life. (Brian and Marjorie reached the parting of the ways in 1947, and daughter Judith Ann was court-assigned to six months with each parent.)

Brian's screen appearances continued in supporting roles. The best of these were that of the assistant district attorney in Twentieth Century-Fox's brutal *Kiss of Death* (1947) and big-time gambler Jim Caighn in *Killer McCoy* (1947). He was more than noticeable in *A Southern Yankee* (1948) and played Brigadier General Clifton I. Garnet in MGM's all-star *Command Decision* (1948).

By the late 1940s, the downward career trend had started for Donlevy, but he continued to find film roles. He was cast with Ella Raines in the plodding *Impact* (1949) and

In *Allegheny Uprising* (RKO '39).

remained at United Artists for *The Lucky Stiff* (1949). In the Fifties, he alternated between leads of anti-heroes, heavies, and straight B picture leads. In late 1950 he made his TV debut on "Pulitzer Prize Playhouse," and on March 10, 1952, he starred as Steve Mitchell, an investigator of espionage, in the teleseries "Dangerous Assignment."

He returned to the stage in the summer of 1954, playing the lead of the drunken, has-been actor in *The Country Girl,* and the next year he toured the straw-hat circuit in the comedy *King of Hearts.* As Dr. Roy Bell, head of Sillman University in the Phillipines, he organized a resistance movement on the video series "Crossroads," returning to that series again in May, 1957, as a Presbyterian minister. He repeated his *Impact* film role for "Lux Video Theatre," and his television assignments continued to outdistance the average of two films per year he was making for the declining Hollywood mills.

From the early Sixties until the end of that decade, Donlevy appeared sporadically on television and made a few quickly forgotten films. Rumors circulated that his drinking had become so heavy that he was often unable to remember his script lines. On February 25, 1966, he remarried. His third wife was Lillian Lugosi, ex-wife of Bela "Dracula" Lugosi. Brian's last film was the quickie *Pit Stop,* released in 1969.

Now well into his sixties, he retired to his Palm Springs home, which he had bought in the early Fifties, and attended to his tungsten mines in the Mojave Desert (acquired in the late Thirties). In 1971 he underwent an operation for throat surgery. In early April, 1972, he entered the Motion Picture Country Hospital at Woodland Hills, California, where he died of cancer on April 5, 1972. Thus concluded a lengthy, if erratic and only spasmodically exciting career, that should have brought much more fulfillment to both the actor and his audiences.

BRIAN DONLEVY

Monsieur Beaucaire *(Par 1924)*
Damaged Hearts *(FBO 1924)*
School for Wives *(Vitagraph 1925)*
A Man of Quality *(Excellent 1926)*
Mother's Boy *(Pathé 1929)*
Gentlemen of the Press *(Par 1929)*
Barbary Coast *(UA 1935)*
Mary Burns, Fugitive *(Par 1935)*
Another Face *(RKO 1935)*
Strike Me Pink *(UA 1936)*
Human Cargo *(20th 1936)*
Half Angel *(20th 1936)*
13 Hours by Air *(Par 1936)*
High Tension *(20th 1936)*
36 Hours to Kill *(20th 1936)*
Crack-Up *(20th 1936)*
Midnight Taxi *(20th 1937)*
This Is My Affair *(20th 1937)*
Born Reckless *(20th 1937)*
In Old Chicago *(20th 1938)*
Battle of Broadway *(20th 1938)*
We're Going to Be Rich *(20th British 1938)*
Sharpshooters *(20th 1938)*
Jesse James *(20th 1939)*
Union Pacific *(Par 1939)*
Allegheny Uprising *(RKO 1939)*
Behind Prison Gates *(Col 1939)*
Beau Geste *(Par 1939)*
Destry Rides Again *(Univ 1939)*
The Great McGinty *(Par 1940)*
When the Daltons Rode *(Univ 1940)*
Brigham Young—Frontiersman *(20th 1940)*
I Wanted Wings *(Par 1941)*
Hold Back the Dawn *(Par 1941)*
Birth of the Blues *(Par 1941)*
South of Tahiti *(Univ 1941)*
Billy the Kid *(MGM 1941)*
The Great Man's Lady *(Par 1942)*
A Gentleman after Dark *(UA 1942)*
The Remarkable Andrew *(Par 1942)*
Two Yanks in Trinidad *(Col 1942)*
Wake Island *(Par 1942)*
The Glass Key *(Par 1942)*
Nightmare *(Univ 1942)*
Stand by for Action *(MGM 1942)*
Hangmen Also Die *(UA 1943)*

The Miracle of Morgan's Creek *(Par 1944)*
An American Romance *(MGM 1944)*
Duffy's Tavern *(Par 1945)*
The Virginian *(Par 1946)*
Our Hearts Were Growing Up *(Par 1946)*
Canyon Passage *(Univ 1946)*
Two Years before the Mast *(Par 1946)*
Song of Scheherazade *(Univ 1947)*
The Beginning or the End *(MGM 1947)*
The Trouble with Women *(Par 1947)*
Kiss of Death *(20th 1947)*
Heaven Only Knows *(UA 1947)*
Killer McCoy *(MGM 1947)*
A Southern Yankee *(MGM 1948)*
Command Decision *(MGM 1948)*
Impact *(UA 1949)*
The Lucky Stiff *(UA 1949)*
Shakedown *(Univ 1950)*
Kansas Raiders *(Univ 1950)*
Fighting Coast Guard *(Rep 1951)*
Slaughter Trail *(RKO 1951)*
Hoodlum Empire *(Rep 1952)*
Ride the Man Down *(Rep 1952)*
The Woman They Almost Lynched *(Rep 1953)*
The Big Combo *(AA 1955)*
The Creeping Unknown *(UA 1956)*
A Cry in the Night *(WB 1956)*
Enemy from Space *(UA 1957)*
Escape from Red Rock *(20th 1958)*
Cowboy *(Col 1958)*
Juke Box Rhythm *(Col 1959)*
Never So Few *(MGM 1959)*
The Errand Boy *(Par 1961)*
The Pigeon that Took Rome *(Par 1962)*
The Curse of the Fly *(20th 1965)*
How to Stuff a Wild Bikini *(AIP 1965)*
The Fat Spy *(Magna 1966)*
Waco *(Par 1966)*
Gammera, the Invincible *(World Entertainment Corp. 1967)*
Hostile Guns *(Par 1967)*
Arizona Bushwackers *(Par 1968)*
Rogue's Gallery *(Par 1968)*
Pit Stop *(Distributors International 1969)*

21

James Dunn

No other actor of the Thirties became a star of the magnitude of James Dunn with his very first motion picture. Gable, Tracy, William Powell, Cagney, Bogart, and others who became the great box-office champs ploughed through many minor roles before they headed the bill. Lew Ayres' career approximated Dunn's but lacked the acclaim of both public and critics that was lavished on the star of *Bad Girl* (1931). Few actors brought to the screen the warmth and talent Dunn exhibited in his first few years, although many hit the skids and plunged downhill more quickly. Dunn took his time, re-emerging in the mid-Forties with a stunning performance in *A Tree Grows in Brooklyn* (1945), which won him an Academy Award.

James Dunn's cinema debut in Fox's *Bad Girl* brought hosannas from the press. Louella Parsons gushed, "I was so completely engrossed in this human, interesting tale that I was lifted out of myself. It's the first time in many a day a motion picture has so completely captivated me. James Dunn is excellent." Harrison Carroll in the *Los Angeles Herald* opinionated, "There is no doubt that James Dunn is a real discovery," and the *Chicago Evening Post* proclaimed, "James Dunn begins his screen career with a performance which is going to put him in the very front ranks of screen favorites." They were all right.

Frank Borzage had wanted Spencer Tracy for the role of Edward Collins, but the studio's excitement over their new Broadway import led them to cast James as the frustrated husband in the screen version of Vina Delmar's *Bad Girl*. Borzage won an Oscar for his perceptive and poignant direction, and Edwin Burke received an Academy Award for his adaptation of the story. Strangely, Dunn was not even nominated for an Oscar for his humanized portrayal of the young husband.

James Howard Dunn was born on Saturday, November 2, 1901, in New York City to stockbroker Ralph Howard and Jessie Louise Dunn. The Dunns lived near 147th Street and Broadway but later moved to New Rochelle, New York, where Jim graduated from school and became friends with a large family of vaudevillians—the seven Little Foys and their father, Eddie. Mr. Foy's encouragement of the younger Dunn in his attempt at

178

With Boots Mallory in *Handle with Care* **(Fox '32).**

show business collided with Dunn, Sr.'s idea for his son's future. To appease his dad, Jim tried his hand at mercurial Wall Street. He became involved in the sale of imitation pullman cars on wheels, and sold enough of them to accumulate some ten thousand dollars, which he promptly lost in the stock market. A helpful acquaintance suggested Jimmy try extra work at Paramount's Astoria studios. He did, finding employment in several Thomas Meighan pictures, a few with Richard Dix, and in many of the early two-reel talkie comedies such as *Retire In,* with Billy House.

Dunn made his Broadway debut replacing Raymond Hackett as the undercover cop in *Nightstick* (1927), continuing on tour with the show. He realized his limited acting experience needed a good deal of polish. To gain finesse he joined a repertory company in Englewood, New Jersey, and furthered his training with a company in Winnipeg, Canada. Jerome Kern's *Sweet Adeline,* starring the great Helen Morgan, opened on September 3, 1929, in Manhattan. Toward the end of the run, John D. Seymour became ill, so Dunn stepped into the role of Sid Barnett and later continued the role on an extensive tour with co-players Miss Morgan and Charles Butterworth. Billed as James H. Dunn he sang "The Sun about to Rise" in Act II of *Sweet Adeline.* After the Morgan show closed he was offered a spot in a vaudeville act with Blanche Sweet, but the salary did not impress him. At this time, MGM offered him a screen test to be made in New York's Fox Studios. When Metro decided not to hire him, Fox did.

As a result of *Bad Girl,* James and Sally Eilers—in the title role—were hailed as Hollywood's newest, hottest love team. But for his second film, Fox tossed him into a tale of rival newspaper reporters in love with Linda Watkins—*Sob Sister* (1931). Critics suggested Fox change the title to *The Young Man with a Smile* to capitalize on the warm, Irish charm exuded by James Howard Dunn. The studio had had great success in teaming Janet Gaynor and Charles Farrell, and was convinced that Dunn and Eilers could duplicate the other pair's success. Thus they were matched together onscreen in *Over the Hill* (1931), a new edition of that perennial tearjerker. Mae Marsh gave a superb performance as Ma Shelby, and Dunn was equally fine as her son going to prison for his father's (James Kirkwood) bootlegging and eventually retrieving his mother from the poorhouse. He was again onscreen with Sally Eilers in *Dance Team* (1932), in which he played a hoofer. His dancing was professional and the film's song "I Saw My Future in Your Eyes" came off well.

The intricate, lengthy dance sequence for *Dance Team* was filmed with Jim and, substituting for the less nimble Miss Eilers, June Knight. Dunn fell in love with lovely Miss Knight, and there appeared announcements of their coming marriage, which never materialized. On January 15, 1932, *Dance Team* opened at the Roxy Theatre in New York. Jim was there in person on the stage doing the poignant scene in the doctor's office from *Bad Girl.* He continued an extensive tour with *Dance Team* in many of the country's major cities.

Jim was never idle during his early months at the studio. He studied dancing with Charles Mosconi, learned to play the piano by ear, and perfected his art, now becoming a well-rounded performer. He was given a new contract with Fox and was romantically linked with most of Hollywood's starlets, from Molly O'Day (whom he had known as a child in New Rochelle) to Jessie Le Sueur (Peggy Shannon's stand-in who had just been divorced from Joan Crawford's brother). His liaison with Miss Le Sueur ended when Jimmy lost control of his car, crashing over an embankment, fortunately not injuring either Dunn or Jessie. Among Dunn's other dates about town were Irene Ware and Maureen O'Sullivan. The studio would have been happy had the situation permitted Jimmy to date Sally Eilers, but she was then wed to Hoot Gibson. Besides, Dunn was resistant to the idea of screen teams. "Teams are bad business. It's hard to please one player—let alone two. A story can't be both a man's and a woman's at the same time. . . ."

After his *Dance Team* tour, Fox cast him in *Society Girl* (1932), in which he was a prizefighter, Peggy Shannon the lady, and Spencer Tracy his fight manager. The picture was a dud, despite the effort Jimmy put into training for the prizefighter part with trainer Nate Slot. Fox's scheduled *Little Teacher,* with Marion Nixon, was cancelled and James found himself assigned to a great, maligned, egocentric genius of a director, Erich von Stroheim, to play the lead in von Stroheim's screenplay (with Leonard Speigelgass) of Dawn Powell's play *Walking Down Broadway.* Von Stroheim cast his favorite actress, ZaSu Pitts, as a lonely, psychopathic woman trying to destroy her roommate's (Boots Mallory) romance with Dunn. There were scenes of sexual aberrations and sequences of blatant, sordid prostitution in which Minna Gombell gave a rousing performance as the whore. When Winfield Sheehan left for Europe and turned the production management at Fox over to Sol Wurtzel, the latter, on viewing over 15,000 feet of von Stroheim's film, fired the director. With Wurtzel's "supervision," *Walking Down Broadway* was largely reshot and reedited to some six thousand feet. What might have been another von Stroheim masterpiece was reduced to a shambles. Released a year later as *Hello, Sister!* (1933), it was hardly a passable programmer.

While Fox scheduled Dunn and Sally Eilers to co-star in *Checkers, Born Wild,* and

Okay!, the couple instead starred in a slapstick affair called *Sailor's Luck* (1933), which was advertised as "The perfect story for the perfect team. . . ." On loan to Paramount he was lost in *The Girl in 419* (1933), playing a surgeon, but for that same studio's *Take a Chance* (1933), filmed in New York, he was superior as a tent show crook. With Lillian Roth co-starring, Jimmy joined with June Knight and Charles "Buddy" Rogers in the song "Turn out the Light."

When he returned to the home lot, Fox put him in several reels of unadulterated tripe, *Arizona to Broadway* (1933), and then indulged him with two amusing pictures with Claire Trevor, *Jimmy and Sally* (1933) and *Hold that Girl!* (1934). The Irishman's career took a sudden leap when he teamed with a new child actress, Shirley Temple, portraying her father in Fox's delightful musical *Stand Up and Cheer* (1934). Jimmy in white tie and tails danced and sang "Baby Take a Bow," with the curly-headed, buoyant, polka dot-dressed Shirley.

After playing opposite Ginger Rogers (Sally Eilers was pregnant), with Janet Gaynor and Charles Farrell, and Miss Temple, in a sugar-coated soap opera, *Change of Heart* (1934), Fox reunited Dunn and Temple in *Baby Take a Bow* (1934). In this song and dance venture the pair sang "On Accounta I Love You." Dunn and Shirley were infectious together, and in *Bright Eyes* (1934) the press was calling them a "team," and Dunn Shirley's favorite partner. This film, which featured Shirley singing "On the Good Ship Lollipop," was enhanced by a brisk performance from Shirley's little nemesis, Jane Withers.

Along with the three Temple delights, Dunn made something called *365 Nights in Hollywood* (1934). He was cast as a has-been Hollywood director who makes a hit

With Alice Faye and John Bradford in *365 Nights in Hollywood* (Fox '35).

181

With Dorothy Wilson in *Bad Boy* (Fox '35).

movie with Alice Faye. The resultant film was a mishmash. Much better was *George White's 1935 Scandals* (1935), which also aligned Jimmy with Miss Faye, but this time in an entertaining musical. By this point in the mid-Thirties, Jimmy had begun to wear out his welcome at Fox. The studio had overexposed his image to the public and the company ran out of variations of his sterotyped roles. With two bottom-of-the-bill items for Fox, he concluded his contract there.

Dunn then went to Universal who reteamed him with Sally Eilers in *Don't Get Personal* (1936), a fairly amusing comedy. The former box-office bonanza team would make one more film together, a year later, entitled *We Have Our Memories,* a cops and robbers number aboard an ocean liner. Republic hired an array of Hollywood's former stars (Henry B. Walthall, Fritz Leiber, Irving Pichel, *et al.*) for Lew Ayres' first directorial effort, *Hearts in Bondage* (1936), in which Dunn and Mae Clarke co-starred against a backdrop of the Civil War.

By 1937, the once carefree bachelor Jimmy Dunn fell in love while making *Living on Love* at RKO. He and co-player Frances Gifford were married a year later, and she joined with him in *Mercy Plane* and *Hold that Woman,* two Producers Releasing Corporation quickies turned out in 1940. By this point he was well past his cinematic prime.

Fortunately for Dunn he was offered a chance on Broadway. The show was Cole Porter's *Panama Hattie* and the leading lady was to be Ethel Merman. The musical debuted on October 30, 1940, and was a big hit. Dunn was well cast as the father of moppet Joan Carroll. With the star, Dunn sang "My Mother Would Love You," and the show boasted of such talent as Betty Hutton, Arthur Treacher, Rags Ragland, Phyllis Brooks, and, in the chorus, June Allyson, Vera-Ellen, Doris Dowling, and Betsy Blair. By

With Sally Eilers in *Don't Get Personal* (Univ '36).

December, 1941, Frances Williams replaced Ethel Merman as Hattie, and James Dunn and Frances Gifford were divorced. *Hattie* continued on tour featuring Treacher, Williams, and Dunn. When it concluded Jimmy returned to Hollywood for minor roles in minor films. Already he was creating a reputation in the film city as an unreliable actor and an irresponsible performer because of his frequent alcoholic bouts, all of which was passed off with the comment, "Sure, and it's the curse of the Irish."

One of those miracles that unexpectedly strikes fallen stars in Hollywood then occurred for Dunn. Casting for the film version of Betty Smith's incisive novel *A Tree Grows in Brooklyn* was nearly completed except for the pivotal role of the tippling, procrastinating, shiftless waiter/father, Johnny Nolan. Elia Kazan was directing his first film and had been provided with an excellent script and cast. Studio head Darryl F. Zanuck knowingly took a chance and, after seeing his test, signed James Dunn for the part of the father. It proved to be the finest portrayal of Dunn's career, winning him the Academy Award for Best Supporting Actor of the Year. Dunn, young Peggy Ann Garner, and other cast members would recreate their roles on radio's "Hollywood Star Time."

The Oscar, unfortunately, did nothing for Jimmy's Hollywood career, and after two program fillers, he returned to the stage. He was cast in Eugene O'Neill's *A Moon for the Misbegotten* in the role of James Tyrone, Jr. The drama went into rehearsal in February, 1947, under the direction of Barry Fitzgerald's brother, Arthur Shields, with the casting conforming to O'Neill's dictum that the play must be totally Irish. At the play's first reading the entire cast dissolved in tears. When the reading was finally completed, Dunn commented, "We're all crying now. I guess it will be the management's time to cry later."

A Moon for the Misbegotten played a tryout in Columbus, Ohio, the week of February

20, 1947, and then moved on to Cleveland. When it reached Detroit it was closed by the local police for "obscenity." By the time the play reached St. Louis, O'Neill and the Guild decided to close it, revise it, and reopen it later with a new cast. (Ten years later *A Moon for the Misbegotten* would open on Broadway with Franchot Tone and Wendy Hiller in the leads.) Dunn returned to Hollywood to portray the disagreeable, embittered father of a boxer (Mickey Rooney),in *Killer McCoy* (1947). After a featherweight fiasco, *Texas, Brooklyn and Heaven* (1948), Jim again fled to the stage.

Harvey had opened on Broadway in November, 1944, with Frank Fay starring as Elwood P. Dowd, later succeeded by Bert Wheeler, James Stewart, Jack Buchanan, and Dunn. Jimmy's Elwood had more wistfulness than his predecessors. In the summer of 1950, teamed with Virginia Sale, he took *Harvey* on a straw-hat tour. Then it was back to Hollywood for two unmemorable films. He lost $40,000 in a theatrical misadventure (and would file for bankruptcy) and returned to the stock circuits in Connecticut with *Death of Salesman* and *Goodbye Again.*

Television provided some employment for the dissipated but still sterling Jimmy Dunn in the Fifties. He appeared on most of the major network dramatic shows and had a recurring role in the 1954 teleseries "It's a Great Life." One of his best performances on the small screen was on a "Ben Casey" episode as an old vaudevillian who brings cheer to hospital patients.

His excursions back to filmland were rarely worth the trip, such as his role of a guilt-ridden alcoholic in *The Bramble Bush* (1960) and the small role of a telegrapher in *Hemingway's Adventures of a Young Man* (1962). His last motion picture was ironically *The Oscar* (1966), one of the worst films yet made about Hollywood. His final television appearance (posthumous) was in the video film *Shadow over Elveron,* in which he had a small part.

In August, 1967, he was admitted to the Santa Monica Hospital for surgery to remove a stomach obstruction. On September 3, he died, leaving a stepson, William Tick, his wife's son by a former marriage. Dunn had married Philadelphia radio singer Edna Rush in March, 1945.

The ups and down of Jimmy Dunn's career are a rich study in an actor's life gone awry. With his sensational movie debut in 1931 he should have gone to the top, instead of the eventual downward slide he took, only to be momentarily elevated again in the mid-Forties with a powerful performance that won him an Academy Award but no further decent movie roles.

JAMES DUNN

Bad Girl *(Fox 1931)*
Sob Sister *(Fox 1931)*
Over the Hill *(Fox 1931)*
Dance Team *(Fox 1932)*
Society Girl *(Fox 1932)*
Handle with Care *(Fox 1932)*
Hello, Sister! [Walking Down Broadway] *(Fox 1933)*
Sailor's Luck *(Fox 1933)*
Hold Me Tight *(Fox 1933)*
The Girl in 419 *(Par 1933)*
Arizona to Broadway *(Fox 1933)*
Take a Chance *(Par 1933)*
Jimmy and Sally *(Fox 1933)*
Hold that Girl! *(Fox 1934)*
Have a Heart *(MGM 1934)*
Stand Up and Cheer *(Fox 1934)*
Change of Heart *(Fox 1934)*
Baby Take a Bow *(Fox 1934)*
365 Nights in Hollywood *(Fox 1934)*
Bright Eyes *(Fox 1934)*
George White's 1935 Scandals *(Fox 1935)*
The Daring Young Man *(Fox 1935)*
The Pay-Off *(WB 1935)*
Welcome Home *(Fox 1935)*
Bad Boy *(Fox 1935)*
Don't Get Personal *(Univ 1936)*
Hearts in Bondage *(Rep 1936)*

Two-Fisted Gentleman *(Col 1936)*
Come Closer, Folks *(Col 1936)*
Mysterious Crossing *(Univ 1937)*
We Have Our Moments *(Univ 1937)*
Venus Makes Trouble *(Col 1937)*
Living on Love *(RKO 1937)*
Shadows Over Shanghai *(Grand National 1938)*
Pride of the Navy *(Rep 1939)*
Son of the Navy *(Mon 1940)*
Mercy Plane *(PRC 1940)*
Hold that Woman *(PRC 1940)*
The Living Ghost *(Mon 1942)*
The Ghost and the Guest *(PRC 1943)*
Government Girl *(RKO 1943)*
Leave It to the Irish *(Mon 1944)*
A Tree Grows in Brooklyn *(20th 1945)*
The Caribbean Mystery *(20th 1945)*
That Brennan Girl *(Rep 1946)*
Killer McCoy *(MGM 1947)*
Texas, Brooklyn and Heaven *(UA 1948)*
The Golden Gloves Story *(EL 1950)*
A Wonderful Life *(Protestant Film Company 1951)*
The Bramble Bush *(WB 1960)*
Hemingway's Aventures of a Young Man *(20th 1962)*
The Oscar *(Par 1966)*

22

Ann Dvorak

If dogged determination, perseverance, and an almost obsessive drive to succeed, coupled with talent and an exotic appearance, were enough for stardom, then Ann Dvorak should have been a major movie personality. But Miss Dvorak was not supported by the expertise of the big studio star-creators. She became a contractual chattel shuttled between Howard Hughes and Warner Bros., with neither party doing the best by her. Moreover, since she was not only a superlative actress but a singer, dancer, and songwriter as well, she rebelled at the assembly-line roles shoved at her; she wanted parts to match her capabilities. Her demands succeeded in alienating her employers, and lost Ann the opportunity to become another (or better) Bette Davis-type star.

Ann McKim was born on Friday, August 2, 1912, in New York City. She was the daughter of stage and silent screen actress Anna Lehr and her husband, sometime Biograph director and actor, Samuel McKim. Before Ann was five, her mother and father separated. With her child, Anna Lehr left for the West Coast to pursue her promising career in silent pictures. Soon earning a reputation there as a good, emotional actress, she appeared in Triangle's *Civilization's Child* (1916), played the lead in *Parentage* (1917) and *The Grafters* (1917), and supervised her daughter's screen debut. The film was W. H. Clune's 1916 production of Helen Hunt Jackson's classic *Ramona,* starring Adda Gleason and Monroe Salisbury. Ann was cast as the four-year-old Ramona Phail and used her mother's name, Anna Lehr, on the credits.

Ann's parents were divorced in 1920 and her mother continued making pictures. In the early 1920s she married a handsome, young Californian named Arthur Pearson. Young Ann was placed in a boarding school, and then eventually transferred to Los Angeles' Page School for Girls where she became editor of *The Pagette,* the school newspaper. She also tutored French and dancing to younger pupils, and became an expert pianist. Her mother knew most of the film colony, and had met or appeared with most of the Hollywood silent greats. When young Ann decided her future as an actress could rise in the studios, Anna Lehr arranged an interview for her with Douglas Fairbanks.

Fairbanks was then preparing his production of *The Iron Mask* (1928). The interview resulted in a screen test, but Ann was never called to join the cast of this swashbuckler.

At Warner Bros. in '34.

Nevertheless, her mother encouraged her daughter's ambitions, telling her to "go on and complete what I have started." Ann answered an ad for chorus girls at Los Angeles' Pom Pom Club. Armed with little experience but a great deal of determination and false confidence, she rejected an offer of twenty-five dollars a week by arguing, "I got $80 for my last engagement."

She received sixty-five dollars a week at the Pom Pom Club, and when that job ended she signed on at MGM as a chorus girl for their supermusical *The Hollywood Revue of 1929*. After being turned down several times by the dance director, she cornered him with, "Are you running this show? Well, I'm as good as the ones you chose. Why didn't you pick me? I'm going to get somewhere. I'm sincere. I work. I have ambition." She stayed at the studio and was delighted with her first pay check for $37.50. Six months later choreographer Sammy Lee inveigled the studio to sign her as his assistant.

At Metro, Ann worked with Joan Crawford on the star's dance routines for *Dance, Fools, Dance* (1931), in which a relatively unknown actor played the gangster heavy. He was Clark Gable. Ann had brief bits and walk-ons in several Metro-Goldwyn-Mayer films in 1930 and 1931, including Miss Crawford's *This Modern Age* (1931). For Ramon Novarro's *Son of India* (1931) she performed a quickly passing flash-dance and taught Conchita Montenegro dances for MGM's Spanish-speaking production, directed by Novarro, *La Sevillana* (1931). Although casting directors at Metro told Ann that her initial screen test was less than good, she made tests at other studios. Although no offers came from Paramount, Ann returned to Culver City with her successful Paramount test. As a result, she was given brief scenes in several Metro pictures.

Her self-imposed, rigorous training never ceased. In her spare time she composed songs such as "Go Tell the Devil," but none of them ever reached publication. Then in 1931, Metro signed a vibrant young actress with whom Ann struck an immediate and lasting friendship. The girl was Karen Morley, whose career skyrocketed after her smooth playing of Liane in Greta Garbo's *Inspiration* (1931). Howard Hughes borrowed Miss Morley from Metro to portray gangster moll Polly in his pending production *The Scar*. Karen alerted Ann that the picture had not been entirely cast as yet. "We're looking for someone to play the part of a little Italian girl about eighteen years old." Through Karen, Ann met director Howard Hawks, won the role of Cesca Carmonte in the now retitled *Scarface* (1932), and earned a Howard Hughes contract.

Scarface started shooting in early summer of 1931, and, along with Warner Bros.' *Little Caesar* (1930) and *Public Enemy* (1931), would become a classic of the gangster film genre. Ann's hyperemotional playing of Paul Muni's sister was a sensational screen performance. Had there been an Oscar category for Best Supporting Actress of the Year in 1932, Ann surely would have been a major contender, if not the winner. As Muni's overly protected sister who sparked with glimmerings of incestual longings for her brother, Ann weds coin-flipping George Raft, only to have her insanely jealous brother kill Raft. Censorship problems would plague *Scarface,* forcing Hughes to reshoot several scenes, delete many others, etc. The film was not released until Ann had already completed her second Hughes assignment.

Six writers, including Robert Benchley, collaborated on Hughes' *Sky Devils* (1932), which used leftover footage from *Hell's Angels* (1930). By this point Howard Hawks had moved over to Warner Bros. for *The Crowd Roars* (1932). Since Hughes had nothing scheduled for the actress, he allowed Hawks to borrow her for this James Cagney vehicle. Her role of Cagney's gal, Lee, could have been played by several members of the Warner stable; however, her sincere, intense performance impressed the Warners who consequently offered to buy her contract from Hughes. A deal was made to retain her services for six months "on-loan." Ann claimed later that Hughes owned her soul

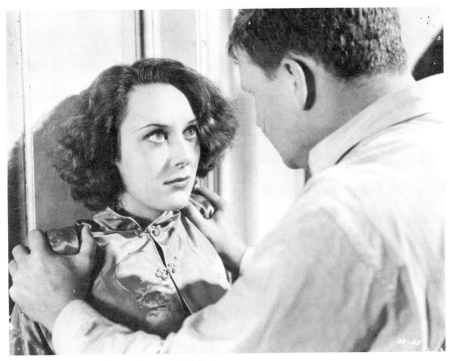

With Barton MacLane in *Dr. Socrates* (WB '35).

and talent, and that he sold her to Warner Bros. for $1,000 a week, while he was only paying her $250 a week under their original pact.

Warner Bros. kept their contractees working at an endless pace. Ann was soon seen in the title role of Michael Curtiz' *The Strange Love of Molly Louvain* (1932), a film that featured one of Ann's own songs, "Gold-Digger Lady." Ann wore a blonde wig as Molly. Playing the villain in the piece was a fine actor who had made his start in the mid-1920s. Leslie Fenton was equally effective on the stage (he had given a brilliant performance in the West Coast production of *An American Tragedy*) as he was on the screen. Ann and Leslie had met casually on New Year's Eve, but by the completion of *Molly Louvain,* they were planning to be wed. With one day off after completing *Molly,* Ann was rushed into a Douglas Fairbanks, Jr. feature, *Love Is a Racket* (1932), while Leslie was completing one of Tallulah Bankhead's deadfalls at Paramount, *Thunder Below* (1932). Fairbanks, Jr. and director William A. Wellman helped Ann complete her scenes for *Love Is a Racket* early in the day, as both of them were privy to the secret of Ann's elopement.

On St. Patrick's Day, March 17, 1932, Ann and Leslie chartered a Stimson cabin plane and pilot, and flew to Yuma, Arizona, where they were wed before going on to Agua Caliente for a brief honeymoon. Fenton was twenty-nine and Ann was nineteen, and it was the first marriage for both.

Back at Warner Bros., Ann was the romantic interest with David Manners in *Crooner* (1932) and *Stranger in Town* (1932). Mervyn LeRoy's *Three on a Match* (1932) was a punchy story blessed with a sterling cast, in which Ann played the lead of Vivian Revere, with Joan Blondell and Bette Davis as her two former school chums.

Jack L. Warner was convinced Ann had a dazzling future and a "dainty unworldly

189

quality that was rare in the actresses around Hollywood at that time." But Ann rebelled at the studio's tyrannical attitude toward their players, refused several dreary roles tossed to her, and left the studio in a rage when she discovered child actor Buster Phelps (of *Three on a Match*) was receiving $500 a week, twice her salary. She secured a doctor's certificate prescribing an extended vacation, presented it to the studio, and, with Fenton, sailed from Los Angeles to New York. In Manhattan she told the press, "I don't like actory people, the so-called 'movie-crowd.' They annoy me with their postures and their falsity. There is nothing real about that set. I stay away from it."

Ann and Fenton sailed for Europe where they stayed for ten months. By the time they returned to Hollywood, Ann had missed a chance to work for Samuel Goldwyn in *Cynara* (1933)—Phyllis Barry got the job instead. Thereafter Ann went to Paramount to replace Sylvia Sidney in Maurice Chevalier's *The Way to Love* (1933).

Later she returned to Warner Bros. to serve out her contract term. The studio would not forgive her for her rebellion, and as the years progressed she was slapped into supporting roles in minor pictures that were quickly made and forgotten. She was Pat O'Brien's neglected wife in *College Coach* (1933), and was Lydia, an Indian girl, in Richard Barthelmess' *Massacre* (1934). She was the most sensitive aspect of *Housewife* (1934) as George Brent's nagging spouse, driving him (temporarily) into the waiting arms of Bette Davis. She returned to dancing and singing as Rudy Vallee's rival and love in *Sweet Music* (1935).

G-Men (1935) had James Cagney on the right side of the law, but it was Ann, with her performance as the nightclub songstress shot to death in a phone booth, who was the outstanding cast member. For William Dieterle's *Dr. Socrates,* Ann returned to support Paul Muni in the tale of a small town doctor who reluctantly becomes the underworld's physician. She added lustre to the role of a lowly burlesque comic's wife in Joe E. Brown's *Bright Lights* (1935). Over at Fox, she returned to her first love, dancing, in *Thanks a Million,* with Patsy Kelly and Dick Powell.

After two Warner Bros. duds, *Midnight Court* (1937) and *The Case of the Stuttering Bishop* (1937), Ann left Warner Bros. She journeyed over to Paramount to appear in *She's No Lady* (1937), directed by Karen Morley's spouse, Charles Vidor. Ann was announced for the lead in the film version of *Dead End* (1937), but it went to Sylvia Sidney. With Phil Regan, Ann joined Republic's modestly described "Miracle Musical," *Manhattan Merry-Go-Round* (1937). She was again at Republic for another flop, James Cruze's *Gangs of New York* (1938).

The huge success of *My Man Godfrey* (1936), with William Powell and Carole Lombard, induced several imitations, one of them a Hal Roach–MGM entry, *Merrily We Live* (1938), in which Ann supported Constance Bennett and Brian Aherne.

On March 21, 1939, while making a bit of trivia at MGM called *Stronger than Desire* (1939), starring Virginia Bruce and Walter Pidgeon, Ann's home was burglarized, and she lost some six thousand dollars in jewelry. Nevertheless she gave an excellent account of her acting abilities in Columbia's *Blind Alley* (1939), with Chester Morris and Ralph Bellamy. After doing *Girls of the Road* (1940), also for Columbia, Ann left for London with Leslie Fenton, who had enlisted in the British Royal Navy.

Ann's stamina kept her in good stead during the London war years, in which, as a member of the British Women's Land Army, she drove an ambulance, became a reporter-columnist for the London *Daily Illustrated* and the London *Herald,* a news commentator on BBC, and, during her spare time, did many shows for the U.S.O. in Ireland and England. While she was filming *This Was Paris* (1942) for Warner Bros.'s British studio, she wrote to Jack L. Warner pleading for more American aid. She stated, "What they don't realize in Hollywood is that it is very important to keep the film business going in England. The money it brings into the country buys all sorts of fighting planes. . . ." She

With John Litel in *Midnight Court* (WB '37).

added that a large sign on the studio's front gate procalimed, "Act Victory, Think Victory, or Damn Well Shut Up!"

Ann's unstinting work for the British war effort continued throughout 1943, but she found time to star in a Nazi spy thriller, *Squadron Leader X* (1943). In the same year's *There's a Future in It,* she played Kitty, in love with bomber pilot Barry Morse, and was directed by her husband, Leslie Fenton. Returning to America, Ann was in *Escape to Danger* (1944) at RKO. Over at Republic, she was Flaxen Terry, singing "Love, Here Is My Heart" and other songs in the better-than-average John Wayne vehicle *Flame of Barbary Coast* (1945). For Paramount's remake of *Midnight* (1939), now titled *Masquerade in Mexico* (1945), Ann played Patric Knowles' bitchy, philandering wife.

The Bachelor's Daughters (1946) cast her as an ambitious pop singer, while in *Abilene Town* (1946), with Randolph Scott, she was Rita, the barroom queen who sings "Snap Your Fingers" and "Everytime I Give My Heart." Her marriage to Fenton, who was back with Paramount, as a director, floundered, and on August 2, 1946, they were divorced. Ann remained at United Artists for the part of Madeleine Forestier in a dud that found George Sanders plodding through *The Private Affairs of Bel Ami* (1947). For RKO's remake of a fine French film, *Daybreak* (1939), which had starred Jean Gabin, Ann generously overacted the role of entertainer Charlene in the prolonged, endless *The Long Night* (1947), with Henry Fonda and Barbara Bel Geddes. Then as Olive she and George Brent made a pleasant thing of Eagle-Lion's *Out of the Blue* (1947). A few weeks before the picture was released, on August 7, 1947, she married Igor (de Navrotsky)

191

Dega, a Russian dancer. On their fourth wedding anniversary, August 7, 1951, Ann divorced dancer Dega for "extreme mental cruelty."

Twentieth Century-Fox's *The Walls of Jericho* (1948) was a well-produced adaptation of Paul Wellman's novel, brightly cast with Cornel Wilde, Anne Baxter, Kirk Douglas, Linda Darnell, and Ann as Wilde's worthless, dipsomaniac wife, Belle. In October, 1948, Ann made her Broadway debut replacing Meg Mundy in the long-running hit of Jean Paul Sartre's *The Respectful Prostitute*. After her success on the Broadway stage, she returned to MGM for *A Life of Her Own* (1950). Director George Cukor guided Ann, Ray Milland, Barry Sullivan, and others through their paces in Metro's continuing (and losing) effort to promote Lana Turner into a topflight dramatic actress.

In 1950 Ann made her television debut on "Silver Theatre's" *Close Up*, and played a weepy woman who abandons her daughter to foster parents Donald Cook and Jane Wyatt in *Our Very Own* (1950). She added class to a better-than-average Western, *The Return of Jesse James* (1950), co-featured in it with John Ireland and Hugh O'Brian. Her ability for honest portrayals brought intensity and reality to her role of Manila nightclub owner Mrs. Claire Phillips in the picture version of that lady's courage and daring during the Japanese occupation of Manila during World War II. This film, *I Was an American Spy* (1951), was modestly produced, but Ann was in excellent form. Her last screen appearance was in Twentieth Century-Fox's *The Secret of Convict Lake* (1951), which offered the talents of such diverse personalities as Gene Tierney, Glenn Ford, Zachary Scott, Ethel Barrymore, and Ann, playing a miner's wife.

Television comprised Ann's major professional appearances in 1952, in which she excelled as the two-timing, tragic wife Anna Maurrant in a video version of *Street Scene* and played the title role of *The Trial of Mary Dugan* on "Broadway's TV Theatre." With Johnny Desmond and Victor Jory, Ann was a guest on the May 3, 1952, "Ken Murray Show." After a few, desultory bids at summer theatre glory, Ann retired from show business. She eventually wed architect Nicholas Wade, and the couple, who have no children, moved to Honolulu in 1959. A good deal of the couple's time is spent in traveling in Europe and in the Orient. Their chief hobby these days is collecting rare first editions.

Strange twists pursued Ann's professional and private life. In the summer of 1934 she had made the nation's headlines in a strange episode that captured the imagination and sympathy of the American public. She appealed to the national press for information regarding her father, Samuel McKim. By August, her uncle, Walter McKim, a Philadelphia resident, read the story in the evening paper and contacted his brother who had become an orange grove farmer in Fort Pierce, Florida. On August 14, 1934, Ann was reunited with her father in Hollywood and was delighted when the dignified Mr. McKim showed her a snapshot of herself as a child that he had carried in his wallet throughout the years.

One can only conjecture what Ann's cinema future might have been had not the talented actress bucked the powerful studio system. Had she not taken that boat through the Panama Canal to New York, what career rewards might have been hers? Nevertheless, she remains one of the best Hollywood players of the Thirties.

192

ANN DVORAK

As: *Baby Anna Lehr:*
Ramona *(Clune 1916)*
The Five Dollar Plate *(Harbough 1920)*
As: *Ann Dvorak:*
The Hollywood Revue of 1929 *(MGM 1929)*
Free and Easy *(MGM 1930)*
Love in the Rough *(MGM 1930)*
Way out West *(MGM 1930)*
Son of India *(MGM 1931)*
Susan Lennox, Her Fall and Rise *(MGM 1931)*
The Guardsman *(MGM 1931)*
Just a Gigolo *(MGM 1931)*
Politics *(MGM 1931)*
This Modern Age *(MGM 1931)*
Sky Devils *(UA 1932)*
The Crowd Roars *(WB 1932)*
The Strange Love of Molly Louvain *(FN 1932)*
Scarface *(UA 1932)*
Love Is a Racket *(FN 1932)*
Crooner *(FN 1932)*
Stranger in Town *(WB 1932)*
Three on a Match *(FN 1932)*
The Way to Love *(Par 1933)*
College Coach *(WB 1933)*
Massacre *(FN 1934)*
Heat Lightning *(WB 1934)*
Midnight Alibi *(FN 1934)*
Friends of Mr. Sweeney *(WB 1934)*
Housewife *(WB 1934)*
Side Streets *(FN 1934)*
I Sell Anything *(FN 1934)*
Gentlemen Are Born *(FN 1934)*
Murder in the Clouds *(FN 1934)*
Sweet Music *(WB 1935)*

G-Men *(WB 1935)*
Bright Lights *(FN 1935)*
Dr. Socrates *(WB 1935)*
Thanks a Million *(Fox 1935)*
We Who Are About to Die (RKO 1936)
Racing Lady *(RKO 1937)*
Midnight Court *(WB 1937)*
She's No Lady *(Par 1937)*
The Case of the Stuttering Bishop *(WB 1937)*
Manhattan Merry-Go-Round *(Rep 1937)*
Merrily We Live *(MGM 1938)*
Gangs of New York *(Rep 1938)*
Blind Alley *(Col 1939)*
Stronger than Desire *(MGM 1939)*
Street of Missing Women *(Col 1940)*
Girls of the Road *(Col 1940)*
This Was Paris *(WB British 1942)*
Squadron Leader X *(RKO British 1943)*
There's a Future in It *(Strand 1943)*
Escape to Danger *(RKO 1944)*
Flame of Barbary Coast *(Rep. 1945)*
Masquerade in Mexico *(Par 1945)*
The Bachelor's Daughters *(UA 1946)*
Abilene Town *(UA 1946)*
Private Affairs of Bel Ami *(UA 1947)*
The Long Night *(RKO 1947)*
Out of the Blue *(EL 1947)*
The Walls of Jericho *(20th 1948)*
A Life of Her Own *(MGM 1950)*
Our Very Own *(RKO 1950)*
The Return of Jesse James *(Lip 1950)*
Mrs. O'Malley and Mr. Malone *(MGM 1950)*
I Was an American Spy *(AA 1951)*
The Secret of Convict Lake *(20th 1951)*

23

Sally Eilers

Gloria Swanson, Carole Lombard, and Phyllis Haver were a few of the famous alumnae of Mack Sennett's Bathing Beauties of the Screen. Another was Sally Eilers who, whether in tandem with popular leading man James Dunn, or on her own, brought a refreshing naturalness to the cinema screen of the Thirties. Although she lacked the sophistication of Dietrich, the electric chemistry of Crawford, or the comedic appeal of snappy Glenda Farrell, there was plenty of room for a congenial, personable miss like Sally. In her pleasant way, she contributed nicely to the output of the decade's products.

Dorothea Sallye Eilers was born on Friday, December 11, 1908, in New York City to Irishman Peter Eilers and his lovely Jewish songstress wife Paula. The Eilers showered an excessive amount of love on their first-born, even following the birth of her brother two years later. This strong parental devotion carried through to Sally's coming of age and instilled in the beautiful young girl a dependence on love and a sensitivity to the slings and slashes of the world. In 1926, because of her brother's ill health, the Eilers moved to California where Sally attended and graduated from Fairfax High School. The family's friendship with former actress Anita Stewart resulted in Miss Stewart arranging a screen test for the young girl. However, the test was a failure. So Sally returned to school and conspired with her chum Jean Peters to invade the movie studios.

It was Jean Peters, later to be known as Carole Lombard, who arranged for Sally's film debut in Marion Davies' MGM version of *The Red Mill* (1927). "I skated around on the ice while Owen Moore chucked me under the chin," Sally later recalled. "I was thrilled. I thought I was a star at last." But she was premature in her estimate. Carole Lombard took Sally to Mack Sennett's Keystone studio where the fun-maker put both girls under contract.

Sally made a batch of Sennett comedies. She appeared with Lombard in such short subjects as *The Campus Vamp, The Campus Carmen,* and *Matchmaking Mammas.* She also had bit roles in features at major studios. When Sennett assigned her to the lead role in his full length film *The Good-Bye Kiss* (1928), Matty Kemp was her leading man. She and Kemp became engaged, an activity for which she exhibited a talent second only to her later screen success. "Getting engaged had always seemed to be about the best thing I did," Sally has admitted. After Kemp, there was a year's betrothal to William

With William Collier, Jr. and Anita Page in *Reducing* (MGM '31).

Hawks, broker brother of directors Howard and Kenneth. After Hawks came director Sutherland; quite obviously, the radiant, witty Sally was a joyful social companion.

At one point Florenz Ziegfeld called Sally "the most beautiful brunette in Hollywood," raving about her expressive brown eyes. The seventh annual Wampas Baby Stars selection listed thirteen potential stars; among them were Lupe Velez and Sally Eilers.

Sennett's production of *The Good-Bye Kiss* was in production for ten months. It seemed Mack could shoot his comedies practically during a lunch break, but his features took an interminable length of time to make. Sally's performance in the film surprised Hollywood, and the flurry of good critical comment seemed to indicate she was *en route* to better screen opportunities. But until her Sennett contract expired, it was he who loaned her to other studios who were offering her good roles. Fox saw her as another vamp type after her performance in *Dry Martini* (1928), and she was "discovered" again after playing in Columbia's *Trial Marriage* (1929). Yet Sally's career did not seem to blossom. Studio executives were leery of her irrepressible behavior and irresponsible ways. Soon she was reduced to playing in the lower standard of productions, such as Universal's *The Long, Long Trail* (1929), a Hoot Gibson Western.

When the troupe went on location to Atascadero for *The Long, Long Trail,* Sally took her mother along. The first night at the hotel, a crib and high chair arrived at the Eiler's room. Attached to it was a note from star Gibson, "Mrs. Eilers—For your little girl, Sally." "Well, I knew I was being kidded but I didn't care," Sally would recall. "But the funny thing was that by the time the picture was finished I found myself on the verge of falling in love with Hoot. He had taken me out quite a lot but he always saw to it that I was brought home early and never once had he attempted to kiss me. That was certainly funny for a man who was supposed to be 'dangerous.' " One day he invited Sally to his

195

ranch for a party, took her aside, and said, "This is your engagement party—and here's your ring!" "Hooter," as Sally called him, became her first husband in a ceremony performed at his Saugus, California, ranch on June 27, 1930. Hoot's young daughter Lois, by his second marriage, became great pals with Sally.

"Before my marriage to Hooter, I never thought for myself," Sally said candidly. "I never had great responsibilities. I lived with my parents, and though we were never wealthy, I did not want for things. Motion pictures were simply a game. I wanted to be a star, but not because it meant a career and accomplishment; my only thoughts were that stars were worshipped by the world, had more money than they could possibly spend, and were the envy of millions of other women." After accompanying Hoot on a personal appearance tour he made in the East, she returned to Hollywood and new offers of film work with a fresh outlook. "I plunged into my work which must have surprised studio officials." It did.

Sally and Hoot had made two more Universal Westerns together, *Roaring Ranch* (1930) and *Trigger Tricks* (1930), before she was signed by MGM for the part of Diane in Norma Shearer's *Let Us Be Gay* (1930). Afterwards at Metro she was with Buster Keaton in *Dough Boys* (1930) and *Parlor, Bedroom and Bath* (1931), and with Marie Dressler in *Reducing* (1930). But Sally and Metro head Louis B. Mayer clashed. The pious Mayer was horrified by Sally's briny, earthy dialogue (second only to pal Carole Lombard's frank language) and did not want her on the lot any more. So after Sally made another Western with Hoot, *Clearing the Range* (1931), for Capital Film Exchange, she went over to the Fox lot.

It was announced that Sally and Spencer Tracy would co-star in *Skyline,* for which George and Ira Gershwin were allegedly contributing the score. That project was dropped, and instead Sally and Tracy were reassigned to *Quick Millions* (1931). It was a hard-hitting tough film, with both players giving good performances under Rowland Brown's direction. Sally was advantageously displayed with featured billing in Warner Oland's second adventure as Charlie Chan in *The Black Camel* (1931).

At this juncture Frank Borzage was seeking an actress with screen experience who had not had a starring role. The role in question was the lead in his proposed production of Vina Delmar's book and successful Broadway play *Bad Girl* (1931). For the male lead Borzage had selected Spencer Tracy, but the studio had just signed young, handsome, talented Irishman James Dunn and decided to give him the star build-up by putting him in *Bad Girl.* Their choice exceeded their fondest hope. The pairing of Dunn and Eilers gave Fox their most successful love team since the all-time great co-stars Janet Gaynor and Charles Farrell.

Bad Girl catapulted both Eilers and Dunn, justifiably, to stardom. Fox modestly proclaimed it "The Greatest Human Interest Picture Ever Made." One critic noted that "Sally Eilers does better than anyone imagined she could do." Following *Bad Girl,* Fox practically married her oncamera to James Dunn. The studio cast the duo in their remake of *Over the Hill* (1931), with James Kirkwood and D. W. Griffith's one-time star Mae Marsh. However, Sally, who had become a blonde, had a rather minor role as son James' girl friend. For *Dance Team* (1932), Dunn received top-billing and Fox now called them "the two greatest new stars of the season." The studio planned to team them in *Checkers, Born Wild,* and *Okay!,* but the pair starred in none of these.

But then for reasons known only to the Fox hierarchy, the Dunn-Eilers team was disbanded. Sally was assigned to replace Linda Watkins in *Disorderly Conduct* (1932) with Spencer Tracy. She completed the year in a dreary program entry, *Hat Check Girl* (1932), in which Ginger Rogers was also involved.

State Fair (1933), the first of three versions of that homespun delight, featured Will Rogers spicing his wife's mince pie and winning a blue ribbon for his prize pig, Blue

With Norman Foster in *State Fair* ('33).

In the late Thirties.

Boy, while his children are beset with falling in love. Sally played trapeze artist Emily Joyce, who is discovered by Rogers' film son, Norman Foster.

Meanwhile, back at the ranch at Saugus, the Eilers-Gibson romance was teetering towards disaster. One of the causes of the marriage's failure was Sally's sudden rise to stardom. Another reason was Sally's inability to subordinate her opinions to those of Hoot. The couple separated several times, with Sally returning to the screen in *Sailor's Luck* (1933) with James Dunn again her leading man.

On July 3, 1933, Hoot Gibson was injured in a plane race, and when interviewed at the hospital, he announced his intention of divorcing Sally and marrying June Gale (she would later marry Oscar Levant). On September 24, 1933, Sally received a Mexican divorce from Hoot in Chihuahua. During this period, Sally turned out several films, including Richard Barthelmess' *Central Airport* (1933) and Metro's *Made on Broadway* (1933), with Robert Montgomery and Madge Evans.

When close friends Bebe Daniels and Ben Lyon asked Sally to go with them on a European trip, she leaped at the chance. Also on board the ship was one of the Lyons' best friends, director Harry Joe Brown. By the time they reached London, Sally had fallen in love with the director. She and Ben made a British film, *I Spy* (1933), but the great adventure of the jaunt was finalizing plans to marry Brown. That was accomplished on September 28, 1933, two days after Brown's fortieth birthday. Not quite a year later, Sally gave birth to a boy whom they named Harry, Jr.

Sally's final major co-starring picture with James Dunn for Fox was *Hold Me Tight* (1933). (Later in the Thirties, Universal would co-star the once hot team in *Don't Get Personal* [1936] and *We Have Our Moments* [1937], two lightweight comedies.) After two rather deadly entries at Fox, including *Three on a Honeymoon* (1934), Sally left that studio.

As a free-lancer she appeared in a declining series of program films. Her performances were often better than her material: as Olga in a Graustarkian fillip with Ben Lyon, *The Morning After* (1934); Daisy, opposite fast-talking Lee Tracy, in *Carnival* (1935); and tough gal Sally, with Ray Milland, in *Alias Mary Dow* (1935). At least Universal's *Remember Last Night?* (1935) had amusing dialogue and a cast that included Edward Arnold, Constance Cummings, Robert Young, and Sally.

By 1936, Sally's career was definitely on the decline. She had a supporting role in Eddie Cantor's *Strike Me Pink,* and was subordinate to Jack Oakie and assorted buffoonery in *Florida Special,* a sort of Grand Hotel on the rails. After being heard on "Lux Radio Theatre" in *Cappy Ricks,* she sailed to England to appear in Gaumont-British's *Talk of the Devil* (1937), with Ricardo Cortez. She then went to Wales as house guest of William Randolph Hearst and Marion Davies at their St. Donat's Castle, keeping Marion in spurts of laughter with her Rabelaisian stories.

Sally's great success of the early Thirties did not repeat itself toward the decade's end. She was seen in a brace of low-budget films such as Republic's *Lady Behave* (1937). In 1938 she signed with RKO for a series of occasionally interesting minor films, such as *Condemned Women* (1938), in which she portrayed a hell-raising convict who falls in love with warden Louis Hayward. Her four-year-old son, whom she called "Poochie," appeared with his mother in *They Made Her a Spy* (1939). After *Full Confession* (1939) with Victor McLaglen, Sally headed for a new field, the legitimate stage.

At the Cape Playhouse in Dennis, Massachusetts, she appeared in *Kiss the Boys Goodbye,* and later that season she joined with Philip Huston for *The College Widow* at the Mohawk Valley Festival. The next year she was back on the straw-hat circuit with *Smilin' Through.* Husband Harry Joe Brown produced a new George Seaton play, *About*

Tomorrow, directed by and starring Frank Craven. It opened in San Francisco in December, 1940, with Sally in a prominent role. The play folded after a week and a half.

After playing Eduardo Ciannelli's unhappy wife in Columbia's *I Was a Prisoner on Devil's Island* (1941), Sally was professionally inactive until she did two quickies in 1944–1945 for poverty row studios. Meanwhile in August, 1943, she and Brown reached a friendly (and financially profitable for Sally) divorce agreement. Two days later (on August 28, 1943) she married Naval Air Force Lieutenant Howard Barney at Santa Fe, New Mexico. That union would also end in divorce and in 1949 she became Mrs. John Hollingsworth Morse. He would leave her in 1958.

Ex-film actor turned producer Johnny Walker engaged Sally for his play *Make Yourself at Home*. The show opened in Philadelphia in August, 1945, but Sally received a critical shelling. She was replaced by Bernadene Hayes, and the play ventured into New York where it lasted only four performances. Sally's last two film performances were in Westerns produced by her ex-husband, Harry Joe Brown: *Coroner Creek* (1948), with Randolph Scott, and *Stage to Tucson* (1950), with Rod Cameron.

Although she was out of film-making by the Fifties, Sally remained a frequent attendee at Hollywood social functions, her bright wit matched by her bright smile. In recent years, due to a recurring illness, she has remained pretty much at home, in her small Beverly Hills home. Her two Yorkie dogs are her constant companions. Now only on late, late show films can one glimpse the Sally of old, whose effervescent personality once led her indulgent father to write in an annual birthday poem for his adored daughter:

"She's my little Dorothea and 'twould
Do you good to see her.
Face so fair and eyes so bright
Haunt me day and haunt me night.
And her baby smile
Does all my cares beguile.
Her image is of one I love,
And long now to embrace;
What's pleasing to me more than all—
She has her mother's face."

SALLY EILERS

The Red Mill *(MGM 1927)*
Paid to Love *(Fox 1927)*
Slightly Used *(WB 1927)*
Sunrise *(Fox 1927)*
Cradle Snatchers *(WB 1928)*
The Crowd *(MGM 1928)*
Dry Martini *(Fox 1928)*
Broadway Daddies *(Col 1928)*
The Good-Bye Kiss *(WB 1928)*
Trial Marriage *(WB 1929)*
Broadway Babies *(WB 1929)*
The Show of Shows *(WB 1929)*
The Long, Long Trail *(Univ 1929)*
Sailor's Holiday *(Pathé 1929)*
She Couldn't Say No *(WB 1930)*
Let Us Be Gay *(MGM 1930)*
Roaring Ranch *(Univ 1930)*
Trigger Tricks *(Univ 1930)*
Dough Boys *(MGM 1930)*
Reducing *(MGM 1931)*
Parlor, Bedroom and Bath *(MGM 1931)*
Clearing the Range *(Capitol Film Exchange 1931)*
Quick Millions *(Fox 1931)*
The Black Camel *(Fox 1931)*
Bad Girl *(Fox 1931)*
A Holy Terror *(Fox 1931)*
Over the Hill *(Fox 1931)*
Dance Team *(Fox 1932)*
Disorderly Conduct *(Fox 1932)*
Hat Check Girl *(Fox 1932)*
State Fair *(Fox 1933)*
Second Hand Wife *(Fox 1933)*

Sailor's Luck *(Fox 1933)*
Made on Broadway *(MGM 1933)*
I Spy *(Wardour 1933)*
Central Airport *(WB 1933)*
Hold Me Tight *(Fox 1933)*
Walls of Gold *(Fox 1933)*
She Made Her Bed *(Par 1934)*
Three on a Honeymoon *(Fox 1934)*
The Morning After *(Majestic 1934)*
Carnival *(Col 1935)*
Alias Mary Dow *(Univ 1935)*
Pursuit *(MGM 1935)*
Remember Last Night? *(Univ 1935)*
Don't Get Personal *(Univ 1936)*
Strike Me Pink *(UA 1936)*
Florida Special *(Par 1936)*
Without Orders *(RKO 1936)*
We Have Our Moments *(Univ 1937)*
Talk of the Devil *(Gaumont 1937)*
Danger Patrol *(RKO 1937)*
Lady Behave *(Rep 1937)*
The Nurse from Brooklyn *(Univ 1938)*
Everybody's Doing It *(RKO 1938)*
Condemned Women *(RKO 1938)*
Tarnished Angel *(RKO 1938)*
They Made Her a Spy *(RKO 1939)*
Full Confession *(RKO 1939)*
I Was a Prisoner on Devil's Island *(Col 1941)*
A Wave, A Wac, and a Marine *(Mon 1944)*
Strange Illusion *(PRC 1945)*
Coroner Creek *(Col 1948)*
Stage to Tucson *(Col 1950)*

24

Frances Farmer

In the midst of Hollywood's Golden Age came a shining, beautiful, supremely talented actress who could have become one of the screen's brightest stars. Instead she remains memorable more for the sensational headlines she made. Few, if any, actresses evoked such antagonism and rancor or were as hell-bent for self-destruction as Frances Farmer. After her first year in Hollywood, a reporter wrote, "Her manners are none too gracious and a lot of people already cordially dislike her." A fellow worker summed up what most of the film colony felt about her: "The nicest thing I remember about Frances Farmer is that she was unbearable!" There were no dissenting opinions to that statement. Yet *Photoplay* magazine could report, "She is Miss Sex-appeal of '37, the prime sensation of the screen and the newest and most original glamour girl to dazzle Hollywood."

The youngest of three children, Frances was born on Saturday, September 19, 1914, at 312 Harvard Avenue in Seattle, Washington. Her parents were Minnesota-born lawyer Ernest Melvin Farmer and Lillian Van Ornums Farmer, a hawklike woman who championed lost causes with all the zeal and fervor of a misguided Messiah. Lillian did nothing in moderation. Unfortunately Frances inherited a good deal of her mother's eccestricities, and the ambivalence between the two women developed into a vortex close to madness.

Frances won a national essay prize of one hundred dollars in her junior year at high school with her piece "God Dies," and the event offered Lillian a golden opportunity to rescue her waning notoriety. In 1931 Frances entered the University of Washington, majoring in journalism, working her way through college with such diverse jobs as a summer camp counselor, a singing waitress at Mount Rainier National Park and an usherette at the local Paramount Theatre. She eventually transferred to the college drama department where, under the method guidance of Sophie Rosenstein, she learned acting. Frances made her debut in the title role of *Helen of Troy*. Then, she was acclaimed for her performance in the college production of *Alien Corn*. It fired her with determination to join the prestigious Group Theatre in New York.

Frances' passage to New York was hampered by a distinct lack of funds, but then she won an all-expense-paid round trip to Moscow, via New York. Her prize work was through a subscription contest for a Communist-indoctrinated Seattle paper, *The Voice of Action*. When Frances won, the headlines of local papers read, "Co-Ed to Act for

With Cary Grant in *The Toast of New York* (RKO '37).

Reds," but it was Lillian who won the day by joining in the hue and cry of the local press against her own daughter. Despite all the turmoil, Frances left Seattle for New York by bus in April, 1935.

After Moscow and Warsaw, Frances returned to the States from Southampton, aboard the *President Harding*. She was determined to remain in Manhattan and gain a foothold in the theatre. She met theatre man Shepard Traube and on June 25, 1935, signed a personal contract with him. Traube arranged a screen test for Frances with Oscar Serlin, Paramount Pictures' New York talent scout. For the audition she did a scene from Katharine Hepburn's Broadway flop *The Lake*. On Miss Farmer's twenty-first birthday, September 19, 1935, she signed a seven-year contract with Paramount starting at one hundred dollars a week with six-month options and proportionate salary increases.

Ten days later she left for the West Coast and first appeared on the screen in a Paramount-produced Community Chest trailer. Her first feature was *Too Many Parents* (1935), featuring Billy Lee and Carl "Alfalfa" Switzer. Frances then supplied the romantic interest in *Border Flight* (1936), a routine programmer film. To acclimate Frances to cinema acting, the studio assigned her to their talent department then headed by drama coach Phyliss Laughton. There Frances met an aspiring actor named William Anderson who had chosen for his screen tag, Leif Erickson. (Frances persisted in calling him Bill.)

Publicity pose c. '37.

Studio publicity department people had discovered early that Miss Farmer was not to be coerced into their usual games of romantic alignments, but when they tentatively suggested she and Erickson made a handsome couple, she surprisingly agreed, although she considered him less than talented and felt their decision to marry was a grave mistake. (She later admitted that she "neither loved him nor was in love with him.") However, on February 8, 1936, they eloped to Huma, Arizona, where they were married by a justice of the peace.

Frances was being given the studio build-up and fighting it every step of the way up to Adolph Zukor, who remonstrated with her about her more than casual dressing habits. She was totally uncooperative and verbalized in the saltiest language possible her disenchantment with Hollywood and everything it represented. The studio next cast her opposite Bing Crosby in *Rhythm on the Range* (1936). This picture, Frances later reflected, she thoroughly enjoyed doing, although she considered it "an absurd movie." However, the carefree ambiance on the set with Crosby, Martha Raye, and Bob Burns made the experience worthwhile.

Her relatively few screen appearances attracted a good press and fan audience, and Samuel Goldwyn borrowed her from Paramount for the screen edition of Edna Ferber's *Come and Get It* (1936).

For the important role of Lotta Bostrom, a bawdy, husky-voiced cafe singer, Frances went to the Red Light district of Los Angeles to observe first-hand the ladies of the evening, studying their mannerisms and steeping herself in creating a fine characterization of the wayward Lotta. The Ferber story of lumbering operations in the Northwest of 1890 provided Frances with dual roles, that of the lusty cafe singer and her sweet innocent daughter, Lotta Morgan. She played both parts to the hilt, and had a rare opportunity to redo her role when Samuel Goldwyn decided that he was dissatisfied with the William Wyler footage of *Come and Get It* and had Howard Hawks refilm most of it. *Photoplay* magazine cited her performance, along with Edward Arnold's masterful portrayal of Barney Glasgow, as one of the month's best and lauded her playing as sensationally brilliant.

On January 4, 1937, Frances was heard on "Lux Radio Theatre" with Spencer Tracy and Virginia Bruce in *Men in White*. In this period she was extremely busy in front of the cameras, making four films within four months. She was loaned to RKO for the showy, if laundered, role of Josie Mansfield, mistress of robber baron Jim Fiske (Edward Arnold), in *The Toast of New York* (1937), sharing the spotlight with Cary Grant. At the same time she was filming *Ebb Tide* (1937) in Technicolor at Paramount. Morning, afternoon, and night she was oncamera, and the tension was building pressure. In *Toast* she was lovely in the period costumes, and critics called her performance "intelligently conceived." Her role of Faith Wishart in *Ebb Tide* was greeted as a masterful performance, and on June 7, 1937, she was back on "Lux Radio Theatre" for *British Agent*, with Errol Flynn. Before *Toast* was in the can, she replaced Carole Lombard in *Exclusive* (1937), and in August she left for the East Coast for her great love, the Theatre.

During this professionally productive period, her anxiety and terrors built up. Lillian did not help the situation. And Frances' marriage to Erickson was quaking, despite their still sharing a small home in Laurel Canyon. Atop of this seething background she opened in her first legitimate stage appearance, at the Westchester Playhouse in *At Mrs. Beams,* co-starring with Mildred Natwick. Reviewing Miss Farmer's debut, writer Douglas Gilbert penned, "Her regular features are as frank as a dollar watch and a superb indication of her attitude. She has no illusions about her talent, freely admitting that what she knows about the art of the legitimate theatre is molecular and, that in using her hard-won studio vacation to make these arduous summer appearances, is simply for study and practice."

Frances' goal was still The Group Theatre. Following another week at the Westport Country Playhouse in *At Mrs. Beams,* she starred with Phillips Holmes in *The Petrified Forest* at the Westchester Playhouse on August 23, 1937. That September she achieved her long-held desire, joining The Group Theatre, by demanding and receiving a release from her Paramount contract. She signed for the role of Lorna Moon in the Group's production of Clifford Odets' *Golden Boy.* Odets describes Lorna as...different. There is a certain quiet glitter about this girl, and if she is sometimes hard it is more from necessity than choice; her eyes often hold a soft sad glance." In several ways he could well have been describing Frances.

Odets was married at the time to Oscar-winner Luise Rainer, but he became romantically involved with Frances. The Farmer-Odets love affair was grist for the gossip columns, and Erickson's arrival in Manhattan to dispel the rumors only resulted in his and Frances' realization that their marriage was a mistake. They agreed to a separation. *Golden Boy* opened on November 4, 1937, at the Belasco Theatre and became one of Odets' biggest hits, running 250 performances and continuing on the road.

Frances planned to leave with the company for her London stage debut but The Group, in response to financial pressures, agreed that actress Lillian Emerson would be Lorna Moon in London. Frances was summarily dismissed. Between the rigors of playing the show, complicated by her strange, emotionally devastating love affair with Odets, she was beset by a $75,000 breach of contract lawsuit by Shepard Traube. Although she won the court battle, the wounds and scars inflicted from diverse sources were compounded when she received a handwritten note from Odets with whom she was to dine that night. It read: "My wife returns from Europe today, and I feel it best for us never to see each other again."

Frances returned to Hollywood and to Paramount who were astonished at her tranquility following her Broadway success. She was assigned to a minor film with, of all people, Leif Erickson. *Ride a Crooked Mile* (1938) was merely a time waster for all concerned. She then returned to New York and began a road tour of *Golden Boy,* with

With Akim Tamiroff and Leif Erikson in a pose for *Ride a Crooked Mile* (Par '38).

Elia Kazan in the lead. In January, 1939, under Kazan's direction, she went into rehearsal for Irwin Shaw's *Quiet City,* which failed quickly on Broadway. In May, 1939, she and Luther Adler appeared on Kate Smith's radio hour in *Men in White.* She again spent the summer on the Eastern straw-hat stages, returning in mid-September for rehearsals in *Thunder Rock* (November 14, 1939). In this Group Theatre production, she was joined by Lee J. Cobb, Franchot Tone, and Luther Adler. *Variety* observed, "Frances Farmer flounders painfully as the pioneer girl out of the past." The Robert Ardrey play lasted only twenty-three performances.

By then her drinking was rapidly getting out of hand. When the Theatre Guild offered her the lead female role in Ernest Hemingway's *The Fifth Column,* she was near an emotional and physical collapse. Under Lee Strasberg's direction she tried to get through the rehearsals, but had to be replaced in Philadelphia by Katherine Locke. She was also fined fifteen hundred dollars for walking out on the show. In February, 1940, she returned to Hollywood.

On March 6 she started work on *South of Pago Pago* (1940), a Universal filler with Jon Hall, and later was heard on radio in *Women in the Wilderness.* She had been quite friendly with John Garfield in New York, and it was he who persuaded Warner Bros. to hire her for *Flowing Gold* (1940). This story about oil drillers was not a successful film, and Hollywood had the smug joy of learning that fourteen retakes were ordered for Frances' fall in the mud in the storyline. She left for another summer season in stock, playing Jo in *Little Women* and then starring with Constance Collier and Ann Andrews in *Our Betters* at the Cape Playhouse, in Dennis, Massachusetts. By the end of summer her drinking was a solitary, dangerous pastime, and when she returned to Hollywood in April, 1941, she rented Dolores Del Rio's home in Santa Monica and started work on Paramount's *World Premiere* (1941).

Her co-star in this film was a fellow alcoholic, the once great John Barrymore, then reduced to a mere caricature of his former self. The following month she started *Among the Living* (1941), a melodramatic film about insanity, with Susan Hayward and Albert Dekker. The title and subject matter of this Paramount potboiler were prophetically applicable to Frances. The day she completed her role in *Among the Living* she moved to Universal to begin *Badlands of Dakota* (1941), a robust Western that paraded most of the fabled heroes and heroines of the Old West. Frances was cast as Calamity Jane, an assignment that was not lost on Louella O. Parsons, who seldom had anything good to write about Frances. By June, Louella was reporting, "The highbrow Frances Farmer, who found Hollywood so beneath her a few years ago, is playing, of all things, Calamity Jane in *Badlands of Dakota* for Universal."

After completing her role of Isobel in Twentieth Century-Fox's *Son of Fury* (1942), starring Tyrone Power and Gene Tierney, Frances retreated into her own personal hell. On October 19, 1942, she was stopped by the California police for driving with full headlights on in a dim-off zone, for driving without a license, and for being drunk. Her declaration to the arresting officer, "You bore me," was augmented by a barrage of abusive language sprinkled with four-letter words in the night court where she was sentenced to 180 days and placed on probation. She signed for a film to be shot in Mexico, but after spending two weeks in Mexico City, she was told there was no script available and she walked off the project.

She returned to Hollywood and moved into the Knickerbocker Hotel where, after the first of the year, she started work on a King Brothers' picture, *There's No Escape.* But on January 6, a warrant was issued for her arrest for failure to pay the remaining half of a $250 police fine. Pictures of her battling arresting officers in the jail became front page items, and her belligerent attitude exploded in court when she hurled an inkwell at the presiding judge. Mother Lillian immediately arrived in Los Angeles to join the fray, calling her own press conference and demanding a sanity hearing. She claimed her daughter was indeed crazy. The Screen Actors Guild was instrumental in installing Frances in a private sanitarium where she was submitted to insulin shock treatment for ninety days straight while Mrs. Farmer arranged to be made her legal guardian. After Frances' release, she returned to Seattle where her mother had her committed to the state insane asylum, some thirty-five miles south of Seattle.

Released back into her mother's domination—who sent her back to the asylum in May, 1945, where she remained for five years—she was released finally in March, 1950. A year later she was certified as fully recovered and adjudged and decreed to have her competency and civil rights restored. On July 27, 1953, Frances secured a court order discharging her mother as legal guardian. Then, in order to have someone help to care for her aging parents, she unemotionally married Seattle engineer Alfred Lobley. (Leif Erickson had divorced Frances on June 12, 1942, and that same afternoon had wed actress Margaret Hayes.)

When life with Lobley became intolerable to Frances, she left Seattle for Eureka, California, the farthest point fifty dollars would take her on the bus. Life in Eureka was spent working in a photographer's shop, and she remained unknown to anyone by using the name Frances Anderson. She isolated herself and indulged in nightly hotel room binges. Then one day she was recognized by Lee Mikesell, a former radio station manager. He took her to San Francisco. There she first worked in the laundry, then as a reservation clerk at the Park Sheraton Hotel. Mikesell alerted Ed Sullivan of her whereabouts and he subsequently offered Frances work on his television show. Meanwhile, Mikesell told San Francisco newspapermen just who the reservation clerk was at the Park Sheraton. There was a good deal of hoopla surrounding the rediscovery of Frances Farmer, now a $75-a-week hotel worker.

For Ed Sullivan she appeared on his highly rated variety show on June 30, 1957, singing the song she had sung in *Come and Get It*. The song was "Aura Lee," which had gained new popularity as "Love Me Tender," as sung by Elvis Presley. One reporter wrote: "An almost forgotten name, an almost forgotten face . . . Frances Farmer. Suddenly she's back looking once again for the fame and stardom she lost fourteen years ago. Suddenly there she is on the Ed Sullivan show singing 'Aura Lee' in a low, soft voice, looking as beautiful as ever."

On August 12, 1957, she returned to the stage at Bucks County Playhouse in *The Chalk Garden,* playing the role of Miss Madrigal, a woman trying to pick up the pieces of her shattered life after fifteen years. Frances understood the role, had lived most of it, and her reviews were fine. She remained at the New Hope, Pennsylvania, playhouse for Michael Ellis' tryout of a new play, *The Jamison Affair.* Her theatre appearance there broke a standing box-office record at the playhouse. When she had completed her Eastern contractual commitments she returned to California to appear with Hugh O'Brian on "Playhouse 90" in the telecast *Reunion.* On March 7, 1958, she was granted a divorce from Alfred Lobley, calmly noting that the marriage had served its purpose.

Her new found fame was well received, and against her better judgment she accepted a prearranged video appearance on "This Is Your Life." Many of Frances' former coworkers and even close friends refused to appear on the show and it was a degrading, dismal affair. On March 27, 1958, she wed Leland at Las Vegas, the week before having appeared with Margaret O'Brien on "Studio One" in *Tongues of Angels.* For her old studio, Paramount, she made a quickie called *The Party Crashers* (1958) and appeared in a segment for TV's "Treasury Agent," with Lloyd Nolan.

By summer she was back in the theatre at Ephrata, Pennsylvania, in *Yes, My Darling Daughter,* and later at Indianapolis' Avondale Theatre for *The Chalk Garden.* Frances had no idea that her remaining years would be spent in Indianapolis. On October 1, 1958, she began a television show every afternoon from five till seven on WFBM-TV called "Frances Farmer Presents," as hostess of a movie show in which she discussed the daily feature and had visiting guests for interviews. During the six-year run of her video program she interviewed, among others, Ginger Rogers, Helen Hayes, Sophie Tucker, Rory Calhoun, and Chet Huntley. At the same time she settled into her own home in Indianapolis, and was named Business Woman of the Year for Indiana. In the spring of 1964 the "Today Show" asked to do an hour profile on her, sending a crew to film her at work in Indianapolis. She agreed and later went to New York for a live portion of the program, being interviewed by John Daly. The show was fine, restoring much of Frances' self-respect, as did an offer from Purdue University to be their actress-in-residence.

There she appeared with glowing success in *Look Homeward, Angel,* and *The Sea Gull,* and was especially effective as the embittered millionairess bent on revenge in *The Visit.* It was a performance Frances felt crowned her gifts as an actress. But her drinking increased and she was becoming more dependent on an escape through the bottle.

Her determination to straighten out her life arrived too late, but she did complete a goodly portion of her memoirs before her death on the afternoon of August 1, 1970, from cancer of the throat. She was not quite fifty-six years old. The title of her autobiography, published posthumously in 1972, was taken from a poem by Emily Dickinson, "Will There Really Be a Morning?" Her staunch and faithful Indianapolis friend Jean Ratcliffe had helped Frances write (and complete) the autobiography, which is dedicated to Jean. Plans to film Frances' life story, to be directed by her friend Ida Lupino, are still under negotiation. Perhaps like the searing book, it will help explain the tormented, tortured life of a brilliant actress who had so much more to offer Hollywood of the Thirties than she or the studios were willing to concede.

FRANCES FARMER

Too Many Parents *(Par 1936)*
Border Flight *(Par 1936)*
Rhythm on the Range *(Par 1936)*
Come and Get It *(UA 1936)*
The Toast of New York *(RKO 1937)*
Exclusive *(Par 1937)*
Ebb Tide *(Par 1937)*
Ride a Crooked Mile (Par 1938)

South of Pago Pago *(UA 1940)*
Flowing Gold *(WB 1940)*
World Premiere *(Par 1941)*
Badlands of Dakota *(Univ 1941)*
Among the Living *(Par 1941)*
Son of Fury *(20th 1942)*
The Party Crashers *(Par 1958)*

25

Glenda Farrell

The all-knowing, wisecracking blonde was a stock feature of many Thirties films and none could compare with the brisk-tongued, arch, acidulous, sparkling Glenda Farrell. In film after film she played the same gold-digging dame, until even a brief appearance by her could add life into a dying script. As the wily, aggressive predatory female she had no equal on the screen.

Although she was never a star in the accepted sense, she gave vibrant support to many a picture with her breezy, undefeatably tough projection. Warner Bros. kept her working in as many as four pictures at the same time. Her lines might vary, but the type of dame she played was almost always the same. She created a singular type on the screen in tandem with another fine actress, Joan Blondell. Nevertheless, there was only one Glenda Farrell, despite casting directors' penchants to find other "Glenda Farrell types." The real Glenda Farrell brightened the screen of the Thirties with her strong presence, sudden radiant smile, and crisp, no-nonsense voice.

She was born on Thursday, June 30, 1904, in Enid, Oklahoma, to Charles and Willamena Farrell. She began her stage career at age seven, playing Little Eva in Virginia Brissac's stock company. Following school she was back in a San Diego, California, stock company playing *Rebecca of Sunnybrook Farm.* In San Diego she met a handsome, blue-eyed boy with curly black hair who had been awarded the Distinguished Service Medal during his Navy duty in World War I. Glenda fell in love with Thomas Richards and in six weeks they were wed in Los Angeles. Together they worked up a poor vaudeville act that paid starvation wages. When Glenda became pregnant, they returned to live in the Farrell household.

"We were so poor," Glenda later recalled, "that I was forced to make my baby's diapers out of old flour sacks which Dad brought home from the store." Her son's (Tommy) arrival was the beginning of the end of her marriage to the ex-war hero who was finding solace in heavy drinking. Divorce was inevitable, and when her son had reached the age of ten, his confusion between living with the Farrell family and being a Richards developed into a trauma. He asked Glenda to change his last name, so she went to court to have her son legally renamed Thomas Farrell.

In the fall of 1928 Glenda came to New York, and within two weeks of her arrival she

Publicity pose c. '32.

replaced Erin O'Brien-Moore in *Skidding,* the domestic drama that eventually became the keystone for the *Andy Hardy* film series. In 1929 Glenda made her screen debut in a bit in George Jessel's part-talking *Lucky Boy* film and appeared as Vina Chase in the forty-performance run of *Divided Honor.* She had three 1930 Broadway plays. She was in the short-lived *Recapture,* and then in March of that year she was billed as "The Young Girl" in the play *Love, Honor and Betray,* which starred Alice Brady, with Clark Gable and George Brent also in the cast. On October 29, 1930, she opened as a tough gangster moll in *On the Spot,* with Crane Wilbur and Anna May Wong. The dramatization of Edgar Wallace's exciting novel had a successful New York run and was continued on tour.

In March, 1931, it was announced that Glenda would wed Jack Durant of the vaudeville act Mitchell and Durant. But the marriage never came about and she continued living at the Hotel Cardinal on West End Avenue while appearing in *On the Spot.* While she was performing on Broadway, her first screen appearance for Warner Bros. was being shown to rousing critical and audience acclaim: the hardhitting *Little Caesar* (1930). In this Edward G. Robinson gangster melodrama, Glenda was barely adequate as Olga, the dancing lover of Douglas Fairbanks, Jr.

Chamberlain Brown's first season with his Players at the Westchester Theatre in Mount Vernon, New York, opened in April, 1931, with a resident company which included among others, Jerome Cowan, Beverly Bayne, and Dorothy Sands, as well as guest stars. On June 29, 1931, Cesar Romero starred in *Strictly Dishonorable* with Glenda Farrell, and on July 6, Glenda was with Romero and Ralph Morgan supporting Judith Anderson in a repeat of her Broadway role in *Cobra.*

Glenda's opportunity to display her supreme talent as a first-rate comedienne came when *Life Begins,* a stark, tragic play centered on events in a hospital maternity ward, opened on Broadway on March 28, 1932. Glenda was admirably cast as show girl Florette Darien vowing there should be a law permitting the sale of kids. It was a showy, stand-out part, and Glenda played it to the hilt, singing "Frankie and Johnny" as a lullaby to her newborn child. Years later she would recall, "I was in a play, *Life Begins,* which Warners bought. I played a wisecracking, hard-boiled dame who drank gin out of a hot water bottle and I really didn't know how to do the part. Arthur Hopkins [then a top Broadway producer] told me to make it very theatrical and I got great laughs and great notices. So Warners wanted me for the picture."

Her film performance was as hilarious as her stage work, and Warners quickly signed her for their hard-working stable of players. Reminiscing about her film career, Glenda would later admit, "It all went so fast. I was making four pictures at a time. The first time I played a newspaperwoman[5] in *Hi, Nellie!* with Paul Muni (and it was one of the hardest roles I ever had), the character was always sitting at the typewriter with a cigarette dangling from her mouth, and I can't type and I don't smoke."

Unlike others who labored for the Brothers Warner with periodic rebellion and later reflections on the slave atmosphere prevalent at the Burbank factory, Glenda was not bitter about her lengthy tenure with the studio. "Warners typed you, but you'd get a starring part in one picture and a small part in another. They built their people fast and it was like a family. All the actors were so loyal, it was our home and we adored it." During her studio stay she had few competitors in her speciality as the all-knowing tough dame. While heavy dramatics would never be her screen forte, she was effective as Paul Muni's wife, betraying him to the law in *I Am a Fugitive from a Chain Gang* (1932).

[5]Actually her first such newspaperwoman role was as tough, saucy Florence, tracking down mad Lionel Atwill in *The Mystery of the Wax Museum* (1933).

With Paul Muni in I Am a Fugitive from a Chain Gang *(WB '32).*

213

To coincide with their opening of their blockbusting musical *42nd Street* (1933), Warner Bros. sent a special "42nd Street Train" across the country with many of their contractees, plus Tom Mix, Jack Dempsey, and Eleanor Holm, to make personal appearances. Aboard the lavishly publicized train were Joe E. Brown, Preston Foster, Lyle Talbot, Bette Davis, Leo Carrillo, Claire Dodd, and Glenda. Along with Laura La Plante, Glenda would sing some of the *42nd Street* songs from the stage preceding the first showing of the Warners musical bonanza in various cities.

Her personal life was pleasantly occupied with a romance shared by writer Robert Riskin (who later wed Fay Wray). Due to her association with Riskin she was borrowed from Warners for Frank Capra's delightful filming of *Lady for a Day* (1933) at Columbia. Glenda played a Texas Guinan-type nightclub owner called Missouri Martin. She and the cast won plaudits for their performances.

During her Warner Bros. heyday, the studio kept her busy working six days a week from six A.M. to seven, eight, or nine P.M., until she wondered on which set she was supposed to be working, if she had the right script in mind, and who her co-players were to be. But her quick, lively mind made her a quick study, and she could fire off lines with a rapidity attained by few actresses (other than her pal Joan Blondell), even pacing such male counterparts as Lee Tracy, Pat O'Brien, James Dunn, and, frequently, Cagney.

In *Bureau of Missing Persons* (1933) she vied with Pat O'Brien as his bigamist wife, and received a well-earned spanking from O'Brien. Even in such feeble fare as *Havana Widows* (1933) and *I've Got Your Number* (1934), she and Blondell injected laughter into laughless scripts with their split-second timing. It was a feat the two blondes duplicated in *Kansas City Princess* (1934) and *Traveling Saleslady* (1935). Glenda decorated and added considerable zest to one of the least successful of the gold-diggers series, *Gold Diggers of 1935,* a film memorable today for Busby Berkeley's stunning staging of "The Lullaby of Broadway" number with Wini Shaw. In this musical, Glenda

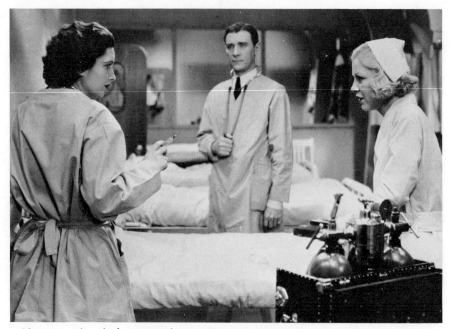

With Kay Francis and John Marston in *Mary Stevens, M.D.* (WB '33).

was a gold-digging stenographer trying to blackmail Hugh Herbert into a breach of promise suit. For *Gold Diggers of 1937* (1936) she was Genevieve Larkin hoping to drive confused Victor Moore to an early grave but coming up with a better plot solution —she marries him. She is the type of character who tosses off such lines as, "It's so hard to be good under the capitalistic system!"

At the end of 1936 Warner Bros. cast her as Torchy Blane, a hard-boiled newswoman, in *Smart Blonde,* which set off a successful low-budget series. The popularity of this series was mostly due to Glenda's performance as the brassy female reporter. Commenting on the cinematic sob sister character, Glenda said, "They were caricatures of newspaperwomen as I knew them. So before I undertook to do the first Torchy, I determined to create a real human being—and not an exaggerated comedy type. I met those who visited Hollywood and watched them work on visits to New York City. They were generally young, intelligent, refined and attractive. By making Torchy true to life, I tried to create a character practically unique in movies."

And Miss Farrell did just that. Her honest playing, speedy delivery of lines—in the series entry *Torchy Gets Her Man* (1938) she rattled off a four-hundred-word speech in forty seconds—and comedy timing added to the buoyancy of the entire project. (For the fifth film in the series, Lola Lane would play Torchy, and in the ninth and final picture, Jane Wyman was cast as the distaff member of the fourth estate.)

Glenda was a frequent radio performer. She did a Flag Day sketch with Phillips Holmes, Genevieve Tobin, and Herman Bing for Mary Pickford's June 14, 1936, broadcast of "Parties at Pickfair." Glenda was heard the following year on "Hollywood Playhouse" in *Vanity and Some Sables* with Tyrone Power. In January, 1938, she did a half-hour broadcast of *Manhattan Latin* with Humphrey Bogart and, in October of that year, gave a strong, emotional performance in a sketch on Kate Smith's radio show.

Glenda went to England in 1937 to make *You Live and Learn.* She was cast as an American show girl believing she has landed a rich lord of the manor only to find he is a widowed farmer with children. Her arrival in England startled her. The English press announced her London entrance with "Tough Baby Arrives." Once she returned to America her roles onscreen were more of the same, sardonic, good dame companions she had played for several years. After she had completed her *Torchy* fling, her Warners' contract ended and she returned to the stage.

Glenda opened the ninth season of the Westport Country Playhouse in July, 1939, starring in *Anna Christie* with Nance O'Neill as Marthy. From her indelibly Farrellesque roles (as they were known and imitated in Hollywood) to O'Neill's fallen *Anna* was quite a leap, but she did an excellent job playing the tarnished heroine. Through the summer she played the straw-hat stages in S. N. Behrman's *Brief Moment,* with Douglass Montgomery as her co-star, at the Cape Playhouse in Dennis, Massachusetts, in this comedy. In March, 1940, Glenda was featured in *Separate Rooms,* which opened in Seattle, Washington, under the title *Thanks for My Wife.* It made the cross-country transplant to Broadway successfully where it ran up 613 performances. Glenda was teamed with Alan Dinehart and Lyle Talbot in the comedy until July, 1941, when her understudy, Virginia Smith, took over the role.

The joys of a Broadway hit became secondary when Glenda found great happiness in her marriage to Dr. Henry Ross on January 19, 1941. He was a West Point alumnus and a Harvard Medical School graduate, and then a staff surgeon at New York's Polyclinic Hospital. The couple were quietly wed at the home of Dr. Ross' friends, Dr. and Mrs. Irving H. Saxe, in Passaic, New Jersey, with police judge Michael Andrus officiating. Glenda's good friend, actress Mary Brian, was the maid of honor. The newlyweds returned to Glenda's apartment in the Essex House in Manhattan, and Mrs. Ross returned to play *Separate Rooms* onstage that night.

Glenda returned to Hollywood in 1941 for a role at MGM in *Johnny Eager*. Although Robert Taylor and Lana Turner were miscast in their lead parts, Van Heflin won a Best Supporting Actor's Oscar for his playing of Taylor's drunken friend, and Glenda received good notices for her part. She then joined George Brent, Joan Bennett, and Mischa Auer in yet another remake of that aged farce, *Twin Beds* (1942). Her role of Regina Bush in *The Talk of the Town* (1942) was overshadowed by the glossier well-played leads of Ronald Colman, Cary Grant, and Jean Arthur. In April of 1942, Glenda was back on Broadway in the short-lived *The Life of Reilly*. In August of that year she was announced for the lead in Louis Verneuil's play *L'Amant de Madame Vidal* (retitled *Item One, Lover*), but the show never materialized.

Commuting between both coasts became a ritual for Glenda through the years. She and her husband settled in a Park Avenue apartment in Manhattan and on a fifty-acre estate at Brewster, New York. In early 1942 Glenda sold her San Fernando Valley home to George "Gabby" Hayes, and thereafter on her Coast trips stayed with her son Tommy. Her Forties' film appearances were hardly milestones, but she received pleasant notices for her journey work. She was luckier on Broadway, joining with Arlene Francis and Jack Whiting in *The Overtons,* directed by Elisabeth Bergner for a February, 1945, opening.

Always proud of her son Tommy, she was very happy when, in the late Forties, he teamed with Peter Marshall (later host of TV's "Hollywood Squares") for a successful nightclub act. In 1948, Glenda was back in filmdom for a supporting role in the whitewashed version of *Lulu Belle,* with Dorothy Lamour. Glenda then jaunted back to New York to open in *Mrs. Gibbon's Boys,* a brief offering in May, 1949, for theatregoers. In the summers of 1949 and 1950 she toured the countryside theatres in *The Fatal Weakness.* After her television debut in February, 1950, on "Silver Theatre" in *Gaudy Lady,* she was a frequent performer in that medium. During the summer of 1952 Glenda starred with Dennis King in an unsuccessful tryout of a new play, *Traveller's Joy,* and on September 22, 1954, she returned to Broadway in *Home Is the Hero.*

Her few Fifties' movies were inconsequential forays for her, and she spent most of her energies on television performances. She was especially good in the typecast-breaking role of John Cassavetes' downtrodden mother in "Elgin TV Theatre's" *Crime in the Streets.* In July, 1957, Glenda inherited the Thelma Ritter role in a Twentieth Century-Fox TV pilot of "The Model and the Marriage Broker" series, which never made the grade.

While working on the West Coast, and staying at her son's home, Glenda would catch up with her brothers, Richard the film editor and Gene the cameraman, and her director-cousin, Jerry Hopper. Wise and wily Glenda liked all of Tommy's wives, claiming, "All three of Tommy's wives are charming girls." Glenda could never be accused of being the interfering mother-in-law. When Tommy and his ex-wife asked her what to do about their seventeen-year-old daughter's marriage to a middle-aged man, calm Glenda told them: "Let her alone. You got through! Whatever they want to do, they do. We have to make our own mistakes and our own successes. I was always rushing down to prep school to get Tommy out of trouble. He was only a kid in college when he first married and when he was breaking up with his wife, I warned him not to be so fast to say you're through and that you want somebody else. All you're changing is the face! I was very young at the time of my first marriage, so how could I really say anything?"

Starring with Donald Cook and Cloris Leachman, Glenda opened in New York on March 16, 1959, in *Masquerade,* a confused charade that closed the same night. Critic Kenneth Tynan offered only a shrug of commiseration to the cast and added, "Glenda

Farrell plays her [Leachman] mother, one of those baleful matrons who throng the annals of American drama, turning their children into psychological messes by using them as ventriloquist's dummies." Glenda later played *The Gift Horse* at the Paper Mill Playhouse in Millburn, New Jersey. She then returned to the screen in a minor but telling portrayal of Mrs. Mueller, with Fredric March and Kim Novak, in *Middle of the Night* (1959).

In October, 1959, she was with Claudette Colbert and Robert Preston in a TV version of *The Bells of St. Mary's.* In November, 1959, Glenda was in the TV adaptation of Hemingway's *The Killers* and in 1961 was in a solid drama, *A String of Beads,* a video entry headed by Jane Fonda, Chester Morris, and George Grizzard. The diversity of roles Glenda found through television would have been impossible for her in the Golden Age of Hollywood. On January fourteenth and twenty-first of 1963 she was featured in a two-part "Ben Casey" entry, *A Cardinal Act of Mercy.* Her expert playing was paced by the sharp performance of Kim Stanley as the drug-addicted attorney Faith Parsons. At the fifteenth annual presentation of the Emmy Awards (May 26, 1963), Kim Stanley won the Best Dramatic Actress Emmy, and Glenda, fifty-two years after making her stage debut, won an Emmy as Most Outstanding Supporting Actress in a dramatic show.

Of all things, Glenda returned to the screen as Elvis Presley's "Ma" in *Kissin' Cousins* (1964). In this Sam Katzman quickie-but-lucrative musical, Glenda showed what a trouper she was. During the hasty production of the film, she suffered an injury that damaged her neck. Rather than be hospitalized she merely donned a neck brace when offcamera, and removed it to suffer through her scenes (but never showing her discomfort). Her last feature was also in 1964, getting involved with zany Jerry Lewis in *The Disorderly Orderly,* one of the more sane of that funnyman's features.

After completing three television shows and spending some time in New Mexico filming, she returned to her Park Avenue home, a very spry lady of sixty-four. But after a few days at home, spending her built-up nervous energies through outlets of painting, needlepoint, and reading, she alerted her husband she thought she had an ulcer. Wise Dr. Ross knew the symptoms, diagnosing her irritability as the old "roar of the greasepaint." "Call your agent," he told his wife, "you need a job." David Merrick engaged her to play Julie Harris' sophisticated, worldly mother in the play *Forty Carats.*

Glenda was delighted. "I've played so many droopy, tired mothers; this one gives me a chance to dress up! I've never really stopped acting. It's the only business I know. I haven't done much on Broadway because I'm married to a doctor, a general practitioner, and it's hard on him when I work in a play. He gave me a mink coat two years ago for *not* doing a play. It upsets our routine. When he comes home, I'm leaving for the theatre. We've been married for twenty-seven years and it's good and I don't want to louse it up. I could be replaced; I don't want to chance it."

When *Forty Carats* opened on Broadway at the Morosco Theatre on December 26, 1968, Glenda's playing of Maud Hayes was a constant joy. But by February, 1969, her failing health forced her to leave the comedy hit, and on February 24, 1969, she was replaced by Violet Dunn. Glenda went to Florida to recuperate. Her illness continued for two years until May 1, 1971, when she died in her Park Avenue apartment.

Knowing her illness was terminal she and her husband chose their gravesites on a mound overlooking the Hudson River at West Point. After a funeral service at Faith, Hope and Charity Chapel, a few doors from her Park Avenue residence, her interment was private at the United States Military Academy at West Point. Glenda Farrell, actress, is the only member of her profession to be buried in the West Point cemetery, in a grave marked with a cross, symbolic of her devout Catholicism. When Dr. (Colonel) Ross eventually rests at West Point, there will be a Star of David next to Glenda's cross.

Today, new generations of film-watchers are growing to know the Glenda Farrell brand and style of humor, as her movies are frequently shown on television. In the current age of women's lib, Glenda's motion picture performances of the Thirties stand out like a beacon, pointing the wry way to the future when a woman can speak her mind and gain respect for her self-sufficient approach to life. Glenda had the good grace to make her pathfinding entertaining as well as instructive.

GLENDA FARRELL

Lucky Boy *(Tiffany 1929)*
Little Caesar *(FN 1930)*
Scandal for Sale *(Univ 1932)*
Three on a Match *(FN 1932)*
Life Begins *(FN 1932)*
I Am a Fugitive from a Chain Gang *(WB 1932)*
The Match King *(FN 1932)*
Mystery of the Wax Museum *(WB 1933)*
Grand Slam *(WB 1933)*
Central Airport *(WB 1933)*
Girl Missing *(WB 1933)*
The Keyhole *(WB 1933)*
Gambling Ship *(Par 1933)*
Lady for a Day *(Col 1933)*
Mary Stevens, M.D. *(WB 1933)*
Bureau of Missing Persons *(WB 1933)*
Havana Widows *(FN 1933)*
Man's Castle *(Col 1933)*
The Big Shakedown *(FN 1934)*
Hi, Nellie! *(WB 1934)*
I've Got Your Number *(WB 1934)*
Dark Hazard *(FN 1934)*
Heat Lightning *(WB 1934)*
Merry Wives of Reno *(WB 1934)*
The Personality Kid *(WB 1934)*
Kansas City Princess *(WB 1934)*
The Secret Bride *(WB 1935)*
Gold Diggers of 1935 *(FN 1935)*
Traveling Saleslady *(FN 1935)*
Go Into Your Dance *(FN 1935)*
In Caliente *(FN 1935)*
We're in the Money *(WB 1935)*
Little Big Shot *(WB 1935)*
Miss Pacific Fleet *(WB 1935)*
Snowed Under *(FN 1936)*
The Law in Her Hands *(FN 1936)*

Nobody's Fool *(Univ 1936)*
High Tension *(20th 1936)*
Gold Diggers of 1937 *(FN 1936)*
Smart Blonde *(WB 1936)*
Here Comes Carter! *(FN 1936)*
Fly-Away Baby *(WB 1937)*
Dance, Charlie, Dance *(WB 1937)*
You Live and Learn *(WB 1937)*
Breakfast for Two *(RKO 1937)*
The Adventurous Blonde *(WB 1937)*
Hollywood Hotel *(WB 1937)*
Blondes at Work *(WB 1937)*
Stolen Heaven *(Par 1938)*
The Road to Reno *(Univ 1938)*
Prison Break *(Univ 1938)*
Torchy Gets Her Man *(WB 1938)*
Exposed *(Univ 1938)*
Torchy Blane in Chinatown *(WB 1939)*
Torchy Runs for Mayor *(WB 1939)*
Johnny Eager *(MGM 1941)*
Twin Beds *(UA 1942)*
The Talk of the Town *(Col 1942)*
A Night for Crime *(PRC 1942)*
Klondike Kate *(Col 1943)*
City without Men *(Col 1943)*
Ever Since Venus *(Col 1944)*
Heading for Heaven *(EL 1947)*
I Love Trouble *(Col 1947)*
Lulu Belle *(Col 1948)*
Apache War Smoke *(MGM 1952)*
Girls in the Night *(Univ 1953)*
Secret of the Incas *(Par 1954)*
Susan Slept Here *(RKO 1954)*
The Girl in the Red Velvet Swing *(20th 1955)*
Middle of the Night *(Col 1959)*
Kissin' Cousins *(MGM 1964)*
The Disorderly Orderly *(Par 1964)*

26

Stepin Fetchit

The history of the black performer in America is sparse, and, until a few years ago, remained largely undocumented. One of the first black actors to gain a foothold in the motion picture field was Stepin Fetchit, who created an enduring stereotype of the slow-moving, slow-speaking servant, forever a slave to the whims of the white race. In later years, this actor was to abhor the image he had created onscreen; but by then it was too late.

Lincoln Theodore Monroe Andrew Perry was named after four presidents of the United States. He was born in Key West, Florida, on Friday, May 30, 1902. His father was a Key West cigar maker, and after his early death Mrs. Perry took in sewing for affluent blacks and whites. When she died, Theodore and his two sisters were adopted by one of Mrs. Perry's customers—a dentist—in Tampa, Florida. The dentist and his wife had problems in particular with young Theodore. After he was expelled from the local school he was packed off to St. Joseph's College in Montgomery, Alabama.

At age thirteen he did a stint with Diamond-Tooth Billy Arnte's Minstrel Show, and was billed as Rastus; later he was known as Jolly Perry or Skeeter Perry. How much of his future characterization was gleaned from minstrel performers, especially imitators of Billy Kersands, is moot. When Perry entered vaudeville with Ed Lee in a comedy buck-and-wing act, they were also known as "Step" and "Fetchit." Legend has it that Perry's theatrical name was inspired by a race horse "Fetch It"; another story states that he wrote a song called "The Stepin Fetchit, Stepin Fetchit Turn Around, Stop and Catch It, Chicken Scratch It to the Ground Rag." (Years later, John Hay Whitney would name a horse after the popular actor.)

From vaudeville, Perry graduated to films, appearing as Highpockets in MGM's *In Old Kentucky* (1927). About his screen debut, the actor told reporters: "Until I came along in 1925, the movies had used only whites mimicking Negroes. But my part in *In Old Kentucky* stole the whole picture. It surpassed anything ever done up to then by a Negro. Me and this girl, Caroline Snowden, who was a star at the Sebastian Cotton Club in Culver City, closed the picture hugging on the screen. This broke the law that the Negro had to look inferior."

After his screen debut, he appeared as the slave husband of Miss Snowden in *The Devil's Skipper* (1928), and he had bits in *Nameless Men* (1928) and *The Tragedy of Youth* (1928).

Fetchit appeared in bit parts in *The Kid's Clever* (1929) and attracted critical attention

With Will Rogers and Evelyn Venable in *David Harum* (Fox '34).

as Christopher Lee in Fox's *The Ghost Talks* (1929). That studio was reluctant to use him in features because he was temperamental and reportedly irresponsible. But when a short subject they made with him turned out so well, they decided to expand it to feature-length. As Gummy, the largest colored gent below the Mason-Dixon line, he was excellent and the highlight of *Hearts in Dixie* (1929). Thereafter he was the janitor in the whodunit *Thru Different Eyes* (1929) and Swifty, the call boy, in *Fox Movietone Follies of 1929*. He was loaned to Universal to appear as Joe in the part-talking 1929 version of *Show Boat*. Then he returned to his home base as Eli in a show business fable starring Lee Tracy and Mae Clarke—*Big Time* (1929). Later came roles as Smoke Screen in John Ford's *Salute* (1929) and as Croup in *Cameo Kirby* (1930).

During his early Hollywood days, Stepin had lived at the Summerville Hotel (otherwise known as the "Colored Ritz") in Los Angeles. Later, as his career progressed, he bought the biggest house on Central Avenue, entertained lavishly, and owned three cars. One of them, a pink Rolls Royce, had his name emblazoned in neon lights on the back and was driven by a liveried chauffeur. He soon owned over fifty suits, some of which had been made for the deceased romantic idol Rudolph Valentino. Some of these suits cost $2,000 a piece. Mr. Perry was living very high. But his insistence on directing, meddling, and complaining about conditions on the set brought Fox to the end of their patience, and the studio released him.

Fetchit left Hollywood and returned to vaudeville in a tour of "in person" shows in small theatres and small towns. In the fall of 1932 he was starred in an all-colored stage production, *Rhapsody in Rhythm,* billed as "The World's Greatest Colored Star." He sang and danced in the show as Speedy Smith, dueting with Reid Hall the song "Where Does the Wind Go."

An apprehensive Fox grudgingly rehired him, signing him to a contract in 1934. They were constantly fearful about his habit of disappearing during filming. His second chance with the studio made his name a household word internationally. He told the Fox executives, "You don't have to worry about me anymore. You're not taking any chances at all. I've been reading history, and I noticed that they all became big guys after they were 32. Napoleon, Washington and Abe Lincoln. You don't have to worry anymore about me. I'm 32 today!"

Fox exploited their black star and Stepin lived up to his "star" status in his personal life. Fetchit sparked such films as Janet Gaynor's *Carolina* (1934). As Scipio in *Stand Up and Cheer* (1934), he sang and danced until it was impossible for an audience not to respond to his talent and amazing body control. One contemporary critic noted, "Mr. Fetchit's feet are like chained lightning as he performs." Donald Bogle in his book *Toms, Coons, Mulattoes, Mammies and Bucks* (1973) wrote, "Even when his characters were flamboyantly exaggerated, the master Fetchit was economic and in command of his movements. Never was there a false footstep. Never was there excessive excessiveness."

Fox fortuitously teamed Stepin with the great Will Rogers and the two of them played together hand in glove. In *David Harum* (1934) Stepin was Sylvester, traded to Rogers in a shady package deal with a horse. The actors complemented one another so well that they were teamed successfully in three more features. For *Judge Priest* (1934) Stepin was paired with sassy Hattie McDaniel. She was Aunt Dilsey and he played Jeff Poindexter. He had two musical numbers in the film, plus leading a street parade dressed in a top hat and fur coat, stepping high and making the scene memorable, strutting to the song "Dixie." The *New York Times* observed, "That cloudy streak of greased lightning, Stepin Fetchit, is riotous as the judge's man of all or no work, and he is always threatening to drop the auditors into the Music Hall's plush aisles."

With Warner Oland in *Charlie Chan in Egypt* (Fox '35).

222

Stepin appeared as Sassafras in Rogers' *The County Chairman* (1935) and as George Lincoln Washington in Rogers' last film, directed by John Ford, *Steamboat 'round the Bend* (1935). After Will Rogers' tragic death in a plane crash, Fetchit's roles were confined mostly to family retainers, and, generally, character-filler parts in lesser releases. After Hal Roach's *Zenobia* (1939), in which Stepin played Zero, and Hattie McDaniel was Alice Brady's faithful servant, he left the screen, for the time being.

In 1937 he made a cross-country "in person" tour, often with Roger Pryor's Orchestra. As part of the act he would make an agonizing shuffle to center stage and tell the audience, "I'm an expert at doing nothing, but the less I do, the more I make. I'm makin' as much as I can now, then, when I get older, I can rest." He termed his cinematic fumbling mumble "audible pantomime." Again, after he left the movies, he played smaller cities in a similar manner.

In the fall of 1939 he was signed for his first Broadway-headed musical. It was the oft-told tale of three gold-digging sisters out to land rich spouses. Stepin was cast as the faithful family retainer, Chesterfield. Simone Simon, Mitzi Green, and Mary Brian were the three heroines. There was a bouncy score by Hoagy Carmichael and Johnny Mercer, but a very dreary book. As *Three after Three* the show closed in Chicago, and Misses Simon and Brian were replaced, with the musical being retitled *Walk with Music.* It opened on June 4, 1940, on Broadway but closed after fifteen performances. During the out-of-town ordeal the producers brought charges against Fetchit with Actor's Equity, complaining about his temperament and non-professional behavior. The charges were later dropped.

In 1943 while playing in a stage revue, *Flamingo Follies,* in Chicago, Stepin was sentenced to thirty days in jail for corrupting the morals of a minor. In 1945, he filed a five-million-dollar bankruptcy suit in Chicago, listing assets of $146. Work in films was stymied by outcries from civil rights groups who claimed that he was debasing his race. Plagued by his battery of trouble, Stepin said: "People don't understand any more what I was doing then, least of all the young generation of Negroes. Maybe because they don't really know what it was like then. Hollywood was more segregated than Georgia. Humor is my only alibi for being there. Show business is a mission for me. I was a 100% black accomplishment." He did return to the screen briefly in 1948 in Screen Guild's *Miracle in Harlem.*

Later he settled down in Chicago. In 1951 he ran an ad in *Variety* calling himself "The Laziest Man in the World." The following year he had a small role in James Stewart's Western *Bend of the River* (1952). He had equally small bits in Joan Crawford's *Sudden Fear* (1952) and John Ford's *The Sun Shines Bright* (1953). Then he dropped from sight. In 1964 he was admitted to Cook County Hospital as a charity patient for a prostate operation. Later that year he formed an unlikely but deep friendship with Cassius Clay, or Mohammad Ali. It was rumored that the actor had converted to the Black Muslim faith.

Stepin made the headlines again in 1969. On the morning of April 6, along a ten-mile stretch of the Pennsylvania Turnpike between Lancaster and Lebanon, the driver of a 1968 blue Pontiac sedan with Missouri license plates shot at cars heading east in the opposite lane with a .30 calibre Army-type carbine. The car was owned by Mrs. Donald Martin Lambright of St. Louis, Missouri, a nurse for the Veterans Administration. Her husband, age thirty-one, had left a $10,000-a-year job with the Ohio State Employment Service to work in the Cleveland, Ohio, Post Office and to attend Lincoln University, where he was to graduate in June. Two years before the shooting spree, Lambright had lived in Philadelphia and attended classes at St. Joseph's College. Before the shooting spree was over, Lambright had killed two and wounded fifteen others. He then pulled

223

his car onto a road siding and shot his wife and then himself. The car contained a great deal of ammunition and black militant literature. His mother, Mrs. Winifred Lee of Cleveland (formerly Winifred Johnson and once a singer with Duke Ellington's band) had married her second husband, Dr. Middleton H. Lambright, and her son was adopted by the Cleveland surgeon. His father was Mrs. Lee's first husband, Lincoln Theodore Perry.

From a hotel in Louisville, Kentucky, Stepin told reporters, "I just can't understand it. He was such a cool, calm, intelligent boy."

On July 2, 1968, CBS-TV telecast a program, *Black History—Lost, Stolen or Strayed,* on which clips from Stepin's old movies were shown over a commentary by Bill Cosby, who described Fetchit as "the white man's Negro, the traditional lazy, stupid, crap-shooter, chicken-stealing idiot." In 1970, Stepin filed a three-million-dollar defamation suit against the Columbia Broadcasting System, the sponsoring Xerox Corporation, Twentieth Century-Fox Studios, and the Indiana Broadcasting Company. Unfortunately, Fetchit did not have the support of his race who felt (and still feel) that he did fit Cosby's description. As a man who was praised by Will Hays, Hollywood's custodian of morals, as "a credit to the industry," Stepin demanded equal time on television to confront his accusers.

Claiming the *Black History* telecast cost him a job on TV's "Sanford and Son," Stepin went on to explain:

"I was the first Negro to stay in a hotel in the South. I was the first Negro to fly coast-to-coast in an airliner. I wiped away the image of rape from the Negro, made him a household word, somebody it was all right to associate with. I opened up all the theatres. Look back in my old pictures, you never see me showing my teeth, lazy, stupid, eye-rolling, breaking down all those things. That was my imitators. . . . I gave hope and opportunity to those that didn't have no skills and education. I was proof that you didn't need an education to be a success. I was proof that all men are created equal."

Stepin felt strongly he should continue with his lawsuit to prevent the same thing happening in the future to other black stars. The legal aspect of the suit dragged on for two more years, and on October 17, 1974, Fetchit lost the lawsuit. The court ruled that unless CBS-TV had maliciously defamed him, there was no case.

But Stepin was and is a hard man to keep down. In late 1974 he appeared onscreen once again, this time in the company of Moms Mabley and Butterfly McQueen in *Amazing Grace* (1974), a senior citizen-black society satire, and he had a cameo in the satirical feature *Won Ton Ton, the Dog Who Saved Hollywood* (1976).

On April 21, 1976, Stepin suffered a stroke and was admitted to Michael Reese Hospital in Chicago, where his condition stabilized, but he had lost the power to speak.

Perhaps the finest tribute to Stepin was paid by fellow black actor Raymond St. Jacques. "People put down Stepin Fetchit. He paid his dues. Because of him there could be Poitier. Because of Poitier, I'm here. It's a question of what you have to do to survive and you had to bend a lot more in 1930 than you do now." Fetchit was well aware of all this and learned to bend, capturing delighted audiences, and becoming the best known black performer in motion pictures here and abroad.

STEPIN FETCHIT

In Old Kentucky *(MGM 1927)*
The Devil's Skipper *(Tiffany-Stahl 1928)*
Nameless Men *(Tiffany-Stahl 1928)*
The Tragedy of Youth *(Tiffany-Stahl 1928)*
Show Boat *(Univ 1929)*
Hearts in Dixie *(Fox 1929)*
Big Time *(Fox 1929)*
Salute *(Fox 1929)*
Fox Movietone Follies of 1929 *(Fox 1929)*
The Kid's Clever *(Univ 1929)*
Thru Different Eyes *(Fox 1929)*
The Ghost Talks *(Fox 1929)*
Cameo Kirby *(Fox 1930)*
The Big Fight *(Sono Art-World Wide 1930)*
Swing High *(Pathe 1930)*
Wild Horse *(Allied 1931)*
Neck and Neck *(Sono Art-World Wide 1931)*
The Prodigal [The Southerner] *(MGM 1931)*
Carolina *(Fox 1934)*
David Harum *(Fox 1934)*
The World Moves On *(Fox 1934)*
Stand Up and Cheer *(Fox 1934)*
Judge Priest *(Fox 1934)*

Marie Galante *(Fox 1934)*
Bachelor of Arts *(Fox 1934)*
Helldorado *(Fox 1935)*
The County Chairman *(Fox 1935)*
One More Spring *(Fox 1935)*
Charlie Chan in Egypt *(Fox 1935)*
Steamboat 'Round the Bend *(Fox 1935)*
The Virginia Judge *(Par 1935)*
36 Hours to Kill *(20th 1936)*
Dimples *(20th 1936)*
On the Avenue *(20th 1937)*
Fifty Roads to Town *(20th 1937)*
Love Is News *(20th 1937)*
His Exciting Night *(Univ 1938)*
Zenobia *(UA 1939)*
Miracle in Harlem *(Screen Guild 1948)*
Bend of the River *(Univ 1952)*
Sudden Fear *(RKO 1952)*
The Sun Shines Bright *(Rep 1953)*
Amazing Grace *(UA 1974)*
Won Ton Ton, the Dog Who Saved Hollywood *(Par 1976)*

27

Preston Foster

Fame is mercurial, often fading more quickly than it arrives and taking on many faces. In the 1954 Thanksgiving Parade, an annual march sponsored by Gimbel Brothers Department Store in Philadelphia, there were shouts from moppets along the parade route, "There's Captain John!"

To the actor leading the procession it was an amusing accolade. "That's all they yelled at me. If you told them that I was Preston Foster, they'd have given you an argument!" Foster, as Captain John, led the teleseries "Waterfront" for two years through seventy-eight episodes, syndicated through 116 outlets starting September 28, 1954. "You know you have a good rating when this sort of thing happens," said Foster, delighted by his "Waterfront" identification. But what the new medium of television had gained in a personality was lost to the theatre and films: that most capable actor—Preston Foster.

He was born on Friday, August 24, 1901, in Ocean City, New Jersey. He sang in the church choir, and completed his education in Pitman, New Jersey, where the family moved when he was thirteen. With school behind him, he struck out for Philadelphia. He had a series of jobs, ranging from bus driver to selling newspaper advertising to briefly wrestling professionally. Along the way he studied singing and became determined to make an entree into opera. He did win a few chorus jobs with the Philadelphia La Scala Opera Company. However, the *Philadelphia Evening Ledger*, where he was then working, took a dim view of his musical activities and fired him.

Therefore, opera it had to be. He eventually won small roles with La Scala, and then, with the Pennsylvania Grand Opera Company he appeared in *Othello, Hamlet, The Masked Ball,* and *La Boheme.* With the Philadelphia Grand Opera he appeared as the father in *Aida,* the baron in *La Traviata,* and then decided to try his baritone in the Broadway musical theatre. He would never sing in a New York musical, but he would develop into a first-rate actor.

His first stage role was a bit in the road company of *The Silent House.* When he returned to Manhattan he augmented his resources by playing a tiny role in Richard Dix's film *Nothing But the Truth* (1929), made by Paramount at their Astoria, Long Island, studios. By the time the picture was released he had opened on Broadway in *Congratulations,* which ran for thirty-nine performances. *The Idol,* with William Farnum and Irene Purcell, tried out in Atlantic City and closed there. In late 1929 he was in two

226

In *The Last Days of Pompeii* (RKO '35).

227

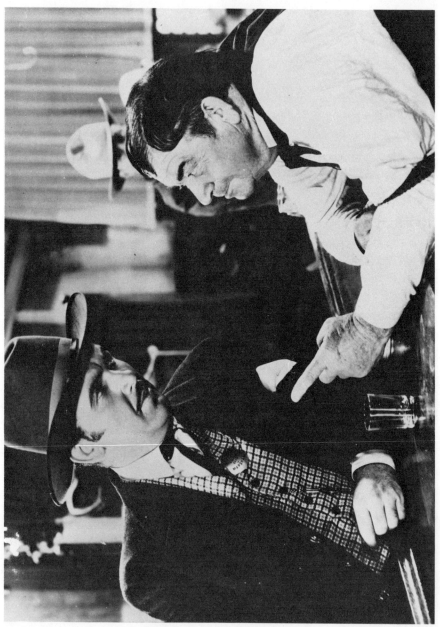

With Russ Powell in *The Arizonian* (RKO '35).

short-runs on Broadway, and then, in July, 1930, he was again back in Atlantic City for the opening of Ladies All, starring Violet Heming and Walter Woolf. That show did move to Broadway where it ran for 140 performances.

During the run of Ladies All, Foster again shuttled to Paramount's Astoria studios, to play a minor role in Heads Up (1930), featuring Charles "Buddy" Rogers, Helen Kane, and Victor Moore. He continued his Astoria employment by playing Two-Gun Terry, a gangster subdued by Ed Wynn in Follow the Leader (1930). It was in the imaginative drama Two Seconds that Preston finally gained Broadway recognition. Critic Robert Garland said of Foster's performance as killer Edward Pawley's best friend, "Mr. Preston Foster is straightforward and likeable," while John Mason Brown found his acting "excellent, direct, likeable and simple and honest." Director Mervyn LeRoy saw Preston in Two Seconds and recommended him to Warner Bros.-First National who were to film the play with Edward G. Robinson as the doomed man. But Foster had contracted for a role in Adam Had Two Sons, which "fortunately" closed after five Broadway performances.

Despite his Hollywood offer, Foster was telling the press during the fiasco of Adam Had Two Sons: "Most people cannot understand why I quit the opera for the legitimate theatre when the average stage artist looks to the opera as the goal of goals. But that, of course, is a point of view. I wanted to give dramatic expression rather than voice expression and this is something you cannot achieve in the opera. I have always loved the theatre and now that I am part of it my love has grown even greater and I hope to remain in the legitimate no matter how tempting the opera may ever be to me." But Foster did go to Hollywood where in 1932 he was seen on screen in a repeat of his Bud Clark role in Two Seconds.

The studio picked up his option after Two Seconds. Preston now felt secure enough to send for his wife, home-town girl Gertrude Warren (he called her "True"), whom he had wed in 1926. He now told the press: "I certainly hoped to get a chance in Hollywood. The talkies seemed just the thing to spread your name over the country. An actor can spend his whole life on Broadway, and never be known outside New York. And, say what they will, actors like to be known far and wide. Oh, don't let any one kid you into believing an actor pays no attention to what's said of him. I have often heard a player say that he never bothers about reviews or fan mail. Tell him he's a liar. The first thing I do the morning after a picture has been released is to read the reviews. If most reports are complimentary, I feel great. If they're not so good, I'm wretched all day."

Warners kept Foster busy on the soundstages. He was the lunatic murdering physician in Doctor X (1932), a sympathetic doctor in the maternity ward melodrama Life Begins (1932), and was the heavy, Pete, in Paul Muni's splendid I Am a Fugitive from a Chain Gang (1932). Then the studio lent him to World Wide for the star role of Killer Mears in Cell 4, where life ends in The Last Mile (1932). Foster gave a superlative bitter performance in the role Spencer Tracy gained fame in on Broadway and that Clark Gable had performed on the West Coast stage successfully. For Universal, Foster was in a good football yarn featuring James Gleason coaching The All-American (1932), and back at Warners he worked on location at Catalina Island, playing the heavy in a hilarious Joe E. Brown romp called You Said a Mouthful (1932).

Fox originally intended Spencer Tracy to play the role of Anton Cermak, mayor of Chicago killed by an assassin's bullet. But Tracy was occupied with another film—The Power and the Glory (1933)—and Fox sought Foster. "I had the time of my life getting that part," Foster later said. "Warners didn't want to lend me out. I begged the casting director to let me go, pointing out it was a lead, a star part." Foster stayed on at Fox for Hoopla (1933), which proved to be Clara Bow's last screen work.

229

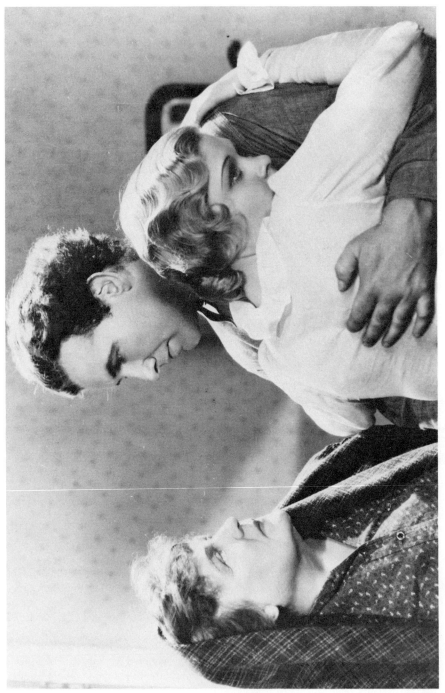

With Alison Skipworth and Dorothy Dell in *Wharf Angel* (Par '34).

Before Fox released this lesser film, Foster returned to Warners to join their spring 1933 *42nd Street* Special Train. It traveled to key cities to promote the opening of the lot's musical extravaganza. All the stars appeared in an "in person" stage presentation prior to the screenings of *42nd Street*. Most audiences were amazed when Preston Foster stepped forward to sing (very well in his near basso voice) "Old Man River."

Back in Hollywood his film roles were varied from hero to heavy, but mostly in a series of quickly forgotten films. Then John Ford assigned him the role of Don Gallagher in Liam O'Flaherty's *The Informer* (1935) at Preston's new home lot, RKO. The film won Ford the New York Film Critics Award, the Academy Award, an Oscar for Victor McLaglen's turbulent playing of Gypo Nolan, a trophy for Dudley Nichols' script, and another for Max Steiner's music scoring. Preston gave a stirring performance as the dashing, reformed bad man in *The Arizonian* (1935), and *Photoplay* called his black-smith-gladiator in *The Last Days of Pompeii* (1935) one of the best performances of the month. It certainly presented Foster in a most virile characterization, one that surprised viewers who only knew him from more routine screen assignments. He was excellent as *Annie Oakley's* nemesis and again he was nominated for *Photoplay's* best performance. On November 8, 1935, he and co-star Barbara Stanwyck did scenes from the film on radio's "Hollywood Hotel" broadcast.

Universal borrowed Carole Lombard from Paramount (in exchange for Margaret Sullavan) and Preston Foster from RKO to cavort in a pleasant comedy *Love before Breakfast* (1936), aided by Cesar Romero and spiritedly directed by Walter Lang. Preston returned to his home lot, RKO, to sympathetically play a police investigator in *We Who Are about To Die* (1936) and then was well cast (with Barbara Stanwyck as his wife) in John Ford's *The Plough and the Stars* (1936). It was Barry Fitzgerald's Fluther Good who overshadowed this production of Sean O'Casey's work. Preston was too dour in *You Can't Beat Love* (1937), a light froth to promote newcomer Joan Fontaine. He returned to Warner Bros. in 1937 to join Kay Francis in a leaden version of *First Lady* and the next year was on the lot there for *White Banners* (1938), which glowed from Fay Bainter's performance in tandem with Claude Rains.

On January 4, 1938, 36-year-old Preston asked for and received his release from RKO. However, his free-lancing status did not improve his roles. Like countless other actors, he was tested for the Rhett Butler part in *Gone with the Wind* (1939). In 1939 Cecil B. DeMille used him with Barbara Stanwyck on "Lux Radio Theatre" in a broadcast of *So Big*. DeMille would employ him again for the movie *North West Mounted Police* (1940), in which Preston wins Madeleine Carroll from Gary Cooper. Also that year Foster made a dud at Paramount entitled *Moon over Burma,* in which Dorothy Lamour was the girl in question, and another Preston, Robert, was his onscreen rival.

His film career stagnated until he signed with Twentieth Century-Fox for *My Friend Flicka* (1943), which proved so popular that he repeated his role in *Thunderhead, Son of Flicka* (1945). One of Foster's best screen portrayals was that of Father Donnelly in 20th's expertly made version of Richard Tregaskis' *Guadalcanal Diary* (1943), with William Bendix and Richard Conte. One of Hollywood's best World War II films, it is today still an exciting, intense picture. In February, 1944, Foster repeated his role on "Lux Radio Theatre," and in November of that year he was back on the program for a broadcast of *Dark Waters,* with Merle Oberon and Thomas Mitchell. In 1945, he played well in two MGM pictures, *The Valley of Decision* especially, and the next year joined with Judy Garland, Ray Bolger, and John Hodiak in *The Harvey Girls* (1946).

It was in 1945, after nineteen years of marriage, that he was divorced by his wife Gertrude, who retained custody of their daughter Stephanie. The next year he married Sheila D'Arcy (stage name for Rebecca Heffener). His succeeding film assignments were pedestrian and, in the early Fifties, Foster and his new wife formed a nightclub act. It featured folk songs, guitar, and Preston's still resonant bass-baritone voice. They played small clubs across the country and state fairs. Their act was successful and elated Foster. "Even when you stop at a gas station out in the middle of nowhere you'll find people know you from pictures!" (Later Foster would do a similar club act with his daughter, Mrs. Stephanie Troulman, of Marina Del Rey, California.)

He entered television in 1953 on an episode of "Schlitz Playhouse" and appeared on several other anthology shows before finding new success with his role of tugboat Captain John Herrick on the "Waterfront" series. Lois Moran played his wife Mae, and Douglas Dick and Harry Lauter were cast as his sons, Carl and Jim. Television became his great enthusiasm.

During the Sixties he made four films, the last, *Chubasco,* in 1968. TV viewers in 1963 saw Foster as a niggardly rich man on an episode of the "Going My Way" series with Gene Kelly, and later he was a big-shot political boss trying to clear his son of a murder charge on a segment of "77 Sunset Strip." Altogether, not counting the "Waterfront" series, Foster appeared in some two dozen television episodes.

In the late Sixties he went into retirement at his home in Pacific Beach, California. There he became actively interested in community projects and devoted considerable time to Coast Guard Auxiliary activities. He held an honorary rank of Commodore, given in recognition of his work for safe boating practices. In the summer of 1970 he was taken ill and was rushed to the Scripps Memorial Hospital at La Jolla, California, where he died on July 14. Funeral services were held on July 18 at 11 A.M. in the La Jolla Presbyterian Church. He was buried at El Camino Memorial Park.

Nothing but the Truth *(Par 1929)*
Follow the Leader *(Par 1930)*
His Woman *(Par 1931)*
Two Seconds *(FN 1932)*
Doctor X *(FN 1932)*
Life Begins *(FN 1932)*
The Last Mile *(World Wide 1932)*
The All-American *(Univ 1932)*
I Am a Fugitive from a Chain Gang *(WB 1932)*
You Said a Mouthful *(FN 1932)*
Ladies They Talk About *(WB 1933)*
Elmer the Great *(FN 1933)*
Corruption *(Imperial 1933)*
The Man Who Dared *(Fox 1933)*
The Devil's Mate *(Mon 1933)*
Hoopla *(Fox 1933)*
Sensation Hunters *(Mon 1933)*
Heat Lightning *(WB 1934)*
Sleepers East *(Fox 1934)*
Wharf Angel *(Par 1934)*
The Band Plays On *(MGM 1934)*
Strangers All *(RKO 1935)*
The People's Enemy *(RKO 1935)*
The Informer *(RKO 1935)*
The Arizonian *(RKO 1935)*
The Last Days of Pompeii *(RKO 1935)*
Annie Oakley *(RKO 1935)*
We're Only Human *(RKO 1936)*
Muss 'em Up *(RKO 1936)*
Love before Breakfast *(Univ 1936)*
We Who Are about to Die *(RKO 1936)*
The Plough and the Stars *(RKO 1936)*
Sea Devils *(RKO 1937)*
The Outcasts of Poker Flat *(RKO 1937)*
You Can't Beat Love *(RKO 1937)*
The Westland Case *(Univ 1937)*
First Lady *(WB 1937)*
Everybody's Doing It *(RKO 1938)*
Double Danger *(RKO 1938)*
The Lady in the Morgue *(Univ 1938)*
White Banners *(WB 1938)*
Army Girl *(Rep 1938)*
The Storm *(Univ 1938)*
Up the River *(20th 1938)*
Submarine Patrol *(Univ 1938)*
The Last Warning *(Univ 1938)*
News Is Made at Night *(20th 1939)*
20,000 Men a Year *(20th 1939)*

Chasing Danger *(20th 1939)*
Society Smugglers *(Univ 1939)*
Missing Evidence *(Univ 1939)*
Geronimo *(Par 1939)*
Cafe Hostess *(Col 1940)*
Moon over Burma *(Par 1940)*
North West Mounted Police *(Par 1940)*
The Round Up *(Par 1941)*
Unfinished Business *(Univ 1941)*
Secret Agent of Japan *(20th 1942)*
A Gentleman after Dark *(UA 1942)*
A Night in New Orleans *(Par 1942)*
Little Tokyo, U.S.A. *(20th 1942)*
Thunder Birds *(20th 1942)*
American Empire *(UA 1942)*
My Friend Flicka *(20th 1943)*
Guadalcanal Diary *(20th 1943)*
Bermuda Mystery *(20th 1944)*
Roger Touhy—Gangster *(20th 1944)*
Thunderhead, Son of Flicka *(20th 1945)*
The Valley of Decision *(MGM 1945)*
Twice Blessed *(MGM 1945)*
The Harvey Girls *(MGM 1946)*
Tangier *(Univ 1946)*
Inside Job *(Univ 1946)*
Strange Alibi [Strange Triangle] *(20th 1946)*
King of the Wild Horses *(Col 1947)*
Ramrod *(UA 1947)*
The Hunted *(AA 1948)*
Thunderhoof *(Col 1948)*
I Shot Jesse James *(Screen Guild 1949)*
The Big Cat *(EL 1949)*
The Tougher They Come *(Col 1950)*
Three Desperate Men *(Lip 1951)*
Tomahawk *(Univ 1951)*
The Big Night *(UA 1951)*
The Big Gusher *(Col 1951)*
Montana Territory *(Col 1952)*
Kansas City Confidential *(UA 1952)*
Face to Face *(RKO 1952)*
I, the Jury *(UA 1953)*
Law and Order *(Univ 1953)*
Destination 60,000 *(AA 1957)*
The Man from Galveston *(WB 1964)*
The Time Travelers *(AIP 1964)*
You've Got to be Smart *(Producers Releasing Organization 1967)*
Chubasco *(WB-7 Arts 1968)*

28

Richard "Skeets" Gallagher

One of the more unusual nicknames in the annals of show business was that given to Richard "Skeets" Gallagher. He once explained it with: "When I was a youngster I was so slender, and quick on my feet, that someone once compared me to a mosquito. The name seemed to apply to me because I was always jumping all over the place. I was particularly agile, especially in dancing. So after I had been compared to a mosquito, my friends, as a joke, used to call me 'Skeets.' " It was a name Gallagher was to adopt for professional use, and it remained with him through much of his show business career.

He was born on Tuesday, July 28, 1891, in Terre Haute, Indiana, educated in that city's public schools, and later attended the Rose Polytechnic School. Eventually he matriculated at the University of Indiana where he drifted from his original career choice, engineering, to the wonderful world of show business. He made his first theatre appearance on Friday night in a Terre Haute vaudeville house, with many of his relatives and friends seated in the first three rows; and, as a result of this experience, he became convinced that the world of show business was for him. With a friend named William Reardon he prepared a vaudeville act that the two young men presented in and around Chicago. But, after a few months, both returned home broke.

"Skeet" next joined two girls, Mary Anne Dentler and Anna Orr, in a vaudeville act that fortunately was booked into New York. Gallagher later admitted, "We made a hit in New York and that was the beginning of the good days for me that have kept up ever since. After playing together a whole season the two girls and I split up and I went into a vaudeville partnership with a Boston girl, Irene Martin." The new act was highly successful, and Gallagher and Martin played about five seasons on the two-a-day. But Gallagher's ambitions extended beyond vaudeville and aimed toward musical comedy.

On January 9, 1922, he opened on Broadway in *Above the Clouds*. The show played six months at Broadway's Lyric Theatre. During the later Chicago run he left the cast to return to New York. Then on November 6, 1922, the musical version of *Too Many Cooks*, called *Up She Goes*, with music by Harry Tierney, opened under the auspices of William A. Brady at his 48th Street Playhouse in New York. The part of Frank Andrews was played by Richard Gallagher. He had decided "Skeet" was not dignified for musical comedy. The show ran 256 performances.

Marjorie opened August 11, 1924, at New York's Shubert Theatre, and Richard

With Lillian Roth in *Honey* (Par '30).

"Skeet" Gallagher provided most of the laughs in a show featuring a newcomer, Ethel Shutta. Next Skeet was signed to play the role of the young man who, with his sister rents their run-down mansion to a wealthy grande dame. The brother and sister stay on to act as her butler and maid. Ruth Chatterton replayed her original role from *Come out of the Kitchen* in this musical comedy, which was retitled *The Magnolia Lady*. With Chatterton, Skeet sang "Liza Jane" and soloed "When the Bell Goes Ting-aling-ling." Six years later Gallagher would play the same role on the screen, in Paramount's *Honey* (1930).

Later Gallagher joined the Chicago company of *No, No, Nanette* and then returned to Broadway to open in October, 1925, in *The City Chap,* in which Irene Dunne was a cast member. The show also included George Raft and Mayor Jimmy Walker's favorite chorine, Betty Compton. Skeet's next Broadway hit was another Jerome Kern-Otto Harbach, Harry Ruby and Bert Kalmar musical called *Lucky,* in which Mary Eaton had the title role, and other performers included Ruby Keeler, Joseph Santley, and Walter Catlett. However, despite the cast, the show ran only seventy-one performances. Then Gallagher signed a term contract with prestigious Paramount Pictures.

During the run of *Above the Clouds,* Skeet had made his movie debut in Equity's *The Daring Years* (1923). In 1927 he first appeared with W. C. Fields in *The Potters* and was judged acceptable in the part of "Red" Miller, although he overacted. As Buck in Paramount's *New York* (1927) he surprisingly reversed himself and gave a portrait of a well-rounded human being. He next joined his old pal Ben Lyon for First National's *For* the Love of Mike (1927), playing the obstreperous Yale coxswain. The picture was made in New York by director Frank Capra, and it provided the screen debut for Claudette Colbert. Miss Colbert still considers the picture the worst of her career, and director Capra was never paid for his services.

From the rigors of New York filming, Skeet went into FBO's *Alex the Great* (1928), carrying off a rather dreary picture with his smart-alecky manner. He then returned to First National as a gangster in *Three-Ring Marriage* (1928) and almost overplayed swaggering Tom Greene in *Stocks and Blondes* (1928). Returning to Paramount his roles increased in scope and excellence. He was fine as the tippling news reporter in *The Racket* (1928) and made an impression with his teaming with Jack Oakie as the singing-comedy team of Barney and Bey in *Close Harmony* (1929). In the summer of 1929 Skeets (the nickname had now been pluralized) married Pauline Mason, with whom he had an off-again, on-again romance since 1924 when they were in a show together. That same year Skeets showed to advantage in teaming with "boop-boop-a-doop" girl Helen Kane in *Pointed Heels* (1929).

Five-foot, seven-and-a-half-inch Gallagher was similar to the one-time Paramount star Wallace Reid, but Skeets never played either the speedy-type comedy or the romantic roles given to Reid. No one ever seemed to take Skeets seriously onscreen or on the lot, often the fate of comedy-and-dance performers. In *Paramount on Parade* (1930) the all-star revue opened with Skeets, Leon Errol, and Jack Oakie acting as the film's masters of ceremonies and singing a song about their chore. Skeets also joined Clara Bow, Oakie, and some forty Marines in singing "I'm True to the Navy Now." *The Social Lion* (1930) found Gallagher reteamed with Oakie yet again. In *Love Among the Millionaires* (1930) he is a railroad detective vying with Stuart Erwin for waitress Clara Bow's affections, but they have gone to Stanley Smith. For Jeanette MacDonald's *Let's Go Native* (1930) he was paired once more with Jack Oakie, and with Clara Bow he did a commendable job of acting in *Her Wedding Night* (1930).

With Norman Foster, Carole Lombard, and Morgan Wallace in *It Pays to Advertise* (Par '31).

It was in October, 1930, that Richard "Skeets" Gallagher, Jr. was born. The actor was telling the press: "I love Broadway. It got into my blood. There's no place in the world like New York. But you couldn't hire me to live there again for all the money in the world. Because I've got something money can't buy. We'll never go back. It took years of heartbreaks, years of kidding each other back and forth, trying to put on the hard pan when our hearts were yearning for each other, before Pauline and I found all this. But we've got it now and all hell can't move us away from it."

Skeets returned to Paramount for *Up Pops the Devil* (1931), with Carole Lombard and Norman Foster, and with these two would reteam in *It Pays to Advertise* (1931). He was less than adequate in a minor role in Paramount's dreadful *Road to Reno* (1931). As for his loan-out to MGM for a role in *Possessed*, which starred Joan Crawford and Clark Gable, *Photoplay* reported, "Skeets Gallagher is the not-so-funny comic." But at Fox, as the radio news commentator who supplies amusing dialogue, he brightened an otherwise dreary courtroom drama, *The Trial of Vivienne Ware* (1932). Back on the home lot he gave a sparkling performance as the irrepressible Buck in *Merrily We Go to Hell* (1932), at one point breaking into a tap dance and enlivening slower sequences. He went to RKO for four 1932 releases, and in May, 1933, he joined his old friend Walter Catlett in a short subject called *Private Wives*.

After RKO's *The Past of Mary Holmes* (1933) he came back to Paramount for a further matching with Jack Oakie, this time in *Too Much Harmony* (1933), a backstage saga of the show-must-go-on variety. Gallagher was a perfect choice for the White Rabbit in the studio's all-star *Alice in Wonderland* (1933). Upon completion of this film, his studio contract concluded and he found himself free-lancing.

At RKO he joined with Pert Kelton in the amusing *Bachelor Bait* (1934) and was paired with acerbic Miss Kelton again in RKO's *The Meanest Gal in Town* (1934), which featured the comic talents of ZaSu Pitts and El Brendel. However, Skeets caused no ripples in Norma Shearer's *Riptide* (1934), and he was an odd choice for the love interest of Lona Andre in *Woman Unafraid* (1934). After two bottom-of-the-bill features, he returned to the stage.

Hollywood Holiday was a farcical comedy staged by actor Thomas Mitchell. The show rehearsed on the West Coast in early 1935 and, with Bebe Daniels, Ben Lyon, and Skeets, took to the road. Mr. and Mrs. Lyon were cast properly as movie stars on holiday, with Gallagher as a slick, amusing wisecracker who becomes the stars' butler. Notices were encouraging during the cross-country shakedown trek, but after playing Chicago in April, the project collapsed.

When Skeets returned to Hollywood he was delighted to be back in California with Pauline and his two children. Nevertheless, his parts for several studios had little variance, although he was good in *Yours for the Asking* (1936), with George Raft, Dolores Costello, and Ida Lupino. Also, his parts grew noticeably smaller, and in 1938 he and his family visited the Ben Lyons, who had resettled in England. While there Skeets made *Mr. Satan* (1938), in which he played the lead role as a war correspondent. In 1939 he was back in Hollywood for a small role in *Idiot's Delight*, made famous by its stars, Norma Shearer and Clark Gable. Two years passed before he gained other movie roles, this time in two quickies in 1941 and then a part in the Hal Roach dud *The Brooklyn Orchid* (1942).

Success might be eluding him onscreen, but he was determined to find continued employment in show business. He was starred in a revised version of that perennial farce *Ladies Night in a Turkish Bath*, which for the spring, 1942, season was retitled *Good Night, Ladies*. From San Francisco, this lampoon moved to Chicago, and it eventually seemed that Skeets, co-starred with Buddy Ebsen, was fated to play the part

In the mid-Thirties.

of Mike Bonner for the rest of his career. Stuart Erwin eventually replaced Ebsen as Skeets' co-lead, and the burlesqued farce remained in Chicago for nearly two years. When the show began a cross-country tour, Erwin was succeeded by younger James Ellison as the shy Professor John Matthews. Finally, nearly three years later, *Good Night, Ladies* ventured into Broadway's Royale Theatre on January 17, 1945. It survived only seventy-eight performances.

With *Good Night, Ladies* years behind him, Skeets returned to California. He was in the cast of Republic's *Duke of Chicago* (1949), with Tom Brown and Grant Withers, and then retired. However, in 1952, he re-emerged to be seen on ABC-TV's "Personal Appearance Theatre" and went to Warner Bros. for his last motion picture, a tired Gloria Swanson vehicle called *Three for Bedroom C.* On May 22, 1955, at the age of sixty-four, he died after suffering a heart attack the previous week. He was buried in Holy Cross Cemetery in Hollywood.

When he first started in show business, Gallagher had answered a press agent's query "Why do you want to become an actor?" as follows: "It's the easiest thing I could think of after unsuccessfully studying Engineering at Rose Polytechnic and the Indiana University." Perhaps it was the easiest for Skeets. But through the years of his career he contributed many bright and happy hours to theatre and movie audiences.

RICHARD "SKEETS" GALLAGHER

The Daring Years *(Equity 1923)*
The Potters *(Par 1927)*
New York *(Par 1927)*
For the Love of Mike *(FN 1927)*
Alex the Great *(FBO 1928)*
Three-Ring Marriage *(FN 1928)*
Stocks and Blondes *(FBO 1928)*
The Racket *(Par 1928)*
Close Harmony *(Par 1929)*
Fast Company *(Par 1929)*
Pointed Heels *(Par 1929)*
Honey *(Par 1930)*
Let's Go Native *(Par 1930)*
Paramount on Parade *(Par 1930)*
The Social Lion *(Par 1930)*
Love Among the Millionaires *(Par 1930)*
Her Wedding Night *(Par 1930)*
Up Pops the Devil *(Par 1931)*
It Pays to Advertise *(Par 1931)*
Road to Reno *(Par 1931)*
Possessed *(MGM 1931)*
The Trial of Vivienne Ware *(Fox 1932)*
Merrily We Go to Hell *(Par 1932)*
The Bird of Paradise *(RKO 1932)*
The Phantom of Crestwood *(RKO 1932)*
The Conquerors *(RKO 1932)*
Night Club Lady *(Col 1932)*
The Sport Parade *(RKO 1932)*

The Unwritten Law *(Majestic 1932)*
Easy Millions *(Freuler Film Associates 1933)*
Reform Girl *(Tower 1933)*
The Past of Mary Holmes *(RKO 1933)*
Too Much Harmony *(Par 1933)*
Alice in Wonderland *(Par 1933)*
In the Money *(Chesterfield 1934)*
Bachelor Bait *(RKO 1934)*
The Meanest Gal in Town *(RKO 1934)*
Riptide *(MGM 1934)*
Woman Unafraid *(Goldsmith Productions 1934)*
The Crosby Case *(Univ 1934)*
Lightning Strikes Twice *(RKO 1934)*
The Perfect Clue *(Majestic 1935)*
Yours for the Asking *(Par 1936)*
Polo Joe *(WB 1936)*
Hats Off *(Grand National 1936)*
The Man I Marry *(Univ 1936)*
Espionage *(MGM 1937)*
Danger in the Air *(Univ 1938)*
Mr. Satan *(British FN 1938)*
Idiot's Delight *(MGM 1939)*
Zis Boom Bah! *(Mon 1941)*
Citadel of Crime *(Rep 1941)*
The Brooklyn Orchid *(UA 1942)*
Duke of Chicago *(Rep 1949)*
Three for Bedroom C *(WB 1952)*

29

William Gargan

The reveling Twenties dissolved into a huge hangover, a decade depressed by millions of unemployed Americans, political scandals, and last rites for the art medium of silent pictures. But William Gargan, a six-foot, bellowing, joyously happy Irishman whose zest for living was bountiful, joyfully bounced from the roaring Twenties into the moribund Thirties with a carefree, resilient approach that would lead him to success on stage, screen, radio, and television. He would win the New York Drama Critics Award, be nominated for an Academy Award, become proficient as a polo player, and, more importantly, as a human being. And he would learn to live out his final years as a laryngectomee. Above all, he was a good actor who stumbled into the theatre without a passion to act or become an actor, only that the theatre provided something he needed momentarily—a job.

William Dennis Gargan was born in Brooklyn, New York, on Monday, July 17, 1905, to William Gargan, a sometime saloon owner and racetrack bookie, and erstwhile acquaintance of the likes of Mayor James J. Walker, Al Capone, and other subnotables of the era. William Jr.'s mother was the former Irene Gertrude Flynn, a retired school teacher. His older brother, Edward Gargan, eventually became the screen's best known, versatile cop, and it was he who was responsible for his kid brother's entrance into the acting profession.

The two Gargan brothers were paid $3.85 each for a day's work in a Vitagraph one-reeler featuring a neighborhood youth, Paul Kelly, jolly John Bunny, and Lillian "Dimples" Walker. Meanwhile, young Bill attended Brooklyn's St. Francis Xavier grade school and St. James High School but left in his last year without graduating. His smiling, happy-go-lucky nature won him a variety of jobs from selling soda pop at Ringling Brothers' Circus to doubling as an ontrack bookie at Saratoga Springs on the family's annual pilgrimage to that famous racing spot each August from 1911 to 1920. He was also a runner for a Wall Street brokerage house, a private detective, and an amateur but proficient bootlegger.

By 1921 brother Ed was singing in the chorus of the Metropolitan Opera Company and knew a large and varied group of theatrical people. During all this time Bill had developed a singular, but superior, talent for getting fired. When Ed introduced him to Le Roy Clemens, co-author of the play *Aloma of the South Seas,* Clemens suggested Bill read for a small part in the show then in rehearsal. The part of the native Boano was

With Marian Marsh in *The Sport Parade* (RKO '32).

small and consisted of one line: "Mr. Bob, Heap big coconuts." At the same time Bill doubled as assistant stage manager and producer of the show's sound effects for a torrential rainstorm. He was paid thirty dollars weekly. The show opened at New York's Lyric Theatre on April 20, 1925, and lasted sixty-six performances. It went on the road for forty weeks, with Gargan in charge of the Eastern road company at seventy-five dollars a week. Twenty-year-old, light-auburn-headed, blue-eyed Bill decided that the theatre had potential for him. He settled down to learn all he could about what would become his lifetime profession.

Earl Carroll's *Laff that Off* was a Broadway hit and, in the late summer of 1926, a road company was formed. Bill won the role of Leo Mitchell and played the show for three weeks on Broadway (with Shirley Booth) before starting on a long tour. After that tour ended, Bill did a brief stint as Sergeant Perkins in the Shuberts' perennial musical revival *My Maryland*. In the summer of 1927 he signed with producer Sam Harris for the part of the photographer, Babe, in the touring company of *Chicago*, starring Francine Larrimore. The tour passed through New York and he called on a spirited young chorine, Mary Kenny, he had been dating between tours. They were married on January 19, 1928, at the Assumption of the Blessed Virgin Mary Cathedral in Baltimore. Following the end of the *Chicago* tour, the Gargans returned to New York where Sam Harris soon offered him a job supporting Richard Bennett in *The People*. However, the play was a colossal dud and it opened and closed in the midwest. Gargan left for Cleveland and a stock company. There he became enamored of a comedy, *Not Herbert*, which failed in Cleveland, and did no better in Chicago while still under Gargan's auspices. (He had borrowed $1,500 from his mother to back the show.)

241

Sam Harris engaged Gargan again in the summer of 1928 for the role of Private James Perkins in *War Song,* starring George Jessel, with Shirley Booth, Lola Lane, and one of Bill's closest friends, Raymond Guion (Gene Raymond). During the run, William Gargan, Jr., called Barrie by his mother, was born. Jessel became the boy's godfather. During a period of unemployment, Bill made a silent film, *The Ghetto,* in which Jessel starred and produced. The film was put together at a studio on 34th Street and Fifth Avenue. The new talkies were becoming the rage and Jessel added a few hundred thousand dollars into reshooting the silent *Ghetto* into *My Mother's Eyes,* after the song he is forever singing off-key. It became known in release as *Lucky Boy* (1929). All the title changes in the world could not have improved the film or Jessel's singing. Gargan found employment in a Max Gordon-produced vaudeville sketch, *The Family Upstairs.* But he obtained his release from that to join former silent screen star William Farnum in a play called *Headquarters.* That production lasted two weeks in New York. Next Bill joined the company of *City Haul,* starring former movie star Herbert Rawlinson. Gargan played a wisecracking, tabloid reporter sniffing out corruption in city hall.

Gargan's income was augmented by brief bits in pictures made by Paramount at their Long Island Astoria Studios. He got his release from *City Haul* to accept the role of the German playreader in an avant-garde German play adapted and directed by Leslie Howard. *Out of a Blue Sky* did not last beyond seventeen performances after its February 8, 1930 opening. But *Out of a Blue Sky* started a lifelong, nearly inseparable friendship between two opposites, urbane Leslie Howard and Big Bill Gargan.

Bounding back from the German dud, Gargan was signed by the Theatre Guild for *Roar China* (1930) and then was in *She Lived Next Door to the Firehouse* (1931) with Victor Moore. He returned to the Theatre Guild for *He,* and while playing the show in Chicago, he read Philip Barry's new play, *The Animal Kingdom* (1932). The role of the wisecracking butler-ex-prizefighter Red Regan seemed tailor-made for Gargan. When he returned to New York he read for the part, after having his hair dyed a fiery red. He won the role and rehearsals began with young Katharine Hepburn in the female lead. After the first week of rehearsals she was replaced by Frances Fuller. The show, starring Leslie Howard, opened in Pittsburgh to loud bravos from the audience and a roar of "We Want Red!" during the curtain calls. Howard led the astonished Gargan to the footlights, leaving him to accept the ovation alone.

Gargan's run-of-the-play contract for *The Animal Kingdom* brought him $450 a week, but his agent kept persuading him to journey to Astoria and Paramount where Gargan had made *His Woman* (1931) and *Misleading Lady* (1932) with Claudette Colbert. An offer from Hollywood created a crisis for Gargan, and he sought his release from the stage show. On May 3, 1932, the Gargan family left for California.

When Paul Kelly was rejected for the role of Sergeant O'Hara in the Joan Crawford version of *Rain* (1932), Bill was substituted. He had little to do in the film, and the part would have been more suitable for Kelly, the actor who had recently been released from San Quentin (and thus was considered an unsafe bet on a big project).

During the shooting of *Rain,*[6] Gargan signed a RKO contract, for that studio had purchased the screen rights to *The Animal Kingdom* and wanted Bill for his original role of Red Regan. [First he was tossed into a minor effort with Joel McCrea called *The Sport Parade* (1932).] *The Animal Kingdom* adapted well to the screen. With Leslie Howard, Gargan, and Ilka Chase in their original roles, the film was enhanced further by the performances of Ann Harding and Myrna Loy.

[6]While *Rain* was shooting, Gargan criticized Crawford's performance to an interviewer. The following year when Clark Gable had an appendectomy, MGM proposed that Gargan replace him as leading man of *Dancing Lady.* Crawford, remembering the earlier slight, flatly refused to work with him.

With Kay Francis in *Women in the Wind* (WB '39).

In 1933 Gargan ground out a series of what he calls "Schlemeil Pictures." Although he hated *Aggie Appleby—Maker of Men* (1933), he was fine as the tough but lovable Red Branahan, overshadowing Wynne Gibson and Charles Farrell (sadly miscast). His one splendid performance was on loan to Paramount where he gave a strong interpretation of the attorney's part in *The Story of Temple Drake* (1933), a whitewashed version of William Faulkner's controversial novel *Sanctuary*.

On June 28, 1933, Mary and Bill Gargan's second son was born at St. Vincent's Hospital. They named him for their close friend, Leslie Howard.

Four Frightened People (1934) put Bill under the directorship of the flamboyant Cecil B. DeMille. The master decided to film the story in the Hawaiian Islands, and the cast and crew departed on the ship *Lurline*. The shooting conditions were extremely hazardous to everyone but DeMille. Claudette Colbert, Herbert Marshall, Mary Boland, and Gargan played out their roles in the jungle regions of Waialulua and Keauchano. The exhausted film-makers returned to the mainland in mid-November, 1933. The picture was a disastrous flop at the box-office, never regaining its production costs.

After making a couple of quickie pictures, Bill was reunited with Leslie Howard in *British Agent* (1934), which co-starred Kay Francis. Again Gargan's playing was of high quality. When Howard was scheduled to film *The Scarlet Pimpernel* (1934) in London, he persuaded Gargan to go to Britain with him for a lark. On board ship Bill met playwright Robert Sherwood who had already persuaded Howard to appear in his new Broadway-bound play, *The Petrified Forest,* after the England film-making. Gargan read the script and told Sherwood he would love to play the role of the heavy, Duke Mantee. While in London, Bill made *Things Are Looking Up* (1935) for Alexander Korda at

With Joan Bennett and Adolphe Menjou in a pose for *The Housekeeper's Daughter* (UA'39).

Gaumont-British. Things were definitely doing that for him, for in the next mail Bill received a seven-year contract from Warner Bros. amounting to close to $1,500 a week, including options. When he returned to New York he decided to accept the Warners' offer and thus lost the stage role of Duke Mantee that made a star out of Humphrey Bogart. "Everyone should—at least once—work for Warner Brothers," Bill later advised. "It is like, except more painful, sleeping on beds of nails; it is like, except more persistent, the Chinese water torture." And he was probably all too right in that he was cast in supporting roles in a batch of hurriedly made fill-the-program pictures. Then Paramount borrowed him for the part of the boxing champ who is clobbered by a meek milkman (Harold Lloyd) in Leo McCarey's funny *The Milky Way* (1936).

Gargan's unhappiness with the dismal roles Warner Bros. tossed his way got his Irish dander up, and he was highly critical of the Burbank studio and the factory-line assembled films. Two weeks after the start of his second contract year, he received his studio release. About this time his lively father died of cancer.

In 1937, Mary and Bill bought a Spanish-styled, seventeen-room home on North Palm Drive in Beverly Hills, which had once been the home of the late Jean Harlow. Then, also in 1937, Bill's mother died.

Free-lancing through the rest of the Thirties, Gargan worked constantly in a long series of forgettable films, frequently enlivening a picture with his fine acting, such as his performance as the tragic ex-champ in MGM's *The Crowd Roars* (1938). In 1939 he was in *Three Sons*, a remake of *Sweepings*, which he had done with Lionel Barrymore in 1933.

The success of series pictures prompted Metro to film Damon Runyon's tale of a married couple's protest to the President of the United States over the firing of their mailman. In *Joe and Ethel Turp Call on the President* (1939), the chief executive was played by Lewis Stone, and Gargan felt the film, which starred him with Ann Sothern, was good enough to warrant a continuation. But the studio disagreed.

While making *Sporting Blood* (1940) at Metro, Bill met Garson Kanin who was preparing a film remake of Sidney Howard's classic play *They Knew What They Wanted*. Gargan was chosen for the role of the foreman, Joe, of a grape ranch who seduces his middle-aged boss' mail-order wife. He and Carole Lombard as Amy made the film memorable despite a contrived performance by Charles Laughton as the ungainly, cuckold-boss. For his work in *They Knew What They Wanted*, Gargan received his first Academy Award nomination for Best Supporting Actor, but he lost to Walter Brennan for *The Westerner*.

Then the Gargans purchased a ranch at San Jacinto, California, and Bill continued in minor roles in such fare as *I Wake Up Screaming* (1941), *Bombay Clipper* (1942), and *Miss Annie Rooney* (1942). After the outbreak of World War II, Bill contacted the U.S.O. and asked for an overseas assignment. This organization put together a small troupe consisting of leader Gargan (rated as a Major in case of capture), Paulette Goddard, Keenan Wynn, and accordionist Andy Arcori. Sent to China, Burma, and India, the group had a harrowing, hilarious, heart-warming, exhausting tour. Prior to leaving for the U.S.O. junket, Gargan had made the final three films in Columbia's *Ellery Queen* series, succeeding Ralph Bellamy in the title role, with Margaret Lindsay and Charlie Grapewin continuing in their series parts.

From his first broadcast as master of ceremonies in the early Thirties for a live coast-to-coast show, radio had intrigued Gargan. In 1943 he did a short-lived series for ABC entitled "Murder Will Out." He continued making substandard pictures and then, through personal friend Frank Folsom, president of RCA who controlled NBC-TV, he became television's "Martin Kane, Private Eye." Bill did eighty-five weeks of "Martin Kane" at $ 4,500 per week, and was later replaced by Lloyd Nolan; then, Lee Tracy; and finally, Mark Stevens. Gargan went through the paces of another private detective for NBC radio, "Barry Craig, Private Detective." In the mid-Fifties, Gargan signed with ZTV Productions to film a television series, "The Return of Martin Kane," in London and in locations all over Europe.

In 1954 Bill was asked to star in the West Coast stage production of *The Desperate Hours*. The thriller opened in August, 1955, in San Francisco, toured in Portland and Seattle, and returned to Hollywood at the Carthay Circle Theatre. Bill played the harassed husband whose family is held hostage by three escaped convicts. Nancy Coleman was his wife onstage. Gargan's final screen appearances were in *Miracle in the Rain* (1956) and in *The Rawhide Years* (1956).

There followed more years of television work, and, in 1958, he joined with Gene Raymond and Leon Ames in the West Coast edition of *The Best Man*. Bill inherited Lee Tracy's role of the ex-President who is dying from cancer. When the show played Los Angeles, the *Los Angeles Times* printed, "Gargan was the head-and-shoulders standout of the ailing ex-Chief." The show then played San Francisco. Unfortunately it was to be Gargan's close-to-final fling at acting.

On November 10, 1960, William Gargan was operated on for a cancerous larynx. The laryngectomy left him with a hole in the throat called a stoma. From the time he returned home ten days later until 1962, his devoted wife Mary constantly prodded him to learn to speak once again, to study the American Cancer Society's pamphlet, "Your New Voice," forcing him to stop whispering and to speak louder. In April, 1962, he addressed a group of laryngectomees at the National Hospital for Speech Disorders in New York City. The persistance of his wife and his own perseverance had paid off, for he could speak again, loud and clear enough to make himself understood by others.

It was like a rebirth, and he was appointed to the board of directors of the National Hospital for Speech Disorders, and traveled extensively for the American Cancer Society. In September of 1962 Pope John made Gargan a Knight Commander of the Holy Sepulchre. Two months later, he received the George W. Buck Memorial Award of the Catholic Actors Guild. He even did a "silent" role as a clown in a TV show featuring Broderick Crawford, entitled *King of Diamonds*.

By November, 1965, Gargan was declared cured of cancer. He received the much-honored Criss Award, following such past recipients as Dr. Jonas Salk and Dr. Tom Dooley. Lieutenant General James H. Doolittle presented him with the gold medal and check for $10,000 on October 26, 1965, at the Beverly Hills Hotel, where virtually all of Hollywood's famous had crowded.

In 1966, the Gargans left the Hollywood area for Carlsbad, some ninety miles south on the California coast. The following year he received the Creighton University Award. But it was 1967 that seemed to crown Gargan's achievement when the Screen Actors Guild selected him as Man of the Year. He accepted the tribute at the Hollywood Palladium, stating, "At times like this it matters very little that I have lost my voice. For what could I do with a voice if I don't have any words?" In 1969, Gargan wrote (with Arnold Hano) his autobiography, tersely titled *Why Me?*, a heart-warming account of the life of a large-hearted man and a fine actor.

Today, William Gargan, the surviving member of the screen's beloved Gargan brothers (Edward died in February, 1964), continues his work for the American Cancer Society. He sponsors the La Costa Golf Tournament and an annual ball in Palm Springs, proceeds going to the Society's fund. He still tours the country, giving pep talks to other cancer victims, encouraging them by his recovery.

WILLIAM GARGAN

Mother's Darling (Vitagraph 1917)
Lucky Boy (Tiffany 1929)
His Woman (Par 1931)
Misleading Lady (Par 1932)
Rain (UA 1932)
The Sport Parade (RKO 1932)
The Animal Kingdom (RKO 1932)
Lucky Devils (RKO 1933)
Sweepings (RKO 1933)
The Story of Temple Drake (Par 1933)
Emergency Call (RKO 1933)
Headline Shooter (RKO 1933)
Aggie Appleby—Maker of Men (RKO 1933)
Night Flight (MGM 1933)
Four Frightened People (Par 1934)
The Line-Up (Col 1934)
Strictly Dynamite (RKO 1934)
British Agent (FN 1934)
Things Are Looking Up (Gaumont 1935)
Black Fury (FN 1935)
Traveling Saleslady (FN 1935)
A Night at the Ritz (WB 1935)
Bright Lights (WB 1935)
Broadway Gondolier (WB 1935)
Don't Bet on Blondes (WB 1935)
Manhunt (WB 1936)
The Milky Way (Par 1936)
The Sky Parade (Par 1936)
Navy Born (Rep 1936)
Blackmailer (Col 1936)
Alibi for Murder (Col 1936)
Flying Hostess (Univ 1936)
You Only Live Once (UA 1937)
Fury and the Woman (Rialto 1937)
Breezing Home (Univ 1937)
Wings over Honolulu (Univ 1937)
Reported Missing (Univ 1937)
She Asked for It (Par 1937)
Behind the Mike (Univ 1937)
Some Blondes Are Dangerous (Univ 1937)
You're a Sweetheart (Univ 1937)
The Crime of Dr. Hallet (Univ 1938)
The Devil's Party (Univ 1938)
The Crowd Roars (MGM 1938)
Personal Secretary (Univ 1938)
Women in the Wind (WB 1939)
Within the Law (MGM 1939)
Broadway Serenade (MGM 1939)

The House of Fear (Univ 1939)
The Housekeeper's Daughter (UA 1939)
Three Sons (RKO 1939)
Joe and Ethel Turp Call on the President (MGM 1939)
Isle of Destiny (RKO 1940)
Double Alibi (Univ 1940)
Star Dust (20th 1940)
Turnabout (UA 1940)
Sporting Blood (MGM 1940)
They Knew What They Wanted (RKO 1940)
Cheers for Miss Bishop (UA 1941)
Flying Cadets (Univ 1941)
Sealed Lips (Univ 1941)
I Wake Up Screaming [Hot Spot] (20th 1941)
Keep 'em Flying (Univ 1941)
Bombay Clipper (Univ 1942)
The Mayor of 44th Street (RKO 1942)
Miss Annie Rooney (UA 1942)
A Close Call for Ellery Queen (Col 1942)
Enemy Agents Meet Ellery Queen (Col 1942)
A Desperate Chance for Ellery Queen (Col 1942)
Destination Unknown (Univ 1942)
Who Done It? (Univ 1942)
No Place for a Lady (Col 1943)
Harrigan's Kid (MGM 1943)
Swing Fever (MGM 1943)
The Canterville Ghost (MGM 1944)
Song of the Sarong (Univ 1945)
She Gets Her Man (Univ 1945)
One Exciting Night (Par 1945)
Midnight Manhunt (Par 1945)
The Bells of St. Mary's (RKO 1945)
Follow that Woman (Par 1945)
Behind Green Lights (20th 1946)
Strange Impersonation (Rep 1946)
Murder in the Music Hall (Rep 1946)
Night Editor (Col 1946)
Rendezvous 24 (20th 1946)
Hot Cargo (Par 1946)
Till the End of Time (RKO 1946)
Swell Guy (Univ 1946)
The Argyle Secrets (Film Classics 1948)
Waterfront at Midnight (Par 1948)
Dynamite (Par 1949)
Miracle in the Rain (WB 1956)
The Rawhide Years (Univ 1956)

30

Wynne Gibson

One of the favorite celluloid prototypes of the Thirties was the brassy, worldly wise, weary gold digger. Usually they were blondes with exhaustible persistence and inexhaustible sex appeal. Every studio had a string of acceptable tough dames who could spark many moribund scripts with their interpretation of the same role in picture after picture. These character actresses made many motion pictures of the decade memorable by their all-too-brief appearances. Several of the more talented women of this type nearly made it to stardom. Wynne Gibson was one such actress.

Winifred Gibson was born on Friday, July 3, 1903, in New York City to Christian Science practitioner Frank W. Gibson and his wife Elaine Coffin Gibson. After graduating from Wadleigh High School for Girls, Wynne decided on a stage career. With two school pals she made her first theatrical audition, trying out for Carle Carleton who was casting for a musical, *Tangerine*. Wynne was given a small part as one of "six little Hawaiian wives." The show opened in Atlantic City, moved on to Baltimore, and later traveled to Washington, D.C. where Mr. Gibson caught the show and his daughter. "You get some clothes on and come with me," ordered Mr. Gibson, and Wynne obeyed. But on the train ride back to Manhattan she persuaded her father that being in show business was not degrading and that it offered sound opportunties for a willing aspirant. By the time they reached home, Wynne had convinced her father that the stage was her true love.

She made her New York City debut at the Knickerbocker Theatre on April 25, 1921, in the chorus of *June Love*. At the same time Ray Raymond was seeking a partner for a new vaudeville act he was forming. He spotted Wynne prancing on stage and hired her. With Raymond's act, "The Melody Charmers," Wynne sang and danced on the vaudeville circuit and even played the mecca of the profession—the Palace. From this stint, she went into *Poor Little Ritz Girl,* playing thirteen small bits in the Shubert hit, and then joined Lew Fields' company for *Snapshots of 1921.* In the 1923 edition of that revue, Wynne did a "Love Tap" dance with another redhead, James Cagney, and the duo appeared in several of the show's sketches with Fields. Wynne went back with her vaudeville partner, Ray Raymond, in a legitimate musical, *When You Smile.* When that show had run its course, she replaced Mary Hay in Marilyn Miller's smash hit *Sunny.*

Energetic Wynne always seemed able to find theatrical work. She joined the national touring company of the musical *The City Chap* and then signed for the West Coast

With William Gargan in _Emergency Call_ (RKO '33).

company of _Castles in the Air_. Ray Raymond, Guy Kibbee, and Wynne (singing "I Don't Blame 'Em") headed the cast. During their eight-week engagement in San Francisco, Erich von Stroheim offered her a role in his _The Wedding March_ (not released until 1928), but her overlapping schedule did not permit her to accept. Her relationship with Raymond ended on April 19, 1927, when he died as a result of a fight with actor Paul Kelly in Hollywood. Kelly was imprisoned at San Quentin for twenty-five months and Raymond's widow served ten months in prison for being an accessory after the fact.

Wynne returned to New York City and success with Richard Bennett (and his daughter Joan in her first stage appearance) in _Jarnegan_. When Wynne's marriage to John Gallaudet proved disastrous, she sailed to Europe for rest and rehabilitation. Back in the States in the early spring of 1930, she left for the West Coast and a contract with Metro-Goldwyn-Mayer. (She had already made her film debut in a Vitaphone short, _Sympathy_, in Manhattan and in Paramount's Long Island studio-filmed _Nothing But the Truth_ [1929], playing Helen Kane's sister.) At MGM she appeared in _Children of Pleasure_ (1930) with Lawrence Gray and Benny Rubin. Then she was offered a role in Cecil B. DeMille's first MGM epic, _Madam Satan_ (1930), but she declined and Metro let her go.

At RKO she played Jack Mulhall's wife in _The Fall Guy_ (1931). At this juncture she was asked to play the lead in the West Coast production of _Molly Magdalene_. Everyone advised her against playing the part, that it was not suitable and could not further her career. Wynne's philosophy of "nothing ventured, nothing gained" led her to accept the part. Paramount was impressed by her performance, and the studio subsequently signed her to a term contract.

In _The Gang Buster_ (1931) Wynne played a gangster's moll, with a cast that included Jack Oakie, and later was with smiling Jack again in the hit by Ring Lardner and George

249

S. Kaufman, *June Moon* (1931). Wynne literally walked away with the picture, getting every line off to advantage with perfect timing. In *City Streets* (1931), with Sylvia Sidney and Gary Cooper, she was cast as Paul Lukas' mistress who kills beer baron Lukas.

Her deft playing of William Powell's assistant editor of an underground scandal sheet in *Man of the World* (1931) should have elevated her to stardom. By rights she should have joined the league of Paramount's other ladies in residence: Nancy Carroll, Miriam Hopkins, Kay Francis, Marlene Dietrich, Carole Lombard, Sylvia Sidney, *et al*. But the studio saw her only as a capable second female lead. Five-feet two-inch Wynne, with gray-green eyes and blonde hair, had an abhorrence of being typecast, and she was aghast to see herself being pegged by Paramount as the bright, slightly soiled, wise-cracking tough dame.

She made the most of her role as a tough-as-nails gal in Clara Bow's *Kick-In* (1931), gave Miriam Hopkins a run for acting honors in *Two Kinds of Women* (1932), and was more than mildly effective as one of the *Ladies of the Big House* (1931), with Sylvia Sidney.

Option time arrived and Paramount decided they could no longer use Wynne's services. Everyone was taking a cut in salary, and the studio brass felt Wynne was overpaid. "Let's not talk about money," Wynne fenced their arguments. "Let's talk about me. Why did you sign me in the first place? Because you thought I had something, didn't you? Because you thought you could do something with me, didn't you? Have you ever tried? Have you ever given me a part where I could really show what I could do? Am I less capable with the experience I've had this past year than I was when you

With John Wray, John Gilbert, Walter Catlett, Victor McLaglen, and Leon Errol in *The Captain Hates the Sea* (Col '34).

signed me." Wynne continued her barrage, "Well, suppose you pay me whatever you can afford for the next six months, give me some decent parts so I'll really have a chance and then, if I click, we'll talk money. How's that?"

Paramount thought "that" was just fine and assigned her to the lead in *The Strange Case of Clara Deane* (1932), a property originally bought for Ruth Chatterton who had since gone over to Warner Bros. The sacrificial mother-love story had all the trappings of mediocre soap opera, but Wynne played the characterization for all it was worth. The picture, which featured Pat O'Brien, failed at the box-office, and Wynne's persuasive powers with the Paramount brass ebbed. She was next cast as Puff Rogers in love with an alcoholic prizefighter (George Bancroft) in *Lady and Gent* (1932) and got to sing "Everyone Knows It But You." This should have given the lot a hint to cast her in musicals; instead, she was drafted as George Raft's tough mistress in *Night after Night* (1932).

Paramount's offbeat, multi-storied *If I Had a Million* (1932) allowed Wynne the chance to work with director James Cruze in a segment featuring her as a weary prostitute who uses her million-dollar check to leave the slums for a Park Avenue apartment. The next year she was seen in an unusual whodunit, *The Crime of the Century* (1933), and then sparkled as a showgirl, covered with jewelry donated by admirers, hiring Edmund Lowe to protect her from producer Edward Arnold in *Her Bodyguard* (1933). She was vivacious in this entry and sang "Where Have I Heard That Melody." Regardless of her efforts, Paramount failed to pick up her option, primarily because the studio was feeling the inroads of the Depression. For a brassy, sexy, acting-and-singing dame they now had glorious Mae West, and did not need Wynne.

As with most perf ners who leave the secure studio fold to free-lance, the movement of her career steadily declined. She appeared in one dismal program picture after another, including Fox's *Sleepers East* (1934) and Columbia's *The Captain Hates the Sea* (1934), which featured John Gilbert in his final screen role. George M. Cohan had gone back East to film his stage play *Gambling* (1934) on Long Island. Wynne was hired to play scarlet lady Maizie. The film resulted as little more than a photographed play.

From Long Island she went to England to appear as an American movie star kidnapped by pirates in *Admirals All* (1935). Her second British film appearance was as an overly busy American newspaper correspondent hiding spies, stealing secret fortification plans, and overcoming villain Fritz Kortner in *The Crouching Beast* (1935). After five months, Miss Gibson decided she had been absent from the Hollywood scene long enough. She hoped, by going back to California, that she could obtain a meaty screen characterization. "What I mean," she explained, "is a real human being. You know I played one once. In *Lady and Gent* with George Bancroft. That 'Puff' was a real woman. I felt she was real. She wasn't just another like the 'girl next door,' nice maybe but not particularly interesting. Have you ever thought how few real human beings get on the screen? Interesting ones, I mean, who are characters not cut from one or another favorite pattern? Yes, I know there are some, but Gibson doesn't get to play 'em.''

When she did reappear in Hollywood she was cast in B pictures in indifferent roles, although she was quite good as the frivolous woman adopting two orphans in *Michael O'Halloran* (1937). The rest of her pictures rarely rose above the double-feature line, and in 1943 she made her last Hollywood try for Republic in *Mystery Broadcast*.

Anxious to keep working she played on the West Coast stage in *Silk Harry* in 1943, and the next summer she co-starred with John Hubbard and Russ Brown in *Good Night Ladies,* a lame farce derived from Avery Hopwood's creaking comedy *Ladies Night in a Turkish Bath.* More fortunate was her radio career. She was heard on most of the major network shows, including a long run on WOR's "My True Story." She was in the serial

With Sidney Blackmer in *Michael O'Halloran* (Rep '37).

drama "Thanks for Tomorrow" and later moved over to television for two seasons of the Martin Kane detective series. She was on various daytime soap operas such as "Valiant Lady," and in 1957 appeared on the thrice weekly telecast of "Three Houses."

Throughout the late Forties and the early Fifties, Wynne did summer stock on the East Coast. For two years (1955-1956) she was chairlady of the Equity Library Theatre in New York, involved in their free-to-the-public (donations accepted) productions at the West 103rd Street Theatre. She occasionally visits with other Paramount alumni like Connecticut-based Sylvia Sidney (with whom she participated in a New York museum tribute to Rouben Mamoulian in the late Sixties). For a time after she retired from acting, Wynne was an actor's agent in Manhattan, her partner another former Thirties' leading lady, Beverly Roberts. They presently share a house in West Babylon, Long Island.

At the height of her Paramount career a fan magazine published an article that theorized, "Wynne Gibson has everything it takes but that elusive lucky break. Luck done her wrong!" It did, indeed.

WYNNE GIBSON

Nothing But the Truth *(Par 1929)*
Children of Pleasure *(MGM 1930)*
The Fall Guy *(RKO 1930)*
The Gang Buster *(Par 1931)*
June Moon *(Par 1931)*
City Streets *(Par 1931)*
Man of the World *(Par 1931)*
Kick-In *(Par 1931)*
Road to Reno *(Par 1931)*
Ladies of the Big House *(Par 1931)*
If I Had a Million *(Par 1932)*
Two Kinds of Women *(Par 1932)*
The Strange Case of Clara Deane *(Par 1932)*
Lady and Gent *(Par 1932)*
Night after Night *(Par 1932)*
The Devil Is Driving *(Par 1932)*
Crime of the Century *(Par 1933)*
Her Bodyguard *(Par 1933)*
Emergency Call *(RKO 1933)*
Aggie Appleby—Maker of Men *(RKO 1933)*
I Give My Love *(Univ 1934)*

The Crosby Case *(Univ 1934)*
Gambling *(Fox 1934)*
Sleepers East *(Fox 1934)*
The Captain Hates the Sea *(Col 1934)*
Admirals All *(Radio 1935)*
The Crouching Beast *(Olympia 1935)*
Come Closer, Folks! *(Col 1936)*
Racketeers in Exile *(Col 1937)*
Trapped by G-Men *(Col 1937)*
Michael O'Halloran *(Rep 1937)*
Gangs of New York *(Rep 1938)*
Flirting with Fate *(MGM 1938)*
My Son Is Guilty *(Col 1940)*
Cafe Hostess *(Col 1940)*
Forgotten Girls *(Rep 1940)*
A Miracle on Main Street *(Col 1940)*
Double Cross *(PRC 1941)*
A Man's World *(Col 1942)*
The Falcon Strikes Back *(RKO 1943)*
Mystery Broadcast *(Rep 1943)*

31

Bonita Granville

The exuberance, sweetness, and joys of being young that were featured on the screen through the Twenties—with an occasional hell-raiser tossed in—continued into the golden Thirties. But then a deeper psychological approach invaded these innocent fields that made the once amusing, normal pranks of *Our Gang* or Mary Pickford seem more fantastic than real. It was in the Thirties that the screen really discovered the true brat, the juvenile villain or villainess who could give full cry to outrageous behavior, often with Freudian undertones. This new and different flowering of juvenilia proved that several of the more talented youngsters in Hollywood were capable of portraying something other than Pollyanna or Rebecca of Sunnybrook Farm. And the best of the lot was Bonita Granville.

She was born in New York City on Friday, February 2, 1923, to Rose Timponi Granville and Bernard "Bunny" Granville. He was an actor-dancer and Broadway star of several editions of the Ziegfeld Follies, and his career had started in 1904 with Al G. Field's Minstrels. Bonita was dubbed "Bun-Bun" at first, but later her father's nickname, "Bunny," became hers. Her show business legacy was a rich one, but it was really her resemblance to actress Ann Harding that started her movie career.

As Little Olivia, Bonita made her feature film debut as Ann Harding's daughter in a pedestrian version of Margaret Ayer Barnes' bestseller *Westward Passage* (1932), in which her father was played by a handsome, relatively unknown English actor, Laurence Olivier. Bonita would later play Miss Harding's child again (this one illegitimate) in a weeper film reminiscent of *Back Street* (1932), namely, *The Life of Vergie Winters* (1934). In the elaborate *Cavalcade* (1933), shot at Fox, Bonita was seen to good advantage as the young Fanny Bridges, played later in the film by Ursula Jeans, who rose to fame in London's music halls. Quick-study Bonita picked up the requisite cockney accent in a day or two and regaled her family at dinner with the sprightly on-set dialogue and imitations of other cast members. Following this triumph, she was charming as Carmen in Paramount's *The Cradle Song* (1933) and then, in 1935, as the young Mildred, Eric Linden's sister, in Metro's *Ah, Wilderness!* At the time she was attending Junior High School in Hollywood, where she succeeded in getting straight A's and remaining unaffected by her new importance.

Bonita's screen performances continued to reach a high professional level equal to her fellow adult players. Then came her role in the highly controversial *These Three* (1936). Samuel Goldwyn's production of Lillian Helman's *The Children's Hour* was

With Catharine Doucet, Merle Oberon, Miriam Hopkins, and Joel McCrea in *These Three* (UA '36).

changed enough for the screen to appease the censors. However, the role of the preco-cious, pitiless, devious adolescent bitch, Mary Tilford, was left intact; and Bonita played the part to a T. As the belligerent, psychological liar knowingly ruining the lives of three people (Merle Oberon, Joel McCrea, and Miriam Hopkins), the part of Mary Tilford is as bitter a portrait as has ever appeared on stage or screen. So convincing was Bonita's playing of this plum role that people on the Goldwyn lot would whisper as she passed them, "There goes the hell-child. That's the Granville kid." For her performance, Bonita was nominated for Best Supporting Actress of the Year (the first year of that category), but lost to Gale Sondergaard of *Anthony Adverse*.

In John Ford's *The Plough and the Stars* (1936) Bonita played a consumptive whose burial saves Preston Foster's life when he hides a gun in her coffin. For Paramount's *Maid of Salem* (1937) she was again cast as the nasty child, herein falsely accusing a black servant of being a witch. She was agonizingly convincing, leading audiences to hope a stake might be lit for her. Next, Warner Bros. paid her $500 a week to play the romantic teenager who says her prayers under a picture of the poet Shelley in Dodie Smith's delightful comedy *Call It a Day* (1937).

For Warner Bros., which had now become her home lot, she was a hellion of a poor little rich girl in *The Beloved Brat* (1938). During the shooting of the film, Bonita was dragged up a flight of stairs by her golden hair—for fifteen takes! (or so the publicity releases would have us believe). She was Kay Francis' brattish daughter in an uneven picture, *My Bill* (1938), and then she was loaned to Metro for the role of the wisecrack-ing daughter in a zany comedy, *Merrily We Live* (1938). Back at Warners, she offered a sincere, natural performance as Claude Rains' daughter in *White Banners* (1938).

Five-feet, two-inch Miss Granville was selected by her studio to be the famous Nancy

At her sixteenth birthday party on the set of *Nancy Drew, Trouble Shooter* (WB '39) with Frankie Thomas.

Drew in what Warners hoped would be a successful series. But neither *Nancy Drew, Detective* (1938) nor the three follow-ups captured the flavor of the book originals. In August, 1939, she obtained her release from Warner Bros. and signed with Metro. It was there that Bonita's steady boyfriend, Jackie Cooper (with whom she appeared in *White Banners*), had his greatest successes as a child actor. She and Cooper were such a steady combination that columnists were predicting an early marriage, or an even earlier elopement. With Jackie she appeared in Metro's *Gallant Sons* (1940), solving a murder which results in releasing the falsely accused Ian Hunter from prison. *The Mortal Storm* (1940) may seem overdramatic by today's standards, but the performances were vivid, including Bonita's as the servant girl beaten by Nazis into revealing the whereabouts of Margaret Sullavan.

Bonita had first appeared on the stage at the age of three with her parents. In 1941 she joined an all-star *Charlot's Revue* for the opening of the El Capitan Theatre on Hollywood Boulevard. Following several more MGM films she joined Jackie Cooper, again, at RKO in *Syncopation* (1942). In the film they are married, and once again real-life columnists were predicting wedding bells for the film star pair. Jackie commented that it was silly to talk about marriage when he was not even old enough to vote; Bonita was even more practical. "Each of us happens to be at a pretty important part in our professional lives. If we are to win the success we want, our first interest must be for those careers, not marriage." They had been dating once every two weeks since making *White Banners,* and the three-year romance was summed by Bonita thusly: "We go together, but we aren't engaged and, as for marriage, 19 is too young for a man to become a husband. For me, it is maybe five years distant."

Following her outing with Jackie at RKO, Bonita made *Now, Voyager* (1942), probably the best of the Bette Davis "romantic" involvements at Warner Bros. At Paramount, she played Brian Donlevy's daughter in the remake of Dashiell Hammett's *The Glass Key* (1942). Early in 1943 Bonita appeared as an American girl of German descent going to school in Nazi Germany in RKO's *Hitler's Children.* It became the exploited sleeper of the year and Bonita nearly attained star status on an adult footing. The picture enjoyed a radio saturation campaign and it remains her favorite film.

Bonita's striving for more adult, romantic parts never seemed to make much headway against the reputation of her early bitchy-brat roles, but she did get a chance at a change in her usual image in *The Beautiful Cheat* (1945) and with Barry Sullivan in *Suspense* (1946). That same year she provided the love interest for Mickey Rooney returning from World War II to Wainright College in *Love Laughs at Andy Hardy,* the fifteenth and next to last of the perennial Hardy series.

John Devereaux Wrather, Jr., a Dallas oil millionaire produced his first picture for Monogram release (March 2, 1947) called *The Guilty.* Before the picture's premiere, 28-year-old Wrather and Bonita (at twenty-four) were wed on February 5, 1947, at a Bel Air Hotel, with Ann Rutherford as matron of honor and Don Castle (her *The Guilty* leading man) as best man. The marriage became one of Hollywood's milestones, and across the years they became the parents of Molly, Jack, Linda, and Christopher. The busy Mrs. Wrather made two more feature films for her husband: *Strike It Rich* (1948), with Rod Cameron, and *Guilty of Treason* (1949), in which Charles Bickford was the persecuted Cardinal Mindszenty.

During 1951 the still beautiful Bonita appeared in three television shows, including the *One Strange Day* episode of "Gruen Theatre" with Steve Brodie. She did four TV shows in 1952, and on February 23, 1953, the small screen gave her a role that might have been written for her. It was the part of psychotic Evelyn Heath in *Guest in the House.* It was a demanding and treacherous part, but proved to be Bonita's greatest triumph on television. She played the characterization for five consecutive nights "live"

In '39.

from New York. Thereafter she averaged about two video appearances a year. In 1958 she was reunited with her former teenage love, Jackie Cooper, in a "Studio One" outing about plagiarism in a movie studio. By then Cooper had been thrice married and had become a success on Broadway and on television.

The television bonanza "Lassie" series started in 1954, survived four or five TV families of actors/actresses, and continued on the air for nearly twenty seasons. Two and a half years after the debut of Rudd Weatherwax's famous collie, Jack Wrather purchased the show. Bonita became associate producer of the famous "Lassie" series, occasionally directing a segment, and also became a member of the board of directors of the Wrather Corporation. In May, 1960, she appeared on an episode and maintained their show sold "morals and soap." Never reticent, Bonita (a grandmother by then) in the Seventies lashed out at the retrogression in entertainment "I don't go to the Movies. I know they're no good from the voyeurs who say they're terrible but have seen each one of them three times. I also have two or three dear friends on committees to clean up movies—and all they see now are dirty pictures. They explain to me they have to see them to know how dirty they are."

Bonita's last appearance to date on the screen was in 1956, twenty-six years after she had made her first screen appearance in a two-reel short subject for Bryan Foy. She played the female lead in, of all things, Warner Bros.' *The Lone Ranger,* with Clayton Moore and Jay Silverheels.

In November, 1974, Bonita Granville Wrather was named a trustee of Loyola Marymount University. Few child actors successfully made the transition into adulthood and maintained their screen or acting careers. Bonita Granville was on the threshold of altering that premise when she became Mrs. John Devereaux Wrather, Jr. and felt the latter role was more important. It still is.

Westward Passage (RKO 1932)
Silver Dollar (FN 1932)
Cavalcade (Fox 1933)
The Cradle Song (Par 1933)
The Life of Vergie Winters (RKO 1934)
Anne of Green Gables (RKO 1934)
Ah, Wilderness! (MGM 1935)
These Three (UA 1936)
Song of the Saddle (FN 1936)
The Plough and the Stars (RKO 1936)
Maid of Salem (Par 1937)
Quality Street (RKO 1937)
Call It a Day (WB 1937)
It's Love I'm After (FN 1937)
The Beloved Brat (WB 1938)
My Bill (WB 1938)
Merrily We Live (MGM 1938)
Hard to Get (WB 1938)
White Banners (WB 1938)
Nancy Drew, Detective (WB 1938)
Nancy Drew, Reporter (WB 1939)
Angels Wash Their Faces (WB 1939)
Nancy Drew, Trouble Shooter (WB 1939)
Nancy Drew and the Hidden Staircase (WB 1939)
Those Were the Days (Par 1940)
Forty Little Mothers (MGM 1940)

Third Finger, Left Hand (MGM 1940)
The Mortal Storm (MGM 1940)
Escape (MGM 1940)
Gallant Sons (MGM 1940)
The People vs. Dr. Kildare (MGM 1941)
The Wild Man of Borneo (MGM 1941)
Down in San Diego (MGM 1941)
H. M. Pulham, Esq. (MGM 1941)
Syncopation (RKO 1942)
Now, Voyager (WB 1942)
The Glass Key (Par 1942)
Seven Miles from Alcatraz (RKO 1942)
Hitler's Children (RKO 1943)
What a Woman! (Col 1943)
Youth Runs Wild (RKO 1944)
Song of the Open Road (UA 1944)
Andy Hardy's Blonde Trouble (MGM 1944)
Senorita from the West (Univ 1945)
The Beautiful Cheat (Univ 1945)
Love Laughs at Andy Hardy (MGM 1946)
Breakfast in Hollywood (UA 1946)
Suspense (Mon 1946)
The Truth about Murder (RKO 1946)
The Guilty (Mon 1947)
Strike It Rich (AA 1948)
Guilty of Treason (EL 1949)
The Lone Ranger (WB 1956)

32

Mitzi Green

Ever since D. W. Griffith had transformed Gladys Smith of Canada into a full-fledged child movie star, dreaming mothers had been offering the studios their offspring as the next Mary Pickford. The public's adoration of talented moppets never ceased and Hollywood was ever watchful for another Mary Pickford or Jackie Coogan. Then in the late 1920s Paramount signed little Mitzi Green. In their musical *Honey* (1930), starring Nancy Carroll, Mitzi emerged as the Thirties' first child star. Her expertise at mimicry had never been seen on the screen and what appeared to many viewers as just preco-ciousness was true unadulterated talent.

Mitzi was born on Friday, October 22, 1920, on Morris Avenue in the Bronx, New York. Her parents, Joe Keno and Rosie Green, were native New Yorkers. Rosie started in show business in the chorus of George M. Cohan's *Little Johnny Jones* and went into vaudeville with the Four Cohans. Her fast dancing brought her a subtitle of "the female George M. Cohan." Joe Keno was originally a member of Keno, Walsh, and Montrose, a group of comedy acrobats who toured America and Europe. He left the troupe and went into such Broadway shows as *Somebody's Sweetheart* and *Honey Girl.* Journalist Jack Lait suggested Joe Keno, "a single," and Rosie Green, a soubrette, as replacements for the temperamental team of Adelaide and Hughes. The new team joined Jerome Kern's musical *Head over Heels,* starring Mitzi Hajos. Keno was featured and Rosie did a specialty dance in the show; later they were married. Their child was named after Miss Hajos.

Keno and Green were highly successful in vaudeville. It was not long after little Mitzi joined her parents' act that she was being called a baby Elsie Janis and receiving headline billing as "Little Mitzi." Her proud father announced, "You know, it's a grand thing to see your youngster take up where you left off." The Kenos had the joy of playing that mecca of all vaudevillians, The Palace Theatre.

However, by the late Twenties, vaudeville was dying, and the Kenos found it more difficult to find advantageous engagements. While traveling to San Francisco, they left their daughter with an old show business friend in Los Angeles, Jack Coogan. Keno and Green returned from the Bay City to find Elsie Janis had interested Paramount in their daughter. Onscreen, Mitzi was to play one of seven children shuttled from pillar to post under the doting care of eldest sister Mary Brian. The picture was *The Marriage Play-*

With Leon Errol and ZaSu Pitts in *Finn and Hattie* (Par '31).

ground (1929) and featured Fredric March, Kay Francis, Miss Brian, and Anita Louise, as well as an excellent young performer, Phillipe De Lacy, and, as Zinnie, little Mitzi Green.

"Little Mitzi" had little to do in her screen debut, but she did it well enough for the studio to sign her to an unprecedented multiple-picture child contract. Meanwhile she developed a tremendous crush on slightly older Phillipe De Lacy. Her second screen appearance made her name a household word, as "Little Mitzi" became Mitzi Green. The film was *Honey,* and it featured Nancy Carroll and Lillian Roth, the latter singing a rousing torch rendition of the picture's best song, "Sing, You Sinners."

Mitzi was cast as Doris, the all-seeing, all-knowing brat who pries and spies on the affairs of a wealthy household from a vantage point up in a tree. Smeared with jam and peanut butter, and consumed with viciousness, she was well-paid by elegant social matron Jobyna Howland every time she began her chant "I know a secret!" Her performance in this film at nine years old was thoroughly professional, and her round, smiling face and black hair cut in bangs gave her the appearance of a female Jackie Coogan. She had traveled a long way since the days of her "youth" when she was a member of Gus Edwards' kiddie troupe.

Paramount next thrust her into their star-studded *Paramount on Parade* (1930), in which she impersonated Maurice Chevalier and Moran and Mack. (Between film assignments she attended the studio's schoolhouse on the lot, with Rachel Smith as her teacher. The law permitted her to work five hours a day, but compelled her to attend classes for three hours daily.) Clara Bow's third 1930 Paramount picture was a would-be musical called *Love among the Millionaires,* in which she plays a railroad-track-cafe waitress who aspires to society. Mitzi was cast as her sister Penelope. She sang "Don't

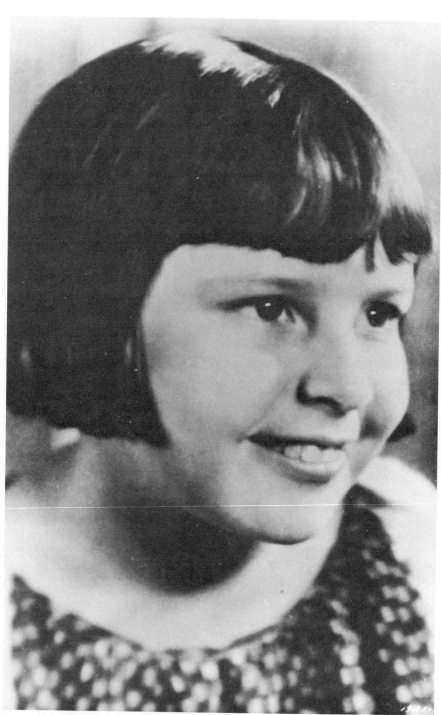

Paramount's child star in '31.

Be a Meanie," and then expertly mimicked Bow's crooning of "Rarin' to Go." After this outing, Mitzi learned to ride a horse in her role of Emily, who helps Richard Arlen save a ranch, while befriending the Indians with help from Junior Durkin, in *The Santa Fe Trail* (1930).

In 1917, Paramount had made Mark Twain's *Tom Sawyer* with Jack Pickford in the title part and in 1930 decided to remake the Twain classic with Jackie Coogan as the irrepressible Tom. What resulted was one of the year's ten best pictures. Also offered in the cast were Junior Durkin, as Huck, and Mitzi, as a blonde Becky Thatcher. The youngsters played the story straight and were delightful, especially Jackie Searl as the obnoxious snitching sissy Sidney. Unintentionally Mitzi was becoming one of the all-time champion scene stealers through her natural reactions to other players and the naturalness of her own performing. Several old troupers despaired of playing with her, and when *Finn and Hattie* (1931) was cast, it was every person for himself/herself. The film sported Leon Errol as Finley Haddock, and ZaSu Pitts as his wife Hattie on holiday with daughter Mildred (Mitzi) and nephew Sidney (Jackie Searl). Lilyan Tashman was cast as the film's femme fatale. Her oncamera scenes with Mitzi called for an understanding and she took the child star aside for a heart-to-heart. Said the elegant Miss T., "Come on, Mitzi, give Aunt Lil a break. Let me get this next scene over and you can have all the rest." Mitzi agreed but as the scene progressed, Mitzi's reaction to Tashman's dialogue drew all attention from the languishing Lilyan.

In *Dude Ranch* (1931) Mitzi gave a clever performance as Alice, part of a theatrical troupe playing the West, in a film that was focused on Jack Oakie's shenanigans. The

With Harrison Greene and Charles Sellon in *Dude Ranch* (Par '31).

263

success of *Tom Sawyer* inspired Paramount to produce *Huckleberry Finn* (1931) with most of the same cast, including Coogan and Mitzi.

Although she had a small part, Eloise, in Paramount's *Skippy* (1931), Mitzi worked well with another Jackie—Jackie Cooper. Also in the film was Jackie Coogan's younger brother Robert. Norman Taurog received the year's Academy Award for Best Director, while Jackie Cooper was Ocar-nominated.

By the end of 1931, Mitzi had run the gamut of roles at Paramount and, as a result, the studio dropped her option.

Papa Keno was able, however, to maneuver a picture deal at RKO for his daughter. There she was assigned to a feeble, dreary version of *Girl Crazy* (1932) that was converted from its Broadway original into a Bert Wheeler-Robert Woolsey screen comedy. In the midst of production, David O. Selnick (who had insisted on Mitzi for her career-making role in *Honey* while he was at Paramount) took charge. Thus Mitzi's role was beefed up and, for five minutes oncamera, Mitzi, as Bert Wheeler's kid sister Tessie Deegan, was given the screen for close-ups. Her impersonations caused audiences to break into applause in a picture that was deserving of none at all. A few years later she would reflect on her *Girl Crazy* experience. "When I played in *Girl Crazy* I thought some of the lines were too broad and many of the lines they wanted me to say were ridiculous—lines that no child would have said."

Following the *Girl Crazy* venture, Mitzi returned to vaudeville. Billed as "The Famous 'I Know a Secret' Girl," she drew a large salary and larger audiences doing her impersonations of Chevalier, Edna May Oliver, and an uncannily accurate impersonation of the venerable George Arliss, complete with monocle. Her long tour ended in the fall of 1932 and she returned to RKO to play *Little Orphan Annie* with explosive Edgar Kennedy as Daddy Warbucks and May Robson as the rich Granny. Mitzi was well cast as Annie, but she was also getting chubby and her body was showing signs of maturity. Five-feet, four-inch Mitzi was entering her teens when she made *Transatlantic Merry-Go-Round* (1934) at United Artists with Jack Benny. The studio offered her a five-year contract, but her parents declined, hoping for a better deal. Then Mitzi was brought back to RKO for a role in *Finishing School* (1934), starring Frances Dee and Ginger Rogers. Suddenly Mr. Keno yanked his daughter out of the production, feeling the role of Billie was not big enough for the "child" star. The studio quickly substituted Dawn O'Day who went on to stardom later that year in *Anne of Green Gables*.

In the spring of 1935, maturing Mitzi was on the vaudeville route doing impersonations of Garbo, Mae West, George M. Cohan, Ed Wynn, and her old standby, George Arliss. Two years later she opened in a stunning club act at New York's swank Club Versailles. There she was seen by Richard Rodgers and Larry Hart who were writing a new musical and needed new faces. This chance viewing led to her being cast in *Babes in Arms*, which opened on Broadway on April 14, 1937, and ran for 289 performances. The enormously talented cast included Mitzi, Alfred Drake, Grace and Ray MacDonald, the Nicholas Brothers, Dan Dailey, and others. Mitzi enjoyed the musical's best numbers, and she introduced "Where or When," led the company in the title song, made memorable her solo of "My Funny Valentine," had a duet with Ray Heatherton, "All at Once," and brought down the house with "The Lady Is a Tramp."

By the next year she was playing the club circuits; somehow her momentum as a Broadway star had halted. RKO announced she would have a co-starring role with Ruby Keeler in something called *Fiddlesticks* and as the femme lead for the Marx Brothers' film version of *Room Service* (1938). The first project never materialized and it was RKO contract player Lucille Ball who joined the zany Marx Brothers romp. During the summer of 1939 Mitzi played summer stock in *The Gentle People, It's a Wise Child,* and

Stage Door. That fall she was signed for the play *Three after Three,* with Simone Simon, Mary Brian, Stepin Fetchit, and Frances Williams. However, the show collapsed on the road in January, 1940. Some of the cast was replaced, but Mitzi, Miss Williams, Stepin Fetchit, and a few others were retained. The show opened on Broadway as *Walk with Music* but lasted only fifteen performances.

The year 1942 was a banner one in Mitzi's personal life, if not professionally. (She was in *My Dear Public* which closed after a few weeks on the road.) On August 25 she wed that show's director, Joseph Pevney, in New York. Pevney was temporarily deferred from the Army to stage the Youth Theatre's production of *Let Freedom Ring.* It opened in October, 1942, but after eight performances closed, and he went into military service. Meanwhile, Mitzi returned to the West Coast to await the birth of her child, born in 1943. That same year Joe Keno died.

After the war, life returned to "normal" for the Pevneys. Mitzi was announced in August, 1945, to start rehearsals for a new musical, *Slightly Perfect.* But she got a much better offer and withdrew from the first show. *Billion Dollar Baby,* directed by George Abbott, cast Mitzi as a Texas Guinan-type nightclub hostess. It opened on Broadway on December 21, 1945, and Mitzi went through 219 performances as the brassy hostess. Six nights after *Billion Dollar Baby* opened, Pevney was on Broadway in Arthur Laurents' *Home of the Brave.* Later Pevney would go to Hollywood to make his film debut in George Raft's *Nocturne* (1946) and by 1950 would become a director at Universal. Mitzi moved to the Coast to be with her husband, and soon the family consisted of four children: Joel, Jan, Jeff, and Jay.

Mitzi made a few forays back into pictures, including Abbott and Costello's *Lost in Alaska* (1952). She was an occasional guest star on television variety shows, and then on January 1, 1955, she made her bow in the teleseries "So This Is Hollywood," co-starring with Jimmy Lydon. Her final fling on the stage was via the summer circuits in 1961 as the domineering mother in *Gypsy.* Her performance was uneven and the spirited vitality of the past seemed faded, although she could still belt out a song.

Then on May 24, 1969, at Huntington Beach, California, cancer claimed the life of Mitzi Green at forty-eight years of age. She was buried in Mount Eden Cemetery near Los Angeles. She had been a performer for forty-five years and during those decades had delighted several generations with her outstanding talent. She is to be remembered fondly.

MITZI GREEN

The Marriage Playground *(Par 1929)*
Honey *(Par 1929)*
Paramount on Parade *(Par 1930)*
Love among the Millionaires *(Par 1930)*
Tom Sawyer *(Par 1930)*
The Santa Fe Trail *(Par 1930)*
Finn and Hattie *(Par 1931)*
Dude Ranch *(Par 1931)*

Newly Rich *(Par 1931)*
Huckleberry Finn *(Par 1931)*
Skippy *(Par 1931)*
Girl Crazy *(RKO 1932)*
Little Orphan Annie *(RKO 1932)*
Transatlantic Merry-Go-Round *(UA 1934)*
Lost in Alaska *(Univ 1952)*
Bloodhounds of Broadway *(20th 1952)*

Richard Greene

While Tyrone Power was Twentieth Century-Fox's prime young leading man, there were other candidates on the lot hoping to take his enviable spot as king of the studio. Among them was Richard Greene, who was extremely handsome, had a flair for swashbuckling pictures, and was being groomed as Power's chief competitor during the late Thirties.

Richard was born on Tuesday, August 25, 1914, at Plymouth, Devonshire, England. His father, Richard Greene, Sr., and his mother, Kathleen Gerrard Greene, stage character actors, were on tour at the time of his birth. Within two weeks of his arrival, his mother had placed him in the care of a nursemaid while she returned to the stage. Young Richard was the product of four generations of actors. His grandfather, William Friese-Greene, pioneered the idea of making photographs move in 1885 with the exhibition on a screen of a flickering moving image known as *Girl with the Moving Eyes.* (1951's film, *The Magic Box,* with Laurence Olivier, Robert Donat and Michael Redgrave honored Friese-Greene and his invention.)

It was inevitable that Richard should become involved with the theatre. After finishing studies at Cardinal Vaughan School at Kensington, he debuted at the Old Vic as a spear carrier in *Julius Caesar.* He was nineteen. Since acting jobs were scarce in those Depression years, he turned to modeling for collar and hat advertisements at one pound a sitting. He roomed in London with three other hopeful actors, but stubbornly refused help of any kind from his parents.

He obtained a small role in a brief revival of *Journey's End* and in 1934 he was given a bit in the film *Sing As You Go,* which starred Gracie Fields. His dialogue consisted of two words, "Not yet," in reply to a question put to him by Miss Fields. He admitted years later: "For me, it was the entire script. I rehearsed for two whole days. I said 'Not yet' in every possible intonation and inflection. I murmured these words and I shouted them until I almost grew hoarse in repeating them. But I said them only once to Miss Fields; the director thought that sufficient."

It turned out that his dedicated efforts were for naught since his scene was clipped in the final editing. As a member of the Brandon-Thomas Repertory Company, he then toured the British Isles for a year, playing everything from a cockney to an Irishman. "It was the best training in the world, because Britons are not slow in expressing their disapproval, and I learned quickly what the audiences liked and what they did not, whether a line had registered or a joke had flopped."

266

With Loretta Young in *Kentucky* (20th '38).

In '39.

At the year's end, he returned to London for a small stage part in a short-lived version of *Anthony and Cleopatra.* However, his next play, *French without Tears,* proved to be a smash hit in London. Alexander Korda was the first to test him for films, but he was unimpressed with the results and made no contract offer. Both Selznick-International and MGM made contract overtures, but Richard rejected them because he did not like the scenarios they offered.

Then, along came Darryl F. Zanuck. Twentieth Century-Fox had a picture in production that urgently required a handsome Britisher. When Zanuck's London scouts cabled laudatory words about Richard's performance as the juvenile lead in *French without Tears,* he gave the signal to offer him whatever he wanted. On Christmas Eve, 1937, Richard was visited by the mogul's representatives. On January 17, 1938, after signing a seven-year pact, he boarded the *Aquitania* bound for New York. From there he flew to Los Angeles. In exactly seven days after leaving London he was thrust into wardrobe fittings, dental caps, photograph sittings, and Fox publicity department interviews. Within thirty-eight hours of arrival in Hollywood he was at work on a soundstage with Loretta Young in a scene for the John Ford-directed *Four Men and a Prayer* (1938).

Of this film venture, Greene would recall, "I was so bewildered. I still don't know how I ever got through the scene. If Loretta hadn't kidded me out of my fright, I might never have made it." John Ford would nickname him "Bouncer" because he seldom sat still. In the story he is one of four brothers (along with George Sanders, David Niven, and William Henry) who clear the good name of their father (C. Aubrey Smith) of a conspiracy charge.

Upon the release of *Four Men and a Prayer,* Richard became a sensation with female fans. Movie magazines publicized his statistics (6'1½", 170 lbs.; dark brown wavy hair, blue-gray eyes) and his likes (American hamburgers, cowboy ballads, Loretta Young). But he found little time to enjoy any of the latter because of a full work schedule. In *My Lucky Star* (1938) he made oncamera love to a skating co-ed (Sonja Henie). In *Submarine Patrol* (1938) he romanced studio starlet Nancy Kelly World War I style as directed by John Ford. In *Kentucky* (1938) he helped to save Loretta Young's family from financial ruin by training her horse to win the Derby. Lush color photography enhanced this entry. In *The Little Princess* (1939) he romanced Anita Louise in the Victorian era while helping Shirley Temple find her papa (Ian Hunter). The sixth Fox film he made was *The Hound of the Baskervilles* (1939), a first-rate adaptation of the Sir Arthur Conan Doyle tale and the first to star Basil Rathbone and Nigel Bruce as Sherlock Holmes and Dr. Watson, respectively. Richard played *the* Baskerville. Fan magazines, at this point, were not alone in discovering his screen attributes. *The Boston Globe's* Mayme Ober Peak wrote, "Richard Greene is the only really romantic leading man since Robert Taylor and Tyrone Power to hover on the horizon," and called him "handsome as the dickens."

For a time, his Hollywood companions were Twentieth Century-Fox's Sonja Henie and Virginia Field, but his attentions were soon exclusively concentrated on a former manicurist and "cinderella girl on the lot"—Arleen Whelan. At the same time he was hoping to obtain more substantial parts. "I would like to get more and more into character roles that have some real meat to them." But Fox continued to cast him as the handsome love interest. In *Stanley and Livingstone* (1939) he wins the girl (Nancy Kelly) while Stanley (Spencer Tracy) is beating the African bush for Livingstone (Sir Cedric Hardwicke).

In *Little Old New York* (1940), however, Richard came closer to the type of portrayal he wanted. He played the determined, glum-faced Robert Fulton who builds a steamboat with the help of Alice Faye (in a non-singing role), Fred MacMurray, and Brenda Joyce. After completing *I Was an Adventuress* (1940), in which he makes an honest woman of jewel thief Vera Zorina, Richard was released from his film contract to return to England to fight for King and country.

In September, 1940, he enlisted as a private in the Royal Armoured Corps of the Twenty-Seventh Lancers and served in France, Holland, and Belgium. In December he became an officer cadet and was commissioned a second lieutenant in May 1941. However, he was relieved of active duty for several days in August to appear in the British war propaganda film *Unpublished Story* (1942). On December 24, 1941, he was married to eighteen-year-old British film actress Patricia Medina, the girl with the flashing, dark eyes. After a two-day Christmas honeymoon, he returned to the army at Yorkshire for a year of training, at the end of which he was promoted to first lieutenant.

He suffered a leg injury in May, 1943, but rather than take a medical discharge he was given a staff liaison post with the rank of captain. During furlough in March, 1943, he starred with Anna Neagle in *The Yellow Canary* for RKO, in which they were a pair of British spies. Finally, in December, 1944, he received his military discharge.

After returning to civilian life, Richard appeared in British films such as *Gaiety George* (1946). Later that year he accompanied his wife to Hollywood where she underwent a screen test at Twentieth Century-Fox. One of the first things he did was renew acquaintances with the American hamburger when he said, "I've been dreaming about this meal ever since I left Hollywood." He was offered various film roles, but he was steadfast in his campaign to obtain other than drawing room, "dimpled" parts. "I don't want to become Lionel Barrymore," he said, "but I would like to get character lines, as actors say, in my face."

Then came the offer of a role that appealed to him. The filming of Kathleen Winsor's 956-page novel of lusting, *Forever Amber* (1947), had previously been shut down for a number of reasons, chief of which was the miscasting of Peggy Cummins as Amber St. Clare. When production resumed (with a blonde Linda Darnell replacing Miss Cummins), Vincent Price, originally signed to enact the role of the worldly Lord Almsbury, had gone on to other cinematic commitments. Richard assumed the vacated role of the cynical bystander-friend of the hero (Cornel Wilde), the sincere love object of the much-seduced Amber. With a wig covering his wavy hair, Richard received third billing in this expensive costume picture. Critics welcomed him to the American cinema. He "justifies his role" *(Los Angeles Times);* "Deserves special attention" *(Variety);* "Is a standout" *(Los Angeles Examiner);* "Has humor and charm" *(Motion Picture). Film Daily* stated simply, "It is good to see Richard Greene again."

He then acted in another Hollywood costume film, *The Fighting O'Flynn* (1948). In this Universal release Richard is the villain to Douglas Fairbanks, Jr.'s hero. (Patricia Medina was also in the cast). Over at Twentieth Century-Fox he appeared in *The Fan* (1949). He is Oscar Wilde's Lord Windemere whose Lady (Jeanne Crain) loses her fan in the chambers of Lord Darlington (George Sanders). In August, 1949, Richard was in Italy making *Now Barabbas Was a Robber* (1949), and then went on location in England and Capri to support Myrna Loy and Roger Livesey in *If This Be Sin* (1949). Again, he was in Italy for *Shadow of the Eagle* (1950), with Valentina Cortesa and Binnie Barnes, and then shuffled back to England for *My Daughter Joy (Operation X)* (1950), with Edward G. Robinson and Peggy Cummins.

Shadow of the Eagle, although released on the Continent in 1950, was not seen in the U.S. until five years later, but it was instrumental in starting Richard on a new career as an onscreen adventurer. "This swashbuckle stuff is a bit rough on the anatomy," he would confess, "but I find it more exhilarating than whispering mish-mash into some ingenue's pink little ear."

From Hollywood on April 15, 1950, Patricia Medina Greene made the announce-

With Nancy Kelly in *Stanley and Livingstone* (20th '39).

ment of their marital separation. "We're quarreling all the time when we're under the same roof," she said. "He doesn't like the way I keep house and I find fault with him, but we both care more for each other than anyone else."

In June, 1950, Richard returned to Hollywood where he bought a house on Mulholland Drive, acquired a 12½-foot dinghy, which he labeled "Arachnid," and went before the cameras at Universal to star in *The Desert Hawk* (1950). In the film he is a blacksmith by trade, but devotes his swashbuckling hours to freeing the people from the nobles' oppression. For all his heroics he wins the love of Princess Shaharazade (Yvonne De Carlo). From the white desert sands, he was then cinematically transported to the English countryside of the seventeenth century as the champion of *Lorna Doone* (1951). In this Columbia economy-minded entry, the entire Doone clan are despicable money-grabbers. But Lorna ends up in his sword-hardened hands, since it develops that she really is not of Doone lineage after all. While Richard was cavorting in these minor cloak-and-sword entries, another Britisher, Stewart Granger, was engaged in prime quality swashbuckling films at MGM, taking over the crown in the genre once held by Douglas Fairbanks, Sr., Errol Flynn, and Tyrone Power.

On June 25, 1951, when Patricia Medina acquired her divorce in Los Angeles, she told Superior Court Judge Thurmond Clarke that her husband had been "moody, cold, indifferent, humiliating and insulting." She was awarded $15,000 in cash, plus $2,400 payable at the rate of four hundred dollars a month. (She would later wed Joseph Cotten.)

Meanwhile, Richard kept busy on television ("Prudential Playhouse," "Robert Montgomery Presents," "Video Theatre," "Studio One," etc.). His films during the ensuing three years were an extension of *The Desert Hawk*, the portrayal of the sword-wielding benefactor of the less fortunate. These films, all of them costumed programmers, evoked enthusiastic Saturday matinee jeers for the villains and cheers for the heroes. In *The Black Castle* (1952) he is befriended by Boris Karloff in league against murderous Stephen McNally. In MGM's *Rogue's March* (1952) Queen Victoria never had a more dashing soldier in her India regiment. *Captain Scarlet* (1953), filmed in Mexico, had him in the title-telling lead. *The Bandits of Corsica* (1954) meet their ultimate defeat at the tip of Richard's three swords (he played three roles in this one).

Richard revealed to the *Los Angeles Daily News'* Howard McClay, "For a long time I've wanted to play a cowboy. Naturally, I kept my trap shut in the past about this desire, because nothing could be more ludicrous than a cowpoke with a British accent." An original story, *The Dude from Montana* (by Don Martin), was one that he was certain could be used for the screen and in which his accent would prove to be an asset. However, he could find no producer interested in backing the venture.

In 1955 he associated himself with Yeoman Films in their plan to make a modestly priced teleseries in England for American audiences. These weekly, half-hour segments, based on the legendary exploits of "Robin Hood," emerged on CBS-TV on September 26, 1955, with Richard in the title role. It revived his professional standing and proved to be a lucrative venture for all concerned. Of this successful show, he said: "Kids love pageantry and costume plays. But the most important single thing is: Robin can be identified with any American hero. He's the British Hopalong." The series lasted four television seasons, through 1959. For theatrical release, Richard produced (with Sidney Cole) and starred as Robin in *Sword of Sherwood Forest* (1951), filmed in Ireland.

After buying an estate in Ireland, Richard went into semiretirement at the age of forty-seven. Occasionally he would appear in a film, such as *The Blood of Fu Manchu* (1968) or *Tales from the Crypt* (1972) or tour on stage, countryside living. By the late Sixties his wavy hair was thinning and his waistline had expanded, but his dimples were still in place.

In 1973 he took as his second wife a wealthy Brazilian girl who was (and still is) devoted to the equestrian life. The Greenes occasionally embark from Ireland with jet-set chums, on trips by yacht and plane to various ports of the world. On a visit to Hollywood in August, 1973, Richard observed the decline of the movie industry with, "The glory of Hollywood will return when they make four-star films, and eliminate the four-letter words in the scripts."

RICHARD GREENE

Four Men and a Prayer *(20th 1938)*
My Lucky Star *(20th 1938)*
Submarine Patrol *(20th 1938)*
Kentucky *(20th 1938)*
The Little Princess *(20th 1939)*
The Hounds of the Baskervilles *(20th 1939)*
Stanley and Livingstone *(20th 1939)*
Here I Am Stranger *(20th 1939)*
Little Old New York *(20th 1940)*
I Was an Adventuress *(20th 1940)*
Unpublished Story *(Col British 1942)*
Flying Fortress *(WB 1942)*
The Yellow Canary *(RKO 1943)*
Don't Take It to Heart *(General Film Distributors 1944)*
Gaiety George [Showtime] *(WB British 1946)*
Forever Amber *(20th 1947)*
The Fighting O'Flynn *(Univ 1948)*
The Fan *(20th 1949)*
That Dangerous Age [If This Be Sin] *(British Lion 1949)*

Now Barabbas Was a Robber *(WB British 1949)*
The Desert Hawk *(Univ 1950)*
My Daughter Joy [Operation X] *(British Lion 1950)*
Shadow of the Eagle *(Independent Film Distributors 1950)*
Lorna Doone *(Col 1951)*
The Black Castle *(Univ 1952)*
Rogue's March *(MGM 1953)*
Captain Scarlet *(UA 1953)*
The Bandits of Corsica *(UA 1954)*
Contraband Spain *(Associated British Producers 1955)*
Beyond the Curtain *(Rank 1960)*
Sword of Sherwood Forest *(Col 1961)*
Dangerous Island *(British 1967)*
The Blood of Fu Manchu *(AA British 1968)*
Kiss and Kill *(Commonwealth United 1969)*
Tales from the Crypt *(Cin 1972)*

34

Phillips Holmes

The Thirties spawned a new breed of young leading men. Many of them were lured from the stage because of a theatre-trained voice and ability to read lines convincingly. Others gained Hollywood prominence because they were handsome male specimens with an aura of the boy-next-door or personified the all-American boy capable of fulfilling the average girl's dream of the ideal lover. One of the more sensitive (some insisted stiff) emigres to movieland in the late Twenties was Phillips Holmes. He was a handsome, six-foot, blond, blue-eyed actor with a dazzling smile. When given good direction and material, he could create a startling fine performance. But without astute guidance, he was capable only of being bland. His best-known celluloid performance was in *An American Tragedy* (1931). Strangely, he became just that.

Taylor Holmes had a sixty-year show business career that started in vaudeville in 1899 and continued until his death in 1959. While playing Rosencrantz to E. H. Sothern's *Hamlet,* he fell in love with Edna Phillips, a co-player. After their marriage they both continued working in the theatre. Taylor had finished a show tour and was playing a brief engagement at Ramona Park outside of Grand Rapids, Michigan, where their first son was born on Monday, July 22, 1907. They gave their first-born their combined names: Phillips Holmes. In the fall of 1907 they deposited their son with his paternal grandmother in Chicago, while Taylor went to New York to appear in *A Grand Army Man* and Edna appeared in a vaudeville sketch, *Lost, a Kiss.*

By the time Phillips was sixteen he had been in many schools and lived on both coasts, and the family had expanded to include brother Ralph (born in 1915) and sister Madeline (born in 1914). At sixteen, Phillips spent half a year at Georgetown Prep School, then transferred to Newman Prep School at Lakewood, New Jersey, where he graduated at seventeen. His decision to enter Cambridge was encouraged by his Canadian-born mother. Thus, in September, 1925, Mrs. Holmes and Phillips sailed for England. Edna left for a holiday in Paris, and Phillips for Tunbridge Wells and a tutoring school, Henley House. He made his first half-term at Cambridge, then transferred to Grenoble University in the south of France. By summer he was back in California with his family, excited about being one of twenty students chosen from 120 applicants to enter Trinity House at Cambridge in the fall. He did well at Cambridge, became a passionate Anglophile, and won his colors on the rowing team.

When he returned home the following summer, his mother was not well, so he

With Kay Francis in *Storm at Daybreak* (MGM '33).

decided to remain in the U.S. to complete his education. He chose Princeton University, where he later joined their rowing team and made his bid for the famous Triangle Club. On December 20, 1927, he made his New York stage debut with the 39th Annual Princeton Triangle Show, *Napoleon Passes,* at the Metropolitan Opera House. He played Sonia, daughter of the empress of Russia, who rejects France's pudgy emperor. "Leading Lady" Holmes received good notices and "stood out well in any assembly of the fairer sex."

In the spring of 1928 "Flip" Holmes (as his classmates had nicknamed him) was asked to report to Dean Stewart's office. There he met another former Princeton man, Frank Tuttle, who had arrived on campus with Charles "Buddy" Rogers and Mary Brian to direct a college story for Paramount Pictures. Dean Stewart had suggested Holmes for the small role of Middlebrook, Buddy Rogers' roommate in the film. When the location scenes were completed, Phillips left with the cast for Hollywood to complete interior shots. Based on his work in *Varsity* (1928), Paramount offered him a contract. After a long favorable consultation with his parents, he was on his way back to Hollywood. He thought that Paramount would offer him important assignments. But after two weeks of being ignored, he went to see Frank Tuttle who gave him a one-scene bit in Adolphe Menjou's *His Private Life* (1928).

Holmes haunted the studio casting office and was finally sent to a new director, John Cromwell. The latter gave Holmes a job—in a play. The Los Angeles Civic Repertory Company was attempting to establish a western Theatre Guild with their 2,500 subscribers and, for their first production, selected *The Silver Cord.* Cromwell directed and his newly acquired wife, Kay Johnson, played Christina Phelps, the daughter-in-law of domineering Nance O'Neil. Phillips was assigned the role of Robert, the unfortunate, victimized, younger son. Paramount executives and directors saw Holmes' performance, and his name suddenly became known at the studio.

In Paramount's proposed production of *The Genius,* Phillips was given the lead, that of a violin virtuoso. Later he reflected on the sudden transition: "This intensive work followed directly on the nervous strain that had carried me through *The Silver Cord.* I had been totally unprepared, technically, for the demands of the role that would have taxed the ingenuity of an experienced, seasoned actor. Because I lacked technical equipment, my one resource had been a complete immersion of myself in the character, a resource which experienced players are never forced to employ by itself."

Paramount decided to shelve *The Genius* and abandoned production. Phillips had what was termed a nervous breakdown. His father was on tour with the road company of a revival of *The Beaux Strategem,* but learning of Phillips' hospitalization, he left the show, and, with his wife, rushed to the West Coast. Paramount suspended Phillips' contract. Rumors spread in Hollywood about his unreliability plus a lot of other bad habits, all equally false.

After some six weeks in the hospital, Phillips returned to the studio and asked to be reinstated. For quite a while, there were no assignments for him, then only a bit in Buddy Rogers' *Illusion* (1929) and the small part of Phil in Clara Bow's first talking picture, *The Wild Party* (1929). Finally he was given the juvenile lead in Paramount's last silent picture, *Stairs of Sand* (1929), starring Wallace Beery and featuring Jean Arthur. The film was rushed through to fill the programming requirements of block-booking and Holmes was glad to see its completion.

His disappointment in this Zane Grey fiasco was alleviated a bit when Paramount sent him to their Astoria, New York, studio for the juvenile lead in *The Return of Sherlock Holmes* (1929). It was made with a predominantly British cast and starred Clive Brook as the famed detective. Before completion of the Long Island picture, Phillips received a wire from director A. Edward Sutherland requesting him to play one of the leads in Paramount's musical *Pointed Heels* (1929), some of which was filmed in Technicolor. He played composer Donald Ogden married to Fay Wray in a fairly well-done backstage story featuring William Powell. With *Pointed Heels,* his billing changed from Phillips R. Holmes to Phillips Holmes and he was announced for a never-made picture called *Youth Has Its Fling* with Jean Hersholt, Fay Wray, and Kay Francis. Instead he played a fiery Confederate captain in Gary Cooper's *Only the Brave* (1930) and appeared in a Technicolor sequence of the old South in *Paramount on Parade* (1930) with Gary Cooper, Fay Wray, Jean Arthur, Richard Arlen, and Virginia Bruce.

Director Edmund Goulding practically fought with Holmes to draw out the requirements of his role in *The Devil's Holiday* (1930) opposite Nancy Carroll. But Goulding's demands produced a fine performance that *Photoplay* liked very much indeed. Holmes credited Goulding with teaching him more in a few weeks than he had learned about acting in years. He had finished *Devil's Holiday* on a Saturday afternoon at five and started *Grumpy* (1930) at nine that night. It was a standard juvenile lead part. Thereafter other studios requested his services, but Paramount refused to lend him for *All Quiet on the Western Front, Journey's End,* or *The Case of Sergeant Grischa.* But they did negotiate a loan-out to Pathé in exchange for one of that studio's players.

Tay Garnett was to direct his version of *Frankie and Johnny* for Pathé and for the role of the rough, tough sailor to play opposite Helen Twelvetrees, Garnett had Dean Jagger in mind. Jagger tested for the part but Garnett was told to use Holmes. Twenty-five years later Jagger saw Garnett for the first time since the Pathé test and greeted him with, "About that part in *Her Man,* I guess you decided to use somebody else!" For Holmes the part of the rugged sailor was a golden opportunity and he credited Garnett's tight direction with being one of his best breaks in pictures. Ricardo Cortez and Marjorie Rambeau took the acting honors in *Her Man,* but Phillips' notices were good. The film required him to sing, but his singing voice was dubbed by Jess Kirkpatrick.

After the Pathé outing, Paramount loaned him to Warners for *Man to Man* (1930), filmed in twenty days. The day following completion of *Man to Man* he went to work at Columbia for their *The Criminal Code* (1931). His sterling portrayal brought more predictions of his bright future, as did his interpretation of the thief in the George Abbott-directed *Stolen Heaven* (1931). Phillips and Nancy Carroll were both better than the story.

Among the more chaotic productions at Paramount was the first rendition of Theodore Dreiser's *An American Tragedy* (1931). Executive Jesse L. Lasky had seen the Broadway adaptation of the mammoth novel, but instead of buying the rights to that, he hired Russian director Sergei M. Eisenstein for the pending Dreiser project. By the time the artistic Russian and his staff had concluded preparing a draft of the novel (some said it was almost as long as the book itself), the studio had spent some $500,000 on the still-unmade production. Adolph Zukor removed Eisenstein from the film and asked Josef von Sternberg to rewrite the script with Samuel Hoffenstein, and to be mindful of a much less expensive production than Lasky had anticipated. The Eisenstein script was discarded. Production started March 3, 1931, while Hoffenstein was in New Orleans discussing the completed script with Dreiser for the first time. As the cameras rolled, Dreiser's displeasure with the screen treatment of his novel became national news. He battled with von Sternberg over the interpretation given the book in the scenario. Dreiser later sued the studio, but the court ruled that the film was a faithful translation of the novel and denied Dreiser's claim at a court cost of ten dollars.

To play the leads in *An American Tragedy,* von Sternberg used Sylvia Sidney and Holmes, both of whom had co-starred in a slushy melodrama, *Confessions of a Co-Ed* (1931), that was so bad that no one would acknowledge authorship. On the other hand, both Phillips and Miss Sidney were lauded for their performance in *An American Tragedy,* as was Irving Pichel as the district attorney. Although some critics found Holmes' performance as Clyde Griffiths rather dolefully pedestrian in the first part of the picture, it was generally agreed that his performing was intense during the trial scenes for his drowning of the pregnant Roberta (Sidney) who stood in his way of his marrying wealthy Frances Dee. Holmes' performance was effective as Griffiths, if not the equal of Montgomery Clift's interpretation in the George Stevens-directed remake, *A Place in the Sun* (1951).

Phillips concluded 1931 with work on Ernst Lubitsch's *The Man I Killed* (1932). Lubitsch's direction was, as ever, fluid, but the public was not expecting a bitter drama of post-World War I. During the second week of release, the studio changed the title to *Broken Lullaby,* but this action was unable to generate any additional box-office activity.

On a much less expert, but more successful, level was the quickie *Two Kinds of Women* (1932), which headlined Miriam Hopkins as a midwestern senator's daughter enthralled with Manhattan and a playboy (Phillips). Holmes played the role well. He then made a guest appearance in *Make Me a Star* (1932) along with other studio contractees. Paramount's *70,000 Witnesses* (1932) cast him as a star quarterback accused of murdering his roommate (Johnny Mack Brown) during a football game. Over at MGM for *Night Court* (1932) Phillips was a taxi driver involved in a quickly paced expose of a corrupt judge (Walter Huston). When Holmes' contract expired with Paramount, he signed with MGM at the end of 1932.

The Secret of Madame Blanche (1933) was another mother-sacrifice drama that found Metro borrowing Irene Dunne from RKO. Phillips was the weakling whom 1890s chorus girl Irene marries, only to have his enraged British aristocratic father (Lionel Atwill) deny him his inheritance and support. Holmes commits suicide, leaving valiant Miss Dunne with child. Phillips was next entrapped, as a son torn between his pacifist mother (Diana Wynyard) and his super-patriotic father (Lewis Stone), in MGM's *Men Must Fight* (1933).

Hard-working Phillips completed seven more MGM features in 1933, most of them run-of-the-studio affairs. But he was included in a two-scene bit with three or four lines in the final reel of the star-studded *Dinner at Eight* (1933) as Madge Evans' fiance.

Phillips returned to Paramount for a dismal comedy trying to be a mystery, or both, called *Private Scandal* (1934). His great promise, as was happening to other "sensitive" young Hollywood leads (David Manners, Douglass Montgomery, Eric Linden) was quickly fading, as the flood of talented young men entering into Hollywood increased. With the end of his Metro contract there were no immediate demands for his services. Then Samuel Goldwyn offered him the plum romantic lead opposite his highly exploited Russian importation, Anna Sten, in *Nana* (1934).

His performance as Lieutenant George Muffat—again beset by Lionel Atwill—was erratic. Fine in some scenes, wooden in others, he never seemed at ease in the role. The making of the film had been turbulent when, halfway through the script, Goldwyn had halted production and started again with a different director and other technical changes. But the exercise of repeating the role did not seem to improve Phillips' performance. Despite his less-than-expert performance in *Nana,* he was selected for the role of dashing, devil-may-care Lieutenant von Tokay in Fox's flowery musical *Caravan* (1934), opposite equally miscast Loretta Young. Only Charles Boyer and Jean Parker managed to brighten the Erik Charell-directed film. Charell would make an English version with the same cast and a French version with Boyer, Annabella, Conchita Montenegro, and Pierre Brasseur, but none of these films were very popular.

During these years, Holmes' personal life was as erratic as his career. On December 29, 1933, an announcement was made of his pending marriage to Grantland Rice's daughter, actress Florence Rice, but he was soon dating other girls from the film colony. On March 25, 1934, Mae Clarke dropped a lawsuit charging negligence in Holmes' driving and seeking damages (he had driven head-on into a tree, whereby she broke her jaw). Mae dropped the $21,500 lawsuit when Holmes paid all her hospital bills.

In 1934 he made two films for Universal, including playing the grown Pip in *Great Expectations.* This version in no way compared to the later English-made edition of the Dickens' novel. After a fairly entertaining programmer, *No Ransom* (1934), he left for England.

For British Lion he appeared as the young man dreaming of a perfect murder in *Ten-Minute Alibi* (1935) and then signed for the role of Vincenzo Bellini in the Italian-British-produced *Casta Diva (The Divine Spark)* (1935) made in Italy. In 1936 he returned to Hollywood to support Anne Shirley in RKO's *Chatterbox,* in which he and Shirley made a pleasant duo. With Mae Clarke he filmed the old play *The House of a Thousand Candles* (1936) and returned to Metro for a Civil War yarn, *General Spanky* (1936), geared to display the talents of Hal Roach's *Our Gang* contingent, including Spanky McFarland, Carl "Alfalfa" Switzer, and Billie "Buckwheat" Thomas. It was to be Phillips' last American film. In June, 1936, he was heard on the broadcast of Pickford's "Parties at Pickfair" in a Flag Day sketch with Glenda Farrell, Genevieve Tobin, and Herman Bing. Then he returned again to England to film *The Dominant Sex* (1937) with Diana Churchill and Carol Goodner.

278

With Jean Parker in a pose for *Caravan* (Fox '34).

In 1937 Holmes was seen with some regularity with torch singer Libby Holman Reynolds, who two years before had been granted seven million dollars by the courts (most of it to be held in trust for her son Christopher Reynolds) in settlement of the estate of her slain husband, Smith Reynolds. During the summer of 1937 Phillips returned to the stage at the Cape Playhouse at Dennis, Massachusetts, in *The Petrified Forest*, with Richard Carlson and a bright, young actress as yet unseen on Broadway, Martha Scott.

He returned to England in 1938 to film *The Housemaster*, with Otto Kruger and Diana Churchill, which was generally ignored by the reviewers. While in London he co-produced Paul Osborn's successful Broadway play *On Borrowed Time*. Although the part of Death, or Mr. Brink, required a much older man, Phillips cast himself in the part. The show opened in October, 1938, but lasted only three weeks.

His London stage debut having been a failure, he came back to America where he subsequently signed to co-star with Jean Muir on a road tour of *Golden Boy*. The Holmes-Muir edition opened on Christmas night, 1938, and closed in Detroit in mid-January, 1939. The gossip columnists still predicted an imminent marriage to Miss Holman, but Phillips joined a newly formed company to give a finely etched performance as Joe Bonaparte on the East Coast in *Golden Boy*, with Betty Furness. The two-year publicized romance exploded when Libby eloped on March 31, 1939, with Phillips' 24-year-old brother Ralph—ten years Libby's junior. (Ralph had appeared briefly off and on Broadway, and in 1940 did summer stock with his wife. On November 15, 1945, a little over a month following Libby and Ralph's separation, he was found dead in his New York apartment, a suicide from barbiturate poisoning. Libby would later remarry. In 1950 her son died on a mountain-climbing expedition and on June 18, 1971 she died of carbon monoxide poisoning, classified as a suicide.)

As a Paramount player in '34.

Phillips starred in a summer production of *The Male Animal*, featuring Celeste Holm, David Wayne, and Lyle Bettger in the supporting cast, that opened June 24, 1941, at the Bronx Windsor Theatre, played another week in Flatbush, and transferred to Atlantic City's Garden Pier Theatre on July 7. His last stage appearance was in the stock production of *The Philadelphia Story* at Pawling, New York, in August, 1941. Father Taylor Holmes was playing the straw-hat circuit that year in *The Man Who Came to Dinner*. In December, 1941, both Phillips and Ralph enlisted in the Royal Canadian Air Force. Ralph became a pilot officer and Phillips attended the Air Ground School at Winnipeg where, as a boy, he had made his only stage appearance with his dad in Taylor's stage hit *The Great Necker*.

Following his graduation from Air Ground School a Leading Aircraftsman, RCAF, Phillips, with six of his classmates, transferred to Ottawa. They never made it. Shortly after take-off en route to Ottawa on Wednesday, August 12, 1942, their plane collided with another craft over Armstrong, Ontario. All were killed. Phillips Holmes was dead at age thirty-five.

PHILLIPS HOLMES

Varsity *(Par 1928)*
His Private Life *(Par 1928)*
Illusion *(Par 1929)*
The Wild Party *(Par 1929)*
Stairs of Sand *(Par 1929)*
The Return of Sherlock Holmes *(Par 1929)*
Pointed Heels *(Par 1929)*
Only the Brave *(Par 1930)*
Paramount on Parade *(Par 1930)*
The Devil's Holiday *(Par 1930)*
Grumpy *(Par 1930)*
Her Man *(Pathe 1930)*
Man to Man *(WB 1930)*
The Dancers *(Fox 1930)*
The Criminal Code *(Col 1931)*
Stolen Heaven *(Par 1931)*
Confessions of a Co-Ed *(Par 1931)*
An American Tragedy *(Par 1931)*
The Man I Killed [Broken Lullaby] *(Par 1932)*
Two Kinds of Women *(Par 1932)*
Make Me a Star *(Par 1932)*
70,000 Witnesses *(Par 1932)*
Night Court *(MGM 1932)*
The Secret of Madame Blanche *(MGM 1933)*

Men Must Fight *(MGM 1933)*
Looking Forward *(MGM 1933)*
Storm at Daybreak *(MGM 1933)*
The Big Brain *(RKO 1933)*
Dinner at Eight *(MGM 1933)*
Penthouse *(MGM 1933)*
Beauty for Sale *(MGM 1933)*
Stage Mother *(MGM 1933)*
Private Scandal *(Par 1934)*
Nana *(UA 1934)*
Caravan *(Fox 1934)*
Great Expectations *(Univ 1934)*
Million Dollar Ransom *(Univ 1934)*
No Ransom *(Liberty 1935)*
The Divine Spark [Casta Diva] *(Italian-British 1934)*
Ten-Minute Alibi *(British Lion 1935)*
Chatterbox *(RKO 1936)*
The House of a Thousand Candles *(Rep 1936)*
General Spanky *(MGM 1936)*
The Dominant Sex *(British International 1937)*
The Housemaster *(Associated British Producers Corporation 1938)*

Ian Hunter

Staunch, sturdy, dependable, and poised. These were the attributes of Ian Hunter whose able acting bolstered many major and minor films. Always more competent than distinctive, Ian's screen portrayals never launched him into true stardom, for being pleasant, sympathetic, and handsome onscreen were qualities taken for granted by both Hollywood and movie fans.

Ian was born on Wednesday, June 13, 1900, at Kenilworth, near Cape Town, South Africa, to wine merchant Robert Hunter and his wife Isabel Gates Hunter. Ian was the youngest of three sons (there were also four daughters). He was educated at St. Andrew's College at Grahamstown, Cape Colony, and after graduation he wed Catherine (called Casha) Pringle. His two older brothers, Colin and Kenneth, had joined the Army, and in 1917, Ian and Catherine left for England where Hunter joined the British army. He saw service in France, and when the war ended, he returned to England instead of South Africa. By then he was obsessed with going into the theatrical profession.

He studied elocution with Miss Elsie Fogerty. He obviously learned his lessons well because one of the most memorable things about Ian Hunter was his well-modulated voice. He made his first professional appearance on the stage of the New Theatre in London on September 4, 1919, in *Jack O'Jingles*, in which he played a peasant, a Dutch and English soldier, and offstage provided the hoof beats of horses. During 1920 he toured in *General Post* and *The Skin Game*, and the following year, in London, he played in *The Blue Lagoon* and *A Bill of Divorcement*. He became quite well known on the London stage and for the next three years was seen in several major plays, including *R.U.R., London Life, Diplomacy*, and *Peter Pan*, the latter two with Gladys Cooper. He made his English film debut in 1924 in *Not for Sale* and continued the practice of making motion pictures during the day and playing in the theatre at night for the next eleven years. For Stoll Films in 1925 he was Mr. Charles Oddy in *Confessions* and Peter Horniman in *A Girl from London* while appearing on the stage in *Spring Cleaning* and *The Show*.

In 1925 American producer George C. Tyler went to England to cast a revival of Richard Brinsley Sheridan's *The School for Scandal*, which he was to produce in the States in the fall of 1925. Basil Dean recommended Ian Hunter, regarded then as one of the best of the younger actors and a matinee idol. Dean thought he would be an excellent choice for the part of the wild, young spendthrift, eighteenth-century Charles Surface. Tyler signed the young actor and Hunter made his American stage debut in the Sheridan role at the Knickerbocker Theatre in New York for one performance only on

With Lupe Velez in *The Morals of Marcus* (Gaumont '35).

With Kay Francis and Paul Lukas in *I Found Stella Parish* (FN '35).

December 6, 1925. Tyler wished only to exhibit his choice company prior to an extensive road tour. Ian returned to London and in 1926 appeared on stage in *The Best People* and *The Gold Diggers*. His popularity on the London stage continued and in 1928 he returned to America as the handsome Hussar captain in Gilbert Miller's production of *Olympia*. The Molnar play, with Fay Compton and Laura Hope Crews, lasted thirty-nine performances.

On the screen Hunter had been busier than in the theatre, appearing in three 1927 releases, including *Downhill* with Ivor Novello and Ursula Jeans. In 1928 he played with Tallulah Bankhead in the British-made *His House in Order* and shot two other features. Hunter continued his film career in America when, after the closing of *Olympia*, he appeared with Morton Downey and his wife (Barbara Bennett) in *Syncopation* (1929).

Hunter was back in London by April 1929, for the opening of *The Stag* and, a month later, played in *Why Drag in Marriage?* During the days of these months, Hunter appeared onscreen in *The Physician* (1930) and as the detective in John Galsworthy's *Escape* (1930). On-stage he was in *The Silver Tassie, The Way Out, A Song of Sixpence,* and *A Pair of Trousers*. Later, on the screen, he was to be seen as Gordon Kingsley absconding with his firm's cash in E. A. DuPont's *Cape Forlorn* [a.k.a. *The Love Storm*] (1931). He joined with Gracie Fields for *Sally in Our Alley* (1931), was with Renate Muller in the musical *Marry Me* (1932), and played with Jessie Matthews in *The Man from Toronto* (1933). Ian was Captain Harper in an unexpectedly riotous screen comedy *Orders Is Orders* (1933), with Cedric Hardwicke, Ray Milland, and two American imports, Charlotte Greenwood and James Gleason. Also for Gaumont-British, he teamed with Leslie Banks in *The Night of the Party* (1934) and was again at Gaumont for *The Silver Spoon* (1934).

Several of Hunter's English-made features crossed the Atlantic, including *Death at the Broadcasting House* (1934), in which he was Inspector Gregory. With Lupe Velez and Adrianne Allen he was the frivolous lead in *The Morals of Marcus* (1935). By this time, he had received further offers from Hollywood. Together with his wife and two sons, Jolyon (born: 1928) and Robin (born: 1931) Ian left his furnished flat in Berkeley Square for America. This latest jaunt to the States lasted eight years.

Although he had all the makings of a major star, there was something about Hunter that suggested the gallant loser, the stalwart friend, or suave would-be rake. His manner was a good deal like Eugene O'Neill's description of good old Charlie Marsden in *Strange Interlude:* "Mild, blue eyes those of a dreamy self-analyst. His manner is cool and poised. He speaks with careful ease as one who listens to his own conversation. The main point about his personality is quiet charm, a quality of appealing, inquisitive friendliness, always willing to listen, eager to sympathize, to like and be liked." In short, Ian was the British counterpart of Ralph Bellamy or the later Gig Young, the perennial "other" man of filmdom.

After he appeared with Bette Davis in *The Girl from Tenth Avenue* (1935), Warner Bros.-First National, his contract employer, loaned him to RKO for *Jalna* (1935), and then he returned to the Burbank lot to play King Theseus in Max Reinhardt's vast production of *A Midsummer Night's Dream*. His final task for 1935 was clearing Kay Francis' name when she is confined to prison for a murder she did not commit. Thus, as newspaper reporter Keith Lockridge, he was the male lead in *I Found Stella Parish,* the first of seven pictures he would make with the chic, soignee Miss Francis.

Unfortunately, Ian's next assignment with Miss Francis was in her watershed vehicle, *The White Angel* (1936), an inconclusive biography of Florence Nightingale which helped convince Warner Bros. that their highest paid actress was no longer worth the salary she commanded. Hunter had the dimly drawn, vague role of Fuller in that stodgy chronicle. Twentieth Century-Fox borrowed Hunter to play in *To Mary, with Love* (1936). He was the other man in love with Myrna Loy who magnanimously saves her marriage to Warner Baxter. Hunter, Loy, and Baxter repeated their roles on radio's "Hollywood Hotel." Metro claimed the services of much-in-demand Hunter for the role of Freddie Bartholomew's dad in *The Devil Is a Sissy* (1936). Ian concluded 1936 by giving a tense performance as the man in pursuit of Kay Francis in *Stolen Holiday,* an early screen rendition of the events surrounding the life and career of the amazing Stavitsky.

Undoubtedly, Hollywood and America's Anglophilia was in part responsible for his success in films, as much as his well-bread manner and refined looks. He played the income tax official involved with a madcap family in *Call It a Day* (1937), but then with a stern upper lip flew off into the sunset and death in *Another Dawn* (1937), a Kay Francis-Errol Flynn love story set at an African-located British outpost. He was back with the well-dressed Miss Francis in a pretentious drama, *Confession* (1937), which benefited more from the performances of Basil Rathbone and Jane Bryan. In *That Certain Woman* (1937) he returned to his first Hollywood leading lady, Bette Davis, to portray her unrequited lover.

There seemed no end to the demands for a pleasant and sympathetic soul who displayed understanding and forebearing. Occasionally he had a saintly role, as, for example, that of King Richard in Errol Flynn's Technicolor *The Adventures of Robin Hood* (1938). *Comet over Broadway* (1938) was a second-rate Faith Baldwin story in which Kay Francis starred and in which Ian offered his usual masculine support. In *The Sisters* (1938) Ian loses Bette Davis to Errol Flynn, and *Secrets of an Actress* (1938) finds him succumbing to his usual and inevitable sacrifice, in this case giving up Kay Francis to George Brent.

In California the Hunters had settled into a lovely home at Santa Monica that they had purchased from Anna Sten. Their two sons attended Hollywood Military Academy. Meanwhile, onscreen, Ian was driven to drink by love for Jeanette MacDonald who

With Pat Paterson in *52nd Street* (UA '37).

remains faithful to composer Lew Ayres in *Broadway Serenade* (1939). Hunter was sterling as Priscilla Lane's perplexed, conservative father in *Yes, My Darling Daughter.* Warner Bros. loaned Ian and Anita Louise to Twentieth Century-Fox for Shirley Temple's *The Little Princess* (1939), and at this juncture he signed a term pact with Metro-Goldwyn-Mayer. But his roles at Culver City were only slightly better than the placid, "dear old friend" parts at Warners.

In 1939, he was loaned to Universal to play King Edward IV to Basil Rathbone's Richard III in *The Tower of London* and later appeared as Clifford Ames, committing suicide over his wife's (Ruth Hussey) endless infidelities, in Metro's series-starter *Maisie.*

Then came the role which showed the true calibre of Hunter's acting acumen. It was the part of Cambreau in *Strange Cargo* (1940), the seventh and final Joan Crawford-Clark Gable film. Hunter offered an impressive performance as the Christ-like figure in this allegorical drama, which has never received its just due as a film. At the time of its initial release there was a great deal of controversy over the subject matter of this religious-oriented drama, and several state censor boards were offended by it, as was the Catholic Church. But as cinema historians have often overlooked, Hunter and Miss Crawford—in the nonglamorous role of a cafe tart—provided sincere characterizations that had great dimension. Ian's interpretation of the role was worthy of an Academy Award nomination, but, sadly, he did not get any Oscar bid.

Metro kept Hunter continually busy, from *Andy Hardy's Private Secretary* (1941) to *Dr. Jekyll and Mr. Hyde* (1941). His best part that year was as Robert Taylor's benefactor in *Billy the Kid* (1941). He was polished as the Reverend Owen Harding in Jeanette MacDonald's *Smilin' Through* (1941) and then left for England to play in MGM's *A Yank at Eton* (1942). For a change of pace he was sought by both Louise Allbritton and Frieda Inescort in *It Comes up Love* (1943) and was one of the many Britishers who donated their services to charity for *Forever and a Day* (1943).

Although he was in his forties, Ian joined the R.N.V.R. in which he served throughout World War II. He returned to British film-making in *Bedelia* (1946), but was off his usual mark in *The White Unicorn* (1947). With Madeleine Carroll and Michael Rennie he made *White Cradle Inn* (a.k.a. *High Fury*) (1947) in Switzerland.

Then he returned, yet again, to Broadway. This time it was *Edward, My Son,* written by and starring Robert Morley. It opened in September, 1948, cost $70,000, and in the course of 260 performances, netted $130,000. Co-starred with Morley were Peggy Ashcroft and, as the man secretly in love with Morley's wife (Ashcroft), Ian Hunter was equally good in the film version of 1949 with Spencer Tracy and Deborah Kerr.

After a West End production of *The Seagull,* in which he was Trigorin, Hunter was in Boston, Massachusetts, in March of 1950 for *The Heart of the Matter.* The tireless actor then reappeared in London for the role of Edward Chamberlayne in *The Cocktail Party.* During the Fifties he was back to his old schedule of playing theatre at night and filming during the day. In 1954 he was onstage in *It's Never Too Late* and in early 1955 succeeded Wilfrid Hyde-White in *Hippo Dancing,* again playing with Robert Morley. The next year he was in front of the footlights in *South Sea Bubble* and onscreen, in a rather lesser role, in the sea drama *Pursuit of the Graf Spee* (1957). He ended the decade by joining Lauren Bacall and Ursula Jeans in *Northwest Frontier* (1959), shown in the U.S.A. as *Flame over India.*

Ian's Sixties' film efforts were minor, although he was shown to advantage in the role of Dr. Swann in *Guns of Darkness* (1962), which also starred David Niven and Leslie Caron. His last feature to date was *Act of Mercy* (1963). He occasionally appeared on British television, including a part of the mid-Fifties teleseries "Robin Hood" as King Richard. In 1970 he co-authored the screenplay for *A Dream of Kings,* directed by Daniel Mann, and starring Anthony Quinn and Irene Papas.

286

On September 24, 1975, Ian Hunter died in London, at age seventy-five.

In whatever show business capacity he performed, it could scarcely ever be said that Ian Hunter was less than substantial and reliable.

IAN HUNTER

Not for Sale *(Stoll 1924)*
Confessions *(Stoll 1925)*
A Girl of London *(Stoll 1925)*
Downhill *(Gainsborough 1927)*
Easy Virtue *(Gainsborough 1927)*
The Ring *(British International 1927)*
His House in Order *(Ideal 1928)*
The Thoroughbred *(Gaumont 1928)*
Valley of the Ghost *(British Lion 1928)*
Syncopation *(RKO 1929)*
The Physician *(Tiffany-Stahl 1929)*
Escape *(Radio 1930)*
Cape Forlorn [The Love Storm] *(Wardour 1931)*
Sally in Our Alley *(Radio 1931)*
The Water Gypsies *(Radio 1931)*
The Sign of Four *(Radio 1932)*
Marry Me *(Gainsborough 1932)*
The Man from Toronto *(Gainsborough 1933)*
Skipper of the Osprey *(Associated British Film Distributors 1933)*
Orders Is Orders *(Gaumont 1933)*
The Night of the Party *(Gaumont 1934)*
The Silver Spoon *(Gaumont 1934)*
Something Always Happens *(First National 1934)*
No Escape *(WB British 1934)*
Death at the Broadcasting House *(Phoenix 1934)*
The Phantom Light *(Gainsborough 1935)*
Lazybones *(Radio 1935)*
The Morals of Marcus *(Gaumont 1935)*
The Church Mouse *(1935)*
The Girl from Tenth Avenue *(FN 1935)*
Jalna *(RKO 1935)*
A Midsummer Night's Dream *(WB 1935)*
I Found Stella Parish *(FN 1935)*
The White Angel *(FN 1936)*
To Mary, with Love *(20th 1936)*
The Devil Is a Sissy *(MGM 1936)*
Stolen Holiday *(WB 1936)*
Call It a Day *(WB 1937)*
Another Dawn *(WB 1937)*
Confession *(WB 1937)*
That Certain Woman *(WB 1937)*
52nd Street *(UA 1937)*
The Adventures of Robin Hood *(WB 1938)*
Comet over Broadway *(WB 1938)*
The Sisters *(WB 1938)*
Secrets of an Actress *(WB 1938)*
Always Goodbye *(20th 1938)*
Broadway Serenade *(MGM 1939)*

Yes, My Darling Daugher *(WB 1939)*
Tarzan Finds a Son! *(MGM 1939)*
The Little Princess *(20th 1939)*
The Tower of London *(Univ 1939)*
Maisie *(MGM 1939)*
Bad Little Angel *(MGM 1940)*
Broadway Melody of 1940 *(MGM 1940)*
Strange Cargo *(MGM 1940)*
The Long Voyage Home *(UA 1940)*
Dulcy *(MGM 1940)*
Bitter Sweet *(MGM 1940)*
Gallant Sons *(MGM 1940)*
Come Live with Me *(MGM 1941)*
Andy Hardy's Private Secretary *(MGM 1941)*
Ziegfeld Girl *(MGM 1941)*
Dr. Jekyll and Mr. Hyde *(MGM 1941)*
Billy the Kid *(MGM 1941)*
Smilin' Through *(MGM 1941)*
A Yank at Eton *(MGM 1942)*
It Comes up Love *(Univ 1943)*
Forever and a Day *(RKO 1943)*
Bedelia *(General Film Distributors 1946)*
White Cradle Inn [High Fury] *(British Lion 1947)*
The White Unicorn [Bad Sister] *(General Film Distributors 1947)*
Edward, My Son *(MGM 1949)*
It Started in Paradise *(General Film Distributors 1952)*
Appointment in London *(British Lion 1953)*
Eight O'Clock Walk *(British Lion 1954)*
Don't Blame the Stork *(Adelphi 1954)*
The Door in the Wall *(Associated British Producers 1956)*
Pursuit of the Graf Spee [Battle of the River Plate] *(Rank Film Distributors 1957)*
Fortune Is a Woman [She Played with Fire] *(Rank Film Distributors 1957)*
Mad Little Island [Rockets Galore] *(Rank Film Distributors 1958)*
Northwest Frontier [Flame over India] *(Rank Film Distributors 1959)*
The Bulldog Breed *(Rank Film Distributors 1960)*
Dr. Blood's Coffin *(UA British 1961)*
The Treasure of Monte Cristo [The Secret of Monte Cristo] *(Regal Film International 1961)*
The Queen's Guards *(Imperial 1961)*
Guns of Darkness *(Cavalcade 1962)*
Act of Mercy *(British 1963)*

36

Josephine Hutchinson

Often a chance observation by a Hollywood movie-maker would suddenly lead to a performer's being signed to a contract, without either party giving careful consideration to whether they were suited for one another. Such was the case of handsome, titian-haired Josephine Hutchinson, the pride and joy of Eva Le Gallienne's Civic Repertory Theatre who was spotted by director Mervyn LeRoy. As a result of his enthusiasm about her performance as Nora in *A Doll's House*, she was signed to a three-film pact at Warner Bros. It was odd, because that studio mainly pushed out fast-paced headline-inspired melodrama or slick-slushy soap opera or gun-hitting gangster epics that hardly required such offbeat casting as this classic actress.

Josephine was born on Sunday, October 9, 1898, in Seattle, Washington, to building contractor Charles James Hutchinson and his wife Leona Doty (known on the stage and in Hollywood as Leona Roberts). During the summer of 1917 "Jo" and Mrs. Hutchinson were in Hollywood where her mother renewed an acquaintance with Douglas Fairbanks, Sr. Fairbanks subsequently arranged for Josephine to work in a picture version of *Sara Crewe* entitled *The Little Princess* (1917), starring Mary Pickford. The young lady was fascinated with film-making, Miss Pickford, and Hollywood, but her mother took her back to Seattle. There she studied acting with three different teachers, including Moroni Olsen; learned dance from George Faurot and Mary Ann Wells; and made her first stage entrance at Seattle's Metropolitan Theatre in *The Little Mermaid* (1920).

For two years Josephine was a member of the Rams Head Playhouse Company in Washington, D.C., and on April 12, 1924, she wed director-coach Robert Bell. When the Rams Head Company went to New York in June, 1925, to do four matinees of *The Bird Cage* at the 52nd Street Theatre, Josephine played Louisette. Later that year (October 13) she made her official Broadway debut at the same theatre in *A Man's Man*, featuring Dwight Frye and Pat O'Brien.

Early in 1926 she appeared in *The Unchastened Woman* and *One Day More*, and later that year (in November) she offered her first performance with Eva Le Gallienne's Civic Repertory Theatre when she succeeded Rose Hobart in *The Three Sisters*. Critics were extolling her talent and one wrote, "She is beautiful, direct and possessed of the emotional reserve that this department has just about decided must be a part of the equipment of any actress who wants the coveted Gold Star Award." Her training with Le

With Ross Alexander in *I Married a Doctor* (FN '36).

Gallienne's troupe was impressive and she played in repertory roles in *John Gabriel Borkman, Twelfth Night, The Cradle Song, The Sea Gull, The Cherry Orchard,* and as Wendy in *Peter Pan*. Her mother, Leona Roberts, also played in many of the Civic productions and, throughout the early Thirties, Josephine was alternating leads with Eva Le Gallienne and supporting her as Louise in *Alison's House* and Nichette in *Camille*.

During the summer of 1931 Josephine was rushed to the hospital along with Eva Le Gallienne and her maid, Marie Coo, when in lighting a water heater, it exploded and ignited Miss Le Gallienne's dress. Josephine and the maid frantically beat out the flames around Eva's dress, both receiving bad burns. The flaming apparel badly scarred Miss Le Gallienne, but all three soon recovered. On December 12, 1932, Miss Le Gallienne opened her delightful staging (with Florida Friebus) of *Alice in Wonderland*. Josephine was Alice with her mother as the Red Chess Queen, Eva as the White Chess Queen, and Burgess Meredith as a duck on roller skates. When the Civic Repertory took to the road for a national tour of *Alice,* that play was eventually replaced on the road by Ibsen's *A Doll House*. It was as Nora in a scene from the Ibsen drama that Josephine made her successful screen test for Warner Bros.

At the time, Kay Francis ruled the roost at the studio. When Josephine was contracted by the Burbank film factory it must have posed problems for their casting department. In fact, it is very evident, for her first assignment was in a musical with Dick Powell.

Mervyn LeRoy directed *Happiness Ahead* (1934) with Josephine as a wealthy girl posing as a poor miss after falling in love with a handsome window cleaner (Powell). Her first day in front of the camera was spent entirely kissing Powell, between rehearsals, retakes, and long shots. Perc Westmore of Warners' makeup department spent hours testing various hairdos and colorings for Josephine. Orry-Kelly did her wardrobe and Warners tried to launch a new star. But *Happiness Ahead* was merely a mildly entertaining musical—certainly nothing that would match the continuous teaming of Powell with tap-dancing Ruby Keeler.

If her initial adult screen introduction to the public was informal, her second Warners feature provided sufficient material to test her acting capabilities. *The Right to Live* started production in September, 1934, and was a remake of W. Somerset Maugham's *The Sacred Flame*. Cast as Stella Trent, she is wed to crippled Colin Clive and falls in love with his brother, George Brent. Although *Variety* tagged the film "sombre and agonizing," the cast carried off the adulterous triangle story extremely well. Director William Keighley said at the time: "If this girl isn't one of the three biggest box-office draws in pictures within the next twelve months, then I'm going to admit once and for all that absolutely nothing in this business can be predicted. She has everything—talent, personality, good looks and one of the clearest and quickest brains with which I have ever come in contact. While we were making *The Right to Live,* I didn't have to tell her anything; she knew beforehand the right thing to do in every instance. She knew the character she was playing inside out. It was a pleasure and a privilege to work with her."

When Josephine had arrived in Hollywood her marriage to Robert Bell had already been dissolved for 2 years (July 7, 1930). She was met at the train by James F. Townsend, an associate of her agent, Leland Hayward. He took charge of her luggage, arranged for pleasant hotel accommodations, and made himself almost indispensable. After she finished her first Warners film, Josephine and Townsend were married on January 12, 1935, in Yuma, Arizona.

Warner Bros. had hoped to sign Claudette Colbert for the role of Hester in *Oil for the Lamps of China* (1935). Since she was unavailable for this Mervyn LeRoy-directed film they put Josephine into the role, in which she played opposite her old Broadway friend, Pat O'Brien. The picture was overlong and overearnest, but it won a strong audience following. Warners then loaned her to United Artists for *The Melody Lingers On* (1935) to play the opera singer who has an affair with an Italian officer (George Houston) during World War I, and years later rediscovers her son to guide his musical career. Her success at portraying Madame Marie Pasteur, Paul Muni's wife in *The Story of Louis Pasteur* (1935), brought an announcment that the studio would film the life of Madame Curie with Josephine in the lead. But it eventually turned out to be Greer Garson at Metro in 1943 who played that role.

First National remade Sinclair Lewis' *Main Street* as *I Married a Doctor* (1936) and reteamed Josephine with Pat O'Brien as her doctor husband. From this story of small-town life, Warners put her into *Mountain Justice* (1937), a thinly veiled account ripped from a headlined story (the Edith Maxwell case). Josephine was top-billed with George Brent, offbeat casting for both players. She seemed an odd choice for the role of Ruth Harkins who kills her sadistic father (Robert Barrat) and is saved from a lynching by Brent. The picture was neither exciting nor successful, and it completed Josephine's Warner Bros. contract.

For "Lux Radio Theatre" Josephine played opposite Clark Gable in the April 5, 1937, broadcast of *A Farewell to Arms,* returning to the same program on June 28 with Walter Winchell and James Gleason in *The Front Page,* and again in February, 1939, with Robert Montgomery for *The Count of Monte Cristo.* She free-lanced at Metro, Columbia, and Universal. At the latter studio she played Elsa von Frankenstein in *Son of Frankenstein* (1939) with Basil Rathbone in the title role. This was the third and longest of that horror series and the last one in which Boris Karloff appeared as the Monster. During the filming Karloff and Josephine became staunch friends through their mutual love of flowers. On May 8, 1939, Josephine was reunited with Paul Muni on "Lux Radio Theatre" for *The Life of Emile Zola,* and that November she was heard on the program with Wallace Beery in *The Champ.*

With Mona Barrie and George Brent in *Mountain Justice* (WB '37).

291

With Ralph Bellamy and William Gargan in *The Crime of Dr. Hallett* **(Univ '38).**

Josephine's superior performance as Nellie Essex, dying and leaving her wretched son (Louis Hayward) to be raised by his father (Brian Aherne), was a polished piece of acting. On March 11, 1940, the four stars of the film *My Son, My Son*, Aherne, Madeleine Carroll, Hayward, and Hutchinson repeated their roles for "Lux Radio Theatre." For RKO's *Tom Brown's School Days* (1940) Josephine was appropriately cast as Cedric Hardwicke's wife. After playing Jane Withers' mother in *Her First Beau* (1941), an unimportant Columbia film, Josephine was off the screen for five years. She returned to give the best performance in Twentieth Century-Fox's *Somewhere in the Night* (1946) and then had a minor role in Metro's Spencer Tracy-Lana Turner starrer *Cass Timberlane* (1946).

With her film career definitely on the wane, she turned to a series of mother roles: Shirley Temple's in *Adventure in Baltimore* (1949). Elizabeth Taylor's in *Love Is Better than Ever* (1952), Jennifer Jones' in *Ruby Gentry* (1952), Eleanor Parker's in *Many Rivers to Cross* (1955), Jeffrey Hunter and Dean Stockwell's in *Gun for a Coward* (1957), and Colleen Miller's in *Step Down to Terror* (1958). For *Sing, Boy, Sing* (1958) she was Tommy Sands' aunt and in *The Adventures of Huckleberry Finn* (1960), with Eddie Hodges, she was the Widow Douglas.

In the mid-Fifties Josephine branched out into television. Her roles were small but always substantially handled. By the end of the Fifties her film appearances averaged about one or two a year, usually in minimum parts, but her video activities increased.

She was seen in four "Perry Mason" episodes, on "The Deputy" series, and in a "Dr. Kildare" segment. The 1968 telefilm *Storm over Elveron* had a powerful cast including in the younger group James Franciscus, Leslie Nielsen, and Shirley Knight, and in the older but superior group of performers, Franchot Tone, James Dunn, Stuart Erwin, and Josephine. That October, Josephine played Robert Stack's mother on a "Name of the Game" episode. Her acting gave Patricia Neal and Richard Thomas excellent support in the winning Christmas classic *The Homecoming,* televised first on December 19, 1971. Josephine still continues in her profession in minor parts. On the new teleseries "Little House on the Prairie" she recently popped up in a segment. On September 23, 1972 she wed Staats Cotsworth with whom she had acted in the Civic Repertory Company forty years earlier. He was the widower of actress Merriel Kirkland.

When Josephine was first approached about a movie career, her mother was less than enthusiastic about it, reluctantly telling her, "All right! Go ahead. But don't come back until you've learned the business." Her presence in any cast was assurance of good performing, but Warners did not work on building her into a major star. (Her beautifully modulated voice in itself was a unique instrument oncamera.) It was everyone's loss.

JOSEPHINE HUTCHINSON

The Little Princess *(Par 1917)*
Happiness Ahead *(WB 1934)*
The Right to Live *(WB 1935)*
Oil for the Lamps of China *(WB 1935)*
The Melody Lingers On *(UA 1935)*
The Story of Louis Pasteur *(WB 1935)*
I Married a Doctor *(FN 1936)*
Mountain Justice *(WB 1937)*
The Women Men Marry *(MGM 1937)*
The Crime of Dr. Hallett *(Univ 1938)*
Son of Frankenstein *(Univ 1939)*
My Son, My Son *(UA 1940)*
Tom Brown's School Days *(RKO 1940)*
Her First Beau *(Col 1941)*
Somewhere in the Night *(20th 1946)*
Cass Timberlane *(MGM 1947)*

The Tender Years *(20th 1947)*
Adventure in Baltimore *(RKO 1949)*
Love Is Better than Ever *(MGM 1952)*
Ruby Gentry *(20th 1952)*
Many Rivers to Cross *(MGM 1955)*
Miracle in the Rain *(WB 1956)*
Gun for a Coward *(Univ 1957)*
Sing, Boy, Sing *(20th 1958)*
Step Down to Terror *(Univ 1958)*
North by Northwest *(MGM 1959)*
The Adventures of Huckleberry Finn *(MGM 1960)*
Walk Like a Dragon *(Par 1960)*
Baby, the Rain Must Fall *(Col 1965)*
Nevada Smith *(Par 1966)*
Rabbit Run *(WB 1970)*

37

Kay Johnson

Kay Johnson had class. A lovely actress whose film career started with Cecil B. DeMille and ended with Mark Twain, she managed to make several interesting pictures. Had she actively pursued a screen career, backed by a studio build-up, Kay could have become a player of major prominence. But at the time she chose to find greater achievement and happiness in being Mrs. John Cromwell.

Kay was, in many ways, reminiscent of a young Judith Anderson and another fine actress Paramount did not develop, Gertrude Michael. Kay's acting had spirit and honesty, with a cool detachment that released an inner fire. While she never found the proper way to enchant the mass public, she did become somewhat legendary in Hollywood by doggedly holding her ground against the great Cecil B. DeMille and telling him to go to hell.

Kay was born as Catherine Townsend in Mount Vernon, New York, on Tuesday, November 29, 1904. She was educated at the Drew Seminary for Young Women, rebelled at seventeen, and determined to become an actress. She enrolled at Sargent's Dramatic School of the American Academy of Dramatic Art, where fellow student Spencer Tracy had graduated to the Theatre Guild's *R.U.R.* When the Guild sent *R.U.R.* on the road, Kay was signed for the part of Helena, the robot. She made her stage debut in that show in Chicago. Her first Broadway appearance was at the Punch and Judy Theatre on November 12, 1923. She was Laura Harper in *Go West, Young Man.* For the George S. Kaufman-Marc Connelly spirited hit, *Beggar on Horseback,* Kay played the role of Cynthia Mason for seven months in New York, four months in Chicago, and then on an extensive road tour with Spring Byington and Roland Young. Among her other appearances were in *The Morning After, All Dressed Up, One of the Family,* and *No Trespassing.* In February, 1927, she joined with Sylvia Sidney, Douglass Montgomery, Chester Morris, Kay Francis, and James Rennie in *Crime.*

During the winter of 1928 Kay was appearing in *A Free Soul* as Jan Ashe when she met actor-producer-director John Cromwell, who was then appearing in *Gentlemen of the Press.* He had just signed a contract with Paramount Pictures to act and direct. Shortly after their meeting, they became engaged. When the Coast sought Cromwell, he asked Kay to marry him and they left for California.

Kay later related her entrance on the Hollywood scene as unplanned and rather strange, with *no* idea of attempting motion pictures. "I said 'yes' and in a single day I'd

With John Mack Brown in *Billy the Kid* (MGM '30).

married and taken a train for Los Angeles. I'd fully made up my mind to quit the stage and just be a loving and devoted housewife but on the way out to Los Angeles, I got a telegram in Chicago asking me if I wouldn't like to play the lead in *The Silver Cord*." The Sidney Howard play was to be directed by Cromwell, who had directed the original New York production, and would be the first play presented to the 2,500 subscribers of the Los Angeles Civic Repertory Company. The cast starred Nance O'Neil, with Phillips Holmes, Philip Strange, and Kay featured.

Kay's astute playing of Christina, battling her husband's domineering mother for his possession and finally cutting "the silver cord," was seen by producer-director Cecil B. DeMille, who had recently (August 2, 1928) signed a contract with MGM to make his first talking picture. In discussing the casting of his first Metro film in his autobiography, Cecil B. DeMille referred to the young actress as, "the lovely Kay Johnson whose beautiful performance in *The Silver Cord* had shown me what talent she could bring to the new medium of talking pictures."

Dynamite (1929) was based on an idea of DeMille's gleaned from an actual death row marriage. Scripter Jeanie MacPherson concocted a tale of a society girl (Kay) wedding a tough miner (Charles Bickford) sentenced to death so that she can fulfill the requirements of her inheritance and be free to wed her lover (Conrad Nagel). But fate intervenes: the miner is reprieved and Kay is forced to live with him as his lawful wife in a wretched mining community. Nagel dies in a mine disaster and Kay eventually realizes her love for Bickford. *Dynamite* was advertised as, "She Denied Him Her Love, So He Took It! She Stole His Name, Tricked Him, Humbled Him and—in the end—Worshipped Him!"

The released film was 11,584 feet long and stretched the slim story to extremes. There was also a new DeMille bathtub for *Dynamite,* this one in glass with a spouting fountain of bath salts. The film also had a theme song that was better for its Jack King music than Dorothy Parker's lyrics. The song was sung in the film by a Mexican prisoner (Russ Columbo) during the marriage ceremony.

If DeMille's *Dynamite* did not blow box-office ratings skyward, there were plenty of fireworks during the filming. One scene Kay found so difficult to handle that she continually muffed her lines. DeMille's patience erupted and he said: "That's all right, Miss Johnson, don't let it bother you. Our production cost is only fifteen thousand dollars a day. Now, would you like a few hours out to study your lines, or shall we try a take?" When Kay fluffed the lines yet again, DeMille's sarcastic remarks hit new highs. Bickford urged Kay to "tell the son-of-a-bitch to go to hell." A further exchange of dialogue revealed that DeMille had picked up on his earphones Bickford's advice to Kay and the master intoned icily, "I'm still waiting, Miss Johnson." Kay's temper had reached its peak at that moment and, in a voice quivering with fury, she said: "You don't have to wait any longer Mr. DeMille. You can start any time. You go to hell!" The take was perfect and the fury Kay accumulated against the director flew at Bickford, making the scene perfect and winning the applause of the crew.

Afterwards, a beaming DeMille approached his two leads and embraced Kay, and told her how great the scene had turned out. He then gave Kay and Bickford each a twenty-dollar gold piece saying, "Those are DeMille medals. They are only awarded for what I consider magnificent performances."

Kay's other problems on *Dynamite* involved being rushed to the Cedars of Lebanon Hospital for an appendectomy and wrenching a kneecap during the filming of an automobile-racing scene. The hazards of Hollywood were beginning to make Broadway seem like heaven!

Metro followed Kay's impressive cinema debut by putting her in a potboiler, *The Ship*

In *The Spy* (Fox '31).

from Shanghai (1930). She and Conrad Nagel were wasted in this tale of mutiny and insanity. Her next film was directed by C. B.'s brother, William De Mille. In *This Mad World* (1930) Kay played the wife of a German general who encounters a French spy (Basil Rathbone) behind the lines. She has an affair with him until she discovers that he was responsible for her nephew's death, and turns him in to the German command. Then, depressed over her betrayal, she commits suicide. In these first three films, the studio released both silent and sound versions, requiring reshootings of parts of each film. Kay's fluency in the sound version did not carry through in the silent counterpart.

Metro loaned her to Paramount for their talking version of *The Spoilers* (1930) and she was more than adequate opposite Gary Cooper. Back at MGM, Louis B. Mayer thought Cecil B. DeMille's second studio film should be a musical. The director cast Kay in the title role. *Madam Satan* (1930) was vaguely culled from the same plot as Ferenc Molnar's *The Guardsman*, exchanging Molnar's jealous husband for a dull socialite wife (Kay) whose husband finds her less alluring than show girl Trixie (Lillian Roth). Masquerading as the mysterious, exotic, and erotic Madam Satan, she (Kay) lures him back during a gigantic party that takes place aboard a zeppelin moored near New York City. She successfully vamps her husband during an incredible ballet mechanique led by Russian dancer Theodore Kosloff that was devised and directed by LeRoy Prinz.

The music score for *Madam Satan* intruded on the story, what with the characters bursting into song without reason. The spectacle was saved for the finale when lightning strikes the dirigible, with the entire cast parachuting to earth in their fantastic ball costumes. *Madam Satan* cost approximately $980,000 and returned less than three-quarters of that investment.

If the score for *Madam Satan* was unmemorable, the costumes designed by Adrian were decidedly not. For Kay, Adrian devised an exotic creation using a flame motif that barely covered her breasts, with a split skirt to reveal her handsome legs. She wore a mask, covered her hair with sequined Mephistophelean horns, and a sharp widow's peak front piece. Her performance both as the dull home-loving wife of Reginald Denny and as the sexy, alluring Madam Satan was a thing of joy, but could not keep the picture from collapsing.

King Vidor's *Billy the Kid* (1930), with Johnny Mack Brown in the title role and Wallace Beery as Sheriff Pat Garrett, is still probably the best film about the famous outlaw. After Lucile Brown proved too inexperienced to play Claire, for whom Billy kills and kills again in order to revenge the death of her near husband, the studio cast Kay in the role. Following the location shooting on *Billy the Kid,* Kay was assigned to a triangular love story penned by Kathleen Norris and directed by William De Mille. *Passion Flower* (1930) did not live up to its title, despite the handsome playing of Kay Francis, Charles Bickford, and Kay Johnson. Years later Bickford would call it the daddy of all stinkeroos and the worst picture he ever made (and he was featured in some deadly entries).

In 1931, stage-loving Kay returned to the theatre for a tour in *The Silver Cord* with the original Mrs. Phelps, Laura Hope Crews. While she was on the road with this vehicle, two further pictures were released. Tiffany's *The Single Sin* (1931) was a miserable double-bill entry in which she was miscast and gave a forced performance. Fox's *The Spy* (1931) did nothing to reestablish her Hollywood career. For the first two months of 1932 she played Roxanne to Richard Bennett's lead in *Cyrano de Bergerac* on the stage.

For the first joint screen effort of writer Robert Riskin and director Frank Capra, Kay appeared to good advantage as Walter Huston's wife in *American Madness* (1932). It was a brave film subject, dealing with the evils and terrors of the country's Depression. Luckily there was a sterling cast of performers to portray the story: Walter Huston,

298

Constance Cummings, Pat O'Brien, Gavin Gordon, and Kay. Then for RKO, Kay played Helen, one of *Thirteen Women* (1932) oriental Myrna Loy sets out to methodically kill for their snubbing of her in finishing school. Kay returned to the stage for the West Coast production of *When Ladies Meet.* Paramount's *Eight Girls in a Boat* had overtones of the much better German film, *Maedchen in Uniform,* but Kay did well with the role of the gym instructress.

John Cromwell transferred to RKO to direct an Irene Dunne vehicle, *This Man Is Mine* (1934), and he cast Kay as Bee McCrea. It was a small but showy role, presenting her as a sardonic, sagacious gal blessed with many of the script's best lines. She tossed them off expertly with pure professionalism. Husband John's next RKO assignment was the superb filming of W. Somerset Maugham's novel *Of Human Bondage* (1934), starring Leslie Howard and Bette Davis. Kay performed the part of Nora, an authoress of romantic novels pursuing a romance with rejected, crippled Leslie Howard. She fades out of his life when he returns to the slatternly ex-waitress (Davis). After completing her role in RKO's *Their Big Moment* (1934), Kay returned to the theatre.

Following a vacation in London, spending a busman's holiday soaking up London's theatre, Kay saw one of the season's West End hits, *Living Dangerously.* When Lee Shubert offered her the role of Helen in the American production, co-starring Conway Tearle, she leaped at the chance. Unfortunately, on Broadway, the show lasted a mere nine performances. Kay refused to be led into the usual comparative trap of preference of theatre over films and cagily told reporters: "Both stage and screen have redeeming qualities. The movies pay better and the work is less exacting. Furthermore, there is a bigness, a completeness about the technical facilities of the films that the stage cannot hope to equal. The stage, on the other hand, offers the actor the thrill of direct contact with his audience. The films can offer nothing to compare with that. I'd almost forgotten what it was like."

Cromwell was assigned to direct RKO's version of *Village Tale* (1935), a Phil Stong novel of frustrated love in rural America. Kay played a farmer's wife loved by Randolph Scott. In *Jalna* (1935), the first of Mazo de la Roche's five novels chronicling the history of the Whiteoaks family, Cromwell directed Kay in the lead, with Jessie Ralph dominating in her performance as the grandmother. It was three years before Kay was onscreen again, this time at Warner Bros. as Claude Rains' fragile wife in *White Banners* (1938).

In March, 1938, after nearly ten years of marriage, Kay and John Cromwell adopted a two-year-old child to start a family. Then in May of 1939 Kay discovered that she was pregnant. Their firstborn, a son, John Oliver arrived on January 28, 1940. During her pregnancy she gave a splendid performance as Mrs. Mabel Manning seeing her Captain husband hacked to death before her eyes by Philippine terrorists in *The Real Glory* (1939).

Kay found motherhood entrancing, but when Darryl F. Zanuck hired Cromwell to direct Twentieth Century-Fox's version of *Benjamin Blake,* called *Son of Fury* (1942), Kay accepted a small role in this Tyrone Power swashbuckler. The next year she accepted a featured part in RKO's *Mr. Lucky* (1943), starring Cary Grant. In this picture she was teamed again with her *Dynamite* co-star, Charles Bickford. The following year, forty-year-old Kay played the mother of Fredric March, Mrs. Jane Clemens, wife of Judge Clemens (Frank Wilcox), in Warner Bros.' *Adventures of Mark Twain.* This 1944 biographical film proved to be her last feature film assignment.

Her years of stage experience did not go untapped; in the summer of 1945 she was offered a meaty supporting role in Howard Lindsay and Russel Crouse's *State of the Union.* Kay was sparkling as the newspaper publisher seeking a presidential candidate. Beautifully gowned, she was excellent in her role of backing Ralph Bellamy for the

With Molly Lamont and David Manners in *Jalna* (RKO '35).

Presidency. After a year Kay left the show and was replaced by Margalo Gillmore. It was Kay's last acting assignment.

In the late Forties Kay and Cromwell were divorced. Later returning more and more to stage acting, Cromwell, who remarried, won the 1952 Tony Award for Best Supporting Actor of the Year for his performance in *Point of No Return.* He later appeared in the hit comedy *Mary, Mary,* and recently has been working on his memoirs.

On November 17, 1975, Kay died at her Waterford, Connecticut, home, her death receiving scant notice in the trade papers.

Early in her career, Cecil B. DeMille recognized the talent Kay Johnson possessed. Sadly, Hollywood never used that talent to its fullest.

KAY JOHNSON

Dynamite *(MGM 1929)*
The Ship from Shanghai *(MGM 1930)*
This Mad World *(MGM 1930)*
Billy the Kid *(MGM 1930)*
The Spoilers *(Par 1930)*
Madam Satan *(MGM 1930)*
Passion Flower *(MGM 1930)*
The Single Sin *(Tiffany 1931)*
The Spy *(Fox 1931)*
American Madness *(Col 1932)*
Thirteen Women *(RKO 1932)*

Eight Girls in a Boat *(Par 1934)*
This Man Is Mine *(RKO 1934)*
Of Human Bondage *(RKO 1934)*
Their Big Moment *(RKO 1934)*
Village Tale *(RKO 1935)*
Jalna *(RKO 1935)*
White Banners *(WB 1938)*
The Real Glory *(UA 1939)*
Son of Fury *(20th 1942)*
Mr. Lucky *(RKO 1943)*
Adventures of Mark Twain *(WB 1944)*

Allan Jones

Irving Thalberg once said there was never such a thing as a silent picture. From the early days of film-making, Hollywood had been fascinated with musicals. When talkies became a commercial reality, the hunt was on for photogenic singers. One such singer to make a vivid impression in the mid-Thirties was Allan Jones. Had MGM not had such a large investment in baritone Nelson Eddy, it is certain that the studio would have endorsed Jones as a major screen talent. Not only could he vocalize exceedingly well, but he was also quite handsome. However, due to its commitment to Eddy the studio never showcased Jones adequately. In the Sixties he was relegated to being known as pop singer Jack Jones' dad. However, in the Seventies, with the resurgence of nostalgia for the Golden Age of Hollywood, Allan has come back into his own once more.

Allan Jones was born on Monday, October 14, 1907, at Old Forge, outside of Scranton, Pennsylvania, the grandson and son of coal miners. His father, Daniel Jones, was foreman of a coal mine. Having a Welshman's innate love of singing, he taught his young son Allan to sing the Welsh folk song "Ar Hyd a Nos" ("All through the Night"). At the age of nine, Allan was the boy soprano soloist at Scranton's St. Luke's Episcopal Church. While going to school, he worked as a messenger boy, ran concessions at Scranton's Central High School sports games, and worked in the school cafeteria. At sixteen he entered the National Welsh Eisteddfod at the Academy of Music in Philadelphia, competing against experienced singers from all over the United States. He won the tenor solo honors.

Determined on a singing career, Allan went to work in the mines until he had accumulated $1,500. Then, in 1926, he received a scholarship from Syracuse University, but soon transferred to New York University where he began studying voice with Claude Warford. Allan became the soloist with the University Glee Club and was engaged as tenor soloist by the University Heights Presbyterian Church. He continued his voice studies with Warford in Paris and studied opera with Felix Leroux, *chef de chant* of the French National Opera. In the fall he went to London to study oratorio with the esteemed British conductor and musicologist, Sir Henry Wood. During the season 1927-1928 he played many singing engagements back in America. It was during this period that he met Dame Nellie Melba, who, until her death, would encourage the one-time coal miner from Old Forge in his chosen career.

With Walter Woolf King and Kitty Carlisle in *A Night at the Opera* (MGM '35).

In April 1929, Allan wed Marjorie Buel but the brief marriage soon ended and the former Miss Buel would retain custody of their son. Later that year he went back to Paris where he became American Church soloist and was signed by composer-conductor Reynaldo Hahn to sing leading roles with the Cannes Opera Company's summer season at Deauville. Two years later he returned to the United States to sing at Carnegie Hall with the combined New York Symphony and Philharmonic Orchestras in their first concert as the New York Philharmonic Orchestra under the direction of Walter Damrosch.

Allan made his Broadway debut in November 1931, playing the title role in an opera comique by Franz von Suppi, *Boccaccio.* Later came singing leads in a variety of operettas with the St. Louis Municipal Opera Company during the summer of 1932. In 1933 he signed with the Brothers Shubert to head their touring companies of *Blossom Time, The Only Girl,* and *The Student Prince.*

That fall the Shuberts mounted a version of Noël Coward's *Bitter Sweet* with Allan and Margaret Carlisle in the leads. After a lengthy road tour, it was brought to the Forty-Fourth Street Theatre on May 7, 1934 with Evelyn Herbert replacing Miss Carlisle. The favorable reviews cited Jones as ''a good actor with a fine voice and an air of friendly amusement,'' but the Coward musical lasted only two weeks. However, Allan was not long unemployed, for the Shuberts then assigned him to *Annina,* a rather complicated Rudolf Friml operetta. Both Jones and Mme. Maria Jeritza were complimented for their duet of the show's best song ''My Heart Is Yours.'' The reviewers termed Allan ''the best young tenor on the stage today,'' and added that he is ''handsome, acting with ease and his excellent voice quietly winning audience favor.'' However, the show, whose cast received plaudits on the road in Boston, Philadelphia, and Chicago, was not brought to Broadway. Along with the more sophisticated critics, the Shuberts decided that Friml's offering was too dated for the contemporary theatre.

With his reputation on the rise, Allan was next cast in a new musical written by Karl Hajos. It was based on the life of Stephen Foster and called *America Sings*. Unfortunately, a stagehand strike prevented its scheduled opening in Philadelphia on October 29, 1934. The curtain never went up, and instead Allan went to Hollywood, where he had been signed by MGM.

Actually Louis B. Mayer's studio had planned to co-star Jones with Jeanette MacDonald in a heavily mounted version of *Naughty Marietta* (1935), but the Shuberts refused to release Allan from his stage agreement, consequently, the studio looked elsewhere, eventually picking Nelson Eddy, who was under Metro contract. When the much-postponed *Naughty Marietta* was finally put into production and released, a new screen team was launched. Eddy and MacDonald became one of the cinema's most endearing acting-singing pairs.

When Allan finally did get to fulfill his MGM contract (he bought out his Shubert pact), he made his screen debut in Jean Harlow's *Reckless* (1935), and sang "Everything's Been Done Before." His next film assignment immersed him in one of the maddest, wildest, and, very possibly, the best of the Marx Brothers-organized chaos ever put on film. Certainly, *A Night at the Opera* (1935) is one of the finest film comedies ever made. The Irving Thalberg production had all the usual MGM gloss, and Sam Wood directed the film at a maddening pace.

On the very first day on the set witty Groucho greeted Jones with, "Hello, Sloucho." Allan asked what that was supposed to mean. Groucho growled, "You're the 4th Marx Brother in this!" Perhaps, the part could have been played by the retired Zeppo, but he lacked Jones' finesse, polish, and superb voice. In the course of the zany plot, Allan got to sing the Arthur Freed-Nacio Herb Brown song "Alone," which became a hit. At the time Groucho felt the song should be cut from the film, but Allan went to Irving Thalberg and pleaded to keep the number in the picture. The legendary Irving agreed, "The Marx Brothers know comedy—you know music. I'll leave it in." The song has become a standard and Allan's other song in the film, his solo, "Cosi Cosa," also enjoyed great popularity.

After these operatic insanities with the Marx Brothers, Allan returned to cinematic grand opera in sequences inserted into Metro's remake of *Rose-Marie* (1936), again starring MacDonald and Eddy. Jones' work in this operetta outing was confined to what he did best—sing. With Miss MacDonald he sang the death scene from *Romeo and Juliet* and did a superb solo of "E lucevan le stelle" in the prison scene from *Tosca*. Other footage of Jones was excised from the film, allegedly because it detracted from the starring team.

Then Allan was loaned to Universal for their grand-scale remake of *Show Boat* (1936), matching him with the versatile Irene Dunne. Also in the cast was Helen Morgan repeating her brilliant stage performance as Julie. To sing "Old Man River" the great Paul Robeson was cast as Joe, doubling in a newly written duet, "Ah Still Suits Me?," with Hattie McDaniel. Allan provided just the right flair for the ne'er-do-well Gaylord Ravenal. Jones and Miss Dunne sang and acted the two leads as well as they would ever be done, including Metro's handsome 1951 color remake with Howard Keel and Kathryn Grayson. Jerome Kern and Oscar Hammerstein II added a new song for Jones' Ravenal, "I Have the Room Above." Allan's screen career would never top *Show Boat*.

Back at MGM, he once again provided the love interest and sang a few songs in the Marx Brothers' milder comedy *A Day at the Races* (1937), which was directed again by Sam Wood. Then working at Metro was a lovely young actress named Irene Hervey. On Sunday, June 26, 1936, she became Mrs. Allan Jones, for the next twenty-one years.

With Irene Dunne in *Show Boat* (Univ '36).

(Allan also inherited Gail Christenson, Irene's five-year-old daughter from her first marriage.)

After Thalberg's death, Louis B. Mayer had the notion of pairing Jeanette MacDonald with someone other than Nelson Eddy, namely, Allan Jones. Together they made *The Firefly* (1937), with Allan cast as Don Diego spying for Napoleon while wooing Nina Maria (MacDonald). *The Firefly* was to become indelibly stamped on Jones' career by Herbert Stothart's musical revision of an early Friml melody, "Chansonette," with lyrics now provided by Bob Wright and Chet Forrest. It was inserted in the film as a solo for Jones and retitled "The Donkey Serenade." After the film's release in 1937 Allan recorded the song for RCA Red Seal Victor with another of his *Firefly* solos, the beautiful "Giannina Mia," on the flip side. The record became the third largest selling single record in RCA's history.

In November, 1937, Allan was master of ceremonies for the new "Metro-Maxwell House Radio Hour" with guests Sigmund Romberg, Rosalind Russell, James Stewart, Mickey Rooney, Fannie Brice, and Judy Garland. With the latter two, Allan would join in *Everybody Sing* (1938), a frivolous account of a wacky theatrical family with Jones as Ricky Zaboni, the crooning chef. Allan reprised "Cosi Cosa" from his first Marxian adventure plus another solo from *Everybody Sing*, "The One I Love," on a Victor recording. The day following the making of these records, on January 14, 1938, he became the father of John Allan Jones.

Unfortunately for Allan, his temperament and that of Louis B. Mayer clashed and he was "benched" for the remainder of his Metro tenure, a prime example of a major talent being wasted. When he was freed from Culver City, he went to Paramount to make *The Great Victor Herbert* (1939), in which Susanna Foster made her film debut. The only thing "great" about the film was the music, as magnificently sung by Jones, Mary Martin, and Foster. Allan's final fling at Paramount—where Bing Crosby was the premier crooner—was a straight role in a dreary affair called *Honeymoon in Bali* (1939), in which he, Fred MacMurray, and Madeleine Carroll were lost in a tropical shuttle. Allan at least got to sing the aria "O Paradiso" from *L'Africaine*.

With Jeanette MacDonald in *The Firefly* (MGM '37).

Still anxious to make his mark in the cinema, Allan joined the ranks of Universal, yet another step downward from his MGM days. The studio brought Rodgers and Hart's *The Boys from Syracuse* (1940) to the screen with Allan playing the dual role of Antipholus of Ephesus and his twin from Syracuse. With Rosemary Lane, Allan dueted "Falling in Love with Love" and soloed in a new number, "Who Are You?" Irene Hervey played the role of Adriana, and it marked the first appearance together on screen of the married couple. "We weren't exactly jittery," Miss Hervey recalls, "just nervous about how we'd react to each other in a scene. It's an unaccustomed feeling to face your husband before the cameras with 100 members of the cast and crew looking on and the credibility of the scene resting on your shoulders. After the first scene we were all right. But all through the first romantic 'mood' I expected Allan or myself to break down and say, 'Oh, be yourself, honey!'" The Eddie Sutherland-directed film was lively and sparkled with comedic performances from Martha Raye, Joe Penner, and Charles Butterworth.

Earl Derr Biggers' *Love Insurance* had been filmed first in 1919 and served for the basis of yet another film. Then Universal persuaded Jerome Kern to set it to music with lyrics by Dorothy Fields. Thus *One Night in the Tropics* emerged in 1940, and it featured a new film comedy team, Bud Abbott and Lou Costello. As the film was in production, the studio heads decided to expand the roles of the funsters at the expense of the rest of the cast. Although Allan had a sparkling Kern song, "Remind Me," to sing, among others, the picture definitely belonged to Abbott and Costello who proved to be a rib-tickling sensation. Allan, once again, became the unheralded straight man.

In November, 1940, Allan was cast in a minor Universal musical, *Las Vegas Nights*, but he contracted the flu and was replaced by tenor Phil Regan. The next year he returned to Paramount for *There's Magic in Music*, which was a showcase for the talents of Susanna Foster.

While Jones was laboring in lesser musicals at lesser studios, MGM was making *Bitter Sweet* (1940), *The New Moon* (1940), and *The Chocolate Soldier* (1941) with Nelson Eddy. All three musicals had been successfully done by Allan on the stage and he would have excelled in the screen versions. However, his final Paramount effort was a preposterous comedy called *True to the Army* (1942) in which the spotlight was on the hyperactive Judy Canova and the spirited Ann Miller. Back at Universal he had the title role in a sleeper, *When Johnny Comes Marching Home* (1942), a feature aided considerably by Donald O'Connor, Gloria Jean, and Peggy Ryan. *Rhythm of the Islands* (1943), with Universal's B-musical queen, Jane Frazee, was nothing to brag about, but neither were the remainder of Allan's contract fodder.

During the war years, Allan entertained with U.S.O. shows and served out his Universal tenure. *Larceny with Music* (1943) joined him with Kitty Carlisle, and the songs, if not leaders on the hit parade, were the decent "Do You Hear Music?," "Please Louise," "Only in Dreams," and "For the Want of You." After two more minor musicals and a quickie guest appearance in Olsen and Johnson's *Crazy House* (1943), Allan returned to Broadway in *Jackpot*, which had a timely wartime background of three G.I.s and their gals. Jones starred with Jerry Lester and Benny Baker in the musical for sixty-nine performances after it opened on January 13, 1944. Nanette Fabray, Betty Garrett, and Mary Wickes completed the sextette. Surprisingly the Howard Dietz-Vernon Duke songs were unmemorable.

While *Jackpot* was trying out on the road in the latter part of 1943, Irene Hervey was recovering from a broken knee cap received in an automobile accident several months before. She joined Allan in the East and was signed for the lead of Dr. Enid Karley in *No Way Out*. That show lasted eight performances in October, 1944.

Still game, Allan returned to the West Coast and finished his Universal contract with three low-budget musicals, the studio specialty. Then he formed his own troupe and toured England for nearly two years. The trek culminated in a command performance at the Palladium in London before the King and Queen of England. During 1947 Irene Hervey toured with the national company of *State of the Union* and in 1948 Allan was on the road with Ed Wynn, Phil Baker, and Sid Silvers. Jones continued thereafter with club work and concert tours, and for Edwin Lester's Civic Light Opera Association he opened as Sky Masterson in *Guys and Dolls*, which had capacity runs in San Francisco and Los Angeles. His performance in the Frank Loesser-Damon Runyon fable was one of his best stage appearances. However, the studios took no notice and did not clamor for his services.

The year 1954 was a disruptive one for the Joneses. On June 17, Irene filed for a divorce, but the couple were reconciled before the decree became final. Three years later, Miss Hervey was again back in the courts, intent on dissolving their 21-year-old marriage on the grounds of "grievous suffering" and demanding custody of their son. The case was transferred to Nevada to speed up the proceedings; she received an uncontested divorce on December 28, 1957. In early 1958, Allan wed Mary Florsheim Picking, heiress to the Florsheim shoe fortune. She made headlines that November when removed from their Westwood, California, home after being found unconscious. Jones denied his second wife had taken an overdose of barbiturates following an argument. She returned home from the Los Angeles Medical Center November 11, 1958.

By the late Fifties Allan and his son Jack were performing a dual club act, but after the divorce the team was disbanded and Allan did a single in Las Vegas. He performed well and his health (he had suffered prior slight heart attacks) was buoyant. While son Jack continued to gain fame as a singer and an often-married performer, Allan continued his stage career mainly in the summer theatre. In 1966 he appeared with Darryl Hickman in *How to Succeed in Business without Really Trying* and for the next five years was to be seen in presentations of *Silk Stockings, Paint Your Wagon, The Fantasticks,* and *The Happy Time.*

It was not until 1971 that he gave the greatest performance of his career. At age sixty-two he had a role that seemed tailored for his talents, both acting and, especially, singing. As the lead of *Man of La Mancha* he was superb. His singing of the almost hymnal "The Impossible Dream" was perfectly pitched with clarity and force that denied his years. In 1972 Allan joined a revue geared to the recurrent wave of nostalgia called *The Big Show of 1936.* He served as master of ceremonies and reprised several of his all-time hit songs in a company that included Sally Rand, Cass Daley, Beatrice Kay, the Ink Spots, Jackie Coogan, and Virginia O'Brien. The show collapsed in Philadelphia in the spring of 1972.

Jones currently resides in New York in the West Sixties with wife number four, dancer Esther Maria Villavincie. (He and Mary Florsheim had divorced in 1964.) Allan continues to make concert and club appearances and has recently recorded a new LP album of trademark songs in England.

No one in Hollywood's Thirties brought to the screen a finer singing voice than Allan Jones. He may have been too jaunty (some said too stiff) as an actor, but no one yet has been able to sing "The Donkey Serenade" quite as well. One can only speculate what might have been his professional lot had not other performers captured the lead spots for which Allan so long contended, and deserved.

ALLAN JONES

Reckless *(MGM 1935)*
The Great Ziegfeld *(MGM 1936—voice only)*
A Night at the Opera *(MGM 1935)*
Ramona *(20th 1936)*
Rose-Marie *(MGM 1936)*
Show Boat *(Univ 1936)*
A Day at the Races *(MGM 1937)*
The Firefly *(MGM 1937)*
Everybody Sing *(MGM 1938)*
The Great Victor Herbert *(Par 1939)*
Honeymoon in Bali *(Par 1939)*
The Boys from Syracuse *(Univ 1940)*
One Night in the Tropics *(Univ 1940)*
There's Magic in Music *(Par 1941)*
True to the Army *(Par 1942)*

Moonlight in Havana *(Univ 1942)*
When Johnny Comes Marching Home *(Univ 1942)*
Rhythm of the Islands *(Univ 1943)*
Larceny with Music *(Univ 1943)*
You're a Lucky Fellow, Mr. Smith *(Univ 1943)*
Crazy House *(Univ 1943)*
The Singing Sheriff *(Univ 1944)*
Honeymoon Ahead *(Univ 1945)*
The Senorita from the West *(Univ 1945)*
Stage to Thunder Rock *(Par 1964)*
A Swingin' Summer *(United Screen Arts 1965)*

39

Victor Jory

Someone once said Ella Fitzgerald could probably sing the telephone book. Likewise, Victor Jory could probably act any impossible piece given him. Ruggedly, angularly, darkly handsome Jory stands six feet, one and one-half inches. He was once the light heavy weight boxing champion of British Columbia. However after fighting nine professional fights he decided acting was less hazardous. In the early Thirties he became something of an acclaimed matinee idol. He has been acting almost fifty years and can still be seen infrequently on television shows.

Victor is of French (Alsace-Lorraine) extraction and was born on Sunday, November 23, 1902, to Edwin and Joanna Snyder Jory at Dawson City, Yukon territory, Alaska. His father became a rancher when the gold fever subsided, and his only child, Victor Edwin Jory, attended schools in Dawson City and Vancouver. Later he graduated from the Pasadena High School, attended Fullerton College for two years, and then joined Gilmor Brown's famed Pasadena Playhouse in 1923.

With the Pasadena Community Players he performed all sorts of roles in a range of plays authored by anyone from Pirandello to Avery Hopwood. He even played Caligula in Eugene O'Neill's *Lazarus Laughed.* Moving eastward Victor joined the Denham Theatre stock company in Denver, Colorado. Four months after meeting his leading lady, Jean Inness, he married her on December 23, 1928, in Burns, Wyoming, returning to Denver to play the company's production of *Stella Dallas.*

In 1930 Jory became leading man for Chamberlain Brown's permanent stock repertory company at the Riviera Theatre in Manhattan. For Brown's second season at the Westchester, New York, theatre, Victor continued as resident leading man. The season opened on September 21, 1931, with *What Every Woman Knows* and he played opposite Pauline Lord. Thereafter he appeared in *Dishonored Lady* with Alice Brady, had the Leslie Howard role in *Berkeley Square,* the lead in *On the Spot* with Agnes Ayres, and was featured in *The Truth Game* with Fannie Ward. Later Jory appeared with stock companies in the Ohio cities of Cincinnati, Columbus, and Dayton, and returned to California to play John the Baptist in Hollywood's *Pilgrimage Play.* In the annual outdoor production at Hemet, California, he appeared as Allessandro in *Ramona.*

Jory entered films in a rather minor way. He had a bit in *Renegades* (1930) at Fox, a picture starring Warner Baxter and featuring Myrna Loy, C. Henry Gordon, and Bela Lugosi. Two years later Victor had a larger role in the Rin Tin Tin, Jr. vehicle, *The Pride*

With Leslie Fenton, Walter Connolly, and Fay Wray in *White Lies* **(Col '34).**

of the Legion (1932). He played a mug in *Handle with Care* (1933) and was lost in a vintage slapstick affair in James Dunn's *Sailor's Luck* (1933). He then signed a term contract at Fox where he was in eleven features in 1933. Will Rogers, Charles Farrell, Warner Baxter, Spencer Tracy, and James Dunn were the studio's top leading men, and Victor was used to fill supporting roles.

Although he was impressive as the garrulous barker in *State Fair* (1933), his role of Stone in *Broadway Bad* (1933) was practically deleted. But his polished, sophisticated performing as the deep-toned married roue pursuing Elissa Landi in *I Loved You Wednesday* (1933) impressed the Fox brass. Studio executive Winfield Sheehan assigned him the lead of Foreign Legion army surgeon Andre in *Devil's in Love* (1933), with Loretta Young. *Photoplay* cited Jory's performance as Andre as one of the best of the month, and word was out that the studio was grooming the lanky Alaskan for stardom. His bright, penetrating eyes and curly black hair, to say nothing of his slightly wistful sardonic smile and emphatic masculinity, were certain to entrance the distaff side of any moviegoing audiences. But the great promise was short-lived. He was assigned roles in minor pictures, with the exception of the part of the tough but soft-spoken bronc buster Clint in *Smoky* (1933).

Jory resided in Pasadena and was not part of the Hollywood colony. He found his own brand of contentment with his wife and two-year-old daughter Jean. He wrote two plays *(Five Who Were Mad, Bodies by Fisher)*, both of which were produced. He was informing the press at the time that his main interest in films was for the money. Early in 1934 it became obvious that Fox, which was undergoing another regime changeover, was not building Jory into star status. He left the studio to free-lance.

311

As Portuguese fisherman Nick Gardella, hoping to marry Joan Blondell, Jory was fine in the seventh and last of the Blondell-James Cagney pictures, *He Was Her Man* (1934). Also at Warner Bros. Victor was cast as d'Aiguillon in Dolores Del Rio's *Madame Du Barry* (1934). He then slid into a series of programmers until Warners recalled him to join their all-star cast for Max Reinhardt's *A Midsummer Night's Dream* (1935). Jory stood out as Oberon, playing the dark and sinister figure with assurance. From Shakespearean fantasy, Jory dropped back into B films until he was assigned to Columbia's Graustarkian musical nonsense with Grace Moore, *The King Steps Out* (1936).

Through the remaining Thirties, Victor slid into a rut of playing oversized Charles Middleton-type sinister roles. He did two films in England, *Glamorous Night* (1937) with Mary Ellis and *Bulldog Drummond at Bay* (1937) with Dorothy Mackaill and John Loder. One of Jory's favorite screen parts came along with *The Adventures of Tom Sawyer* (1938) as Injun Joe. His screen portrayals thereafter varied from heavies (Yancy in *Dodge City*, 1939) to straight supporting fare (Lieutenant Parsons in *Wings of the Navy*, 1939) to even playing Wolf Pelt in Shirley Temple's *Susannah of the Mounties* (1939). The most memorable of his eleven 1939 assignments was his role as Jonas Wilkerson, former overseer and outraged carpetbagger in *Gone with the Wind*.

Victor's career seemed to take an upswing in the new decade, when he went to Columbia for two serials. In the fifteen-episode *The Shadow* (1940) he played three roles: Lamont Cranston, Lin-Chang, and the Shadow. For another fifteen-chapter cliffhanger, *The Green Archer* (1940), he had the lead of Spike Holland. But his career continued to be erratic. Although he was a fine actor, capable of playing any role given to him (and he did), his screen career ran a strange, almost inexplicable course of ups and downs, but always in a minor key. He tuned up as Clay Beaudine in *The Lone Wolf Meets a Lady* (1940) and did three Westerns in 1940 for Paramount, including the fourth remake of Zane Grey's *The Light of Western Stars*. At Warners, he was in their third remake of James Oliver Curwood's *River's End* (1940) and remained on the lot to support Miriam Hopkins in a commercial disaster called *Lady with Red Hair* (1940).

From 1941 through 1943, seasoned Victor appeared in seven of William Boyd's Hopalong Cassidy features, was seen in *Charlie Chan in Rio* (1941), and then returned to the Warren William detective series in *Secrets of the Lone Wolf* (1941). He then gravitated back to the stage. In Chicago he was in *Angel Street,* and on August 3, 1943, he was featured as Geoffrey in *The Two Mrs. Carrolls,* starring Elisabeth Bergner. Jory's fascination with the footlights had never abated and during his film years he had kept in touch by producing and starring in Los Angeles in *Shadow and Substance, Kind Lady,* and Elmer Rice's *Not for Children*. He also continued his association with the Pasadena Playhouse as a special counsellor.

The Two Mrs. Carrolls seemed destined to run forever with Victor as the husband intent on murdering his wife. The show finally closed on February 3, 1945, after 585 performances. By then Jory had left the production to take the role of Dale Williams, the husband of Miriam Hopkins, in *The Perfect Marriage*. The Samson Raphaelson comedy opened on October 26, 1944, at Broadway's Barrymore Theatre and lasted 92 performances.

With his resonant speaking voice, it was natural that Victor should be involved with radio. He had his own show, "Matinee Theatre," and played such diversified roles as Lord Essex, Sir Walter Raleigh, and Francois Villon. Elsa Maxwell became one of his great radio fans and proclaimed, "He is the first radio star to link the spoken voice with sex-appeal." The Jory family, including wife and daughter, son Jon, and the family cook Elvira Jensen, moved East where it was obvious that Victor's career would keep him.

With Grant Mitchell, Anita Louise, Kay Francis, Henry O'Neill, Preston Foster, and Verree Teasdale in *First Lady* (WB '37).

313

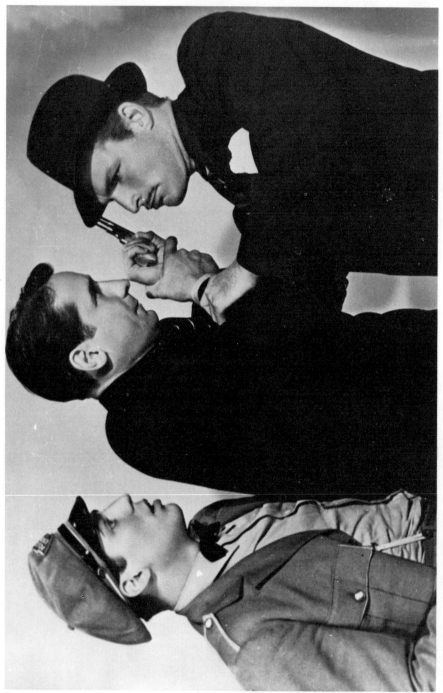

With Billy Halop and Buster Crabbe in *Call a Messenger* (Univ '39).

314

In the spring of 1945 he had a short out-of-town opening and closing in Rachel Crothers' *Bill Comes Back*. That autumn he starred with Eva Le Gallienne and Dame May Whitty in *Therese*, directed by Dame May's daughter, Margaret Webster. The show debuted on October 9, 1945, and lasted ninety-six performances on Broadway. Thereafter it was announced that Victor had been selected as leading man for Miss Le Gallienne's American Repertory Theatre, with its play productions to be directed by Margaret Webster.

Victor was providing additional news to the press. "I left the film with only one pride. I never used a double for any of my riding scenes." He spoke with pleasure about learning to ride a horse in Hollywood and was not bitter about specializing in Westerns and "heavies" onscreen. He was happy to be one of the few screen players who could ride and act. Regarding the new American Repertory Theatre, Jory said, "I consider myself lucky to be connected with three women I most admire in the Theatre. Cheryl Crawford is the best business woman, Peggy Webster the best director and Eva Le Gallienne the most artistic and brilliant actress." After all of *this* it seemed unlikely that he would ever be asked back to Hollywood. But he was.

With the American Repertory Theatre, Jory starred with Miss Le Gallienne, Walter Hampden, June Duprez, Ernest Truex, Richard Waring, Philip Bourneuf, and Margaret Webster in *Henry VIII*. (The company also included Efrem Zimbalist, Jr., Eli Wallach, and William Windom.) Through March, 1947, Victor also played the lead in *John Gabriel Borkman*, Ferrovius in *Androcles and the Lion*, and James Carroll in *Yellow Jack*. In the latter part of the year he toured in *The Girl of the Golden West*. He then came back to California where he played three more years of supporting roles in films. Then in January, 1950, he was back in New York with the New York City Theatre Company's production of *The Devil's Disciple*, starring Maurice Evans, Dennis King, and Marsha Hunt. Jory played Minister Anthony Anderson. In the summer of 1950 Victor, with his wife and daughter in the same cast, toured the summer theatres in *The Spider*. In 1951 he toured in *Mr. Barry's Etching*, and the next summer played in *Private Lives* with Alexis Smith. In June of 1952 he took over the part played by Richard Whorf on Broadway in *Season in the Sun* and later that year toured in the play with Nancy Kelly. The summer of 1953 found him paired with Alexis Smith again, this time in *Bell, Book and Candle*.

With his wide media experience, Victor did several television shows in 1950. In 1952 he was excellent in a telecast of *Angel Street*. By the Fifties his film appearances declined to two a year, but the versatile Mr. Jory tackled a new medium: records. He started recording children's albums with "Story of the Confederacy" and continued in this field. His video appearances through the decade were highlighted by playing Captain Ahab on "Hallmark Hall of Fame's " *Moby Dick*, and joining in *A Connecticut Yankee in King Arthur's Court*, playing the marvelous wily magician, Merlin.

In 1955 Jory tried out a new play, *The Fairly Fortune*, and that September he debuted in the teleseries "Kings Row" as Dr. Tower. He made three more films in 1956 and was seen on Senator John F. Kennedy's "Profiles in Courage" series on Kraft television as Thaddeus Stevens involved in impeachment proceedings against President Andrew Johnson. In the summer of 1958 he was back on the straw-hat stage in *The Happiest Millionaire* and that fall starred in the "Manhunt" teleseries as a San Diego detective lieutenant. He told the press, "I can think of at least 40 actors who could play this part better than I can. Hollywood is full of fine, young actors who aren't working and young non-actors who are."

Jory was effective as the cancer-riddled husband of Anna Magnani in *The Fugitive Kind* (1960), a Marlon Brando film dud. Tennessee Williams' dramas were no stranger

315

to Victor, as he and his wife had toured in 1958 in Williams' *Cat on a Hot Tin Roof.* While his television work escalated and excelled in the Sixties, he was only rarely seen in feature films. From playing Helen Keller's father in *The Miracle Worker* (1952) he went to playing yet another Indian in John Ford's *Cheyenne Autumn* (1964).

His son, Jon, joined the Long Wharf Theatre at New Haven as a director and in 1965 directed a wide range of diversified plays. After a second season there, he transferred his talents to Princeton's McCarter Theater and to the Charles Playhouse in Boston. By 1970 he was at the Actor's Theatre in Louisville, Kentucky, and, that February, directed his father in *Cat on a Hot Tin Roof* and *Tobacco Road.* Meanwhile Victor continued with occasional movie roles. He was the narrator for *Mackenna's Gold* (1969) and was Wounded Bear Mr. Smith in Anthony Quinn's *Flap* (1970). Also in 1970 Victor, this time with his wife Jean, was directed by son Jon in *Our Town* in Louisville and, not directed by Jon, appeared with the Actor's Theatre there in December in *A Thurber Carnival.*

The Jorys were back in Louisville with the Actor's Theatre in 1972 for *A Man for all Seasons.* On November 16, Victor took over the directorial reins for *You Can't Take it With You,* with his wife in the cast. In April, 1972, Victor excelled as Willy Loman in *Death of a Salesman,* directed by son Jon for the Louisville Theatre. *Tricks,* with book by Jon Jory and music by Jerry Blatt (with Jon directing), opened on Broadway in January, 1973, but lasted just one week.

Even now, in his mid-seventies, Victor continues to act whenever the opportunity presents itself. In recent years, he was on television episodes of "Banacek" and "Nakia," in the latter playing an American Indian. He is still one of the most versatile actors Hollywood has known: a player with great talent, not just a star with personality.

VICTOR JORY

Renegades *(Fox 1930)*
The Pride of the Legion *(Mascot 1932)*
Handle with Care *(Fox 1933)*
Sailor's Luck *(Fox 1933)*
State Fair *(Fox 1933)*
Infernal Machine *(Fox 1933)*
Broadway Bad *(Fox 1933)*
Trick for Trick *(Fox 1933)*
Second Hand Wife *(Fox 1933)*
I Loved You Wednesday *(Fox 1933)*
My Woman *(Fox 1933)*
Devil's In Love *(Fox 1933)*
Smoky *(Fox 1933)*
He Was Her Man *(WB 1934)*
I Believed in You *(Fox 1934)*
Murder in Trinidad *(Fox 1934)*
Madame Du Barry *(WB 1934)*
White Lies *(Col 1934)*
Pursued *(Fox 1934)*
Mills of the Gods *(Col 1935)*
Party Wire *(Col 1935)*
Streamline Express *(Mascot 1935)*
A Midsummer Night's Dream *(WB 1935)*
Escape from Devil's Island *(Col 1935)*
Too Tough to Kill *(Col 1935)*
Hell-Ship Morgan *(Col 1936)*
The King Steps Out *(Col 1936)*
Meet Nero Wolfe *(Col 1936)*
Glamorous Night *(Associate British Pictures 1937)*
First Lady *(WB 1937)*
Bulldog Drummond at Bay *(Rep 1937)*
The Adventures of Tom Sawyer *(UA 1938)*
Blackwell's Island *(WB 1939)*
Dodge City *(WB 1939)*
Wings of the Navy *(WB 1939)*
Man of Conquest *(Rep 1939)*
Women in the Wind *(WB 1939)*
Susannah of the Mounties *(20th 1939)*
Men with Whips *(Hoffberg, 1939)*
Each Dawn I Die *(WB 1939)*
I Stole a Million *(Univ 1939)*
Call a Messenger *(Univ 1939)*
Gone with the Wind *(MGM 1939)*
The Shadow *(Col serial 1940)*
The Green Archer *(Col serial 1940)*
Knights of the Range *(Par 1940)*
The Light of Western Stars *(Par 1940)*
The Lone Wolf Meets a Lady *(Col 1940)*
River's End *(WB 1940)*
Girl from Havana *(Rep 1940)*

Cherokee Strip *(Par 1940)*
Lady with Red Hair *(WB 1940)*
Give Us Wings *(Univ 1940)*
Border Vigilantes *(Par 1941)*
Wide Open Town *(Par 1941)*
Charlie Chan in Rio *(20th 1941)*
Bad Men of Missouri *(WB 1941)*
Secrets of the Lone Wolf *(Col 1941)*
Riders of the Timberline *(Par 1941)*
The Stork Pays Off *(Col 1941)*
Shut My Big Mouth *(Col 1942)*
Tombstone, the Town Too Tough to Die *(Par 1942)*
Hoppy Serves a Writ *(UA 1943)*
Buckskin Frontier *(UA 1943)*
The Leather Burners *(UA 1943)*
The Kansan *(UA 1943)*
Bar 20 *(UA 1943)*
Colt Comrades *(UA 1943)*
The Unknown Guest *(Mon 1943)*
Power of the Press *(Col 1943)*
The Loves of Carmen *(Col 1948)*
The Gallant Blade *(Col 1948)*
A Woman's Secret *(RKO 1949)*
South of St. Louis *(WB 1949)*
Canadian Pacific *(20th 1949)*
Fighting Man of the Plains *(20th 1949)*
The Capture *(RKO 1950)*
The Cariboo Trail *(20th 1950)*
The Highwayman *(AA 1941)*
Cave of Outlaws *(Univ 1951)*
Flaming Feather *(Par 1951)*
Son of Ali Baba *(Univ 1952)*
Toughest Man in Arizona *(Rep 1952)*
Cat Women of the Moon *(Astor 1953)*
The Hindu [Sabaka] *(Ferrin 1953)*
The Man from the Alamo *(Univ 1953)*
Valley of the Kings *(MGM 1954)*
Manfish *(UA 1956)*
Blackjack Ketchum, Desperado *(Col 1956)*
Death of a Scoundrel *(RKO 1956)*
The Man Who Turned to Stone *(Col 1957)*
Last Stagecoach West *(Rep 1957)*
The Fugitive Kind *(UA 1960)*
The Miracle Worker *(UA 1962)*
Cheyenne Autumn *(WB 1964)*
Jigsaw *(Univ 1968)*
Mackenna's Gold *(Col 1969)*
Flap *(WB 1970)*
A Time for Dying *(Etoile 1971)*
Papillon *(AA 1974)*

40

Arline Judge

Intermittently Arline Judge had a career in motion pictures. Between films she married. And married. And married. In the Hollywood marital sweepstakes she was equaled only by another perpetual bride, Lana Turner. Arline emerged on the screen in the early Thirties, a refreshing comedienne who could be effective in more serious roles. But she was also an anachronism even for the Thirties. Her proper niche should have been the Twenties, the era of jazzy flappers, flaming youth, a time of alleged utter nonsense when she would have been considered normal. But despite this anachronism, Miss Judge sparkled and glowed on the Thirties' screens with a perky personality, displaying overtones and undertones of a young Clara Bow, Sue Carol, or Helen "Boop-Boop-a-Doop" Kane.

Arline was born in Bridgeport, Connecticut, on Wednesday, February 21, 1912. Her father, a newspaperman, moved his family to New York City where Arline attended parochial schools and later Ursuline Academy in the Bronx. At the latter she was voted the girl most likely to succeed. While at Ursuline she studied dancing with Jack Donahue, did a brief stint in vaudeville, and, through Donahue's influence, won a chorus job in Ruth Selwyn's *Nine-Fifteen Revue* (1929). Petite Arline (5', brunette, brown eyes, and curvaceous body) landed another Broadway show thereafter. It was *The Second Little Show* (1930), with sketches directed by Monty Woolley and music and lyrics mostly by Howard Dietz and Arthur Schwartz. The song hit of the show was contributed by Herman Hupfield, with Arline as one of three girls selected to sing the bouncy "Sing Something Simple." Her romance with West Point cadet Hugh Warner Stevenson ended with his graduation from the Academy. But popular and pursued Arline was never without another romance waiting in the wings. Also waiting in the wings was an RKO talent scout with a Hollywood contract.

Arline's film debut was predictable. She was cast as a "whoopee girl" in Lowell Sherman's *Bachelor Apartment* (1931). Then RKO loaned her to Paramount for the role of Bella Griffiths in Josef von Sternberg's *An American Tragedy*, in which Sylvia Sidney and Phillips Holmes had the leads. The first real impact Arline made on the screen was in Wesley Ruggles' stinging indictment of the youth of that day. It was all bitterly captured and delineated in his scripted-directed *Are These Our Children?* (1931). She played the role of Florence, a wild gin and jazz-mad teenager obsessed with fast living and the glitter of cheap dance halls. In her first serious acting assignment, Arline was

With Eddie Nugent in *College Scandal* (Par '35).

particularly effective, but Eric Linden's superior performance (also his screen debut) overshadowed Miss Judge. So did Mr. Wesley Ruggles, to whom she was married by Judge Fletcher Bowron in Ruggles' home at noon on October 15, 1931. The newlyweds honeymooned in British Columbia.

Arline returned to RKO for the Wheeler-Woolsey comedy version of *Girl Crazy* (1932), played a minor role of Maisie in *Love Starved* (1932) featuring the studio's champion weeper, Helen Twelvetrees, and was again directed by her husband in *Roar of the Dragon* (1932). Her comedic talent was evident in *Is My Face Red?* (1932), and she was excellent as the vixenish college campus waitress leading Richard Cromwell astray in *The Age of Consent* (1932). But then after she played Ralph Bellamy's two-timing wife in love with Eric Linden in *Flying Devils* (1933), RKO chose not to renew her contract. But she became a mother of a son, Wesley Ruggles, Jr.

Arline's annual birthday parties for Wesley, Jr. brought the famous offspring of top stars out *en masse*. The galas were imaginative and well publicized. All appeared to be content and well within the Ruggles menage. Between making an obvious success of marriage and motherhood, Arline free-lanced. She was in Monogram's *Sensation Hunters* (1934), a cheap tale set in Panama. She then teamed with Jack Oakie in *Looking for Trouble* (1934), a bad offbeat film that was directed, strangely enough, by William A. Wellman, and featured the likes of Spencer Tracy. Arline and Oakie were teamed again in *Shoot the Works* (1934), she making once again a splendid balance for his mugging. But for every good role, such as the vindictive office clerk in *One Hour Late* (1934), there were duds such as Monogram's cutesy *Million Dollar Baby* (1935). She went to Fox for their economically produced *George White's 1935 Scandals*. Although she was amusing as the bird-brained Midgie playing Cleopatra to Cliff "Ukelele Ike" Edward's Mark Anthony, the film was redeemed by the picture debut of the cinema's all-time best tap dancer, Eleanor Powell.

Spunky Arline continued to play a brace of shady ladies. In 1935 she was reunited with the ebullient Oakie for Twentieth Century-Fox's *King of Burlesque,* in which she was the ever-available, hell-bent-for-matrimony gal in hot pursuit of the elusive Oakie. However, it was Alice Faye, the star of the picture, who received all the audience notice. Arline remained at Fox to give a smooth performance in the George Raft-Rosalind Russell entry *It Had to Happen* (1936) and then to cavort in reels of slapstick episodes in *Here Comes Trouble* (1936).

Paramount assigned Wesley Ruggles to direct the screen version of Barry Benefield's challenging novel *Valiant Is the Word for Carrie* (1936), with Gladys George as the tarnished lady from the Louisiana bayous who "adopts" two waifs. Arline and John Howard were cast as the adult "children" of the sacrificial Miss George. But it was as a sharp-tongued comedienne that Arline was seen to best advantage. She returned to Twentieth Century-Fox to sparkle as a chorus girl in *Star for a Night* (1936) and then played Adolphe Menjou's justly suspicious, trombone-playing wife in Sonja Henie's *One in a Million* (1936).

Then Miss Judge started a new career for varying runs in two acts: marriage and divorce. On February 4, 1937, she sued Wesley Ruggles for divorce in Los Angeles charging he left home for long periods and humiliated and embarrassed her in front of their friends. She was soon courted by Daniel Reid Topping who defended Arline in a fist fight with Pat di Cicco. Director W. S. Van Dyke II, who witnessed the fight claimed both Topping and di Cicco missed one another so often it got to be a dull bore. But Arline left for Reno on February 25, 1937, and, a few hours after her divorce from Ruggles was granted (April 9, 1937), she married Topping at Virginia City. The couple had one child, Daniel, Jr.; but by September, 1939, Arline left Topping, taking both sons with her. She moved in with her chum, Sally Haines, Bert Wheeler's ex-wife.

With John Howard in *Valiant Is the Word for Carrie* (Par '36).

With Tony Martin and Dixie Dunbar in *Pigskin Parade* (20th '36).

By April 20, 1940, Arline was relating the horrors of her marriage to Topping to State Referee John W. Banks in her home town of Bridgeport, Connecticut. She claimed the volatile Topping had crashed through her bedroom door in a Palm Springs hotel the previous year, broke a bed, splintered furniture around the room, and had to be re-strained from assaulting her by her mother. According to Arline, the climax came when the hotel maid told Miss Judge she had seen Topping kissing a young, luscious female guest. The referee recommended divorce. On grounds of cruelty, Arline was freed from Topping on May 3, 1940, in Bridgeport, Connecticut. She left the next day to attend the Kentucky Derby at Churchill Downs in Louisville. Her companion was James M. Bryant, an executive of the Hotel Pierre in New York City.

On the morning following the big race, Arline and Mr. Bryant returned to Louisville and announced to the press that somewhere in Kentucky between six o'clock the previous evening and three o'clock that morning they had been married. Arline admit-ted the rite culminated a long romance.

During 1941 Arline hoped to land the *Tillie the Toiler* film series, but instead joined Wendy Barrie, Lola Lana, and Lou Holtz in a variety show that toured presentation houses. Each of them played the mandolin, Miss Lane sang "The Last Time I Saw Paris," and Arline, in her little girl voice of persuasive innocence, told a ribald tale of hunting rabbits at night. Whether Arline was married to Mr. Bryant at the time is debatable, but in 1941 she was dating Huntington Hartford III. However, that relationship was short-lived.

In July, 1941, she rented Corinne Griffith's Malibu Beach home, living there with her two sons and planning to return to the legitimate stage in something called *Daylight Saving*. But after an abortive return to the screen in some very low-budget pictures, she decided another fling at wedlock was better than one with the cameras.

On October 4, 1942, in Santa Barbara, California, she and Royal Air Force Captain James Ramage Adams signed for a marriage license which they used on October 7 in Montecito. During the ceremony Arline was served by a local constable with a writ for $2,100 filed by the Fifth Avenue Realty Corporation of New York City for rental and legal fees. (This pertained to her auctioning of the furnishings from her 876 Fifth Avenue apartment.) Eight days following the marriage, Capt. Adams left for R.A.F. duty in England. On July 24, 1945, Arline divorced her eight-day husband for desertion. There was a not-so-small war going on in Europe, but to Arline that constituted desertion.

Attended by her brother and sister-in-law, Mr. and Mrs. John Armond Judge, Arline wed Vincent Morgan Ryan, a Chicago advertising executive on August 3, 1945, in Las Vegas. On August 9, former husband James R. Adams contested their divorce, claiming Arline had given false testimony to the judge in May 1945. Arline retaliated, stating that she had established legal residence in Chicago for three years and the divorce from Adams was perfectly legal. At any rate, the Ryan union was short-lived. On April 29, 1947, in Miami Beach, Arline became Mrs. Henry J. (Bob) Topping. Her sixth husband, brother of Dan Topping, her second, had an even briefer reign with Arline. After their divorce, and less than a year later, he married Lana Turner.

Arline made a few more brief movie forays. She was the manicurist in Harold Lloyd's comeback and swan song film, *Mad Wednesday* (1947), produced, directed, and written by Preston Sturges. The Sturges "comedy" was Arline's last important film, although she returned to the screen in 1964 to be strangled by *The Crawling Hand*.

If Arline's cinema days had ended, her matrimonial ones had not. On January 18, 1949, at Fort Lee, New Jersey, she wed George Ross III. The ceremony was officiated by Mayor Charles Heft. Arline was delighted with her latest marriage, but complained to the press that she felt ecclesiastically impure since all of her "I do's" were performed in civil ceremony. At the end of the Ross tenure, Arline was off and running again, marrying inventor Edward Cooper Heard of Beverly Hills, California. But in January, 1960, Mr. Heard left Arline with the closing statement, "Divorce is our only answer." On November 2, 1960, she was granted a divorce from Heard with a court-awarded $12,000 alimony payable at $400 a month. She claimed "too many celebrations" ruined this latest marriage. But when asked if she would consider marriage again, she quipped, "Why not? You gotta keep trying!" And that was something that Arline certainly did.

However, Miss Judge eventually retired from stage, screen, and matrimony. She accepted spot commercials on television and continued her zest for living until Thursday, February 7, 1974, when she was found dead in her West Hollywood apartment. The Los Angeles Coroner's office ascribed her death to aspiration of gastric contents. Her death was ruled to be of natural causes. On February 12, 1974, at nine A.M., a mass was said for the actress at St. Victor's Church in Los Angeles. Sixty-one-year-old Arline was buried in Bridgeport, Connecticut.

If Arline's passion for marriage could have been harnessed in other directions, she might have been one of the screen's more memorable comediennes. When she first arrived in Hollywood she told a reporter: "It makes me a little dizzy to think how quickly things have happened to me. Just three short years ago I was hopping to college proms and suffering through schoolgirl infatuations. Wesley [Ruggles] gets an awful kick out of looking at my collection of fraternity pins and rings and so forth. He says I was too fickle to have been so popular. If he had been one of the collegians he swears he would have shot me! I'm glad I didn't marry a collegian—as cute as they are and they are so 'hot-cha.' " Arline, on and off screen, was quite "hot-cha" herself.

Bachelor Apartment *(RKO 1931)*
An American Tragedy *(RKO 1931)*
Are These Our Children? *(RKO 1931)*
Everything's Rosie *(RKO 1931)*
Girl Crazy *(RKO 1932)*
Love Starved *(RKO 1932)*
Roar of the Dragon *(RKO 1932)*
Is My Face Red? *(RKO 1932)*
The Age of Consent *(RKO 1932)*
Flying Devils *(RKO 1933)*
Sensation Hunters *(Mon 1933)*
Looking for Trouble *(UA 1934)*
Shoot the Works *(Par 1934)*
The Party's Over *(Col 1934)*
Name the Woman *(Col 1934)*
When Strangers Meet *(Liberty 1934)*
Bachelor of Arts *(Fox 1934)*
One Hour Late *(Par 1934)*
The Mysterious Mr. Wong *(Mon 1935)*
Million Dollar Baby *(Mon 1935)*
George White's 1935 Scandals *(Fox 1935)*
College Scandal *(Par 1935)*
Welcome Home *(Fox 1935)*

Music Is Magic *(20th 1935)*
Ship Cafe *(Par 1935)*
King of Burlesque *(20th 1935)*
It Had to Happen *(20th 1936)*
Here Comes Trouble *(20th 1936)*
Valiant Is the Word for Carrie *(Par 1936)*
Pigskin Parade *(20th 1936)*
Star for a Night *(20th 1936)*
One in a Million *(20th 1936)*
Law of the Jungle *(Mon 1942)*
The Lady Is Willing *(Col 1942)*
Harvard, Here I Come *(Col 1942)*
Smith of Minnesota *(Col 1942)*
Wildcat *(Par 1942)*
Song of Texas *(Rep 1943)*
Girls in Chains *(PRC 1943)*
The Contender *(PRC 1944)*
Take It Big *(Par 1944)*
G. I. Honeymoon *(Mon 1945)*
From This Day Forward *(RKO 1946)*
Mad Wednesday [The Sin of Harold Diddle-bock] *(UA 1947)*
The Crawling Hand *(AIP 1964)*

41

Paul Kelly

F. Scott Fitzgerald's era of wonderful nonsense was never better symbolized than by Hollywood of the Twenties. Beauty-contest winners, chorus girls, handsome young men, college athletes, and demi-mondaines sprang from anonymity to stardom. Their screen images often captured a sex appeal, an unusual personality, and a surprising well of talent that registered with the public. Many of these newly invented star-personalities gradually believed the volumes of fantasy glorifying their artistic gifts. Their ascension in the film colony increased. They took up residence in palatial homes where, as Anita Loos observed, their servants were their peers in everything but sex appeal.

One of those "lucky" individuals whose career was on the rise in the Twenties was Paul Kelly. But then a scandal in 1927 was to throw the performer's life into disarray. He emerged into the Thirties professionally scarred, but game enough to accept a more modest position in the hierarchy of screen players.

Paul Michael Kelly was born in Brooklyn, New York, to Michael D. and Nellie Therese Murphy Kelly on Wednesday, August 9, 1899, the ninth child of a family of ten. The early death of Mr. Kelly forced the children into earning money at odd jobs. It was Paul who provided the largest contribution to the family fund. Young Paul had made his theatrical stage debut at the age of eight on Broadway with David Warfield in *The Grand Army Man,* then toured with Robert Mantell in Shakespearean repertory, and was on the road in *The Confession* with Wallace Reid's father, Hal.

But his steadiest employment was found practically next door to the Kelly home at Vitagraph Studios. He started his film career there in such early one-reelers as *Captain Barnacle, Diplomat* (1911), with Vitagraph's star and matinee idol, Maurice Costello. Mr. Costello's two daughters, Dolores and Helene also worked at that studio, as did a young William W. Reid who later attained stardom as the ill-fated Wallace Reid.

Paul vied with young child actor Bobby Connelly as resident juvenile. After four years Paul was featured in Vitagraph's *Buddy's First Call* and starred with Constance Talmadge in *Buddy's Downfall*. Vitagraph started the first of the famous *Family* series in 1915. They were turned out at a rate of three or more reels a month. The first of the one-reel series, *The Jarr Family Discovers Harlem,* was released on March 8, 1915, and

With Peggy Conklin in *The President Vanishes* **(Par '34).**

featured Harry Davenport and Rose Tapley as Mr. and Mrs. Jarr, with Paul as their son, Willie. The Jarrs continued their adventures throughout 1915 and Paul alternated between his Jarr assignments and a variety of other roles in one-reelers, until 1917. In 1918 he made a U.S. Army propaganda film with Raymond McKee called *Fit to Fight.*

On January 22, 1918, talented, ambitious Paul joined Stuart Walker's Broadway production of Booth Tarkington's *Seventeen.* He played George Crooper, with Ruth Gordon as the baby-talking Lola Pratt. Relinquishing his part to Ben Lyon, Paul left *Seventeen* to open in another Tarkington stage comedy. *Penrod* debuted on September 2, 1918, with Paul as Robert Williams. The cast of this show was filled with several bright youngsters, including Ben Grauer, Lillian Roth, Helen Chandler, and Helen Hayes.

Kelly's first "grown-up" romantic lead was that of Gilbert Blythe, with Mary Miles Minter, in Paramount's *Anne of Green Gables,* directed in late 1919 by William Desmond Taylor. Then he was on the screen in 1920 in *Uncle Sam of Freedom Ridge,* and the next year joined with Lionel Barrymore in *The Great Adventure,* based on Arnold Bennett's *Buried Alive.* At the age of twenty-two he returned to Broadway, confident that his ambition and drive, along with his untapped talent, would find him a lofty place in the theatre.

Kelly's first leading man role on Broadway was in *Up the Ladder,* which opened on March 6, 1922, with Doris Kenyon as his leading lady. His success in this show brought him an offer of the pivotal role in *Whispering Wires.* He left *Up the Ladder* to star in the new play which opened on August 7, 1922, at the 49th Street Theatre. During his Broadway shuttling, he became reacquainted with a lovely young actress, Dorothy Mackaye, who had married a rising musical comedy performer, Ray Raymond, the previous year. Paul was often invited to the Raymonds' home in Forest Hills, Long Island.

By 1925 Paul was starring on Broadway as the rum-running ladykiller in *The Sea Woman,* with Blanche Yurka in the title part. In 1926 the Raymonds went to Hollywood, while Paul went to Florida to play in Paramount's satire on the booming Florida trade in swamp land, *The New Klondike* (1926). After returning to Broadway, Kelly also left for Hollywood to join William Haines in MGM's *Slide, Kelly, Slide* (1927). His friendship with the Raymonds was again renewed and they became constant companions. By now Paul's feelings for Mrs. Raymond had gone far beyond friendship. While he was appearing in Eddie Cantor's Paramount silent *Special Delivery* (1927), he and Dorothy realized that they were deeply in love. Dorothy had joined her husband in San Francisco where he was appearing in a musical. Paul and Dorothy exchanged daily telegrams which she would sign "Dot E. Mrs. K" (which translated "Dot, Elegant Mrs. Kelly"). In turn he made frequent telephone calls to her from the Paramount set.

Raymond's alcoholic excesses became slyly sadistic and his quick and violent temper created many problems for Dorothy. His fury at her solicitation of Kelly's understanding and sympathy sent him into a blinding rage and he beat her severely. Raymond rented San Francisco's Wilkes Theatre and invited some two hundred people to a gala "separation and divorce" party, with his wife as "guest of honor."

While the party was being planned, Dorothy received a letter from Paul dated March 28, 1927: "Oh, I am so terribly in love with you—so terribly—I am miserable here without you. I love you—love you—love you. I thought I would die last week; haven't had a civil word for anyone when they speak to me—was always thinking of you and dreaming of you—oh, God it was awful. Your first letter nearly drove me crazy—almost drank myself to death. Take good care of yourself darling, for my sake as well as your own. I want you. Glad you got the roses. Now, you must have received my wire telling you I would wait. But, sweetheart, it is bad enough not seeing you without thinking I'll have to wait much longer than I thought. Don't make it long dear. I want you so much, my little wife, I love you so much, really I do."

Dorothy wired back: "Letter received. Arrive Monday by motor. Expect visit. Crazy to get home. OUR home, love, and everything that goes with it."

On Saturday afternoon, Kelly's Japanese houseboy had served several rounds of gin drinks to Kelly, Dorothy, Helen Wilkinson, and Kelly's roommate, Max Wagner. About 6:30 Kelly called Raymond and warned him to cease his constant gossip concerning him and defamation of his character. The well-liquored Raymond responded, "You're damn right I have, and I wish you were here right now so that I could give you what you deserve." Paul, unfortunately, obliged the alcoholic singer, and after his arrival at the Raymond home, a violent argument over Paul's affection for Dorothy began in earnest. Kelly's fighting Irish flared and he slapped Raymond several times. Raymond's profane crescendo ignited Kelly's rage and he started pummeling Raymond. Valerie, the Raymonds' five-year-old daughter watched the fight as the 33-year-old Raymond was felled thrice by Kelly. Raymond's black housemaid, Dorothy Lee, kept Valerie at a safe distance from the brawling six-foot, 180-pound Kelly. Miss Lee later claimed Kelly kicked the fallen Raymond and beat his head against the wall. Saturday, April 16, 1927, was a landmark for Paul Kelly.

Removed to a hospital, Raymond suffered from a damaged left eye, two fractured ribs, two contusions on the forehead, bruises on the left arm, shins, and chest—although, following the fracas, Raymond had managed to rise from the battleground and get to his bed. On Tuesday morning, April 19, 1927, Ray Raymond died. That evening Paul Kelly was arrested and charged with murder. The next day the *New York Times* gave it front page coverage, "HOLLYWOOD ACTOR KILLED, RIVAL HELD. PAUL KELLY IS ARRESTED AFTER FIGHTING RAY RAYMOND IN THE LATTER'S HOME." The coroner's cause of death was stated as hypostatic pneumonia following extensive subdural hemorrhage on right side of brain, and the contributing cause was given as acute alcoholism.

Paul fainted when put under arrest for murder, but he remained composed throughout the lurid trial which exposed his relationship with Dorothy. Dorothy and Dr. W. J. Sullivan were indicted on charges of compounding a felony and being accessories after the fact in an alleged plot to conceal the true facts involving Raymond's death. During the trial a search of records in Gretna Green, Maryland, produced no evidence that Dorothy and Raymond had been married there. To add further confusion to the lack of a marriage registration, Raymond's first wife, Florence Bain Raymond, claimed that they were never divorced. On May 25, a jury found Paul Kelly guilty of manslaughter, and Judge Burnell sentenced him to one to ten years in San Quentin. Kelly's only comment was, "I guess the jury said what they thought was right." On June 30, Dorothy was convicted and, for the benefit of reporters, sang and danced on the boat taking her to San Quentin.

The movie colony underwrote a huge amount of money for Paul and Dorothy's defense. Thomas Meighan alone contributed ten thousand dollars toward the fund. Dorothy was able to sever ten months from her conviction. On August 2, 1929, two years and one month after his entrance to San Quentin, Paul Kelly was released— paroled for excellent behavior. The lovers left for New York. Concerning her future career plans, Dorothy told the press, "If I'm coming back to the stage it is because it is my profession, not to indulge in any cheap capitalization on my life in prison. I want to win my way back on my own ability." Likewise, Dorothy let Paul recapture the limelight as a brilliant, professional actor.

After a brief stint in the *9:15 Revue* early in 1930, Paul opened on Broadway in

October, 1930, in *Bad Girl*. Kelly and co-star Sylvia Sidney received far better notices than Vina Delmar's play. The critics raved that a real actor had come to town, and Paul's theatre career seemed to be launched successfully, all over again. After *Bad Girl*, for which he received only thirty dollars per week salary (the maximum permitted under the terms of his parole), he was seen in the short-lived *Hobo* (1931) and, in September, 1931, in *Just to Remind You.*

Dorothy and Paul were wed in 1931 when his parole permitted. On January 20, 1932, he appeared in *Adam Had Two Sons* as a brawling, fighting sailor. It lasted five performances. Then he made a quickie film with Fifi D'Orsay called *The Girl from Calgary* (1932) and returned to the stage in December, 1932, for the flop *The Great Magoo.*

Word of Paul's stature on Broadway reached Hollywood. He received offers from several of the major studios, and these bids were helped a good deal by the statement of the czar of movie censorship, Will Hays. He said of Paul, "Any man who comes out of prison has the right to earn his living in whatever honest way he knows how to earn it." The film colony listened to Hays, and Kelly, who might have achieved greatness on the New York stage, chose to return to movie-making.

Seeking a forceful actor to portray Sergeant O'Hara in the remake of *Rain*, Lewis Milestone hired Paul for the role. But United Artists executive Joseph Schenck thought Somerset Maugham's controversial story would be subjected to enough censorship problems without the added burden of possible unfavorable publicity about Kelly's past. Thus Kelly was replaced by another Irishman, William Gargan, in the Joan Crawford vehicle.

Instead Kelly's screen return was in *Broadway Thru a Keyhole* (1933), based on a screen treatment by Walter Winchell. Former actor Lowell Sherman directed the opus with Kelly as square-dealing gangster Frank Rocci. One reviewer noted of the player, "Paul Kelly gives a startling performance that should be judged on its own merits. This man is a real actor, with power, repression and passion." The film was a big money-maker for Darryl F. Zanuck's new Twentieth Century company. The rave notices should have established Paul as a star, but they did not.

Kelly's future screen performances—whenever he was given a playable role—were always fine, well-shaded, truly realized characterizations. He was on target in *The President Vanishes*, (1934) matching talent with the fine work of Edward Arnold and Arthur Byron. But thereafter followed a long series of supporting roles, occasional leads in quickly forgotten class-B movies, with all-too-infrequent chances to display his varied talents. George M. Cohan's *The Song and Dance Man* was remade by Twentieth Century-Fox in 1936. Although Paul had never before been asked to sing or dance professionally, he approached the role of Hap Farrell with his usual thoroughness. He tap danced in the film and sang "On a Holiday in My Play Room," once again proving his versatility.

Paul and Dorothy had settled down and led a quiet life within the film colony. Then, on January 5, 1940, Dorothy was killed in an automobile accident. Nearly overwhelmed with grief, Paul plunged into work. Left with two daughters, he felt remarriage would solve his personal life. Luckily he met, fell in love with, and wed Mardelle Zurcker in 1941. As the years passed Kelly worked continuously in front of the cameras, often making a minor role a good deal better than it had been conceived by the scriptwriters. He worked for most of the major studios, even to making a fifteen-episode serial for Columbia, *The Secret Code* (1942), masquerading as "The Black Commando" (in reality Police Lieutenant Dan Barton).

With Warren Hymer in *Join the Marines* (Rep '37).

With James Cagney in *The Roaring Twenties* (WB '39).

The bulk of Paul's screen career for the next several decades was divided between playing gangsters or criminals: a wide variety of army, navy, and marine officers; innumerable gentlemen of the law (from judge to district attorney to plain cop); and a few newspaper reporters and doctors. Despite this typecasting, his performances were never shoddy. After playing rustler Roy Stuart, owner of the notorious Bella Union Hall, with Errol Flynn in *San Antonio* (1945), he went back to Broadway.

Beggars Are Coming to Town arrived at the Coronet Theatre in New York on October 27, 1945, and Paul played reformed gangster Frankie Madison. Despite a cast that included E. G. Marshall, Dorothy Comingore, and Luther Adler, the play quickly folded. Paul returned to the West Coast, earning his keep in a clutch of B pictures until 1947. Then he aroused critical attention, as did the entire cast and production of RKO's *Crossfire*. This bitter, bravely done indictment of prejudice was expertly directed by Edward Dmytryk, and featured three Roberts: Ryan, Young, and Mitchum.

After starring in a tacky remake of *Ebb Tide* (1937), called *Adventure Island*, Paul again returned to New York to assume the finest role of his career. William Wister

Haines' play *Command Decision* opened at the Fulton Theatre on October 1, 1947. Paul was the hard-boiled but deeply compassionate Brigadier General K. C. Dennis. He played the part for 408 performances. Kelly's conveyance of the inner heartbreak and struggles of this general with his hard-core exterior, as he knowingly sends men off into war and certain death, was a gem of acting. When the drama was bought by MGM for filming, Clark Gable inherited Kelly's stage role.

The ballroom of the Waldorf Astoria Hotel in New York on March 28, 1948, was the setting for the second annual Antoinette Perry (Tony) Awards. For the first and only time in the history of the Tony Awards to date, *three* actors were selected for best performance: Henry Fonda for *Mister Roberts*, Basil Rathbone for *The Heiress*, and Paul for *Command Decision*. The men received gold money clips inscribed with the honor of the award. Paul also won the Donaldson Award for outstanding achievement in the theatre as Best Actor. When he completed his tour in *Command Decision*, Paul once more returned to Hollywood. However, the best the industry could offer him were supporting roles. He completed two ridiculous assignments in 1950 and went back East.

"Clifford Odets has gone straight to the heart of three characters in a vivid and stinging play about theatre people, and written about them with pitiless integrity," Brooks Atkinson wrote of *The Country Girl*. Paul Kelly was starred as the seedy, ingenious actor Frank Elgin who is forced back into the limelight and eventual success by the courage of his wife (Uta Hagen) and the confidence of the play's director. After much out-of-town rewriting, *The Country Girl* opened on November 10, 1950, at New York's Lyceum Theatre for a 235-performance run. Paul's once black hair had now turned white, and his physical appearance and stage presence could not have been improved for the choice of the devious, alcoholic actor. Paul's superior performance, unfortunately, lost out in the Tony Award sweepstakes that year. Claude Rains of *Darkness at Noon* won. (When *The Country Girl* was filmed in 1954 by Paramount, Bing Crosby, in an astonishing and astute piece of casting, played the Frank Elgin role—and did it well.)

By the time *The Country Girl* had ended its Broadway run, Paul had appeared on television in a version of *Street Scene* with Ann Dvorak. Returning to Hollywood, he was assigned to support Lassie in *The Painted Hills* (1951) at MGM. But he delighted in being back in California and able to pursue his game of golf. In 1952 he supported Gary Cooper in *Springfield Rifle,* and was a wounded outlaw in Dick Powell's first directorial effort, *Split Second* (1953). On March 19, 1953, Kelly suffered a heart attack and entered St. John's Hospital in Santa Monica, California. His return to the screen seemed a striking source of irony.

Warner Bros. cast Paul, of all people, as the legendary Warden Clinton Duffy in their picture *Duffy of San Quentin* (1954). In twenty-five years he had gone from inmate in reality to warden in fiction.

Some of his better roles were on television, such as the video version of *One Foot in Heaven.* When the "Crossroads" series made its television debut on October 7, 1955, Paul played Father Riggs in the opening episode. He returned to the series again, once more as Father Riggs, in April, 1956.

He played detective Jim McBride in *The Square Jungle* (1955), with Tony Curtis; continued to serve the law as Judge Robert Ellerbe in *Storm Center* (1956), with Bette Davis; and made his last television appearance on April 8, 1956, in *Instant of Truth,* with Angela Lansbury. He then completed his role of Colonel Hughes in *Bailout at 43,000* (1957). After return from voting with his wife, Mardella, on November 6, 1956, Paul had a fatal heart attack.

Few actors could have survived the trauma, publicity, and heartbreak Paul Kelly

333

withstood in the late Twenties. How many others would have had the stamina, will power, and talent to remain in show business for a few months short of fifty years under the strain Paul did? With his death, the theatre lost one of its great stars, and Hollywood, one of its most talented featured actors.

PAUL KELLY

Fit to Fight *(War Department—American Social Hygiene Ass'n 1918)*
Anne of Green Gables *(Par 1920)*
Uncle Sam of Freedom Ridge *(Levey Productions 1920)*
The Great Adventure *(Associated FN 1921)*
The Old Oaken Bucket *(Warren Corp. 1921)*
The New Klondike *(Par 1926)*
Slide, Kelly, Slide *(MGM 1927)*
Special Delivery *(Par 1927)*
The Girl from Calgary *(Mon 1932)*
Broadway Thru a Keyhole *(UA 1933)*
Side Streets *(WB 1934)*
Blind Date *(Col 1934)*
Death on the Diamond *(MGM 1934)*
The Love Captive *(Univ 1934)*
School for Girls *(Liberty 1934)*
The President Vanishes *(Par 1934)*
When a Man's a Man *(Fox 1935)*
Public Hero Number One *(MGM 1935)*
Star of Midnight *(RKO 1935)*
Silk Hat Kid *(Fox 1935)*
Speed Devils *(J. H. Hoffberg 1935)*
My Marriage *(20th 1935)*
It's a Great Life *(Par 1936)*
Here Comes Trouble *(20th 1936)*
The Song and Dance Man *(20th 1936)*
The Country Beyond *(20th 1936)*
Women Are Trouble *(MGM 1936)*
Murder with Pictures *(Par 1936)*
The Accusing Finger *(Par 1936)*
Parole Racket *(Col 1937)*
Join the Marines *(Rep 1937)*
It Happened out West *(20th 1937)*
The Frame-Up *(Col 1937)*
Fit for a King *(RKO 1937)*
Navy Blue and Gold *(MGM 1937)*
The Nurse from Brooklyn *(Univ 1938)*
Torchy Blane in Panama *(WB 1938)*
Island in the Sky *(20th 1938)*
The Devil's Party *(Univ 1938)*
The Missing Guest *(Univ 1938)*
Juvenile Court *(Col 1938)*
Adventure in Sahara *(Col 1938)*
Forged Passport *(Rep 1939)*
The Flying Irishman *(RKO 1939)*
Within the Law *(MGM 1939)*
6,000 Enemies *(MGM 1939)*
The Roaring Twenties *(WB 1939)*

Invisible Stripes *(WB 1940)*
Queen of the Mob *(Par 1940)*
The Howards of Virginia *(Col 1940)*
Wyoming *(MGM 1940)*
Girls under 21 *(Col 1940)*
Flight Command *(MG 1940)*
Ziegfeld Girl *(MGM 1941)*
I'll Wait for You *(MGM 1941)*
Parachute Battalion *(RKO 1941)*
Mystery Ship *(Col 1941)*
Mr. and Mrs. North *(MGM 1941)*
Call out the Marines *(RKO 1942)*
Tarzan's New York Adventure *(MGM 1942)*
Tough as They Come *(Univ 1942)*
Flying Tigers *(Rep 1942)*
The Secret Code *(Col serial 1942)*
The Man from Music Mountain *(Rep 1943)*
The Story of Dr. Wassell *(Par 1944)*
Dead Man's Eyes *(Univ 1944)*
Faces in the Fog *(Rep 1944)*
China's Little Devils *(Mon 1945)*
Grissly's Millions *(Rep 1945)*
Allotment Wives *(Mon 1945)*
San Antonio *(WB 1945)*
The Cat Creeps *(Univ 1946)*
The Glass Alibi *(Rep 1946)*
Deadline for Murder *(20th 1946)*
Strange Journey *(20th 1946)*
Fear in the Night *(Par 1947)*
Spoilers of the North *(Rep 1947)*
Crossfire *(RKO 1947)*
Adventure Island *(Par 1947)*
The File on Thelma Jordan *(Par 1949)*
Side Street *(MGM 1949)*
Guilty of Treason *(EL 1949)*
The Secret Fury *(RKO 1950)*
Frenchie *(Univ 1950)*
The Painted Hills *(MGM 1951)*
Springfield Rifle *(WB 1952)*
Gunsmoke *(Univ 1953)*
Split Second *(RKO 1953)*
Duffy of San Quentin *(WB 1954)*
Johnny Dark *(Univ 1954)*
The High and the Mighty *(WB 1954)*
The Steel Cage *(UA 1954)*
The Square Jungle *(Univ 1955)*
Storm Center *(Col 1956)*
Bailout at 43,000 *(UA 1957)*

42

Elissa Landi

"There is a depth of the ages in her eyes, today in her body and tomorrow in her spirit." So spoke Cecil B. DeMille of Elissa Landi, whom he would cast as Mercia, the Christian woman, in his spectacle *The Sign of the Cross* (1932). It would be her most memorable screen appearance and would insure her place in the Thirties' cinema.

Elissa Landi had, by 1931, risen, momentarily, to great prominence at the Fox Film lot. She needed no pretentions of royalty for her lofty spot. She was, supposedly, the granddaughter of one of history's most beautiful monarchs, Elizabeth of Austria. Elissa's mother, the Countess Karoline Franziska-Marie, had been born in 1882, reputedly the daughter of Elizabeth and Emperor Francis Joseph. (The countess would later write a book of her bizarre regal existence, a volume published in the United States in 1915 as *The Secret of an Empress*.) The countess was kept away from the royal palaces because the empress did not want her last-born to be "an empty-headed, empty-hearted princess!" Often the princess resided with a family called Kaiser.

It was on January 26, 1902, that Richard Kuhnelt, doctor of law and the son of court councillor Kuhnelt, married "Miss Kaiser." On November 17, 1902, a son, Anthony-Francis was born and on December 6, 1904,[7] Elizabeth-Marie-Christine was born. By this time, the former "Miss Kaiser" had learned that her husband knew her true identity all along and that the marriage had been planned to ward off any claims to the Austrian throne that she might have. Eventually Kuhnelt departed the scene, for a time, and went to Abbazzia.

In May, 1906, Karoline, with her two children and their nurse, left for Canada, settling in Sault-au-Recollet near Montreal. Kuhnelt soon arrived on the scene, but the marriage was unsalvageable and he returned to Vienna in 1908. Karoline moved to Vancouver, and worked as a cook at the Yale Hotel and then in a successful Viennese confectionery shop. During this time she met Count Charles Zanardi-Landi. In 1911, Karoline, accompanied by Landi, returned to Austria to obtain a second divorce, supplementing the United States decree that had permitted her marriage to Zanardi-Landi. She again attempted to pursue her demands for recognition, mainly for her children. But the Imperial Court successfully intimidated her attorney so that the case was dropped. The Zanardi-Landis finally returned to, and established residence in, London, sent for their children, and entered the children in private schools.

---

[7]Elissa would always insist she was born in Venice rather than on a farm called Kleinhart outside of Vienna, as her mother, the countess, had detailed.

With Ronald Colman in *The Masquerader* (UA '33).

Elissa and her brother Anthony bore a startling resemblance to the Hapsburgs, and, in profile, the similarity of Elissa to the Empress Elizabeth was clear.

The Landi acting career grew from her interest in writing. She joined a repertory company to study play structure and decided acting was a thrilling experience. She made her stage debut in Oxford, England, in April, 1924, as Sheba in *Dandy Dick*. In London, on August 13, 1924, she had the title role of *Storm*. American producer Gilbert Miller wanted to transfer it to Broadway with Elissa, but she refused. Instead, she continued to play various roles on the London stage and completed her first novel, *Neilsen,* published in 1925.

Her motion picture debut was made the next year as Dorothy Gish's benefactress in the English-made picture *London* (1926). In the next two seasons she played a variety of stage roles, including parts in *Lavender Ladies,* with Herbert Marshall, and *The Constant Nymph,* with Noël Coward and Edna Best. During 1928 she resumed her film career by joining Brian Aherne in *Underground,* by playing a dual role in *Bolivar,* and by going to Sweden to film *Brott Och Brett* (with Lars Hansen) that became *Sin* (1929) when released in England. In France she made *Le Leur sur La Cime* (1928), which was shown in London as *The Betrayal* (1929). In the meantime she wed London barrister John Cecil Lawrence.

By April, 1929, Elissa was back on the stage in *The Stag* with Ian Hunter, Adrianne Allen, and Reginald Owen, and was seen onscreen in *The Inseparables* (1929). In January, 1930, she left for Paris to film *Mon Gosse de Pere,* shot in six weeks in English and French simultaneously, with Elissa for the English version (*The Parisian,* 1930), Alice Cocea for the French version, and Adolphe Menjou playing the lead in both. Back in England, Elissa survived two screen flops, both written by that oracle of Twenties' sex, Elinor Glyn. The films were *Knowing Men* (1930) and *The Price of Things* (1931).

Elissa's second novel, *The Helmers,* was published in England before Rouben Mamoulian, after appraising some forty other English actresses, cabled producer Al Woods in New York that he had signed Miss Landi for the Broadway version of *A Farewell to Arms.* In that production Crane Wilbur was Rinaldi, Glenn Anders was Lieutenant Henry, and Elissa was Nurse Catherine Barkley. Lawrence Stalling's woeful adaptation of Ernest Hemingway's work met with disapproval from reviewers and audiences alike. Nevertheless, critic John Mason Brown reported, "In the playing of Elissa Landi, the charming Englishwoman Mr. Woods has imported to act Catherine, it gains its moments of glamour and conviction. For Miss Landi alone among the members of the large and sprawling cast suggests the quality that made *A Farewell to Arms* so fine and poignant a novel." The play lasted a mere twenty-four performances.

Fox Films was impressed by Elissa's stage presence and signed her to a term contract. Her first American picture was *Body and Soul* (1931), in which she portrayed the widow of heroic aviator Humphrey Bogart. Next she played with Lewis Stone and John Garrick in *Always Goodbye* (1931). Turgid was the best that could be said of *The Yellow Ticket* (1931), a Raoul Walsh-directed remake of a prior stage and film work. Within this film Elissa played the Russian who kills government official Lionel Barrymore to protect her British journalist lover (Laurence Olivier). In 1931, she had made *Wicked* with Victor McLaglen, and in 1932, the two appeared in *The Devil's Lottery*.

It was after completing two emotional and capably played roles in *The Woman in Room 13* (1932) and *A Passport to Hell* (1932) that Cecil B. DeMille paged her for *The Sign of the Cross.* Charles Laughton had been assigned to play Nero and originally Elissa, who had specialized in fallen, deceived, and semi-wicked women at Fox, was cast as the sensuous Empress Poppaea. But then upon actually meeting her, director DeMille decided she would be more appropriately cast as Mercia, whose love for a

At Columbia Pictures in '34.

With Edmund Lowe in *Mad Holiday* (MGM '36).

Roman centurion (Fredric March) converts him to Christianity. Eventually both Landi and March are led to the lions in the Coliseum. For the now vacant role of Poppaea, both Pola Negri and Norma Talmadge were considered until the director spotted Claudette Colbert on the lot and gave her the part of "the wickedest woman in the world."

Fox took advantage of the publicity given *The Sign of the Cross* and continued to promote Elissa as "The Empress of Emotion." The studio touted her too much and overestimated her screen appeal. There were plans for her to star in *Red Dancer, Glamorous,* and then *The Last Trick,* an unpublished and unproduced play by Noel Coward. In the meantime, she continued writing and in 1932 her third novel, *House for Sale,* received considerable critical attention.

Besides writing and acting, she would go horseback riding after working hours. She delighted in talking breeding and horses with the grooms and owners of stables. The Hollywood social life held little interest for her. She was fond of music, was herself an accomplished pianist, and was fascinated with ballet, which she had studied in England. She also enjoyed dabbling with oils and canvas. With her knowledge of languages, she was a great favorite with the cosmopolitan set in Hollywood.

At Fox, she inherited Katharine Hepburn's stage role of Antiope in *The Warrior's Husband* (1933). But then she was stuck in a dull version of the play *I Loved You Wednesday* (1933), cast as a ballerina. When Fox came up with another dreary part in *I Am a Widow,* Elissa rebelled and the studio cancelled her contract.

Free-lancing, she accepted a part in Columbia's *Sisters Under the Skin* (1934), the showgirl role Carole Lombard had rejected. It was not a good part for Landi either. Then

340

she overplayed the part of Marie in *By Candlelight* (1934), displaying the gushy trait that too often invaded her characterizations. For Francis Lederer's film debut in RKO's *Man of Two Worlds* (1934) she was the far-fetched love interest. She was much better in *The Great Flirtation* (1934) as Adolphe Menjou's temperamental actress wife. Probably the finest screen performance Elissa offered was as Mercedes, surrounded by a superlative cast and the excellent Robert Donat, in *The Count of Monte Cristo* (1934).

Nina Koshetz dubbed for Elissa's operatic sequences in Paramount's *Enter Madame!* (1934), but Miss Landi supplied her own radiance in the scenes with Cary Grant. After a low-budget entry, *Without Regret* (1935), she returned to the Broadway stage for twenty-four performances of *Tapestry in Grey*, with Melvyn Douglas.

When that show closed she returned to England for the first production of Criterion Films founded by Douglas Fairbanks, Jr. and two co-partners. In *The Amateur Gentleman* (1936), Douglas Jr. played opposite Elissa. Her performance was described as lovely and regal, but not always suitable for the film itself. It would be on May 9, 1936 that Elissa and her husband, John Cecil Lawrence, would divorce in California. She testified that his unconventional views on married life included extramarital affairs on his part with recommendations that she avail herself of an equal freedom of expression. (It would be Douglas Fairbanks, Jr. in 1939 who, with his new bride, Mary Lee Epling, would purchase Landi's former California home on Amalfi Drive in the Pacific Palisades. The two-story Spanish-style house was sold to the Fairbanks for an unbelievable bargain price of $25,000.)

Irving G. Thalberg at MGM thought that Elissa had never been properly showcased and consequently signed her to a MGM contract. She appeared in *Mad Holiday* (1936), a satire on murder mysteries, for the studio, then was given the pivotal role of Selma Landis in what many consider the best of the *Thin Man* series, the second one, called *After the Thin Man* (1936). She appeared as Myrna Loy's cousin whose husband is killed by her rejected suitor, James Stewart. Elissa's portrayal of Princess Aurore in the bilingual British-made *Koenigsmark* (1936) was her last film effort in England.

She returned to work once again for Cecil B. DeMille, not at Paramount but on his "Lux Radio Theatre." She played with Robert Montgomery in an airing of *The Grand Duchess and the Waiter*.

In January, 1937, with her mentor, Thalberg, dead, she returned to Metro, not as an actress but as staff technical adviser for, of all things, The Marx Brothers' wild *A Day at the Races*. The studio had rented her horse Tristan for the film, and Elissa, so to speak, went along for the ride. She did play Helen Trent in MGM's remake of an old thriller *The Thirteenth Chair* (1937), with Dame May Whitty as the Medium.

From Hollywood she journeyed to Broadway to open in *The Lady Has a Heart* with Vincent Price as her co-star. The promotional use of cut-rate tickets and performing scenes on radio did much to keep the mild comedy going for ninety-one performances. Her next production, the well-produced flop of *Empress of Destiny*, with Glenn Hunter as Peter, survived only five performances in March, 1938.

On May 19, 1938, Elissa was a guest on Connie Boswell's radio show and then spent the summer touring the Eastern coast straw-hat circuit in a tryout of a new play, *Veronica*, as well as versions of *The Warrior's Husband*, *The Lady Has a Heart*, and her own *Holiday House*. Under the pseudonym of Mady Francis she authored *Rebellion in Shadow*, in which she starred in a Maplewood, New Jersey, tryout in March, 1939. She plied the lucrative summer circuits again in 1939. While she would discuss her writings, including her fourth novel, *The Ancestor* (1934), she would not talk of her romance with Nino Martini. In 1940 she was only heard on radio and represented in bookshops (by her fifth novel, *Women and Peter*). But the next year she played *Romance* in Kansas

City, Missouri, and spent the summer starring in East Coast productions of *Candida* and *The Shining Hour.* She was among those who participated in the *Let Freedom Sing* revue held at the Imperial Theatre in New York on Sunday Night, May 25, 1941. The show was sponsored by the National Women's Division of the Committee to Defend America by Aiding the Allies.

March, 1943, brought her to the Mansfield Theatre as The Lecturer in an appropriately named flop, *Apology.* Her last flight at Hollywood was at the front lines of *Corregidor,* a junky film turned out by the poverty row studio, PRC. On August 28, 1943, she married Curtiss Thomas, a writer-teacher from Newburyport, Massachusetts, and she became an American citizen. She closed the year by accepting the lead in the road company of *Tomorrow, the World,* in which she would again tour in 1945. Eight weeks after the birth of her daughter, Caroline Maude, on December 11, 1944, she opened in *Dark Hammock* on Broadway, but it lasted only two performances. Her new novel, *The Pear Tree,* was also published that year.

Actually Elissa retired from both stage and screen, but continued writing on her 123-acre farm, Bright Acres, in complete contentment with her husband and daughter. Occasionally she would come into New York to join Paula Stone and Maggi McNellis on a panel show, or in July , 1945, to appear in the summer theatres in *This Is a Woman.* (In August, 1945, she was seen in *Another Language* at Bass Rocks Theatre in Gloucester, Massachusetts.)

Early in 1948, Dr. Kenneth Lefever, who had been treating Elissa for some time for a "chronic condition," told her husband that the "condition" was terminal cancer. It was decided to keep the negative prognosis from the vital, lively 43-year-old Elissa. On October 21, 1948, following ten days of intensive care, she died in the Kingston, New York, Hospital.

For all her talents, Elissa never actually became the great star of films or theatre, which was surprising. Her life objectives were multiple and varied. Her writing was even more important to her than her acting, and, in later life, her family became more vital than her career. There were a few sparks of glory throughout her career but she remained a *name* in the acting profession and, certainly, a large mystery in the annals of royal lineage.

ELISSA LANDI

London *(Par British 1926)*
Underground *(Pro Patria 1928)*
Bolivar *(Pro Patria 1928)*
The Inseparables *(Warner Bros. British 1929)*
The Betrayal [Le Leur sur la Crime] *(British International 1929)*
Sin [Brott Och Brett] *(British International 1929)*
My Kid of a Father *(British 1930)*
The Parisian *(UA British 1930)*
Knowing Men *(UA British 1930)*
The Price of Things *(UA British 1931)*
Children of Chance *(British International 1931)*
Body and Soul *(Fox 1931)*
Always Goodbye *(Fox 1931)*
Wicked *(Fox 1931)*
The Yellow Ticket *(Fox 1931)*
The Devil's Lottery *(Fox 1932)*

The Woman in Room 13 *(Fox 1932)*
A Passport to Hell *(Fox 1932)*
The Sign of the Cross *(Par 1932)*
The Masquerader *(UA 1933)*
The Warrior's Husband *(Fox 1933)*
I Loved You Wednesday *(Fox 1933)*
Sister under the Skin *(Col 1934)*
By Candlelight *(Univ 1934)*
Man of Two Worlds *(RKO 1934)*
The Great Flirtation *(Par 1934)*
The Count of Monte Cristo *(UA 1934)*
Enter Madame! *(Par 1934)*
Without Regret *(Par 1935)*
The Amateur Gentleman *(UA 1936)*
Koenigsmark *(General Film 1936)*
Mad Holiday *(MGM 1936)*
After the Thin Man *(MGM 1936)*
The Thirteenth Chair *(MGM 1937)*
Corregidor *(PRC 1943)*

Francis Lederer

The phenomenon of the Broadway matinee idol had virtually vanished after the halcyon days of John Barrymore. But then a young, handsome, Czech actor made his American stage debut on November 19, 1932. The play was *Autumn Crocus* and the male was Francis Lederer. His bright charm kept the play going for 210 performances. After each run-through, crowds of wilting females would gather at the Morosco Theatre stage door to glimpse their new idol, fawn over his autograph, and often rapturously have their hand kissed by the continental charmer. Away from the theatre, Lederer attempted to live a systematic, well-regulated life at the New York Athletic Club, riding a horse through Central Park and maintaining a rigorous physical training program. New York hostesses vied for his attendance at their parties and were astonished to discover the current toast of Broadway neither smoked nor drank.

The day after *Autumn Crocus* opened, RKO signed Francis to a motion picture contract to start contingent on the run of the play. In the studio's publicity for forthcoming releases, it was announced, "Hollywood rolls down the red carpet to welcome Francis Lederer, Idol of Millions, in a glittering musical romance, *Nights Are Made for Love* with Irene Dunne." That picture was never made, and RKO had to wait two years before claiming Lederer's screen services.

Frantisek Lederer was born on Tuesday, November 6, 1906, in Karlin, Prague, Czechoslovakia to Rose Ornstein and Joseph Lederer. He was educated at Handelsacademie, Academie Für Musik, and Darstellende Kunst in Prague. Although only a young boy he served as a corporal during World War I with the Austrian artillery. He won a scholarship to the Prague Academy of Dramatic Arts and was an apprentice student with the New German Theatre where he made his stage debut in a walk-on part in *The Burning Heart*. He appeared in many of their productions until 1922 when he toured Moravia and Silesia with a repertory company, returning to his country eventually.

In 1925 he went to Germany. While playing in Noël Coward's *Hay Fever* in Breslau, he was persuaded by German star Kathe Dorsch to go to Berlin to play Shaw's *Man and Superman*. By a variety of plays in the German capital, Lederer established himself as one of Berlin's most popular stage actors, under the name of Franz Lederer, and under contract to theatrical manager Saltenburg.

344

With Lionel Stander, Frances Dee, Ferdinand Gottschalk (hidden), Akim Tamiroff, and Lennox Pawle in *The Gay Deception* **(Fox '35).**

When Max Reinhardt planned to produce *Romeo and Juliet* starring Elisabeth Bergner, the actress insisted that no one but Lederer should be cast as Romeo. Miss Bergner's demand ignited a singular revolt in the theatre. Saltenburg refused to release Lederer, either as a concession to art or a service to the public. Each faction took out large advertisements in the Berlin newspapers, all of which served to heighten public interest in Franz. Eventually Reinhardt finally won and the Shakesperean tragedy went into rehearsal. Lillian Gish, then (1929) a guest at Reinhardt's home, was invited to attend the rehearsals, and she was so impressed with Lederer that she signed him to a three-film contract. But silent pictures were to be a thing of the past. *Romeo and Juliet* was lavishly praised when it opened, and Lederer's interpretation of the star-crossed lover is still considered one of the greatest performances in German stage history.

During his Reinhardt days, Lederer started appearing in German films, one of the best being *Die Wunderbar Luge der Nina Petrovna* (1929) with Brigitte Helm, and also another, *Die Buchse der Pandora* (*Pandora's Box,* 1929), with American actress Louise Brooks. The latter film was banned in Munich but has established itself as a film classic. Then Franz made *Ihre Majestat Die Liebe* (1929) with Kathe von Nagy, and the German-English *Atlantik* (1929). He was rapidly becoming a screen personality.

Max Reinhardt next used Lederer in a role that required acting, singing, and dancing. Franz's success as the gigolo in *Die Wunderbar* brought the actor offers from all over Europe, and he accepted an offer from England. With six weeks of intensive study, he learned enough English to speak the role of Fleuriot in *My Sister and I,* which debuted on the London stage in February, 1931. Then came vast acclaim for his performance in *Autumn Crocus,* followed by his role of Mosca in *Volpone* and his joint appearance with Peggy Wood in the London production of Jerome Kern's *The Cat and the Fiddle.* He then returned to Germany to film *Das Schicksal der Renate Langen* (1933), in which he was cast as a demi-villain opposite Mady Christians. In the fall of 1932 he arrived in the United States.

When Broadway's new matinee idol closed in *Autumn Crocus,* he reopened the play in Los Angeles in January, 1934, with Julie Haydon as the school teacher. The show played later in San Francisco, and then Lederer reported to RKO to start his American film career. For his Hollywood movie debut, RKO selected *A Man of Two Worlds* (1934) and cast the charming Czech as a blubber-eating Eskimo! Despite this unlikely casting, Francis, armed with his Reinhardt training, insisted on mouthing the Eskimo language phonetically, eating raw fish, and creating a realistic portrait of the icebound native who falls in love with a picture of Elissa Landi and invades London's drawing rooms with disastrous results. Then Paramount borrowed Lederer for the role of a charming young Hessian, Max, who decides that "bundling" with Joan Bennett is far preferable to fighting the Colonials. This role in *Pursuit of Happiness* (1934) was ideal for Lederer, allowing him to display all the gusto and charm he had used in *Autumn Crocus.*

Returning to RKO he played a bewildered immigrant who finds *Romance in Manhattan* (1934) with Ginger Rogers. During the filming of this picture he was guest speaker at several local clubs, expounding his theories on world peace. His involvement in, and dedication to, an International League for Peace started years before when he went to that declining organization to promote his plans for an actively nonpolitical, worldwide anti-war movement.

Lederer still vividly recalled his involvement in World War I: "My older brother was killed. I loved him and was fired with desire to avenge his death. I ran away and joined the army. There were boys of eight at the front and twice I was decorated for extraordinary bravery. One of the medals came because I braved artillery fire to bring the men in the trenches their food. So I got a medal. Perhaps it cost the government $2.00 and for that symbol of misguided patriotism you risk your life. I saw the war in all its horror and emerged from it unscathed physically but with an ambition to do whatever I could to prevent future purposeless waste." Hollywood was taken aback. Here was an actor who was a thinking man and could articulate without a script or agent's prompting.

For Francis the year 1935 began with a lawsuit filed by European playwright Jack Quatero demanding $250,000 for Lederer's alleged pirating and submission to a studio of a film plot Quatero had outlined verbally to the actor. On top of this the gossip columnists were making snide remarks about Francis' refusal to play the romantic lead in Katharine Hepburn's *Break of Hearts* (1935). Charles Boyer had accepted the role. RKO announced they were reading Dumas' *The Three Musketeers* (1935) for their new star, but it was Walter Abel and not Lederer who played D'Artagnan. Francis left the confusion of RKO in 1935 to free-lance, never to return to that studio. Adding to his legal hassles, a British theatrical agent claimed that by way of an oral agreement, Lederer owed him fifteen percent of his movie earnings.

At Fox, Francis starred as a frisky, prank-prone Prince masquerading as a bellhop in the bubbling *The Gay Deception* (1935) with Frances Dee. That same year officials of the San Diego Exposition invited Lederer to speak to a group of two hundred educators at the World Peace Day meeting of the Institute of World Affairs. His fervent speech and enthusiastic response from the educators impelled him to form the World Peace Federation, dedicated to outlawing war. Lederer was passionately preaching his theories across the land but not endearing himself to Hollywood when he announced that acting was practically a useless art. ("Anything I do toward advancing peace is futile unless I am a public figure. So I remain an actor in order to keep in the public spotlight.") Cecil B. DeMille set off respondent fireworks by denouncing Lederer's remarks as "nonsense!" Outspoken Carole Lombard observed, "Mr. Lederer is a little confused. The only kind of acting that's useless is bad acting."

United Artists made *One Rainy Afternoon* (1936), an amusing version of Rene Pujal's

With Ann Sothern in *My American Wife* **(Par '36).**

story, *Monsieur Sans Gene,* with Francis as a French actor romancing Ida Lupino. While Lederer was filming *My American Wife* (1936) at Paramount, he was dating Margo, who was then filming *Winterset* at RKO. In August, 1936, on the "Hollywood Hotel" radio show he and Margo were heard in a scene from *Liliom.* Later that year it was announced that Francis would star in a life of Chopin to be directed by Frank Capra, but the project never materialized.

In 1937 Francis wed Margo and he went back to the theatre, starring in Clifford Odets' *Golden Boy* with Betty Furness. He played the title role with much fire, but some critics thought he was miscast. In July, 1938, Ruth Selwyn signed Lederer for the lead in a play, *The King and the Umbrella,* wanting Margo for his co-star, but the show never came to be. During 1938 he made *It's All Yours* (1938) and, while still at Columbia, played Michael Lanyard in *The Lone Wolf in Paris.* Over at Paramount he joined Claudette Colbert, Don Ameche, John Barrymore, and Mary Astor in *Midnight* (1939), which was labeled as "one of the best of all Hollywood comedies—with a script [by Charles Brackett and Billy Wilder] of diamond brilliance." In contrast was Francis' performance in *Confessions of a Nazi Spy* (1939) as the German-American dupe of the fifth columnists. By now Lederer's days as a continental matinee idol in leading screen roles were over.

In the late spring of 1939, Margo and Francis left for a brief tour in *Seventh Heaven.* When Laurence Olivier was forced to relinquish his role opposite Katharine Cornell in *No Time for Comedy* on Broadway, Lederer succeeded Olivier in the role of Gaylord

With Frances Drake in *The Lone Wolf in Paris* (Col '38).

Easterbrook, and the role was renamed for the change in accents to Gai Esterbruch. Despite unfavorable critical comparisons to Olivier's performance, Francis was more than adequate in the role and played it both in New York and later on tour to enthusiastic audience response.

The front page of the *New York Times* on August 15, 1940, blared "HOLLYWOOD STARS ACCUSED AS REDS BEFORE GRAND JURY IN LOS ANGELES." Accused as either members, sympathizers, or contributors to the Communist parties were such "dangerous Reds" as Franchot Tone, Fredric March, Humphrey Bogart, James Cagney, and Francis. All the actors denied the ridiculous charges. Lederer stated, "I am not a Communist and have never been one. I am violently opposed to Communism and everything it stands for." Shortly thereafter, a Congressional committee cleared Francis of all Communist-related charges.

In 1940 Lederer and Margo divorced, and in July, 1941, he wed for the third time. (He had been married for a year and a half during his Prague student days to opera singer Ada Nejedly.) His new bride was Marion Ivrine of Toronto, Canada; they were wed at Las Vegas' Immanuel Community Church.

When George Sanders refused an assignment for Twentieth Century-Fox as the lead in *The Man I Married* (1940), Francis replaced him, playing Joan Bennett's German-

348

American husband who converts to the Hitler movement during a visit to Germany. However, by this time his screen personality was no longer a novelty and he found it harder and harder to find decent roles. He was forced to accept a role in a Judy Canova movie, *Puddin'head* (1941), and then left the screen for three years, having become involved in real estate.

If movies were not much interested in Lederer, stage audiences still were. He played the juvenile lead in a West Coast revival of *Music in the Air* in mid-1942 with Jan Clayton, and returned to the Eastern stages with *Pursuit of Happiness* and *The Play's the Thing*, among others. With Gloria Swanson he appeared in an evening of three one-act plays entitled *Three Curtains*, which toured throughout the spring of 1943.

In 1944 he returned to the West Coast to resume his film career in what was hoped to be a milestone film version of Thornton Wilder's *The Bridge of San Luis Rey* (1944). The film offered him in two roles as twin brothers. Despite a strong cast (Nazimova, Akim Tamiroff, Louis Calhern, Blanche Yurka), the production was inferior to MGM's 1929 edition. Then Francis spent thirteen days shooting *Voice in the Wind* (1944) in which he portrayed a Czech pianist tortured and persecuted by the Nazis. His scenes of mental derangement were well executed, but the whirlwind project made on too tight a budget ($50,000) lost money at the box-office.

Again the screen had proved unfulfilling for him, and he went back to the stage to star and tour in a West Coast production of *A Doll's House*. He was Torvald Helmer in a cast that included Jane Darwell, Philip Merivale, and Lyle Talbot. He toured in Angel Street in mid-1946 with Bramwell Fletcher. Occasionally a screen role would come his way, as the part of the homicidal artist in Republic's *The Madonna's Secret* (1946) or as the embittered, sadistic valet in *The Diary of a Chambermaid* (1946), starring Paulette Goddard and directed by Jean Renoir. These were to be his last worthwhile screen performances. In the summer of 1948 he received co-billing with Janet Blair in a tour of *For Love or Money*.

At the start of the new decade he was in three films. There was a dull Western with Vera Ralston, *Surrender* (1950); a colorless role as Rosalind Russell's suitor in *A Woman of Distinction* (1950); and a part as Barone Rocco De Greff supporting a seemingly disenchanted Alan Ladd in an uninteresting picture, *Captain Carey, U.S.A.* (1950). By the time of the Ladd bore, Francis, although only in his mid-forties, had obviously aged. He tried television on "TV Playhouse" and spent the summer touring in such diverse stage fare as *The Silver Whistle* and *Arms and the Man*.

He reappeared on the English stage in 1951 in *Collector's Item* at Manchester, England, and then went on to Berlin for the plays *Relative Values* and *Nina*. From there he went to Vienna to film *Stolen Identity* (1951), a competently made postwar romantic melodrama. He was satisfactorily cast as a famous pianist in this Turhan Bey production. Back on American TV he was exuding his old charm on a "Robert Montgomery Presents" segment. In February, 1955, he succeeded Anton Walbrook as Evelyn Laye's leading man in *Wedding in Paris* at London's Hippodrome, stopping en route in Lisbon to play Claude Rains' sinister henchman in *Lisbon* (1956). He closed the year by playing a prince in Olivia de Havilland's *The Ambassador's Daughter* and then was on the stage in Los Angeles in *The Sleeping Prince* with Shirley MacLaine and Hermione Gingold.

Francis' activities in civic affairs have not lessened over the years, and he has been a member of various committees for the improvement of the Los Angeles area. His film career ended with a Cornel Wilde production, *Maracaibo* (1958), and two horror films, *The Return of Dracula* (1958) and *Terror Is a Man* (1959). His private ranching interest and business occupies his advancing years, but in 1960 he performed exceptionally well as Dr. Gottlieb in a telecast of *Arrowsmith* with Farley Granger in the title role.

Infrequent video appearances occurred throughout the Sixties; one joyous occasion was a guest spot on Marlo Thomas' "That Girl" series.

As his acting career declined, his civic interests expanded. He became mayor of Canoga Park, California, was one of the founders of the Hollywood Museum, and raised a constant voice for the cause of world peace. Today he also lectures and teaches courses in acting. (He recently founded The American International Academy of Performing Arts.)

After making *The Gay Deception* with Lederer in 1935, Frances Dee commented on his screen work by saying: "He hasn't touched yet what he can and will do. Why won't people see the genius in this man? Certainly it is there!" It was there but Hollywood was reluctant to see it.

FRANCIS LEDERER

Die Wunderbar Luge der Nina Petrovna
(German 1929)
Zuflucht *(German 1929)*
Die Buchse der Pandora [Pandora's Box]
(German 1929)
Ihre Majestat die Liebe *(German 1929)*
Atlantik *(German 1929)*
Maman Ceribri *(French 1929)*
Haitang *(French 1930)*
Susanne Macht Ordnung *(German 1931)*
Das Schicksal Der Renate Langen *(German 1933)*
A Man of Two Worlds *(RKO 1934)*
Pursuit of Happiness *(Par 1934)*
Romance in Manhattan *(RKO 1934)*
The Gay Deception *(Fox 1935)*
One Rainy Afternoon *(UA 1936)*
My American Wife *(Par 1936)*
It's All Yours *(Col 1938)*

The Lone Wolf in Paris *(Col 1938)*
Midnight *(Par 1939)*
Confessions of a Nazi Spy *(WB 1939)*
The Man I Married *(20th 1940)*
Puddin'head *(Rep 1941)*
The Bridge of San Luis Rey *(UA 1944)*
Voice in the Wind *(UA 1944)*
The Madonna's Secret *(Rep 1946)*
The Diary of a Chambermaid *(UA 1946)*
Million Dollar Weekend *(EL 1948)*
Captain Carey, U.S.A. *(Par 1950)*
A Woman of Distinction *(Col 1950)*
Surrender *(Rep 1950)*
Stolen Identity *(Ainsworth 1953)*
The Ambassador's Daughter *(UA 1956)*
Lisbon *(Rep 1956)*
Maracaibo *(Par 1958)*
The Return of Dracula *(UA 1958)*
Terror Is a Man *(Valiant 1959)*

44

Eric Linden

Public clamor for the new talkies featuring new personalities kept Hollywood scouts on the prowl for performers who could act, handle dialogue, and perhaps even reach stardom. In the summer of 1931 director Wesley Ruggles was making an extensive search for the youthful lead role in *Are These Our Children?* (1931), a story which he had written and would direct for RKO. Among those tested was a young New York actor named Eric Linden. He won the part of Eddie Brand and subsequent national recognition.

He was born in New York City on Wednesday, September 15, 1909, to Swedish parents. His mother had married Philip Linden, an actor in Stockholm's Royal Theatre, and as their family grew they migrated to America. When the Linden family had grown to include four sons and a daughter, Mr. Linden abandoned his brood. One son was later killed by a truck on a New York street. Young Eric developed a lasting bitterness toward his father. "None of us ever heard of him again. He was a weakling and I do not see why I should be expected to do anything but despise him."

Eric worked at odd jobs from an early age, hawking newspapers ("I was the most raucous-voiced newsie on Tenth Avenue"), to earning two dollars a week as an errand boy for a hat shop, and washing dishes in his uncle's 56th Street restaurant. All these jobs occurred while he was attending the Paul Hoffman, Jr. School. Later he achieved high academic records while attending DeWitt Clinton High School, where he made his first stage appearance in the school's production of *If I Were King*. During the summer he worked as a filing clerk at Columbia University.

"There were two things which have driven me on ever since I can remember. I hated my father, so I made up my mind to make something out of myself, just to show him we could do without him. The other was my love for my mother. I had to succeed so that I could make up those long, hard years when she had to take me to work with her." Mrs. Linden was companion to a grande dame in Manhattan and for seven years kept the parish house of Trinity Chapel in New York on 126th Street. For a time, the Lindens lived in a room above the choir loft.

After Eric left school, he was a bank messenger, then worked in the mailing department of a medical concern, and later was employed by the foreign travel bureau at the Biltmore Hotel. He also ushered at the Riverside and Riviera Theatres on West 96th Street and took courses in English and literature at Columbia University. Next came a post as usher at the Roxy Theatre where he worked every day, including midnight

With Dorothy Jordan in *The Roadhouse Murder* (RKO '32).

shows, for eighteen dollars a week. There his former English teacher and drama coach discovered her star pupil and lectured him on wasting his talents. She had her former college chum, lyricist Dorothy Fields, write a letter of introduction for Eric to Cheryl Crawford at the Theatre Guild.

When Eric did reach Hollywood, the studio would promote him as "The Boy Sensation of the Theatre Guild." Actually, Eric's connection with the prestigious Guild was rather unglamorous. He made his first appearance on the stage of the Guild Theatre on January 9, 1928, as a slave and in six other minor parts in *Marco's Millions*. During the summer of 1928 Eric was assigned as assistant to stage manager Maurice McRae for the Guild's production of Eugene O'Neill's *Strange Interlude*. That fall he was cast as the He-Ape in their version of Goethe's *Faust,* as well as doubling as a villager in a cast that included Helen Chandler and Douglass Montgomery.

After his tenure with the Guild, Eric was in and out of two minor Broadway casualties, *Buckaroo* and *One Way Street.* He did summer repertory with the Berkshire Players in Stockbridge, Massachusetts. Through a chance meeting with Carrol Sax, Eric went to Paris for a year and a half to perform with the American Players in an assortment of roles. He was paid eighteen dollars a week, out of which he saved eleven dollars. Following the completion of the Paris engagement, he bought a second-hand bicycle for two dollars and toured the continent. He worked his passage home from Marseilles aboard a cattle ship.

Back in New York he was signed by NBC as one of their first radio juveniles as the lead in "The Adventures of Dick Trever." He opened in two plays that never reached Broadway, *Hilda Cassidy* and *Reunion,* and then came his audition for *Are These Our*

Children? "You know I won my Hollywood contract on the Lord's Prayer," says Eric. "I was broadcasting on a Tuesday when they sent for me for a test. They told me to do something dramatic. So the most dramatic thing I could think of was the Lord's Prayer. The test was sent to Hollywood by air and I left for Hollywood on Thursday and went to work the following Monday."

Eric's screen debut as the egomaniac Eddie Brand was greeted with loud bravos from the critics. *Motion Picture Herald* announced: "Ruggles was fortunate in his selection of his lead. Eric Linden's remarkable performance as the boy who gets into bad company and lands in the shadow of the electric chair does much to give the story compelling realism. We will be seeing more of this Linden boy. He has the goods." For the closing scene of the film, Linden, his arms clinging to the iron bars of his prison cell, recited the Lord's Prayer so effectively it brought tears to the eyes of most filmgoers. Many critics thought that his most impressive scene in the film was his pleading of his own case in court on the charge of murdering his best friend during a drunken brawl, and the registered shock he projected on being sentenced to death. The film closed with a spoken query to the audience to decide Linden's punishment and justice.

Of his career-making role, Eric has said: "I played the real me in the end. The boy who said the prayer was Eric Linden. That was a very simple thing. I've said the Lord's Prayer ever since I was old enough to say it. It has linked up every experience in my life up to now. We said it regularly when we lived over the church."

As part of his five-year RKO contract, Eric was next paired with the studio's champion weeper, Helen Twelvetrees, in *Young Bride* (1932). He was wasted in the worthless *The Roadhouse Murder* (1932), and then was loaned to Warner Bros. to play the hero-worshipping brother of auto-racing star James Cagney in Howard Hawks' *The Crowd Roars* (1932). Along with Richard Cromwell, Arline Judge, and Dorothy Wilson, Eric had a lead in *The Age of Consent* (1932), a campus story.

Linden fared much better on loan to Warner Bros. He was the country bumpkin salvaged by hard-boiled Joan Blondell in *Big City Blues* (1932). Then came his best screen portrayal, the hysterical young father in *Life Begins* (1932). Loretta Young was cast as his pregnant wife who had been imprisoned on a murder charge. Later in this story about events in a maternity ward, Eric's character is torn between anger and grief when the surgeon saves his child rather than his wife. He finally agrees to accept his fatherhood. Eric was fine in the demanding role, but admitted, "I had to live everything I did. I didn't know any other way. They said I took it all too seriously, but I had to take it that way!"

Since RKO had no immediate assignments for Eric they loaned him to Universal for *Afraid to Talk* (1932), the screen version of a controversial play entitled *Merry-Go-Round.* The story blatantly depicted municipal corruption. The film edition featured Eric as the unfortunate bellhop hero, with Edward Arnold as the gangland chief and Louis Calhern as the crooked district attorney. Back on his home lot he was cast as Lionel Barrymore's high-living, dissolute son in *Sweepings* (1933) and later Eric was the young inventor and Irene Dunne the long suffering, deceived wife of Charles Bickford in *No Other Woman* (1933).

Eric was being tagged as "the tragic boy actor of the screen." This designation was underscored by the studio handing him the male lead in a remake of *The Goose Woman* entitled *The Past of Mary Holmes* (1933). But the picture lacked the verve of the original Rex Beach drama, and the direction was erratic. Linden was much more fortunate with John Cromwell's direction in *The Silver Cord* (1933), which featured Laura Hope Crews (repeating her Broadway role) as the domineering mother, and the combined talents of Irene Dunne, Joel McCrea, Eric, and Frances Dee. The main complaint lodged against this prestige production was that it emerged as too stagey. Eric then made an air circus epic for RKO, *Flying Devils* (1933), and announced his retirement from the screen and Hollywood.

His disappointment with his past several film assignments was reduced when George Cukor singled him out to play Laurie in RKO's Katharine Hepburn version of *Little Women* (1933). But then there was a corporate shake-up at RKO and Kenneth Macgowan was put in charge of the project. He informed Eric that he was unsuited for the role of Laurie and that a very important member of the cast felt he was not equipped to portray the role properly. Douglass Montgomery was given the part and Eric, heartbroken and distraught, left Hollywood. He flew to New York and sailed for France. He rented a small villa near Monte Carlo and determined to write. After six months he returned to America, just at about the time *I Give My Love* (1934), a picture he had made for Universal, was being released. In New York, Eric signed for George Abbott's *Ladies' Money*, which opened on November 1, 1934, and lasted for thirty-six performances.

Then, Eric returned to Hollywood. After three programmers, he had the good fortune to sign a contract with MGM for the role of Richard Miller in *Ah, Wilderness!* (1935). Joining with Lionel Barrymore, Wallace Beery, and Mickey Rooney, Eric did an excellent job in this adaptation of Eugene O'Neill's play. Hollywood's columnists spoke of Eric's screen return as a comeback. Actually it was the slow beginning of a downhill slide.

Metro advertised their *The Voice of Bugle Ann* (1936) as "featuring the stars and

With Richard Arlen and Ian MacLaren in *Let 'em Have It* (UA '35).

With Bruce Cabot and Edgar Kennedy in *Robin Hood of El Dorado* (MGM '36).

producer of *Ah, Wilderness!*" Lionel Barrymore played crusty Springfield Davis and Eric
was his son Benjy. The movie was offbeat and well-directed by Richard Thorpe. After
two top performances, Eric was tossed in the middle of the cast of a saga of Mexican
outlaw Joaquin Murietta, *Robin Hood of El Dorado* (1935), starring Warner Baxter.
Linden supplied the romantic lead opposite Cecilia Parker in Wallace Beery's *Old
Hutch* (1936) and again played opposite Miss Parker in Grand National's fiasco *In His
Steps* (1936).

After a supporting role with Claire Trevor in *Career Woman* (1936) at Twentieth
C. ntury-Fox, Eric returned to MGM for a B picture called *A Family Affair* (1937). The
film turned out to be the beginning of a bonanza series for Metro-Goldwyn-Mayer on
the Hardy Family. Linden appeared in this initial installment as Wayne Trent, the beau
of Mickey Rooney's sister, Cecilia Parker. This was Eric's only participation in the series.

Eric and Cecilia Parker made a trio of dull quickies at Grand National that did nothing
to install the duo as a new screen love team. His final Metro picture under contract was
in support of Wallace Beery in *Good Old Soak* (1937). After a few other assignments
Eric again left Hollywood and the United States.

He went to London where he made his stage debut there by succeeding Luther Adler
in the role of Joe Bonaparte in *Golden Boy.* Later Eric's agent persuaded his client to

accept a small role in *Gone with the Wind* (1939). It was a tiny but showy part as an amputation case in the Atlanta hospital sequence. What was left of the scene onscreen was less than Eric had anticipated. He then returned to his first studio, RKO, for a minor role in *Everything's on Ice* (1939), which showcased juvenile ice skater Irene Dare.

In September, 1940, he began an extensive tour in the lead of *Golden Boy*, an itinerary that would include over seventy U.S. and Canadian cities. *Criminals Within* (1941) was Eric's last motion picture and a weary finale to his screen career. In the summer of 1941 he returned to the stage at Gloucester, Massachusetts, in *Another Language* with Fritzi Scheff, and later in *The Philadelphia Story* with Diana Barrymore. He went to Bradford, Connecticut, to play *Mr. and Mrs. North* with Claire Luce, doubling for a suddenly ill juvenile in their current week's *My Sister Eileen* while rehearsing his own show. The following summer he co-starred with Gloria Stuart in *Sailor, Beware!* on the New York subway circuit and was involved in the Washington, D.C., production of *Brighton Rock*. In the mid-Forties, after leaving the Armed Services, he was seen on the West Coast stage in *Trio*, which had a brief run.

At the Church of St. Mary's in Laguna Beach, on October 7, 1955, Eric was married at forty-six years of age. He and his creative artist wife Jo became the parents of Karen, David, and Andrea. For the past decade he has been employed by the County of Orange and is retiring this October (1976), contemplating picking up some of lucrative TV money—if he can take the pace.

Reflecting recently on his film career, Eric is most proud of his work in *Are These Our Children?*, *Life Begins*, and *Ah, Wilderness!* They were exceptional performances, but much of his work in the films of the Thirties was good. As a dramatic juvenile there were few who could outshine him on the screen.

ERIC LINDEN

Are These Our Children? *(RKO 1931)*
Young Bride *(RKO 1932)*
The Roadhouse Murder *(RKO 1932)*
The Crowd Roars *(WB 1932)*
The Age of Consent *(RKO 1932)*
Big City Blues *(WB 1932)*
Life Begins *(FN 1932)*
Afraid to Talk *(Univ 1932)*
No Other Woman *(RKO 1933)*
Sweepings *(RKO 1933)*
The Past of Mary Holmes *(RKO 1933)*
The Silver Cord *(RKO 1933)*
Flying Devils *(RKO 1933)*
I Give My Love *(Univ 1934)*
Let 'em Have It *(UA 1935)*
Ladies Crave Excitement *(Mascot 1935)*
Born to Gamble *(Rep 1935)*

Ah, Wilderness! *(MGM 1935)*
The Voice of Bugle Ann *(MGM 1936)*
Robin Hood of El Dorado *(MGM 1935)*
Old Hutch *(MGM 1936)*
In His Steps *(Grand National 1936)*
Career Woman *(20th 1936)*
A Family Affair *(MGM 1937)*
Girl Loves Boy *(Grand National 1937)*
Good Old Soak *(MGM 1937)*
Sweetheart of the Navy *(Grand National 1937)*
Here's Flash Carey *(Grand National 1937)*
Midnight Intruder *(Univ 1938)*
Romance of the Limberlost *(Mon 1938)*
Gone with the Wind *(MGM 1939)*
Everything's on Ice *(RKO 1939)*
Criminals Within *(PRC 1941)*

45

Margaret Lindsay

The influx of talent pouring into Hollywood in the early 1930s was phenomenal. That even a small percentage of the newcomers obtained screen work was amazing; that some of them achieved a degree of popularity was incredible. Few who made the grade to cinema note were as personable or as pleasantly talented as Margaret Lindsay.

She was born Margaret Kies in Dubuque, Iowa, on Monday, September 19, 1910. She attended the National Park Seminary in Washington, D.C., and later persuaded her parents to let her enroll at the American Academy of Dramatic Arts in New York. When she graduated she found she could not obtain any desirable stage spots. Determined to succeed, she booked passage for England and subsequently made her stage debut there, appearing in such plays as *Escape, Death Takes a Holiday, By Candlelight, The Middle Watch,* and *The Romantic Age.*

Coming back to America she expected to score on the Broadway stage. But the show for which she had signed kept being delayed by production problems, so she encouraged her agent to arrange screen tests for her. Several studios tested her, but it was Universal which signed the "English" Miss Lindsay for a role in their forthcoming *The Old Dark House* (1932). But when she arrived in Hollywood, Universal had cast Gloria Stuart in the film. Instead Margaret was assigned to play a kidnapping victim in a diverting picture with Lew Ayres and Maureen O'Sullivan, *Okay, America!* (1932). She did two minor roles in *The All-American* (1932) and *Afraid to Talk* (1932), and then became Tom Mix's leading lady, Molly, in *The Fourth Horseman* (1932). She was saddled in Monogram's dull *West of Singapore* (1933) and then learned that Fox was seeking English actors for their all-British production of Noël Coward's *Cavalcade* (1933).

The engaging hazel-eyed brunette was a fast study, not only on lines for filming but also on the fictionalized fantasies of Hollywood's overworked press agents. She arrived at the Fox lot armed with a fake biography that included, among other whimsies, that she was born in Kenley, an austere suburb of London, and her father, a London broker, had her educated by private tutors in a London convent. The fact that Margaret, eldest of a family of five of a pharmacist who died in 1930 was really from Dubuque, where her three younger sisters and brother were still in residence with their mother, could have been easily checked; but Fox bought Miss Lindsay's phony background and assigned her the brief but showy role of Edith Harris in *Cavalcade.* In the second half of the film,

With James Cagney in *The Frisco Kid* (WB '35).

set aboard the deck of an Atlantic liner, Margaret is shown with John Warburton. They are on their honeymoon, dressed formally for dinner and stopped momentarily on the promenade deck to plan their future. Margaret declares they could never in their whole lives be happier than they are at the present. At the end of their dialogue she takes up her cloak from the railing and they walk out of the scene. A spotlight picks up a lifebelt hanging under the railing whose black letters spell out S.S. *Titanic*. Critics applauded the picture, and the "all-British" cast, including Margaret, was singled out for its expert performance.

After the panoramic excellence of *Cavalcade*, Margaret was signed to a term contract by Warner Bros. Explaining her hoodwinking of Hollywood, Margaret later admitted: "I was in a quandary. Although I looked and talked English, to tell them I was actually from Iowa would have lost the assignment for me. Yet, I was conscience-stricken at fooling them. The upshot was that I resolved to investigate the rest of the cast. If any of the leads were not English, I'd go through with it. Who do you suppose was less authentic than I? None other than Beryl Mercer. She was born in Spain!"[8]

As a Warner Bros. contractee, Margaret played anything the studio assigned to her. Her best role in 1933 was in *Captured!*, in which she was fourth-billed as "the radiant beauty of *Cavalcade*," playing in support of Leslie Howard, Douglas Fairbanks, Jr., and Paul Lukas. She also had a good role in George Arliss' *Voltaire*. But because of *Caval-*

[8]Actually Beryl Mercer was born of British parents in Spain, but her entire career was spent in Britain until she came to America. The one who was less authentic was Bonita Granville who had a fairly sizeable role as Fanny as a young girl. Bonita had been born in New York City of American parents. It is really more to her credit that nobody ever questioned her being in the film. Betty Grable can also be glimpsed during the Twentieth Century Blues sequence at the end, but she did not have a speaking role in *Cavalcade* like Lindsay, Mercer, and Granville.

cade, critics were forever saying about her that she was being cast in roles more suited to an *American* actress. Fox borrowed her for Janet Gaynor's *Paddy, the Next Best Thing* (1933) to play Janet's older sister. (Actually she was four years younger than Miss Gaynor.) She returned to Warner Bros.-First National for Paul Muni's *The World Changes* (1933), a profile and study of a wealthy American family. In *Lady Killer* (1933) she was very good as a movie star in this James Cagney vehicle. Her work was competent during 1934 in minor Warner films, but showed to advantage in their *Bordertown* (1935) with Bette Davis and Paul Muni. Offscreen, Louella Parsons was linking her romantically with singer Dick Powell as an arch rival of Mary Brian for his affection.

James Cagney won Margaret in *Devil Dogs of the Air* (1935), but her performance was uneven, in fact uneasy to the point of making her seem bored by the whole thing. The studio continued to keep her busy during 1935, often in two pictures in production at the same time. Uusually she had the second female lead, but occasionally rose to the distaff top slot, as in James Cagney's *G-Men* (1935). But 1936 was eventful and racking for Margaret for reasons beyond the Warner Brothers.

In January of 1936, Warner released Margaret from an assigned role in *Murder by an Aristocrat* and replaced her with Marguerite Churchill. The normally calm and cool Miss Lindsay was in a state of nervous exhaustion and emotionally spent. The reason was the mystery death of her actress friend Thelma Todd on December 17, 1935, who was found dead in her sports car, due, it was supposed, to carbon monoxide asphyxiation. The death occurred after the ice cream blonde, Thelma, had returned from a party given in her honor by Ida Lupino's father, Stanley. Margaret had attended the gathering and was the dinner companion of Pasquale Di Cicco, to whom Thelma had been married in 1932 but divorced in 1934. The intense investigation by a grand jury included Margaret's being subpoenaed as a witness. The outlandish publicity and the rigors of testifying undermined the Lindsay nervous system.

After recuperating, she returned to the studio and was given generally minor assignments. After completing *Isle of Fury* (1936) she sailed to Hawaii, but on her arrival in Honolulu she was met by a company representative who told her she had to return to the studio for retakes on the film with Humphrey Bogart. The retakes amounted to one line of dialogue that, when the picture was released, had been cut from the film.

In 1937 she was fine as Frances Ogilvie with Errol Flynn in *Green Light.* A group of sound engineers, commenting on Lindsay's husky tones, claimed she had "the most pleasant voice in pictures." Warners loaned her to Metro for two features in 1937, *Sinner Take All* and *Song of the City.* In mid-June of that year she was rushed to a local hospital for arsenic poisoning due to eating unwashed, ill-prepared vegetables.

One of Margaret's best screen appearances came in *Jezebel* (1938). She played the unwelcome Yankee bride of Henry Fonda who agrees to permit Bette Davis to take yellow-fever victim Fonda to an isolated island where they are consigned to death as an anti-plague measure. Unfortunately, after *Jezebel* Margaret was tossed into such hack films as *When Were You Born?* (1938).

As the Thirties drew to a close, Margaret was reduced to programmers, and she was romantically linked with Edward Norris with whom she made *On Trial* (1939). In December, 1939, she started filming *The Devil Is Yellow,* which Universal released the next year as *Double Alibi* (1940). When *The House of Seven Gables* (1940) was released, in which Margaret played Hepzibah to Vincent Price's Clifford, Louella Parsons was gushing in print that Margaret and actor William Lundigan were "talking" wedding rings.

In 1940 Margaret signed with Columbia for the continuing role of free-lance mystery writer Nikki Porter, secretary to master detective Ellery Queen in a series of seven

In the mid-Thirties.

With Richard Bond in *Broadway Musketeers* (WB '38).

celluloid mysteries solved by Mr. Queen. Four of these films featured Ralph Bellamy as the famed sleuth and the final three had William Gargan as the elite gumshoe. Between the making of the series entries, Margaret appeared in Universal's remake of *The Spoilers* (1942), and the columns were reporting her romance with Charles Wendling (Claudette Colbert's brother) and with Forrest Tucker. Margaret lived with her sister Helen in Hollywood and considered Cesar "Butch" Romero one of the town's best dates and, beyond equal, the best ballroom dancer in Hollywood. She enjoyed dancing with him at the Club La Bomba with its Cuban band.

In 1943 Columbia started another new mystery series with fading Warner Baxter as Dr. Robert Ordway, the Crime Doctor. But Margaret appeared only in the first *Crime Doctor* entry, cast as Grace Fielding. Throughout the Forties, Margaret appeared mostly in B-film leads in programmers that sated the film market with its continual demand for double features. Infrequently she would land a good supporting role in films which were considered more prestigious, such as MGM's *Cass Timberlane* (1947) or their *B. F.'s Daughter* (1948). But most of the films she graced were quickly forgotten.

In late spring of 1950, Margaret, who still had a "name" with some segments of the entertainment-craving audience, left for the East Coast and a return to the legitimate stage. Directed by Jean Dalrymple, she co-starred with Franchot Tone in a revival of S. N. Behrman's *The Second Man*. The show, which featured Cloris Leachman in a supporting role, played the straw-hat circuit. During that summer Margaret made her television debut on "Masterpiece Theatre" in a telecast of *The Importance of Being Earnest,* giving her a chance to rework her British dialect. Throughout the decade, she was seen in a variety of supporting roles in films and in better parts on television, including *The Martha Crockett Story* on "The Millionaire" series in February, 1958.

For Ross Hunter and Universal, Margaret appeared as nurse Coleman in love with Dr.

Macdonald Carey in *Tammy and the Doctor* (1963), a secondary lead to Sandra Dee. It was Margaret's last screen appearance to date.

Margaret Lindsay, who has never married, flirted often with stardom but never really attained it. Her memorable performance as the doomed bride in *Cavalcade* should have been followed with more such striking and enduring assignments. Instead, she became a capable supporting actress at Warner Bros.' Burbank factory. The penalty for such secondary status was the loss of top-ranking assignments, pay, and prestige; the reward was letting her continue in acting when many other faster-rising screen ingenues had fallen by the wayside, having used up their brief moments as leading ladies.

MARGARET LINDSAY

Okay, America! *(Univ 1932)*
The All-American *(Univ 1932)*
Afraid to Talk *(Univ 1932)*
The Fourth Horseman *(Univ 1932)*
West of Singapore *(Mon 1933)*
Cavalcade *(Fox 1933)*
Christopher Strong *(RKO 1933)*
Private Detective 62 *(WB 1933)*
Baby Face *(WB 1933)*
The House on 56th Street *(WB 1933)*
Captured! *(WB 1933)*
Voltaire *(WB 1933)*
Paddy, the Next Best Thing *(Fox 1933)*
The World Changes *(FN 1933)*
From Headquarters *(WB 1933)*
Lady Killer *(WB 1933)*
Merry Wives of Reno *(WB 1934)*
Fog over Frisco *(FN 1934)*
The Dragon Murder Case *(FN 1934)*
Gentlemen Are Born *(FN 1934)*
Bordertown *(WB 1935)*
Devil Dogs of the Air *(WB 1935)*
The Florentine Dagger *(WB 1935)*
The Case of the Curious Bride *(FN 1935)*
G-Men *(WB 1935)*
Personal Maid's Secret *(FN 1935)*
Frisco Kid *(WB 1935)*
Dangerous *(WB 1935)*
The Lady Consents *(RKO 1936)*
The Law in Her Hands *(FN 1936)*
Public Enemy's Wife *(WB 1936)*
Isle of Fury *(WB 1936)*
Sinner Take All *(MGM 1936)*
Green Light *(WB 1937)*
Song of the City *(MGM 1937)*
Slim *(WB 1937)*
Back in Circulation *(WB 1937)*
Jezebel *(WB 1938)*
When Were You Born? *(WB 1938)*
Gold Is Where You Find It *(WB 1938)*
There's That Woman Again *(Col 1938)*

Broadway Musketeers *(WB 1938)*
Garden of the Moon *(WB 1938)*
Hell's Kitchen *(WB 1939)*
On Trial *(WB 1939)*
The Under-Pup *(Univ 1939)*
20,000 Men a Year *(20th 1939)*
Double Alibi *(Univ 1940)*
British Intelligence *(WB 1940)*
Honeymoon Deferred *(Univ 1940)*
The House of Seven Gables *(Univ 1940)*
Meet the Wildcat *(Univ 1940)*
Ellery Queen, Master Detective *(Col 1940)*
Ellery Queen's Penthouse Mystery *(Col 1941)*
There's Magic in Music *(Par 1941)*
Ellery Queen and the Perfect Crime *(Col 1941)*
A Close Call for Ellery Queen *(Col 1942)*
A Tragedy at Midnight *(Rep 1942)*
The Spoilers *(Univ 1942)*
Enemy Agents Meet Ellery Queen *(Col 1942)*
A Desperate Chance for Ellery Queen *(Col 1942)*
Crime Doctor *(Col 1943)*
Let's Have Fun *(Col 1943)*
No Place for a Lady *(Col 1943)*
Alaska *(Mon 1944)*
The Adventures of Rusty *(Col 1945)*
Scarlet Street *(Univ 1945)*
Club Havana *(PRC 1945)*
Her Sister's Secret *(PRC 1946)*
Seven Keys to Baldpate *(RKO 1947)*
Louisiana *(Mon 1947)*
Cass Timberlane *(MGM 1947)*
The Vigilantes Return *(Univ 1947)*
B. F.'s Daughter *(MGM 1948)*
Emergency Hospital *(UA 1956)*
The Bottom of the Bottle *(20th 1956)*
The Restless Years *(Univ 1958)*
Please Don't Eat the Daisies *(MGM 1960)*
Jet over the Atlantic *(Inter-Continent 1960)*
Tammy and the Doctor *(Univ 1963)*

46

Anita Louise

Artist McClelland Barclay described Anita Louise as "a piece of Dresden china and probably the most beautiful woman in the movies." No overstatement!—she looked like a model for the angelic figures in Renaissance paintings. There was about her a cool detachment and an unearthly radiance that constantly evoked the comment that she was the most ethereal ingenue in pictures.

Anita Louise Fremault was born on Saturday, January 9, 1915, in New York City to antique dealer Louis Fremault and his wife Anne. From the very beginning her life was intended for the arts. Acting, singing, and playing the harp and piano were some of the goals the ambitious Mrs. Fremault had for her daughter. Anita was enrolled in New York's famous Professional Children's School and at the age of six made her stage debut with Walter Hampden in *Peter Ibbetson*. As a child she had golden curls and sparkling blue eyes. Her education was combined with training in music, stage, and dancing, and she studied the latter with Mme. Nijinska.

Anne Fremault's long-range plans for her lovely daughter included all areas of theatrical endeavor, so when Anita turned seven, Anne took her to New England for a brief bit in *Down to the Sea in Ships* (1922). Director Elmer Clifton noticed the beautiful girl in the oncamera crowd and later asked her, "Are you Swedish?" Little Anita answered, "No, I'm Catholic!"

In 1924 she made two films for William Christy Cabanne at studios in Astoria, New York: *The Sixth Commandment* and *Lend Me Your Husband*. Cabanne became one of Anita's closest friends throughout her life. At Fox's 56th Street Studios in New York she made *The Music Master* (1927) with Alec B. Francis, and that same year, Mrs. Anne Beresford (formerly Fremault) took her gifted daughter to Hollywood. There Anita was entered at the Lawlor Prep School. According to classmate Mickey Rooney, no child broke down under "Ma" Lawlor's curriculum, which was just as well since Mother Anne had daughter Anita studying dancing with Helen Meuller, intently practicing piano and harp, and learning three languages.

Fox's *Four Devils* (1928) was released as a silent picture, and then recalled to have sound and talking sequences added. In the first section, or prologue, kindly old clown J. Farrell MacDonald rescues four children, raising them to become circus acrobats. The children portraying the young "Four Devils" were: Dawn O'Day, Anita Fremault, Phil-

At Warner Bros. c. '36.

lipe De Lacy, and Jack Parker. For Tiffany, Anita appeared in the silent *The Spirit of Youth* (1929) and had a bit in the part-talkie *Wonder of Women* (1929).

By the end of 1929 Anita had adopted a new surname, Louise, for her professional career, and she was parading forth in a series of minor roles for various studios. At the age of fifteen, Anita was assigned her first leading role, as Mimi, who becomes a Parisian dancer, in *Just Like Heaven* (1930). For the same studio she had the lead in *The Third Alarm* (1930), this time being rescued from an orphanage fire by the man she loves, James Hall.

Helen Twelvetrees underwent endless betrayals, seductions, and heartbreaks that climaxed in shooting her former lover, within *Millie* (1931), all to protect her daughter's (Anita) virginity. Here, as in other ventures, Anita's playing was sincere. If her roles were frequently vacuous, her acting and natural beauty offset some of the coyness. One exception was Universal's misguided *Heaven on Earth* (1931), in which she played "Cowhead" opposite Lew Ayres. Both Ayres and Anita were badly miscast. *Motion Picture Herald* kindly described Anita's performance as "Just blah," noting her attempted southern accent was merely terrible.

Anita's roles were usually a blend of romantic background. Thus, she was thrilled when RKO considered her for the demanding dramatic role of Sidney Fairfield in David O. Selznick's production of *A Bill of Divorcement* (1932). But director George Cukor insisted on a new actress named Katharine Hepburn. Anita fared better at RKO the next year when director Cukor was agreeable to her being cast in *Our Betters* (1933) as Constance Bennett's lovely and talkative sister. Anita remained friends with Miss Bennett for years; no mean feat, since Constance preferred masculine company and could not abide the girl-talk syndrome.

One of Anita's great joys was working with Will Rogers in *Judge Priest* (1934), in which she was in love with Rogers' screen son, Tom Brown. Offscreen, the Brown-Louise romance attracted considerable attention. Their engagement was finally announced and eventually broken. After a year-and-a-half romance with attractive Tom Brown and reteaming on the screen with him in *Bachelor of Arts* (1934), Anita declared, "He's the dearest friend I have and I miss him dreadfully when I'm away from Hollywood." Although Anita and Tom made a handsome couple, they both decided their youth and careers would be too conflicting and confining for a successful marriage.

Anita had come into her cinematic own with her striking performance as a very lovely Marie Antoinette in Warner Bros.' *Madame Du Barry* (1934). She later confessed to a preference for period and costume pictures. And little wonder, for her natural beauty was enchantingly enhanced by the bustled gowns and sweeping silks and taffetas of earlier days (which also hid her slight limp, due to one leg being a little shorter than the other).

Her best films were for Warner Bros., and when that studio decided to bring Max Reinhardt's superbly staged *A Midsummer Night's Dream* to the screen in 1935, Anita was selected for the role of Titania, Queen of the Fairies (played by Julie Haydon in Reinhardt's stage rendition). Anita gave a stunningly beautiful performance in the Shakespearean classic, in addition to making personal appearances with the film's opening in key cities. But the film was uneven and the studio's decision to use their stable of stars—from James Cagney to Joe E. Brown—was unfortunate.

Since her performance as the young murderess in *The Firebird* (1934) Anita had been under contract to Warner Bros. They loaned her to Fox as dancer Lydia Lubov in *Here's to Romance* (1935). Nino Martini starred in that film and the Fox publicity department created a romance between Anita and the Italian tenor. Anita rebuffed the gossip columns with: "I'm eighteen [sic], and as old as the hills because I've played grown-up parts since the age of thirteen. And, as to romance, there is no time in my life for it at present. That talk about Mr. Nino Martini and me was silly. We became acquainted on the set of *Here's to Romance* and I showed him around Hollywood because he was a stranger. Those rumors that we'd be married were quite ridiculous. I'm not in love with Mr. Martini in the first place, and anyway, I intend to devote myself entirely to my career for a while. A girl can't be eighteen forever and I've been in pictures so long that people are already beginning to count on their fingers."

Besides her extensive film work, Anita had graduated from the Greenwood School for Girls and had become a member of Delta Phi Alpha Sorority. In September of 1936, she and her mother Mrs. Anne Beresford took a course in American literature thrice weekly at the University of California, and multi-talented Anita continued her studies on the harp.

As Paul Muni's daughter Annette in *The Story of Louis Pasteur* (1935), Anita was a vision of loveliness, and the next year she was equally picturesque as the less than virtuous mother of illegitimate *Anthony Adverse* (1936), sired by Louis Hayward to whom passion-struck Anita whispers, "I'm yours now! I'm all yours!"

It was not unusual for Anita to shuttle from one set to another, whenever her picture schedules at the Burbank studio overlapped. She rushed from the soundstage of *Call It a Day* (1937), in which she was the gorgeous girl next door, to the sets of *The Go-Getter* (1937). Between these multiple activities she was heard on "Radio Theatre" as Jean Hersholt's daughter in *The Music Master*. And later that May (of 1936) she was photographed receiving blue ribbons for her prizewinning Irish setters in a local dog show. This lady obviously kept busy. On Easter Sunday, March 28, 1937, Anita opened the sunrise service at Hollywood Bowl, reciting a "Salute to Dawn." The golden-haired, five-foot, six-inch young lady who had been chosen a Wampas Baby Star in 1931 was becoming a welcome fixture in filmdom.

Her performances continued to be screenworthy. She starred with Errol Flynn in a tale of a dedicated doctor, *Green Light* (1937), and she was classy as Kay Francis' niece in *First Lady* (1937). In the remake of Gloria Swanson's *The Trespasser* (1929) retitled *That Certain Woman* (1937), Bette Davis was the star. However, as the crippled wife of Henry Fonda, Anita gave a telling performance, especially in the final reel when she was confined to a wheelchair.

Metro's posh production of *Marie Antoinette* (1938) starred Norma Shearer as the tragedy-prone queen. Cast in the role of Princesse de Lamballe was Maureen O'Sullivan. By the time the shooting started, it was discovered that Miss O'Sullivan (wed to writer-director John Farrow) was pregnant, and could not perform. A frantic call to Warners provided Anita with the showy role. Back on the home lot she joined Dick Powell in *Going Places* (1938), a remake of *The Hottentot,* and she was the loveliest of *The Sisters* (1938), a period tearjerker that starred Bette Davis. This film was really Anita's last well-rounded, fulfilling screen role. It was also the end of her Warners contract, although she was initially announced for *All This and Heaven Too* which went to Bette Davis.

As a free-lancer, Anita was her usual lovely self, but only shared the romantic background with Richard Greene in Shirley Temple's *The Little Princess* (1939) at Twentieth Century-Fox. On the other hand, she had more of a variety of roles on radio, being heard in the *Silver Dollar* and *A Man to Remember* episodes of "Lux Radio Theatre" in 1939.

If her screen career was being dissipated by the rise of celluloid newcomers, Anita did quite nicely on the domestic front. On May 10, 1940, she and Buddy Adler applied for a marriage license and were wed the following Saturday, May 17. Their marriage became one of the happiest of Hollywood's unions. It would be in that year that 31-year-old

With Edward Norris and Art Miles (as the gorilla) in *The Gorilla* (20th '39).

Adler, a graduate of the University of Pennsylvania's Wharton School, would win an Academy Award for his first screen effort, a Pete Smith short subject, *Quicker 'N a Wink*. (Later Adler would become a perspicacious producer and in the mid-Fifties rose to production chief at Twentieth Century-Fox.)

Anita continued her screen career in a string of lackluster programmers, in most of which she was miscast. By the summer of 1941 she returned to the stage, co-starring with Owen Davis, Jr., in *Mr. and Mrs. North*. The straw-hat tour was so successful the management decided to continue the production into the new season. But the summer success was not repeated on the road and it folded in Detroit by October.

During the war years, Adler served as an army lieutenant in the photographic unit of the Signal Corps while Anita made a few pictures. Perhaps her best of this period was *Casanova Brown* (1944), in which she is left at the altar by Gary Cooper. Later that year she played the heavy of Gamma Theta sorority who is murdered in *Nine Girls*, a clever whodunit with Ann Harding, Evelyn Keyes, and Nina Foch. In 1940 David O. Selznick had tested Anita for the Joan Fontaine role in *Rebecca*, and in 1945 he gave her a featured role in the Jennifer Jones-Joseph Cotten soggy romance tale *Love Letters*.

The Partridge Club at a luncheon in New York's Hotel Abbey honored Anita in January 1944 for her tireless efforts in the city's paper salvage campaign; she was crowned "Paper Doll of the Salvage Campaign." On October 17, 1945, she was back in Manhattan to greet nearly twelve thousand returning war veterans aboard HMS *Queen Mary*, participating in a "Welcome Home" show hosted by Ed Sullivan at the end of the pier.

With David Holt in *Hero for a Day* (Univ '39).

In 1946 Anita did three double-bill items with Michael Duane for Columbia and was back in costume as lady-in-waiting Catherine Maitland, with Cornel Wilde, in *The Bandit of Sherwood Forest*. After two more quickies for Harry Cohn's studio, she retired from the screen to become the mother of daughter Melanie, born August 10, 1947. Three years later, Anita and Adler had a son, Anthony. That same year she ventured into television, first appearing on Ken Murray's variety show in a nine-minute dramatic sketch and, of course, playing her harp. Over the next few years she was a guest on several anthology series and then, on September 30, 1955, she made a debut in what became a hit teleseries, "My Friend Flicka," co-starring with Gene Evans and Johnny Washbrook. In the summer of 1957 and 1958 she was lead-in hostess for reruns of Loretta Young television programs, and looked appropriately gorgeous.

At the Cedars of Lebanon Hospital on July 12, 1960, Buddy Adler died of lung cancer at the age of fifty-one. Anita and her children attended the funeral at Los Angeles' Temple Israel with a goodly portion of the Hollywood colony. George Jessel delivered the eulogy. Two years later Anita married importer Henry L. Berger, and she became active in philanthropic causes, devoting a large portion of her time to the National Hemophilia Foundation and to the Children's Asthma Research Institute. The Bergers became close friends with President and Mrs. Richard Nixon, often celebrating Anita's and Mr. Nixon's mutual birthday together, January 9.

On Tuesday, April 21, 1970, Anita and Henry Berger celebrated their eighth wedding anniversary. Daughter Melanie had moved to New York and son Tony Adler was a student at Claremont, California, College. On April 25, 1970, Anita was to appear at a

369

charity ball for which she was chairman, but earlier in the day she complained of a violent headache. A doctor was summoned to her Holmby Hills home. By nightfall she was dead of a massive cerebral stroke. The golden-haired, lovely Anita was gone at the age of fifty-five.

This ending was a sad postscript to the glory that once was Anita's. In February, 1975, part of her estate was auctioned off at the Starlight Garden of the International Hotel, near Kennedy Airport. The bidding was spotty and the auctioneer told the press, "You're witnessing auction history today. . . . These people are setting new records for low bids." Most of the people who attended the auction were browsers. Some did not know whose possessions were being sold. One woman was asked if she knew who Anita Louise was. She replied, "My husband said the name registered a little with him. . . . But I don't even recognize the pictures [of her]."

ANITA LOUISE

As: *Anita Fremault:*

Down to the Sea in Ships *(W. H. Hodkinson 1922)*
The Sixth Commandment *(Associated Exhibitors 1924)*
Lend Me Your Husband *(C. C. Burr 1924)*
The Music Master *(Fox 1927)*
Four Devils *(Fox 1928)*
A Woman of Affairs *(MGM 1928)*
The Spirit of Youth *(Tiffany 1929)*
Wonder of Women *(MGM 1929)*

As: *Anita Louise:*

Square Shoulders *(Pathé 1929)*
The Marriage Playground *(Par 1929)*
What a Man! *(Tiffany 1930)*
The Florodora Girl *(MGM 1930)*
Just Like Heaven *(Tiffany 1930)*
The Third Alarm *(Tiffany 1930)*
Millie *(RKO 1931)*
The Great Meadow *(MGM 1931)*
The Woman Between *(RKO 1931)*
Everything's Rosie *(RKO 1931)*
Heaven on Earth *(Univ 1931)*
The Phantom of Crestwood *(RKO 1932)*
Our Betters *(RKO 1933)*
Most Precious Thing in Life *(Col 1934)*
Are We Civilized? *(Raspin Productions 1934)*
I Give My Love *(Univ 1934)*
Cross Streets *(Chesterfield 1934)*
Judge Priest *(Fox 1934)*
Madame Du Barry *(WB 1934)*
The Firebird *(WB 1934)*
Bachelor of Arts *(Fox 1934)*
Lady Tubbs *(Univ 1935)*
Here's to Romance *(Fox 1935)*
A Midsummer Night's Dream *(WB 1935)*
Personal Maid's Secret *(WB 1935)*

The Story of Louis Pasteur *(WB 1935)*
Brides Are Like That *(FN 1936)*
Anthony Adverse *(WB 1936)*
Call It a Day *(WB 1937)*
Green Light *(WB 1937)*
The Go-Getter *(WB 1937)*
First Lady *(WB 1937)*
That Certain Woman *(WB 1937)*
Tovarich *(WB 1937)*
My Bill *(WB 1938)*
Marie Antoinette *(MGM 1938)*
Going Places *(WB 1938)*
The Sisters *(WB 1938)*
The Gorilla *(20th 1939)*
Hero for a Day *(Univ 1939)*
Reno *(RKO 1939)*
These Glamour Girls *(MGM 1939)*
Main Street Lawyer *(Rep 1939)*
The Little Princess *(20th 1939)*
Wagons Westward *(Rep 1940)*
The Villain Still Pursued Her *(RKO 1940)*
Glamour for Sale *(Col 1940)*
The Phantom Submarine *(Col 1941)*
Two in a Taxi *(Col 1941)*
Harmon of Michigan *(Col 1941)*
Dangerous Blondes *(Col 1943)*
Nine Girls *(Col 1944)*
Casanova Brown *(RKO 1944)*
Love Letters *(Par 1945)*
The Fighting Guardsman *(Col 1945)*
Shadowed *(Col 1946)*
The Bandit of Sherwood Forest *(Col 1946)*
The Devil's Mask *(Col 1946)*
Personality Kid *(Col 1946)*
Blondie's Big Moment *(Col 1947)*
Bulldog Drummond at Bay *(Col 1947)*
Retreat, Hell! *(WB 1952)*

47

Paul Lukas

Paramount's Jesse Lasky celebrated his forty-sixth birthday in Budapest, Hungary, seeing a performance of a play *Antonia* at the Vigszinhaz Comedy Theatre. Although Lasky understood no Hungarian, he was a good judge of fine acting. After the show he went backstage to congratulate the young, forceful actor, Paul Lukas, and, through an interpreter, offered him a contract to make motion pictures in America.

To the screen of the Thirties, Paul Lukas brought a suave personality, exceptional acting ability, poise, charm, and sincerity. Paul called this versatility of talent "Gesellschaftspiel." He equated the term to a parlor game, played with partners, that was translated into acting and that cannot be done alone. "When I speak lines in a play, I mean them; I am talking to someone. It is all real. But how can I say real things to someone who talks back to me like a bad actor—you know, with a big voice from the throat? I can't. It is impossible. So there cannot be true acting unless everyone in the cast is true." His explanation was valid, if not always applicable, to films made in Hollywood, or even to life itself.

Paul claimed he was born on a railroad train as it pulled into the Budapest Station on Saturday, May 26, 1894. He was the only son of Janos and Maria Lukacs. When the First World War erupted, he went into the service in August 1914. Six months later he was back in Budapest, shell-shocked and torn by shrapnel. His career with the Fifth Dragoons, Hungarian Cavalry, was ended. In 1915 he entered the Royal Academy of Acting and fell in love with an actress, but the marriage was brief. By 1917 he returned to war service, joining the Aviation Corps and piloting a plane, a talent he never lost.

When Paul had been a student at the Piarista Gymnasium, his father had assumed he would eventually join the family advertising and music publishing business. But the boy had different ideas. In 1912 he joined the wrestling team for the Olympic Games in Stockholm, and after the war he tried the theatre. "Whatever I know about acting I owe to one man, Daniel Job, the director of the Comedy Theatre in Budapest." Before he joined that troupe, Paul had appeared in more than fifty roles with a repertory company in Kassa, Hungary. In Budapest he appeared in *Liliom, The Swan, Uncle Vanya, The Cherry Orchard,* and other plays by Wilde, Shakespeare, and Molnar. He also appeared in a series of Hungarian-made movies and the German-made feature *Derumberkanuta Morgen.* Prior to coming to America he married Gizella Benes on June 4, 1927.

In typical working clothes of the Thirties.

Paul arrived in Hollywood with no knowledge of English. He began his American film career as Commander Ramon de Linea in Samuel Goldwyn's *Two Lovers* (1928) with another Hungarian, Vilma Banky, and very British Ronald Colman. His Paramount contract started with two Pola Negri features: playing Count Dietrich Wallentin in *Three Sinners* (1928) and Dr. Durande in *Loves of an Actress* (1928).

At Paramount he was becoming an efficient and effective contract player when the ogre of sound quaked the foundations of Hollywood. Most of the foreign stars and contract players could not make the transition to sound. Negri and Banky faded and Paramount's great star, Emil Jannings, returned to Germany. Six feet, one and one-half inches tall, suave, and attractive (although he wore a toupee even during the silent screen days), Paul spoke little, if any, English. Paramount offered to buy back his contract. Lukas asked for a chance to learn English and in eight months he was speaking well enough, despite an accent that he never really lost. Now he was ready to tackle the beast called talkies. (However, for his initial sound films Paramount had Lawford Davidson dub his voice.)

After a few minor parts, Paul gave the only real performance in Paramount's *Young Eagles* (1930) as von Baden. In *The Benson Murder Case* (1930) it was suave William Powell who appeared as Philo Vance, with Paul in a subordinate role. Five years later at MGM in *The Casino Murder Case* (1935), it would be Paul who impersonated the gentleman sleuth for film audiences. Lukas' accent was still rather thick in his early talkie efforts, but his performances were rarely bad. However, he was miscast in the Sylvia Sidney-Gary Cooper *City Streets* (1931) as an underworld beer baron. Usually he was cast, although not always successfully, in tales of illicit loves or as unfaithful husbands, as in two Ruth Chatterton melodramas where her stage-trilled vocal cords clashed with Paul's Hungarian overtones. He was in a remake of *Daddy's Gone-a-Hunting* with the charming Eleanor Boardman, *Women Love Once* (1931), and then, oddly, loaned to Universal and cast as Gus in the film version of Preston Sturges' great hit *Strictly Dishonorable* (1931). He had difficulty with several of the brighter lines, but his comedic timing and sly humor put the part across, although the play was well laundered for the cinema.

When William Powell left Paramount for Warner Bros., Paul was handed down "Powell-type" roles, which he played expertly. *Photoplay* cited him for his deeply sincere performance as Major Stephen Lucarno in *The Vice Squad* (1931) and he received applause for his playing of sculptor Michael Morda in *The Beloved Bachelor* (1931). He was with Ruth Chatterton again in the screen version of Philip Barry's *Tomorrow and Tomorrow* (1932) and then tried to cope with Tallulah Bankhead and a bad script in *Thunder Below* (1932). *A Passport to Hell* (1932) at Fox was not much better, even with Elissa Landi in the cast.

By now Paul's Paramount contract had expired, and that studio felt that his vogue as a continental had passed. But expert player that he was, he continued to make much of lesser roles in often mediocre pictures. He offered a finely shaded performance as the doctor who shoots his wife (Gloria Stuart) in her lover's (Walter Pidgeon) arms in *The Kiss before the Mirror* (1933). As Ehrlich, commander of a German prisoner-of-war camp, he was fine in *Captured!* (1933) with Leslie Howard and Douglas Fairbanks, Jr. It was in this period that he received his final citizenship papers and enlisted in California's National Guard.

Professor Fritz Bhaer who finally marries Jo (Katharine Hepburn) provided Paul with a fine characterization in the well-received *Little Women* (1933). He justifiably received star billing over Elissa Landi in a charming film version of *By Candlelight* (1934) via the

With Judith Wood in *Working Girls* (Par '31).

With Nils Asther in *By Candlelight* (Univ '34).

part that Leslie Howard had played on Broadway—as the elegant butler masquerading as his employer.

His "Gesellschaftspiel" often penetrated his American films, such as his performance as Athos in RKO's classy remake of Dumas' *The Three Musketeers* (1935). Then, on December 27, 1937, Paul made his American stage debut on Broadway, with Ruth Gordon, in an excellent revival of Ibsen's *A Doll's House*. He enjoyed a 144-performance run as Dr. Rank in Ibsen's drama as adapted by Thornton Wilder. Before this venture, Paul had gone abroad for film-making, appearing in such productions as the British-made *Dinner at the Ritz* (1937), with Annabella.

His return to Hollywood produced nothing outstanding on the screen, although he was splendid as Dr. Kassel in *Confessions of a Nazi Spy* (1939) and the next year was outstanding as the wife-killer Hessler in the offbeat Joan Crawford film *Strange Cargo* (1940). Then, at the Martin Beck Theatre in New York on April 1, 1941, Paul opened in Lillian Hellman's *Watch on the Rhine*. His performance encased him in theatrical glory after twenty-five years of acting.

If ever a role and actor were truly mated, it was Paul Lukas and Hellman's anti-Nazi German, Kurt Mueller. The press scrambled for superlatives to describe Lukas' interpretation. Brooks Atkinson glowed in the *New York Times,* "As the enemy of fascism, Mr. Lukas' haggard, loving, resourceful determination becomes heroic by virtue of his sincerity and his superior abilities as an actor." Herman Shumlin's staging of Hellman's pre-Pearl Harbor drama brought the power and force of the playwright's work into focus and Paul found all the "Gesellschaftspiel" he would ever require in his fellow players: Lucile Watson, Mady Christians, and George Coulouris. Paul deprecated the loud hosannas with, "The writing is so right you don't have to learn the part; it sticks to you. I amuse myself by changing a gesture occasionally." (Paul was becoming accustomed to being "discovered" each decade. On June 15, 1941, he was heard on radio's "Inner Sanctum Mystery Theatre" portraying a psychiatrist who becomes his own patient in a broadcast of *Murder in Mind*.)

On May 9, 1941, at a luncheon at the Hotel Pierre in New York, the Drama League of New York awarded Paul the Delia Austrian Medal for the most distinguished performance of the season. Accepting the Award from former winner Raymond Massey, Lukas praised the League, the American Theatre, etc. as examples of democracy at work.

Warner Bros. acquired the screen rights to *Watch on the Rhine* and wisely cast Paul in his original role. Bette Davis was assigned to play his American-born wife to insure the box-office potential of the vehicle. Paul repeated his splendid characterization of Kurt Mueller to ever-growing acclaim. Bosley Crowther *(New York Times)* wrote, "Mr. Lukas re-creates his stage role—out of a richly written part to be sure—which will live in the memory of this reviewer so long as it is possible to recall." The New York Critics named Paul the best actor of 1943; the National Board of Review announced, "Paul Lukas here has a chance to be indisputably the fine actor he has always shown plenty of signs of being"; James Agee wrote, "Very belatedly I want to say that *The Watch on the Rhine* seemed much better on the screen than it did, almost identically on the stage—though I still wished Henry James might have written it, and that I join with anyone whose opinion of Paul Lukas' performance is superlative."

In the spring, the Academy of Motion Picture Arts and Sciences awarded Paul Lukas the coveted Oscar. Paul had shown Hollywood that he was not washed up as a major force in the arts. Unfortunately his follow-up roles were in conventional productions that were entertaining but not memorable. He was excellent as the harassed detective trying to return escaped convict Errol Flynn to prison in *Uncertain Glory* (1944) and he gave a noteworthy performance as the radical, devout Nazi Martin Schultz in *Address Unknown* (1944). Hedy Lamarr was a bit vague in *Experiment Perilous* (1944) at RKO, but Paul was on his usual mark as her insanely jealous husband. He was heard on the "Lux Radio Theatre" in May, 1944, with Olivia de Havilland in *Appointment for Love*, and for Danubia Pictures, Paul did the narration for a 45-minute Russian-filmed documentary, *Capture of Budapest*.

But with the end of World War II, the vogue for continental villains diminished and, unlike Charles Boyer who still continued to play romantic leads, Paul was forced to continue with supporting roles in some less than spectacular films. One sturdy entry was the European-lensed *Berlin Express* (1948), starring Merle Oberon and Robert Ryan. By this point, Paul looked very much like the middle-aged man that he was.

During the summer of 1949 he took to the straw-hat stages in a brace of plays: *Accent on Youth, The Play's the Thing,* and *The Heiress.* In 1950 he offered a nicely wrought characterization of the Lama in MGM's *Kim,* starring Errol Flynn and Dean Stockwell. Then Paul shifted from Kipling to Ethel Merman, of all people. Such were the whims of show business.

Irving Berlin's infectious musical *Call Me Madam* opened on Broadway on October 12, 1950. An unusual, but exacting piece of casting was that of the role of the statesman-diplomat-prime minister, Cosmo Constantine. For this part the producers signed Paul Lukas for his first musical. He sang "Lichtenburg" and joined Miss Merman (if that is possible) in "Marrying for Love" and "The Best Thing for You Would Be Me!" Lukas' singing threatened no one in the musical arena, but his presence and fine acting were major contributions. *Variety* reported, "Paul Lukas provides a suave, ingratiating assist as a charming Lichtenburg diplomat, despite severe limitations as a singer." Brooks Atkinson *(New York Times)* penned, "But it would be unforgivable not to express appreciation for the taste and warmth of the acting of Paul Lukas." (When Twentieth Century-Fox filmed *Call Me Madam* in 1953, Ethel Merman was joined by George Sanders, the latter assuming Lukas' stage role.)

Paul left *Call Me Madam* late in the run to join the cast of *Flight into Egypt,* which opened on March 18, 1952, for thirty-nine performances. Others in the George Tabori play about Viennese refugees were Jo Van Fleet, Gusti Huber, and Zero Mostel.

Paul and his wife went abroad in 1953, and at the Edinburgh Festival he played Dr. Bartok in *Night of the Fourth*. He returned to Hollywood to film *20,000 Leagues under the Sea* (1954) at Buena Vista, a surprisingly urbane rendition of the Jules Verne tale that also featured Kirk Douglas, James Mason, and Peter Lorre.

A few years before Paul had ventured into the world of television, appearing as a guest on Ken Murray's variety show. With Signe Hasso he was in the telecast of *Something to Celebrate*, a 1910 Viennese tragedy tale. In January, 1955, he appeared on the small screen with Mary Astor and Diana Lynn in "U.S. Steel Hour's" telecast of Henri Bernstein's play *The Thief*.

Paul returned to Broadway in 1955 in *The Wayward Saint*, an Irish romp. William Hawkins reported in the *New York World-Telegram and Sun*, "Paul Lukas is caught in the unfortunate position of being starred in what is obviously not a starring role." Paul was cast as the Baron Nicholas de Balbus, an emissary of the devil out to taunt Irish clergymen. The show lasted for twenty-one performances.

Darryl F. Zanuck, producing independently for Twentieth Century-Fox release, kindly used Paul in two vehicles, neither of them very successful. One was the African-lensed *The Roots of Heaven* (1958) with Errol Flynn; the other was *Tender Is the Night* (1960) with a too mature Jennifer Jones and a too lethargic Jason Robards, Jr. in the leads of the F. Scott Fitzgerald novel. Lukas was one of the few good items in the latter picture, as Dr. Dohmler. Much more successful was Paul's participation in the television version of *Judgment at Nuremberg* on "Playhouse 90." He had the role of Ernst Janning, a part played two years later on the screen by Burt Lancaster. The year 1960 found Paul participating in Michael Todd, Jr.'s disaster in widescreen and with Smell-O-Vision called *Scent of Mystery*.

MGM unwisely chose to remake *The Four Horsemen of the Apocalypse* (1962) starring the king of remakes at that time, Glenn Ford. The two Pauls (Lukas and Henreid) in the cast gave the least embarrassing performances. As Dr. Steinfeldt in *55 days at Peking* (1963), Paul was showing his nearly seventy years. For "Chrysler Theatre's" *Four Kings*, by the now infamous Clifford Irving, Paul was Dr. Krug, with Peter Falk and Susan Strasberg also starring. Then, the once mighty European star and Oscar winner was found supporting Elvis Presley and Ursula Andress in *Fun in Acapulco* (1963).

In 1962 his wife, Gizella (he called her Daisy), died. On November 7, 1963, Paul married Annette Driesens.

After *Holiday in Spain* (1966) and *Sol Madrid* (1968), Paul went into semi-retirement. He made two appearances as Von Wolfgang, a billionaire inventor of a secret rocket formula, on Robert Wagner's teleseries "It Takes a Thief" and was to be seen in the 1970 telefilm *The Challenge*. During that year he chose to retire to Palma de Mallorca, Spain.

In the late spring of 1971 he left Palma for Tangiers and in April was admitted to the Italian Hospital there for treatment of a heart condition. On August 15, 1971, he died at the Tangiers Hospital of a heart attack. He was seventy-six years old and had spent nearly sixty of those years in the theatre and films, offering his best, which was very good indeed.

PAUL LUKAS

Man of the Earth *(Hungarian 1915)*
Sphinx *(Hungarian 1917)*
Song of the Heart *(Hungarian 1917)*
The Yellow Shadow *(Hungarian 1920)*
Little Fox *(Hungarian 1920)*
The Castle without a Name *(Hungarian 1920)*
The Milliner *(Hungarian 1920)*
The Actress *(Hungarian 1920)*
Telegram from New York *(Hungarian 1921)*
Love of the 18th Century *(Hungarian 1921)*
The Lady in Grey *(Hungarian 1922)*
Samson und Delila *(Austrian 1922)*
Lady Violette *(Hungarian 1922)*
Eine Versunkene Welt *(Austrian 1922)*
The Glorious Life *(Hungarian 1923)*
A Girl's Way *(Hungarian 1923)*
Derumberkanuta Morgen *(German 1923)*
Two Lovers *(UA 1928)*
Three Sinners *(Par 1928)*
Loves of an Actress *(Par 1928)*
Hot News *(Par 1928)*
The Night Watch *(FN 1928)*
Manhattan Cocktail *(Par 1928)*
The Wolf of Wall Street *(Par 1929)*
The Shopworn Angel *(Par 1929)*
Illusion *(Par 1929)*
Half-Way to Heaven *(Par 1929)*
Slightly Scarlet *(Par 1930)*
Behind the Make-Up *(Par 1930)*
Young Eagles *(Par 1930)*
Grumpy *(Par 1930)*
The Benson Murder Case *(Par 1930)*
The Devil's Holiday *(Par 1930)*
Anybody's Woman *(Par 1930)*
The Right to Love *(Par 1930)*
City Streets *(Par 1931)*
Unfaithful *(Par 1931)*
The Vice Squad *(Par 1931)*
Women Love Once *(Par 1931)*
Strictly Dishonorable *(Univ 1931)*
The Beloved Bachelor *(Par 1931)*
Working Girls *(Par 1931)*
No One Man *(Par 1932)*
Tomorrow and Tomorrow *(Par 1932)*
Thunder Below *(Par 1932)*
A Passport to Hell *(Fox 1932)*
Rockabye *(RKO 1932)*
Downstairs *(MGM 1932)*
Grand Slam *(WB 1933)*
The Kiss before the Mirror *(Univ 1933)*
Sing Sinner Sing *(Majestic 1933)*
Captured! *(WB 1933)*
Secret of the Blue Room *(Univ 1933)*

Little Women *(RKO 1933)*
By Candlelight *(Univ 1934)*
Glamour *(Univ 1934)*
The Countess of Monte Cristo *(Univ 1934)*
Affairs of a Gentleman *(Univ 1934)*
I Give My Love *(Univ 1934)*
The Fountain *(RKO 1934)*
Gift of Gab *(Univ 1934)*
Father Brown—Detective *(Par 1935)*
The Casino Murder Case *(MGM 1935)*
Age of Indiscretion *(MGM 1935)*
I Found Stella Parish *(WB 1935)*
The Three Musketeers *(RKO 1935)*
Dodsworth *(UA 1936)*
Ladies in Love *(20th 1936)*
Espionage *(MGM 1937)*
Dinner at the Ritz *(20th British 1937)*
Brief Ecstasy *(Associated British Film Distributors 1937)*
The Mutiny on the Elsinore *(Associated British Film Distributors 1938)*
The Lady Vanishes *(Gaumont 1938)*
Dangerous Secrets *(Grand National 1938)*
Confessions of a Nazi Spy *(WB 1939)*
Lady in Distress *(Times 1939)*
Captain Fury *(UA 1939)*
The Ghost Breakers *(Par 1940)*
Strange Cargo *(MGM 1940)*
The Monster and the Girl *(Par 1941)*
They Dare Not Love *(Col 1941)*
Chinese Den *(Film Alliance of the U.S. 1941)*
Watch on the Rhine *(WB 1943)*
Hostages *(Par 1943)*
Uncertain Glory *(WB 1944)*
Address Unknown *(Col 1944)*
Experiment Perilous *(RKO 1944)*
Deadline at Dawn *(RKO 1946)*
Temptation *(Univ 1946)*
Whispering City *(EL 1947)*
Berlin Express *(RKO 1948)*
Kim *(MGM 1950)*
20,000 Leagues under the Sea *(BV 1954)*
The Roots of Heaven *(20th 1958)*
Scent of Mystery *(Mike Todd, Jr. 1960)*
Tender Is the Night *(20th 1960)*
The Four Horsemen of the Apocalypse *(MGM 1962)*
55 Days at Peking *(AA 1963)*
Fun in Acapulco *(Par 1963)*
Lord Jim *(Col 1965)*
Holiday in Spain *(Todd 1966)*
Sol Madrid *(MGM 1968)*

48

David Manners

To remain an essentially private person in Hollywood in the Thirties (or any other decade) is a feat few people accomplished, hoped for, or diligently pursued. David Manners was one of the few actors who managed to achieve both a career in pictures and to remain his own man in his own private world. His entire film career lasted for one decade, the Thirties, and was replete with both ups and downs. If he was not noted for exceptional acting brilliance or screen charisma, he was never less than dapper and well-mannered, an appropriate leading man for any type of showy actress who required a very refined, handsome vis-a-vis.

He was born Rauff de Ryther Duan Acklom in Halifax, Nova Scotia, on Wednesday, April 30, 1902. He attended Collegiate Grammar School in Windsor, and received a B.S. degree in forestry from the University of Toronto. Young Rauff was ancestrally distinguished, tracing his lineage vaguely back to William the Conqueror. On his mother's side, the family tree included the likes of Lady Diana Cooper and the Duke of Rutland. The Acklom blood lines also included Arthur Conan Doyle, W. H. Homing, and Morley Aklom, all three writers, a profession David deeply reveres. (He himself has published novels, *Convenient Season* and *Under Running Laughter* and, recently, completed work on *The Dreamer Awakes* and *The Divine Fool*, delving into philosophical themes and involving metaphysics.)

Following school Rauff held a profusion of jobs from that of foreman of a Canadian lumber camp to a post in London in an art-antique shop. Later he contracted pneumonia and was shipped to Arizona to convalesce. There he became a cowboy guide and met (and later married) Suzanne Bushnell. While at the University of Toronto, David had studied for the stage under the late Bertram Forsyth of the Hart House Theatre, where he played two seasons of repertory theatre. David made his stage debut in the title role of Euripides' *Hippolytus*. The event decided him on his future choice of a profession.

While Rauff's parents left Canada in the early 1920s to settle in a home high in the Hudson Heights section of Hastings-on-the-Hudson, New York, David went to Manhattan to try his luck in the theatre. In January, 1924, he joined Basil Sydney's touring company. For this repertory group, the young actor took on a variety of assignments from Alfred Bezano, a bareback rider, in *He Who Gets Slapped*, to Solveig's father (as well as a courtier and a keeper) in *Peer Gynt*. He made his Broadway debut in the Helen Hayes hit *Dancing Mothers*, which premiered on August 11, 1924.

With Helen Chandler and Dorothy Peterson in *Mother's Cry* (FN '30).

Eventually David made his way to Hollywood where friends introduced him to director James Whale. The latter offered him a fine acting role, that of Second Lieutenant Raleigh, in the film version of the classic war drama *Journey's End* (1930). David's portrayal of the young, hero-worshipping, mortally wounded Raleigh was on a par with Colin Clive's finely etched playing of Captain Stanhope. The movie *Journey's End* was on most of the year's ten best lists. Using his mother's maiden name of Manners, David received critical praise for his astute acting.

Well-bred and congenial, David was then signed by RKO for their screen version of S. N. Behrman's play *The Second Man*. The movie, retitled *He Knew Women* (1930), starred silent screen actress Alice Joyce (in her final movie role) and featured Lowell Sherman and David. The film did not equal the success of the Broadway rendition of *The Second Man*, which had starred Alfred Lunt, Lynn Fontanne, Margalo Gillmore, and Earle Larimore, but it was an amusing early talkie and Manners was more than adequately cast as Austin Lowe.

Warner Bros.-First National had its share of tough-guy actors (such as James Cagney and Edward G. Robinson), but needed bolstering in the gentle leading man category, in which Douglas Fairbanks, Jr. was then their mainstay. The studio cast David in the role of Jimmy opposite Alice White's burlesque queen in a sub-melodrama, *Sweet Mama* (1930). David's six feet, brown hair, and hazel eyes were put to good advantage in the romantic and colorful role of Caliph Abdallah in love with the daughter (Loretta Young) of the beggar Hajj (Otis Skinner) in *Kismet* (1930).

With Ruth Chatterton in *The Right to Love* **(Par '30).**

First National's low-budgeted *The Truth about Youth* (1930) teamed David again with Loretta Young but more directly to sexy-vamp Myrna Loy. But within the story line, he loses both women and heads West to forget the whole affair (and probably the picture as well). In an unabashed tearjerker, *Mother's Cry* (1930), David was the only believable and successful one of a group of four children.

By this point he had made a reputation in the film industry as an up-and-coming leading man who was *not* a scene-stealer. Paramount borrowed David for the small but vital role of Joe Copeland, Ruth Chatterton's secret lover, in *The Right to Love* (1930). He is the character who meets an untimely death by a harvesting machine, leaving Miss Chatterton with child. (She conveniently weds Irving Pichel in the photoplay before giving birth and apoplexy to any would-be censors.)

Today, David is perhaps best remembered for his performance in the frequently shown *Dracula* (1931), the Tod Browning-directed Gothic thriller which starred Bela Lugosi as the vampire. While Lugosi naturally commanded the bulk of audience attention, David was present as Jonathan Harker who stands in love-struck awe of Helen Chandler.

Back at Warner Bros., David was featured in *The Millionaire* (1931), a prestige production starring George Arliss. Manners was cast as the partner of millionaire-in-disguise Arliss in a gas station venture. Then came a rather dramatic role in the studio's *The Last Flight* (1931). Other studios seemed to do better by the young actor. Columbia used him in *The Miracle Woman* (1931), a Barbara Stanwyck vehicle in which blind aviator David abandons suicide after hearing evangelical hustler Stanwyck give her pitch on the radio.

Of his next loan-out, to United Artists for *The Greeks Had a Word for Them* (1932), *Motion Picture World* reported, "David Manners gives a distinctly pleasant performance. A handsome fellow of pleasantly cultured diction quite adequate for his job and doubtless capable of bearing up well for heavier assignments." David's performance was a bright one, even alongside such pros as Ina Claire, Joan Blondell, and Madge Evans. RKO borrowed both Ben Lyon and David for Constance Bennett's *Lady with a Past* (1932). Commenting on his working with the tempestuous Miss Bennett, David said, "People either adore her madly or hate her—no half-way measures about it. Yet, if those in the latter category could know what a thoroughly good scout she really is and how hard she works at the studio, they'd undoubtedly react differently towards her."

When he returned to the Burbank studio, he was tossed into their stock leading man roles: opposite Marian Marsh in *Beauty and the Boss* (1932), an uninspired bit of nonsense as Kay Francis' secretary in *Man Wanted* (1932), and then as a city boy romancing Ann Dvorak in *Stranger in Town* (1932). With admirable courage he played the sudden rise and fall of Teddy via the title role of *Crooner* (1932), with his singing voice dubbed in this dreary picture.

Out on loan again, David was more than competent as Katharine Hepburn's rejected fiancé in RKO's *A Bill of Divorcement* (1932), in which John Barrymore, as Hepburn's insane father, gave one of his greatest screen portrayals. The film, directed by George Cukor, was prestigious and did well by the entire cast. As a "reward" for his RKO work, Warner Bros. gave him a deadly supporting role, again with Loretta Young, in a mediocre picture titled *They Call It Sin* (1932).

David's contract with Warner Bros. expired in mid-1932 and he started free-lancing in pictures little better than his home-lot fare. He played the romantic lead opposite Zita Johann in Karl Freund's classic horror picture, *The Mummy* (1932), with Boris Karloff as the ancient Imhotep. Manners was a scenario writer sleuthing a studio murder mystery in *The Death Kiss* (1932) and was among the occupants of a racetrack hotel in Para-

With Kay Francis in *Man Wanted* (WB '32).

mount's *From Hell to Heaven* (1933). For Fox he played the commander of the Greek army, Othesus, vying with Amazon Elissa Landi in their sprightly film version of *The Warrior's Husband* (1933). His legs were as shapely as Miss Landi's and their playing was well timed. Stock leading man parts in several quickly forgotten pictures led him to the role of the wealthy and handsome Josephus, adoring a princess and buying a personal slave (Eddie Cantor), in *Roman Scandals* (1933). For Universal's *The Black Cat* (1934) he was a bridegroom escaping a storm with his bride (Jacqueline Wells) and finding shelter with those warm, friendly characters Bela Lugosi and Boris Karloff.

In the film version of Gregory Ratoff's story *The Great Flirtation* (1934), David was again cast as Elissa Landi's inamorata, and offered an ingratiating performance. Despite a poor script and poor direction by Reginald Barker, David turned out a satisfactory portrayal of Franklyn Blake in *The Moonstone* (1934). In the title role, he was strangled on Christmas Eve and buried in quicklime by Claude Rains in *The Mystery of Edwin Drood* (1935). His last three pictures were in minor appearances in RKO's history of the Whiteoaks family in *Jalna* (1935), in Republic's *Hearts in Bondage* (1936), and as the last in the cast of RKO's *A Woman Rebels* (1936), in which Katharine Hepburn fought for women's liberation in Victorian England.

Having exhausted his screen appeal, David retired from the cinema to write in 1936, but there were rumors of one or more nervous breakdowns. However, he remained in retirement until ten years later when he was coaxed by actor's agent Alan Brock into returning to the stage in Maxwell Anderson's new play *Truckline Cafe,* which tried out in Baltimore and opened in New York at the Empire Theatre on February 27, 1946. As directed by Elia Kazan, the show was blasted by the critics and died, but not without an unprecedented furor, after thirteen performances. The one bright thing about Anderson's immobile, unexciting, if well-written, play was a young actor named Marlon Brando. As Wing Commander Hern, David received two hundred dollars a week for his Broadway return.

Manners remained in New York City and took the role of Smith in the short-lasting London success *Hidden Horizons.* His co-star was Diana Barrymore. The September, 1946, show lasted only a dozen performances at the Plymouth Theater. That summer he appeared in the lead of *The Male Animal* in Maine.

In December 1946, David replaced Henry Daniell as Lord Windemere in a most successful revival of Oscar Wilde's *Lady Windemere's Fan.* With David were Cornelia Otis Skinner, Bramwell Fletcher, and Estelle Winwood, and the stylish production as designed by Cecil Beaton was a terrific hit. David's reviews were glowing and he fit the role of Lord Windemere admirably. The comedy was as popular on tour as in New York. By June of 1948 the company had reached San Francisco where it had opened in August, 1946, and had played virtually every major city across the land.

Manners definitely retired after the tour of the Wilde play to concentrate on his writing. He enjoys his retirement from the world of acting. He likes to paint for fun, and runs an art gallery not far from his Pacific Palisades home, which he shares with fellow writer William Mercer.

For David the present is real and he has no love affair with the past. His Hollywood years were filled with good friends like the Fairbankses at Pickfair, and he enjoyed talking with Mary Pickford of their youthful days in Canada. "Tried and true friendships," says Manners, 'That's what this old world needs plenty of. Personally, I love people. And value friendship above everything else. I made some very wonderful friends in Hollywood—for instance, George Arliss and his wife, the William Seiters [then Laura La Plante], Mary and Doug Fairbanks, Ruth Chatterton and Constance Bennett. I guess I've been extremely lucky."

DAVID MANNERS

Journey's End *(Tiffany-Gainsborough 1930)*
He Knew Women *(RKO 1930)*
Sweet Mama *(FN 1930)*
Kismet *(FN 1930)*
Mother's Cry *(FN 1930)*
The Truth about Youth *(FN 1930)*
The Right to Love *(Par 1930)*
Dracula *(Univ 1931)*
The Millionaire *(WB 1931)*
The Last Flight *(FN 1931)*
The Miracle Woman *(Col 1931)*
The Ruling Voice *(FN 1931)*
The Greeks Had a Word for Them *(UA 1932)*
Lady with a Past *(RKO 1932)*
Beauty and the Boss *(WB 1932)*
Stranger in Town *(WB 1932)*
Crooner *(FN 1932)*
Man Wanted *(WB 1932)*

A Bill of Divorcement *(RKO 1932)*
They Call It Sin *(FN 1932)*
The Mummy *(Univ 1932)*
The Death Kiss *(World Wide 1932)*
From Hell to Heaven *(Par 1933)*
The Warrior's Husband *(Fox 1933)*
The Girl in 419 *(Par 1933)*
The Devil in Love *(Fox 1933)*
Torch Singer *(Par 1933)*
Roman Scandals *(UA 1933)*
The Black Cat *(Univ 1934)*
The Luck of a Sailor *(Wardour 1934)*
The Great Flirtation *(Par 1934)*
The Moonstone *(Mon 1934)*
The Perfect Clue *(Majestic 1935)*
The Mystery of Edwin Drood *(Univ 1935)*
Jalna *(RKO 1935)*
Hearts in Bondage *(Rep 1936)*
A Woman Rebels *(RKO 1936)*

Burgess Meredith

That quiet, persuasive voice one hears over radio and television suggesting you fly the friendly skies of United Airlines belongs to a five-foot, seven-inch, blue-green-eyed actor with tousled hair. His theatrical career spans more than four decades. Attempting to compress his professional years within the confines of a single chapter, as well as portraying his dexterity and talent as an actor, is itself a tough feat.

Burgess Meredith was born on Monday, November 16, 1908, in Cleveland, Ohio, to Dr. William George and Ida Beth (Burgess) Meredith. He became a prizewinning boy soprano at Cathedral Choir School and gave many solos at the Cathedral of St. John the Divine in New York City. He then went to Hoosac Falls, New York Prep School, and later attended Amherst College. From there he joined Eva Le Gallienne's Student Repertory Group at her Civic Repertory Theatre. He made his professional debut in their production of *Romeo and Juliet* as a servant, a drummer, and a page. When the repertory company opened at their theatre on April 21, 1930, in *Peter Pan*, Burgess was one of the four wolves.

During that summer he played Marchbanks opposite Vera Allen's *Candida* at Mount Kisco, New York, later playing the same part with leading ladies Edith Barret and Pauline Lord at Philadelphia's Garrick Theatre, and then with Peggy Wood at the Millbrook Theatre. Meredith remained with the Le Gallienne troupe for nearly three years, and then left to play Crooked Finger Jack in *The Threepenny Opera*, with Steffi Duna, Robert Chisholm, and Rex Weber, at the Empire Theatre on April 13, 1933.

Burgess would obtain his release from that show to play reform school kid Red Barry in *Little Ol' Boy*, for which he dyed his hair a flaming red. The critics hailed his performance, but the play lasted only twelve performances. His ambition and drive for perfecting his abilities as an actor kept him playing dissimilar challenging roles throughout the summer of 1933. His first big hit arrived on November 20, 1933, at the 46th Street Theatre when he played the madcap, tap-dancing Princeton student in the hit comedy *She Loves Me Not,* which ran 248 performances.

After brief excursions into *Hipper's Holiday* and *Battleship Gertie,* he went into rehearsal for his most successful and most identifiable role in Maxwell Anderson's poetic drama *Winterset.* The playwright had written the part with Burgess in mind, and the actor excelled as the doomed Mio, seeking vengeance for his father's death only to find death himself. The play was dramatically staged and played to perfection by an

With Ann Sothern in *There Goes the Groom* (RKO '37).

expert cast that included, besides Burgess, Margo, Richard Bennett, and Eduardo Ciannelli. The Anderson drama kept Burgess occupied from its opening (September 25,
1935) through 195 performances and an extensive road tour.

Winterset also took Meredith to Hollywood for the film version. Meredith's screen
portrayal of Mio for RKO established him as a new cinema personality.

Prior to the opening of the stage *Winterset*, Meredith divorced Helen Berrian Derby,
his wife of three years. On Friday afternoon, January 10, 1936, he would wed Margaret
Perry, the elder daughter of Antoinette Perry, actress and director of Preston Sturges'
Strictly Dishonorable. Margaret and Burgess were married at his rented home at Snee-
den's Landing, New York, by the Reverend Darrow Raymaker, and Burgess returned to
playing *Winterset* that evening. During the summer of 1938, after Burgess had been
elected acting president of Actor's Equity, Margaret made her second trip to Reno,
Nevada (she had divorced her first husband Winsor Brown French II there in 1935), and
divorced Meredith on July 19, 1938.

While Burgess' first film, *Winterset,* was in national distribution, he opened (January
9, 1937) in another Maxwell Anderson play, *High Tor,* with Peggy Ashcroft and Hume
Cronyn. This fantasy, set upon a mountain top, charmed the drama critics. Again
Anderson had written a part for Meredith, and his playing of Van Van Dorn was a
delight for 171 performances. On July 13 of that year he was heard on CBS' inaugural
Shakespearean broadcast as *Hamlet,* a part he had played on radio the previous season.
(Burgess had made his broadcasting debut in October, 1934, as Red Davis, a three-
times-weekly show.)

387

Following his first film venture, Burgess steadfastly refused to sign a long-term contract with any Hollywood studio. But he did owe RKO another film. The studio presented him with the part of Dick Matthews, with Ann Sothern and Mary Boland, in *There Goes the Groom* (1937). It was a part obviously intended for a big football type, like Joel McCrea. Burgess could not believe the company's ill-advised assignment. When he finished this RKO fiasco he went over to MGM for *Spring Madness* (1938) with Lew Ayres and Maureen O'Sullivan. It was a project he was delighted to do. However, he was not pleased with Hollywood (and made it quite well known in his own acid-tinged wordage), and the film colony felt the same way about this maverick actor.

He returned joyfully to New York for yet another Maxwell Anderson play, this one co-starring him with Lillian Gish. In *The Star Wagon* they opened in the show as a 65-year-old couple who later in the proceedings revert to sudden youth, age eighteen. The play opened in September, 1937, ran through 223 performances, and then had an extensive road tour. In early 1939, Burgess joined forces with multi-talented genius Orson Welles for a combined Theatre Guild-Mercury Theatre production of *Five Kings*, based on the Shakespearean chronicle plays. The opening night in Boston was a shambles long to be remembered, and by the time it reached Philadelphia, the Theatre Guild decided to call off the costly venture.

Burgess crossed the continent again, returning to MGM to play with Norma Shearer and Clark Gable in *Idiot's Delight* (1939). Within the film he was the confused pacifist. He created much commotion offcamera when he dated the lot's Queen, Miss Shearer. Meredith's reputation as a Don Juan flourished from coast to coast.

With Lew Ayres in *Spring Madness* (MGM '38).

With Betty Field in *Of Mice and Men* **(UA '39).**

Lewis Milestone's fine direction of *Of Mice and Men* (1939) gave Burgess his best celluloid role since *Winterset*. He sympathetically played George to Lon Chaney, Jr.'s excellent near-imbecilic Lennie. On October 22, 1939, Burgess became master of ceremonies for CBS radio's drama-music-variety show "Pursuit of Happiness." At Warner Bros. he joined John Garfield in a remake of *20,000 Years in Sing Sing* (1933) entitled *Castle on the Hudson* (1940). He then moved over to Paramount for a musical with Fred Astaire. He was trumpet player Hank Taylor (dubbed by Billy Butterfield) in *Second Chorus* (1940). His co-star was Paulette Goddard, then Mrs. Charles Chaplin. The charming actress was bewitched by the wit and growing reputation of Meredith. She had already separated from Chaplin and she began dating Burgess. (She would divorce Chaplin in June, 1942, and marry Burgess on May 21, 1944.)

Following the zany *Second Chorus*, Buzz (as he was known to his pals) made a program filler for Universal. *San Francisco Docks* (1940), shot in eleven days, was a trifle, and it was certainly a comedown for the once-lofty stage actor. His next film was Ernst Lubitsch's *That Uncertain Feeling* (1941), a remake of a silent film. Meredith played a slightly demented and ponderous pianist, giving a hilarious performance that stole the limelight from stars Merle Oberon and Melvyn Douglas. If Hollywood had any doubts about Burgess' acting abilities they should have been dispelled when he strolled merrily away with RKO's *Tom, Dick and Harry* (1941), directed by Garson Kanin and starring a rather coy Ginger Rogers. His final film performance before being drafted into the Armed Services was as an amnesia victim accused of murder in *Street of Chance* (1942), a double-bill item for Paramount.

A three-month draftee stationed at the Santa Ana Air Force Base in California, Burgess was applying his vast talent to cleaning latrines when a call from Katharine Cornell interrupted his vital military duties. General George Marshall backed Miss Cornell's idea of a revival of *Candida,* in which the proceeds would go to the Army-Navy Relief Fund. Meredith was her choice for Marchbanks and within two hours of her call, the commanding officer at the Santa Ana base was reading a telegram to Private Meredith reassigning him on temporary duty to Miss Cornell for *Candida.*

Tickets for the limited engagement (April 1942) of the Shaw play were going at $50 to $100 apiece, and following the Manhattan run, the company with Miss Cornell, Raymond Massey, Dudley Digges, Mildred Natwick, Stanley Bell, and Meredith moved on to Washington, D.C. for two weeks. The critics were ecstatic about the revival, and the public showed their positive enthusiasm. The engagement brought $122,247.50 into the treasury of the Army-Navy Relief Fund.

In the Air Force Meredith progressed from private to lieutenant, and he was transferred to the Office of War Information where his multiple talents were put to a good purpose, that of making films for G.I.'s. The first, *Welcome to Britain* (1943), was a two-reel effort he directed. Robert Sherwood and Ernest Hemingway called it the most effective orientation film made during the war. For *Salute to France* (1944), Burgess enlisted the help of Garson Kanin and Jean Renoir with the direction and the services of Claude Dauphin and Phillip Bourneuf as players. The film ran thirty-five minutes. Before returning to the States, the British government invited him to make a film which he wrote, appeared in, narrated, and co-directed with Colin Dean. However, *A Yank Comes Back* (1947) was not a success.

William Wellman's classic *The Story of G. I. Joe* (1945) was Meredith's first film after his war service. He offered an uncanny portrayal as war correspondent Ernie Pyle (an old friend he had visited in Albuquerque, New Mexico, before the famed writer returned to the Pacific and his death). His resemblance to Pyle was noticeable and no actor in Hollywood could have played the role better than Meredith. Robert Mitchum was equally fine as the disillusioned Captain, for which he received an Academy nomination for Best Supporting Actor of the Year. Hollywood, which had never forgiven Meredith for being a Thirties' upstart, did not even nominate him for *G. I. Joe.*

With Benedict Bogeaus, Burgess produced his own screenplay, based on a novel by Octave Mirbeau, *The Diary of a Chambermaid* (1946). Directed by Jean Renoir, the film starred, in addition to Meredith, Paulette Goddard as a nineteenth-century French maid. From this French foray, Meredith became the president (James Madison) of the United States in an unbelievable concoction directed by Frank Borzage, *The Magnificent Doll* (1946), starring Ginger Rogers in the title role. Her lame performance proved her oft-quoted remark, "Great acting's not my line."

Again with Bogeaus, Meredith produced another film. This time it was a multi-episode picture shared by directors King Vidor and Leslie Fenton for United Artists called *A Miracle Can Happen* (1948), which fared no better when it was nationally distributed as *On Our Merry Way.* Goddard also acted in this venture, as did Meredith. In England for Twentieth Century-Fox and Alexander Korda, Burgess played a psychiatrist in *Mine Own Executioner* (1948) and then filmed a project with Jean-Pierre Aumont which was released in the U.S. in 1953 as *The Gay Adventure.* He then did a bit as a "guest" appearance in *Jigsaw* (1949), starring Franchot Tone and filmed largely in New York City.

If Burgess was no longer the burning young light of the entertainment field, he continued to work with great frequency. For RKO he directed and starred in a grand guignol tale filmed in Paris, *The Man on the Eiffel Tower* (1949), which also featured

Franchot Tone and Charles Laughton. Meredith and Laughton became close friends and the English star would turn the tables on Burgess in October, 1956, by directing him on Broadway in an all-star revival of *Major Barbara* for a smashing run of 232 performances.

The Meredith-Goddard marriage was more than drifting and when he returned from Paris, Paulette divorced him on June 6, 1949, in Cuernavaca, Mexico. In 1952 he would marry ballet dancer Kaja Sundsten, and they would become the parents of Jonathan and Tala. A year after his marriage to Kaja, Burgess sued his ex-wife to account for some $400,000 in community property. Paulette promptly brought a countersuit testing the validity of their Mexican divorce and the legality of this fourth marriage. (In March 1976, Burgess and Kaja would separate.)

After his fling at the Parisian adventure and the Goddard Mexico-divorce trek, Burgess returned to the East. In 1950 he directed and played the lead in *Happy as Larry,* made his television debut in *Our Town,* and toured the summer circuits as Elwood P. Dowd in *Harvey.* He also directed a summer tryout of *Season in the Sun,* a comedy by Wolcott Gibbs that opened to good notices and a long run on Broadway. Through 1951 Burgess never stopped the constant rush of work: he directed *Let Me Hear the Melody* that collapsed in Philadelphia, toured the summer theatres in *The Silver Whistle,* directed the hit *Lo and Behold!,* and on June 9, 1952, replaced Hume Cronyn in *The Fourposter,* with Betty Field substituting for Mrs. Cronyn, Jessica Tandy.

The theatre kept the indomitable Burgess occupied throughout the early Fifties, with spare time spent in television assignments, directing a new play *The Frogs of Spring,* and then co-starring with Martha Scott in *The Remarkable Mr. Pennypacker.* Thereafter he directed *Macbeth* at Hamilton, Bermuda, in 1954 and succeeded David Wayne on Broadway as Sakini in the long-running riotous hit *The Teahouse of the August Moon,* heading the national touring company. With Courtneay Burr he produced *Speaking of Murder* at the Royale Theatre in New York in December, 1954, and then journeyed to Tokyo for the title role in the film *Joe Butterfly* (1957). The final product was not worth the trip. After directing a version of *Ulysses in Nighttown* in New York and London, he was in the out-of-town flop *Enrico.* Through the next two years he alternated between directing and acting and appearing on television. Then he turned in an impressive performance on "Hallmark Hall of Fame" in *Ah, Wilderness!* playing the tippling ne'er-do-well Sid Miller, with Helen Hayes, Lloyd Nolan, and Betty Field also in the memorable cast.

The new decade gave resilient Burgess the opportunity to align himself with a kindred spirit, James Thurber. For his direction of *A Thurber Carnival* he would receive a special Tony Award in April, 1960. Burgess then had less luck with Mary Chase's *Midgie Purvis.* Despite a cast which boasted Tallulah Bankhead, Alice Pearce, and Audrey Christie, it quickly closed. He returned to acting in *Mr. Kicks and Co.,* which closed in Chicago, and then narrated the Canadian government documentary *Universe.*

It was director Otto Preminger who gave Burgess a new cinema lease, hiring him for *Advise and Consent* (1962) to join the likes of Walter Pidgeon, Charles Laughton, Don Murray, and Gene Tierney in a study of politics-saturated Washington, D.C. Preminger used him again for the tedious *The Cardinal* (1963), this time casting him as the aging priest, Father Ned Halley. Later that year Burgess had the title part of *Hughie* on the London stage, doing full justice to the Eugene O'Neill play. Beginning their sixth TV season, "77 Sunset Strip" did a five-part story called *Five* in which Burgess had the recurring role of an antique dealer strangely settling his dead brother's estate. This cameo-star-studded tale ran from September 20 through October 18, 1963.

Burgess' excursions to Hollywood were either for minor, supporting, or cameo roles.

391

Otto Preminger used him again in the World War II picture *In Harm's Way* (1965), but it was a comic strip series that offered him a more popular outing. Both on television and in the Twentieth Century-Fox feature-length version of *Batman*, Burgess excelled as the mad Penguin, arch fiend and foe of Batman and Robin. Meanwhile, he appropriated a southern drawl to appear as one of the luckless performers in Otto Preminger's sugar-and-sex-coated *Hurry Sundown* (1967). It was a rather unrestrained Meredith who popped up in the multi-episode horror film *The Torture Garden* (1968). Work was work and he accepted a part in Elvis Presley's *Stay Away, Joe* (1968), and later was part of Otto Preminger's fiasco, *Skidoo* (1968), which proved that what the director thought was comedy was not that at all.

Preminger had never been noted for his good taste, but it was a surprise to find Burgess appearing in a nude scene for the director's *Such Good Friends* (1971). The *New York Daily News* thought it should be "recorded as the screen's most embarrassing moment." When Hume Cronyn proved unavailable due to a conflicting work schedule, Burgess was hired to play seedy ex-vaudevillian Harry Green in the bizarre *The Day of the Locust* (1975), an indulgent study of the fringes of Hollywood in the Thirties. He was one of the more satisfying ingredients in this overrated feature, wrongly directed by Britisher John Schlesinger. (He won a Best Supporting Actor's nomination, but lost the award.) In *Burnt Offerings* (1976) he is matched with Bette Davis and Karen Black in a Gothic thriller.

With his son Jonathan doing graduate work at the University of the Pacific and daughter Tala attending the San Francisco Art Institute, Meredith and wife of two-and-one-half decades revel in contentment in their Malibu Beach home. This aging elf of show business is far from retirement. He recently signed as narrator for a new ABC-TV children's series, and is always available for guest roles on television and in films. In his "spare" time he is writing a book on wine appreciation.

Proving that the busy person finds time for everything (and anything?) he recently toured college campuses across America in a two-hour routine of reading (from anthropologist Carlos Castaneda's *Tales of Power)*, music on a flute synthesizer and Tibetan oboe by flutist Charles Lloyd, and an eight-minute chant using the word "cogitate." "It's heavy going," Meredith has admitted, "but we've struck a minefield of enthusiasm."

BURGESS MEREDITH

Winterset *(RKO 1936)*
There Goes the Groom *(RKO 1937)*
Spring Madness *(MGM 1938)*
Idiot's Delight *(MGM 1939)*
Of Mice and Men *(UA 1939)*
Castle on the Hudson *(WB 1940)*
Second Chorus *(Par 1940)*
San Francisco Docks *(Univ 1940)*
That Uncertain Feeling *(UA 1941)*
Tom, Dick and Harry *(RKO 1941)*
Street of Chance *(Par 1942)*
The Story of G. I. Joe *(UA 1945)*
The Diary of a Chambermaid *(UA 1946)*
Magnificent Doll *(Univ 1946)*
On Our Merry Way [A Miracle Can Happen] *(UA 1948)*
Mine Own Executioner *(20th 1948)*
Jigsaw *(UA 1949)*
The Man on the Eiffel Tower *(RKO 1949)*
The Gay Adventure *(UA 1953)*
Joe Butterfly *(Univ 1957)*
Advise and Consent *(Col 1962)*
The Cardinal *(Col 1963)*
The Kidnappers [Man on the Run] *(Manson 1964)*

In Harm's Way *(Par 1965)*
Crazy Quilt *(Walter Reade 1966) [narrator]*
A Big Hand for the Little Lady *(WB 1966)*
Madame X *(Univ 1966)*
Batman *(20th 1966)*
Hurry Sundown *(Par 1967)*
The Torture Garden *(Col 1968)*
MacKenna's Gold *(Col 1968)*
Stay Away, Joe *(MGM 1968)*
Skidoo *(Par 1968)*
Hard Contract *(20th 1969)*
There Was a Crooked Man *(WB 1970)*
Such Good Friends *(Par 1971)*
Clay Pigeon *(MGM 1971)*
The Man *(Par 1972)*
8 Must Die *(Taurean Films 1974)*
Golden Needles *(AIP 1974)*
The Day of the Locust *(Par 1975)*
92 in the Shade *(UA 1975)*
The Hindenburg *(Univ 1975)*
Burnt Offerings *(UA 1976)*
The Sentinel *(Univ 1977)*
Remember Those Poker Playing Monkeys *(Cinema III 1977)*

50

Douglass Montgomery

Douglass Montgomery's last starring appearance on the New York stage was in a drama, originally written for television and expanded into a full-length play, that had two performances at the 54th Street Theatre in February, 1959. In *The Legend of Lizzie,* his performance as district attorney Sewell, prosecutor of the murderess, was mannered, self-conscious, and abruptly played. The final scene left the actor on stage taunted by a group of Fall River children while he walks to the footlights and explains wearily to the audience, "They don't understand—it would take a lifetime." He sadly shakes his head and bites his underlip—gestures he had been employing through the years to express sorrow and frustration.

Montgomery was then fifty-one years old and he *had* spent a lifetime seeking and realizing understanding as an actor.

He was born on Tuesday, October 29, 1907, in the fashionable Berkeley Square district of Los Angeles to Leona Smith and Chester Arthur James Montgomery. Their only son was christened Robert Douglass Montgomery. Mr. Montgomery was a prominent jeweler in Pasadena and society-conscious Mrs. Montgomery helped found the Los Angeles Symphony Society. The family spent their summers in Altadena on their estate, Edgecliffe, in a huge, nineteenth-century house.

By age six, young Douglass was improvising plays and performing them before the servants and reluctant neighbors. His desire to become an actor never wavered, although at the age of ten his indulgent family had published a book of poems he had written. Of *Pipe Dreams,* he later said, "The verses were seemingly sophisticated and vicious. Oh, they were dreadful! I must have been a terrible kid—self-centered and ruthless and conceited. I can tell by the things I wrote at the time how pretentious and nasty I was. I must have been precocious for my age. Everything I did was conspicuous —and self-conscious."

He entered Los Angeles High School at thirteen, where he organized a dramatic club, enlisting a large segment of the student body. At the end of the school day he rushed to the Pasadena Community Playhouse for rehearsals and to become resident juvenile in one of the country's greatest training schools for actors. After Montgomery's performance in the Playhouse's production of *Lady with a Lamp,* Joseph Schildkraut rushed backstage to congratulate "that remarkable kid who'd given such a soul-searching performance." To impressionable young Douglass the great Schildkraut said, "You have grease paint in your veins."

With Mae Clarke in *Waterloo Bridge* **(Univ '31).**

Reflecting on those early years Douglass admitted: "It was an education for me. The theatre is the only education I've had really—I never went to college. I was a juvenile at the Pasadena Playhouse where they gave me every sort of play from classics to musical comedy and I also joined every experimental theatre that happened to be in existence out there. When I'd come home from school and see Charlie Ray making scenes for a picture right on our street, I didn't even stop to watch." He grew up watching movies being made but also maintained the stage actor's dismal view of flickers. The theatre had become his entire world.

Montgomery made his professional debut at the Orange Grove Theatre in Los Angeles in December, 1925, in *Hell Bent for Heaven.* He appeared as Lionel Barrymore's son in *The Copperhead,* Bert Lytell's son in *Silence,* and toured in these and other West Coast productions *(Kempy, Desire under the Elms).* His ambition was boundless. His parents agreed reluctantly to use funds set aside for his college education to finance his dream of a Broadway career. He arrived in New York in August, 1926, and made his Broadway debut that October in *God Loves Us.*

Douglass' arrival in New York was in the middle of the greatest revitalization the American theatre had ever had. The renaissance had started after World War I with the emergence of great new playwrights, exciting experimental theatre groups, and a constant flow into Manhattan of gifted young players fired with enthusiasm; and all were caught up in the burgeoning vitality of the arts. When *God Loves Us* closed, Montgomery went into Pauline Lord's *Daisies Won't Tell,* which folded in Boston. Then in January, 1927, he signed for *Crime,* advertised as "A Melodrama, Depicting Life in New York's Underworld." The play opened in February starring James Rennie and featuring such newcomers as Douglass, Sylvia Sidney, Chester Morris, Kay Johnson, Jack La Rue, and Kay Francis.

By the end of his first few months in New York, the young blond Montgomery had aroused the attention of critics and audiences alike, and never again did the family have to send "Dougsie" (as they called him) an allowance. The young man had arrived. With Mary Boland he opened in *Women Go on Forever* (1927), in which James Cagney was featured. Douglass left that show to appear with Alison Skipworth in the comedy *The Garden of Eden,* which only survived twenty-three performances. His friends were theatre people and his popularity as a party guest was on the rise. Leonard Sillman invited him to be a part of a new concept for Sunday show concerts at the Klaw Theatre. Douglass and Helen Chandler did a scene from a Pierre Louys' novel, Blanche Yurka read poetry, Imogene Coca and Sterling Holloway provided comedy, and Libby Holman sang. By January, 1928, Montgomery had signed for a new melodrama, *Kidnapper,* that was tested in Scranton, Pennsylvania, in February of that year, but closed in Philadelphia in early March.

For any actor of any calibre, joining the Theatre Guild organization was a prestigious and career-advancing goal. Douglass was intent on becoming associated with the Guild and practically besieged the office of executive director Theresa Helburn. Later he would recall, "I went to Miss Helburn's office at the Theatre Guild every day. I sat there so much she had to give me a job to get me out of her office."

He entered the Guild's services in the spring of 1928, assigned as understudy to Alfred Lunt as Mosca in *Volpone.* When Claude Rains took over the title role from Dudley Digges, Montgomery succeeded Lunt as Mosca. Dudley Digges as Mephistopheles, Helen Chandler as Margaret, George Gaul in the title part, and Douglass as Valentine opened the Guild's production of Goethe's *Faust* on October 8, 1928. From that project, Douglass was next summoned to join the Lunts in *Caprice,* a soufflé of endless, if amusing, adultery. Douglass' role of Lunt's teenage illegitimate son had originally been planned for another Montgomery, Robert, then an impressionable, rising young actor.

No opportunity for a young actor starting in the theatre could compare with working with the Lunts at their peak. For a less poised and confident actor than Douglass, the constant experimental acting perfected by the Lunts would have dented his composure and performance. But Douglass proved his merit during the New York, and later London, engagement of *Caprice*.

Returning to New York, Douglass went into rehearsal for S. N. Behrman's weak play *Meteor*, again with the Lunts. But by the time the play had reached Broadway (on December 23, 1929), Montgomery had relinquished his role to Franchot Tone. Montgomery informed the press that he was leaving the Guild because it had given him insufficient opportunity to develop his talent. In early February, 1930, he found other theatre work: featured billing with Sylvia Sidney in a mild comedy, *Many a Slip*. Then, after a brief stock season in Baltimore, he underwent a sinus operation and decided to return to Pasadena to recuperate and to vacation with his doting family.

"If I thought of pictures at all, it was to imagine how hideous I'd be in them. Certainly I never dreamt that they would want me or even know of my work in the East. I was astounded when I got several offers from movie companies. I went into pictures because I was flattered and because I needed the money. The movie offers came from Paramount and Metro-Goldwyn-Mayer who, like the other major studios, were signing stage-trained actors for the relatively new talkies that had dissipated their contract logs and demolished several top stars."

Douglass came to an agreement with MGM. Their first crisis with the new player was his coloring. Hollywood leading men were traditionally dark and handsome. The lot decided Montgomery had a "black-haired personality," and dyed his hair only to discover he appeared to better advantage as his natural blond self. Metro's next crisis was his name. The studio had signed Robert Montgomery in 1929 and was in the process of building him into one of their top leading men. Two Montgomerys on the lot would not do. Douglass dug into his family tree and discovered a Kent Douglass, a name that delighted the studio. So he became Kent Douglas.

Paid (1930) was his initial Metro vehicle. It was a remake of the taut drama *Within the Law* and featured Joan Crawford in a meaty role. "Kent" was her husband who was unaware that she had married him out of revenge for his father's criminal action against her, which had resulted in an unjust prison sentence. Any personable young contract player could have handled the part, and Miss Crawford dominated the picture.

From *Paid* he went on to *Daybreak* (1931) as Ramon Novarro's Viennese officer buddy. Because of his blond good looks and his obvious talent, Marion Davies asked that he play her brother in *Five and Ten* (1931), a new studio offering to be based on a Fannie Hurst work. As the wretchedly unhappy brother who takes to drink and later crashes his private plane, Douglass had a showy part. He played it well, if occasionally overly hysterical in manner. However, the film caused no great excitement when released. He felt stymied by his Metro tie and asked to be released. Instead, they loaned him to Universal for two of his best movies.

Montgomery's most memorable cinema appearance was the first film version of Robert E. Sherwood's *Waterloo Bridge* (1931). As the young American serving with the Royal Canadian forces, he returns to London on sick leave and meets a heart-of-gold prostitute (Mae Clarke). Despite her confession of her profession he remains in love with her. William Wyler directed the actor's next production, *A House Divided* (1932), in which Douglass was Walter Huston's gentle but rebellious son who falls in love with his father's mail order bride (Helen Chandler).

At about this time he told the press, "I'm not proud of the roles I've played in *Paid* with Joan Crawford and in *Five and Ten* with Marion Davies. At the time I felt pretty bad about them and asked to be released from the contract I had signed." Although the two

Universal ventures met with his approval, he still felt he was unsuited to motion pictures and finally won his studio release. He left Hollywood at 3 A.M. by plane, to arrive later in New York and join the cast of *Nikki,* a Hemingwayesque tale of a group of aviators afloat in Paris after World War I. The company of seventy in the show included a piano playing, singing Englishman who went on to Hollywood to become Cary Grant. Also featured in *Nikki,* was Fay Wray, the wife of the author (John Monk Saunders), in her stage debut. *Nikki* opened on September 29, 1931, and lasted thirty-nine performances.

Universal now offered Douglass a $1,200-a-week contract, in addition to replacing all advertising on the billings for the two pictures with his real name. But Douglass remained in the East. He enjoyed theatre people; he was always "on," and he knew how to take entrances on and off stage. Prominently displayed in his apartment was a signed photograph of actress Lois Moran with whom there was a close friendship but no real thoughts of any impending nuptials, despite theories of such action in the press.

During late November, 1931, he was in Philadelphia with the Mae Desmond Stock Company, but by Christmas Day, 1931, he was back on Broadway in the short-lasting *Fata Morgana.* Later came roles in *Men Must Fight* and a return to the Theatre Guild for *An American Dream* with Claude Rains, Josephine Hull, and Gale Sondergaard.

Returning to California to see his family, he rejoined the Pasadena Playhouse with an all-Montgomery production (sets, direction, and title role) of *Peer Gynt.* RKO offered him the part of Laurie in *Little Women* (1933). "It wasn't exactly the sort of role I wanted —I'm somewhat tired of being the sweet boy who doesn't win out—but I knew it would be a sensational picture and I was eager to work with Katharine Hepburn." In the Louisa May Alcott story he was well cast as Laurie, who is able to transfer his affections from Jo (Hepburn) to Amy (Joan Bennett). It was a step downward from this vehicle to appear in Paramount's *Eight Girls in a Boat* (1934).

By now the actor was using his Douglass Montgomery name for screen credits, and in 1934 appeared in the American movie of the potent anti-fascist novel *Kleiner Mann, was nun?* In the Universal picture, titled *Little Man, What Now?,* he was well cast as Margaret Sullavan's hopelessly life-discouraged husband who needs constant morale bolstering. While the press heaped praise on both performers, the two stars were busy informing reporters how much they detested movie-making! After his authentic *Little Man* performance, Montgomery transferred to Fox for his first screen musical. It was Jerome Kern's *Music in the Air* (1934), which was transformed to the screen as a Gloria Swanson comeback vehicle. The music score remained the only memorable item of this rather forced venture.

During the 1934–1935 season Montgomery played the leading role in the West Coast production of *Merrily We Roll Along* and then went into Universal's well-directed *The Mystery of Edwin Drood* (1935), in which Claude Rains offered a strikingly repellent performance as jealous John Jasper who kills his nephew Edwin (David Manners) and accuses hot-tempered Neville Landless of the crime. Montgomery as Landless, if over-shadowed by the fire of Rains' acting, maintained pace with the inestimable Claude. But this good film was followed by the pedestrian *Lady Tubbs* (1935) in which Douglass had a run-of-the-studio romantic lead opposite Anita Louise. An ambitious effort for the smaller Mascot studio fascinated Montgomery and he gave a carefully shaded charac-terization of the tragic composer Stephen Foster in *Harmony Lane* (1935). Hoping for better luck in England, he made two features there: a quickie, *Tropical Trouble* (1936), and a vehicle with Constance Bennett, *Everything Is Thunder* (1936), in which he was a sensitive youth trying to save his own life. Returning to Hollywood he made two program films for Columbia, banked his money, and returned once again to the stage in November, 1937. In Baltimore he was part of the cast of *Merely Murder,* but when the

In *Music in the Air* (Fox '34).

On the set of *Life Begins with Love* (Col '37) with his assistant, Atkins.

play reached Princeton on its pre-Broadway tour, Montgomery withdrew from the cast and was replaced by Rex O'Malley.

Universal had made a silent film version of the scary *The Cat and the Canary* and had refilmed it in 1930 as a talkie. Paramount, in 1939, revamped the play for more laughs and chills as a Bob Hope-Paulette Goddard vehicle, with Douglass performing as the innocent-appearing but slightly insane "cat." It was to be his last American film. Returning to New York he joined what Leonard Sillman hoped to be a sensational New York Drama Festival, reviving past Broadway hits with top stars for a two-week run per play. Sillman persuaded Montgomery to appear with June Walker in *They Knew What They Wanted,* but the production fared poorly with Italian actor Giuseppe Sterni as Tony.

Following a 1941 American tour as the charming maniac in *Night Must Fall,* Douglass joined the Canadian Army, serving through the war. After World War II he remained in England, making a film with Michael Redgrave and John Mills. In *Johnny in the Clouds* (a.k.a. *The Way to the Stars,* 1945) he portrayed an emotionally upset flyer depressed by the many deaths of his fellow aviators. He returned to the stage in Edinburgh in *Now the Day Is Over* and, in May 1946, he appeared on the London boards as the Captain in *The Wind Is Ninety.* It was during this period that he married a lovely actress-designer, Kathleen (Kay) Tamor Young.

For British National he played an amnesia victim of the war in *Woman to Woman* (1946), a tearjerker that had been filmed twice before. The 1946 version was not an improvement. In the late autumn of 1946, Douglass went to Italy where, during the winter, he made *Sinfonia Fatale* (1947) with Sarah Churchill and Tullio Carminati; the film was later shown in England as *When in Rome*. His last screen appearance was in *Forbidden* (1948) as a man tormented in the misbelief he has killed his wife for love of another woman. The English press labeled this production as one of his best films.

After 1948, Montgomery concentrated on the English stage playing such diverse roles as Dick Dudgeon in *The Devil's Disciple,* Peter Standish in *Berkeley Square,* Oswald in *Ghosts,* and the hard-bitten, revenge-seeking Captain McLeod in *Detective Story.* He toured the British Isles in all his plays except *Detective Story.*

Montgomery returned to the States in 1951, settling in Connecticut and calling his place Eagle Rock. His summers, thereafter, were spent touring New England's straw-hat theatres in revivals of tested Broadway successes. His initial television appearance in 1952 was in one of his favorite roles as *Peer Gynt,* and he was seen in the telecast of *The Way of Courage.* For "Hallmark Hall of Fame" in 1954 he depicted James Oglethorpe's battle against England's debtors' prisons. He also played Robert Louis Stevenson seeking a healthy climate with his wife (Martha Scott) on "TV Reader's Digest." His final video role was an actor's dream in which he could let loose all of his array of acting tricks, nuances, and dramatic expression as *Dr. Jekyll and Mr. Hyde.*

Two of the Lunts' proteges died on July 23, 1966. Large newspaper columns were devoted to the death of Montgomery Clift. In Norwalk, Connecticut, on the same day, Douglass Montgomery passed away almost without press coverage or comment. Both Montgomerys were excellent performers, but their personalities were worlds apart. The exuberant, extroverted, constantly onstage Douglass was the exact opposite of the problematical and plagued Clift. Much of their acting experience they had learned from the incomparable Lunts. Both fluctuated in a passion for stage versus screen.

The English press noted Douglass Montgomery's death with memories of the Forties when his voice was Britain's second favorite American voice, heard constantly over the BBC—Franklin Delano Roosevelt took first honors. Following the war years the British government had bestowed upon Douglass the full rights of an English subject, except the vote, in recognition of his contributions to Anglo-Saxon solidarity.

There was seldom a time in the life of Douglass Montgomery when the question *Little Man, What Now?* was valid. He usually knew.

DOUGLASS MONTGOMERY

As: *Kent Douglas:*
Paid *(MGM 1930)*
Daybreak *(MGM 1931)*
Five and Ten *(MGM 1931)*
Waterloo Bridge *(Univ 1931)*
A House Divided *(Univ 1931)*
As: *Douglass Montgomery:*
Little Women *(RKO 1933)*
Eight Girls in a Boat *(Par 1934)*
Little Man, What Now? *(Univ 1934)*
Music in the Air *(Fox 1934)*
The Mystery of Edwin Drood *(Univ 1935)*
Lady Tubbs *(Univ 1935)*

Harmony Lane *(Mascot 1935)*
Everything Is Thunder *(Gaumont 1936)*
Tropical Trouble *(General Film Distributors 1936)*
Counsel for Crime *(Col 1937)*
Life Begins with Love *(Col 1937)*
The Cat and the Canary *(Par 1939)*
Johnny in the Clouds [The Way to the Stars] *(UA British 1945)*
Woman to Woman *(British National 1946)*
Sinfonia Fatale [When in Rome] *(Scalera 1947)*
Forbidden *(British Lion 1948)*

Dickie Moore

He was a late starter in pictures. Baby LeRoy began his screen career at eight months. Dickie Moore began his when he was eleven months old. Baby LeRoy was washed up, a has-been at age three; Dickie Moore spent his entire childhood in picture after picture, becoming the busiest and one of the most talented moppets in Hollywood.

He was born John Richard Moore, Jr. to banker John R. and Nora Eileen (Orr) Moore on Saturday, September 12, 1925, in Los Angeles. It was a secretary of movie executive Joseph Schenck who persuaded Dickie's mother to let him appear in John Barrymore's *The Beloved Rogue* (1927). It was the beginning of a long career. Despite the unusual attention he would soon be given, Dickie would remain a totally unspoiled, natural boy.

His cherubic face, an appealing pout, and natural boyish acting made him one of the most popular young actors of the Thirties. His rosy cheeks, light brown hair, and luminous, large brown eyes, coupled with a placid, if somewhat serious, disposition, endeared him to those with whom he worked and most of the studio employees.

Dickie hit his stride at the beginning of the Thirties as Tommy Wallace in a dreary triangle affair, MGM's *Passion Flower* (1930), starring Kay Francis and Charles Bickford. In Tiffany's *Aloha* (1931) the action centers on Dickie as Junior Bradford. In *Seed* (1931) he is one of five children of Lois Wilson and John Boles. As Ned Leeds in Warner Bros.' *The Star Witness* (1931) he and Chic Sale stole the movie from old pros Walter Huston and Frances Starr. The young boy and Sale were teamed again by Warners in *The Expert* (1932), a lively screen version of Edna Ferber's *Old Man Minick*. In Cecil B. DeMille's remake of *The Squaw Man* (1931) Dickie was Little Hal.

Between the dozen features in which Dickie appeared in 1932, he also became a member of Hal Roach's *Our Gang* two-reel comedies, appearing in such short-subject entries as *Birthday Blues*, *Free Wheeling*, and *A Lad An' a Lamp* in 1932, and in *Forgotten Babies* and three others in 1933. His frequent teammates on the *Our Gang* entries were Stymie Beard, Spanky McFarland, Dorothy De Borba, and Bobby "Wheezer" Hutchins.

As Spencer Tracy's nephew Timmy, Dickie was a bright spot in Fox's *Disorderly Conduct* (1932), in which he is killed by gangsters while decked out in a specially made policeman's uniform. For Warner Bros., Moore played Barbara Stanwyck's young son, Dirk, in *So Big* (1932), and his scenes with the actress were charming. Once again he demonstrated how natural he could be onscreen, eschewing the artificiality that so often ruined moppets' oncamera performances.

Child star of the Thirties.

Warner Bros.' *Winner Take All* (1932) starred Moore with James Cagney, and the critics extolled Dickie as "the screen's most precious baby actor." From Cagney, Dickie went to the glamorous Marlene Dietrich to play her son, Johnny Faraday, in Josef von Sternberg's overblown drama *Blonde Venus* (1932). This exotic melodrama flaunted the censorship code of Hollywood where prostitution was permissible oncamera if done through mother love and sacrifice. It was a plot that kept many children performing in front of the cameras in many steamy, questionable photodramas. Dickie was seen as James Gleason and Lois Wilson's son in *The Devil Is Driving* (1932), in which a hit and run driver leaves him a cripple. He was again Miss Wilson's son, Dickie Chester, helping Leo Carrillo become a good naturalized American citizen, in *Obey the Law* (1933).

Dickie's largest screen role arrived in 1933 when he was chosen to play the title role in Monogram's surprisingly well done version of Charles Dickens' *Oliver Twist*. Moore was a constant delight and Irving Pichel, director and actor, was excellent as Fagin. Dickie gave a poignant performance as dying Bill Malone living to meet his idol, big league baseball player Wallace Ford, in *Called on Account of Darkness*; the film was made in 1933 but not released by Columbia until 1935, and then under the title *Swell Head*. Dickie was again a crippled boy in *Man's Castle* (1933), with Loretta Young and Spencer Tracy, and in *Gallant Lady* (1933) he was Ann Harding's illegitimate son. As Demi in Mascot's *Little Men* (1934), Master Moore performed extremely well, and for Warner Bros.' *Upper World* (1934) he became the son of Mary Astor and Warren William. Critics claimed *The World Accuses* (1935), a maudlin mother-love tale with Vivian Tobin and Mary Carr, rested almost entirely on Dickie Moore's boyish pout and acting.

403

With Elsa Buchanan in *Peter Ibbetson* (Par '35).

Dickie walked away with the acting honors in *Without Children* (1935), surpassing by far the acting of the picture's adults, Bruce Cabot, Marguerite Churchill, and Evelyn Brent. *The Story of Louis Pasteur* (1935), which brought Paul Muni an Oscar, saw Dickie turn in a first-rate job as the boy stricken with hydrophobia, leading Dr. Pasteur to unethically test his unproven vaccine against the disease. When Warner Bros. filmed *The Life of Emile Zola* (1937), a film highlighted by Zola's (Paul Muni) defense of the falsely accused French traitor, Alfred Dreyfus (Joseph Schildkraut), Dickie played the role of Dreyfus' son. Possibly the best screen work Dickie contributed to the Thirties was his playing of Kay Francis' youngest son in *My Bill* (1938). Warner Bros. was delighted with his work in this maudlin story, and the studio began talking about a long-term contract for the young actor who was now thirteen.

But Dickie had reached that gangling, indeterminate stage of adolescence, and the studio was afraid to chance having an awkward teenager under pact. Film roles became scarcer for Moore, as he saw younger, fresher talent taking the roles he once would have had. Occasionally he had a more-than-a-bit role, as in *Miss Annie Rooney* (1942), in which he gives Shirley Temple her first romantic screen kiss. For Los Angeles' KMPC radio broadcast "Time and the Play" in 1942, Dickie directed the series.

Until he enlisted in the U.S. Army in 1944, Dick's screen appearances were in minor roles, such as for Twentieth Century-Fox in *The Eve of St. Mark* (1944) as William Eythe's brother, or in RKO's *Youth Runs Wild* (1944), a quickie. During the war, he served in the Pacific theatre of war operations as a correspondent for the army newspaper *Stars and Stripes,* holding the rank of sergeant. After spending twenty-five months on Saipan, Dickie was returned to the States toward the end of the war with an insular disease that had paralyzed him from the waist down. Sent to Sawtelle Veteran's Hospital, he was visited regularly by his former screen mother, Barbara Stanwyck, who interceded for him to get writing assignments during his recovery.

Following his rehabilitation, the adult Dick Moore made his stage debut as Jigger in *The Stone Jungle* at Los Angeles' Coronet Theatre in August 1948, having already made three rather brief screen appearances in the past year. On December 14, 1949, after making *Bad Boy* (1949) with Lloyd Nolan and *Tuna Clipper* (1949) with Roddy McDowall, Dick married Patricia Dempsey. The same year he produced on his own a splendid

With Bob Burns in *The Arkansas Traveler* (Par '38).

short film, *The Boy and the Eagle,* which was nominated for an Academy Award, and he played the title role of Marco Polo in a Children's Theatre production of *The Adventures of Marco Polo* that opened in Chicago.

For Monogram in 1950 Dick made *Killer Shark* and played the title role in a fifteen-episode Columbia serial, *Cody of the Pony Express,* in which he stopped gun-smuggling to the Indians and recovered stolen gold. In 1951 he returned to the stage at Chicago's Tenthouse Theatre in *Hay Fever,* and, with Fredric March, Florence Eldredge, and Theodore Newton, he appeared in the national touring company of *The Autumn Garden.* Dick was now the father of a son, Kevin, and returned to the screen for Stanley Kramer's *Eight Iron Men* (1952), a World War II story with Lee Marvin and Richard Kiley.

Dick returned to Stanley Kramer's film unit in 1952 to play the lonely, drunken soldier who tries to console and make love to Julie Harris in *The Member of the Wedding* (1952). Despite the fact that Ethel Waters, Brandon de Wilde, and Miss Harris were repeating their stage roles, the film lacked the stage show's magic. In summer stock, Dick played the maniacal murderer, Danny, in a production of *Night Must Fall* in Birmingham, Alabama; and in 1954, he did a four-month tour as Michael in *The Fourposter.* During the summer of that year he played Lachie in *The Hasty Heart* at Myrtle Beach, South Carolina, and he and Patricia were divorced.

His studies at Los Angeles' Actor Lab plus another year with Florence Enright had given him a greater command and appreciation of acting, and he accordingly sought additional stage work. Directing became more appealing than playing, and in 1955 at Glens Falls, New York, he directed *Bell, Book and Candle* and *The Fourposter.* At the summer theatre in Cincinnati, Ohio, he directed *The Rainmaker,* returning the following summer to pace the actors through *Dial M for Murder, On Borrowed Time,* and *Goodbye, My Fancy.* He returned to Glens Falls to perform the same service for *The Hasty Heart* and *Dial M for Murder.*

Siobhan McKenna's *Saint Joan* tried out in the summer theatres before opening September 11, 1956, at the Phoenix Theatre. In the cast were Kent Smith, Ian Keith, Peter Falk, and, making his broadway debut as Brother Martin Ladvenu, Dick Moore.

In April, 1957, Dick became the editor of *Actors' Equity Magazine,* published by the players' union. In addition he served as public relations director and legislative liaison officer for AEA, working closely with Equity president Ralph Bellamy and his several-times screen mother Lois Wilson, who was then a member of Equity's executive board. In Manhattan, Dick studied acting with Uta Hagen and voice with Marion Rich. In 1957 he, too, taught acting and lectured at the American Academy of Dramatic Arts, continuing his directing activities by staging *No Exit* at Brooklyn's Academy of Music and by directing *Angel Street* and *The Fourposter* for an Equity-U.S.O.-sponsored overseas tour.

Dick had been seen on television in 1954 on the series "Man Behind the Badge" and "The Web." In September, 1958, he wrote *The Jewel Box* for NBC-TV's "Matinee Theatre." He was also seen on television as falsely accused check forger Harry Mead, cleared by Herbert Rudley, on NBC-TV's "Treasury Men in Action." As Ranger Hillary he was part of the cast of the space series "Captain Video."

On November 8, 1959, he remarried. He second wife was the former Eleanor Donhowe Fitzpatrick and they became the parents of a son. Moore's professional growth was commendable and his versatility was displayed in 1962 when he published his first book, *Opportunities in Acting,* followed in 1963 by *The Relationship of Amateur to Professional in the American Theatre,* written under a grant and commission from the Rockefeller Foundation. On May 4, 1964, Dick became creative director of the meetings and show department of the S.C.I. division of Communications Affiliates, Inc, having given up his editorship of the Equity's magazine.

Dick's home base these days is New York City where he manages his own public relations firm, Dick Moore and Associates. Dick is editor and publisher of the AFTRA Quarterly magazine for the American Federation of TV and Radio Artists that started in 1971. Considering Dick's contemporaries, few have made the mature decisions and readjustments needed for great accomplishments in life better than John Richard Moore, Jr. He started in the trade earlier than most child actors and withstood the adulation and lost childhood far better than most of other past Hollywood studio-bred children.

For a recent interview with *Film Fan Monthly*, Moore was asked, "Do you feel you've been lucky?" His response: "Incredibly. I've had good friends, I've been in the right place at the right time, and I was lucky in the sense that I never really liked acting that much. The big problem, the big floundering for me was to get the hell out of the bag and take the contents with me."

DICKIE MOORE

The Beloved Rogue *(UA 1927)*
Object—Alimony *(Col 1928)*
Timothy's Quest *(Gotham 1929)*
Son of the Gods *(FN 1930)*
Passion Flower *(MGM 1930)*
Lawful Larceny *(RKO 1930)*
The Matrimonial Bed *(WB 1930)*
Aloha *(Tiffany 1931)*
Seed *(Univ 1931)*
Confessions of a Co-Ed *(Par 1931)*
Three Who Loved *(RKO 1931)*
The Star Witness *(WB 1931)*
The Squaw Man *(MGM 1931)*
Manhattan Parade *(WB 1931)*
Union Depot *(FN 1932)*
Husband's Holiday *(Par 1932)*
Fireman, Save My Child! *(FN 1932)*
The Expert *(WB 1932)*
Disorderly Conduct *(Fox 1932)*
So Big *(WB 1932)*
No Greater Love *(Col 1932)*
Million Dollar Legs *(Par 1932)*
Winner Take All *(WB 1932)*
Blonde Venus *(Par 1932)*
The Devil Is Driving *(Par 1932)*
The Racing Strain *(Maxim Productions 1932)*
Deception *(Col 1933)*
Oliver Twist *(Mon 1933)*
Obey the Law *(Col 1933)*
Gabriel over the White House *(MGM 1933)*
Cradle Song *(Par 1933)*
Man's Castle *(Col 1933)*
Gallant Lady *(UA 1933)*
This Side of Heaven *(MGM 1934)*
Little Men *(Mascot 1934)*
In Love with Life *(Chesterfield 1934)*
Upper World *(WB 1934)*
The Human Side *(Univ 1934)*
Tomorrow's Youth *(Mon 1935)*
The World Accuses *(Chesterfield 1935)*
Swell Head *(Col 1935)*

Without Children *(First Division 1935)*
Peter Ibbetson *(Par 1935)*
So Red the Rose *(Par 1935)*
The Story of Louis Pasteur *(WB 1935)*
Timothy's Quest *(Par 1936)*
Star for a Night *(20th 1936)*
The Little Red Schoolhouse *(Chesterfield 1936)*
Madame X *(MGM 1937)*
The Life of Emile Zola *(WB 1937)*
The Bride Wore Red *(MGM 1937)*
Love, Honor and Behave *(WB 1938)*
My Bill *(WB 1938)*
The Gladiator *(Col 1938)*
The Arkansas Traveler *(Par 1938)*
Hidden Power *(Col 1939)*
The Under-Pup *(Univ 1939)*
A Dispatch from Reuter's *(WB 1940)*
The Blue Bird *(20th 1940)*
The Great Mr. Nobody *(WB 1941)*
Sergeant York *(WB 1941)*
The Adventures of Martin Eden *(Col 1942)*
Miss Annie Rooney *(UA 1942)*
Heaven Can Wait *(20th 1943)*
The Song of Bernadette *(20th 1943)*
Happy Land *(20th 1943)*
Jive Junction *(PRC 1943)*
The Eve of St. Mark *(20th 1944)*
Youth Runs Wild *(RKO 1944)*
Sweet and Low Down *(20th 1944)*
Out of the Past *(RKO 1947)*
Dangerous Years *(20th 1947)*
Sixteen Fathoms Deep *(Mon 1948)*
Behind Locked Doors *(EL 1948)*
Bad Boy *(AA 1949)*
Tuna Clipper *(Mon 1949)*
Cody of the Pony Express *(Col serial 1950)*
Killer Shark *(Mon 1950)*
Eight Iron Men *(Col 1952)*
The Member of the Wedding *(Col 1952)*

Chester Morris

Chester Morris was among the vanguard of leading men imported from Broadway who gained stardom in the Thirties, providing the screen with impressive, understated, virile performances. These were the men who appeared opposite a growing list of movie queens who eventually dominated the male sex on the screen during the Depression years.

Morris was a handsomely rugged and supremely talented actor who, by the mid-Thirties, was destined to be a B-picture lead, being unable to compete with the newer breed of more handsome, more flexible younger performers.

Later he would become a solid stage and TV actor. His strong facial features —dominated by a square-cut jaw and expressive eyes—and straight black hair led him to be compared to earlier actor Richard Dix or to cartoon hero Dick Tracy. Today Chester is largely remembered as the screen's (and radio's) Boston Blackie. However, the impact of his early screen career should not be minimized, for in the fledgling talkie period he was a man with whom to reckon.

John Chester Brooks Morris was born in New York City on Saturday, February 16, 1901. His parents, William Morris of Boston and Etta Hawkins of Minnesota, were well-known stage performers. William's career had begun in 1876 and he later became leading man for Olga Nethersole, Mrs. Fiske, and Modjeska. Etta Hawkins was a member of Charles Frohman's famous theatre company and in 1886 was the ingenue in a road company of *The Young Mrs. Winthrop* with Henry C. and Beatrice De Mille, who had arranged for Etta's mother to take care of their two sons, William Churchill and Cecil Blount DeMille, at their home in Echo Lake, New Jersey, while they toured in the play.

Young Chester made his theatrical debut in several productions of the Westchester Players at Mount Vernon, New York, in 1917. While playing hooky from school he made his movie debut that year as Dick, with Gladys Leslie, in Thanhouser's *An Amateur Orphan*. It was on February 18, 1918, that Chester made his Broadway debut with Lionel Barrymore's production of *The Copperhead*, and that year he found another film job playing Dan in Mae Marsh's *The Beloved Traitor* (1918) for Goldwyn.

During the early Twenties Chester concentrated on learning his family's profession of acting, playing in *Thunder, So This Is London, The Exciters* in 1922 and *Extra* in 1923. While his parents were playing in *Partners Again*, Chester made another motion picture,

With Dolores Costello in *Second Choice* **(WB '30).**

taking the part of Tom O'Hara in Vitagraph's *Loyal Lives* (1923), with Mary Carr and Brandon Tynan.

For the next two years the Morris family, including Chester, brothers Gordon and Adrian, and sister Wilhelmina, made a national tour in vaudeville in a comedy sketch entitled *All the Horrors of Home*. When their act played Los Angeles, Mrs. Morris introduced Chester to her old friend Cecil B. DeMille. Promised a role in DeMille's first independent picture, Chester was elated with dreams of instant movie fame and stardom in future DeMille photoplays. The dream was quickly shattered when he was given but one fleeting scene, as a party guest, in *The Road to Yesterday* (1925). He returned to Broadway under the personal management of George M. Cohan, appearing in *The Home Towners* and in *Yellow.*

It would be *Crime*, a melodrama of New York's underworld, that would establish Chester as an authoritative actor headed for greater theatrical triumphs. The play opened at the Eltinge Theatre on February 22, 1927, with a cast no producer could have afforded five years hence: Sylvia Sidney, Chester, Douglass Montgomery, Kay Johnson, James Rennie, Jack La Rue, and Kay Francis. Morris' *Crime* success continued through the Broadway run and on tour through January 1928. In the middle of the play's run, on September 30, 1927, he wed Suzanne Kilborn. He was back on Broadway in February 1928, in *Whispering Friends* and later that year with Claudette Colbert and Crane Wilbur in *The Fast Life,* in which his own father, William, played his stage father. Then Hollywood beckoned him.

Morris' first try at the new talking picture medium was a resounding success. In *Alibi* (1929), a film version of *Nightstick,* he played a gangster married to a policeman's daughter who kills an undercover agent (Regis Toomey) and uses his wife for a cover-up. In his first movie lead he was Oscar-nominated, but lost to Warner Baxter who won the Best Actor Award for *In Old Arizona*. Morris would never again be nominated for an Academy Award.

Warners filmed Chester's Broadway show *Fast Life,* and he was signed for the 1929 release. Then he moved to Paramount for *Woman Trap* (1929) in which he was cast as a hardened criminal who commits suicide before being captured by his police captain brother (Hal Skelly). Morris returned to Warners for an appearance with that studio's entire contract company in their revue *The Show of Shows* (1929). He stayed on at the Burbank studio to play yet another gangster in *Playing Around* (1930) and *She Couldn't Say No* (1930). In *Second Choice* (1930) he was Dolores Costello's romantic interest. Then RKO signed Chester for the lead in Herbert Brenon's filming of *The Case of Sergeant Grischa* (1930), an overlong, highly publicized film in which Morris stalked through a muddled mass of intrigue and gave a performance that bordered on hysteria and considerable excessive emoting.

MGM signed Chester for two features that should have assured him future important leads. Irving Thalberg's wife, Norma Shearer, insisted on a more daring role than had been her lot and she persuaded her husband to film Ursula Parrott's ode to sexual freedom, *Ex-Wife*. It emerged on the screen as *The Divorcee* (1930) and she had three leading men: Chester, Robert Montgomery, and Conrad Nagel. As directed by Robert Z. Leonard, it became one of the year's biggest hits and won Norma her only Oscar. *The Divorcee* was also one of the first of "women's pictures" that skirted censorial damnation by having the lead characters find ultimate redemption from their loose morals.

Thalberg's second assignment for Morris was the lead in an intense, brutal film, *The Big House* (1930), which rescued the faltering career of Wallace Beery who had been recently dismissed from Paramount. In Chester's lengthy career, his role of Morgan in *The Big House* remained his favorite, and it was one of his best characterizations.

Director George Hill was greatly responsible for the excellent playing of his cast, threatening them with the statement "The first person that acts gets canned." In addition, any actor given to overplaying would be informed, "You played that like an actor in New York." Hill tolerated no makeup and the cast gave their best to Hill's dictum of underplaying. *The Big House* was imaginative and inventive, the first important crime film of the talkie era. Years later Chester would recall, "We all gave our roles the best that was in us, and the virility and truthfulness of the picture was more satisfying than anything else I've done." Metro made *The Big House* in German, Spanish, and French versions, the latter directed by Paul Fejos, with Charles Boyer in Chester's role of Morgan.

Then came the lead in a remake of *The Bat,* entitled *The Bat Whispers* (1931), followed by an overly imaginative tale of an ex-football hero turned to piracy on the high seas. However, *Corsair* (1931), with Thelma Todd, proved to be just another adventure movie. Paramount's remake of *The Miracle Man* starred Chester in the Thomas Meighan silent screen role, but his forceful, hard playing was less sympathetic than Meighan's and the talking version was not equal to the 1919 edition. After playing in the lackadaisical comedy *Cock of the Air* (1932) and being Carole Lombard's romantic interest in *Sinners in the Sun* (1932), Chester was back at Metro to film *Red-Headed Woman* (1932). Anita Loos revamped F. Scott Fitzgerald's attempt at adapting Katherine Brush's risque novel, and the resultant production turned out to be a stylish film which provided sex goddess Jean Harlow with one of her greatest screen successes.

With Boris Karloff in *The Miracle Man* (Par '32).

With Helen Morgan in *Frankie and Johnny* (RKO '35).

However, after *Red-Headed Woman,* Chester descended to less-than-major pictures, but he maintained his professionalism in most of them, often raising the level of lower-case B films to first-class entertainment. His performance in John Ford's *The Three Godfathers* (1936) was a fine bit of acting, and he was notable in such pictures as *Blind Alley* (1939) and John Farrow's *Five Came Back* (1939). Chester was even convincing as twin brothers in Republic's *Wagons Westward* (1940). Then he hit upon unexpected fame when he was signed for Columbia's *Boston Blackie,* a role he would play frequently on screen and on radio (later replaced by Richard Kollmar).

On a personal level, in November, 1939, Suzanne Kilborn sued Morris for divorce, retaining custody of their two children, Brooks and Cynthia. A year later, on November 30, 1940, Chester wed the original Chesterfield Cigarette Girl of national advertising, Lillian (Lili) Kenton Barker, by whom he would have another son, Kenton.

During the war years Morris did nearly four hundred shows for the U.S.O., using a vaudeville act which highlighted his prowess as an exceptionally clever magician. Although Cecil B. DeMille never invited Chester to join the cast of his screen epics, he did appear on DeMille's "Lux Radio Theatre" in June, 1943, with Barbara Stanwyck in *The Great Man's Lady,* and later in the year, with Rosalind Russell in *Flight to Freedom* and with Pat O'Brien in *The Navy Comes Through.* The next year on the same program he would be heard in *The Hard Way* with Miriam Hopkins, and with Dorothy Lamour and Alan Ladd in *Coney Island.* (Morris' initial radio performance had been with Mary Pickford in October, 1934, in *Saturday's Children.*)

With the Boston Blackie adventures completed at Columbia, Morris took his vaudeville magic act to London in 1948 and returned to the States to head the national road company of *Detective Story* in 1949.

As the Fifties began, Chester concentrated on theatre and television. If Hollywood had found no major source for his talent, he managed to carve new, productive, and notable careers in the other two entertainment media. He appeared on most of the major television network dramatic shows, with especially able performances on "Studio One" in two segments, *Jack Sparling* and *Death and Life of Larry Benson.* He hosted the "Gang Buster" teleseries and was fine as Warden Garry caught in a prison revolt on *Blow Up at Cortland,* also for "Studio One."

In the summer of 1952 he played the theatre circuits as Max in *The Dark Tower* and returned to Broadway in September, 1954, when he succeeded Richard Whorf in the comedy hit *The Fifth Season.* After the Broadway run, Chester went on an extensive road tour with the comedy.

His television appearances stopped for the year 1958 and he spent the season in the theatre playing in *Blue Denim.* A role which sustained him for several stock seasons was that of Eddie Carbone in *A View from the Bridge.* He proved his talent for deep characterization on "Play of the Week" in the splendid telecast of *Morning's at Seven,* in a cast that included Ann Harding, Dorothy Gish, Eileen Heckart, and Beulah Bondi. After the April 25, 1960, telecast of this John Osborne play, critics seemed to rediscover the Morris talent. Chester would be sixty years old within a year of this triumph, and Hollywood was no longer interested in him.

He did a successful ten-week summer season in the TV series "Diagnosis: Unknown" in 1960, and then was seen on Broadway (November 17, 1960) as Senate Majority Leader Bob Munson in the play *Advise and Consent* that ran for 212 performances. In the road tour, Chester replaced Ed Begley in the starring role of Orrin Knox. In late 1962 he was seen on television in episodes of "The Defenders" and "Eleventh Hour."

In the early Sixties Chester became a member of the Drama Panel for the Bureau of Education and Cultural Affairs of the Department of State in Washington, D.C. His video appearances in 1964 included guest roles on "Route 66," "The Name of the Game," and "Dr. Kildare." Then on June 1 he was off to the summer stages for *Time Out for Ginger* with Liza Minnelli. When Edgar Lansbury, producer of the Broadway hit *The Subject Was Roses*, decided to send the show on the road, Chester joined Maureen O'Sullivan and Walter McGinn in the tour. Chester was splendid in the difficult role of the father that Jack Albertson had made so individually his own in New York. In the summer of 1968 he toured with Barbara Britton in *What Did We Do Wrong?*. Thereafter frequent illness would force Morris to recover his strength at his Manhattan home on East 77th Street, and, except for a television outing or two, he did not appear professionally again till 1970.

At the end of the summer of 1970 he returned to Bucks County Playhouse in New Hope, Pennsylvania, appearing as Captain Queeg in *The Caine Mutiny Court Martial*. He preferred playing unsympathetic characters and said of Captain Queeg: "He is a complete paranoiac. He is a strange man, so offbeat. I like that kind of role. Anybody can play nice boys." He was excellent as the neurotic Queeg, but his illness had taken its toll and he had grown frail.

Lee R. Yopp, producer-director of the Bucks County Playhouse, had a luncheon engagement with Morris on September 11, 1970. Unable to reach him by telephone, he checked the actor's room at the Holiday Inn and found Morris dead on the floor. County Coroner Samuel B. Williard registered Morris' death as the result of an overdose of barbiturates. Morris was sixty-nine years old. His last screen role as Pop Weaver in *The Great White Hope* (1970) was seen after his death.

For fifty-three years he had been a performer and his intense, professional playing seldom faltered during those many decades. Ironically, for all his extensive, versatile career, the thirteen *Boston Blackie* pictures made for Columbia have remained his greatest testament to fame. Today, the memory of *Blackie* still invokes the image of Chester Morris.

CHESTER MORRIS

An Amateur Orphan (Thanhauser 1917)
The Beloved Traitor (Goldwyn 1918)
Loyal Lives (Vitagraph 1923)
The Road to Yesterday (PDC 1925)
Alibi (UA 1929)
Fast Life (WB 1929)
Woman Trap (Par 1929)
The Show of Shows (WB 1929)
Playing Around (WB 1930)
She Couldn't Say No (WB 1930)
Second Choice (WB 1930)
The Case of Sergeant Grischa (RKO 1930)
The Divorcee (MGM 1930)
The Big House (MGM 1930)
The Bat Whispers (UA 1931)
Corsair (UA 1931)
The Miracle Man (Par 1932)
Cock of the Air (UA 1932)
Sinners in the Sun (Par 1932)
Red-Headed Woman (MGM 1932)
Breach of Promise (Sono Art-World Wide 1932)
Infernal Machine (Fox 1933)
Blondie Johnson (WB 1933)
Tomorrow at Seven (RKO 1933)
Golden Harvest (Par 1933)
King for a Night (Univ 1933)
Embarrassing Moments (Univ 1934)
Let's Talk It Over (Univ 1934)
Gift of Gab (Univ 1934)
The Gay Bride (MGM 1934)
Princess O'Hara (Univ 1935)
I've Been Around (Univ 1935)
Public Hero Number One (MGM 1935)
Frankie and Johnny (RKO 1935)
Society Doctor (MGM 1935)
Pursuit (MGM 1935)
Moonlight Murder (MGM 1936)
The Three Godfathers (MGM 1936)
Counterfeit (Col 1936)
They Met in a Taxi (Col 1936)
The Devil's Playground (Col 1937)
I Promise to Pay (Col 1937)

Flight from Glory (RKO 1937)
Law of the Underworld (RKO 1938)
Sky Giant (RKO 1938)
Smashing the Rackets (RKO 1938)
Pacific Liner (RKO 1939)
Blind Alley (Col 1939)
Five Came Back (RKO 1939)
Thunder Afloat (MGM 1939)
The Marines Fly High (RKO 1940)
Wagons Westward (Rep 1940)
The Girl from God's Country (Rep 1940)
No Hands on the Clock (Par 1941)
Confessions of Boston Blackie (Col 1941)
Meet Boston Blackie (Col 1941)
Alias Boston Blackie (Col 1942)
Boston Blackie Goes Hollywood (Col 1942)
Canal Zone (Col 1942)
I Live on Danger (Par 1942)
Wrecking Crew (Par 1942)
Tornado (Par 1943)
The Chance of a Lifetime (Col 1943)
Aerial Gunner (Par 1943)
After Midnight with Boston Blackie (Col 1943)
High Explosive (Par 1943)
Gambler's Choice (Par 1944)
Secret Command (Col 1944)
One Mysterious Night (Col 1944)
Double Exposure (Par 1944)
Boston Blackie Booked on Suspicion (Col 1945)
Rough, Tough and Ready (Col 1945)
Boston Blackie's Rendezvous (Col 1945)
One Way to Love (Col 1946)
A Close Call for Boston Blackie (Col 1946)
The Phantom Thief (Col 1946)
Boston Blackie and the Law (Col 1946)
Blind Spot (Col 1947)
Trapped by Boston Blackie (Col 1948)
Boston Blackie's Chinese Venture (Col 1949)
Unchained (WB 1955)
The She-Creature (AIP 1956)
The Great White Hope (20th 1970)

53

Wayne Morris

Big (6'2"), blond, blue-eyed Wayne Morris flirted with stardom in Hollywood in the mid-Thirties, but it forever eluded him. His projection of the affable, boyish, none-too-bright average American Boy was likable but too predictable. The public soon found other less-than-average American boys more to their liking. But Morris persisted. Had not the intrusion of World War II claimed a large portion of his youthful life, it is possible he might have accomplished far more than he did on the motion picture screen.

Bert De Wayne Morris was born on Tuesday, February 17, 1914, in Los Angeles, California. He attended Los Angeles City College where he became a star football player and won a scholarship to the Pasadena Playhouse. There he studied acting and appeared in their productions of *The Trial of Mary Dugan* and *Yellow Jack.* A Warner Bros.' talent scout was impressed with his performance in the latter play and arranged a screen test. The studio signed him to a long-term contract and tested his camera appearance and acting acumen in several minor roles.

His first screen appearance was the tiny part of the navigator in *China Clipper* (1936) with Pat O'Brien and Humphrey Bogart. He was slipped into five other brief roles in as many pictures and then the studio decided it was worth featuring him in their production of *Kid Galahad* (1937). It was this Michael Curtiz-directed feature which established Morris as a new cinema find. After seeing Wayne's performances as Ward Guisenberry, the bellhop who rises to championship in the fight game, the author of the story, Francis Wallace, wired the young actor, "Thank you for bringing our boy over the border of fiction into reality." *Photoplay* magazine selected the picture as one of the best of the month and Morris' performance as one of the top acting jobs. Frank S. Nugent in the *New York Times* wrote, "Assisted no little by the comforting presence of Edward G. Robinson, Bette Davis and Harry Carey in his corner, young Wayne Morris, the Warners' latest astronomical discovery, comes through with a natural and easy performance in *Kid Galahad* . . . a promising debut for a new star and a good little picture as well." Humphrey Bogart played Robinson's rival fight promoter climaxing the feature with a gun battle in which "Little Caesar" is killed.

The studio was so impressed with their new boy that they started negotiations with Clifford Odets to purchase his Group Theatre play, *Golden Boy.* In March 1938, Odets was asking one hundred thousand dollars for the screen rights. Warners did not buy it, but Harry Cohn of Columbia did and the film launched another film actor to stardom, William Holden.

Publicity photo.

417

Warners placed Morris into their exciting sea drama of the maiden voyage of *Submarine D-I* (1937) as "Sock" McGillis; Pat O'Brien and George Brent had the two top roles. *Photoplay* was still applauding smiling Morris in print with, "This is a part that will do much to make him an independent star." But Warners paired him with Priscilla Lane in a cheaply produced potboiler. In *Love, Honor and Behave* (1938) he is a perennial good sport, a role he seemingly never stopped playing. Then followed another attempt at recapturing the success of *Kid Galahad. The Kid Comes Back* (1938) featured Wayne as a heavyweight contender who fights Barton MacLane and loses! He was back with stalwart Miss (Priscilla) Lane in a dreary affair called *Men Are Such Fools* (1938) rather lackadaisically directed by Busby Berkeley.

As Bill Cardigan, Morris was well cast in *Valley of the Giants* (1938), a picture the studio first had filmed in 1927 with Milton Sills. As briskly directed by William Keighley, this color feature was called by the *New York Times* "a rip-snorting, sinewy flashback to the days of the strong and silent 'thrillers.'" The old-fashioned cliff-hanger was highly enjoyable and on September 9, 1938, Morris opened the film at New York's Strand Theatre with an in-person stage appearance.

Wayne seemed headed for a period of good luck. He was one of the three Virginia Military Institute cadets involved in high-jinks in *Brother Rat* (1938). The other two young men were played by Ronald Reagan and Eddie Albert, the latter making his screen debut in his original stage role. (The studio tried to capitalize on the film's popularity by making a sequel in 1940, but *Brother Rat and a Baby* did not match its predecessor.) *The Kid from Kokomo* (1939) had Wayne as a mother's boy straight from the farm. Although he was convincing in this dreary affair, it was May Robson as his hell-raising substitute mother who walked away with the film's honors.

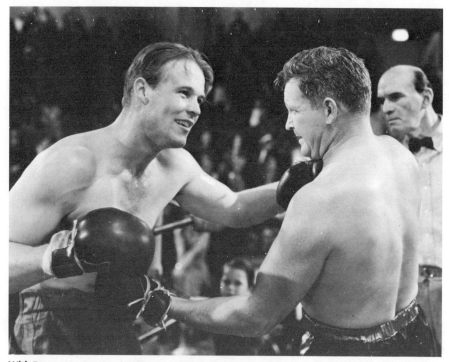

With Barton MacLane and Bob Perry in *The Kid Comes Back* (WB '38).

With Priscilla Lane in a pose from *Love, Honor and Behave* (WB '38).

With Claire Trevor in *The Valley of the Giants* (WB '38).

Thereafter the great promise predicted for Morris was not realized by the studio's assignments. In *The Return of Doctor X* (1939) Morris had a bland role as a reporter, with Humphrey Bogart, of all people, as a murdering zombie. During the making of *Flight Angels* in 1940, Morris became interested in flying. He had taken flying lessons during the making of the picture, which starred Dennis Morgan and Virginia Bruce. Warners had originally made a successful early talkie of George M. Cohan's play *The Hometowners*. In 1940, the studio revised this tale of a farm boy falling for a nightclub singer to accommodate the talents of Wayne and Rosemary Lane. The new version was called *Ladies Must Live*. Then Paramount borrowed Morris for the part of Jimmy Jones in *The Quarterback* (1940), a role which relied on his pre-movie college gridiron experience.

However, his personal life did not include as many goals, fun, or games. In January 1939, he wed tobacco heiress Leonora "Bubbles" Schinasi, but the stormy marriage erupted by June. Wayne filed a petition in Judge Ben B. Lindsey's Court of Reconciliation but his efforts failed, although the couple reunited briefly. Their son, Bert De Wayne Morris III, was born in December, 1939. However, "Bubbles" pursued a divorce which was granted in September, 1940. She latered married Arthur Hornblow, Jr. who once had been wed to Myrna Loy.

Oddly enough Morris was borrowed by Paramount in 1941 for the Arthur Hornblow, Jr. production of *I Wanted Wings*, in which he played the role of the ex-football star who joins the Army Air Corps and dies in a plane crash. (It was the film that really launched Veronica Lake as a major star of the Forties.) Returning to home base, Wayne played one of the infamous Younger Brothers (Dennis Morgan and Arthur Kennedy were Cole and Jim Younger) in *Bad Men of Missouri* (1941). After a dull comedy-mystery, *The Smiling Ghost* (1941), Wayne enlisted in the Navy Air Corps in the summer of 1941. It was on February 25, 1942, that Ensign Bert De Wayne Morris married Patricia Ann O'Rourke of Beverly Hills in an evening ceremony attended by a guard of honor of his flying mates at the Long Beach Naval Air Base.

Morris' war record was far more thrilling than anything he had played in on the screen and he was destined to become Hollywood's hero. He was assigned to Fighting Squadron Fifteen (commanded by Patricia's uncle, Captain David S. MacCampbell) aboard the carrier *Essex* in the Pacific. He flew *fifty-seven* combat missions and was part of the squadron's raids on Wake, Iwo Jima, and Okinawa. He shot down seven Japanese planes and was rated as an ace. Three F-6F Hellcat airplanes that he piloted in the course of military action were so bullet-riddled that they had to be jettisoned. Morris was credited also with sinking a Japanese gunboat, two enemy destroyers, and helping to destroy a submarine. On the side of his plane were painted seven Japanese flags, signifying his "hits" in combat.

While on duty in the Pacific, his daughter Patricia (called "Pam") was born. He wrote his wife: "Hello, Little Mother: Well, I feel a lot better today. Yesterday it was kind of rugged for me but I'll have to start right in from the beginning. As you know, we left the little island No. 2 on the morning of the sixth real early and the night before I had written you a letter saying I hadn't had a word of the baby yet. Well, I surely did feel bad, 'cause I just knew that it had been born, so I figured that I wouldn't hear for three or four weeks more. Well, anyway, after we were quite a way out to sea they brought out the mail that had been brought aboard the night before, and I hurriedly read through your letters both postmarked the 30th. It was the same old story. But one from my mother P.M. 'd the 31st gave me the smooth news of my daughter. Needless to say, I was elevated from a very morose young man to the happiest guy in the fleet and, really, secretly, I was just a little bit happier that it was a girl."

Morris won four Distinguished Flying Crosses and two Air Medals, returning home a Lieutenant Commander. Studio head Jack L. Warner gave him a big welcome-home luncheon, and Hollywood hosted him at numerous cocktail and dinner parties. "Bubbles" Schinasi arrived from the East with the five-year-old son and remained friends with both Wayne and Patricia. At one point shortly after his return, Mrs. Morris asked her spouse whether he had ever been afraid while in the service. Morris gave her his warmest, wide grin and cracked, "I sure was honey. Every time they showed a picture aboard the *Essex* I was scared to death it would be one of mine. That's something I could never have lived down." Wayne remained in the Naval Reserve and toured air bases and veteran hospitals as an entertainer.

And he returned to Warner Bros.' film factory. The studio cast him in a rather dismal production, *Deep Valley* (1947), that was distinguished only by the playing of its polished cast (Ida Lupino, Fay Bainter, and Wayne). He was then given a supporting role as Eve Arden's beau, Commander Ned Burling, in Warners' classy and frequently hilarious filming of the stage hit *The Voice of the Turtle* (1947), starring Eleanor Parker and Ronald Reagan. He was borrowed by the Cagney Brothers for their United Artist production of *The Time of Your Life* (1948). He turned in a fine performance as James Cagney's best pal and "guy-Friday" Tom.

Following a supporting part in *John Loves Mary* (1949), which spotlighted Patricia Neal and Ronald Reagan, he was the third part of a triangle featuring David Niven and Jane Wyman in *A Kiss in the Dark* (1949). Coming nearly full circle he was another of the Younger brothers, this time Cole, in *The Younger Brothers* (1949), a Western in which Janis Paige tries to form her own gang of outlaws. Again cast with Miss Paige, he appeared in a sluggish comedy, *The House Across the Street* (1949). Warners seemed to have used up all the residual and surplus ammunition from World War II in their *Task Force* (1949), a well-made feature starring Gary Cooper, with Wayne as McKinney. It was also Morris' last picture under his studio contract. Along with several other players, he was let loose to free-lance.

Once again after leaving the Burbank lot, his screen work deteriorated, as he starred in a clutch of B Westerns. However, in *Stage to Tucson* (1950), in which he was a Union trouble shooter, he and the film were a notch above the average sagebrush affair.

The Morris family had settled in suburban Studio City and the household now included another daughter, Melinda. Wayne kept working and in 1952 co-produced and starred in *Desert Pursuit* and *Arctic Flight*. In 1953 he made several Westerns and returned to the stage at Ivoryton, Connecticut, in June, starring in *Mister Roberts* and finishing the summer with *The Tender Trap*. At age forty he was simultaneously losing his boyishness and gaining weight. Yet he continued making Westerns.

He made his television debut in 1955 in *The Mink Doll* episode of "Damon Runyon Theatre" and left for England to make a saga of jewel smuggling in *Cross Channel. The Gelignite Gang* (shown in the U.S. as *The Dynamiters* in 1956) was another jewel yarn. In *The Crooked Sky*, made in 1957 but not released in America till 1959, he was involved in a story about counterfeiting.

When he returned from abroad, Wayne starred with Robert Sterling and Tom Tully in *The Clay Pigeon* on "Ford TV Theatre." On October 17, 1957, he made his Broadway debut in William Saroyan's *The Cave Dwellers*, with Eugenie Leontovich and Barry Jones. Morris played a former prizefight champion known as "The Duke" and made the simple-hearted character attractive and real. The play lasted ninety-seven performances. That same year he was seen onscreen in Stanley Kubrick's disturbing, haunting film, *Paths of Glory*, dealing with French military corruption in World War I. Morris' last film work was *Plunder Road* (1957), a story of a train robbery geared to a minor level.

During 1958 he concentrated on television, appearing on episodes of "Gunsmoke," "Wagon Train," and "Maverick." In 1959 he was a guest on additional teleseries, ranging from "Wanted: Dead or Alive" to "Bat Masterson" to "Playhouse 90" and "Ellery Queen."

On September 14, 1959, Morris had been invited by his wife's uncle (and former commanding officer) to watch air maneuvers from the U.S.S. *Bonhomme Richard* off Monterey, California. While he and Captain David MacCampbell were watching the planes, the actor collapsed from a heart attack. He was forty-five years old when death claimed him. His performances in segments of "Adventure in Paradise" and "They Went Thataway," a Western pilot, were telecast after his death.

One can only wonder what Morris' professional future might have been had he been pushed to higher thresholds of acting by his studio or had not the war intervened. His vintage Thirties' features are a hint of a promise never fulfilled.

WAYNE MORRIS

China Clipper *(WB 1936)*
King of Hockey *(WB 1936)*
Polo Joe *(WB 1936)*
Here Comes Carter *(WB 1936)*
Smart Blonde *(WB 1936)*
Once a Doctor *(WB 1937)*
Kid Galahad *(WB 1937)*
Submarine D-1 *(WB 1937)*
Love, Honor and Behave *(WB 1938)*
The Kid Comes Back *(WB 1938)*
Men Are Such Fools *(WB 1938)*
Valley of the Giants *(WB 1938)*
Brother Rat *(WB 1938)*
The Kid from Kokomo *(WB 1939)*
The Return of Doctor X *(WB 1939)*
Brother Rat and a Baby *(WB 1940)*
Double Alibi *(Univ 1940)*
An Angel from Texas *(WB 1940)*
Flight Angels *(WB 1940)*
Ladies Must Live *(WB 1940)*
The Quarterback *(Par 1940)*
Gambling on the High Seas *(WB 1940)*
Three Sons O'Guns *(WB 1941)*
I Wanted Wings *(Par 1941)*
Bad Men of Missouri *(WB 1941)*
The Smiling Ghost *(WB 1941)*
Deep Valley *(WB 1947)*
The Voice of the Turtle *(WB 1947)*
The Big Punch *(WB 1948)*
The Time of Your Life *(UA 1948)*
A Kiss in the Dark *(WB 1949)*

John Loves Mary *(WB 1949)*
The Younger Brothers *(WB 1949)*
The House Across the Street *(WB 1949)*
Task Force *(WB 1949)*
Johnny One-Eye *(UA 1950)*
The Tougher They Come *(Col 1950)*
Stage to Tucson *(Col 1950)*
Sierra Passage *(Mon 1951)*
The Big Gusher *(Col 1951)*
Yellow Fin *(Mon 1951)*
The Bushwhackers *(Realart 1952)*
Desert Pursuit *(Mon 1952)*
Arctic Flight *(Mon 1952)*
The Fighting Lawman *(AA 1953)*
The Marksman *(AA 1953)*
The Star of Texas *(AA 1953)*
Master Plan *(Astor 1954)*
Riding Shotgun *(WB 1954)*
The Desperado *(AA 1954)*
Two Guns and a Badge *(AA 1954)*
Port of Hell *(AA 1954)*
Lord of the Jungle *(AA 1955)*
The Green Buddha *(Rep 1955)*
Cross Channel *(Rep 1955)*
Lonesome Trail *(Lip 1955)*
The Dynamiters [The Gelignite Gang] *(Astor 1956)*
Paths of Glory *(UA 1957)*
Plunder Road *(20th 1957)*
The Crooked Sky *(J. Arthur Rank 1959)*

54

Lloyd Nolan

If Spencer Tracy is the actor's actor, the runner-up in less prestigious pictures would most likely be Lloyd Nolan. He has been described as "an American dependable leading man," "the finest actor in Hollywood," and, in 1969, Robert de Roos, writing in *TV Guide* about Nolan, called him "the unforgettable man from many forgettable movies."

Lloyd was born in San Francisco on Tuesday, August 11, 1903, to shoe manufacturer James Nolan and his wife Margaret (Shea) Nolan. Lloyd graduated from Santa Clara Prep School in California and then attended Stanford University. Years later he would say: "I really don't know why I kept on going to college: I was not really interested in the academic life, and while perfectly able to study I didn't enjoy the prospect of working my way through Stanford. The one thing I really enjoyed was the Dramatic Club, in which I played leading roles, succeeding Lester Vail who graduated the year I came in. Finally, upon the advice of one of my professors, I gave up scholastic pursuits and went to acting as my whole occupation."

In 1924 he played the Keith-Albee vaudeville circuit in a sketch called "The Radio Robot." After that it was an actor's life for him. He joined the student body of the famed Pasadena Playhouse. There he appeared with Edward Everett Horton in *The Queen's Husband* and acted in twenty-seven other productions. "It was there," recalls Nolan, "I came to know Victor Jory who, before he was a success in films, took part in many of the Pasadena productions." After a year there Lloyd decided the time was right to head east, conquer the world of theatre, and build a reputation as a stage actor.

Three seasons at the Cape Playhouse in Dennis, Massachusetts, gave him a firm base in the theatre, where he learned his trade along with fellow students Henry Fonda and Robert Montgomery and got to know a young apprentice serving as an usher, Ruth Elizabeth Davis, who later became movie queen Bette Davis. In 1929 Nolan made his Broadway debut with *Cape Cod Follies* which had been transferred from the summer theatre to New York. It lasted thirty performances. On December 23, 1929, Lloyd appeared at the Old Rialto Theatre in Hoboken, New Jersey, in *The Blue and the Gray, or War Is Hell* and toured with Edna Hibbard in *High Hat*. Then he joined the Chicago company of *The Front Page*.

Billed as Lloyd B. Nolan he returned to Broadway in October, 1930, as Holloway the office boy in *Sweet Stranger*. One of the others in the cast was Mel Efird who eventually would become Mrs. Lloyd Nolan. One of Nolan's first prestigious assignments was

With Claire Trevor in _King of Gamblers_ (Par '37).

acting with the Lunts in _Reunion in Vienna_ (November 16, 1937), playing the role of the inquiring student Emil for 264 performances on Broadway and then participating in the road tour.

Nolan was part of the revue _Americana_ which debuted on October 5, 1932, and which introduced the hit song "Brother, Can You Spare a Dime?" Lloyd played in four of the sketches. While attending a performance of _Autumn Crocus,_ with his agent, Nolan was asked by the latter to the lobby to meet producer Leslie J. Spiller and director Lee Bulgakov. They requested Lloyd to read for them for an upcoming show.

"I studied the script and found that the part for which I was destined was that of Hugo Barnstead. Frankly, I didn't care for it, but in Biff Grimes, I saw exactly what I wanted. I finally argued myself into the role and the young actor who had been rehearsing Biff for three weeks became my understudy and played a tiny part. It was a cruel thing for him but he took it splendidly, even coming to me afterward to say that it made it easier for him to lose the part when he saw how well it was being done." As the blustering, inarticulate, conceited young dentist, Biff Grimes, Nolan was perfection in _One Sunday Afternoon._ He played the part for 322 performances.

Established successfully in the theatre, Lloyd married Mel Efird on May 23, 1933. Following his success in _One Sunday Afternoon_ (February 15, 1933), Nolan played two performances in _Ragged Army,_ and then was in the short-lived Group Theatre project _Gentlewoman_ with Stella Adler and Claudia Morgan.

Following a successful screen test, Lloyd returned to his native state, California, this time to Hollywood, where he made his film debut in *Stolen Harmony* (1935) at Paramount. He was in another George Raft film that year, *She Couldn't Take It,* a semi-comedy with Joan Bennett co-starred. By the time Lloyd played Capper Stevens with Chester Morris in *Counterfeit* (1936), *Photoplay* was writing, "You'll appreciate Lloyd Nolan as the modern, well-educated bandit and killer." That same year he was outstanding as the bad man in *The Texas Rangers,* starring Fred MacMurray and Jack Oakie.

He had signed a pact with Columbia, but in 1936 he negotiated a term contract with Paramount, who kept him occupied playing heavies. In the first of the *Dr. Kildare* pictures, *Internes Can't Take Money* (1937), Lloyd played big shot bookie Hanlon so realistically that he overshadowed the work of the leads, Barbara Stanwyck and Joel McCrea. He gave a zesty performance as a yellow journalist in *Exclusive* (1937) and was memorable as the murderous Attwater, king of a lonely island, in the Technicolor feature *Ebb Tide* (1937). He was considered for the George Raft role in *Souls at Sea* (1937), until Raft decided the part had been sufficiently enlarged to accommodate his singular talents. Instead Lloyd made the villainous Slade of *Wells Fargo* (1937) a memorable experience for viewers. For Mae West's final Paramount picture, *Every Day's a Holiday* (1937), Lloyd played a corrupt politician, Honest John Quade, the type of character Mae described as being "so crooked he uses a corkscrew for a ruler."

By this time, however, Paramount was more concerned with building the careers of Ray Milland, Dorothy Lamour, and others, so the studio relegated Lloyd to a series of quickie films. Nevertheless, he gave fine performances, such as the escaped murderer Joe Albany ("I'm no bigger than the gun in my hand") in *Hunted Men* (1938), and Raymond Grayson, the ship's wireless man, in *King of Alcatraz* (1938), a film that had nothing to do with the famous Rock. He also took over George Raft's intended role in *St. Louis Blues* (1939), which starred Dorothy Lamour.

With Mae West in *Every Day's a Holiday* (Par '37).

Posing with Dorothy Lamour for *St. Louis Blues* (Par '39).

On April 11, 1938, Lloyd was heard on a radio broadcast of *Mary Burns, Fugitive* with Miriam Hopkins, Henry Fonda, and Mary Astor. At about that time, in another part of Hollywood, two Johns, Ford and Wayne, were having an all-night card and drinking session. Director Ford pestered Wayne to recommend the right actor for the role of the Ringo Kid in the planned *Stagecoach* (1939). Wayne said the only actor in Hollywood who could play the part was Lloyd Nolan. Wayne actually wanted the role for himself but would not suggest it to Ford. Eventually Ford used Wayne in the part anyway.

At Paramount, earnest Lloyd continued working in B films such as *Undercover Doctor* (1939), as a G-Man, and *The Magnificent Fraud,* as Akim Tamiroff's right-hand man. By July, 1939, he could not bear the lowercase assignments anymore, so he left Paramount. He signed with Twentieth Century-Fox where he gave a superlative performance as Joe Monday in the studio's remake of *The Valiant* (Paul Muni's debut film in 1929), which was retitled *The Man Who Wouldn't Talk* (1940). But following this fine role his parts at Fox were much the same as those he had been given at Paramount.

Lloyd was always an assured actor capable of immersing himself in any role and making trite dialogue seem clever, or at least respectable. Fox assured him of better assignments and he was withdrawn from the cast of Fritz Lang's *Western Union* (1941) and began a series of detective stories, the first being *Michael Shayne, Private Detective* (1940). Including the opener, he made six such *Shayne* entries: *Sleepers West* (1941), *Dressed to Kill* (1941), *Blue, White and Perfect* (1941), *The Man Who Wouldn't Die* (1942), *Just Off Broadway* (1942), and *Time to Kill* (1942). Between the *Shayne* opuses, which were as snappy as Columbia's *Boston Blackie* (Chester Morris) or *Crime Doctor* (Warner Baxter) or *Lone Wolf* (Warren William) segments, Lloyd returned to Paramount to play, first, gangster Ricky Dean for straight laughs in *Buy Me that Town* (1941) and then Del Davis, a notorious gangster-roadhouse owner, in Warners' fine *Blues in the Night* (1941). With his fast-clipped speech and pugnacious look, Lloyd seemingly could not escape being typecast as either a hardened criminal or a breezy law enforcer.

In November, 1942, he was heard with George Raft and Janet Blair on "Lux Radio Theatre" in *Broadway* and the same year he gave a terrific performance as Frank Maguire, manager of a baseball team, in Twentieth Century-Fox's *It Happened in Flatbush.* The next year Fox loaned dependable Nolan to MGM and Tay Garnett for *Bataan,* shot on Metro's Stage 16, in which Lloyd played Corporal Barney Todd. The *New York Times* thought his performance overdone, but admitted "he comes thru nicely at the climax." He returned to the home lot to play Gunner O'Hara in the intense filming of *Guadalcanal Diary* (1944), and then to repeat his role on "Lux Radio Theatre."

Because of his age, Lloyd did not serve in World War II, but the absence of such Fox top leading men as Tyrone Power, Victor Mature, and George Montgomery still did not allow him to push into the front rank. While never a star, he was, and is, a fine actor. Along with James Dunn's memorable comeback performance in *A Tree Grows in Brooklyn* (1945), there was Lloyd's kindly neighborhood cop, McShane, bringing drunken Dunn home and pursuing a credo of "and wasn't it an officer's duty to look after the ladies?" His brief but outstanding role of city detective Kendall in *Somewhere in the Night* (1946) is illustrative of the creative, capable, and outstanding work he turned in on the screen, as was his crooked detective in Robert Montgomery's *Lady in the Lake* (1946).

Lloyd returned to Paramount and director Tay Garnett for *Wild Harvest* (1947), a picture shot largely on location near Bakersfield, California. Alan Ladd and Dorothy Lamour were that film's stars, but Nolan's presence greatly enhanced the credibility of the proceedings.

As the Forties wore on, Lloyd's screen work diminished and he returned to the stage to head the national touring company of *The Silver Whistle*. He portrayed the raffish charlatan Oliver P. Erwent (played on Broadway by José Ferrer). His reviews were excellent: "It is a genuine pleasure to meet Mr. Nolan—too long relegated to Hollywood's B-hive—in a footlight role both he and the customers can enjoy." The play traveled to the West Coast and Lloyd's children, nine-year-old Melinda Joyce and seven-year-old Jay Benedict, first saw their father onstage. The twelve-week tour was a success for Nolan and its producers, the Theatre Guild.

If Hollywood had ill-used his talents, he rose above it, as he did with personal tragedy. The Nolans discovered their son was autistic (an emotional-biological condition which causes children to be unresponsive to the world about them). "We first noticed something was wrong when he was about two years old. Jay wouldn't react to people and I thought, 'My God, he's deaf!' But doctors said he wasn't. . . . When Jay was three years old, he refused to feed himself. Acting under a doctor's suggestion, we didn't feed Jay even though the food was in front of him. As the days wore on, he got thinner and thinner. . . . Poor Mel was getting thinner each day too, from worry. Finally, on the ninth day, Jay picked up his spoon and fed himself. After that, we never had to feed him again." (Eventually Jay was placed in special schools, first on the West Coast, then in Philadelphia where he stayed for over eleven years. In 1969 he choked to death on a piece of food that stuck in his throat. Thereafter, Nolan has been a good will ambassador for the National Society for Autistic Children, serving as honorary chairman.)

In the early spring of 1951 Lloyd signed with James Russo and Michael Ellis to star in their musical production of *The Farmer's Wife*, called *Courtin' Time*. Staged by Alfred Drake, with dances by George Balanchine, it had all the trappings of a hit. However, it was not. Lloyd had just completed a role in Bob Hope's *The Lemon Drop Kid* (1951) and he was billed in the tryout venture as the star. In the middle of the Philadelphia run he developed acute laryngitis and Alfred Drake substituted for him until it was decided to close the show for repairs. Then Nolan's role was recast, and Joe E. Brown got the starring part. The show reached Broadway and closed after thirty-seven performances.

In August, 1951, Nolan replaced William Gargan on television's "Martin Kane, Private Eye" series and he became a Broadway-to-Brentwood (California) commuter, managing to get home once every six weeks. "Frankly, radio gives me mike fright," he commented after assuming Gargan's sleuth role, "but I suppose because of my work on both stage and screen I do feel more at home in front of the video camera. Luckily, I'm aided in both mediums by the fact that Martin Kane is the kind of quiet, calculating character that I genuinely love to play." He continued as Martin Kane until May 22, 1952, and was replaced the following week by Lee Tracy.

Paul Gregory produced *The Caine Mutiny Court-Martial,* directed by Charles Laughton and starring Henry Fonda, John Hodiak, and, as the paranoid Lieutenant Commander Philip Francis Queeg, Lloyd. The show opened on the West Coast in October, 1953, and played sixty-seven cities before reaching Broadway in January, 1954. Praise for the three stars was overwhelming, with the bulk of the accolades going to Nolan for his outstanding performance as the psychotic skipper. He basked in his success, believing it came at just the right time. "Man most needs a lift at fifty!" For his sterling performance he received the year's Donaldson Award—the Variety New York Drama Critics poll as best actor of the season. However, it was David Wayne who received the Tony Award that year for his playing in *The Teahouse of the August Moon*. Lloyd would tour with the show in 1955, and on November 19, 1955, on "Ford Star Jubilee" he repeated his part in an outstanding video presentation. He was given an Emmy for his work. On June 13, 1956, Lloyd made his London stage debut by starring in and directing *The Caine Mutiny Court Martial* with an English cast and himself as Queeg. Kenneth

Tynan in his review wrote, "I shall never forget the skill with which Lloyd Nolan . . . outlined the collapse of Queeg: the glib plausibility with which he took the stand, and the self-justifying hysteria with which he left it."

Nolan returned to Hollywood where it was still agreed that he was not a marquee name. He played Stewart Granger's partner in *The Last Hunt* (1956), joined with Tyrone Power in the British-produced *Abandon Ship!* (1957), and provided an outstanding interpretation of John Pope, Sr., the father of drug addict Don Murray, in Twentieth Century-Fox's *A Hatful of Rain* (1957). He gave substance to his role of Dr. Matthew Swain, the dedicated and kindly physician of *Peyton Place* (1957).

But it was television that continued to bring Lloyd his best recognition. In the April, 1959, "Hallmark Hall of Fame" telecast, he was fine opposite Helen Hayes, Burgess Meredith, and Betty Field in O'Neill's *Ah, Wilderness!* He also made twenty-six install-ments of a series called "Secret Agent 7," which never made the major networks. He was a frequent guest star on teleseries and during the Sixties appeared on most of the major dramatic network shows.

Occasionally he would return to film-making, as when he played the cameo role of the bedridden shipping magnate conveniently killed off by Lana Turner and her lover (Anthony Quinn) in *Portrait in Black* (1960). He and Dorothy McGuire added mature conviction to their roles in the soap opera *Susan Slade* (1961), another showcase for the talents of Troy Donahue and Connie Stevens. For Warner Bros., *The Double Man* (1967) he gave a sound acting job as Bill Edwards, and in 1968 he became Admiral Garvey ordering a nuclear submarine to a weather station at the North Pole in *Ice Station Zebra*. Then Lloyd was seen as General Amos Bailey granting defector Ryker (Lee Marvin) a stay of execution, a new trial, and eventual acquittal in *Sergeant Ryker* (1968), which had originally been a two-part "Kraft Television Suspense Theatre" telecast.

Lloyd was always returning to television. The role of Dr. Morton Chegley in the "Julia" series kept him occupied from the fall of 1968 through 1970. The recurring part did as much for Lloyd's national image and recognition as had *Caine Mutiny*. His actual filming time on "Julia" required only one day a week. His crusty, rough-exterior, heart-of-gold physician character became as well known as Lionel Barrymore's elder doctor had been in the *Dr. Kildare* series.

In 1970 Lloyd was back in front of the camera in Hollywood playing a U.S. Customs Inspector in *Airport* and confronting an elegant grande dame smuggler (Jessie Royce Landis). Occasionally Hollywood makes films so bad they can never recover their negative or distribution costs. Lloyd made one of these bombs, *Ankles Away,* that still is on the shelf. He continued in television after the demise of "Julia," and, in 1975, was seen as Cornwall, with Pat O'Brien, in an amusing tale of a grandfather's persistence in rehabilitating an old biplane to give his grandson a true flying experience. This was for "The World of Disney" and the episode was titled *The Sky's the Limit.* In January, 1976 Lloyd turned up on an episode of "Ellery Queen," the TV detective series, playing a gym doctor who murders a would-be boxing champ. Nolan, as usual, was the most convinc-ing performer in the show.

Lloyd's last Broadway appearance to date was on March 18, 1960, in *One More River.* It led one local critic to assess, "Mr. Nolan is a believable man, slow of move-ment and speech, serious and lonely but the play is more like a [weak] TV script." It lasted three performances.

Despite the irony of television providing him with national acclaim, instead of his long years in films, Lloyd admits of his video success, "It makes me feel good. When someone says, 'Thank you for all the pleasure you've given me over the years'—that's an extra dividend."

LLOYD NOLAN

Stolen Harmony *(Par 1935)*
G-Men *(WB 1935)*
Atlantic Adventure *(Col 1935)*
She Couldn't Take It *(Col 1935)*
One Way Ticket *(Col 1935)*
Lady of Secrets *(Col 1936)*
Big Brown Eyes *(Par 1936)*
You May Be Next *(Col 1936)*
The Devil's Squadron *(Col 1936)*
Counterfeit *(Col 1936)*
The Texas Rangers *(Par 1936)*
15 Maiden Lane *(20th 1936)*
Internes Can't Take Money *(Par 1937)*
King of Gamblers *(Par 1937)*
Exclusive *(Par 1937)*
Ebb Tide *(Par 1937)*
Wells Fargo *(Par 1937)*
Every Day's a Holiday *(Par 1937)*
Dangerous to Know *(Par 1938)*
Tip-Off Girls *(Par 1938)*
Hunted Men *(Par 1938)*
Prison Farm *(Par 1938)*
King of Alcatraz *(Par 1938)*
St. Louis Blues *(Par 1939)*
Ambush *(Par 1939)*
Undercover Doctor *(Par 1939)*
The Magnificent Fraud *(Par 1939)*
The Man Who Wouldn't Talk *(20th 1940)*
The House across the Bay *(UA 1940)*
Johnny Apollo *(20th 1940)*
Gangs of Chicago *(Rep 1940)*
The Man I Married *(20th 1940)*
Pier 13 *(20th 1940)*
The Golden Fleecing *(MGM 1940)*
Michael Shayne, Private Detective *(20th 1940)*
Charter Pilot *(20th 1940)*
Behind the News *(Rep 1940)*
Sleepers West *(20th 1941)*
Mr. Dynamite *(Univ 1941)*
Dressed to Kill *(20th 1941)*
Buy Me that Town *(Par 1941)*
Blues in the Night *(WB 1941)*
Steel against the Sky *(WB 1941)*

Blue, White and Perfect *(20th 1941)*
It Happened in Flatbush *(20th 1942)*
Apache Trail *(MGM 1942)*
Just off Broadway *(20th 1942)*
Manila Calling *(20th 1942)*
Time to Kill *(20th 1942)*
The Man Who Wouldn't Die *(20th 1942)*
Bataan *(MGM 1943)*
Guadalcanal Diary *(20th 1943)*
A Tree Grows in Brooklyn *(20th 1945)*
Circumstantial Evidence *(20th 1945)*
Captain Eddie *(20th 1945)*
The House on 92nd Street *(20th 1945)*
Somewhere in the Night *(20th 1946)*
Two Smart People *(MGM 1946)*
Lady in the Lake *(MGM 1946)*
Wild Harvest *(Par 1947)*
Green Grass of Wyoming *(20th 1948)*
The Street with No Name *(20th 1948)*
Bad Boy *(AA 1949)*
The Sun Comes up *(MGM 1949)*
Easy Living *(RKO 1949)*
The Lemon Drop Kid *(Par 1951)*
Island in the Sky *(WB 1953)*
Crazylegs *(Rep 1953)*
The Last Hunt *(MGM 1956)*
Santiago *(WB 1956)*
Toward the Unknown *(WB 1956)*
Abandon Ship! *(Col 1957)*
A Hatful of Rain *(20th 1957)*
Peyton Place *(20th 1957)*
Portrait in Black *(Univ 1960)*
Girl of the Night *(WB 1960)*
Susan Slade *(WB 1961)*
We Joined the Navy *(Dial 1962)*
The Girl Hunters *(Colorama Features 1963)*
Circus World *(Par 1964)*
Never Too Late *(WB 1965)*
An American Dream *(WB 1966)*
The Double Man *(WB 1967)*
Ice Station Zebra *(MGM 1968)*
Sergeant Ryker *(Univ 1968)*
Airport *(Univ 1970)*
Earthquake *(Univ 1974)*

55

Jack Oakie

Everyone loves a clown, and this basic knowledge dawned on the motion picture industry at its meagre start. Roscoe "Fatty" Arbuckle, Buster Keaton, Harry Langdon, Charlie Chaplin were just some of the first famous funnymen of the silent screen. There were Mack Sennett's pie-throwing films, the derring-do escapades of Harold Lloyd of the horn-rimmed eyeglasses, and the wondrous antics of Mabel Normand among many, many others. The talkies brought their own breed of laugh-makers. One of the most amusing was Jack Oakie.

He was born Lewis Delaney Offield in Sedalia, Missouri, on Thursday, November 12, 1903. His father died when Lewis was relatively young. Schooling never much appealed to him so as soon as he could he headed to New York. There he worked as a telephone clerk for a brokerage house, successfully resisting any interest or knowledge of the complex business world. He left Wall Street for Broadway and changed his name to Jack Oakie.

He landed a job as a chorus boy in George M. Cohan's *Little Nelly Kelly*. Then, on January 8, 1924, he opened at Atlantic City as one of the Moulin Rouge Boys in *Innocent Eyes,* a show starring Mistinguett, Cecil Leon, Cleo Mayfield, and Frances Williams. Thereafter Oakie pranced as a chorus boy in the Shuberts' *Artists and Models* that enjoyed a 411-performance run after its June 24, 1925, opening. His next hoofing job on Broadway was in Rodgers and Hart's musical *Peggy-Ann* (December 27, 1926) with Helen Ford, Edith Meiser, and Lulu McConnell, the last with whom he frequently partnered over the years.

Years later Oakie would recall of *Peggy-Ann:* "Now I have always wanted to be the man with the love, the guy with so much swoon to him that maidens flock around him closer than income-tax collectors around a million-dollar income. However, I recognized some few things as impossible and every time I shaved, the mirror told me the truth about my pan. Therefore I tried to make ruins out of the Romeos and one night in *Peggy-Ann,* I mimicked our hero so completely, behind his back but before his public, that I brought down the house . . . and also brought down Seymour Felix on my head, who in turn brought me down on my posterior in the alley outside the stage door. Seymour told me he'd see to it that I never got another job on Broadway. That didn't faze me. I didn't have that much sense. I took all the money I had, bought a ticket on a freighter that was going through the Canal and headed for Hollywood.

432

With Ginger Rogers and George Barbier in *The Sap from Syracuse* **(Par '30).**

"Three weeks after, there I met Wesley Ruggles, the director, told him how funny I was and through him got a job at Paramount, which I kept for nine solid years. That meant I started in silent pictures, of course, but when talkies came in I went right on with them." Jack never returned to Broadway.

Actually Oakie's first Hollywood exposure was in the Wesley Ruggles-directed Universal film *Finders Keepers* (1928), in which he played a small part. After a quickie role in Fox's *Road House* (1928) he joined Paramount's contract players as Searchlight Doyle in Clara Bow's lively *The Fleet's In* (1928). (He would again play naval boxing champ Searchlight Doyle in 1930 in *Sea Legs*, with Lillian Roth.) Jack was loaned to Cecil B. DeMille's Pathé pictures to play "Chicken" O'Toole in *Sin Town* (1928) and returned to Paramount to play in Clara Bow's talkie debut with Fredric March, *The Wild Party* (1929). In *Close Harmony* (1929) it was Nancy Carroll who broke up the singing team of Oakie and Skeets Gallagher, and in the remake of *The Dummy*, with Ruth Chatterton and Fredric March, it was Jack who played the part of Dopey Hart. Oakie finally received his first important lead role when Paramount filmed *Elmer, the Great*, retitled *Fast Company* (1929), with Jack as the village baseball hero who rises to the big leagues and wins the world series.

Oakie was becoming an anticipated feature in Paramount Pictures, and his versatility ranged from acting to singing to dancing to eventually becoming Hollywood's greatest mugger. Edward Everett Horton would perfect the double-take, but Oakie went one better with a triple-take that compounded astonishment. There were several great muggers in pictures, including Lionel Barrymore, but no one outdistanced Oakie in that specialty.

Paramount had loaned Oakie to RKO to play opposite Betty Compson in *Street Girl* (1929) and to Warner Bros. to appear with Louise Fazenda and Jimmy Finlayson (another expert double-take artist) in *Hard to Get* (1929). Then Jack was brought back to his home studio to sing "Alma Mammy" in *Sweetie* (1929). His roles at Paramount were constant and never-ending, until it seemed that few of that studio's pictures did not contain Oakie footage. In 1930 he won Ginger Rogers in *The Sap from Syracuse* and in

433

1931 he was a stupid insurance salesman from Arkansas getting involved with gangsters and Jean Arthur in *The Gang Buster*. But it was Wynne Gibson who walked away with *June Moon* (1931), in which Jack was a not-very-bright songwriter.

Jack was first-billed in a wacky comedy about athletics from mythical Klopstockia, where the President was W. C. Fields, in the well-remembered *Million Dollar Legs* (1932). George Kaufman's satire on Hollywood, *Once in a Lifetime* (1932), provided a tailor-made role for Oakie's talents, the dumb but successful Hollywood producer George Lewis. In the Grand Hotel-style story of racetrack addicts, *From Hell to Heaven* (1933), Jack was the radio crooner, and then in a barrelhouse romp, *Sailor Be Good* (1933), he was a prizefighting gob. For one of these seemingly endless entries in the co-ed fun and games pictures, *College Humor* (1933), he was Midwest University's most unique freshman, winning the big football game and scoring a huge personal success.

In *Too Much Harmony* (1933) Jack was teamed again with Skeets Gallagher. The two clowns made a first-rate duo and the picture also marked the screen debut of Jack's mother; she played his oncamera mama. He sang and danced in *Sitting Pretty* (1933)—one song became a standard, "Did You Ever See a Dream Walking?"—and he was Tweedledum to Roscoe Karns' Tweedledee in Paramount's *Alice in Wonderland* (1933). Spencer Tracy was on loan from Fox to join with Jack and Arline Judge in *Shoot the Works* (1934) at Darryl F. Zanuck's Twentieth Century Productions for United Artists release. *Shoot the Works* (1934) gave Jack the role of a sideshow barker, and the film was released after the death of two of the picture's principals, Lew Cody and Dorothy Dell.

On April 14, 1934, Jack was among the several guests on a special one-hour broadcast from Hollywood featuring George Arliss, Loretta Young, Constance Bennett, Ronald Colman, Russ Columbo, *et al.* Later that year Jack made a recording of "Take a Number from One to Ten" and the title song from his *College Rhythm*. The next year he would record "Miss Brown to You" and "Why Dream?" from his film *The Big Broadcast of 1936*. Of his picture-making in the mid-Thirties, Jack would reminisce years later: "A lot of newcomers came along and made their first pictures with me. There was a chap named Bing Crosby, and a cute little trick named Alice Faye. I also gave the old debut treatment to Lanny Ross, Burns and Allen and Lily Pons."

During 1935 Jack kept busy playing Clark Gable's sidekick in Alaska in *The Call of the Wild* and then was excellent with Warner Baxter and Alice Faye in Fox's *King of Burlesque*. Among his other entries during 1936 was *That Girl from Paris*, his first film under his RKO pact. (It was a remake of his 1929 *Street Girl*.) Hollywood observers insisted that Oakie's career had hit the skids and that he would soon disappear from the scene. They did not count on his game qualities and his capacity to survive as a second banana, now that his stardom days were gone.

His roles at RKO were not as good as those he had played at Paramount, although he walked off with *Fight for Your Lady* (1937) and he was just right as Lucille Ball's wacky press agent in *The Affairs of Annabel* (1938), which spawned a sequel, *Annabel Takes a Tour* (1938). But there were rumors on the set that Oakie's ego had not adjusted to his reduced status.

As a matter of fact, Jack would admit that his quick success in Hollywood had distorted his perspective: "I went around Hollywood calling myself its 'insurance man. With Oakie in the cast, it's insurance the film will be gigantic,' I'd boast. I got so sure of myself that, with my wife, I went on a long tour of Europe in 1938. I hadn't signed a new contract." RKO dropped Jack from their contract list in October, 1938.

The comedian also recalled, "I didn't quite see how Hollywood could get along without me, but still I felt it was the moment for me to go over and give European culture the old brush-off." When Jack returned to "Sex Appeal Junction" (his term for Holly-

With Clark Gable in *The Call of the Wild* (UA '35).

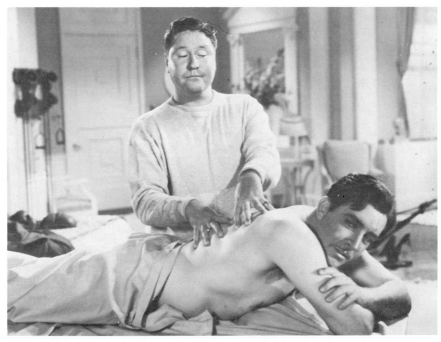

With John Boles in *Fight for Your Lady* (RKO '37).

wood) he discovered his absence had not been missed. "I suddenly found out that I was the little man who wasn't there. No producer sent for me. No telephone rang for me. No script writers begged for me. At first I thought it was an accident. I don't blame Hollywood for those two black years I went through when I couldn't get a job of any sort. The cup that cheers turned traitor, as it always does when you begin to rely on it. Some of it was my own fault. I'd got careless in my work. My mother had died. All I had was my wife, my conviction that I was still a handler when it came to comedy lines, and my dogs—I began eying their meals warily." But after a couple of inconsequential pictures for Twentieth Century-Fox, Jack earned the part of his lifetime.

"It was Charlie Chaplin, the greatest comedian there will ever be, who broke the Oakie drought. He sent for me to play the Italian Dictator in his untitled production. When Chaplin called me and asked me to play Mussolini in *The Great Dictator* I was shocked and puzzled and said, 'Charlie, why me? Get an Italian actor.' And he said a pretty smart thing, 'What's funny about an Italian playing Mussolini?' " Jack made a superb "Il Duce" and Chaplin was at the height of his genius as mad Adolph doing a ballet with a world atlas balloon. Chaplin was nominated as Best Actor of the Year and Jack was nominated by the Academy as Best Supporting Actor of the Year, but each lost (Chaplin to James Stewart of *The Philadelphia Story* and Oakie to Walter Brennan of *The Westerner*). Jack was crushed by losing his bid for Oscar glory. He had gained forty-five pounds for the role, all of which added to his disappointment at losing the prize.

Nevertheless, he returned to RKO for an excellent performance in *Little Men* and was fine as Harry Calhoun teamed with Betty Grable in *Tin Pan Alley* (1941). In June of 1941 he purchased Barbara Stanwyck's Marwyck Ranch. For his recitation of "The Shooting of Dan McGrew" in *The Great American Broadcast* (1941) he read the poem from blackboard cues *a la* John Barrymore. On the first day on the set of Warner Bros.' *Navy Blues* (1941) he gave star Ann Sheridan a tub filled with flowers. Ann had once played a bit as a washwoman in an early Oakie vehicle.

He returned to Twentieth for *Song of the Islands* (1942) and for *Hello Frisco, Hello* (1943), the latter starring Alice Faye and John Payne. By then his marriage was floundering, and Venita, in January, 1943, moved away from the ranch and returned to Hollywood where she was dating Alan Curtis. Mrs. Eva Kemper, Venita's mother, kept house for Jack while her daughter socialized. In March, 1943, the gossip columns were linking Oakie romantically with actress June Haver. In 1944 he made four mediocre pictures and on February 16, 1945, Venita Varden divorced him.

Through the remaining years of the Forties Jack's pictures were less than spectacular, and shortly after the Fifties began, he married Victoria Horne. On March 17, 1955, he appeared in *Burlesque* on television's "Shower of Stars" with Dan Dailey, Marilyn Maxwell, and Dick Foran; and, the next year, was among the cameo performers in *Around the World in 80 Days*. After some video guest spots, he reemerged in feature films, playing in *The Wonderful Country* (1959), an overly ambitious Robert Mitchum Western. The excessively self-assured performances of Debbie Reynolds and Tony Curtis did not aid *The Rat Race* (1960), a fitful screen adaptation of Garson Kanin's play, but Jack Oakie as Mac was his refreshing self, even if his hair had turned white. His final screen appearance to date was in Doris Day-Rock Hudson's *Lover Come Back* (1961), in which he succumbs to the delights of a candy product laced with alcohol.

Even though he suffered from a hearing problem, Jack appeared on television throughout the early Sixties in various series. In 1963 he filmed three episodes of the "Real McCoys" program. In 1966 he made a segment of the "Daniel Boone" show, and his last TV appearance, to date, was in December, 1972, on Rod Serling's "Night Gallery." He refuses to do TV talk shows for they only pay scale salary.

Jack lives on a ten-acre estate in the San Fernando Valley of California and is still wed to Victoria Horne. He claims he will not act again until the pay and the scripts get better. He spent nearly thirty-five years in films, and now in his seventies, he is one of the industry's wealthier men. Unfortunately, now he is almost completely deaf.

Once Oakie was asked to define his art of comedy. He said: "You learned [in vaudeville] what not to do from the audience. If they didn't laugh you never repeated that joke again. Scene stealing tricks was one labeled the 'triple fade,' or an extension of the double-take. We learned long ago that if a situation was funny, don't you be funny. You be funny when the situation isn't."

Jack Oakie was usually right.

JACK OAKIE

Finders Keepers *(Univ 1928)*
Road House *(Fox 1928)*
The Fleet's In *(Par 1928)*
Someone to Love *(Par 1928)*
Sin Town *(Pathé 1928)*
Chinatown Nights *(Par 1929)*
The Wild Party *(Par 1929)*
Close Harmony *(Par 1929)*
The Dummy *(Par 1929)*
The Man I Love *(Par 1929)*
Fast Company *(Par 1929)*
Street Girl *(RKO 1929)*
Hard to Get *(WB 1929)*
Sweetie *(Par 1929)*
Paramount on Parade *(Par 1930)*
Hit the Deck *(RKO 1930)*
The Social Lion *(Par 1930)*
Let's Go Native *(Par 1930)*
The Sap from Syracuse *(Par 1930)*
Sea Legs *(Par 1930)*
The Gang Buster *(Par 1931)*
June Moon *(Par 1931)*
Dude Ranch *(Par 1931)*
Touchdown *(Par 1931)*
Dancers in the Dark *(Par 1932)*
Sky Bride *(Par 1932)*
Make Me a Star *(Par 1932)*
Million Dollar Legs *(Par 1932)*
Madison Square Garden *(Par 1932)*
If I Had a Million *(Par 1932)*
Once in a Lifetime *(Univ 1932)*
Uptown New York *(Sono Art-World Wide 1932)*
From Hell to Heaven *(Par 1933)*
Sailor Be Good *(Par 1933)*
The Eagle and the Hawk *(Par 1933)*
College Humor *(Par 1933)*
Too Much Harmony *(Par 1933)*
Sitting Pretty *(Par 1933)*
Alice in Wonderland *(Par 1933)*
Looking for Trouble *(UA 1934)*
Murder at the Vanities *(Par 1934)*
Shoot the Works *(Par 1934)*
College Rhythm *(Par 1934)*

The Call of the Wild *(UA 1935)*
The Big Broadcast of 1936 *(Par 1935)*
King of Burlesque *(Fox 1935)*
Collegiate *(Par 1935)*
Colleen *(WB 1936)*
Florida Special *(Par 1936)*
The Texas Rangers *(Par 1936)*
That Girl from Paris *(RKO 1936)*
Champagne Waltz *(RKO 1937)*
Super Sleuth *(RKO 1937)*
The Toast of New York *(RKO 1937)*
Fight for Your Lady *(RKO 1937)*
Hitting a New High *(RKO 1937)*
Radio City Revels *(RKO 1938)*
The Affairs of Annabel *(RKO 1938)*
Annabel Takes a Tour *(RKO 1938)*
Thanks for Everything *(20th 1938)*
Young People *(20th 1940)*
The Great Dictator *(UA 1940)*
Tin Pan Alley *(20th 1940)*
Little Men *(RKO 1940)*
Rise and Shine *(20th 1941)*
The Great American Broadcast *(20th 1941)*
Navy Blues *(WB 1941)*
Song of the Islands *(20th 1942)*
Hello Frisco, Hello *(20th 1943)*
Wintertime *(20th 1943)*
Something to Shout About *(Col 1943)*
It Happened Tomorrow *(UA 1944)*
The Merry Monahans *(Univ 1944)*
Sweet and Low Down *(20th 1944)*
Bowery to Broadway *(Univ 1944)*
That's the Spirit *(Univ 1945)*
On Stage Everybody *(Univ 1945)*
She Wrote the Book *(Univ 1946)*
Northwest Stampede *(EL 1948)*
When My Baby Smiles at Me *(20th 1948)*
Thieves' Highway *(20th 1949)*
The Last of the Buccaneers *(Col 1950)*
Tomahawk *(Univ 1951)*
Around the World in 80 Days *(UA 1956)*
The Wonderful Country *(UA 1959)*
The Rat Race *(Par 1960)*
Lover Come Back *(Univ 1961)*

56

Gail Patrick

Many roads led to Hollywood and one of the most-trodden highways was the route of the beauty contest where the winner was assured of a movie contract, fame, and a career in pictures judged by measurements, beauty, and scarcely any talent. In 1932 Paramount sponsored a contest that was reminiscent of Theda Bara's "vampire" heydays and was almost as ridiculous. Each state in the union was to select its own "Panther Woman." From Alabama came a lovely young Miss Margaret Fitzpatrick who was born in Birmingham on Tuesday, June 20, 1911. Luckily Miss Fitzpatrick lost. The winner was Kathleen Burke who made *Island of Lost Souls* (1932) for which the "Panther Woman" contest was a gimmick.

Paramount liked the tall, slim Birmingham loser who wore her long black hair in a bun. After giving her a screen test they were impressed and offered her a contract. Miss Fitzpatrick was less than enthusiastic about a movie career and was planning to head back home for law school when the Paramount officials offered a standard seven-year option contract, renewable every six months.

Paramount renamed her Gail Patrick. Law student Gail read every word, including the fine print, on Paramount's document. When she reached the clause, included in virtually all studio stock contracts, that guaranteed twenty-weeks pay within the six-month period, she went screaming to the front office that twenty weeks was *not* six months. She elected to return to Birmingham. When the studio contractors realized the lady was actually going back to Alabama, actress Gail Patrick received the first beginner's contract guaranteeing pay for every week within six months.

Actually Gail had only entered the bizarre contest in order to win enough money to help her with her law school education. Her major ambition was someday to be the first woman governor of Alabama. But when she signed her Paramount pact, these dreams became impractical. Even Gail had to admit, after she saw the first studio publicity pictures which highlighted her well-formed legs, that, "I want to be the governor of Alabama! How can I be governor of Alabama if everyone sees my legs!"

Gail was an unusual challenge to Hollywood. She would later recall, "I came to Hollywood in borrowed clothes; refused to take cheesecake pictures so everyone thought I was crazy." While paying her seventy-five dollars a week, Paramount put her through an extensive six-month training course in deportment, drama, grooming and

In *The Preview Murder Mystery* (Par '36).

speech, especially, to eradicate the "Y'all" drawl in her diction. Happily, after the deep-south dialogue disappeared, Gail was still the possessor of a stimulating low-pitched contralto voice that added as much allure to her screen presence as her beauty. Cautious Gail would retain her return railroad ticket to Birmingham for twelve years before finally destroying it.

Paramount tried her out onscreen in the small role of a secretary in their episodic *If I Had a Million* (1932), a few featured parts in Westerns, and then as the zoo keeper's daughter in *Murder in the Zoo* (1933), a film that also featured the Panther Woman, Kathleen Burke. Gail's assignments continued to be small, but she was noticed as the lovely Maria Luccia in *Cradle Song* (1933) and as Rhoda in *Death Takes a Holiday* (1934).

Gail's career picked up in 1935. Along with Katherine De Mille, Gertrude Michael, Ann Sheridan, Grace Bradley, and Wendy Barrie, she was chosen as one of Paramount's Protegees of 1935, a gimmick designed to gain press coverage for their rising young starlets. She was assigned to Paramount's second remake of Booth Tarkington's play *Magnolia*, which was retitled *Mississippi* (1935). Lanny Ross, Evelyn Venable, and Grace Bradley and W. C. Fields were the original choices for the picture, but when it was made, it proved to be Bing Crosby, Joan Bennett, Gail, and Fields. The latter offered one of his fuller-bodied characterizations as Commodore Jackson, the prevaricating river boat captain. As Elvira, Gail was asked to use her once-southern drawl to portray the fiery, coquettish Elvira Rumford. Fox then borrowed Gail for their hilarious adaptation of George Kelly's *The Torchbearers*, retitled *Doubting Thomas* (1935), in which Will Rogers and veteran actresses Billie Burke and Alison Skipworth filled the screen with laughter. Gail was stylishly perfect as Therese in MGM's *No More Ladies* (1935), which starred Joan Crawford, but the acting kudos were stolen by Edna May Oliver as a cocktail-drinking grandmother. It was Miss Crawford who had requested Gail for the part of the husband-stealing, intellectual girl.

For someone seemingly disinterested in an acting career, Miss Patrick enhanced more than her share of movies of the Thirties with several smart performances. Since 1933 Gail had dated steadily Robert Howard Cobb, manager of the famed Brown Derby Restaurant. After returning from a personal appearance tour in the South and escorting her friends the Maharajah and Maharanee of Indore in New York City for Paramount's Silver Jubilee, the couple eloped and were married in Tijuana, Mexico, on December 16, 1936. Gail's secretary Jean Edwards and Cobb's close friend Charles Seymore were the witnesses at the ceremony.

Meanwhile Gail's screen roles varied from supporting parts to romantic leads in the studio's *Wanderer of the Wasteland* (1935), with Dean Jagger, and *Two Fisted* (1935), a revamping of *Is Zat So?* She appeared as Marcia Stuart, the woman in the case, in the first of the all-talking *Lone Wolf* series for Columbia, *The Lone Wolf Returns* (1936), in which Melvyn Douglas played the gentleman sleuth.

Gail's best film roles came from studio loan-outs. She was fortunately cast as the bitchy, bad-tempered, brattish Cornelia Bulloch in Universal's bright screwball comedy *My Man Godfrey* (1936). As the icy, ill-tempered Cornelia, Gail was beautifully cast and held her own against such scene-stealing pros as Carole Lombard, William Powell, Alice Brady, and Mischa Auer. Gail's marvelous performance was certainly worthy of Academy Award consideration, but she did not receive any nomination.

After her expert playing in *My Man Godfrey,* Gail was rewarded by Paramount with stock roles in *Murder with Pictures* (1936), *Artists and Models* (1937), and *John Meade's Woman* (1937). She did have a chance to perform "No More Tears" and "You Gambled with Love" as the nightclub singer in *Her Husband Lies* (1937), a remake of *Street of Chance* (1930) with William Powell and Kay Francis. Again on loan-out, Gail was a standout in a topnotch cast in RKO's *Stage Door* (1937). As producer Adolphe Menjou's ex-mistress she gives unsolicited advice and feline know-how to Menjou's current infatuation, Ginger Rogers. On August 16, 1937, Gail was heard as Celia on WABC's radio broadcast of *As You Like It* with Frank Morgan and Dennis King. Onscreen she brightened Universal's *Mad about Music* (1938) as Deanna Durbin's actress-mother, repeating the role on Cecil B. DeMille's "Lux Radio Theatre" in April of 1938.

Because Paramount had its array of top-string leading ladies (from Claudette Colbert to Carole Lombard and Dorothy Lamour), the studio continued to assign Gail to run-of-the-mill productions. In fact, she was usually cast in bottom-of-the-bill quickies, such as *Dangerous to Know* (1938). But even in these low-budget items, she managed to be striking and sometimes effective, as in *King of Alcatraz* (1938) in which she was a nurse who performs an operation at sea guided by morse code from a surgeon on another vessel. Much more frequently it was on radio that she received superior roles, as on Woodbury's Hollywood broadcast of *Algiers* in October, 1938, with Charles Boyer and Joseph Calleia.

In May, 1939, Helena Rubinstein selected the ten most glamorous women in Hollywood: Norma Shearer, Claudette Colbert, Loretta Young, Hedy Lamarr, Barbara Stanwyck, Carole Lombard, Dorothy Lamour, Irene Dunne, Joan Bennett, and Gail Patrick— "for her warmth, graciousness and sincerity."

In 1940, Garson Kanin directed Samuel and Bella Spewack's hilarious script *My Favorite Wife,* which was certainly among the best of the screwball comedies. The film, starring Irene Dunne and Cary Grant, cast Gail as Grant's second wife whose honeymoon is destroyed when Grant discovers his first wife (Dunne) did not die at sea. The

With Ricardo Cortez in *Her Husband Lies* (Par '37).

With Preston Foster and Otto Kruger in a pose for *Disbarred* **(Par '39).**

film was brisk and comic, definitely superior to Twentieth Century-Fox's 1963 remake with Doris Day, James Garner, and Polly Bergen, called *Move Over, Darling*. Strangely, Gail was badly miscast as baby-talking Marilyn Thomas in Columbia's breezy comedy *The Doctor Takes a Wife* (1940), starring Ray Milland and Loretta Young. Gail usually played the epitome of cold sophistication, but she was forced here to enact a simpering nincompoop. Gail's forte, as some casting directors forgot, was the dame of poise, sophistication, and feline bitchery, all enmeshed in an aura of dulcet-toned dialogue.

During the late Thirties Gail's marriage to Robert "Bob" Cobb disintegrated and she won a divorce from him on November 14, 1940, charging mental cruelty. In 1941 the gossip columns were linking her with Lieutenant Harold Hastings, but the actress remained single until July 11, 1944, when she wed Lieutenant Arnold Dean White in Jacksonville, Florida, at the All Saints Protestant Chapel at the naval air station. She must have thought her personal life was a rerun of *My Favorite Wife* when on July 13, her bridegroom was confined to his quarters in Miami for ten days, a sentence imposed for going to Jacksonville for his marriage without permission.

After 1939 Gail free-lanced. She was a home-wrecker in the Myrna Loy-William Powell comedy *Love Crazy* (1941), and was jilted by Herbert Marshall in Shirley Temple's *Kathleen* (1941). In the episodic *Tales of Manhattan* (1942) she woos Cesar Romero on the rebound when his love, Ginger Rogers, runs off with his best friend, Henry Fonda. At MGM, Gail was Melvyn Douglas' sexy old flame complicating Norma Shearer's life in the tepid *We Were Dancing* (1942). Her last radio appearance for "Lux" was on February 8, 1943, in *The Maltese Falcon* with Edward G. Robinson and Laird Cregar.

In 1945 Gail made a film for Metro, *Twice Blessed,* a story involving parents with twins; at the same time in her personal life she experienced a tragedy. While her husband, Navy Lieutenant Arnold D. White, was on flight duty in the Pacific, Gail gave birth to twins who, born prematurely, lived only a short time. In October, 1945, the grieving Gail and her friend Helen Moore opened their "Enchanted Cottage for Children," in Beverly Hills, featuring clothing, books, toys, and furniture for the younger citizens. Her husband joined in the project, building doll houses fully equipped with electric lighting, windows, flower boxes, and doorbells. Relating to "Enchanted Cottage," Gail said: "I had to do something like that. Otherwise, when you've lost children, you could become a complete neurotic if you allow yourself to. I started the shop for my own therapy. Losing your babies can ruin the rest of your life if you just keep thinking about it. Your first reaction is 'Why did it have to happen to me?' I had to feel there was a reason. My faith in God helped me tremendously. I couldn't live without it. I'm not sure I'd want to live without it, because it is such a strength for me." A year later Gail and Lieutenant Arnold Dean White were divorced.

Gail returned to the screen as one of the victims of artist Francis Lederer in *The Madonna's Secret* (1946). Then she supported Dorothy McGuire, Robert Young, and Mary Astor in *Claudia and David* (1946), and played a villainess who joins Joseph Schildkraut in stopping the 1859 Pony Express operation in *The Plainsman and the Lady* (1946).

On July 25, 1947, Gail married advertising man Cornwall Jackson. The wedding was performed by the Reverend Thatcher Jordan in Gail's home. "We'd known each other as friends for many years. But I wasn't eager for marriage after two failures and he'd been a bachelor for 45 years." But, after her marriage to Jackson the still very attractive Gail virtually retired from the screen. Her last theatrical feature was Republic's *The Inside Story* (1948), a small town saga.

Shortly after her marriage to Cornwall Jackson, Gail discovered she was a diabetic. "I learned to pace myself. I also learned to give myself injections. You have to learn; without them you're dead in 36 hours, so you learn very fast and very happily." Gail and Jackson also adopted two children, Jennifer and Thomas. Gail admits adopting the two children brought great joy to their lives. "I loved being a mother while the children were growing up. I love the sounds of children."

In September, 1957, the first telecast of a highly successful series, "Perry Mason," had Gail Patrick Jackson as executive producer. (Her husband was Erle Stanley Gardner's literary agent.) The series, which won many Emmys for Raymond Burr and his co-worker Barbara Hale, ran for 271 episodes and is still being shown in syndication. In 1973, "The New Perry Mason Show" debuted with Monte Markham in the lead, but it did not have the crisp, tight story lines of the original. In discussing the "New" Perry Mason show, Gail said: "I negotiated the deal for the series but decided this time I would just be a consultant on it. I enjoyed the last series but worked very hard; this time I wanted to be on the sidelines. Now, Mr. Jackson will be the executive producer." This new position would also give Gail time for her duties as chairman of the board of the American Diabetes Association and the advisory council for the National Institute of Health.

After twenty-two years of marriage Gail received another divorce. In 1969 she explained: "The children didn't want the divorce; I didn't want it and Mr. Jackson didn't want it, but sometimes things are unavoidable. There has to be a reason for everything. Sometimes it's hard to see at the time, but later, looking back, you can usually understand it. Of course I was devastated and baffled when I lost my twin babies, but even then I felt there had to be a reason. Now I realize that if it hadn't been for that, it's most unlikely I would have adopted Thomas and Jennifer, who are wonderful."

Thomas majored in music at Pepperdine College and Jennifer is a successful artist. Neither of her children have displayed any interest in show business because, says Gail: "I myself have no great interest in pictures. I enjoyed working in pictures, but had no great ambition. It was just a means to an end. I never felt that I was a good actress. You really had to be more emotionally involved than I could be. Fortunately, the main thing for movies at that time was personality. I just hit the time right. I had Gail Patrick parts. I guess that was a part of my Irish luck."

Marriage again? "Who knows? I am a fatalist. I've told the children I hope they get married and have children—and hope that they do it in that order!" Recent news items teamed Gail Patrick Jackson with Dr. George Mueller, but on September 28, 1974, she married Illinois business executive John E. Welde, Jr. in Neuilly, France. In late 1975 she appeared on TV in one of "those" Bicentennial Minute programs.

Recently, Gail, who claims to have never bothered watching herself on the big screen, saw a print of one of her Thirties' movies. "I always felt self-conscious as an actress because I'm tall. I see that it came over as haughtiness. I just don't have an actress' soul. I think mine has a dollar sign on it."

GAIL PATRICK

If I Had a Million *(Par 1932)*
The Mysterious Rider *(Par 1933)*
Mama Loves Papa *(Par 1933)*
Pick-Up *(Par 1933)*
The Phantom Broadcast *(Mon 1933)*
Murder in the Zoo *(Par 1933)*
To the Last Man *(Par 1933)*
Cradle Song *(Par 1933)*
Death Takes a Holiday *(Par 1934)*
Murder at the Vanities *(Par 1934)*
Wagon Wheels *(Par 1934)*
The Crime of Helen Stanley *(Col 1934)*
Take the Stand *(Liberty 1934)*
One Hour Late *(Par 1934)*
Rumba *(Par 1935)*
Mississippi *(Par 1935)*
Doubting Thomas *(Fox 1935)*
No More Ladies *(MGM 1935)*
Smart Girl *(Par 1935)*
The Big Broadcast of 1936 *(Par 1935)*
Wanderer of the Wasteland *(Par 1935)*
Two Fisted *(Par 1935)*
Two in the Dark *(RKO 1936)*
The Lone Wolf Returns *(Col 1936)*
The Preview Murder Mystery *(Par 1936)*
Early to Bed *(Par 1936)*
My Man Godfrey *(Univ 1936)*
White Hunter *(20th 1936)*
Murder with Pictures *(Par 1936)*
Her Husband Lies *(Par 1937)*
Artists and Models *(Par 1937)*

John Meade's Woman *(Par 1937)*
Stage Door *(RKO 1937)*
Mad about Music *(Univ 1938)*
Dangerous to Know *(Par 1938)*
Wives under Suspicion *(Univ 1938)*
King of Alcatraz *(Par 1938)*
Disbarred *(Par 1939)*
Man of Conquest *(Rep 1939)*
Grand Jury Secrets *(Par 1939)*
Reno *(RKO 1939)*
My Favorite Wife *(RKO 1940)*
The Doctor Takes a Wife *(Col 1940)*
Gallant Sons *(MGM 1940)*
Love Crazy *(MGM 1941)*
Kathleen *(MGM 1941)*
Tales of Manhattan *(20th 1942)*
Quiet Please Murder *(20th 1942)*
We Were Dancing *(MGM 1942)*
The Hit Parade of 1943 *(Rep 1943)*
Women in Bondage *(Mon 1943)*
Up in Mabel's Room *(UA 1944)*
Brewster's Millions *(UA 1945)*
Twice Blessed *(MGM 1945)*
The Madonna's Secret *(Rep 1946)*
Rendezvous with Annie *(Rep 1946)*
Claudia and David *(20th 1946)*
The Plainsman and the Lady *(Rep 1946)*
Calendar Girl *(Rep 1947)*
King of the Wild Horses *(Col 1947)*
The Inside Story *(Rep 1948)*

57

Roger Pryor

The multi-talented Roger Pryor was a good actor, musician, and singer who was successful in these various entertainment formats. In the pursuit of these varied interests and fulfillment of his abilities he lost the chance of standing out in any one endeavor. He was an earnest screen worker in the Thirties, but never gained that certain image that might have insured real stardom.

Roger was born on Tuesday, August 27, 1901, to Maud Russell and Arthur Pryor in New York City. Mr. Pryor was a bandleader, trombonist, and composer who became a soloist with John Philip Sousa's great band at Chicago's 1893 Fair. He then organized his own band in 1903, and played twenty-five summer seasons at Asbury Park, New Jersey, eleven winter seasons in Miami, Florida, and, in 1905, composed the delightful "The Whistler and His Dog." Roger and his older brother, Arthur Jr., grew up meeting many great personages in music, vaudeville, and the theatre. Following his education, he felt it was natural that he should seek success in a profession he knew and loved, although his father was opposed to his entering show business.

At twenty-three, Roger made his Broadway stage debut on April 11, 1925, as Douglas Lane in *The Backslapper.* He spent the rest of 1925 playing with Blanche Yurka and Paul Kelly in *The Sea Woman* and opened and closed quickly in *The Winner Loses* and *Paid.* His first personal success arrived in Maxwell Anderson's *Saturday's Children* (1927), in which Ruth Gordon was his co-player. He played the part for 150 performances before being replaced by Humphrey Bogart. Pryor had been tempted by the musical stage and the prospect of appearing in a new Gershwin show with an innovative book by George S. Kaufman. The show was *Strike Up the Band* and the cast included Blanche Ring, Morton Downey, Jimmy Savo, Vivian Hart, and Roger. It tried out in Long Branch, New Jersey, in August, 1927, and a month later opened in Philadelphia to devastating notices. The book was before its time and the show just did not work. It closed in that city, only to be revised, rewritten, and recast (without Roger) for a successful January, 1930, bow on Broadway.

After the fiasco of *Strike Up the Band,* Roger went on to a solid part in *The Royal Family* (1927) and then succeeded Lee Tracy, who left for Hollywood, as brash newspaper reporter Hildy Johnson in *The Front Page.*

Pryor was becoming one of Broadway's most personable and talented leading men, proving himself in *See Naples and Die* (1929), with Claudette Colbert, and in *Up Pops the Devil* (1930), with Brian Donlevy. After a brief fling with Margaret Sullavan in *A*

With Mae West in *Belle of the Nineties* (Par '34).

Modern Virgin, he hit stardom as the high-powered, Walter Winchell-like character in *Blessed Event* (1932). Later in that year Warner Bros. would make a screen version of the play, but Pryor was not asked to repeat his brittle Broadway performance. Instead, the part went to Lee Tracy.

Next Roger replaced Herbert Marshall in John Van Druten's *There's Always Juliet* and toured with the show with Violet Heming until the spring of 1933 when he signed with the Shuberts for a role in *A Trip to Pressburg,* a resounding flop that Lee Shubert closed in Philadelphia. (It was later resurrected without Roger.) While playing in the Chicago touring company of *Riddle Me This,* he signed with Universal Pictures. It was at this point he dissolved his first marriage, to Priscilla Mitchell, and headed westward.

While never known for producing top-grade musicals, Universal cast Pryor in an unexpectedly entertaining diversion with an unlikely title, *Moonlight and Pretzels* (1933). His resourceful talent was apparent in *I Like It that Way* (1934), with Gloria Stuart, and in the often hilarious *Romance in the Rain* (1934), which cast him as a true-confession writer beset with addled Victor Moore. Universal's diverting *Wake Up and Dream* (1934) paired Roger with vaudeville pal June Knight, and was sparked by Russ Columbo's singing.

Roger's best opportunity on the screen came on a loan-out to another studio. Mae West was preparing her third major film which was to feature George Raft as the Midwest boxing champ, The Tiger Kid. But when the film censorship office pared down Raft's part before production began, he bowed out of the proceedings. At that point Mae, who dominated the selection of her casts, chose Roger Pryor. She later explained her decision, stating he was "the son of the well-known military bandleader, Arthur Pryor. He was a new face, with very curly hair; he'd had Broadway training and possessed an acting talent that made him believable." She made an excellent choice.

With Carole Lombard in *Lady by Choice* (Col '34).

Although the Hays Office had an official censor on Miss West's set every day, some scenes were filmed which were later deemed objectionable. The studio was forced to pare down the feature, ruining much of the continuity and almost ruining the film. Although final shooting on *Belle of the Nineties* (1934) was completed in June, 1934, Mae and Roger were recalled by Paramount to placate the censors by reshooting the final scene to include a moralistic wedding ceremony. (By this point in the plot, villain John Miljan had been shoved out of the storyline.) Despite all the censorship restrictions, the $800,000-lush, lively *Belle of the Nineties* burst with life. Mae's shrewd insistence on having Duke Ellington and his band backing her oncamera singing added immeasurably to the production. The picture opened at the Paramount Theatre in New York on September 21, 1934. It played there for four weeks and racked up close to a quarter of a million dollars in box-office receipts. Although the film dealt mostly with Miss West, Roger received his share of credit in this commercial success.

During 1934 Roger varied his activities between screen and stage. He was in the West Coast productions of *Men in White, The Petrified Forest,* and *Her Master's Voice.* Universal loaned him to Columbia to play opposite Carole Lombard in *Lady by Choice* (1934), but it was bustling May Robson, as a reformed actress and alcoholic who stole the picture.

Roger made eight films in 1935. He received plaudits for his performance with Jackie Cooper and Mary Astor in *Dinky.* He made Columbia's *The Girl Friend* seem a lot better than it was, most likely because he had fallen in love with his co-star, Ann Sothern. Although the following year was not a good one for Roger on the screen, it was important in other ways. On September 26, 1936, he and Ann Sothern were guests on

With Jackie Cooper and Mary Astor in *Dinky* (WB '35).

449

the Olsen and Johnson radio show, and at 12:01 Sunday morning, he and Ann were married at Hollywood's Congregational Church. Arthur Pryor was on hand to congratulate the couple. The newlywed Pryors honeymooned in Chicago where Roger and his previously formed orchestra were booked.

While Ann made several second-string musicals with Gene Raymond, liking neither the films nor Jeanette MacDonald's husband, Roger was playing supporting roles with occasional leads in a series of B and filler pictures. Roger and Ann had adopted a son, David, to repair the potentially nasty inroads in the marriage due to the distances constantly separating them. (Roger and his orchestra had made extensive tours in 1937 and 1938.)

In 1940 Roger more or less settled in Hollywood and he became master of ceremonies for radio's "Screen Guild Players," which dramatized well-known plays and movies. Roger also directed the shows and frequently took a role in the productions. In January, 1940, Roger and Ann lost their son David, who was reclaimed by his large family. The marriage could not withstand the many separations and despair of losing their adopted child. In 1942, the same year that Arthur Pryor died, Ann and Roger were divorced.

Roger's film career teetered between leads in minor features to supporting roles in a few above-average entries, such as Warner Bros.' *Gambling on the High Seas* (1940) and the same studio's *She Couldn't Say No* (1941) which featured the acerbic comedy of Eve Arden. He continued playing roles in a long string of double feature fodder while serving twenty-seven months as a civilian flight instructor for the Army Air Force at Blythe, California.

Then, Roger returned to the stage with another Hollywood compatriot, Kay Francis. The year was 1945. *Windy Hill* was a strange concoction written by former silent screen actress Patsy Ruth Miller, the ex-wife of director Tay Garnett. The play was produced and directed by actress Ruth Chatterton and opened in Montclair, New Jersey, in August. Roger appeared as a war correspondent, and the cast included Judy Holliday. *Windy Hill* underwent a long road tour both in summer theatres and in larger cities, with Eileen Heckart eventually joining the cast. But the poorly conceived play closed in Chicago in May, 1946.

Having lost a good deal of his own money backing his orchestra/band tours, Roger returned to Hollywood. He directed three features, all so poorly mounted that he refused to allow his name to appear on the credits. At the same time, his radio activities continued. He produced radio's "Cavalcade of America" broadcasts, narrated the NBC Symphony programs, and was narrator-master of ceremonies for "Theatre Guild of the Air" for five years, frequently playing a role in their broadcasts. He took the role of Justice Oliver Wendell Holmes in *Yankee from Olympus* for the "Theatre Guild" broadcast the night before he opened at the Plymouth Theatre in New York on April 16, 1947. It was a new play by James Parish [no relation to this book's co-author] entitled *Message for Margaret*. It starred Mady Christians and Miriam Hopkins, with Roger featured. It proved to be a dull and driveling piece of nonsense, and was Roger's last Broadway appearance.

From 1947 until 1962 Roger was affiliated with a large New York advertising firm and was in charge of their broadcasting activities. (Pryor's late brother held a similar post with another large Manhattan advertising firm.) In the early 1960s Roger retired completely from business and later moved with his third wife and daughter to Pompano Beach, Florida. He was once asked if he missed his former show business days. He replied, "No . . . and especially not acting. I never felt I was very good and in seventy-two [sic] features I don't think I improved very much."

450

En route to Puerto Vallarta, Mexico, for a vacation, Roger suffered a heart attack and died on January 31, 1974, at the age of seventy-two. With his death, a brand of multi-talented performer passed forever from the scene.

ROGER PRYOR

Moonlight and Pretzels (Univ 1933)
I Like It That Way (Univ 1934)
Romance in the Rain (Univ 1934)
I'll Tell the World (Univ 1934)
Wake Up and Dream (Univ 1934)
Gift of Gab (Univ 1934)
Belle of the Nineties (Par 1934)
Lady by Choice (Col 1934)
Strange Wives (Univ 1935)
Straight from the Heart (Univ 1935)
Headline Woman (Mascot 1935)
Dinky (WB 1935)
To Beat the Band (RKO 1935)
A $1,000 a Minute (Rep 1935)
The Girl Friend (Col 1935)
The Case of the Missing Man (Col 1935)
The Return of Jimmy Valentine (Rep 1936)
Sitting on the Moon (Rep 1936)
Ticket to Paradise (Rep 1936)
Missing Girls (Chesterfield 1936)
The Man They Could Not Hang (Col 1939)
Sued for Libel (RKO 1940)
The Man with Nine Lives (Col 1940)
The Lone Wolf Meets a Lady (Col 1940)
Money and the Woman (WB 1940)

Gambling on the High Seas (WB 1940)
Glamour for Sale (Col 1940)
She Couldn't Say No (WB 1941)
Bowery Boy (Rep 1940)
South of Panama (PRC 1941)
Power Dive (Par 1941)
Bullets for O'Hara (WB 1941)
Richest Man in Town (Col 1941)
Flying Blind (Par 1941)
Gambling Daughters (PRC 1941)
The Officer and the Lady (Col 1941)
I Live on Danger (Par 1942)
Smart Alecks (Mon 1942)
So's Your Aunt Emma [Meet the Mob] (Mon 1942)
Submarine Alert (Par 1943)
Lady Bodyguard (Par 1943)
Thoroughbreds (Rep 1944)
Scared Stiff (Par 1945)
The Kid Sister (PRC 1945)
High Powered (Par 1945)
Identity Unknown (Rep 1945)
The Cisco Kid Returns (Mon 1945)
The Man from Oklahoma (Rep 1945)

Gene Raymond

America became ultra-conscious of platinum blonde hair after Jean Harlow's emergence in Howard Hughes' *Hell's Angel* (1930). By 1931 when she made a movie called *Platinum Blonde,* almost everyone knew it referred to Miss Harlow. Nationwide there was a sudden transformation in hair coloring, but even Hollywood was unprepared for a male counterpart when Paramount signed a young, handsome actor named Raymond Guion. They made his first name his last and added Gene from the name of a character (Gene Gibson) he had successfully played on Broadway in *Young Sinners.*

Gene was born to LeRoy and Mary Smith Guion in Brooklyn, New York, on Thursday, August 13, 1908. Almost from the start, Mrs. Guion was convinced her son was destined for a stage career. He made his first stage appearance at age five. In summer stock he appeared in children's roles in such plays as *Mrs. Wiggs of the Cabbage Patch, Mother Carey's Chickens,* and *The Crowded Hour.* He also participated with the Bramhall Players in repertory.

His parents enrolled him in New York's Professional Children's School where he was among the first pupils of that establishment on West 48th Street. Among the first students at the school were Mary Miles Minter, Lila Lee, and Georgie Price. While attending the school Raymond made his Broadway debut at the Fulton Theatre on March 19, 1920, in *The Piper.* Other classmates (Helen Chandler, Lillian Roth, and Raymond Hackett) were then also on Broadway.

From *The Piper,* young Guion played a shepherd boy in *Eyvind of the Hills* and then Billy Thompson in *Why Not.* When *The Potters* (1923) arrived for 208 performances, his name was well known on Broadway. Two years later he was at the Music Box Theatre in *Cradle Snatchers* as one of three college boys (Gene, Raymond Hackett and Humphrey Bogart) pursued by Mary Boland, Edna May Oliver, and Margaret Dale. The comedy remained on Broadway for 332 performances and then toured the States for another year. When he returned to New York he appeared in *Take My Advice,* had a brief stand with Sylvia Sidney in *Mirror,* and, later in 1928, played with Robert Warwick and Frank Keenan in a revival of *Sherlock Holmes.* In the fall of 1928 he joined the company of *The War Song,* which starred George Jessel, as well as Lola Lane, Shirley Booth, and William Gargan. Raymond played another Swede.

Before his twenty-first birthday he was receiving excellent notices for his portrayal in *Jonesy.* However, it was *Young Sinners* that offered him his most challenging stage role

Double O camera study at Paramount in '32.

to that time. As a result of this show, he was known as "the nearly perfect juvenile" on Broadway, and Hollywood was offering picture contracts.

He signed with Paramount through the persistence of Jesse L. Lasky. Of his new screen name, he admitted: "Changing an established name is looked upon with horror by professional people. But after having suffered with a difficult handle for so long, I appreciated the chance of getting rid of it. I've spent hours trying to have people understand it over the telephone. I once worked for a producer for two years—and at the end of that time he called me 'Ginion.' "

Paramount cast him as a wealthy, staid fellow in *Personal Maid* (1931), in which his "father," Donald Meek, from *The Potters* and *Jonesy* became his first screen father. His movie mother was Mary Boland, one of the *Cradle Snatchers*. The Nancy Carroll *Personal Maid* made no huge waves at the box-office and Gene's screen debut was not heralded as the coming of a second Barrymore. In Sylvia Sidney's *Ladies of the Big House* (1931), Gene had a subordinate role as a man condemned to hang for the killing of a policeman. Then he was another killer, this time one who, while awaiting execution, becomes the recipient of a million-dollar check in *If I Had a Million* (1932).

For *Forgotten Commandments* (1932), Paramount imported Sari Maritza and used spectacular footage from Cecil B. DeMille's silent *The Ten Commandments*. Their efforts helped to spice the tale of communal living in modern Russia. Over at MGM, Gene, who was being promoted as the platinum blond leading man, was pitted against Clark Gable in *Red Dust* (1932), which boasted a torrid performance by sassy Jean Harlow.

Gene's acceptance as a new leading man was reflected in his assignments. He appeared to advantage in *Ex-Lady* (1933) at Warner Bros., convinced by Bette Davis that love is better than marriage. It was a glossy potboiler, but his next assignment remains one of his favorite films. It was Jesse L. Lasky's first independent production for Fox release, *Zoo in Budapest* (1933). It was a beautiful, atmospheric film directed by Rowland V. Lee, with Gene as animal lover Zani and Loretta Young as his human devotion. He then did two conventional roles for Columbia, including playing a wealthy playboy opposite Carole Lombard's torch singer in a less than satisfactory screen adaptation of S. N. Behrman's stage hit *Brief Moment* (1933).

RKO's "musical extravaganza staged in the clouds," *Flying Down to Rio* (1933) is remembered today for the first screen pairing of Fred Astaire and Ginger Rogers, the hit song "The Carioca," and the highly imaginative choreography by David Gould and Hermes Pan. In this film Gene replaced the originally announced Joel McCrea in the male lead opposite Dolores Del Rio. He had the pivotal role in a triangular romance that got lost in the music and sensational dancing of Astaire and Rogers. Then for Lasky at Fox, Gene had an excellent role as a puppeteer in a gentle, poignant story of a crippled acrobat (Lilian Harvey) in *I am Suzanne!* (1934).

Although Gene was never known as a singer, he suddenly became a creditable crooner introducing "All I Do Is Dream of You" in his role of Tommy in MGM's *Sadie McKee* (1934), which starred Joan Crawford. A few years later Gene would do a series of personal appearances to promote RKO's *Love on a Bet* (1936). The act was originally an eight-minute spot, but grew to over twenty minutes as Gene sang "Nearer and Nearer," "All I Do Is Dream of You," "I Couldn't Do It without You," and "Will You." The latter was a song Gene wrote and sang in RKO's *The Smartest Girl in Town* (1936), one of several mildly entertaining minor musicals he made with Ann Sothern.

The first musical Gene made with Ann Sothern was *Hooray for Love* (1935) for his new contract employer, RKO. The studio felt the combination of Raymond and Sothern was a good match for their B musicals and reteamed them in *Walking on Air* (1936), *The*

With Lilian Harvey in *I Am Suzanne!* (Fox '34).

With Margaret Callahan in *Seven Keys to Baldpate* (RKO '35).

Smartest Girl in Town (1936), *There Goes My Girl* (1937), and *She's Got Everything* (1938). RKO's enthusiasm for their second-string musicals was not shared by the talented Miss Sothern who liked neither her roles in them nor working in harness with Raymond. During these forgotten reels of musical RKO comedy, Gene was busily courting the prima donna of Culver City, Jeanette MacDonald. In November, 1936, he recorded his song "Will You" for Brunswick Records, and returned to the soundstages to play a jazz band leader who wins prima donna Lily Pons in *That Girl from Paris* (1936).

Hollywood had witnessed many weddings, but for sheer opulence and magnitude nothing had equalled the Vilma Banky-Rod La Rocque nuptials in 1927; that is, until ten years later when Miss MacDonald became Mrs. Gene Raymond. Their plans for a "quiet" wedding became a major event when approximately 15,000 fans assembled near the church, creating problems for a 150-man police riot squad who had to rope off three city blocks. The 1,000 invitations that were sent out brought most of Hollywood's famous personalities to the Wilshire Methodist-Episcopal Church. Jeanette's screen co-star Nelson Eddy sang "I Love You Truly" and "Perfect Love," and then Jeanette, preceded by her bridesmaids (Ginger Rogers, Fay Wray, Helen Ferguson, Mrs. John Mack Brown, and matron of honor Marie MacDonald Blake), walked down the aisle. The Reverend Willsie Martin read the service on that 16th day of June, 1937.

Following the reception Gene took his bride to their new home on the Claudell Estate in Bel Air, and the next day Jeannette returned to Metro to complete *The Firefly* (1937). It was not until June 26 that the newlyweds sailed to Honolulu for their delayed honeymoon. After they returned, Jeanette was back with Nelson Eddy in *The Girl of the Golden West* (1938) and Gene reported to Paramount for *Stolen Heaven* (1938). He was miscast as a crook, giving an uneasy, stiff performance, almost as if he had studied acting from George Raft. In 1939 Jeanette made an extensive concert tour using a song "Let Me Always Sing" that Gene had written for her. She would later record it for Victor Records in September, 1939, and then re-record the song accompanied by Gene at the piano on October 5, 1939.

In 1940, RKO picked up Gene's option and he made a screwball comedy, *Cross-Country Romance,* his first film after a year's absence from the screen. Gene's once overly publicized platinum blond hair was noticeably darker. As long-suffering Jeff Custer in RKO's *Mr. and Mrs. Smith* (1941), Gene struggled and failed to get laughs out of the role of Robert Montgomery's boorish law partner in Alfred Hitchcock's one and only attempt at broad-screen comedy. That the film appeared at all amusing can be credited to Norman Krasna's smiling script and to the deft comedic talents of Carole Lombard and Montgomery. Well aware of the box-office potential of casting Jeannette with her husband in a film, Metro added Gene to the cast of *Smilin' Through* (1941), and both man and wife contributed decent performances in the bitter-sweet, archaic play. (They would repeat their roles on Cecil B. DeMille's "Lux Radio Theatre" in January, 1942.)

In 1941, Gene enlisted in the U.S. Air Force Intelligence Service. He trained at Randolph and Kelly Fields in the States and later served as Captain Gene Raymond with the 97th Heavy Bombardment Group as a B-17 pilot in England. While Gene was in uniform, Jeannette joined the American Women's Voluntary Service, entertained frequently for the U.S.O., made her operatic debut with Armand Tokatyan in *Romeo and Juliet* in Montreal, and completed her Metro contract with two forgettable features, *I Married an Angel* (1942) and the lower-budgeted, but more enjoyable, *Cairo* (1942).

Gene returned to America and to RKO for *The Locket* (1946), and then switched to tough guy parts in *Assigned to Danger* (1948) and *Sofia* (1948). He directed (and appeared in) Eagle-Lion's *Million Dollar Weekend* (1948), with Francis Lederer and Stephanie Paull (formerly Osa Massen). None of these films, however, were notable successes.

Raymond had returned to the stage in August, 1946, at the Cape Playhouse at Dennis, Massachusetts, in *The Man in Possession.* By early 1949, with the release of *The Sun Comes Up* which Jeannette made at Metro with Lassie co-starred, it seemed that the Raymonds were retired. But later in the year they flew to West Germany to entertain American troops, with Jeannette singing and Gene acting as master of ceremonies. He then tried television in 1950 with an appearance on the "Pulitzer Prize Playhouse." A year later he and Jeannette toured for six months in *The Guardsman* and made a brief appearance that August on Ed Sullivan's "Toast of the Town" TV show. As an encore to their stage work in *The Guardsman* Jeannette would always sing a few of her identifiable songs at the end of the comedy.

During 1952 Gene appeared regularly on television. When the "I Like Ike" movement swelled throughout America, Gene and Jeannette, both of whom were staunch Republicans, joined a large group of Hollywood stars to beat the drum for General Eisenhower. Gene spent the summer of 1952 on the straw-hat circuit in *The Voice of the Turtle,* with Audrey Christie and Geraldine Brooks, and played the Boston Summer Theatre in *The Petrified Forest,* again with Miss Brooks. That fall Gene and Jeannette joined George Murphy, John Wayne, Irene Dunne, and Ward Bond for three days in Dallas, Austin, and Fort Worth, Texas, campaigning for the election of Eisenhower and Nixon. The Raymonds were guests of President and Mrs. Eisenhower at the Inaugural Ball.

In 1953, Gene returned to Dallas to perform in the stage production of *Call Me Madam.* That summer he co-starred with Peggy Ann Garner in a summer stock version of *The Moon Is Blue,* as well as trying out a new play, *Be Quiet, My Love,* with Vicki Cummings. The fall of 1954 found Gene becoming the host of the TV "Fireside Theatre" series, and the next year he returned to Metro for their remake of *Hit the Deck.* He continued to host "Fireside Theatre" (and later "Reader's Digest TV Theatre") and in the spring of 1957 won critical acclaim for his playing of Mercutio in Albert McCleery's production of *Romeo and Juliet,* with Margaret O'Brien and John Drew Barrymore. He was briefly on Broadway that December with Ed Begley in *A Shadow of My Enemy,* giving an illuminating characterization of an icy, inscrutable man who leans toward Communism.

His television work decreased after he signed for the part of Joseph Cantwell in the national touring company of Gore Vidal's biting comedy *The Best Man,* in which he co-starred with Leon Ames and William Gargan. When United Artists filmed the play in 1964, Cliff Robertson played Gene's stage role, with Gene playing the character's brother, Don Cantwell. Gene's last onscreen appearance to date in Hollywood was in that colossal bomb of a film from Ross Hunter, *I'd Rather Be Rich* (1964).

Ever since Jeanette's health worsened in mid-1963, Gene had tried to remain close to home and near his beloved wife. After her two-and-one-half-month hospital confinement in 1963 for open heart surgery, she returned to a newly acquired apartment near Hollywood in mid-January, 1964. Just before Christmas of that year, she was admitted to the UCLA Medical Center in Los Angeles for abdominal surgery for adhesions. On January 12, 1965, she and Gene flew back to Houston, Texas (where she had been operated on in November, 1963), and she was again a patient of Dr. Michael DeBakey. On Thursday, January 14, 1965, Jeanette looked at her husband of nearly twenty-eight years and said, "I love you." Gene smiled and answered, "I love you, too." There were no other words. She died at 4:32 P.M.

Final rites were performed at the Church of the Recessional in Forest Lawn Memorial Park on January 18. A recording of Jeanette singing "Ah, Sweet Mystery of Life" was played. Lloyd Nolan, her co-star in *The Sun Comes Up,* delivered the eulogy. To Gene and to The Jeanette MacDonald International Fan Club, thousands of letters of sympathy poured in from all parts of the world. From New York, her former co-star Maurice Chevalier wrote, "I worked with Gene Raymond in *I'd Rather Be Rich* and found him the picture of a fine artist and also a fine man. After so many years it is always wonderful to see somebody you admire growing older so well." The beloved Frenchman continued to recall Jeanette and their artistic association which he so deeply treasured.

To occupy himself in the summer of 1965, Gene, with Anne Baxter, tried out a new play at Ogunquit, Maine. It was entitled *Diplomatic Relations.* Also in the Sixties he chose several challenging roles on some of television's top-rated dramatic shows. In 1970 he narrated *Five Bloody Graves,* a low-budget Western written by Richard Dix's son, Robert. On March 24, 1974, Gene, who later that year (September 8th) would wed Mrs. Bentley Hees of Pacific Palisades gave a striking, well-shaded character study of an easy-going aging coach on the teleseries "Apple's Way." It was one of Raymond's richest performances.

Clearly here is an actor who has improved with time, now eschewing those bland characterizations which were so typical of his leading man period.

GENE RAYMOND

Personal Maid *(Par 1931)*
Ladies of the Big House *(Par 1931)*
If I Had a Million *(Par 1932)*
The Night of June 13th *(Par 1932)*
Forgotten Commandments *(Par 1932)*
Red Dust *(MGM 1932)*
Ex-Lady *(WB 1933)*
Zoo in Budapest *(Fox 1933)*
Ann Carver's Profession *(Col 1933)*
Brief Moment *(Col 1933)*
Flying Down to Rio *(RKO 1933)*
The House on 56th Street *(WB 1933)*
Coming Out Party *(Fox 1934)*
I Am Suzanne! *(Fox 1934)*
Transatlantic Merry-Go-Round *(UA 1934)*
Sadie McKee *(MGM 1934)*
Behold My Wife *(Par 1934)*
The Woman in Red *(FN 1935)*
Hooray for Love *(RKO 1935)*
Transient Lady *(Univ 1935)*
Seven Keys to Baldpate *(RKO 1935)*
Love on a Bet *(RKO 1936)*

The Bride Walks Out *(RKO 1936)*
Walking on Air *(RKO 1936)*
The Smartest Girl in Town *(RKO 1936)*
That Girl from Paris *(RKO 1936)*
There Goes My Girl *(RKO 1937)*
The Life of the Party *(RKO 1937)*
She's Got Everything *(RKO 1938)*
Stolen Heaven *(Par 1938)*
Cross-Country Romance *(RKO 1940)*
Mrs. and Mrs. Smith *(RKO 1941)*
Smilin' Through *(MGM 1941)*
The Locket *(RKO 1946)*
Assigned to Danger *(EL 1948)*
Sofia *(Film Classics 1948)*
Million Dollar Weekend *(EL 1948)*
Hit the Deck *(MGM 1955)*
Plunder Road *(20th 1957)*
The Best Man *(UA 1964)*
I'd Rather Be Rich *(Univ 1964)*
Five Bloody Graves *(Independent International 1970)* [narrator]

Gilbert Roland

Some years ago there appeared a quasi-confessional blatantly called *Latins Are Lousy Lovers.* By 1968 the authoress, Helen Lawrenson, felt compelled to publish a sequel, *Latins Are Still Lousy Lovers.* Obviously she had never met handsome, six-foot, green-eyed, black-haired Gilbert Roland. For over fifty years he has aroused and stimulated most of the world's female film audience. Even today, now in his seventies, he commands attention from impassioned members of the supposedly weaker sex. He has been called "the most virile actor in movies." That testimonial has remained unchallenged for fifty years onscreen and off.

Luis Antonio Damaso Alonso was born on Monday, December 11, 1905, in Chihuahua, Mexico, the third of six sons born to Consuelo and her husband, Francisco, who had migrated from Spain to Mexico. Young Luis was raised in Juarez, Mexico, where his father owned a bull ring (he had been a matador in Spain), and the youth became familiar with the corridas de toros. The boy became an aficionado of bullfighting, learning the intricate art. He worked at the bullring distributing programs, selling cushions, and watching and assisting the matadors. When Pancho Villa's rampages throughout Mexico became a menace, the Alonso family crossed the border and settled in El Paso, Texas, where Luis continued his education. When his father returned to Spain for a tour of corridas, young Luis found his fascination with bullfighting dimmed by the allure of motion pictures. At the age of fourteen and with less than three dollars in his pocket, he caught a freight train going west in order to become an actor.

Disillusion with Hollywood and acting set in early and he found various menial jobs. He eventually worked as a stevedore unloading boats on Catalina Island and later worked in a battery plant, and then for a lithographer. His dark, sensuous good looks were noticed in Hollywood where a predominance of Latin types had migrated hoping to become second Rudolph Valentinos. Natacha Rambova, Valentino's egocentric wife, selected Luis for the part of Valentino's valet in her projected superproduction of *The Hooded Falcon,* but the film was never made. He finally landed a small part in First National's *The Lady Who Lied* (1925). Producer B. P. Schulberg liked the eager, intense young Luis and offered him a small role amounting to four days' work in Clara Bow's *The Plastic Age* (1925) along with fellow extra Clark Gable.

Years later, Gilbert said, "Ah, we were really eager in those days. The assistant directors used to call us 'the iron circle.' Everytime there would be a close-up of the star

With Robert Elliott, Margaret Mann, and Barbara Leonard in *Men of the North* **(MGM '30).**

we would cluster around him—to get our faces in the camera range. It's too bad the extras of today do not have that ambition. They sit around playing cards or else hide from the assistant director, but I guess they realize that extras don't get to be stars any more. I was an extra with Gable, Janet Gaynor, Charles Farrell and Richard Arlen." For the role of Carl Peters in *The Plastic Age*, Schulberg wanted to change Luis' name to John Adams, but he declined, settling instead for a combination of his two favorite performers, John Gilbert and Ruth Roland. Hence, Gilbert Roland.

Brooklyn-born Clara Bow, whom Schulberg was promoting as "the hottest jazz baby in films," was noted for her romances, and in short order she was having a well-publicized affair with Roland. Gilbert received fifty dollars a week as a stand-in for Ramon Novarro in Metro's *The Midshipman* (1925), filmed at Annapolis, then played in Bebe Daniel's *The Campus Flirt* (1926), and later had the part of Annibale in First National's *The Blonde Saint* (1926). His torrid romance with the alluring Miss Bow ended by the time the actress was dubbed the It Girl, and he met Norma Talmadge.

Miss Talmadge was touted as the screen's first lady, and offcamera she was Mrs. Joseph Schenck. Producer Schenck had guided her career and he had accepted their marriage as a matter of convenience. His tolerance of Norma's love affairs was remarkable, especially her falling in love with Gilbert and having him cast in the important role of Armand opposite her Lady of the Camellias in *Camille* (1927). Roland's roles noticeably improved on the screen and he was seen opposite Mary Astor in *Rose of the Golden West* (1927) and with Billie Dove in *The Love Mart* (1927). When Norma Talmadge joined United Artists, Gilbert went along as her leading man in *The Dove* (1927) and in *The Woman Disputed* (1928), her last silent picture. Gilbert's talkie debut in Norma's first talking venture, a fiasco called *New York Nights* (1929), proved his resonant voice supported his Latin image. Although Gilbert survived his participation in that film, Miss Talmadge's harsh Brooklynese destroyed her romantic image, and after one more misadventure (in which Gilbert did not appear), she retired from the screen.

461

By this point the Roland-Talmadge affair was waning and he went to Metro for both the English and Spanish versions of *Men of the North* (1930). He made a Spanish version of *Resurrection* (1931) with Lupe Velez (who had filmed the English edition with John Boles).

On the West Coast stage he co-starred with Jane Cowl in *Camille*. The Hollywood Latin craze disappeared and Roland had small, unimportant parts in pictures until cast as Clara Bow's half-breed lover Moonglow in Fox's *Call Her Savage* (1932), in which he is whipped by Miss Bow until romance prevails for the climax. There was no recurrence of the former romance and Gilbert stated, "We were a heavy thing for some time. Everybody knew about it so I'm not telling tales."

Roland was advantageously cast as a South American gigolo in Mae West's rousing hit *She Done Him Wrong* (1933). In the film he kissed her hand and whispered, "I've heard so much about it," to which La West retorted, "You can't prove it!" In 1933 he was seen around Hollywood with Constance Bennett with whom he had made *Our Betters* (1933) and with whom he then was filming *After Tonight* (1933). Although she was still married to Gloria Swanson's import from France, the Marquis de la Falaise de la Coudray, whom she had married a few weeks after Swanson's divorce from the noble "Hank" in November, 1931, Roland and Bennett became quite an item.

Norma Talmadge philosophically had announced, "Gilbert was [12½ years] too young for me," and in 1934 divorced Joseph Schenck to wed George Jessel, who, forty years later, still considers her the most exciting woman he has ever known. There were many in the industry who insisted Gilbert's decline in filmdom during the Thirties was due largely to delayed retribution from Schenck. It is true that Gilbert's Hollywood films were few and then only in minor roles. Occasionally he made a few Spanish-speaking features. In 1937 he went to Paramount for a minor Western, *Thunder Trail,* and then received good notices for his playing in the exploitive *Last Train from Madrid* (1937). By then he was dating Simone Simon, the petite, charming French import that Darryl F. Zanuck had ensconced at Twentieth Century-Fox.

After a supporting role in Twentieth's *Gateway* (1938) Gilbert made Columbia's Spanish *La Vida Bohemia* (1939) and was excellent as the traitorous Colonel Miguel Lopez in Warner Bros.' *Juarez* (1939). The following year he was Captain Lopez capturing the elusive *The Sea Hawk* (Errol Flynn).

With Frances Drake in *Midnight Taxi* (20th '37).

On November 14, 1940, Constance Bennett divorced the Marquis de la Falaise and on April 20, 1941, Gilbert and Miss Bennett drove to Yuma, Arizona, to be wed by the Reverend J. C. Bobb. It was Roland's first marriage and Constance's fourth. Gossip columnists were quieted when they "adopted" a child named Linda. Then, on December 11, 1941, Constance gave birth to Gyl Christina, who was christened at Our Lady of the Valley Church on Sunday, April 12, 1942, as Christina Consuela. By then (February 13, 1942) Gilbert had become a U.S. citizen and had enlisted in the U.S. Air Force, where he later became a second lieutenant. The marriage to the tempestuous, egocentric Miss Bennett was a stormy affair with the actress' undisguised impatience and the actor's Latin masculine superiority conflicting at every turn. The couple separated in September, 1944, after Gilbert's Army Air Corps discharge. He gave Constance an uncontested divorce on June 13, 1945, plus a court-approved property settlement and custody of their two daughters. Following the divorce Roland was linked with Rita Hayworth and Doris Duke, but he deflated rude questions from columnists by saying, "We are only good friends."

While many of Gilbert's contemporaries from the Twenties had passed into flabby middle age, he was at the peak of his physical form. However, the Good Neighbor Policy to South America was over in both Washington and Hollywood, and Gilbert could hardly find any screen work. He did make a fifteen-episode serial for Columbia, *The Desert Hawk* (1944), in which he played twin brothers. Then Monogram, a poverty-row studio, saw Roland's potential for the part of The Cisco Kid in their popular and profitable series. Roland was the fourth actor (after Warner Baxter, Cesar Romero, and Duncan Renaldo) to play the Western bandit hero. Roland's portrayal of the Mexican hero was probably the most authentic and richly played and closest to O. Henry's original characterization. Astride his horse Diablo, Roland played The Cisco Kid six times during 1946 and 1947, concluding with *King of the Bandits*. His career then took a sharp upward surge after meeting irascible John Huston.

Huston was casting *We Were Strangers* (1949) for Columbia and suggested Roland for a key role. Columbia asked, "Who wants that long-haired Cisco Kid in a straight dramatic role." Huston bellowed in his strongest, most outraged voice, "I do!" The picture and Roland's part of Guillermo reestablished him on the screen as the fine actor he was. His career developed into a series of showy performances including the Mexi-

With Donald Crisp, Brian Aherne, Mickey Kuhn, and Bette Davis in *Juarez* (WB '39).

can-filmed *The Bullfighter and the Lady* (1951) and the role of the prison kingpin in *My Six Convicts* (1952).

One Roland role of which he is still proud was the lead in Warner Bros.' *The Miracle of Our Lady of Fatima* (1952). To this day he yearly receives an invitation to return to Fatima, where the film was made, to participate in the October religious services commemorating The Miracle. If he had been swaggering as Victor "Gaucho" Ribera in MGM's all-star *The Bad and the Beautiful* (1952), he was substantial as the cavalier sponge fisherman in Twentieth Century-Fox's CinemaScope excursion *Beneath the Twelve-Mile Reef* (1953), filmed at Florida's Tarpon Springs. He told the press, "I don't want to be a star. I've had it before and I know what it's like. Let the young kids have it now." Concerning his seeming lasting youthfulness, he admitted: "I play tennis every day of the year. I have the same waistline—20 inches—that I had when I started in pictures as an extra in 1925. And then, I do not worry. I do not eat myself up inside by fretting about things. That's what makes people old!"

In 1954 Gilbert wed Guillermina Cantu and the marriage has been a successful one. He entered television the same year and, after two dreary films with Jane Russell, appeared on TV's "Fireside Theatre." He added Latin flavoring to both *That Lady* (1955), with Olivia de Havilland, and *Bandido* (1956), with Robert Mitchum. Then, in *Around the World in 80 Days* (1956), Gilbert appeared in a scene with another former Cisco Kid, Cesar Romero.

Roland was especially impressive as the killer in Tony Curtis' *The Midnight Story* (1957) and offered a contrasting performance on television's "Schlitz Playhouse" in *Rich Man, Poor Man,* playing a humble peasant suddenly overwhelmed with wealth. In 1958 he went to Cuba to make *El Señor y La Cleopatra,* which was not released in America until 1967. He played a high-wire artist in *The Big Circus* (1959). Financially secure he seemed to choose his roles for some particular appeal. He made an excellent Indian in John Ford's *Cheyenne Autumn* (1964), and in *The Poppy Is Also a Flower* (1966) he portrayed the charming but villainous drug dealer whose wife (Rita Hayworth) is a drug addict.

Roland continued to appear sporadically on television shows that he had personally selected, but insisted he did not like the medium because the good parts were too few. His career veered strangely at times. He was signed for the role of Marino Bello in Joseph E. Levine's *Harlow* (1965), but was replaced by Raf Vallone. (It had happened before: he and Rita Hayworth were once scheduled to appear in a remake of *Ramona,* but before the project got underway, Twentieth Century-Fox emerged and it was Don Ameche and Loretta Young who played the leads in the 1936 film.)

Gilbert continued to appear in films and during the later Sixties made four so-called "spaghetti" Westerns in Italy and Spain. In the Seventies he appeared in a special two-hour segment of the series "High Chapparal." He recently completed a deep-sea thriller for Royal Productions-Twentieth Century-Fox, *The Black Pearl,* on location in the Bahamas and in Spain. In 1973 he was cited by the League of United Latin American Citizens for championing the cause of Chicanos in motion pictures and television. He continues in his belief that after knowing yesterday, today is vital, and that one should not fear the future.

Roland wears a gold ring engraved with his mother's last words to him, "Hijo mio, no te apuces, no te asustes, adios alma mia" or, "My son, don't rush yourself, don't worry yourself, goodbye my soul." In the mid-Fifties he appraised his career with: "I'm afraid I don't have any delusions about myself as an actor. I'm grateful for being able to find enough work all these years. I'm happy, naturally with the activity of the past three or four years, but I'm not going to get excited or worry about the future. We say in Spanish that death comes soon enough so why kill yourself crying about it?"

GILBERT ROLAND

The Lady Who Lied (FN 1925)
The Plastic Age (B. P. Schulberg 1925)
The Midshipman (MGM 1925)
The Campus Flirt (Par 1926)
The Blonde Saint (FN 1926)
Camille (FN 1927)
Rose of the Golden West (FN 1927)
The Love Mart (FN 1927)
The Dove (UA 1927)
The Woman Disputed (UA 1928)
New York Nights (UA 1929)
Men of the North (MGM 1930)
Monsieur Le Fox [Spanish language version of Men of the North] (MGM 1930)
Resurrection [Spanish language version of Resurrection] (Univ 1931)
Hombres en Mi Vida [Spanish Language version of The Men in Her Life] (Col 1931)
The Passionate Plumber (MGM 1932)
No Living Witness (Mayfair 1932)
Life Begins (FN 1932)
A Parisian Romance (Allied 1932)
Call Her Savage (Fox 1932)
The Woman in Room 13 (Fox 1932)
She Done Him Wrong (Par 1933)
Tarnished Youth (World Wide 1933)
Our Betters (RKO 1933)
Una Viuda Romantica (Fox 1933)
Yom, Tu y Ella (Fox 1933)
Gigolettes of Paris (Equitable 1933)
After Tonight (RKO 1933)
Elinor Norton (Fox 1934)
The Mystery Woman (Fox 1935)
Ladies Love Danger (Fox 1935)
Julieta Compra un Hijo (Fox 1935)
Midnight Taxi (20th 1937)
Thunder Trail (Par 1937)
Last Train from Madrid (Par 1937)
Gateway (20th 1938)
Juarez (WB 1939)
La Vida Bohemia (Col 1939)
The Sea Hawk (WB 1940)
Gambling on the High Seas (WB 1940)
Isle of Destiny (RKO 1940)
Rangers of Fortune (Par 1940)
Angels with Broken Wings (Rep 1941)
My Life with Caroline (RKO 1941)
Isle of Missing Men (Mon 1942)
Enemy Agents Meet Ellery Queen (Col 1942)
The Desert Hawk (Col serial 1944)
Captain Kidd (UA 1945)
The Gay Cavalier (Mon 1946)
La Rebellion de Los Fantasmas (Azteca 1946)
South of Monterey (Mon 1946)
Beauty and the Bandit (Mon 1946)
Riding the California Trail (Mon 1947)

High Conquest (Mon 1947)
The Other Love (UA 1947)
Pirates of Monterey (Univ 1947)
Robin Hood of Monterey (Mon 1947)
King of the Bandits (Mon 1947)
The Dude Goes West (AA 1948)
We Were Strangers (Col 1949)
Malaya (MGM 1949)
The Torch (EL 1950)
Crisis (MGM 1950)
The Furies (Par 1950)
Ten Tall Men (Col 1951)
The Bullfighter and the Lady (Rep 1951)
Mark of the Renegade (Univ 1951)
My Six Convicts (Col 1952)
Glory Alley (MGM 1952)
The Miracle of Our Lady of Fatima (WB 1952)
Apache War Smoke (MGM 1952)
The Bad and the Beautiful (MGM 1952)
Beneath the Twelve-Mile Reef (20th 1953)
The Diamond Queen (WB 1953)
Thunder Bay (Univ 1953)
The French Line (RKO 1954)
Underwater! (RKO 1955)
The Racers (20th 1955)
That Lady (20th 1955)
The Treasure of Pancho Villa (RKO 1955)
Bandido (UA 1956)
Around the World in 80 Days (UA 1956)
Three Violent People (Par 1956)
The Midnight Story (Univ 1957)
The Last of the Fast Guns (Univ 1958)
The Wild and the Innocent (Univ 1959)
The Big Circus (AA 1959)
Guns of the Timberland (WB 1960)
Samar (WB 1962)
Cheyenne Autumn (WB 1964)
The Reward (20th 1965)
The Poppy Is Also a Flower (Comet 1966)
Catch Me If You Can [El Senor y La Cleopatra] (Goldstone Films 1967)
Each Man for Himself [The Ruthless Four] (PCM 1968)
Vado L'Anmazzo e Torna [Any Gun Can Play] (Italian-Spanish 1968)
Johnny Hamlet (Italian 1969)
Entre Dios y El Diablo [Between God and the Devil] (Spanish-Italian 1969)
The Christian Licorice Store (Cinema Center 1971)
Running Wild (Golden Circle 1973)
The Black Pearl (1975)
The Pacific Connection (1975)
Island in the Stream (Par 1976)

60

Cesar Romero

Since the death of Rudolph Valentino in August, 1926, Hollywood has always awaited with great anticipation the arrival of a new Latin lover. Each new male lead became a potential replacement for the great Rudolph. Throughout the Thirties there was still hope that a new celluloid "sheik" would appear on the film scene. The reincarnation never occurred, but the search brought to the screen a clutch of handsome, sexy males who carved their own special niches in screen history. Many of them possessed sufficient talent to weather several decades of movie-making. One of the most outstanding of these actors was a Latin from Manhattan named Cesar Romero.

He was born in New York City on Friday, February 15, 1907, to concert singer Maria Maniela and her Italian-born husband and importer-exporter of sugar refining machinery Senor Romero. They named their son Cesar, and his godfather was Jose Marti, the great Cuban patriot. Following his education at Riverdale Country School and Collegiate School, six-foot, two-inch, black-haired Cesar decided a job in the National City Bank was not for him. The great love of his life was dancing. Janette Hackett, a vaudeville headliner, engaged Cesar as a dancer and, after an extensive tour in the two-a-day, he formed a dance team with Elizabeth Higgins, debutante and heiress to the Higgins Ink fortune.

Their graceful ballroom dancing was booked into most of New York City's finest supper clubs, including Club Richman, the St. Regis Roof, the Ambassador Roof, and the Montmartre Cafe. Their popularity never equalled that of the Castles nor of Veloz and Yolanda, but they were well received and were thereafter hired for the Broadway revue *Lady Do,* featuring America's foremost black female impersonator, Karyl Norman. Elizabeth and Cesar waltzed, tangoed, and did a fast foxtrot and a bit of Apache dancing for fifty-six performances after the show opened on April 18, 1927, at Manhattan's Liberty Theatre.

Later with Nita Vernille as his dancing partner Cesar was booked into the Club Montmartre. During one performance—an acrobatic tango—he raised his partner atop his shoulders and started a series of swirls. He was seized suddenly by a violent pain in his side but managed to finish the number. "I fell to the floor in more pain than I have ever suffered. Finally I was carried to my dressing room. For two weeks I danced with the same pain gripping me but I'd rush off the floor and slap an ice bag over my appendix. It was agony but we fulfilled our contract although I knew it spelled the end of my dancing career."

With Rochelle Hudson, Edward Morris, and Ed Brophy in *Show Them No Mercy* **(Fox '35).**

However, he found another career—the legitimate stage. On September 17, 1929, he opened in the musical produced and directed by Busby Berkeley, *The Street Singer,* with Queenie Smith and Andrew Tombes. It ran for 191 performances. Thereafter, Brock Pemberton, seeking a replacement for the road company of *Strictly Dishonorable,* saw Romero onstage and signed him for the lead role of Count Di Ruvo that had been played by Tullio Carminati on Broadway. Romero was an excellent choice for the romantic part and had great success on the tour.

In the summer of 1931 Chamberlain Brown's Westchester Theatre in Mount Vernon, New York, was continuing as a successful venture. On June 29, 1931, Cesar repeated his Count Di Ruvo role for Brown's company which included Glenda Farrell and Jerome Cowan. Cesar stayed on for the next week's production of *Cobra* starring Judith Anderson, with Ralph Morgan and Glenda Farrell. Then Romero returned to the *Strictly Dishonorable* tour. In January, 1932, Cesar replaced Alan Edwards in *The Social Register,* and in the early autumn he started rehearsal for *Dinner at Eight.* In this George S. Kaufman-Edna Ferber hit, he played Ricci, the chauffeur who is insanely jealous of the maid who weds the butler. The show had a 232-performance run in New York and then went on a successful road tour.

At this point, Cesar decided to try motion pictures. His debut was a bit part in the low-budget independent film *The Shadow Laughs* (1933). Then he moved over to MGM for a small part in the first *The Thin Man* (1934) feature. After a telling performance in Kay Francis-Leslie Howard's *British Agent* (1934), Cesar went back to work for Preston Sturges, the author of *Strictly Dishonorable.* It was Sturges who was assigned by Universal to revamp the spicy and witty comedy *The Good Fairy* (1935) for the screen. The censor-approved script was watered down, but with Margaret Sullavan in the lead it was still a sprightly affair. Cesar played a cheap romantic hustler in the film, the man who tries to teach the heroine a few of the rawer facts of life. Two subsequent films with

United Artists established Romero as a great potential performer of the screen. He was Mir Jaffir in *Clive of India* (1935), with Ronald Colman, and then he played Andre De Pons having a love affair with Maureen O'Sullivan, the ward of *Cardinal Richelieu* (1935).

The artistically successful combination of Marlene Dietrich and director Josef von Sternberg climaxed in the remake of Pierre Louys' *La Femme et le Pantin (The Woman and the Puppet)* that had been filmed in 1920 by Samuel Goldwyn, with Geraldine Farrar and Lou Tellegen in the leads. The picture started filming with Joel McCrea playing opposite Marlene, but within a week McCrea found working for von Sternberg impossible and left the picture. Unperturbed, von Sternberg sought the services of Cesar. Romero recalls: "I wanted the role terribly because I knew how much it could do for me. But I didn't think I had a dog's chance of getting it. I thought so less after Miss Dietrich and von Sternberg eyed me up and down like a prize piece of cattle and then jabbered excitedly in German, which I could not understand. Finally, they told me to get a uniform from wardrobe and let them see me in that. I was both scared and burned up about this thing. When I paraded in front of them in uniform, I felt a lot of I-don't-give-a-damn-about-this-thing. Maybe it was that insolence, maybe it was my apparently not caring what happened, but, anyway, I got the role." The picture was *The Devil Is a Woman* (1935).

The resultant film showed Marlene as never lovelier, but the film was an artistic bore. Its $800,000 cost was never recovered. Additionally, the Spanish government demanded that Paramount withdraw the feature from circulation since it "insulted the Spanish armed forces." Seven months after the film's initial release, the studio withdrew it. On its own terms, the film probably would have been unsuccessful anyway. Romero's acting was nearly inanimate, thanks to von Sternberg's slow-paced direction that was more concerned with providing a variety of alluring poses and close-ups of Dietrich. Thus being Marlene's leading man did not boost Cesar's career, but it did lead to good supporting roles in *Diamond Jim* (1935), *Metropolitan* (1935), and other films. In 1937 he signed with Twentieth Century-Fox and stayed there for thirteen years.

Romero would later reflect on his studio stay: "In the thirties there were places all over this country for a kid to learn to act. Stock companies in Detroit, Pittsburgh, Dallas, regular repertory theatres where you played a different role not only every week, but sometimes every night. You learned your trade—you learned how to act." About Fox, "We were like a family there." And the roles he played at Darryl F. Zanuck's studio were colorful. He was rarely anything but fine in all of them. He was Khode Khan in Shirley Temple's *Wee Willie Winkle* (1937), and Ramdass in her *The Little Princess* (1939). He added zest to Sonja Henie's *Happy Landing* (1938) and *My Lucky Star* (1938). Like many of the featured players of the Thirties, Cesar was as much a drawing card for film audiences as the star.

In 1939 he and Joan Crawford did a magazine feature on dos and don'ts of ballroom dancing, and Miss Crawford declared "Butch" (as his close friends called him) Romero was the best ballroom dancer she had ever known or seen. Cesar was certainly the *most* eligible bachelor in Hollywood. He squired Betty Furness from her earliest years in Hollywood, and dated practically every star or starlet of any importance.

Warner Baxter had won an Oscar for portraying the Cisco Kid in *Old Arizona* (1929), and he played the beloved rogue twice more. In the *Return of the Cisco Kid* (1939), Cesar played his henchman Lopez, complete with an oversized hat, deplorable clothes, and a makeup that would have embarrassed a drunken embalmer. When it was decided that Baxter had grown out of his role, Romero succeeded him for six more entries in the popular series, ranging from *The Cisco Kid and the Lady* (1940) to his finale, *Ride On,*

With Margaret Lindsay in *Public Enemy's Wife* (WB '36).

Vaquero (1941). Between the Cisco adventures he was effective in a musical, *Tall, Dark and Handsome* (1941), and when Duncan Renaldo replaced him as the Cisco Kid, Cesar was cast in a series of pleasant musicals: *The Great American Broadcast* (1941), *Dance Hall* (1941), and *Week-End in Havana* (1941). If he was not in the same league with the studio's top-starring Tyrone Power, Don Ameche, John Payne, or Victor Mature, he was indeed a popular figure on the lot. Romero was particularly effective in the all-star *Tales of Manhattan* (1942) and received glowing praise for his deft playing of Sinjin, pianist with Glenn Miller's Orchestra, in *Orchestra Wives* (1942). (His keyboard playing was dubbed by Chummy McGregor.) Cesar enjoyed working with Betty Grable in *Springtime in the Rockies* (1942) and as carnival pitchman Joe Rocco in her *Coney Island* (1943). Sonja Henie's *Wintertime* (1943) was his last feature before he enlisted in the service.

He joined the U.S. Coast Guard at San Pedro, California, on October 13, 1942, after being a lieutenant in the California State Guard and a member of the Evacuation Corps, as well as an air raid warden and a worker on a government radio program. When he returned from military service in 1946, he repossessed from his family his Pennsylvania Dutch farm house built in 1940 as a potential marriage lair. Eventually most of his relatives departed and he shared the home—and still does—with his sister Maria.

Twentieth Century-Fox decided to send Romero and Tyrone Power (one of his closest friends) on a good-will tour of South America. Tyrone flew a twin engine Beechcraft plane and they arrived in Managua, Nicaragua, on August 26, 1946, and proceeded on their South American jaunt. In Argentina, Juan Peron presented Cesar with an elaborate scabbard holding a knife for use as a letter opener and gave both actors a miniature sword of San Martin. In 1947 the two returned to Hollywood to film *Captain from Castile,* in which the still handsome Cesar made much of the role of the highly colorful Spanish explorer, Cortez.

Since Ernst Lubitsch's *That Lady in Ermine* (1948), which included Cesar in its cast, was half-finished when the producer-director died, Otto Preminger completed the film. The latter proved to lack the famed "Lubitsch touch" and the resultant film died at the box-office. After this Betty Grable fiasco, Cesar was loaned to MGM for the Greer Garson-Walter Pidgeon comedy *Julia Misbehaves* (1948), in which he played a creditable limey (complete with a close-to-Bow Bells accent). He returned to Fox and Preston Sturges for a dismal screen comedy, *The Beautiful Blonde from Bashful Bend* (1949), which did nothing for Betty Grable's career. Cesar's final film for Fox was *Love that Brute* (1950), with Paul Douglas. After that he left his "home" to free-lance.

It was in 1951 that Romero made his video debut on "Bigelow TV Theatre" in *The Big Hello* with Jeanne Cagney. Thereafter he popped up in a variety of guises, as actor, dancer, guest star, or bon vivant. He would be especially good as Desi Arnaz' partner in a sightseeing service on the TV special *Lucy Takes a Cruise to Havana,* with Rudy Vallee, Ann Sothern, and Hedda Hopper. Romero sang "Our Ship Is Coming In" and brought a good deal of charm and vitality to the show. His many talents were given free rein on television and he fluctuated between drama, comedy, variety, and musicals with his usual professional ease.

At the same time Cesar continued to average about two films a year in the Hollywood studios, none of which were especially notable, save for the underrated *Once a Thief* (1950), a gangster study featuring June Havoc. He added considerable color to the star-splashed *Around the World in 80 Days* (1956) playing Gilbert Roland's henchman from Tangier. The following year Cesar headed the *Havana Mardi Gras Revue* at the Las Vegas Dunes Hotel. His old stand-by play, *Strictly Dishonorable,* was his frequent choice for the summer stock circuit, and on the Hollywood party scene he was con-

At Twentieth Century-Fox in '38.

stantly called upon to escort the famous and near famous. It was well known that Cesar could be counted on to be charming, to be an excellent dance partner, and to be discreet.

Oddly enough, one of Romero's most famous roles was via a comic strip, but he both wildly and expertly played that clown prince of crime, The Joker, on the highly successful teleseries "Batman" for two years (1966 and 1967), making his exit by stealing Gotham's art treasures and replacing them with his own paintings. He repeated his boisterous Joker role in the 1966 film feature with Adam West as Batman and Burt Ward as the Boy Wonder, Robin.

By 1968 a *TV Guide* article was describing Romero as one of the most beautiful men in the world, still handsome, erect, and alert, with hair the color of stainless steel. In 1969 he made the films *Skidoo, Midas Run,* and two features which were pushed off onto TV in America, *A Talent for Loving* and Warner Bros.' *Sophie's Place,* the latter with Dame Edith Evans and Telly Savalas.

After over forty years in films, Romero has decided: "It's not fun anymore. Studios used to keep you working every day. You finished one movie and went right into another. It is so very different now. When I started we were all under contract to a studio and were all like a big family. You worked with the same people year in and year out. Your studio was like a second home. And that's all gone."

Gone, too, are many of Cesar's closest friends. "My good friend, my dear friend Tyrone Power, lived right down the street from me." And he continued calling the necrology roll: Carole Landis, Betty Grable, Carole Lombard, Robert Taylor, Gary Cooper, Paul Douglas, and Carmen Miranda. A few of the oldsters are still left. Cesar happily recalls: "George Murphy and his wife Julie and I started in the business together. They were a dance team in a club in Greenwich Village when my partner and I were at the Park Central Roof in New York. We came to Hollywood at the same time. I lived with George and Julie for a while until I got my first apartment."

Retirement? Ridiculous. In his late sixties, Cesar defies Father Time, and recently he underwent acupuncture treatment to cure his injured back and was off to Chicago for a six-week run in *My Three Angels* with Vera Miles (in her stage debut). Also, he continues to pop up in Walt Disney features, such as *The Strongest Man in the World* (1975). And he still can be seen on television in cameo roles. (Part of his acting activity is to recoup losses from his chain of eight men's clothing stores in California.)

Few players from the Thirties had such a reservoir of talents in as many fields as Romero, nor have many endured as well. He may not have become the *new* Valentino, but he was and is a constant delight onscreen.

CESAR ROMERO

The Shadow Laughs *(Invincible 1933)*
The Thin Man *(MGM 1934)*
Cheating Cheaters *(Univ 1934)*
British Agent *(WB 1934)*
The Good Fairy *(Univ 1935)*
Strange Wives *(Univ 1935)*
Clive of India *(UA 1935)*
Cardinal Richelieu *(UA 1935)*
Hold 'Em Yale *(Par 1935)*
The Devil Is a Woman *(Par 1935)*
Diamond Jim *(Univ 1935)*
Metropolitan *(Fox 1935)*
Rendezvous *(MGM 1935)*
Show Them No Mercy *(Fox 1935)*
Love before Breakfast *(Univ 1936)*
Nobody's Fool *(Univ 1936)*
Public Enemy's Wife *(WB 1936)*
15 Maiden Lane *(20th 1936)*
She's Dangerous *(Univ 1937)*
Armored Car *(Univ 1937)*
Wee Willie Winkie *(20th 1937)*
Dangerously Yours *(20th 1937)*
Happy Landing *(20th 1938)*
My Lucky Star *(20th 1938)*
Always Goodbye *(20th 1938)*
Five of a Kind *(20th 1938)*
Wife, Husband and Friend *(20th 1939)*
The Little Princess *(20th 1939)*
Return of the Cisco Kid *(20th 1939)*
Charlie Chan at Treasure Island *(20th 1939)*
Frontier Marshal *(20th 1939)*
Viva Cisco Kid *(20th 1940)*
Lucky Cisco Kid *(20th 1940)*
He Married His Wife *(20th 1940)*
The Cisco Kid and the Lady *(20th 1940)*
The Gay Caballero *(20th 1940)*
Tall, Dark and Handsome *(20th 1941)*
Romance of the Rio Grande *(20th 1941)*
Ride On, Vaquero *(20th 1941)*
The Great American Broadcast *(20th 1941)*
Dance Hall *(20th 1941)*
Week-End in Havana *(20th 1941)*
A Gentleman at Heart *(20th 1942)*
Tales of Manhattan *(20th 1942)*
Orchestra Wives *(20th 1942)*
Springtime in the Rockies *(20th 1942)*
Coney Island *(20th 1943)*
Wintertime *(20th 1943)*
Captain from Castile *(20th 1947)*
Carnival in Costa Rica *(20th 1947)*
Deep Waters *(20th 1948)*

That Lady in Ermine *(20th 1948)*
Julia Misbehaves *(MGM 1948)*
The Beautiful Blonde from Bashful Bend *(20th 1949)*
Love that Brute *(20th 1950)*
Once a Thief *(UA 1950)*
Happy Go Lovely *(RKO 1951)*
FBI Girl *(Lip 1951)*
The Lost Continent *(Lip 1951)*
Scotland Yard Inspector *(Lip 1952)*
The Jungle *(Lip 1952)*
Prisoners of the Casbah *(Col 1953)*
Shadow Man *(Lip 1953)*
Vera Cruz *(UA 1954)*
The Americano *(RKO 1955)*
The Racers *(20th 1955)*
Around the World in Eighty Days *(UA 1956)*
The Sword of Granada *(Manson Distributing 1956)*
The Leather Saint *(Par 1956)*
The Story of Mankind *(WB 1957)*
Villa! *(20th 1958)*
Ocean's 11 *(WB 1960)*
Pepe *(Col 1960)*
7 Women from Hell *(20th 1961)*
If a Man Answers *(Univ 1962)*
We Shall Return *(United International 1963)*
Donovan's Reef *(Par 1963)*
The Castilian *(WB 1963)*
A House Is Not a Home *(Emb 1964)*
Two on a Guillotine *(WB 1965)*
Sergeant Deadhead *(AIP 1965)*
Marriage on the Rocks *(WB 1965)*
Batman *(20th 1966)*
Hot Millions *(MGM British 1968)*
Skidoo *(Par 1969)*
Sophie's Place *(WB 1969)*
Midas Run *(Cin 1969)*
A Talent for Loving *(Par 1969)*
The Computer Wore Tennis Shoes *(BV 1970)*
Latitude Zero *(National General 1970)*
Madigan's Millions *(AIP 1970)*
Soul Soldier *(Fanfare 1972)*
Now You See Him, Now You Don't *(BV 1972)*
The Proud and the Damned *(Prestige 1972)*
Timber Tramp *(Alaska Pictures 1973)*
The Spectre of Edgar Allan Poe *(Cin 1974)*
The Strongest Man in the World *(BV 1975)*
Won Ton Ton, the Dog Who Saved Hollywood *(Par 1976)*

61

Simone Simon

If Russian Anna Sten was Samuel Goldwyn's most expensive import, Simone Simon was one of Darryl F. Zanuck's most spectacular failures at home or abroad. Advertised as the star discovery of 1936, tempestuous Mlle. Simon never really ascended into Hollywood's firmament, although several of her performances were excellent. After she signed a contract with Twentieth Century-Fox at $2,000 a week, there began an astonishing campaign in the press to educate the non-bilingual American public in the proper pronunciation of her French name. Before she had made her first appearance on America's silver screen, few members of the moviegoing public were *not* aware that Simone Simon was pronounced "Seemoan, See-moan."[9] This excessive drive to educate the unsuspecting masses that were anticipated to throng to her photoplays eventually became more than laughable in its patronizing dictatorial emphasis. Herbert Marshall, with whom Simone made her American film debut in *Girls' Dormitory* (1936), answered his telephone, "This is Herbert Marshall speaking—pronounced 'See-moan, See-moan!' "

Petite Mlle. Simone stood five feet, two inches, a pert childlike beauty who could fascinate even those who could not pronounce her name. She started life in Marseilles on Saturday, April 23, 1910 (some sources would later claim it was 1914 and in Lille, France). Before her twenty-first birthday, she had made her Paris stage debut (March 3, 1931) at the Apollo Theatre in the operetta *Balthazar*. She entered motion pictures, so the publicity releases claim, as the result of exiled Russian director Tourjansky spotting her one day, while she was drinking coffee at the Cafe de la Paix. He hired her for a role in his Paris-made *Le Chanteur Inconnu* (1931). She made four other features in 1931 and three in 1932. In 1933 she returned to the stage in *O Mon Bel Inconnu* and made two films. In 1934 she concentrated on the theatre, appearing in another operetta, *Toi, c'est Moi,* and continued in French films where she soon developed a name, had many starring roles, and developed a sizable European following. When she completed the French film *Les Beaux Jours* (1935) she left for America and a contract with Twentieth Century-Fox.

While Fox was promulgating the histrionic virtues of *la sauvage tendre,* rumors flitted

---

[9]Simone always laughed about the earnest campaign Twentieth Century-Fox carried out on the proper pronunciation of her name. She could be quite jovial about it. "They didn't know how to pronounce it," she said. "See-moan, See-moan, indeed! If you're going to spell it phonetically, it should be 'See-mun See-mown.' And that's not even right," she added, "because you go easy on the final 'n's, you know."

With Herbert Marshall in *Girls' Dormitory* (20th '36).

around the film colony that Miss Simon was actually the daughter of Marion Davies and William Randolph Hearst.[10] What was known was that the powerhouse personality had had a most adventurous childhood, having lived in Madagascar as a toddler, and later attending schools in Turin, Berlin, and Budapest.

Zanuck, who momentarily forgot protegees Alice Faye and Shirley Temple in his enthusiasm to push Simone, planned to use the lovely little French actress as Cigarette in his remake of *Under Two Flags* (1935). It soon became apparent that her talents did not extend to playing the role and Claudette Colbert was persuaded to substitute for the French import. Fox then announced Simone for the lead opposite Warner Baxter in *White Hunter*. Instead she was cast as Marie Claudel in *Girls' Dormitory*, which also presented Tyrone Power in an early role. Fox surrounded Simon with an excellent cast for such an unpretentious small story (Ruth Chatterton, Herbert Marshall, and Constance Collier). Miss Simon's reviews were surprisingly good and *Photoplay* called her performance one of the best of the month. "In the person of Simone Simon, a young French actress, comes a new screen personality so vibrantly alive and youthfully charming she completely overshadows the story itself, and forces into secondary place such stars as Herbert Marshall and Ruth Chatterton."

Obviously, Simone had arrived. For her second try at national enchantment she was cast with Janet Gaynor, Constance Bennett, and Loretta Young in an oft-told tale of three gals pooling resources to land affluent gentlemen. This time the story was called *Ladies in Love* (1936), and the script had Simon steal wealthy Paul Lukas from wise and wily Constance Bennett.

[10]Since Miss Simon was born in 1910 and Miss Davies was born in 1897 and did not start "going with" Hearst until 1915, it is impossible to make any logical connection.

The studio's difficulties in finding proper vehicles for their mercurial French soubrette were not helped by her outbursts to the press. She claimed she disliked most of Hollywood where the men talked of nothing but themselves. She insisted she was terribly bored with it all. But she did become enamoured of composer George Gershwin, and Oscar Levant later recalls that pretty Simone was at Gershwin's home quite often. (Supposedly the great composer was coaching and accompanying her in some Massanet operas at his North Roxbury Drive abode, which he shared with his brother Ira and Ira's wife, Lee.) After Gershwin's untimely death on July 11, 1937, there was much clamor in the press about one of Simone's gold keys being found among the late composer's possessions. (Later investigation revealed that the "gold key" scandal was instigated by a Fox executive disgruntled with self-willed Simone.)

Zanuck decided that a remake of *Seventh Heaven* (1937) was just the vehicle to display Simone's talents. It had been a sensational hit a decade earlier with Janet Gaynor and Charles Farrell, and he was determined that it would be just that again. Tyrone Power was originally scheduled to play Chico opposite Simone's Diane, but eventually gangly James Stewart was borrowed from MGM for the role of the remarkable fellow, the sewer cleaner. But his flat, nasal speech was far removed from that usually associated with the braggart Chico. (Simone had wanted her pal Tyrone Power to play the role.)

Fox arranged for Simone to watch several showings of Gaynor's *Seventh Heaven* and the French actress was enchanted by the star's interpretation of the part. But she wisely made no attempt to duplicate it. After more cast shuffling—with John Carradine replacing Don Ameche as Father Chevillion—Henry King's direction brought a surprisingly good performance from Simone. Using her innocent, little-girl voice to advantage, Simone was captivating. However, her performance could not erase the memory of Gaynor's superb, sensitive portrayal. A new title song was written for the picture by Lew Pollock and Sidney Mitchell, but it never caught on, nor could it compare with the haunting theme song from the 1927 version, "Diane," written by Pollock with Erno Rapee. The next year on October 17, 1938, "Lux Radio Theatre" would offer a rendition of *Seventh Heaven*, but Jean Arthur and Don Ameche would be in the lead roles.

During the filming of *Seventh Heaven*, there were unpleasant rumors regarding the chameleonlike Miss Simone who was so hard to please on the set. When the picture opened in March, 1937, she hit the news again when French publisher Francois Louis Dreyfus flew from Paris to Hollywood to persuade Simone to marry him. She said no.

As Yvette-Yvette, Simone received third billing after Walter Winchell and Ben Bernie in the entertaining *Love and Hisses* (1937), in which she sang "The Bell Song" from *Lakme;* a pop tune, "Sweet Someone"; and the ballad "Just a Little Love, a Little Kiss." After *Love and Hisses,* and after hearing several recordings Simone had made in France, Zanuck was ecstatic about his French star's singing voice, and he became determined to star her in a musical. For the book of the proposal musical he selected an aged but delightful comedy by Andre Picard. *Kiki* had been a stage success in 1920 with Lenore Ulric, then Norma Talmadge made a silent film version in 1926. Five years later Mary Pickford made a talkie of it. Zanuck paid Miss Pickford $60,000 for the screen rights to *Kiki* and announced the musical version would be called *The French Doll.* This proposed project was designed for the now French nightingale Simone Simon and was to feature Bert Lahr and Joan Davis. However, it was never made, and, instead, the trio were placed in *Josette* (1938), which co-starred Don Ameche. It was a less than successful feature.

In June, 1938, Simone was in the news when her former secretary Sandra Martin was brought to court for forging some six thousand dollars worth of checks in Simone's

At Twentieth Century-Fox in '36.

In *Seventh Heaven* (20th '37).

name. In order to prevent her from revealing details of Miss Simon's private life, an arrangement was made for her to serve a nine-month jail term and accept a ten-year probation period. On September 1, 1938, Simone's contract with Fox expired and the option for renewal was not taken up by the studio.

She returned to France to appear to good advantage with Jean Gabin in *La Bete Humaine* (1939). By mid-1939 she had arrived back in America and by the fall was signed for a new Broadway musical that would star her with Mitzi Green, Mary Brian, Frances Williams, Art Jarrett and others, including Twentieth Century-Fox's one-time favorite black comedian, Stepin Fetchit. The book of the musical was based on an "original" play by Guy Bolton called *Three after Three*. Simone played Vivi Gibson, who poses as an heiress, with sister Mitzi Green masquerading as her maid and sister Mary Brian as her personal secretary. All three hope to land a millionaire for Simone.

The show tried out in Baltimore and then moved to Philadelphia for the Christmas season. In Chicago it collapsed. The producers withdrew the show and reopened it in June with Kitty Carlisle replacing Simon, Betty Lawford in for Brian, and Jack Whiting replacing the romantic lead Earl Oxford. Mitzi Green, Frances Williams, and Fetchit were retained, and the show finally opened on Broadway where it endured for fifteen performances.

Mlle. Simon returned to Hollywood and on May 30, 1940, she was a guest on Rudy Vallee's radio show and was signed by RKO for one of their more spectacular failures. Stephen Vincent Benet's short story *The Devil and Daniel Webster* had defied adaptation in other theatrical media. Nevertheless, RKO had Dan Totheroh write a screenplay of the Benet story in which Mr. Scratch (Walter Huston) tries to win the soul of young New Hampshire farmer James Craig, with famed orator Daniel Webster (Edward Arnold) arguing against Scratch.[11] Simone was cast as Belle Dee, Mr. Scratch's assistant from "over the mountain" who suddenly appears to keep Faust-like Craig in line with his covenant with the Devil. Simone was fetching if too "foreign" and the film itself was a commercial disappointment, even with the alternate title, *All that Money Can Buy*.

In 1941 Simone appeared at Hollywood's El Capitan Theatre in *Charlot's Revue,* an all-star brief engagement featuring many of the film colony's top names. She was one of the highlights singing a Noël Coward ditty. She then went on a lengthy vaudeville tour, doing the "in person" bit and warbling a few songs while collecting handsomely for her stint. She returned to Hollywood for an unusual and well-made horror film considered one of the minor classics in that genre, Val Lewton's low-budgeted *Cat People* (1942). It was briskly directed by Jacques Tourneur from DeWitt Bodeen's imaginative, well-constructed script. Simone was Irene Dubrovae, bride of young naval designer Kent Smith, who turns into an evil cat destroying those she hates. Psychiatrist Tom Conway pays with his life in his efforts to help her. The film generated a good deal of understated terror, and Simone was exceptionally good as the mysterious Serbian feline. Filmed on a $135,000 budget it grossed about five million dollars. Two years later RKO made a sequel called *The Curse of the Cat People* (1944) in which Simone as a ghost attempts to save Kent Smith's lovely daughter from escaping into a fantasy world. The follow-up did not equal the original. Between the two *Cat* films, Simone made three quickies, all clinkers. By 1945 she was ready for another onslaught on the stage.

Simone signed for the lead in a new play by John Colton and Robert Harris called *Emily,* featuring Ralph Forbes, Margaret Wycherly, and Weldon Heyburn. The show opened and closed in Philadelphia in September, 1945, lasting a mere week. For Simone it was her last attempt to reach Broadway. She returned to Europe to continue

[11]Thomas Mitchell had done some shooting as Daniel Webster, but he unfortunately broke a limb and Arnold had to replace him. In a few of the crowd scenes that RKO did not bother to reshoot, Mitchell can still be spotted.

her film career in the French film *Petrus* (1946), and to play the role of Camelia in Pathé-British's *Temptation Harbour* (1947), with Robert Newton and Marcel Dalio. Her stage career fared better in Paris in 1948 when she played in *Le Bonheur Mesdames!, Le Roi Pasuole,* and *Au Petit Bonheur,* and succeeded in the operetta *Le Square de Perou.*

Flirtatious Simone did not make another American film, but she found a measure of success in the Italian-made *Donna Senza Nome* (1949) and in the French-made *Olivia [Pit of Loneliness]* (1950). Max Ophuls' *La Ronde* (1950) has become a classic. Historian Paul Rotha called the film, "a charming, witty and penetrating essay on the unchanging ways of love." This merry-go-round of *l'amour* backed by Strauss' lovely waltz "La Ronde de l'Amour" was expertly made with an all-star cast including Anton Walbrook, Simone Signoret, Danielle Darrieux, Fernand Gravet, Isa Miranda, Jean-Louis Barrault, and Simone Simon. It was set against the background of 1900 Vienna. As the pert parlor maid, who is seduced with some regularity, Simone provided one of her best screen appearances. Her last film for some years was *The Extra Day* (1956), a British-made entry dealing with the lives of motion picture extras.

In 1966, at the age of fifty-six, she returned to the Paris stage with Jean Meyer in *La Courte Paille.* The short engagement proved she still had retained her charm and looks. Her most recent feature is *La Femme en Bleu* (1973).

Today, still unmarried, she lives a pleasant life in Paris, where her favorite pastimes include painting and playing gin rummy. She maintains a lovely apartment in the French capital and often goes to a studio at Barbizon where she paints.

Not too long ago, she was asked if she would ever return to Hollywood. Like a true French woman, she responded, "I would go back, yes, if the money were good—but it is a terrible place." She later admitted that her California years had been very frustrating, and generally unhappy. "It is what the front-office bosses do to you," she explained. "If you do not do as they say, they treat you like dirt. They try to break your spirit. First they destroy your dreams and break your heart, and then they try to change and make over what is you. They don't want you to have any real identity except the one they impose upon you."

SIMONE SIMON

Le Chanteur Inconnu *(French 1931)*
Un Opere sans Douleur *(French 1931)*
La Petite Chocolatiere *(French 1931)*
Mam'zelle Nitouche *(French 1931)*
Le Pere sans Douleur *(French 1931)*
Un Fils D'Amerique *(French 1932)*
Le Roi Des Palaces *(French 1932)*
L'Etoile De Valence *(French 1932)*
Prenez Garde de La Peinture *(French 1932)*
Tire-au-Flanc *(French 1933)*
Le Voleur *(French 1933)*
Les Yeux Noirs *(French 1935)*
Les Beaux Jours *(French 1935)*
Lac Aux Dames *(French 1936)*
Girls' Dormitory *(20th 1936)*
Ladies in Love *(20th 1936)*
Seventh Heaven *(20th 1937)*
Love and Hisses *(20th 1937)*
Josette *(20th 1938)*

La Bete Humaine *(French 1939)*
The Devil and Daniel Webster [All that Money Can Buy] *(RKO 1941)*
Cat People *(RKO 1942)*
Tahiti Honey *(Rep 1943)*
Johnny Doesn't Live Here Anymore *(Mon 1944)*
Mademoiselle Fifi *(RKO 1944)*
The Curse of the Cat People *(RKO 1944)*
Petrus *(French 1946)*
Temptation Harbour *(Pathé-British 1947)*
Donna Senza Nome *(Italian 1949)*
La Ronde *(French 1950)*
Olivia [Pit of Loneliness] *(French 1950)*
Le Plaisir *(French 1951)*
I Tre Ladri *(Italian 1954)*
Double Destiny *(German 1955)*
The Extra Day *(British Lion 1956)*
La Femme en Bleu *(French 1973)*

62

Penny Singleton

One of America's favorite comic strips has been Murat B. "Chic" Young's *Blondie*. From 1930 onward the adventures of Dagwood Bumstead, his zany wife, children, and dogs have been identifiable by millions of the world's comic strip readers. By 1973 (when Young died—but the strip continued), the Bumstead adventures appeared in 1,623 newspapers and in sixty countries. In 1938 Columbia Pictures hired Arthur Lake and Penny Singleton to portray the Bumsteads onscreen, little realizing they would be spawning a series that would last for twenty-eight entries through to 1950. The two players became so associated with their comedy parts that few viewers could recall how extensive a career each had in non-Blondie vehicles.

Penny was born Mariana Dorothy Agnes Letitia McNulty on Tuesday, September 15, 1908, in Philadelphia, Pennsylvania, to Irish newsman Bernard (Barney) Joseph McNulty and his wife of German ancestry, Maria Louisa. When dark-haired, blue-eyed Dorothy was six years old she was singing and dancing with youngsters Raymond Guion (Gene Raymond), Milton Berle, and Jerome Mann. She attended the Alexander McClure School and continued singing in local theatres for illustrated songs in the silent screen houses. At age fifteen she landed a job in the chorus of the Broadway musical *Innocent Eyes* (Jack Oakie was in the male chorus), but the Gerry Society packed Miss McNulty back to Philadelphia and school.

When *Sky High* opened on Broadway at the Shubert Theatre on March 2, 1925, it starred Willie Howard and, in the small role of the cloak room girl, Dorothy McNulty. With five other girls she sang "Trim Them All But the One You Love" and "We Make the Show." The Shuberts signed her to a contract. After a tour with *Sky High,* she joined the Shuberts' production of *Sweetheart Time,* leaving that successful show for the revue *The Great Temptations.* That production provided her with an opportunity to display her varied talents. She appeared in a skit with Billy Van, and sang "Any Step" with Roy Sedley and "Dancing Town" with Florenz Ames and the chorus. But the greatest recognition for her in the revue was when she received equal billing with Jack Benny as his stooge in a specialty number. The revue remained on Broadway for thirty-eight performances, then played a successful tour of major cities.

In August, 1927, Dorothy was in Atlantic City for *Artists and Models.* After this tryout the show moved to New York that November, but without Dorothy and Peggy Hopkins Joyce. Dorothy transferred to the road company of *Good News,* playing opposite Jack

With Cliff Edwards (right) in *Good News* (MGM '30).

Haley in the Chicago engagement. *Follow Thru* had opened at the 46th Street Theatre on January 9, 1929. Midway through its run, Dorothy replaced Zelma O'Neal. Again she was opposite Jack Haley with whom she sang "Button Up Your Overcoat," "I Could Give up Anything But You," and with the chorus she had the solo "I Want to Be Bad!" After this job she left for Hollywood to film Metro's 1930 version of the musical *Good News*. She played Flo, a freshie, and led the lilting title song while Bessie Love played Dorothy's stage role of Babe O'Day. For MGM's *Love in the Rough* (1930), a remake of *Spring Fever*, Dorothy played Virgie in a romance on the golf course with interpolated music. She then returned to New York.

Advertised as "The Hit of the Summer," *Hey, Nonny, Nonny!* opened on June 6, 1932, on Broadway, starring Frank Morgan and featuring Anne Seymour and Dorothy McNulty. Dorothy drew critical applause for her singing of "Wouldn't That Be Wonderful" and "For Better or for Worse." The revue had a meagre run and she was seen in *Walk a Little Faster* (December 7, 1932). In 1934 she started rehearsals of *Annina* with Allan Jones, but she dropped out of the show, which folded before it reached New York.

The energetic Miss McNulty decided to try Hollywood again. In the sequel to *The Thin Man* (1934), called *After the Thin Man* (1936), Dorothy portrayed a tough cabaret songstress and belted out "Smoke Dreams" and "Blow that Horn." Her bright performance in this mystery-comedy was followed by an erroneous announcement on December 3, 1936, that MGM had signed her to a long-term contract. After appearing as Miss Simms in the Technicolor *Vogues of 1938* (1937) and a quickie for Republic, she changed her screen name to Penny Singleton. Earlier in 1937 she had married Dr. Lawrence Scogga Singleton, a Los Angeles dentist. The actress' passion for collecting pennies provided the "Penny" to go along with her new surname.

As Penny Singleton she signed with Warner Bros. In 1938 she made eight pictures for

With William Powell in *After the Thin Man* (MGM '36).

that studio in supporting roles and was loaned to RKO for Barbara Stanwyck's *The Mad Miss Manton* (1938). Penny's career-making role of Blondie was originally intended for Shirley Deane (who played the eldest daughter in Fox's *Jones Family* series). However, Miss Deane became ill (some said she was fired because she couldn't work naturally with the baby) and Columbia called Penny to test for the title role. The studio decided she was a perfect Blondie and had her chestnut-brown hair bleached to bright gold. Miss Singleton has remained a blonde ever since.

Columbia had originally planned the *Blondie* series to be a three-installment package, but its popularity with the public led studio head Harry Cohn to continue it onward and onward. With two exceptions, *Go West, Young Lady* (1941) and *Young Widow* (1946), Penny remained Blondie oncamera exclusively through the remainder of her screen career.

On July 3, 1939, Penny and Arthur Lake shifted the trials and tribulations of the Bumsteads to radio as a summer filler. The show caught on as enthusiastically as the *Blondie* series, and after Penny departed, other Blondies were Alice White, Patricia Van Cleve, and Ann Rutherford, while Lake remained as Dagwood throughout. Penny later had her own radio show, "That Williamson Widow," with Bea Benaderet, Jim Backus, Hal March, and others. For Hollywood's two-hour-and-twenty-minute broadcast for the Red Cross, Penny and Lake were heard in a "Blondie" sketch followed by Charles Laughton's brilliant reading of "The Gettysburg Address."

In March of 1940 Penny was injured in an automobile crash with Robert Sparks. She recovered quickly. About this time Louella Parsons confirmed in print rumors of a full-fledged romance between the two. When Penny, who had divorced Dr. Singleton, and Sparks eloped to Goldfield, Nevada, in 1941 only Louella knew! Sparks, producer of the *Blondie* series, joined the Marine Corps at the outbreak of the war and Penny, with daughter Dorothy Grace, spent thirteen weeks with him at his post in Quantico, Virginia (the only time that "Blondie" was off the airwaves in nearly eight years). While at Quantico, Penny's second daughter, Robin Susan Sparks, was born there in the naval hospital.

When the *Blondie* series had run its course by 1950, Penny took her talents to clubs and later returned to the musical stage in the Midwest playing leads in *Gentlemen Prefer Blondes, Bells Are Ringing Call Me Madam,* and *Happy Hunting.* Although "Blondie" was transferred to television, Penny was not part of the package. (Pamela Britton played the role opposite Arthur Lake.) However Penny made her TV debut in 1950 on "Ford Theatre" in *Cause for Suspicion.* In 1962 she did a voice-over for a recurring character in "The Jetson" series. On April 3, 1964, she was seen on television's "Twilight Zone" and that same year made her last film appearance to date, as Mrs. T. T. Claypoole in Gore Vidal's *The Best Man.* The following year, she teamed with Lyle Talbot, made a national tour in the comedy *Never Too Late.*

It was in 1963, after twenty-two years of marriage, that Bob Sparks died. Resourceful Penny sprang back into more theatre activities and devoted more and more time to her career with the American Guild of Variety Artists (AGVA).

Her old friend from *Good News* and *Follow Thru,* Jack Haley, AGVA's executive vice-president, has said, "Penny found she had a latent talent for negotiation and for business acumen." If her expertise in this field came as a surprise to show business followers, it would have created small notice within the McNulty family. Her father was a raging apostle for good politics, using his position as a newspaperman to expound them. Penny is known to many today as "the brains of the whole union [AGVA]." And she is a champion of women's rights.

It was in 1957 that she was first elected as a national board member of AGVA, and in

With Arthur Lake and Larry Simms in *Blondie* (Col '38).

1969 she was chosen as its president. She received a great deal of publicity in 1966 when she led a strike for Radio City Music Hall's Rockettes (the first in their history) that lasted twenty-seven days but won better working conditions for the women.

Her abilities at organization, at coping with trade unions, and at testifying at the House of Representatives' investigations of union activities have been notable. She is the first woman to head an AFL-CIO union. She is adamant about her position, saying: "Women are really leaders. A lot of them don't even know they are leaders. But they are. A woman can handle just about anything she puts her mind to . . . if she puts her mind to it. Our great trade union people—a lot of them—are getting well along in years. They are not what you would call young men. Now where are the young men who are going to come into this business? And, furthermore, isn't it time that the young women came into it along with the young men?" She is proud of the gains she has accomplished for her union.

As executive president of the American Guild of Variety Artists, she received an honorary Doctor of Fine Arts degree from St. John's University on May 6, 1974. Later that month she filled in for Ruby Keeler while the star of *No, No Nanette* took a vacation. (Penny later teamed with Arthur Lake for a few weeks of *No, No Nanette*.) She had lost none of her stage presence by arguing over bargaining tables or battling for better deals for her AGVA membership. She maintains: "Women sit and are quiet and analyze things more than men. There is no yelling and screaming because men can't very well do that with ladies present! Besides, women are better at that. Careers are

486

wonderful and there are women who can take things in their stride and who can have careers and also be wonderful mothers and wives and homemakers and all the rest of it.''

With her daughters now grown, Penny refuses to retire into any corners. ''What happened to me can happen to anybody else. If you want it to happen. It takes a lot of work, a lot of study, a lot of reading.''

In the early summer of 1974 Penny ousted the elected board of AGVA, and from her action a great schism developed within the union. She was accused of hiring a guard to keep out the elected board members and of misusing her office to oust elected officials. By August, Judge Margaret J. Mangan of the New York Supreme Court issued a preliminary injunction prohibiting comic Eddie Roy (who had been functioning as the union's president) from interfering with the performance of Singleton's official duties. To insure the judge's decision, Penny changed the locks to her office. She underscored her liberated women's approach. Elections, under the auspices of the U.S. Department of Justice, were rerun, and although Penny came out a victor (the losers unsuccessfully contested), her union problems are still *not* concluded. One result of the conflict is that Penny is certainly one of the better known public figures of the Seventies.

Over the years, Penny's preoccupation with the *Blondie* series kept her from playing many roles that might have increased her fame as a musical comedy talent or as a major comedienne onscreen. One has only to review *Swing Your Lady* (1938) which, despite Humphrey Bogart calling it the worst film he ever made, shows Miss Singleton at her hilarious best, a combination of dumb Marie Wilson and sharp-mouthed Jane Wyman. In this feature she sang and danced and tried to explain the facts of life to dull-brained Nat Pendleton. What the movement for women's liberation and union politics has gained, the public at large has lost.

PENNY SINGLETON

As Dorothy McNulty:
Good News *(MGM 1930)*
Love in the Rough *(MGM 1930)*
After the Thin Man *(MGM 1936)*
Vogues of 1938 *(UA 1937)*
Sea Racketeers *(Rep 1937)*
As Penny Singleton:
Outside of Paradise *(Rep 1938)*
Swing Your Lady *(WB 1938)*
Men Are Such Fools *(WB 1938)*
Boy Meets Girl *(WB 1938)*
Mr. Chump *(WB 1938)*
The Mad Miss Manton *(RKO 1938)*
Garden of the Moon *(WB 1938)*
Secrets of an Actress *(WB 1938)*
Hard to Get *(WB 1938)*
Racket Busters *(WB 1938)*
Blondie *(Col 1938)*
Blondie Meets the Boss *(Col 1939)*
Blondie Takes a Vacation *(Col 1939)*
Blondie Brings up Baby *(Col 1939)*
Blondie On a Budget *(Col 1940)*
Blondie Has Servant Trouble *(Col 1940)*
Blondie Plays Cupid *(Col 1940)*

Blondie Goes Latin *(Col 1941)*
Blondie in Society *(Col 1941)*
Go West, Young Lady *(Col 1941)*
Blondie Goes to College *(Col 1942)*
Blondie's Blessed Event *(Col 1942)*
Blondie for Victory *(Col 1942)*
It's a Great Life *(Col 1943)*
Footlight Glamour *(Col 1943)*
Leave It to Blondie *(Col 1945)*
Life with Blondie *(Col 1946)*
Young Widow *(UA 1946)*
Blondie's Lucky Day *(Col 1946)*
Blondie Knows Best *(Col 1946)*
Blondie's Holiday *(Col 1947)*
Blondie's Big Moment *(Col 1947)*
Blondie in the Dough *(Col 1947)*
Blondie's Anniversary *(Col 1947)*
Blondie's Reward *(Col 1948)*
Blondie's Secret *(Col 1948)*
Blondie Hits the Jackpot *(Col 1949)*
Blondie's Big Deal *(Col 1949)*
Blondie's Hero *(Col 1950)*
Beware of Blondie *(Col 1950)*
The Best Man *(UA 1964)*

63

Anna Sten

Samuel Goldwyn's mid-Twenties success with Hungarian actress Vilma Banky was outshone by MGM who soon thereafter brought over Greta Garbo and by Paramount who in 1930 lured Marlene Dietrich to Hollywood. This situation led Goldwyn into trying to create his own bright international light in the Thirties. His choice was Russian-born Anna Sten, who became known as Goldwyn's Folly.

Anjuschka Stenski Sujakevitch was born on Thursday, December 3, 1908, in Kiev, the daughter of a Swedish mother and an Ukrainian father who taught ballet and folk dancing. When Anna was twelve her father was killed, leaving his wife and two daughters with a large string of debts. The young Anna found menial jobs in restaurants, and in her spare time joined an amateur theatre group. When a state-endowed theatrical company arrived in Kiev, Anna applied for a role in Gerhard Hauptmann's *Hennels Himmelfahrt*. When the great Stanislavsky arrived to direct the play, Anna was assigned the lead. The director's interest in the young performer resulted in her joining the Soviet Film Academy when she was fifteen. She learned film techniques in several minor films but mainly studied acting, eventually joining the famed Moscow Art Theatre where she appeared in repertory in plays by Ibsen, Pirandello, Maeterlinck, and Wedekin.

After a small role in a Sovkino film made in the Crimea, Anna was assigned the lead in *The Girl in the Hat Box* directed by Boris Barnet in 1927. Then, she won international recognition in *Zluta Knizka (The Yellow Ticket)* (1927) directed by Fyodor Otsep. As Maria Varenka, Sten gave a remarkably true portrayal that equaled Elissa Landi's playing of the tragic Maria in Fox's 1931 version. The success of the Meschaprom Studio film led Anna to play the lead in Vsevolod I. Pudovkin's masterful *Potomok Chingis-Khana (Storm over Asia)* (1928), a film that is today cited as one of the classics of Russian film-making.

Anna followed her experience with Pudovkin with *Moskva V Oktjabre* (1928), a slight comedy for Boris Barnet that was released in England and America as *Moscow Laughs and Cries* and *When Moscow Laughs,* respectively. In *Belyi Orel (The White Eagle)* (1928), based on Andreyev's *The Governor,* Anna was poorly photographed but gave a good performance as the governor's nurse in the Protazanov-directed feature which was called *The Lash of the Czar* in America. Meschaprom Studios later sent Anna and director Fyodor Otsep to Berlin to make films with the improved German equipment and facilities. There she learned to speak German and French, and she renewed her

With Lawrence Grant in *Nana* (UA '34).

acquaintance with Dr. Eugene Frenke. They recalled their first meeting in Moscow when Frenke had literally knocked her over on a Moscow Street and unsuccessfully sought her through mutual friends. Soon he became her mentor and guardian, and, in the fall of 1930, Anna became his wife and a stepmother to his thirteen-year-old daughter. In appearance Frenke resembled von Sternberg in that he had a persuasive jaw and piercing black eyes. He was an architect and a widower, and he devoted his time to Anna's career.

One of Anna's ambitions was to play Gruschenka in Dostoievsky's *The Brothers Karamazov*. To ensure that Anna's wish was fulfilled, Frenke produced the film, *Der Morder Dimitri Karamosoff* (1931), starring Anna and Fritz Kortner, with Otsep directing. It was flmed in both German and French versions. The picture was a tremendous success in Europe and Anna signed with the German studio UFA.

For Ewald Andre DuPont, Anna appeared as a seductive, defiant aerialist in *Salto Mortale* (1931), released to generally good reviews in the U.S. as *Trapeze*. For UFA she made *Bomben Auf Monte Carlo* (1931) and *Sturme Der Leidenschaft (Storms of Passion/The Tempest)* (1931), her last German film. The latter picture was with Emil Jannings and directed by Robert Siodmak. Her performance as Anya was remarkably lifelike and totally enhanced the film. She also sang two songs.

By this point Samuel Goldwyn had decided he wished to import Anna to Hollywood, hoping that she could become as big a star as his 1920s Hungarian import, Vilma Banky. He had seen Anna's *Der Morder Dimitri Karamosoff* and was enchanted with the Russian actress. The producer cabled his European representative to approach the stunning Miss Sten and offer her a screen test. Anna was given two pages of dialogue from Gloria Swanson's picture, *Indiscreet* (1931). She learned the lines by rote, and the test was fine. Mr. Goldwyn signed her and brought her to Hollywood, having her escorted from New York City by his hard-working press agent, Lynn Farnol.

Goldwyn instructed Farnol to make America "Anna Sten conscious," and Farnol did his job with commendable, if overzealous, enthusiasm. For two years the American press and fan magazines were deluged with copy on the passionate peasant of Kiev while Goldwyn was paying a small faculty of teachers to polish his Russian import who, alas, could speak no English.

It was first announced that Anna would recreate her triumph as Gruschenka in an English version of *The Brothers Karamazov*. Her costar was to be Ronald Colman. The *Karamazov* project was later abandoned in favor of co-starring Colman and Sten in *Way of a Lancer* to be directed by Richard Boleslawski. When Colman left Goldwyn's company that idea was dropped. Finally Goldwyn selected Zola's *Nana* (1934) to introduce his Soviet star. To direct Willard Mack and Harry Wagstaff Gribble's bowdlerized screen treatment of Zola's prostitute, Goldwyn assigned former great silent film director George Fitzmaurice, who had guided Ronald Colman and Vilma Banky through several pictures. Fitzmaurice had completed half of the expensively mounted *Nana* when Goldwyn decided to abandon Fitzmaurice's footage that had been filmed in an atmosphere of temperamental clashes between Sten and scene-reshooting Fitzmaurice. Goldwyn scrapped the $411,000 of exposed film and hired Dorothy Arzner to assume control of the project. Gregg Toland was retained as cameraman.

Nana was finally completed and broke first day attendance records when it opened at Radio City Music Hall in New York on February 1, 1934. Farnol's super-Sten campaign had produced a hit until the reviews appeared the following day. Critically Anna was well received, but the laundered version of Zola's famed character met with scoffs from the reviewers. Included in the final release print was an effective love scene between Sten and Phillips Holmes, filmed by Fitzmaurice, and Anna was heard singing a Rodgers and Hart song, "Kiss Me and Say Goodbye."

Sam Goldwyn and Phillips Holmes attended the *Nana* premiere in New York. Mr. Goldwyn expanded to reporters after the showing: "Only a woman with her emotional experience could interpret Zola. She has known hunger and cold and the fear of death. When I saw her in a Soviet film two years ago I knew that she had something real and new to give the screen. We have been training her for a year, teaching her English and technique. Hers is a very strange and remarkable story. During the Revolution, Miss Sten learned the meaning of misery. All day she served soup to the boisterous soldiers, hearing shots in the distance and seeing other women dragged screaming through the streets. And at night, along with the other poor of Moscow, she huddled in a pile of rags for warmth. Russia was suffering then for an ideal." Anna's version of her past was probably more accurate: "Then came the galloping Ukrainian revolutionists, brandishing lance and saber, then the storming White Army, followed by the mad attacks of the Bolshevists, the gaunt Polish warrior singing wild songs of victory. I stayed indoors and peeked out the window. I was a fly speck on the page of history!"

After the *Nana* debacle, rumors of the film's actual loss swept through Hollywood. According to columnist Dorothy Manners, it "came out on the wrong side of the financial ledger to the tune of about two-hundred thousand dollars!" Added to the fiasco were recurrent film colony tales of "La" Sten's demands and outbursts of temperament compared only with her nearest contemporary rival in the art of hell-fire-and-bedamned fireworks, RKO's effervescent Czech, Francis Lederer.

Of *Nana*, Anna later said: "I feel toward Nana as a mother toward a sick baby, a crippled child. Full of sadness, full of affection, borne with love. The first version, the one that was discarded, was not a bad picture. But it wasn't good enough to satisfy Mr.

In *We Live Again* (UA '35).

Goldwn, or myself either. It is hard to say just what was wrong, because everything was wrong. When I saw the rushes and the rough cut I was amazed to see that not only I but all the players reflected their unhappiness upon the screen. Even the gay scenes seemed clouded with woe. Believe you me, there was plenty of it." Anna was splendid in the opening scenes as an earthy laundress, but as she rose towards luxury the part seemed to throw her. Dr. Frenke insisted for years that Anna's greatest ability was to portray women of the earth. Perhaps he was correct.

Goldwyn next announced that his Soviet star would be co-starred with Gary Cooper and Edward G. Robinson in *Barbary Coast* (1935), suggested by Herbert Asbury's best-seller and adapted liberally for the screen by Ben Hecht and Charles MacArthur. Miss Sten was less than enraptured at adding another harlot to the cinema's endless hall of whores. Filming began under William Wyler, but after a few days, the production was shut down. Miss Sten obviously was miscast in the role of the infamous lady "Swan." It was announced Gloria Swanson might return to the screen as the soiled lady, but it was Miriam Hopkins who joined Joel McCrea and Edward G. Robinson when the project got underway again, this time under Howard Hawks' direction.

As for Anna, she was to return to Russia, at least on the screen. Showman Goldwyn set the likes of Preston Sturges, Maxwell Anderson, and Leonard Praskins to adapt Tolstoy's *Resurrection* for the next Sten vehicle. It was to be called *We Live Again* (1934) and was to co-star Fredric March under Rouben Mamoulian's direction. (While waiting for the drama to begin production, the Frenkes were delighted when Richard J. Neutra, one of the world's leading modern architects, was awarded a special prize by *House Beautiful* for his design of their home in Santa Monica Canyon.)

Anna was ecstatic about her new Goldwyn assignment. "It is Tolstoy whom I have always worshipped. It is a scene and a character with which I am familiar. It is a part I have always wanted to play. I am content with the production. Not that it matters what I think of it. The estimate of the public is important, not mine. Of course, one always feels that the next picture will be better. It is impossible to live in the past, to consider a completed accomplishment as the paramount achievement of one's career. But I feel that Mr. Goldwyn has done justice to this new *Resurrection*. And I, at least, have tried."

Anna was right on both counts. Goldwyn produced an excellent version of the Tolstoy novel and Sten seemed perfectly fine as the long-suffering Katusha Maslova whose lover, Prince Dimitri Nekhlyudov, deserts her for the riotous living of Russian officers, only to rejoin her for a five-year sentence to Siberia. *Photoplay* magazine selected Anna and March as the best performers of the month, along with *We Live Again* as one of the best pictures of the month. Of the five American movie versions of the story, the Sten-March combination proved the best of the lot.

Goldwyn next selected *Broken Soil,* a story by Edwin Knopf, in which to team Anna with Gary Cooper, tossing in Ralph Bellamy for good measure. Leonard Praskins, who had collaborated with Anderson and Sturges on the *Resurrection* project, called the third picture "Goldwyn's last Sten." It was. King Vidor, who directed what would be called *The Wedding Night* (1935), would later recall that Gary Cooper and Anna were valiantly struggling with the insipid dialogue and losing the battle when Goldwyn's patience erupted. He launched into an eloquent plea for effort and cooperation, elaborating on his box-office poverty and claiming his entire career was staked on the success of this project. He concluded his tirade with, "And I tell you that if this scene isn't the greatest love scene ever put on film, the whole goddamned picture will go right up out of the sewer!"

In *The Wedding Night,* Anna played Manya who flings herself down a flight of stairs and dies rather than marry a man she does not love. The astute Mr. Goldwyn knew of

With Gary Cooper in *Wedding Night* (UA '35).

what he spoke and his tirade of fear was realized at the box-office where the picture flopped. The fiasco of *The Wedding Night* ended the Goldwyn-Sten association under mutual consent.

"We parted friends," said Anna. "I admire Mr. Goldwyn. I respect Mr. Goldwyn. I wish him well. But I will sign no more long contracts." She also denied a good deal of the publicity-generated stories about her and then left with her husband for England. There she made *Two Who Dared* (1936) directed by her husband. She played Maria, a Russian peasant done wrong by Henry Wilcoxon. The film was also known as *A Woman Alone,* but did little business under either title.

The Frenkes returned to Hollywood, and Anna made her radio debut on Tuesday, July 21, 1936, on Caravan's broadcast of *I Love an Actress,* with Walter Abel. In September, 1936, she was a guest star with Jack Oakie on Bob Burns' variety show, and on February 8, 1937, she was heard on "Lux Radio Theatre" with Gene Raymond in *Graustark.* In early summer of 1936 Dr. Frenke announced he would produce a film for Universal starring his wife. It was to be called *The Witch.* But Anna's next film appearance was not until 1939 in a United Players Production (produced by Dr. Frenke) Grand National release called *Exile Express,* a confused tale of a foreigner's (Anna) problems in obtaining her U.S. citizenship through a hodgepodge of spies and murders.

Twentieth Century-Fox's *The Man I Married* (1940) gave Anna the striking supporting role of an ardent Nazi, who converts Joan Bennett's half-Jewish, half-German, American-born husband (Francis Lederer) to Nazism. Following another well-done supporting role in a tale of Jewish refugees, *So Ends Our Night* (1941), Anna struck out in a new venture, the American stage. During the summer of 1941 she appeared alternately from June until mid-August in *Smart Women* and *Nancy's Private Affair.* Then Alan Dinehart, seeking a name replacement for Glenda Farrell in *Separate Rooms,* saw Sten perform; she joined the long-running Broadway show on August 24, 1941. Anna played sixteen

493

performances on Broadway and when the show closed on September 6, 1941 (after 613 performances), she continued on an extensive road tour with the comedy.

In 1943 Anna returned to Twentieth Century-Fox as the wife of freedom fighter Philip Dorn in *Chetniks,* a modestly produced story of Yugoslavia's underground warfare. Then Anna came through with excellent work as the wife of a Nazi whom George Sanders is impersonating in *They Came to Blow up America.* She completed the year by being reunited with her old friend and one of her best directors, Fyodor Otsep (billed as Fedor Ozep), in a minor United Artists release, *Three Russian Girls,* in which she performed well as a nurse bravely volunteering for duty on the Russian front and saving the life of downed American flyer Kent Smith.

During the 1944-1945 season Anna returned to the stage at Hollywood's Jewel Box Theatre in *Black Savannah,* a new play that expired after a brief run. Dr. Frenke and actor Robert Cummings produced a slapstick comedy for Eagle Lion in 1948 called *Let's Live a Little.* During its inane progress, Cummings flings cold cream at Anna and seeks the help of femme psychiatrist Hedy Lamarr, of all people.

Anna reappeared on the nation's screen as Mme. Dupree in Twentieth Century-Fox's Clark Gable-Susan Hayward starrer *Soldier of Fortune* (1955). She did an unbilled bit in her husband's production filmed in the British West Indies on the island of Tobago. Frenke co-produced *Heaven Knows, Mr. Allison* (1957) with Buddy Adler for Twentieth Century-Fox, and the two credited cast members, Deborah Kerr and Robert Mitchum, were directed by John Huston. In the midst of these occasional film bits, Anna appeared as Jenny (Lotta Lenya's role) in the Marc Blitzstein adaptation of *The Three Penny Opera* at the Marine's Memorial Theatre in San Francisco. She was quite effective. Anna's last screen appearance to date was in her husband's production for United Artists, *The Nun and the Sergeant* (1962), a routine Korean War melodrama with Anna as the nun and Robert Webber as the sergeant. While her husband continued producing films, Anna started dabbling with paint and canvas, and in a few years attained recognition as an artist, having her paintings shown (and sold) on both coasts in one-woman shows.

If Anna Sten's screen career was not as memorable as many other ladies of the Thirties, it was surely the most publicized and overblown. Goldwyn Pictures rarely backed flops, and the public associated topflight professionalism with the Goldwyn name. After his experience with Miss Sten—finally tagged "The Edsel of the motion picture industry"—the former Samuel Goldfish, within two years, was again beating the publicity drums for another "new" discovery, this one from Norway and hailed as the new exotic importation. She was Sigrid Gurie from the fjords of Brooklyn.

> "Regardless of every other consideration Anna Sten is the outstanding showmanship asset of *Nana.* Temptation to compare her to Garbo or Dietrich should be ignored. She promises so much in her right as to merit introduction to the public exclusively as herself."
>
> —*Motion Picture Herald*

> "She will dazzle the eyes of the most blase theatregoer. She is not only beautiful, she is breathtaking."
>
> —*Louella O. Parsons*

ANNA STEN

Devushka a Korobkoi *(Russian 1927)*
Zluta Knizka [The Yellow Ticket] *(Russian 1927)*
Potomok Chingis-Khana *(Russian 1928)*
Moskva V Oktjabre [Moscow Laughs and Cries/When Moscow Laughs] *(Russian 1928)*
Belyi Orel [The White Eagle] *(Russian 1928)*
Moj Syn *(Russian 1929)*
Zolotoj Kljuv *(Russian 1929)*
Der Morder Dimitri Karamosoff *(German 1931)*
Salto Mortale [Trapeze] *(German 1931)*
Bomben Auf Monte Carlo [Storms of Passion/The Tempest] *(German 1931)*
Sturme Der Leidenschaft *(German 1932)*

Nana *(UA 1934)*
We Live Again *(UA 1934)*
The Wedding Night *(UA 1935)*
Two Who Dared [A Woman Alone] *(Grand National 1936)*
Exile Express *(Grand National 1939)*
The Man I Married *(20th 1940)*
So Ends Our Night *(UA 1941)*
Chetniks *(20th 1943)*
They Came to Blow up America *(20th 1943)*
Three Russian Girls *(UA 1943)*
Let's Live a Little *(EL 1948)*
Soldier of Fortune *(20th 1955)*
Heaven Knows, Mr. Allison *(20th 1957)*
The Nun and the Sergeant *(UA 1962)*

64

Gloria Stuart

A great number of film appearances as an ingenue may make an actress popular, but it does not guarantee stardom. Such was the case of Gloria Stuart who, in the Thirties, made over forty features while under contract first to Universal and then later in the decade to Twentieth Century-Fox, but never made it to the high pinnacle of star status.

Gloria was born on Monday, July 4, 1910, in Santa Monica, California. Her grandfather, Von Dietrich, had sailed around the Horn in 1846 and had settled in Grass Valley in northern California. He changed his name to Vaughan and was noted as the inventor of the Fresco scraper, used extensively in road building. Pioneering grandfather Vaughan's daughter, Alice, married a Texas oil man by the name of Finch, and they eventually settled in Santa Monica where daughter Gloria grew up. After completing high school she entered the University of California at Berkeley, where she majored in philosophy and joined the Berkeley Players.

At college she met handsome, talented sculptor Blair Gordon Newell. In one of Santa Monica's more elaborate weddings, she married the San Francisco artist in June, 1930. They moved to Carmel, California, and settled into a bohemian life, two intense, vital young people pursuing culture in a hillside shack. Newell created wood carvings and sculpturing that produced some twenty dollars a month, while Gloria wrote for the local weekly newspaper, *The Carmelite,* for twenty-five dollars a month while continuing her studies in acting. She worked with the Theatre of the Golden Bough under the direction of Morris Ankrum and Sam Kuster.

Gilmor Brown, director of Pasadena's famed Community Playhouse, saw Gloria at the Golden Bough and invited her to appear with his company of players. At Pasadena she played Olivia in *Twelfth Night* and repeated her role of Masha in *The Sea Gull* which had impressed Brown in Carmel. Carl Laemmle, Jr. and Universal's casting director Phil Friedman saw her Chekhovian performance and gave her a screen test. Paramount also invited the lovely, natural-blonde actress to make a test, and, liking the results, quickly offered a contract. Serene, poised Gloria was a revelation to the studios before ever appearing in a film. Here was an attractive, native-born blonde with brains, charm, and talent, who fended off Paramount with, "I'll let you know tomorrow. They've asked to see me at Universal and I have to go there before I decide."

Since Universal was offering her far more money than Paramount, the two studios became engaged in a battle of priorities on her tests and contractual commitments. Then

With Claude Gillingwater and Warner Baxter in *The Prisoner of Shark Island* (20th '36).

Will Hays, the dean of censors, was asked to officiate in the matter before an arbitration committee. Paramount contended it was a matter of principle. Universal countered with first claim rights, reinforcing their argument by Paramount's lost opportunity at signing her. The deadlock persisted until Laemmle suggested tossing a coin for her. Paramount lost. Thus, there remains the unanswerable question of whether her career would have been better at Paramount than Universal. However, the coin-tossing Laemmle had great plans for the film colony's unseen, highly publicized dark horse.

Laemmle, Jr. glowed over her screen potential. "This girl is, well I never have seen such poise, such delicate beauty, such depth, why she almost scares you. We'll have to find some truly distinguished stories for her, in fact, the finest, because, you see, nothing else would be quite fitting. It would be foolish, and rather embarrassing all around, to put her in—well, a trivial story." But with minor exceptions, Universal never gave her a role that could have established her potential star status.

Meanwhile Gloria did make her screen debut with Kay Francis in Warner Bros.' *Street of Women* (1932), playing a sweet ingenue role. Universal cast her in much the same mold in their football tale, *The All-American* (1932). She was little more than decorative, registering constant alarm and fright in *The Old Dark House* (1932), a Universal classic which boasted a remarkable cast: Charles Laughton, Melvyn Douglas, Raymond Massey, and Boris Karloff.

Laemmle's elaborate plans for Gloria continued to drift off course. Her first year at Universal constituted little threat to Greta Garbo, to whom she was strangely compared (although she more closely resembled Jeanne Eagels both in appearance and acting mannerisms). In 1932 Gloria was wasted in *Laughter in Hell*, but, in 1933, she was chosen as one of Hollywood's future Wampas Baby Stars, along with Ginger Rogers, Mary Carlisle, Patricia Ellis, Evelyn Knapp, June Clyde, Lillian Bond, and other personalities most of whom never made the grade. For Universal, Gloria played YMCA worker Mary Gregg married to Donald Cook and loved by *Private Jones* (Lee Tracy), one of her

497

lighter 1933 offerings. She was loaned to RKO for a superior role in John Cromwell's *Sweepings* (1933). As Lionel Barrymore's headline-making daughter, Gloria was excellent. Her performance was a declaration that she was capable of playing women of depth far beyond the sweet innocent ingenue roles that Universal had tossed to her.

James Whale directed an unusual Universal picture, *The Kiss before the Mirror* (1933), with Gloria as the bitchy, bored wife of professor Paul Lukas. The film was an exercise in decorous adultery in which all the principals were caught between jealous husbands and lovers. Gloria is killed for her philandering, but lawyer Frank Morgan, having similar problems with his wife Nancy Carroll, gets an acquittal for Lukas.

Gloria's personal life was undergoing more than a period of adjustment. She and Blair Gordon Newell agreed their careers were in conflict and that a trial separation might save their marriage. Gloria was telling the press, "We are both at the formative period of our careers, and we have felt that we should be free to pursue them unfettered by obligations toward each other. We both feel sure that by the time a year has rolled by we shall have found ourselves and become better established and each better able to understand and appreciate the problems of the other."

Gloria gave an impressive performance in *The Invisible Man* (1933), which was Claude Rains' film debut under James Whale's direction. Offscreen, Gloria was further explaining her experiment in marital meliorism: "We are lovers again! Instead of being staid, old married people, we are back already to our courting days! Life flows on happily and there is hardly an evening that we are not together at my apartment, or at a show or some social affair. But if the evening begins to pall on either one of us, Blair goes home to his studio apartment and there is not some meaningless and totally reasonless clash of temperament."

In 1933 Universal loaned Gloria to United Artists for Eddie Cantor's frantic farce *Roman Scandals,* in which she had the romantic lead opposite David Manners. She was quite lovely in white flowing togas. Samuel Goldwyn, the film's producer, was intrigued with her classic beauty and talent, claiming: "The old-fashioned method of picking up an ingenue and a juvenile from the back lot won't do. We must have people who not only can act, but who look right in the characters they portray. Especially in the case of women, for there they must be exceptionally attractive." During the filming of *Roman Scandals* Gloria met writer Arthur Sheekman, former drama and music critic in Chicago and St. Paul who had become scenarist for a few Marx Brothers' films as well as a writer for Eddie Cantor. The erudite, witty, and charming Mr. Sheekman found Mrs. Newell supremely attractive and blessed with a lively, active mind. She soon instituted a peaceful divorce from Blair Newell and, on July 29, 1934, wed Arthur Sheekman in Agua Caliente, Mexico.

The Sheekmans soon became one of Hollywood's most popular couples. On June 10, 1935, their daughter Sylvia was born, and their home on De Longpre Avenue was a constant gathering place for the intelligentsia of Hollywood. When they moved into The Garden of Allah in 1943, the Sheekmans became the entertaining catalysts for the various assorted oddball residents of the Garden, among whom were Dorothy Parker, Robert Benchley, Charles Butterworth, Louis Calhern, and George S. Kaufman. Gloria became renowned for her gourmet cooking.

Her screen work at Universal varied between lead roles and being part of the prescribed romantic background for several films. She was especially good in a cavalcade of music and romance of the 1800s with John Boles, *Beloved* (1934), but Universal's other assignments for her were in generally weak features. For Warners she played Pat O'Brien's sister, who is desired by his arch rival James Cagney, in *Here Comes the Navy* (1934). She instilled some sparkle in a none-too-exciting remake of *Saturday's Children*

At Twentieth Century-Fox in '37.

With Michael Whalen in *Change of Heart* (20th '38).

by First National called *Maybe It's Love* (1935). In one of Warner Bros.' lesser *Gold Diggers* entries, that *of 1935,* she played Alice Brady's daughter and joined Dick Powell in the song "I'm Going Shopping with You." And at RKO she was the nice young woman torn between her caste-minded father (Donald Crisp) and her love for John Beal in *Laddie* (1935).

By now her Universal days were finished and Gloria signed a term pact with Twentieth Century-Fox, where Darryl F. Zanuck's predilection for blonde stars would make celebrities of Alice Faye, Shirley Temple, and Betty Grable, but not Gloria. She was the wife of Dr. Mudd (Warner Baxter), the physician who administered to John Wilkes Booth's wounds following the actor's assassination of President Lincoln in John Ford's *The Prisoner of Shark Island* (1936). She supplied distaff decoration for *Professional Soldier* (1936) and for Shirley Temple's *The Poor Little Rich Girl* (1936). She played the lead in an adventurous picture on mercy killing, *The Crime of Dr. Forbes* (1936). Her successful marriage and growing fame as a hostess made her film work virtually a secondary career, although she gave her best in a long series of lesser roles in similar pictures, including two adventures with the Ritz Brothers, *Life Begins in College* (1937) and *The Three Musketeers* (1939). In the latter she was an exquisite Queen Anne.

On September 20, 1938, Gloria was elected to the Board of Directors of the Screen Actors Guild under President Ralph Morgan and Vice-Presidents Joan Crawford, James Cagney, and Edward Arnold. With the Communist witch hunt beginning in Hollywood, Gloria joined the Committee of 56 and signed their Declaration of Democratic Independence along with Claude Rains, Henry Fonda, Paul Muni, Cagney, Laemmle, Sr., Groucho Marx, and many others.

Her contract with Twentieth Century-Fox ended in 1939 and enabled her to return to the stage. During the summer of 1940 she went East to appear on the straw-hat circuit in *The Night of January 13th*, co-starred with Donald Brian in *Accent on Youth*, and finished the summer season at the Amherst Drama Festival by joining Francis Lederer in *Pursuit of Happiness*. The summer of 1941 became her most active season on the stage. On June 9 she replaced Madge Evans in *Man and Superman* at the University of Michigan Summer Festival; on July 7 opened in *Mr. and Mrs. North* in Suffern, New York; and played in the American premiere performance of Ivor Novello's British play *Comedienne*, retitled *Curtain Going Up*, with Constance Collier, Violet Heming, Mel Ferrer, and Jinx Falkenburg at the Cape Playhouse on Cape Cod, Massachusetts. She closed the season by starring with Warren Hull in the tryout of a new Ward Morehouse play, *U.S. 90*, at the Paper Mill Playhouse in New Jersey.

The following summer (in 1942) Gloria was back on the boards at Brattle Hall, Cambridge, Massachusetts, in *The Dark Tower*, and later she played the New York City subway circuit in Brooklyn and Flatbush with Eric Linden in *Sailor Beware*. Her last four motion pictures were hardly notable, including *The Whistler* (1944), part of the Columbia-Richard Dix series. She returned to her first studio for her final film, *She Wrote the Book* (1946). It was a minor comedy with Joan Davis and Jack Oakie.

Thereafter she retired from the entertainment scene, content to be a wife and mother. She later developed her interest in painting and created several one-woman shows of her work. Her daughter, Sylvia, became a successful author, and, as Mrs. Vaughn Thompson, the mother of four children, lives in Malibu beach, California.

Recently Gloria, who lives in Brentwood with her husband, returned to acting, this time on television. She appeared in an episode of "The Waltons" and on such telefeatures as *The Legend of Lizzie Borden* and *Adventures of the Queen*. Such is the endurance of the actress who was once touted as the bright light of Universal Pictures.

GLORIA STUART

Street of Women *(WB 1932)*
The Old Dark House *(Univ 1932)*
The All-American *(Univ 1932)*
Airmail *(Univ 1932)*
Laughter in Hell *(Univ 1932)*
Roman Scandals *(UA 1933)*
The Kiss before the Mirror *(Univ 1933)*
Private Jones *(Univ 1933)*
The Girl in 419 *(Par 1933)*
It's Great to be Alive *(Fox 1933)*
The Invisible Man *(Univ 1933)*
Secret of the Blue Room *(Univ 1933)*
Sweepings *(RKO 1933)*
Beloved *(Univ 1934)*
I Like It that Way *(Univ 1934)*
I'll Tell the World *(Univ 1934)*
Here Comes the Navy *(WB 1934)*
The Love Captive *(Univ 1934)*
Gift of Gab *(Univ 1934)*
Maybe It's Love *(FN 1935)*
Gold Diggers of 1935 *(WB 1935)*
Laddie *(RKO 1935)*
The Prisoner of Shark Island *(20th 1936)*

Professional Soldier *(20th 1936)*
The Poor Little Rich Girl *(20th 1936)*
36 Hours to Kill *(20th 1936)*
The Girl on the Front Page *(Univ 1936)*
Wanted: Jane Turner *(RKO 1936)*
The Crime of Dr. Forbes *(20th 1936)*
The Lady Escapes *(20th 1937)*
Girl Overboard *(Univ 1937)*
Life Begins in College *(20th 1937)*
Rebecca of Sunnybrook Farm *(20th 1938)*
Change of Heart *(20th 1938)*
Island in the Sky *(20th 1938)*
Keep Smiling *(20th 1938)*
Time Out for Murder *(20th 1938)*
The Lady Objects *(20th 1938)*
The Three Musketeers *(20th 1939)*
It Could Happen to You *(20th 1939)*
Winner Take All *(20th 1939)*
Here Comes Elmer *(Rep 1943)*
The Whistler *(Col 1944)*
Enemy of Women *(Mon 1944)*
She Wrote the Book *(Univ 1946)*

65

Genevieve Tobin

Sophisticated, witty, and possessing a remarkable versatility that Hollywood rarely used (she sang, danced, played both the piano and harp, and was a brilliant actress), Genevieve was a recurrent figure in features of the Thirties. During her peak period in Hollywood she remained aloof from the film colony regulars, numbering among her closer friends the expatriates of Broadway who had come to California for greater riches. After her sixth film she told the press: "I have been making money for years. My family and my friends have amused me when I wasn't working. I love acting but I don't expect to go on emoting indefinitely. Oh, no! When the time comes that I need the companionship of a husband, I'll retire." On September 20, 1938, she wed director William Keighley. She made only four more pictures after that marriage, and that marriage still flourishes today.

Thomas Jerome Tobin and his wife Genevieve (White) Tobin had four children. George was the eldest, followed by Genevieve, Bobby, and Vivian. Genevieve was born on Friday, November 29, 1901. Although there was no theatrical heritage in the family, the Tobin children began acting careers rather early in their lives. Genevieve made her stage debut on Broadway with brothers George and Bobby in David Belasco's production of *The Grand Army Man*, starring David Warfield. Then it was back to school. Genevieve was soon back on the stage at Wallack's Theatre in April, 1912, in a special children's production of *Disraeli*. Her next stage venture was as a boy in *As a Man Thinks* starring John Mason and Chrystal Herne. After playing a bit in the Chicago company of *The Polish Wedding*, Genevieve and her sister were sent to school, first in Brittany, then to Paris where for two years they attended a convent, L'Institute de l'Etoile.

When the girls returned to America after the outbreak of World War I, they adapted a playlet, *The Age of Reason*, into a vaudeville act. Later Genevieve won a role in *Oh, Look!*, a musical starring comedian George Sidney. The show ran for sixty-eight performances following its New York opening on March 7, 1918. Later Genevieve toured in *My Country Cousin* and was back on Broadway in October, 1919, in *Palmy Days*. Her largest assignment at this time was in *Little Old New York* (September 8, 1920), produced by Sam Harris, who borrowed Miss Tobin from her contractual employer, producer Arthur Hopkins. The role of Patricia O'Day was to keep her occupied for two years on Broadway and on the road. Next came *Polly Preferred* (1923) and then the musical *Dear Sir* (1924), featuring Walter Catlett and Oscar Shaw.

With Jack Holt in *The Wrecker* (Col '35).

With Effie Shannon and Henry Hull, Genevieve played in Philip Barry's *The Youngest* (1924) and was thereafter seen in *Treat 'Em Rough* (1926) and *This Woman Business* (1926). Star-playwright Leslie Howard was her leading man in *Murray Hill* (1927), but the farce lasted a mere twenty-eight performances. Finding new roles increasingly difficult to obtain, Genevieve sailed for England where she subsequently made her London stage bow in the West End production of *The Trial of Mary Dugan* (March 2, 1928). *The Bystander* reported "As Mary Dugan, she gives a performance of admirable restraint, and her humours on the witness stand are very rich."

It was back in America that one of her best theatrical parts awaited her. On November 27, 1929, she starred in *Fifty Million Frenchmen*. It was Cole Porter's first smash hit and it was aided a great deal by acerbic Helen Broderick and exuberant, extroverted William Gaxton. With the latter, Genevieve sang the show's hit tune, "You Do Something to Me." Ironically when Warner Bros. purchased the screen rights and made a film of *Fifty Million Frenchmen,* they imported Broderick and Gaxton to repeat their roles, but did not use Genevieve. By then she was under contract to Universal, churning out hasty screen items.

Her first screen encounter had been for Fox in 1923 in a flop entitled *No Mother to*

503

Guide Her. Advertised as "a human drama of life's pitfalls," the script drew generously from *Tess of the Storm Country* and convinced Genevieve, for the time being, that the cinema was *not* for her. But in 1930 she signed with Universal and was put into two steamy properties. *A Lady, Surrenders* (1930), with Conrad Nagel and Basil Rathbone, was advertised as, "an ultra modern romance of smart set love." *Free Love* (1930) had Conrad Nagel and Ilka Chase supporting Genevieve in a film that was advertised nationally as "Risque! Frank! Should a Wife have Affairs?" Unfortunately Miss Tobin offered a rather affected performance in the role of Hope Ferrier.

Universal continued her in the same mold, casting her in *Seed* (1931) as John Boles' ex-flame who returns to inspire him to write. That he is married, with a wife and five children, seemed to be a moot point. Over at RKO she joined Betty Compson, Ivan Lebedeff, and Ilka Chase in the amusing *The Gay Diplomat* (1931). *Motion Picture Herald* reported, "Genevieve Tobin is very rapidly getting to be our favorite actress." If anyone doubted her expert timing and droll playing, Paramount's *One Hour with You* (1932) should have dispelled that wonder. The picture was started by George Cukor, but after two weeks of directing the picture, he was relieved by Ernst Lubitsch, although he did remain on the set as dialogue director. Within the saucy plot line, Maurice Chevalier is pursued by a delightful sexpot (Genevieve) only to have her insanely jealous husband (Roland Young) file for divorce, naming Chevalier as co-respondent. *Photoplay* selected Genevieve's supporting role (Jeanette MacDonald was *the* co-star) as one of the best, while the *New York Times* offered, "Genevieve Tobin gives a very pleasing perform-ance as the flirt, Mitzi." After the film's New York opening at the Rivoli and Rialto Theatres in March, 1932, one cosmopolitan critic was led to write, "Until she appeared as the naughty but alluring Mitzi in *One Hour with You,* a lot of us were immune to the Tobin charm."

From her huge success in the Chevalier picture, Genevieve made a quickie for Columbia, *Hollywood Speaks* (1932), and left for England to contribute a fine support-ing performance as Kitty in the production of *Perfect Understanding* (1933), which starred Gloria Swanson and Laurence Olivier. Back in America her screen roles were less than spectacular, such as Elinor in *Infernal Machine* (1933) and the flirting wife in Frank Tuttle's *Pleasure Cruise* (1933), in which Roland Young was again a frenetic husband. *The Wrecker* (1933) had Genevieve trapped with lover Sidney Blackmer during an earthquake, and *Goodbye Again* (1933) featured her as Warren William's old college sweetheart who proves to be his current nemesis. Later that year she played, with quiet restraint and a good deal of charm, the role of the ignored wife while husband Edward G. Robinson is having an affair with opera star Kay Francis in *I Loved a Woman.*

By this point it was becoming apparent to the film industry hierarchy that Miss Tobin's special charms were not strong enough to warrant major stardom. Yet in Paramount's *Golden Harvest* (1933), she played a difficult role very cleverly. For Warner Bros.' *Easy to Love* (1934) she was able to resolve the anxieties of middle age and marriage with Adolphe Menjou and Mary Astor. This film was directed by the charming, personable William Keighley. Then, as prim and prudish Marge Mayhew, Genevieve offered an offbeat characterization opposite Edward G. Robinson in *Dark Hazard* (1934).

Kiss and Make Up (1934) found her full of delight and charm as Eve who divorces Edward Everett Horton for the much more attractive beauty specialist, Cary Grant. She was back with Frank Morgan again as his spouse guiding him through male menopause and listening to his plight of wanting a "final fling" in *By Your Leave* (1934). As the sharp-clawed, sharper-tongued predatory widow, Nicko, Genevieve was marvelously bitchy in *The Woman in Red* (1935), adding fuel to the explosive marriage of Gene Raymond to wrong-side-of-the-tracks Barbara Stanwyck. After a loan-out to Fox to play

At Warner Bros. in the mid-Thirties.

a wealthy patroness in Nino Martini's *Here's to Romance* (1935), she was back on the Warners lot (where she had a contract) to play one of the many cinema Della Streets in the Perry Mason mystery *The Case of the Lucky Legs* (1935). This was followed by a sub-program picture, *Broadway Hostess* (1935). It was the studio's way of saying they had little regard for her talents.

Nevertheless, Genevieve was superb as the frustrated, bitter, and wealthy Mrs. Chisholm in Warner Bros.' excellent filming of *The Petrified Forest* (1936), in which Bette Davis, Leslie Howard, and Humphrey Bogart had the key roles. After a routine assignment with George Brent in *Snowed Under* (1936), a mindless farce, she returned to the stage in a tryout of a new play by Michael Sheridan. It was *Tomorrow We Live* and was presented at the El Capitan Theatre in Hollywood. Minor Watson and Helen Mack were her co-stars. After two more supporting film roles in the Hollywood production mill, she left for England to film *The Man in the Mirror* (1936) with Edward Everett Horton and Ursula Jeans, and then Edgar Wallace's *Kate Plus Ten* (1938), in which she is loved by a police inspector and successfully manages a gang of train robbers. (The latter picture was released in 1941 by Film Alliance of America as *The Queen of Crime*.) Back in the States, Miss Tobin signed with Metro for the role of Gina Bertier in their less-than-top-calibre *Dramatic School* (1938), which was a vehicle for Luise Rainer.

George Cukor always had a fond spot for Genevieve and saw to it that she had a role in *Zaza* (1939), in which Claudette Colbert was the replacement lead for Paramount's import Isa Miranda. However, Genevieve seemed forced and ill-at-ease as Florianne. Then she was the alluring divorcée, Aunt Connie, hunting any available man in *Yes, My Darling Daughter* (1939), with Priscilla Lane, Jeffrey Lynn, and Fay Bainter. Even though the Broadway play had been laundered for the screen it was banned in, of all places, New York City. However, with judicious pruning, Warner Bros. finally opened the comedy there at two theatres, and business was very brisk. From the great publicity given *Yes, My Darling Daughter,* Fay Bainter and Genevieve transferred to Paramount for *Our Neighbors, the Carters,* an unpretentious film that was rumored to be the pilot for a series that never developed. (Bainter and Frank Craven were the Carters, with Genevieve and Edmund Lowe as their neighbors—it was all a sort of middle-aged *Andy Hardy* venture.)

Genevieve's final acting fling before the cameras was in Warner Bros.' *No Time for Comedy* (1940). As Amanda Swift, self-created, if foolish, patroness of the arts, with a little amour on the side, Miss Tobin and her patient, amused husband in the film, Charles Ruggles, overshadowed Rosalind Russell and James Stewart, who had the key roles. William Keighley had directed both *Darling Daughter* and *No Time for Comedy*.

After her marriage to Keighley, Genevieve kept to her original intent of retirement. She was a wealthy, resourceful woman who accumulated a sizeable fortune through thrift and wise investments. During the World War II years, the Keighleys lived in Washington, D.C., and then from 1945 to 1955, William was Cecil B. DeMille's successor as host-supervisor of "Lux Radio Theatre" (on which talented Genevieve never appeared). Thereafter the Keighleys moved to Paris to live in an ultrafashionable apartment on Avenue Foch. They traveled extensively, with Keighley giving lectures with his travel films. (He has produced an extensive series of slides which have become a very valuable collection.) Following a stroke in 1972, Mr. Keighley's activities slowed considerably, but early in 1974 they returned to New York City where Keighley presented some 70,000 of his slides to the Metropolitan Museum. While in Manhattan, the couple attended the Warner Bros. film festival at the Museum of Modern Art, and the devoted duo were able to tell acquaintances in the theatre audience anecdotes about the pictures being screened. Some forty years after her cinema peak, Genevieve remains as delightful and charming as ever.

With Cary Grant and Helen Mack in *Kiss and Make Up* (Par '34).

GENEVIEVE TOBIN

No Mother to Guide Her *(Fox 1923)*
A Lady Surrenders *(Univ 1930)*
Free Love *(Univ 1930)*
Seed *(Univ 1931)*
Up for Murder *(Univ 1931)*
The Gay Diplomat *(RKO 1931)*
One Hour with You *(Par 1932)*
Hollywood Speaks *(Col 1932)*
The Cohens and Kellys in Hollywood *(Univ 1932)*
Infernal Machine *(Fox 1933)*
Perfect Understanding *(UA 1933)*
Pleasure Cruise *(Fox 1933)*
The Wrecker *(Col 1933)*
Goodbye Again *(FN 1933)*
I Loved a Woman *(FN 1933)*
Golden Harvest *(Par 1933)*
The Ninth Guest *(Col 1934)*
Easy to Love *(WB 1934)*
Dark Hazard *(FN 1934)*
Uncertain Lady *(Univ 1934)*

Success at Any Price *(RKO 1934)*
Kiss and Make Up *(Par 1934)*
By Your Leave *(RKO 1934)*
The Woman in Red *(FN 1935)*
The Goose and the Gander *(WB 1935)*
Here's to Romance *Fox 1935*
The Case of the Lucky Legs *(WB 1935)*
Broadway Hostess *(FN 1935)*
The Petrified Forest *(WB 1936)*
Snowed Under *(FN 1936)*
The Man in the Mirror *(Wardour 1936)*
The Great Gambini *(Par 1937)*
The Duke Comes Back *(Rep 1937)*
Kate Plus Ten [The Queen of Crime] *(General Film Distributors 1938)*
Dramatic School *(MGM 1938)*
Zaza *(Par 1939)*
Yes, My Darling Daughter *(WB 1939)*
Our Neighbors, the Carters *(Par 1939)*
No Time for Comedy *(WB 1940)*

66

Lee Tracy

Hollywood's publicity mills did not have to create glamorized fiction or imaginative legends for Lee Tracy. He lived at a pace that defied a publicist's dream and seemed to approach life with a perpetual thumb to his nose. He had an unconcealed contempt for many of Hollywood's pretentions of genius and an insatiable thirst that would have astounded Alcoholics Anonymous. He was tall and slim and possessed of an electric energy that ignited many fine performances on both stage and screen. In a town that had more than its quota of oddball characters, he managed to be tagged "the Bad Boy of Hollywood." And he was a good actor to boot.

William Lee Tracy was born on Thursday, April 14, 1898, in Atlanta, Georgia, to William Lindsay Tracy and Rachel Griffith Tracy. His father was general superintendent of motive power for the Lehigh Valley Railroad and his mother was a retired school teacher. The demands of his father's occupation kept the Tracy clan on a constant move and young Lee attended Western Military Academy in Alton, Illinois. He worked with his father on the railroad during summer vacations. The family then moved to Schenectady, New York, and Lee matriculated at Union College in 1918.

While at Union College in Schenectady he attended two performances of *Way Down East.* After the show, he went backstage to compliment the star, Walker Whiteside, who, after encouraging the stagestruck youth to read part of the script, offered him an opening in the company. William's brief tour was interrupted by World War I, but his appetite for the theatre had been whetted. He entered the Army Information Branch as a Second Lieutenant and spent his brief military career in Camp Lee, Va. After his Army discharge he gave up any further pursuit of the theatre to become a U.S. Treasury Agent for almost two years.

In 1919 he sent his father a telegram, "Going on the stage. Have engagement with Harry Horton, who used to play in *The Old Homestead.* We're in vaudeville." He played the Loew's vaudeville circuit in this sketch until he bought a playlet for himself. It was called *Bonded Stock* and lasted a quick five weeks on the road. He then joined stock companies in St. Louis, Dallas, and Baltimore, and in September, 1923, played Jackson of the Drew Agency in a road tour of *Whispering Wires.*

While appearing with the Pierre Watkins Players in Baltimore, Tracy was signed for his first Broadway role, as Joe in George Kelly's *The Show Off.* Tracy followed his main stem debut with appearances in *The Book of Charm; Glory, Hallelujah;* and then

508

With John Barrymore in *Dinner at Eight* (MGM '33).

succeeded Hugh O'Connell in the roles of Kellogg and Elliott in *The Wisdom Tooth*. But it was Philip Dunning and George Abbott's *Broadway* in 1926 that made a star of Tracy. The play, which soon was so imitated that it became a cliche itself, concerned a bootlegger, an actress, and a hoofer (Tracy). The New York Critics Association gave Lee their Award for the season's best performance.

No one was more amazed than Tracy who said: "I did not realize it that night at the Broadhurst Theatre, September 16, 1926. There had been so many rehearsals and so much breaking in, that is a kind of breakage of the spirit, on the road; there had been so many things to do and to remember that I was numb. I only had a sense that there would be one more act and it would be over. Then a card came back from my mother, she had come without my knowledge as a guest of the management. She wrote, 'I'm having the thrill of my life.' When she came back and the dressing room was crowded with friends, I was still numb. They said pleasant things but I only half believed them. I kept on reminding myself that it was a first-night and first-night audiences are kind." *Broadway* accumulated a run of 603 performances. Lee Tracy's star burned bright.

Following the run of *Broadway*, Tracy and the heavy from that show, Robert Gleckler, appeared in a vaudeville sketch at the famed Palace Theatre. In the summer, Lee was offered a role that would become virtually his stock-in-trade, that of a bustling and fast-talking newspaperman, the harassed reporter of Charles MacArthur and Ben Hecht's controversial, enduring, and brilliant play *The Front Page* (August 14, 1928). Tracy played Hildy Johnson with split-second timing and an explosive, machine-gun delivery of lines that would make him forever a totally individual performer. Tracy's nasal twang and rapid-fire delivery would eventually become a professional entrapment, for no one could do it better than he.

During the run of *The Front Page*, Lee never missed a performance, despite his nightly carouses at most of Manhattan's livelier night spots. He later claimed he lived in clubs and was nourished by booze throughout his Broadway career. There were no dissenters to that opinion. It was inevitable that Hollywood, always seeking new, different personalities, especially those with stage experience, would put Tracy under contract.

Fox signed him, and his screen debut was in Kenneth Hawks' *Big Time* (1929). He played Eddie Burns who breaks up a successful husband-and-wife vaudeville team. Eddie later hits the skids, only to then become an extra in his movie star-wife's picture. Mae Clarke and Tracy made a good team. In *Born Reckless* (1930), which starred Edmund Lowe, Lee played his first of many newspaper reporters (in film). His next was an adaptation of *Liliom* (1930), in which Tracy was cast as the agitating, evil Buzzard who leads Charles Farrell into a robbery that costs his life. James Cruze directed his ex-wife Betty Compson in a ribald comedy, *She Got What She Wanted* (1930), but Tracy was already showing his temperament and walked off the picture in a high dudgeon.

Disenchanted by Hollywood he returned to the New York Stage and went with Donald Meek into *Oh, Promise Me* (November 24, 1930), which ran for 145 performances. After *Louder Please* (November 12, 1931), he was talked into signing another picture contract, this time with Warner Bros. His newspaperman, Scotty, was an asset to the muddled soap opera *The Strange Love of Molly Louvain* (1932). In Warner Bros.' very successful horror film *Doctor X* (1932), Lee was again an inquisitive news reporter, here one who heroically battles the monster of synthetic flesh. Any doubts about his comedic gifts were dispelled when he burst on the screen as the Walter Winchell-like scandal-mongering columnist in *Blessed Event* (1932). Tracy's performance was hilarious, upstaging Louella Parsons by printing birth announcements before the event.

Offscreen, his drinking increased and his reputation as a ladies' man was on the rise. Isabel Jewell was hopelessly in love with Tracy, but he managed to avoid any excursions to the altar. With his Warners commitments completed, he was summoned by irascible Harry Cohn of Columbia Pictures. He was offered a three-picture deal if he could promise to avoid drinking. Lee said he had refused to promise his mother on her deathbed never to take another drink because he knew he could not keep it, and he did not consider Cohn superior to his mother. Cohn agreed and Tracy made the films for the studio.

Lee was well cast as a fearless neo-politician in *Washington Merry-Go-Round* (1932), and then as Mayor Bobby Kingston he chooses chorine Evelyn Knapp in *The Night Mayor* (1932). Three years later he returned to Columbia to appear as ex-con "Fingers" Chick Thompson, owner of a traveling marionette show, in *Carnival* (1935), a film which also featured Jimmy Durante and Sally Eilers.

The role of a long-winded barker was an ideal part for Tracy in RKO's *The Half-Naked Truth* (1932), but midway through production the studio brought charges against him for "inexcusable delays" caused by his absence. Tracy's doctor told the Conciliation Committee of the Academy of Motion Pictures Arts and Sciences that Tracy had had a nervous breakdown. When the studio countered that drinking was the fault, Lee reminded them that while on Broadway he had never missed a performance. A compromise was eventually reached in the $10,000 suit. For Universal he gave a surprisingly appealing performance in the title role of *Private Jones* (1933). Then Irving Thalberg paged him to join the studio of stars, Metro-Goldwyn-Mayer.

Arriving at Thalberg's Culver City office, Lee encountered Joan Crawford patiently waiting to see the young genius of Metro as well. When he was told he could go in, Lee gallantly suggested Miss Crawford had been waiting longer and should go first. Tracy's salary was eventually settled at two thousand dollars a week. His tenure at MGM should have established him as one of their brightest stars, but his continued drinking bouts

With Gloria Stuart in *Wanted—Jane Turner* **(RKO '36).**

511

nearly cost him his career, created an international incident, and labeled him as tinsel town's naughty boy. His romantic adventures attracted as much press coverage as his drinking. Early in 1933 he was linked with the ubiquitous Peggy Hopkins Joyce. When asked about the relationship he quipped, "It must be love. Last night she gave back a $10,000 bracelet I bought for her!" Nevertheless, Tracy soon returned to dating Isabel Jewell on a steady basis.

His role in Bella and Samuel Spewack's screenplay of *Clear All Wires* (1933) was almost prophetic. He played a high-powered newspaper correspondent creating news when there was a lack of it and precipitating an international incident. Lee was perfect in his rattling off the dialogue at the rate of forty words in ten seconds. He explained his talent with. "To give the impression of speed I always slow up my speech very consider-ably just before I let go rapidly. Thereby the contrast is very great."

In *The Nuisance* (1933) he was an ambulance-chasing shyster lawyer staging fake accidents. David O. Selznick then cast Tracy in MGM's all-star entertainment package *Dinner at Eight* (1933). Tracy enthused to the press about his joy in working with John Barrymore. Metro then used him to play a man reliving his life while under ether in *Turn Back the Clock* (1933), which reunited him with Mae Clarke. For *Bombshell* (1933) he was a splendid foil for Jean Harlow's not very bright movie queen, Lola Burns. As Space Hanlon, her press agent, he almost dominates the Victor Fleming-directed feature. Metro loaned him to Twentieth Century for their United Artists release *Advice to the Lovelorn* (1933) in which he was a gutsy columnist known as "Miss Lonelyhearts."

Then, his next assignment nearly ruined him. Metro sent cast and crew to Mexico to film *Viva Villa!* (1933), starring Wallace Beery, with Tracy in the role of an American reporter following Villa's activities. In Mexico City on Sunday, November 19, 1933, there was a parade of some 30,000 Mexican athletes honoring the anniversary of the revolution. Tracy had been drinking heavily and went out on his hotel balcony to add a good deal more than "ole" to the passing parade. As the Chapultepec Military Cadets passed beneath his balcony his "ovation" was a screech of expletives, the defamatory bellowing accompanied by obscene gestures; and later he literally "rained" on the parade. Lawyer Jose Esparsa filed a complaint with the police that Tracy had offended public morals, witnessed by himself and his twelve-year-old daughter. He insisted that during the actor's animated gesturing a blanket Lee had wrapped around himself fell off and that he was quite nude. At the police station Tracy told Police Chief Mendez that he remembered nothing of the incident. He was fined five hundred pesos and released on his promise not to leave Mexico until the federal district attorney could investigate the charges.

On November 21, Tracy, accompanied by Jack Price and Gustavo Ducieux, flew to Juarez, Mexico, in a private plane piloted by Fritz Bieler. Mexican Attorney General Heracleo Rodriguez claimed he would be re-arrested before the actor crossed the border. U.S. Ambassador Josephus Daniels refused to intercede for Tracy and an-nounced the star should be punished if found guilty. Lee made it across the border and back to Hollywood.

On November 22, Metro-Goldwyn-Mayer cancelled Tracy's five-year contract. Louis B. Mayer wired President of Mexico Abelardo Rodriguez: "The insult offered by this actor to the Mexican Cadet Corps has embarrassed and shocked the Metro-Goldwyn-Mayer organization as deeply as it has the Mexican people. As a result of this actor's deplorable behavior MGM has removed him not only from the film *Viva Villa!* but has dismissed him entirely from its employ and cancelled his long-term contract. The offi-cials of this Company wish to take this opportunity of apologizing for the wretched conduct of one of its employees and assuring the Mexican people and the Cadets

With Ed Gargan in *The Spellbinder* (RKO '39).

against whom this indignity was visited. MGM is grateful to the Mexican people for its forebearance in this matter and to the countless Mexican actors, singers, artists and assistants used in the filming of the motion picture for their talented co-operation."

The Mexican press unanimously continued an all-out attack on MGM's *Viva Villa!*, claiming it was derogatory to Mexico and demanding that the picture not be completed. Nevertheless it was, with Stuart Erwin replacing Tracy and reshooting all his scenes. *Viva Villa!* was one of twelve pictures nominated for Best Picture of the Year. *It Happened One Night* won that honor that year.

Tracy later denied the Mexico City incident saying: "It was wildly exaggerated and published that I had stood on a hotel balcony, naked, and deliberately insulted the Mexican Flag. That was a lie. But, on the other hand, it wasn't a lie that I was drunk. And it was true that I struck a Mexican officer who came to the hotel room where we were drinking to ask that we make less noise." Strangely the American people rooted for Tracy with a deluge of fan mail advising him to "Keep a stiff upper lip, kid. We're for you."

He went to work for Universal as another newsman, this time in *I'll Tell the World* (1934). For Paramount he appeared opposite Helen Morgan in *You Belong to Me* (1934) and then showed up in a dreary adaptation of Damon Runyon's *The Lemon Drop Kid* (1934). Tracy's expert playing as Edward Arnold's friend in Universal's *Sutter's Gold* (1936) was called "superb." In the midst of his continued picture-making, he returned to Broadway for Philip Barry's *Bright Star*, which only survived for seven performances in October, 1935. He returned to Hollywood for a set of forgettable entries and on July 19, 1938, married Mrs. Helen Thoms Wyse in Yuma, Arizona. At that point the couple left for England.

Robert Sherwood's *Idiot's Delight* was a huge success in London, produced and acted by Raymond Massey. But when Sherwood summoned Massey back to New York to play *Abe Lincoln in Illinois*, a West End replacement was needed. Tracy was considered risky, but the producers gambled on him. As Harry Van he strutted through the role for over one hundred performances. (He would repeat his Harry Van role at New York's City Center in 1951.)

Lee returned to Hollywood in 1939 and, from then to 1943, he made five bottom-of-the-bill quickies. He returned to Manhattan for three performances on the Guild Theatre stage in *Every Man for Himself.* At the outbreak of World War II, he reentered the service as a United States Army captain, C.M.P. in the Allied Military Government. One of his duties was to interrogate the Japanese-Americans interned in a Utah detention camp. After the war Tracy made three unimportant screen appearances and returned to Broadway.

On April 4, 1949, he opened in Herman Wouk's play *The Traitor,* giving an amusing performance as the Chief Intelligence Officer, Captain Gallagher. He would make his TV debut in September, 1950, in his *The Traitor* role with co-star Walter Hampden. Neither of his next plays, *Metropole* or *Mr. Barry's Etchings,* had much of a run on Broadway. On the other hand, television occupied his time for the next several years. He played in the video series "The Amazing Mr. Malone" and in May, 1952, replaced Lloyd Nolan as television's "Martin Kane, Private Eye." In the spring of 1955 he was in Australia to play Captain Queeg in the Sydney production of *The Caine Mutiny Court Martial.*

When he returned from "down under," he appeared on "Kraft TV Theatre" and then became occupied with another series, "New York Confidential," that lasted through 1958. The role that was the icing on his long, tumultuous career was the part of ex-President Arthur Hockstader in Gore Vidal's biting *The Best Man* (March 31, 1960). Tracy was Tony-nominated, but his fellow starring actor, Melvyn Douglas, won it. When United Artists filmed the property in 1964, they wisely allowed Lee to repeat his superlative performance as Hockstader, and he received an Oscar nomination. (He lost the Best Supporting Actor Award to Peter Ustinov of *Topkapi.*)

During the run of *The Best Man* in 1961, he was honored by his peers at a dinner in New York, celebrating his nearly forty years in show business. President Kennedy, among others, personally congratulated Lee on his interpretation of Hockstader in the play. Tracy appeared in three television shows during 1962, the best of which was on "87th Precinct." On October 7, 1965, he made his last Broadway appearance in the unlikely role of a horse-playing priest in *Minor Miracle.* The play lasted two performances.

In the summer of 1968 Tracy underwent surgery for cancer and was recuperating at his Pacific Palisades, California, home on Rivas Canyon Road. But then on October 16 he reentered St. John's Hospital in Santa Monica. Two days later, on October 18, he died at age seventy. He was buried beside his parents at Shavertown, Pennsylvania. For all of his playboy antics, he was an astute businessman. At his death, his estate was estimated at approximately three million dollars.

LEE TRACY

Big Time *(Fox 1929)*
Born Reckless *(Fox 1930)*
Liliom *(Fox 1930)*
She Got What She Wanted *(Tiffany 1930)*
The Strange Love of Molly Louvain *(WB 1932)*
Love Is a Racket *(WB 1932)*
Doctor X *(WB 1932)*
Blessed Event *(WB 1932)*
Washington Merry-Go-Round *(Col 1932)*
The Night Mayor *(Col 1932)*
The Half-Naked Truth *(RKO 1932)*
Clear All Wires *(MGM 1933)*
Private Jones *(Univ 1933)*
The Nuisance *(MGM 1933)*
Dinner at Eight *(MGM 1933)*
Turn Back the Clock *(MGM 1933)*
Bombshell *(MGM 1933)*
Advice to the Lovelorn *(UA 1933)*

I'll Tell the World *(Univ 1934)*
You Belong to Me *(Par 1934)*
The Lemon Drop Kid *(Par 1934)*
Carnival *(Col 1935)*
Two Fisted *(Par 1935)*
Sutter's Gold *(Univ 1936)*
Wanted—Jane Turner *(RKO 1936)*
Criminal Lawyer *(RKO 1937)*
Behind the Headlines *(RKO 1937)*
Crashing Hollywood *(RKO 1938)*
Fixer Dugan *(RKO 1939)*
The Spellbinder *(RKO 1939)*
Millionaires in Prison *(RKO 1940)*
The Payoff *(PRC 1942)*
Power of the Press *(Col 1943)*
Betrayal from the East *(RKO 1945)*
I'll Tell the World *(Univ 1945)*
High Tide *(Mon 1947)*
The Best Man *(UA 1964)*

67

Helen Twelvetrees

If, in actuality, suffering could produce nobility, Helen Twelvetrees would have been the Grande Dame of filmdom, First Lady of the Thirties' cinema, and a tragedienne rivalling any actress on the screen, including blonde Miss Ann Harding. But such was not the case for Helen. Her name has filtered down through recent generations as an analogy to monumentally poor acting. This reputation is ill-deserved, because many of her screen performances were above average and she was an integral part of that decade in which sob stories were very much in fashion.

Oncamera, poor Helen was betrayed, seduced, demoralized, raped, and manhandled more often than any other screen heroine, including Sylvia Sidney and Mae Clarke. In her films, Helen would smile through her tears at her early loss of virginity, or her reduction to being a mere plaything for the particular man in question. She suffered through various stages of degradation and shame with astonishing inner fortitude that radiated purity of heart, if not of purpose. Her screen characterizations were generally seasoned with a commendable, indomitable spirit.

Helen was born on Friday, December 25, 1908, at 145 Ridgewood Avenue in the East New York section of Brooklyn. Her parents were Helen Seward and William Jurgens, the latter having come from Portage, Wisconsin, to become advertising manager for the Brooklyn edition of the *New York Evening Journal*. Miss Seward's father, Robert, was a horse-racing buff.

Helen Marie Jurgens was sent to Public School # 119, and after the family moved to Avenue I in Flatbush, where her brother was later born, she attended Brooklyn Heights Seminary. After graduation from the Seminary, Helen enrolled at New York's Art Student League, spending a year studying music, painting, and drama. While there she was noticed by a faculty member, noted artist George Bradshaw Crandall, who later chose to paint a portrait of her for a cover of the *Saturday Evening Post*. The publicity from this cover produced offers from several stage producers, including Gus Edwards. This theatrical interest in her prompted Helen to persuade her parents to enroll her in the American Academy of Dramatic Art, where she met and fell in love with a fellow student, Clark Twelvetrees. His artist father, Charles, was well known for his remarkable sketches of children.

With John Barrymore in *State's Attorney* (RKO '32).

Helen and Clark eloped in 1927 to Greenwich, Connecticut. When he was offered a job with the Stuart Walker Stock Company in Cincinnati, she went along with him. They later returned to New York where Helen soon contracted minor roles in several Broadway shows and Clark picked up a few jobs as stage manager. Helen signed for the part of Sondra in the Chicago company of *An American Tragedy*, played opposite former silent screen star Charles Ray in *Yen*, and then appeared in a series of flops that never got as far as Manhattan.

While Helen's career was slowly building, Clark's never got off the ground. Their marriage was stormy and his drinking habits contributed to violent quarrels. Helen augmented her brief engagements in the theatre by posing for artists. Nothing seemed to improve on the home front. During one alcoholic fracas, Clark leaped onto a window sill. Helen grabbed frantically at his coat, but he managed to wriggle free, leaving it clutched in his wife's hands as he leaped through the window from their seventh floor room. An awning on the second floor broke his fall to the street. The tabloids played up the tragedy of the "artist's model and her drunken husband," accusing Helen of pushing Clark out of the window. When he regained consciousness in the hospital and was able to tell what really happened, Helen was released. Her decision to leave Clark was dispelled through his father's pleading. After Clark's hospital release, the couple left for California and her new career in motion pictures, for she had signed a studio contract with Fox prior to her husband's attempted suicide.

Helen's first screen appearance was as an obtuse blonde, Miriam Holt, in Fox's *The Ghost Talks* (1929). The part required her to lisp, and in the film when asked if she always lisped, Helen replied, "No, only when I talk." Immediately rumors flew around Hollywood and the studios that the New York actress with the strange name had a serious speech impediment. She made two more films for Fox, an orphanage romance, *Blue Skies* (1929), with Frank Albertson, and *Words and Music* (1929), one of the first of an endless parade of college musicals. She played the semi-heavy who does not help the school's problems in staging a show. That year she was elected one of the annual thirteen Wampas Baby Stars and tried her luck at Pathé. This was a more fortunate move for her, as Fox had not done anything significant to help her find her niche in filmdom.

She was well cast in Pathé's *The Grand Parade* (1930), in which she was the long-suffering wife of minstrel singer-alcoholic Fred Scott. In the same company's *Swing High* (1930), directed by Joseph Santley, she gave a good account of herself as Maryan, a trapeze flyer. She made a national personal appearance tour in conjunction with the film's major city openings and won a five-year contract from Pathé. *Photoplay* cited her performance in *Swing High* and the comparisons with Lillian Gish continued to turn up in the press.

• Helen's growing success in Hollywood did not improve the shaky marriage to Clark, who was unable to get anything but minor jobs in the studios. He soon became disenchanted with the film colony and left permanently for New York City. (In August, 1938, Clark Twelvetrees died of acute alcoholism after a streetside fist fight.) Years later, Helen would tell a reporter that her capacity for dramatic fare came from having had sorrow as her primary teacher.

Following her success in *Swing High,* Helen took a major spot in Pathé's lineup for 1930–1931 productions. Among the pictures forecast was *Beyond Victory*, which would deal with women's part in the war. The cast was scheduled to include the company's entire, if tiny, roster of players (other than Carole Lombard): Helen, Ann Harding, William Boyd, James Gleason, Robert Armstrong, ZaSu Pitts, and Laura Hope Crews. Other vehicles projected for her were *The Price of a Party, Prodigal Daughter,* and *Miracle Night.* The studio's publicity department insisted, "Her pictures breathe love and life of millions."

While the above-named projects never came to light, Tay Garnett's *Her Man* (1930) was produced. This version of *Frankie and Johnny* permitted Helen to overact, yet her notices were universally good as the buffeted, lowly saloon heroine. The *New York Evening Graphic* declared that the picture was worth seeing twice for the thrilling, surprising performance from Helen; the *New York American* felt she was "a revelation in the role of the dance-hall moll," while *The New York Post* glowed, "Her work is enough in itself to lift the picture out of the ordinary." The *New York Evening Journal* considered Helen as one of the most promising young actresses of the new film generation. Others in the cast of *Her Man* included Ricardo Cortez as Johnny, Phillips Holmes in an offbeat sailor-lover role, and Marjorie Rambeau in a wonderful performance as drunken Havana Annie.

Her Man was lavishly advertised as "Born in the Scarlet Streets, this hard-boiled woman of the night knew no ten commandments—taking· suckers was her game!" Following her adventurous Frankie, Helen was loaned to Universal for *The Cat Creeps* (1930), another remake of *The Cat and the Canary,* in which Helen was properly terrified as heiress Annabelle West. She returned to RKO-Pathé and an ingenue part in support of William (Hopalong Cassidy) Boyd in *The Painted Desert* (1931), featuring a ruggedly handsome, charming villain, Clark Gable.

Helen's next assignment assured her a place in movie history. It remains a prime example of the salacious themes in which movies of the Thirties abounded. The film version of Donald Henderson Clark's risque novel *Millie* was proclaimed as "the Screen Sensation of 1931." Helen was lauded for her playing of the title role of the right girl who meets the wrong men and later shoots a former lover to protect her daughter's (Anita Louise) virginity. *Photoplay* enthused over her performance, claiming "she proves her right to stardom," while the *Los Angeles Record* rather overstated its enthusiasm with, "Helen Twelvetrees is a better actress than [Ruth] Chatterton!" *Motion Pic-*

ture Daily considered the film a personal triumph for Helen, and her personal life was as blissfully rewarding as reviews for *Millie*. She had met and fallen in love with ex-stunt man, Los Angeles realtor Frank Woody.

On March 21, 1931, Helen and Frank Woody eloped to Reno, Nevada, and were secretly married, only to discover her divorce from Clark Twelvetrees would not become final for another ten days. Telling the press it was "just an unfortunate misunderstanding of dates," Helen and Woody were remarried on April 17, 1931. A year later Helen became the mother of Frank Woody, Jr. Her new husband's fascination with the great outdoors had Helen telling the press: "I had to learn to like the Great Outdoors. I'm really a city person—and I guess I always will be, at heart. But Frank likes the open spaces and I want to go with him wherever he likes. Between pictures we go away. I think that is the best way to achieve happiness in Hollywood, the only way to keep one's perspective. If you stay too close to the motion picture colony you lose your sense of values."

In *A Woman of Experience* (1931) Helen was a tarnished fräulein in espionage-ridden Vienna, playing her role with great charm alongside Lew Cody and William Bakewell. But even director Tay Garnett admits *Bad Company* (1931), in which she tries to be convincing as a woman unaware her husband and brother are both gangsters, left too much to be desired. From Garnett's fiasco, she went on to *Young Bride* (1932), in which she marries dance-hall sheik Eric Linden, suffers a good deal, and becomes pregnant, but ends up happily in a typical Hollywood finale.

Helen's stereotyped fallen woman was less than endearing and soon Helen was telling the press: "I'm tired of taking the blame if the picture wasn't good. A star's years on the screen are limited. The featured players have many years. A star has too much footage in the picture." As for her sordid roles, she observed, "It seems to me I'm the perpetually pure-at-heart street-walker, always drooping over bars while some director says, 'Now, Helen, you must be very sweet about this naughty line. Remember, you haven't the faintest idea what it means!' "

But she was back again playing an intelligent little sinner in Gene Fowler and Rowland Brown's script *State's Attorney* (1932). As directed by George Archainbaud, John Barrymore starred in a stock role, but the Great Profile was lauded for his acting while Helen received kind notices for her poorly defined part. It was one of the six Box-office Champions for the month of May, 1932, along with *Grand Hotel, Letty Lynton, The Rich Are Always with Us, Scarface,* and *The Miracle Man*. Her final RKO picture, *Is My Face Red?* (1932), reunited her with Ricardo Cortez, who portrays a Walter Winchell-type reporter to whom Helen, as a follies girl, feeds inside theatre gossip.

David O. Selznick had become head of RKO Studio production in October, 1931, when RKO and Pathé became one and the corporate structure was greatly changed in the bankruptcy proceedings. Katharine Hepburn became the reigning star and Irene Dunne, Constance Bennett, Ginger Rogers, and fading Ann Harding were far outpacing Helen in box-office draw and appeal to the public. After *Is My Face Red?* her contract was allowed to expire.

At this point Helen moved into the uncertain world of free-lancing. Her first role was at MGM. The studio fashioned *Unashamed* (1932) out of a headlined society murder case in which a wealthy playboy shot his sister's lover. Helen appeared as Jean Ogden, with Robert Young as her brother and Lewis Stone as their perplexed father. About her role in the Bayard Veiller story, Helen said, "I enjoyed the picture hugely because it was a far different type of role from any in my experience." At Paramount, Helen joined Maurice Chevalier in *A Bedtime Story* (1933), which was stolen by an eight-month-old charmer named Baby LeRoy.

With Ricardo Cortez in *Is My Face Red?* (RKO '32).

Helen remained at Paramount as brave, weepy, self-sacrificing model Gay Holloway trying to take the blame for her father's killing of her lover (Bruce Cabot) in *Disgraced!* (1933). For Columbia's *My Woman* (1933) she was back in the melodramatic mold again as a woman leading and goading her ego-ridden husband (Wallace Ford) to radio success. After he deserts her, she winds up in a Panama dive as a barsinger tearfully moaning "I Knew I Couldn't Hold You." Following this outing she was betrayed, led to killing her lover, and then protected by her brother (Chester Morris) in *King for a Night* (1933) at Universal.

She then returned to Fox for three pictures, sporting a new auburn-toned hair style. *All Men Are Enemies* (1934) and *She Was a Lady* (1934) were lowercase entries that failed to generate any public interest. However, *Now I'll Tell* (1934) proved to be a popular success. Edwin Burke's scenario for the film was based on Mrs. Arnold Rothstein's account of marriage to her famous gambler-husband and his career and death. Spencer Tracy played the Rothstein character, with Helen as his wife. A moppet, later to become Fox's brightest star, Shirley Temple, played their daughter, with Alice Faye as Tracy's girlfriend.

Helen was in a well-paced comedy, *One Hour Late* (1934), and in 1935 was the heroine of the first of the Ellery Queen film series, *The Spanish Cape Mystery*, with Donald Cook as the refined sleuth. An invitation to make a film in Australia intrigued Helen and provided an exit from her collapsing marriage to Frank Woody. She left Woody in January, 1936, and went "down under" to film a racing story, *Thoroughbred.* Then she sailed back to the States in March with her three-year-old son.

She made the nation's headlines on April 13, 1936, while dining with a friend, Ed Forest. Frank Woody with two male companions passed by their table and dropped a few well-chosen, offensive remarks. Helen later told the press: "I begged him [Forest]

On the set of *She Was a Lady* (Fox '34).

not to make a fuss and we decided to leave. As we neared the exit, two men grabbed Mr. Forest by his arms and swung him around. Mr. Woody struck him and blackened his eyes. That was all there was to it."

Helen's divorce suit was heard on April 15, 1936, and the judge gave her a quick hearing and custody of her son. Later in the year Helen was heard on "Lux Radio Theatre" with Jack Oakie and Alan Hale in a broadcast of *One Sunday Afternoon.* In 1937 she supported Buck Jones in Columbia's *Hollywood Round-Up,* and in the summer of 1939 opened at Olney, Maryland, in their stage production of *Twin Beds.* Later that season she was in *No More Ladies* and *The Greeks Had a Word for It.* Her film return, after an absence of two years, was undistinguished, being only two cheapies at Paramount, including *Persons in Hiding* (1939), which was based in part on J. Edgar Hoover's book.

In 1940 she returned to the summer stages in *His Wife's Holiday* and *The Man Who Came to Dinner* (which toured in Europe). Her stage experience finally led her to a starring role on Broadway. In February, 1941, she joined Taylor Holmes and Else Argal in *Boudoir,* written by Jacques Deval, the author of *Tovarich* and the husband of Miss Argal. The play folded after only eleven performances. Later in the mid-Forties, Helen married Captain Conrad Payne and moved to Harrisburg, Pennsylvania, where her spouse was stationed at nearby Olmstead Air Force Base.

Blanche Du Bois in *A Streetcar Named Desire* is one of the most challenging roles ever conceived for an actress and Helen played the part to good advantage in August, 1951, at Sea Cliff, Long Island. It was one of her last professional appearances.

At her home in Harrisburg on February 13, 1958, she was found ill and was rushed to the Olmstead Air Force Base Hospital. However, it was too late; within a few moments after arrival she was dead. An autopsy was performed by the county coroner and it revealed that Helen, at the age of forty-nine, had killed herself with an overdose of sleeping pills.

It is strange that even before the current nostalgia renaissance, actresses given to overemotional performing would inspire critics to comment, "She acts like she's studied acting with Helen Twelvetrees." Comics delighted in calling her Rin Tin Tin's favorite actress because she retained her unique surname. It is an ironic finish to a personality who had, and gave, so much to Depression-weary audiences.

HELEN TWELVETREES

The Ghost Talks *(Fox 1929)*
Blue Skies *(Fox 1929)*
Words and Music *(Fox 1929)*
The Grand Parade *(Pathé 1930)*
Swing High *(Pathé 1930)*
Her Man *(Pathé 1930)*
The Cat Creeps *(Univ 1930)*
The Painted Desert *(RKO 1931)*
Millie *(RKO 1931)*
A Woman of Experience *(RKO 1931)*
Bad Company *(RKO 1931)*
Panama Flo *(RKO 1932)*
Young Bride *(RKO 1932)*
State's Attorney *(RKO 1932)*
Is My Face Red? *(RKO 1932)*
Unashamed *(MGM 1932)*

A Bedtime Story *(Par 1933)*
Disgraced! *(Par 1933)*
My Woman *(Col 1933)*
King for a Night *(Univ 1933)*
All Men Are Enemies *(Fox 1934)*
Now I'll Tell *(Fox 1934)*
She Was a Lady *(Fox 1934)*
One Hour Late *(Par 1934)*
Times Square Lady *(MGM 1935)*
She Gets Her Man *(Univ 1935)*
The Spanish Cape Mystery *(Rep 1935)*
Frisco Waterfront *(Rep 1935)*
Thoroughbred *(Australian 1936)*
Hollywood Round-Up *(Col 1937)*
Persons in Hiding *(Par 1939)*
Unmarried *(Par 1939)*

68

Jane Withers

In the Twenties, every movie producer was seeking another Jackie Coogan. In the Thirties, movie-makers were on the prowl for a carbon copy Shirley Temple. Jane Withers won her initial cinema prominence as little Miss Temple's pint-sized nemesis in *Bright Eyes* (1934). She was signed by Shirley's studio, Fox, as a backup child star performer. However, she soon developed her own sturdy following of moviegoers, and she offered the public a distinctive brand of moppet charisma. While there are a great many film viewers who recall Jane's screen work in the Thirties and Forties, newer generations know the adult Miss Withers as that irrepressible Josephine the plumber, of TV commercials fame.

Jane was born in Atlanta, Georgia, on Monday, April 12, 1926. Walter Withers agreed with his wife, Lavinia Ruth, that their daughter should have an artistic career, since the infant exhibited such a remarkable talent for imitating everyone in sight. Mrs. Withers registered Jane at Atlanta's Boston Academy to study ballet, tap, and character dancing. At the age of three Jane made her stage debut at a local theatre's amateur night. She sang "Little Pal." A year later she had her own radio program, singing and performing accurate impersonations. She was soon dubbed "Atlanta's Sweetheart" and "Dixie's Dainty Dewdrop."

When Mr. Withers was transferred by his firm to the West Coast, ambitious Mrs. Withers enrolled their talented four-year-old daughter in Lawlor's Professional School. Between classes, Jane was heard on radio, modeled, entertained at benefits, and with her mother, made the rounds of the studios. Director David Butler made a screen test of Jane at Fox, where she had done small bits in films such as *Handle with Care* (1932). Butler saw her as a fine counter-balance to Fox's new moppet bonanza Shirley Temple. Thus freckled, "cute" Miss Withers made her first screen impression as a hell-raising, brattish, but wonderfully comic, Joy Smythe in Shirley's *Bright Eyes*. Whereas in the film Shirley asks Santa Claus for a doll at Christmas, ebullient Jane demands a machine gun and proceeds to deftly imitate her choice by revolving her body and screeching "ra-ta-ta-ta." As one critic reported the impact of Jane's appearance, "This appalling child kicked and yowled and bit her way through the film so magnificently that millions roared with glee. . . ." As more astute observers of the time noted, Jane was not just another would-be Shirley Temple, but rather a successor to Paramount's Mitzi Green, who by this point had outgrown her tyke's stardom in Hollywood.

In *Can This Be Dixie?* (20th '36).

After Jane's success in *Bright Eyes,* the studio starred her in *Ginger,* in which Fox teamed her opposite the screen's leading male brat, Jackie Searl. *Photoplay* magazine cited her performance as one of the month's best. Critic Richard Watts, Jr. thought Jane should not be forced into sweet, sugary roles, but should instead be left to demonstrate her natural talents, such as impersonating Garbo, ZaSu Pitts, or tossing off a rendition of the balcony scene from *Romeo and Juliet* (as she did in *Ginger*). *Ginger* was the first of Jane's films under her long-term Fox pact signed on December 7, 1934. Her contract called for $125 weekly salary for her first six-month period.

Thereafter she played Della in the Janet Gaynor-Henry Fonda *The Farmer Takes a Wife* (1935), and sang three songs in *This Is the Life* (1935). As *Paddy O'Day* (1935) she sang "Keep a Twinkle in Your Eye," and audiences were delighted by her whirlwind performance. Her contract with Fox at $150 a week had been raised to $1,500 weekly at the end of 1935, but Fox refused her mother's request for Jane to sign radio contracts that would have amounted to nearly $400,000. Instead the studio agreed to increase her weekly pay check to $2,000.

Booth Tarkington's *Gentle Julia* (1936) featured Jane as the impish Florence Atwater. Teamed again with Jackie Searl, Jane (who could have been tagged Little Miss Fix-it) saves the romance of Marsha Hunt and Tom Brown. In 1936 Jane's best film was *Pepper,* in which she was the tomboy leader of a tough gang of tenement-district kids taken to heart by philanthropist Irvin S. Cobb. Her films continued to delight the public, who generally found time and money to see both Jane's pictures and those of higher-ranking Shirley Temple. In *Angel's Holiday* (1937) she played the precocious daughter of a detective-story writer and gave a hilarious imitation of Martha Raye. At the close of 1937 the former "Dixie Dew-Drop" emerged as number six in the Motion Picture Exhibitors' annual poll of the ten top box-office favorites. Shirley Temple held the first position and Clark Gable was number two.

Irvin S. Cobb enthused over Jane's talent, stating, "If Jane Withers is a sample of what a movie career does for children, a law should be passed forcing all youngsters to have such an experience. I have yet to know a sweeter, more well-bred, gently considerate and wholly natural little girl." Jane's naturalness was given notice through such comedies as *Wild and Woolly* (1937), *Forty-Five Fathers* (1937), and *Rascals* (1938), the latter featuring Rochelle Hudson and Borrah Minovitch and His Harmonica Rascals. As Jane Rand in *Keep Smiling* (1938) she rehabilitated her drunken ex-Hollywood director-uncle (Henry Wilcoxon) and did an hilarious satirical imitation of her contemporary, boy soprano Bobby Breen.

Through 1939 her pictures were often B entries with script problems even Jane could not solve. In *Boy Friend* (1939) she received her first screen kiss, awkwardly administered by George Ernest. Her imitation of madcap Eva Tanguay in the Ritz Brothers' *Pack up Your Troubles* (1939) was one of the film's brightest moments. In December, 1939, she bought a hundred-acre ranch near Calabasas, California, jokingly telling reporters it was to house her many pets.

Just as Shirley Temple was outgrowing her popularity as she developed into a young woman, so Jane suffered as a result of her physical-emotional maturing. She was in that awkward stage of beginning adolescence, which caused Fox to cut back even more on the budgets for her features. In 1940 she made *Shooting High* with Gene Autry, the cowboy star on loan from Republic. The next year she was featured in a remake of Simone Simon's *Girls' Dormitory* (1936) entitled *Her First Beau* (1941). Using the name Jerrie Walters, she received screen credit for the story line of her *Small Town Deb* (1941) and was awarded $3,000 extra for her scripting services.

On June 15, 1941, Jane entertained in one of the first U.S.O. shows at Camp Roberts,

At Twentieth Century-Fox c. '37.

along with Laurel and Hardy, Virginia O'Brien, and Ella Logan. Meanwhile, Louella Parsons was busy reporting Jane's many dates with Robert Carroll and Buddy Pepper (the latter had made an arrangement of the "Hut Sut Song" for her). On her sixteenth birthday, Jane was escorted by Freddie Bartholomew to the Biltmore Bowl, followed by a hayride and a barn dance.

In the early Forties, Darryl F. Zanuck decided to clean house and inaugurate a new range of film stars. Among those dropped were Shirley Temple and Jane Withers, the latter leaving the studio in July, 1942. That same year Jane went on an extensive vaudeville tour accompanied by her mother, doing uncannily accurate imitations of ZaSu Pitts, Katharine Hepburn, Carmen Miranda, and Shirley Temple, and singing "Three Little Sisters" and "Franklin D. Roosevelt Jones" backed by the Mitchell Ayres Orchestra. At the time the columns were reporting that Jane was dating A. C. Lyles.

Jane's publicist reported later in 1942 that Valley Forge Military Academy had named her their pin-up(!) girl, and that she had signed a three-year deal with Republic Pictures for a reported $225,000. Between her adolescent roles at Republic, none of which had the sparkle of her past Fox efforts, Jane appeared in the meritorious *The North Star* (1943) produced by Samuel Goldwyn for RKO release. This World War II, Russian-set feature proved that Jane had a gift for dramatic acting.

Shirley Temple proved she was no longer a little girl when in September, 1945, she wed John agar. On September 20, 1947, at Los Angeles Congregational Church, Jane married wealthy Texas oil man William P. Moss, Jr. It was the same year of her last picture of the decade, Paramount's low-budget *Danger Street*. Jane retired from the screen to become a housewife and within a few years the Moss family included children William, Wendy, and Randy. But the marriage collapsed after nearly six years when Moss left her. Jane filed for divorce in Santa Monica, California. Testifying that he drank and gambled excessively, she received her divorce from Moss on June 14, 1954. She received $1,000 monthly in alimony and a $100,000 trust fund for her three children, plus a $24,000 insurance policy for their education. Her share of their community property netted her approximately $500,000. (When Jane had reached the age of twenty-one, her parents had transferred to her the deed to the family home valued at $250,000, other real estate estimated at $75,000, an annuity of $10,000, plus a cash total of $375,000.)

Despite the near-million-dollar divorce settlement, Jane had an emotional post-reaction to the affair and was sent to the hospital completely paralyzed. "The paralysis was, at least, partially induced by negative emotions. I didn't cry, or scream, or yell. But I stifled myself right into paralysis." Three specialists predicted she would be paralyzed for at least three years and that complete recovery seemed doubtful. Medically she was a victim of rheumatoid arthritis. However, Jane's religious convictions and the inestimable help of Dr. Edmund Bowlin had her back home at peace within nine months.

Jane showed enormous emotional strength in her recovery period. "I don't have time to be sick because I have a family to raise. I'd always raised my own children and I wasn't about to spend my life lying in bed. I asked the doctors to use me as a guinea pig —to use any new methods they could, and I promised to do everything I possibly could to help." Years later Jane would say: "I believe with all my heart that arthritis has a lot to do with emotions. I happen to be a very emotional person and had gone through a lot of strain just before the arthritis attack. . . . I had to change my whole life, and it wasn't easy, believe me. I'm still emotional but I just don't let itty-bitty things get me down as much as they used to."

In 1955 Jane remarried. Kenneth Errair was one of the successful singing group The Four Freshman. Jane, in her breathless wonder, said, "I was terrified that I liked him so

In *Wild and Woolly* (20th '37).

well. He was marvelous to me and I wasn't looking for a husband, so I married him!" Jane and Errair had two sons, Kenneth and Kendall. Thirteen years later, in 1968, Errair was killed in a private plane crash. His death left Jane with five children to raise, but, again her deep religious convictions supported her. "The minute the pain came so did God's help. I felt his strength supporting me." In the spring of 1974 Jane received $200,000 in settlement of a superior court suit she brought after her husband's death. "That marriage was truly meant to be," Jane recently admitted. "It almost takes one to find out what it's all about. My first husband, William Moss, and I had a lot of growing up to do. He's been married to four other women since, so it wasn't just me!"

Back in 1944, in between her programmers at Republic, Jane had decided to try Broadway. She signed for the musical *Glad to See You*, directed by Busby Berkeley. Co-starring with Jane were Eddie Foy, Jr. and June Knight. Jane sang, danced, and received glowing personal notices, but the show was a theatrical embarrassment which closed out of town in Boston in January, 1945.

After an absence of nearly ten years from the screen, Jane returned in 1956 to play the lusty, gauche Vashti in George Stevens' massive *Giant*. Rumors flew around Hollywood that Jane's performance was equalled only by that of Mercedes McCambridge in the Warner Bros. epic motion picture starring Rock Hudson, Elizabeth Taylor, and James Dean. Reportedly some of Jane's best scenes were cut from the final print due to the excessive length of the feature. Nevertheless, Jane's gutsy Vashti is still a sterling, outstanding performance.

Jane made her television debut on the "U.S. Steel Hour," live from New York, in *The Pink Burro*, co-starring with June Havoc and Edward Andrews in this July, 1959, epi-sode. Later that summer Jane was to be seen in episodes of "Peck's Bad Girl," on which her young son, Kenneth Edward Errair, II, made his debut. She also taped segments of "Bachelor Father" and "Wagon Train," and later in the Sixties was to be seen on "Pete and Gladys," "Alfred Hitchcock Theatre," and "The Munsters." Actually Jane had been scheduled to make her television debut in the mid-Fifties as co-star of "Love that Bob," starring Robert Cummings. However, for physical and personal reasons she declined and Ann B. Davis took over the part of Schulzie that had been conceived with Jane in mind.

In 1961 Jane was in Twentieth Century-Fox's *The Right Approach* and two years later joined Gregory Peck and Tony Curtis in *Captain Newman, M.D.* She made an interest-ing impact playing Lieutenant Grace Blodgett.

However, most of contemporary America came to know Jane as lovable Josephine the Plumber. It seems while Jane was attending a church revival in Ontario, Canada, in 1968, a few months after Errair's death, an advertising executive handling the Comet cleanser account was in New York planning her future. A spokeswoman was needed for the product and Jane was his choice. As Miss Withers recalls it: "Glamor has never been my cup of tea. I'm not the leading lady type. When they called me in Canada, I asked the man if I'd have to say anything like, 'Oh, hello there! I'm Jane Withers! I have a Product for you!' I told him to forget an endorsement and, incidentally, asked him what the product was. When he told me it was Comet I said, 'Good gravy, I've used that product for years, 'so I said, 'Amen, that's peachy-dandy!' " Twenty different episodes of one-minute installments of Josephine, the Plumber, pushing Comet have survived for the past several seasons.

In late 1974 she gave up the Comet job to return to serious acting (of sorts). She was on a Mitzi Gaynor Television special in 1974 and in February, 1975, she was featured in the telefeature *All Together Now* as Aunt Harriett convincing her husband to permit four orphaned children to stay together as a family unit.

530

Beyond her television activities, Jane is active on the Board of Los Angeles Cancer Society and the Chamber of Commerce, where she was the prime exponent of Hollywood's Walk of Fame—bronze stars encased in the sidewalk of Hollywood Boulevard commemorating the names of Hollywood's present and past greats. Jane has raised her "little people" (her terminology for her children) admirably, and she is a trustee and diligent worker of Hollywood's Church of Religious Science. When she is working in New York, she attends Marble Collegiate Church run by her close friend, Dr. Norman Vincent Peale. Her deep religious convictions astound any viewers when she says grace before eating in public restaurants.

Jane has come a long way since the days of *Bright Eyes* when she shouted, "I don't want a dollie! I want a machine gun!" Her brash good humor dispelled a great deal of gloom during the Depression years of the Thirties.

JANE WITHERS

Handle with Care *(Fox 1932)*
Bright Eyes *(Fox 1934)*
Ginger *(Fox 1935)*
The Farmer Takes a Wife *(Fox 1935)*
This Is the Life *(Fox 1935)*
Paddy O'Day *(Fox 1935)*
Gentle Julia *(20th 1936)*
Little Miss Nobody *(20th 1936)*
Pepper *(20th 1936)*
Can This Be Dixie? *(20th 1936)*
The Holy Terror *(20th 1937)*
Angel's Holiday *(20th 1937)*
Wild and Woolly *(20th 1937)*
Forty-Five Fathers *(20th 1937)*
Checkers *(20th 1937)*
Rascals *(20th 1938)*
Keep Smiling *(20th 1938)*
Always in Trouble *(20th 1938)*
The Arizona Wildcat *(20th 1938)*
Boy Friend *(20th 1939)*
Pack up Your Troubles *(20th 1939)*

Chicken Wagon Family *(20th 1939)*
Shooting High *(20th 1940)*
High School *(20th 1940)*
Youth Will be Served *(20th 1940)*
The Girl from Avenue A *(20th 1940)*
Golden Hoofs *(20th 1941)*
A Very Young Lady *(20th 1941)*
Her First Beau *(Col 1941)*
Small Town Deb *(20th 1941)*
Young America *(20th 1942)*
Johnny Doughboy *(Rep 1942)*
The Mad Martindales *(20th 1942)*
The North Star *(RKO 1943)*
My Best Gal *(Rep 1944)*
Faces in the Fog *(Rep 1944)*
Affairs of Geraldine *(Rep 1946)*
Danger Street *(Par 1947)*
Giant *(WB 1956)*
The Right Approach *(20th 1961)*
Captain Newman, M.D. *(Univ 1963)*

Anna May Wong

Tsong Liu Wong (or Wong Liu Tsong according to Chinese custom) means "Frosted Yellow Willow," but in any language, Anna May Wong was an enchanting actress. Ironically the American-born performer had to go abroad to gain fame before Hollywood in the Thirties realized it had a native source of talent in its midst. She was frequently referred to as "the world's most beautiful Chinese girl," with her high cheekbones, heavy-lidded eyes with penciled eyebrows under black horizontal bangs, and full, sensuous mouth that quickly expanded into a lovely smile.

Anna May was born on Thursday, January 3, 1907, in Los Angeles to Wong Om Tsing and his wife. They lived on Flower Street, and she was the second child of a family of seven who resided in a two-room flat. She first appeared in pictures at the age of twelve when she was one of some three hundred lantern bearers in Nazimova's 1919 film *The Red Lantern*. She missed classes at school to do another bit, carrying a tea tray in a scene from Sessue Hayakawa's *The First Born* (1921). That same year she had a bit in Marshall Neilan's *Dinty*. She received her first screen credit in Neilan's *Bits of Life* (1921), in which she played Toy Sing, with Lon Chaney as her husband. In John Gilbert's *Shame* (1921) at Fox, she was Lotus Blossom. At the end of 1922, Anna became a part of the history of the motion picture industry by appearing in the first Technicolor Motion Picture Company production, *The Toll of the Sea*. In this Metro film, Frances Marion's script switched the *Madame Butterfly* story to conform to an old Chinese folk tale of the sea claiming twice in pain for the joy it bestows. Anna was radiant in color as the girl who drowns herself in the sea.

Douglas Fairbanks' exquisitely mounted (by William Cameron Menzies) *The Thief of Bagdad* (1924), as directed by Raoul Walsh, is still impressive to view. It brought Anna national recognition as Julanne Johnston's Mongol slave girl. Thereafter Anna went to the Canadian Rockies to play Keok in *The Alaskan* (1924), with Thomas Meighan and Estelle Taylor. In Paramount's *Peter Pan* (1924) she was a delightful Tiger Lily.

Unfortunately for Anna, Hollywood film-makers held to the tenet that players of particular ethnic backgrounds could not be stars in the accepted sense. Not only did this apply to Blacks but also to Orientals. Sessue Hayakawa, who became a major star in the late 1910s and early 1920s, was a rare exception, but his Hollywood fame was rather brief. Thus, Anna should have risen to prominence on a continuous level, but she was forced to accept the dictates of the studio system, and only provide exotic atmosphere

With Marlene Dietrich in *Shanghai Express* (Par '32).

for other players' vehicles. She was Loo Song in *Mr. Wu* (1927), with French Renee Adoree in the female lead as Lon Chaney's Chinese daughter. Then in *Old San Francisco* (1927) Anna supported Swedish Warner Oland who was villainously persecuting the Bay City's Chinese. (Ironically Oland later would become identified as the best known "Chinese" player onscreen.) *The Chinese Parrot* (1927) was the second in a long series of Charlie Chan adventures, here with Japanese Kamiyama Sojin as the Chinese detective. In this entry, Anna played a nautch dancer. She had a much showier role as Sada, with Gilda Gray, in *The Devil Dancer* (1927), but then she provided only background in the Joan Crawford-Ramon Novarro *Across to Singapore* (1928). At Warner Bros., in *The Crimson City* (1928), Anna had a minor role as Su, whereas the lead of the Chinese girl Onoto was played by Myrna Loy from Montana. After playing Sojin's sweetheart in *Chinatown Charlie* (1928), Anna conceded to the whims of filmland.

There was a good deal more to Hollywood's casting system than showed on the surface. Interest was high not only in cast but caste, reflecting one of many unwritten taboos rampant in the industry. Some of these no-nos were inspired by national prejudice; others began under Hollywood's self-imposed code of morals. Later, while in Europe, Anna would say: "I see no reason why Chinese and English people should not kiss, even though I prefer not to. If two people are in love it does not matter what their races are. There seems little for me in Hollywood, because, rather than real Chinese, producers prefer Hungarians, Mexicans, American Indians for Chinese roles." There were many movie roles in which Anna May would have excelled. Others would have been beyond her scope and depth as an actress.

Disgusted with Hollywood's treatment of her, Anna went abroad. Her career leaped toward stardom after her first foreign film, *Song* (1928). Directed by Richard Eichberg in Germany, the film was based on the work by Dr. Karl Vollmoeller who had authored *The Miracle* and *Grosstadt Schmetterling.* She learned to speak German fluently and amazed new German friends who believed her dialogue had been dubbed by carrying on a full conversation in their language. But it was in England that Anna really found success. On March 14, 1929, she made her stage debut at the New Theatre in London in Basil Dean's production of *The Circle of Chalk,* an adaptation of an old Chinese play by James Laver. She played the role of Chang Hi-Tan, and Laurence Olivier was cast as Prince Po. At Elstree Studios she was excellent as Shoshe in E. A. DuPont's *Piccadilly* (1929), with Gilda Gray, Jameson Thomas, Cyril Ritchard, and Charles Laughton.

From her flat in Park Lane Anna was feted by all of London. She became known as one of the best dressed women in Mayfair and was a shining success in England. On the British screen she excelled in *Elstree Calling* (1930). Her proficiency with language was evident in the British International release *The Flame of Love* (1930) made at Elstree in three languages: English, French, and German. Anna made all three versions, beautifully playing the role of Hai-Tang, leader of a Russian dance troupe. In the English-speaking version the leading man was John Longden, with Percy Standing supporting. For the French version Marcel Vibert and Robert Ancelin played opposite her and the film was known as *L'Amour Maitre des Choses.* In the German edition, entitled *Hai-tang,* Francis Lederer was her male lead.

When the film opened in September, 1930, in Paris, she was in Vienna making her German-speaking stage debut in the leading role of *Tschuin Tschi (Springtime).* The Austrian critics were enraptured with her acting and wrote, "Fraulein Wong had the audience perfectly in her power and the unobtrusive tragedy of her acting was deeply moving, carrying off the difficult German speaking part very successfully." However, Anna did have a moment of panic, and later confessed her feelings to the press. "I suffered stage fright the moment I started speaking German and felt as if it were my first appearance anywhere, but now, after this wonderful reception, I cannot get back to earth!" But she did return to earth and to America, knowing that her appearance in the Viennese operetta, in which she acted, sang, and danced, had been widely acclaimed.

Her desire to return to Los Angeles was forced into a detour when Lee Ephraim, casting a new Broadway show, cabled Anna May on the *Aquitania* in mid-Atlantic to beg her to accept the role of Minn Lee in Edgar Wallace's dramatization of his novel *On the Spot.* As directed by Ephraim and Carol Reed, *On the Spot* was a melodrama of Chicago racketeering. Crane Wilbur was cast as the underworld figure who keeps his Chinese mistress in a cathedral apartment where he plays Verdi on a pipe organ between murdering rival gangsters. Wilbur, Anna May, and Glenda Farrell, as a two-timing broad, starred in the play for 167 performances after its October 29, 1930, Broadway bow and then made an extensive road tour in the show. Anna's performance was well shaded. Interestingly, Miss Wong's ideas about presenting a Chinese woman differed considerably from those of Lee Ephraim, who insisted her stage crossings should be made in short, hesitant steps *a la* Butterfly. But Anna argued her point that Chinese women did not walk in such a manner and her projection of the tragic Minn Lee (who commits suicide) benefited from her innate knowledge.

Returning to Hollywood she signed with Paramount for the excellent film of Sax Rohmer's *Daughter of Fu Manchu,* which reached the screen as *Daughter of the Dragon* (1931). She portrayed the alluring Ling Moy, daughter of the insidious Dr. .Fu Manchu (Warner Oland), vowing to her dying father to kill his enemies. But she is stopped by Scotland Yard investigator Ah Kee (Sessue Hayakawa). Then came Anna's most memo-

With Elizabeth Allan in _Java Head_ (First Division '34).

rable American film, Josef von Sternberg's _Shanghai Express_ (1932), in which she gave an exotic performance as an American-educated Chinese girl, Hui Fei, of dubious virtue, who stabs to death the rebel leader (Warner Oland) of the Chinese revolution. The film was one of von Sternberg's finest (he was Oscar-nominated for it). Lee Garmes' atmospheric photography won an Academy Award for the year's best cinematography. Had there been a Best Supporting Actress category in 1932, Anna May Wong would certainly have been a contender.

Leaving California en route to England, Anna May played at presentation houses from coast to coast. In Philadelphia at the Mastbaum Theatre, after an introduction by master of ceremonies Dick Powell, she sang "Boys Will Be Girls and Girls Will Be Boys" and thanked an appreciative audience in five languages, including Yiddish. In July she was at New York's Capitol Theatre with Jack Benny, Una Merkel, Lew Cody, Jean Hersholt, Armida, and Abe Lyman's Orchestra for a mammoth stage show. Then she sailed for England to portray sinister but spicy Mrs. Pyke in _A Study in Scarlet_ (1933), with Reginald Owen as Sherlock Holmes. While making _Tiger Bay_ (1933) for Wyndham Studios she was being entertained about London town. At Paul Hyde Bonner's party for Alfred Lunt and Lynn Fontanne she became so flustered at meeting the Prince of Wales she forgot to curtsey, but did manage a feeble "Sir!" Other parties provided as table companions Somerset Maugham, Edward Knoblock, and Wellington Koo, Chinese Ambassador to Great Britain. Anna played a highly successful nightclub engagement at London's swank Embassy Club. London was charmed by her.

Chu Chin Chow was a theatrical legend that had been made as a silent film in 1925 with Betty Blythe and Jameson Thomas. It was decided to revive the project as a new British-made movie with Walter Forde as director. Anna was the luscious slave Zahrat-Al-Kulub, with George Robey as Ali Baba, Fritz Kortner as Abu Hassan, and John

Garrick as the romantic lead. The $500,000 production had its American bow at Broadway's Roxy Theatre on September 21, 1934, and was a great success. Before leaving England, Anna made *Java Head* (1934), playing the part of Taou Yuen that had been performed by Leatrice Joy in Paramount's 1923 silent version.

When Anna returned to Hollywood it was for the role of Tu Tuan, in which she was beautifully gowned and gave an intriguing performance as a dancer in love with half-caste owner of the Lily Garden Club, George Raft, who foolishly discards her for Jean Parker. When this film, *Limehouse Blues* (1934), was completed, Anna returned to Europe for a tour of theatres in Italy, Switzerland, Spain, and Scandinavia. She came back to Los Angeles and then in January, 1936, left for China to visit her father's first wife and his family there. Enchanted as she became with her father's native land, she said upon returning: "I am convinced that I could never play in the Chinese Theatre. I have no feeling for it. It's a pretty sad situation to be rejected by Chinese because I'm 'too American' and by American producers because they prefer other races to act Chinese parts."

When no new film roles developed at home or abroad, Anna returned to tour in her vaudeville act in early 1937. At Paramount, for the low-budget unit she made several releases. In *Daughter of Shanghai* (1937) she played with consummate skill the role of Lin Ying Lin who masquerades as an entertainer in Charles Bickford's dive. She is beset with split-hair adventures, but maintains a cool demeanor as the hounded heroine. In October, 1937, gossip columns carried a report of her engagement to actor Philip Ahn, a childhood friend appearing with her in *Daughter of Shanghai*. Anna was amused with the news item and remarked, "It's like reading the announcement of your engagement to your cousin!" Anna May never married.

Paramount filmed the Edgar Wallace play *On the Spot,* retitling it *Dangerous to Know* (1938), with Akim Tamiroff as the gangster and Anna repeating her original role (called Mme. Lan Yin in the film version). On February 9, 1938, she reported to Warner Bros. to start filming a story by Dr. Manley P. Hall (President of the Philosophical Research Society) and Anthony Coldeway. In the resultant film, *When Were You Born?* (1938), she played an ersatz female Charlie Chan, known as Mei Lee Ling, the famed astrologist. The completed film was a talky bore, and for the first time on the screen, so was Anna. In July, 1938, Mrs. Warner Oland painted her portrait while Anna appeared onscreen in *King of Chinatown* (1939) as Dr. Mary Ling (Hollywood had a fascination with the name Ling), who saves the life of Chinatown racket czar Akim Tamiroff.

While Anna was making *Island of Lost Men* (1939), Paramount hired her to coach Dorothy Lamour who was to play a Eurasian girl in *Disputed Passage.* However, Anna's coaching did not help Miss Lamour's performance as the half-caste. In the summer of 1937, Anna had appeared at Westport Country Playhouse in *Princess Turandot;* in the summer of 1940 she was on the straw-hat circuit in *Turandot* with Vincent Price and later made personal appearances in Australia. In 1941 she played Lois Ling, with Ralph Bellamy as the sleuth, in *Ellery Queen's Penthouse Mystery.* World War II reawakened Hollywood's interest in Oriental subjects and Anna found new prominence, although she was forced to ply her craft at a poverty row studio, PRC, for whom she made *Bombs over Burma* (1942) and *Lady from Chungking* (1942). She did not return to the screen till 1949 for Brian Donlevy's *Impact,* in which Anna was little more than decorative.

In October, 1951, Anna made her video debut in *The Gallery of Mme. Liu;* however, it was not until October, 1956, that she was allowed a role in the medium that was worthy of her. For "Producer's Showcase" she played the Eurasian Mrs. Hammond, the blackmailing, treacherous possessor of the fatal piece of evidence in William Somerset Maugham's *The Letter.* The TV drama was directed by William Wyler, who had directed

With J. Carrol Naish, Ernest Truex, and Anthony Quinn in *Island of Lost Men* (Par '39).

the 1940 Bette Davis film version in which Gale Sondergaard played Mrs. Hammond. Later that year, Anna was seen on "Climax" in *The Chinese Game*. She was an infrequent video performer throughout the end of the decade. On March 15, 1960, she was helping Hugh O'Brian fight prejudice against the Chinese people on an episode of "Wyatt Earp."

It was producer Ross Hunter who lured Anna back to the screen. In the Lana Turner-Anthony Quinn potboiler *Portrait in Black* (1960), she was cast in the part of Tani, but her guest appearance was not enough to make a deadly dull screen drama viable entertainment. Hunter also cast her for a role in his *Flower Drum Song* (1961), but ill health prevented her from appearing in it. (For the record, the 1960 release *The Savage Innocents,* a bilingual film starring Anthony Quinn in a tale of Alaska, does not feature the Anna May Wong of this chapter.)

Anna had converted her home at 326 San Vincente Boulevard in Santa Monica into four apartments, calling her former home "Moongate Apartments." In 1956 she had sold that house and purchased a smaller home just around the corner. She shared that dwelling with her brother Richard.

In January, 1961, she appeared as Barbara Stanwyck's servant on the latter's teleseries. Then on February 3, 1961, two days after completing her last television performance, an episode of "Danger Man," she died of a heart attack. She was fifty-four years old.

During her lifetime Anna accomplished a stunning career against near impossible odds. Her belief in Christian Science, reinforced by her constant search for wisdom, sustained her for many years. Her search led her to the philosophy of Lao Tzu, which she found fascinating. She believed, "Life is too serious to be taken seriously." She thought that her professional life should please the public, but that her personal life should satisfy herself. Anna believed that her stay on earth was but one of many reincarnations. She wished as an epitaph for her life, "I died a thousand deaths."

ANNA MAY WONG

The Red Lantern (Metro 1919)
The First Born (Robertson Cole 1921)
Dinty (Associated FN 1921)
Shame (Fox 1921)
Bits of Life (Associated FN 1921)
The Toll of the Sea (Metro 1922)
Thundering Dawn (Univ 1922)
Drifting (Univ 1923)
The 40th Door (Pathé serial and feature 1924)
Lilies of the Field (Associated FN 1924)
The Thief of Bagdad (UA 1924)
The Alaskan (Par 1924)
Peter Pan (Par 1924)
Forty Winks (Par 1925)
Fifth Avenue (PDC 1926)
A Trip to Chinatown (Fox 1926)
The Desert's Toll (MGM 1926)
The Dragon Horse [The Silk Bouquet] (Fairmount 1926)
Driven from Home (Chadwick 1927)
Mr. Wu (MGM 1927)
Old San Francisco (WB 1927)
The Chinese Parrot (Univ 1927)
Streets of Shanghai (Tiffany 1927)
The Devil Dancer (UA 1927)

The Crimson City (WB 1928)
Chinatown Charlie (FN 1928)
Across to Singapore (MGM 1928)
Song (German 1928)
The City Butterfly (German 1929)
Piccadilly (World Wide 1929)
Elstree Calling (Wardour 1930)
The Flame of Love (British International 1930)
Daughter of the Dragon (Par 1931)
Shanghai Express (Par 1932)
A Study in Scarlet (Fox-World Wide 1933)
Tiger Bay (Wyndham 1933)
Chu Chin Chow (Gaumont 1934)
Java Head (First Division 1934)
Limehouse Blues (Par 1934)
Daughter of Shanghai (Par 1937)
Dangerous to Know (Par 1938)
When Were You Born? (WB 1938)
King of Chinatown (Par 1939)
Island of Lost Men (Par 1939)
Ellery Queen's Penthouse Mystery (Col 1941)
Bombs over Burma (PRC 1942)
Lady from Chungking (PRC 1942)
Impact (UA 1949)
Portrait in Black (Univ 1960)

70

Fay Wray

For an actress whose movie career has spanned four decades, from silents to sound to television, and who has applied her talent to the stage and Broadway, as well as co-authored a play with Nobel Prize winner Sinclair Lewis, it is ironic that Fay Wray's multiple accomplishments are overshadowed by her one-time performance as the inamorata of an ape. For she was the blonde, shrieking heroine of *King Kong* (1933).

The lovely Miss Wray, whose greenish-blue, almond-shaped eyes reminded many viewers of Gloria Swanson, was born on Sunday, September 15, 1907, on her father's ranch called Wrayland near Cardston, Alberta, Canada. Her family, which contained three girls and three boys, migrated first to Arizona and then to Bingham, Utah, and finally settled in Hollywood where Fay was to be seen in a Hollywood High School pilgrimage play. Then she signed for a series of movie shorts, starting with *Gasoline Love* in 1923. From two-reelers she went to the Western range with Art Acord in *Lazy Lightning* (1926), played with Hoot Gibson in *The Man in the Saddle* (1926), and was Jack Hoxie's heroine-in-distress in *The Wild Horse Stampede* (1926). After two more Westerns, Fay was chosen with Dolores Costello, Dolores Del Rio, Joan Crawford, Janet Gaynor, Mary Astor, Mary Brian, and others for predicted stardom in 1926 as a Wampas Baby Star.

Then she was discovered by the maddening though brilliant Erich von Stroheim, who was then planning to direct and play the lead in his own story of a melodrama set in 1914 Vienna. It was called *The Wedding March* (1928). "The Man You Love to Hate" envisioned the project as being filmed in two parts. He spent months on minor details of the thirty-six different sets that included remarkably reconstructed scenes of old Vienna. His casting for this ambitious production was complete except for the lead. Having spent months coping with the egocentric and self-indulgent Mae Murray in *The Merry Widow* (1925), he determined that his crippled Viennese heroine required an unknown actress rather than the originally suggested Miss Murray. Talen scout Mrs. Schley brought him Fay Wray. The austere perfectionist appraised the frightened young girl and inquired, "Are you sure you can do the part?" She answered, "I know I can." Von Stroheim accepted her assurance and dismissed her with, "Goodbye Mitzi." Fay dissolved into tears. Years later Stroheim recalled, "As soon as I had seen Fay Wray and spoken to her, in a few minutes I knew I had found the right girl. I didn't even take a test of her."

With Charles "Buddy" Rogers in *The Lawyer's Secret* (Par '31).

The Wedding March began shooting in early June, 1926, and continued until February, 1927. Fay had the wistful innocence required for the role, and von Stroheim was pleased with her habit of catching her lower lip between her teeth. "Do that every time you meet me," said von Stroheim, who was playing her lover Prince "Nicki," "it will do more to characterize Mitzi than anything else." Fay would spend several years erasing the enthusiasm for Mitzi's trademark in later films. For a young actress with limited experience, her performance ultimately became the best in the interminable feature.

The first part of *The Wedding March* included many of the director-scripter-star's penchant for picturing in detail orgies and sexual aberrations, as well as beautifully effective scenes including a Corpus Christi procession with thousands of extras, filmed in primitive Technicolor. Before its release in 1928, Part One was cut from fourteen to eleven reels. Midway through Part Two of this mammoth project, Paramount and producer Patrick Powers, horrified by the enormous production costs, decided to remove von Stroheim and turn the film over to Josef von Sternberg. Part Two, called *The Honeymoon,* was released in Europe as *Mariage de Prince.* Before his death in 1957 von Stroheim recut *The Wedding March* and *The Honeymoon,* which had been edited by others. But the second half of his marathon tale was destroyed by fire.

If Paramount was disenchanted with von Stroheim, they were delighted with Fay, and Jesse Lasky rewarded her with a long-term studio contract. She was then cast opposite a shy, uneasy performer the company was grooming for stardom. He was Gary Cooper and the film was *The Legion of the Condemned* (1928). Paramount envisioned them as a new "team," but they failed to click with the paying public.

Offscreen, Fay fell in love with John Monk Saunders of Minnesota—a second lieutenant in the Air Force, a graduate of the University of Washington, a Rhodes scholar at Oxford, and the author of *The Legion of the Condemned, Wings* (1928), and Josef von Sternberg's excellent film *The Docks of New York* (1928). On Friday, June 15, 1928, Fay and Saunders were married by the Reverend Edgar T. Read at Calvary Methodist Church in Easton, Maryland, with Fay's mother, Gary Cooper, and Rowland V. Lee as witnesses. A wedding party was given aboard an oyster boat in St. Michael's harbor, and the following Monday Fay returned to playing her role of Anna Lee in Paramount's $200,000 location epic, *The First Kiss* (1928). The film was a flop.

She continued her contract with Paramount, playing to advantage in a series of dramas opposite Emil Jannings, Clive Brook, Richard Arlen, and William Powell. She was reteamed with Cooper in a brief Civil War-period Technicolor sequence in *Paramount on Parade* (1930) and that same year played in Cooper's Western, *The Texan.* Three years later the studio would couple them for the last time in *One Sunday Afternoon* (1933). (They would have one more joint acting fling, in May, 1938, when they were heard together on "Lux Radio Theatre" in *The Prisoner of Shark Island.*)

Near the end of 1930 *Liberty* magazine started a series of weekly episodes written by John Monk Saunders that carried a subtitle of *Nikki and her War-Birds,* eventually published as a novel, *Single Lady.* Saunders later converted the episodes into a screenplay for Warner Bros.-First National, filmed as *The Last Flight* (1931). To complete the cycle Saunders turned his offbeat World War I Hemingway-like tale into a play called *Nikki* that opened on September 29, 1931, on Broadway with Fay making her New York City stage debut. The show was spasmodically delightful, but had been set to music by Philip Charig, with lyrics by James Dyrenforth. The play required neither one nor the other. The "musical" version of *Nikki* was ill-timed since the film version of *The Last Flight,* with Richard Barthelmess, Helen Chandler, and John Mack Brown, was being shown locally. *Nikki,* with Fay, Douglass Montgomery, Louis Jean Heydt, and Cary Grant, lasted only thirty-nine performances.

With Ralph Graves and Jack Holt in *Dirigible* (Col '31).

Fay returned to Hollywood, where she had opportunities as a screaming heroine in *Doctor X* (1932) and *Mystery of the Wax Museum* (1933). Then Merian C. Cooper who had produced such classics as *Grass* (1925), *Chang* (1927), and *The Four Feathers* (1929), the last of which had Fay as the heroine, approached her about a new film venture. He informed her, "You will have the tallest, darkest leading man in Hollywood." Her throbbing vision of playing opposite Clark Gable exploded when Cooper showed her a thirteen-inch-high ape that, he explained, would be enlarged on the screen to appear fifty feet high [staged by animation expert Willis O'Brien who had created the prehistoric animals years before for *The Lost World* (1925)]. Cooper also advised her she would have to be a blonde in contrast to her dark leading man.

Everyone concerned with the *Kong* project worked diligently. Fay spent twenty-two hours of consecutive filming on one sequence. While this hard work was progressing, RKO producer David O. Selznick was paring budgets on other studio projects to complete one of the most memorable, talked about, written about, analyzed, and exhibited films ever made.

The fascination of *King Kong* continues today and Fay Wray's immortality is assured for those future generations who have yet to discover the strange love of the great Kong for the blonde screamer. Miss Wray has frequently appeared over the years in support of the rereleased picture, serenely explaining to the next generation how it was all done. "Pre-filmed animation of Kong and/or the prehistoric animals was projected onto a full-size screen or 'transparency.' Working in front of the large screen, we became mini-people by comparison. Kong's hand and arm in which my close-ups were made was

543

about eight feet in length. Inside the furry arm there was a steel bar and the whole contraption (with me in the hand) could be raised or lowered like a crane. The fingers would press around my waist while I was in a standing position. I would then be raised about ten feet into the air to be in line with an elevated camera. As I kicked and squirmed and struggled in the ape's hand, his fingers would gradually loosen and begin to open. My fear was real as I grabbed onto his wrist, his thumb, whatever I could, to keep from slipping out of that paw! After all the filming was finished we went into a sound room where I recorded an outpouring of various screams."

The long ten months required to shoot *King Kong* were taken up with preparations of filming of background animation, and during that time Fay made other films, including *The Most Dangerous Game* (1932), in which she portrayed Eve Trowbridge being hunted by a mad Russian, Count Zaroff (Leslie Banks), with bow and arrow. After the premiere of *King Kong* at Grauman's Chinese Theatre in Hollywood, Fay was offered in more horror features, screaming her way through *The Vampire Bat* (1933), with her *Wax Museum* co-star, villainous Lionel Atwill.

As a free-lancer Fay gained further reputation as a champion screamer and bedeviled heroine in a bevy of studio products. She was a stunning leading lady coping with Wallace Beery and Jackie Cooper, while George Raft jumps off the Brooklyn Bridge, in *The Bowery* (1933). She was a calm and calculating Russian spy in *Madame Spy* (1934) and a crisply perfect nurse supervisor in *Once to Every Woman* (1934). Her parts were improving and she and Paul Lukas made *The Countess of Monte Cristo* (1934), uplifting the proceedings greatly. Then she signed for the role of Teresa in MGM's super production of *Viva Villa!* (1934), with Wallace Beery playing to the hilt his favorite role of Pancho Villa.

The promise of forthcoming better roles, after Fay played the intended mistress of Benvenuto Cellini (Fredric March) in *The Affairs of Cellini* (1934), did not materialize. "I was standing still in Hollywood doing picture after picture. Oh, I'm grateful for it all. I needed as much experience. In the past two years, however, my roles have been so much of the sameness." On June 14, 1935, Fay received her U.S. citizenship papers and with her husband left for England to make *Bulldog Jack* (1935), also known as *Alias Bulldog Drummond,* with Jack Hulbert and Ralph Richardson. She then played with Jack Buchanan in *Come out of the Pantry* (1935) and later created one of her best roles as Rene, with Claude Rains, in *The Clairvoyant* (1935). She loved England and the easier pace of the British studios. Saunders joined Alexander Korda to write a story of the history of flying from 57 A.D. to 1936 and he helped to co-direct *Conquest of the Air* (1936), starring Laurence Olivier.

Meanwhile Fay had returned to Hollywood to fulfill an obligation to make a picture for Columbia, the low-budget *Roaming Lady* (1936); however, she soon traveled back to England for another film with Jack Buchanan, *When Knights Were Bold* (1936). Later, on September 24, 1936, back in California, she and John Monk Saunders became the parents of a daughter whom they named Susan and who would, in another three years, become contested in a bitter divorce suit between Fay and Saunders.

From 1936 to 1938 Fay's screen activity included a series of programmers for Columbia. On January 1, 1938, she and Tyrone Power did a broadcast of *Story of Natchez* on "Hollywood Playhouse," and later she and Edward Arnold were heard in *The Boss* on "Lux Radio Theatre." By the summer of 1938 her marriage was falling apart and she decided more stage experience was required. She left to play the East Coast straw-hat circuits in *The Night of January 16th, The Petrified Forest,* and *There's Always Juliet,* repeating the latter show during the summer of 1941 before going into the Broadway production of *Golden Wings* (which lasted six performances in December of that year).

With Sinclair Lewis she had written a play, *Angela Is Twenty-Two,* which opened in

On the set of *King Kong* (RKO '33. Note Bruce Cabot's picture on magazine cover.)

Detroit in February, 1939, with co-author Lewis playing the leading role. However, Lewis soon relinquished the part to Philip Merivale. The show proceeded to Chicago with Merivale and Barry Sullivan and closed at the Selwyn Theatre in March, 1939. The project was not a total loss, for the playwrights sold the property to Universal Studios. There it was revamped for Susanna Foster's *This Is the Life* (1941). The resultant production proved the thesis that a bad play does *not* necessarily make a good movie. While *Angela* was dying in Chicago, Fay was rehearsing a new melodrama, *The Brown Danube*, in which she starred with Dean Jagger upon its opening in April, 1939 in Philadelphia. In the second week of the run, Fay was replaced by Jessie Royce Landis, and the show limped into New York for twenty-one performances.

After bitter divorce proceedings with Saunders, Fay won custody of daughter Susan and went to Skowhegan, Maine, for summer stock at the Lakewood Theatre, playing in *Family Portrait,* in *The White Steed,* and, with her *The Brown Danube* replacement, Jessie Royce Landis, in a new play, *Indian Summer.*

On Monday, March 11, 1940, Fay received the news that John Monk Saunders had committed suicide at his Fort Myers, Florida, home. Despite her depression she opened two weeks later in the West Coast production of *Margin for Error.* In December of 1940 she was again heard on "Lux Radio Theatre," this time in *Knute Rockne—All American,* with Pat O'Brien, Donald Crisp, and Ronald Reagan.

545

Ironically as Fay's rigorous, self-imposed training as an actress showed results, Hollywood became less interested in her. In August of 1941 Fay became involved with the wildly ubiquitous Alexander Woollcott. He was then to play in *The Yellow Jacket* and persuaded Harpo Marx to come to Marblehead, Massachusetts, to join him in the theatrical venture. The romantic leads in the show were assumed by Fay and Alfred Drake. Then Fay was called to New York to play in the George S. Kaufman produced-doctored-directed vehicle, *Mr. Big*, with Hume Cronyn in the title role. However, the play fumbled through only seven performances. At the same time, she was seen in such films as Charles Vidor's *Adam Had Four Sons* (1941) and the fifth of the Dr. Christian series with Jean Hersholt, *Melody for Three* (1941).

Physically, artistically, and emotionally, Fay was at her peak at the age of thirty-four in 1941, but she had fallen in love and her career became a secondary, less important element of her new life. On Sunday afternoon, August 23, 1942, Supreme Court Justice Ferdinand Pecora married playwright-scripter-producer Robert Riskin and Fay at the St. Regis Hotel in New York. The witnesses included Mr. and Mrs. Irving Berlin, Mr. and Mrs. William Paley, and David O. Selznick. Riskin became chief of the overseas branch of the Motion Picture Bureau of War Information for three years. While stationed in Washington, shortly after their marriage, the Riskins faced their first dilemma. Fay was under the impression that Robert wanted her to continue her career. But then, says Fay, "It wasn't until it came out accidentally that we each learned neither of us wanted me to act." She became solely Mrs. Robert Riskin.

In 1947 Riskin produced his less than *Magic Town* for RKO and in 1949 formed his own Equitable Pictures. Then tragedy struck in December, 1950, when a surgeon removed a blood clot from Riskin's brain, leaving the patient paralyzed and bedridden until his death at a San Fernando Rest Home on September 20, 1955. Fay was left with her son, Robert Riskin, Jr., daughter Victoria, and her first-born, Susan.

Fay returned to the screen in 1953, and on television became the mother of Bobby Hyatt and Natalie Wood, and wife to addled Paul Hartman in the teleseries "Pride of the Family." Between minor film assignments, she continued doing two or three television shows a year. In one of the few personally directed Alfred Hitchcock television thrillers, Fay appeared with Keenan Wynn in a telecast adaptation of Roald Dahl's short story *A Dip in the Pool*. She appeared in several "Perry Mason" episodes, having made her last (to date) screen appearance in the inauspicious *Dragstrip Riot* (1958) for American International. A few years ago, Fay, single once again, wed neurosurgeon Sanford Rothenberg and today they live in Century City, California.

"Hollywood has changed," Fay reflects. "Pictures used to be fun. They had a magical quality." Over recent years she has attended a few film festivals as guest of honor with the showing of *King Kong*. She observes laughingly, "When I'm in New York, I look at the Empire State Building and feel as though it belongs to me . . . or vice-versa?"

FAY WRAY

The Coast Patrol (Barsky 1925)
A Cinch for the Gander (Univ 1925)
Lazy Lightning (Univ 1926)
The Man in the Saddle (Univ 1926)
The Wild Horse Stampede (Univ 1926)
Loco Luck (Univ 1926)
A One Man Game (Univ 1926)
Spurs and Saddles (Univ 1927)
The Wedding March (Par 1928)
The Legion of the Condemned (Par 1928)
The Street of Sin (Par 1928)
The First Kiss (Par 1928)
The Four Feathers (Par 1929)
Pointed Heels (Par 1929)
Thunderbolt (Par 1929)
Behind the Make-Up (Par 1930)
The Border Legion (Par 1930)
Captain Thunder (WB 1930)
Paramount on Parade (Par 1930)
The Sea God (Par 1930)
The Texan (Par 1930)
The Finger Points (WB 1931)
The Conquering Horde (Par 1931)
Not Exactly Gentlemen (Fox 1931)
Dirigible (Col 1931)
The Lawyer's Secret (Par 1931)
The Unholy Garden (UA 1931)
Stowaway (Univ 1932)
Doctor X (WB 1932)
The Most Dangerous Game (RKO 1932)
The Vampire Bat (Majestic 1933)
Mystery of the Wax Museum (WB 1933)
King Kong (RKO 1933)
Below the Sea (Col 1933)
Ann Carver's Profession (Col 1933)
The Woman I Stole (Col 1933)
The Big Brain (RKO 1933)
One Sunday Afternoon (Par 1933)
Shanghai Madness (Fox 1933)
The Bowery (UA 1933)

Master of Men (Col 1933)
Madame Spy (Univ 1934)
Once to Every Woman (Col 1934)
The Countess of Monte Cristo (Univ 1934)
Viva Villa! (MGM 1934)
The Affairs of Cellini (UA 1934)
Black Moon (Col 1934)
The Richest Girl in the World (RKO 1934)
Cheating Cheaters (Univ 1934)
Woman in the Dark (RKO 1934)
White Lies (Col 1934)
Bulldog Jack (Gaumont 1935)
Come out of the Pantry (UA 1935)
Mills of the Gods (Col 1935)
The Clairvoyant (Gaumont 1935)
Roaming Lady (Col 1936)
When Knights Were Bold (General Film Distributors 1936)
They Met in a Taxi (Col 1936)
It Happened in Hollywood (Col 1937)
Once a Hero (Col 1937)
Murder in Greenwich Village (Col 1937)
The Jury's Secret (Univ 1938)
Smashing the Spy Ring (Col 1938)
Navy Secrets (Mon 1939)
Wildcat Bus (RKO 1940)
Adam Had Four Sons (Col 1941)
Melody for Three (RKO 1941)
Not a Ladies' Man (Col 1942)
Treasure of the Golden Condor (20th 1953)
Small Town Girl (MGM 1953)
The Cobweb (MGM 1955)
Queen Bee (Col 1955)
Hell on Frisco Bay (WB 1955)
Rock Pretty Baby (Univ 1957)
Crime of Passion (UA 1957)
Tammy and the Bachelor (Univ 1957)
Summer Love (Univ 1958)
Dragstrip Riot (AIP 1958)

Jane Wyatt

To date there have been two career peaks in Jane Wyatt's acting years—her role in the classic *Lost Horizon* (1937) and the indelible impression she created playing Robert Young's wife in the long-running teleseries "Father Knows Best." She has had a most erratic, if interesting, career in the theatre, motion pictures, and television. But anyone on the Hollywood scene in 1934 would hardly have expected that the petite young actress would enjoy such a long-range career that has spanned five decades and shows no sign of abating.

Jane was born on Monday, August 12, 1912, in Campgaw, New Jersey, to Euphemia Van Rensselaer and Christopher Billopp Wyatt. Her father was an investment banker and her mother a playwright, drama critic, and editor. The family was in the New York Social Register, from which they were dropped after the stock market crash of 1929.

Inclusion in the Register meant little, if anything, to Jane, but after her marriage to Edgar Bethune Ward in Santa Fe, New Mexico, on November 9, 1935, she was reinstated. She had met Harvard student Ward on a train en route to Hyde Park for a weekend house party while she was playing on Broadway in *The Joyous Season,* a Philip Barry fiasco starring Lillian Gish.

Jane had left Barnard College after two years to begin a theatre career, acting as understudy to Rose Hobart in a trifle called *Tradewinds* that closed en route to New York. She later understudied the ingenue in Mary Boland's *The Vinegar Tree,* which opened on Broadway on November 19, 1930. Her official Broadway debut was made on March 4, 1931, as Freda Mannock in A. A. Milne's *Give Me Yesterday,* featuring Louis Calhern and Gladys Hansen. After playing with Charles Laughton in the quick-folding *The Fatal Alibi* in February, 1932, Jane decided to learn more of her trade at the Westport Country Playhouse. That second season of the new theatre, the acting company was headed by June Walker and Osgood Perkins. Co-founder Lawrence Langner would recall, "Our ingenue was a young girl, Jane Wyatt, who came to see me wearing a very pretty hat with violets, which seemed to be the same color as her eyes, and despite the protestations of my director, after testing her acting talents, I insisted on engaging her. She responded with a very creditable job of making a career for herself, both then, and later on, in motion pictures."

In December, 1932, Jane was in the flop *The Mad Hopes,* and then appeared in a succession of unsustaining Broadway shows: *Evensong, Conquest,* and *For Services Rendered,* the latter with Fay Bainter. Then in May, 1933, Jane replaced Margaret

548

With Phillips Holmes in *Great Expectations* (Univ '34).

Sullavan in the touring company of *Dinner at Eight*. In December, 1933, she signed with producer Joseph Verner Reed to appear in S. N. Behrman's *Love Story*. The show tried out and closed in Philadelphia. A young actor in the cast, Henry Fonda, went unnoticed in the reviews, but Jane was given recognition for her brave try at the role of Ellen Willeke.

Then came *The Joyous Season* (January 29, 1934), which was also a flop, but her marriage to Edgar Ward more than compensated. It was at this time that she signed a picture contract with Universal, which generously gave her a concession to continue with her stage career. For Universal she made her screen debut as Dinny in *One More River* (1934), with Diana Wynyard and Frank Lawton, that was based on one of the later volumes of *The Forsyte Saga*. As mad Miss Havisham's ward, Estella, in Universal's edition of *Great Expectations* (1934)—not so expertly done as David Lean's 1946 English production—Jane was excellent, keeping pace with old pros Florence Reed and Henry Hull.

Then Jane returned to Broadway to play the suicidal Janet Evans in *Lost Horizons*, which opened on October 15, 1934. Critics were enthusiastic about her character interpretation and decided that her past stage work had been nothing compared to this performance. But the show did not enjoy a long run, and by February, 1935, she was joining Walter Connolly in *The Bishop Misbehaves*. This play provided Jane with her longest tenancy on Broadway.

After making *We're Only Human* (1936) at RKO, Universal starred her in her fourth film, *The Luckiest Girl in the World* (1936). She was Pat Duncan, a debutante and heiress who is determined to live her own life in Manhattan on $150 a month and who later discovers that sharing a kitchen and facilities with fellow tenant Louis Hayward is more than just a bit of fun. When the film arrived at New York's Roxy Theatre in late 1936, Universal's advertisements proclaimed Jane Wyatt as "your newest star" and predicted her vibrant, refreshing personality was destined for great screen glory.

It was at this point that Frank Capra was looking for a relatively new screen face and selected Jane for the romantic lead of Sondra, opposite Ronald Colman, in the telling adaptation of James Hilton's *Lost Horizon* (1937). In his autobiography Capra recalls he felt lucky to sign "a Barnard College young lady, a stage actress whose exposure to films was limited to a couple of minor parts. . . ." Despite the director's delight with Jane, cinematographer Joseph Walker discovered photographing Miss Wyatt's retrousse nose a vexing problem, but he eventually surmounted his dilemma.

Lost Horizon was road-shown by Columbia and became one of the year's ten best pictures (after the film's first two reels were discarded upon reconsideration). Its success was phenomenal and added much prestige to Harry Cohn's Poverty Row studio, although the classic picture garnered only one Academy Award.

Jane immersed herself in the *Lost Horizon* project, practicing the violin three hours a day for four weeks before shooting began. She faced the cameras ready to give a full-dimensional, charming interpretation of Sondra. Sadly, when the film was remade in 1972 as a Ross Hunter-controlled musical, it became a ponderous bore, and Liv Ullmann was lost in the poorly conceived, updated role of Sondra.

Three months following the release of *Lost Horizon,* Jane gave birth to her first son, Christopher Ward, on Tuesday, June 16, 1937. (He would grow up to become an engineer and would wed Gretchen Van de Kamp, of the California bakery Van de Kamps. They would have three children, Nicholas, Andrew, and Laura, and in September, 1974, he would become treasurer of Kaiser Steel Corporation.)

By the beginning of 1938 Jane was back on stage rehearsing a mild Graustarkian comedy produced by Max Gordon, *Save Me the Waltz.* Along with Mady Christians, Leo G. Carroll, Laura Hope Crews, John Emery, and Martha Sleeper, she opened on Broadway on February 28, 1938. However, since no one was then interested in the waltzing of ersatz monarchs, the show folded after only eight performances. During the summer of 1938 Jane took to the straw-hat circuits, playing leads in *Biography, Coquette,* and the Carmel, New York, production of *Romeo and Juliet,* in which her Romeo was Douglass Montgomery and her nurse Blanche Yurka. She finished the season touring in *Stage Door.*

Unfortunately, Jane's screen career, which should have picked up after *Lost Horizon,* did not improve. Her next Hollywood effort was Republic's *The Girl from God's Country* (1940), and then she hurried back to the theatre (February 22, 1940) to play Fay Tucker in *Night Music,* and, in November, 1940, Carol Adams in *Quiet Please.* Clifford Odets' *Night Music* was a wordy, soap opera mishmash about the saving of a Hollywood actor through the love of a Broadway actress. It shut down after twenty performances. *Quiet Please,* co-produced by Jesse Lasky and Henry Duffy, quietly closed after sixteen performances and another play Jane joined, *No Code to Guide Her,* folded on the road. Its title seemed to indicate the progress of her career. She spent the war years in Hollywood filming a spate of run-of-the-mill pictures that included such sheer nonsense as *Kisses for Breakfast* (1941), with Dennis Morgan, and then had the leads in a few Westerns, including *Buckskin Frontier* (1943) and *The Kansan* (1943). Yet she only had a secondary part in Clifford Odets' screen adaptation of *None But the Lonely Heart* (1944), in which Cary Grant and Ethel Barrymore's performances outdistanced the rest of the cast.

Finally, on February 7, 1945, Jane opened in a comedy by William McCleery, *Hope for the Best,* which gave her and co-star Franchot Tone a 117-performance run. Return-

At Universal in '34.

ing to Hollywood, she soon found an improvement in the quality of her film assignments as well. In *Boomerang* (1947), a documentary style drama delineating the repercussions and solving of a murder, director Elia Kazan filmed it largely on location in Stamford, Connecticut, and White Plains, New York. Next, Jane had a rather tiny role as Dorothy McGuire's sister in the prizewinning *Gentleman's Agreement* (1947), also directed by Kazan. In 1949 she was well cast and gave a glowing performance as Gary Cooper's wife in Warner Bros.' ammunition-riddled weak story, *Task Force.*

Her Hollywood career was inexplicably going nowhere, forcing her to play roles that any capable actress could have handled. But Jane stuck with her craft, declaring, "If you're going to go the distance, you must have guts and be able to take it!" And she took several she could have lived without. During 1950 she made four movies. She played Louis Hayward's terrified wife in Fritz Lang's tepid *House by the River,* and then David Wayne's wife in support of Betty Grable and Dan Daily in *My Blue Heaven.* As a woman whose placid life with three daughters erupts when one (Ann Blyth) discovers she has been adopted, Jane gave a warm, pleasant performance in Samuel Goldwyn's *Our Very Own;* but as rich, spoiled Lois Frazer, shooting her husband and being protected by her San Francisco police detective lover (Lee J. Cobb), Jane was obviously ill at ease and was unconvincing in *The Man Who Cheated Himself.*

However, her persuasive playing was evident when she entered the new medium of television. She appeared in *Kitty Foyle* on "Robert Montgomery Presents" and, again for that program, in *The Awful Truth* with Lee Bowman. After struggling with the rest of the cast, including Pat O'Brien, in the poor *Criminal Lawyer* (1951), Jane centered her talents on television. She returned for brief engagements in West Coast stage productions of *The Skin of Our Teeth* and *The Winslow Boy,* and commuted to New York for live television as a panelist on "It's News to Me." For that medium she also appeared with Lloyd Nolan on "Ford Theatre" in *Protect Your Honor* and then returned to "Robert Montgomery Presents" in *The Inward Eye.*

Just as Frank Capra's casting of Jane in *Lost Horizon* assured her of cinema immortality, so her decision to join the cast of "Father Knows Best" did much to make her famous throughout America to new generations. She was not sure she wanted to play in the domestic comedy series and it required strong persuasion from her husband, who knew Robert Young and convinced her that he was a most likable fellow. The show made its debut on October 3, 1954, and lasted for six seasons. Jane won three Emmy Awards for her performance as Margaret Anderson, wife to small town insurance man Young and the mother of three children (Elinor Donahue, Billy Gray, Lauren Chapin). Young was producer and owner of the successful series filmed by Screen Gems at Columbia Studios on a six-days-a-week schedule and he became a wealthy man from the long outing.

Regarding her prizewinning participation in "Father Knows Best," Jane has said: "To begin with I love to act and the moment I get something to do I'm enchanted. But I would *never* do another series. By the time we got to the third year I thought I was going to die, and the six years were so hard to get through! The series was at the top of its ratings, but we began to feel we might have come to the end of the good stories over those six years, during which time I was able to read the entire Old Testament between takes." Besides receiving an Emmy in 1960, she was given a citation by the California State Assembly for "consistency in outstanding performance as Margaret Anderson in *Father Knows Best.*"

From 1956 to 1960 Jane served as governor of the Hollywood chapter of the National Academy of Television Arts and Sciences and during layoffs from her chores as Margaret Anderson on "Father Knows Best" she appeared on most of the major network drama showcases. She had one small motion picture role during those VIP years, that of June

With Ronald Colman in *Lost Horizon* (Col '37).

Allyson's pal in *Interlude* (1957). But mainly, due to her TV series, Jane was labeled as America's perfect mother, and could not escape the responsibilities of the task. It reached the point where she hated to go out to dine, because hardly would a meal pass without some television watcher coming up to tell her some personal problem which they felt sure "Margaret Anderson" could solve.

In 1962 Jane received the Poverello Award Medal "in recognition of the great benefactions to humanity—exemplifying the best mankind offers in providing aids and succor to less fortunate people." For years, Jane had worked quietly, industriously, and with great dedication for the March of Dimes and other charities. In 1963 the Association of Marquette University Women awarded her the McElligott Medallion "for the woman of national prominence who has emulated the ideals of our founders in advancing the educational and cultural interests of women."

Jane would later reflect: "I never should have gone to Hollywood at all! I should have stayed on Broadway—perhaps developed into a good actress. Later I loved live TV!"

If Jane did not return to Broadway, she did venture back to stock company theatre where her "Father Knows Best" years made her a top box-office attraction. At the Sombrero Playhouse in Phoenix, Arizona, in 1961, Jane played a commendable *Candida,* and she spent the summer touring the Eastern straw-hat stages in *Oh, Mistress Mine,* with Tom Helmore and Billy Gray. She also did a telecast of *The Wingless Victory* for "Play of the Week." Her television work became an annual affair after doing the telefilm *See How They Run* in 1964. She was back on the stage at the Pasadena Playhouse in 1966 in a tryout of a new marital comedy, *The Decent Thing,* with John Lupton. However, it was television that continued to offer her the versatile range of parts Hollywood never gave her. In the ABC-TV telefilm *Weekend of Terror* (1970), her work was fine. A year later, the "Andersons" were reunited again as guests on a television "Kraft Music Hall" special. Robert Young and Jane Wyatt had become television's ideal man and wife, inheriting the laudatory nuptial niche once held by William Powell and Myrna Loy in the cinema.

Jane's admiration for Robert Young as a fellow actor and as a man is enormous. Thus she accepted a guest starring spot on his "Marcus Welby, M.D." series, in the episode *Designs,* in which she played a sophisticated fashion designer who falls impulsively in love with Welby. Jane's playing of the romantic, fluctuating Edwina was brisk and believable. In addition, during her scenes with Young, Marcus Welby almost disappeared into Jim Anderson of "Father Knows Best."

In 1971 Jane became Chairman of the Women's Activities for the National Foundation of the March of Dimes, traveling hundreds of thousands of miles, speaking to the public about birth defects. She has become one of the Foundation's greatest assets, steadfastly refusing any reimbursement for any of her work and extensive time. Her quiet, persuasive power with audiences, blessed with her pure diction, composure, and warmth, has vastly enriched the various charities to which she has lavishly given her time. Petite Miss Wyatt has always been open to new challenges. She appeared on the concert stage in September, 1951, in Edith Sitwell's *Facade,* and then, nine years later, in Pasadena, she was the narrator in a performance of Benjamin Britten's *A Young Person's Guide to the Orchestra.* Throughout her professional life she has prepared for any eventuality from studying diction with Frances Robinson Duff to studying acting with Lee Strasberg and, later in Hollywood in 1949, with Charles Laughton.

In the Thirties, Jane added several polished performances on the screen and more than a little class to that hard-boiled era. A recent big-screen appearance was in the subordinate role of the friend who offers Maureen O'Sullivan encouragement about her pending pregnancy in *Never Too Late* (1965). On TV, however, Jane has had more luck.

She has appeared with surprising frequency in the medium. Recently she was seen in one of the lead parts in *Ladies of the Corridor* for "Hollywood Television Theater," guested on a "Medical Center" episode, and, in the telefeature *Katherine* (1975), portrayed the wealthy mother of a young girl (Sissy Spacek) who has become a terrorist. In Walt Disney's feature, *Treasure of Matecumbe* (1976), Jane provides support for star Peter Ustinov and the telefeature *Amelia* (Earhart). Miss Wyatt will appear as Susan Clark's mother.

Although Jane was a resident in Hollywood for many years she never really found her Shangri-La in California until television's ideal wife, Margaret Anderson in "Father Knows Best," found her.

JANE WYATT

One More River *(Univ 1934)*
Great Expectations *(Univ 1934)*
We're Only Human *(RKO 1936)*
The Luckiest Girl in the World *(Univ 1936)*
Lost Horizon *(Col 1937)*
The Girl from God's Country *(Rep 1940)*
Hurricane Smith *(Rep 1941)*
Weekend for Three *(RKO 1941)*
Kisses for Breakfast *(WB 1941)*
The Navy Comes Through *(RKO 1942)*
Army Surgeon *(RKO 1942)*
Buckskin Frontier *(UA 1943)*
The Kansan *(UA 1943)*
None But the Lonely Heart *(RKO 1944)*
Strange Conquest *(Univ 1946)*
The Bachelor's Daughters *(UA 1946)*

Boomerang *(20th 1947)*
Gentleman's Agreement *(20th 1947)*
Pitfall *(UA 1948)*
No Minor Vices *(MGM 1948)*
Bad Boy *(AA 1949)*
Canadian Pacific *(20th 1949)*
Task Force *(WB 1949)*
House by the River *(Rep 1950)*
My Blue Heaven *(20th 1950)*
Our Very Own *(RKO 1950)*
The Man Who Cheated Himself *(20th 1950)*
Criminal Lawyer *(Col 1951)*
Interlude *(Univ 1957)*
The Two Little Bears *(20th 1961)*
Never Too Late *(WB 1965)*
Treasure of Matecumbe *(BV 1976)*

Staff

JAMES ROBERT PARISH, California-based free-lance writer, was born in Cambridge, Massachusetts. He attended the University of Pennsylvania and graduated as a Phi Beta Kappa with a degree in English. He is a graduate of the University of Pennsylvania Law School and has been the president of Entertainment Copyright Research Co., Inc., as well as a reporter for Manhattan film trade papers. He is the author of *The Great Movie Series, The Fox Girls, Hollywood's Great Love Teams,* and *Elvis!* He is the co-author of *The MGM Stock Company, Liza!,* and *Film Directors Guide: The U.S.* and many other books on the media. Mr. Parish is also a film reviewer for national magazines.

WILLIAM T. LEONARD, currently research director for the Free Library of Philadelphia Theatre Collection, has devoted many years to theatrical and cinema research, contributing articles to such publications as *Films in Review* and *Classic Film Collector.* During World War II he wrote and appeared in *Hurry Up and Wait* in Italy. He has also written reports for proposed Culture Centers including Lincoln Center for the Performing Arts. He was one of the principal contributors of data for the American Film Institute's catalog volume, *Feature Films 1921–30* and (with James Robert Parish and Lennard DeCarl) is co-author of *Hollywood Players: The Forties.*

DeWITT BODEEN was born in Fresno, California. After graduation from UCLA, he was an actor and playwright at the Pasadena Playhouse. In 1941 he was placed under contract at RKO as a screenwriter. His first project, *Cat People,* was a hit. Two other films that he wrote for producer Val Lewton—*Curse of the Cat People* and *Seventh Victim*—are highly regarded today as cult films. Among his other film-writing credits are: *The Yellow Canary, The Enchanted Cottage, Night Song,* and *I Remember Mama,* the last three for producer Harriet Parsons. He has collaborated on the scenarios for *Mrs. Mike* and *Billy Budd* and has written more than fifty teleplays. He is co-author of *The Films of Cecil B. DeMille* and *The Film of Maurice Chevalier.* He was final associate editor for the reference volume *Who Wrote the Movie (and What Else Did He Write)?* His first novel, *13 Castle Walk,* has recently been published.

T. ALLAN TAYLOR, godson of the late Margaret Mitchell, is presently production manager of the largest abstracting and technical indexing service in the United States.

He was editor of *The Fox Girls, The Paramount Pretties, Vincent Price Unmasked, The Jeanette MacDonald Story, The Great Spy Pictures,* and other volumes.

Brooklyn-born JOHN ROBERT COCCHI is one of America's most respected film researchers. He is the New York editor of *Boxoffice* magazine. He was research associate on *The American Movies Reference Book: The Sound Era, The Fox Girls, Good Dames, The Swashbucklers,* and many other books. He has written cinema history articles for *Film Fan Monthly, Screen Facts,* and *Films in Review.* He is the author of *The Western Picture Quiz Book* and is co-founder of one of New York City's leading film societies.

DON E. STANKE in the past few years has interviewed more than forty American film and stage personalities and has had career articles published on most of them in cinema journals. Interviewing and writing is avocational, since Mr. Stanke is a full-time administrative manager with a medical X-ray firm in San Leandro, California. With Mr. Parish, he is the co-author of *The Glamour Girls, The Debonairs, The Swashbucklers,* and *The All Americans,* and has contributed to *The Real Stars # 2* and *The Tough Guys.*

New York-born FLORENCE SOLOMON attended Hunter College and then joined Ligon Johnson's copyright research office. Later she was director for research at Entertainment Copyright Research Co., Inc., and is currently a reference supervisor at AS-CAP's Index Division. Ms. Solomon has collaborated on such works as *The American Movies Reference Book, TV Movies, The Great Western Pictures,* and others. She is the niece of the noted sculptor, the late Sir Jacob Epstein.

Index

Abandon Ship!, 430
Abilene Town, 191
Above the Clouds, 36, 151
Across to Singapore, 533
Act of Mercy, 286
Actors and Sin, 122
Adam Had Four Sons, 546
Address Unknown, 377
Admirals All, 251
Adventure in Baltimore, 292
Adventure Island, 332
Adventures of a Young Man, 184
Adventures of Huckleberry Finn, 292
Adventures of Marco Polo, The, 54
Adventures of Mark Twain, 299
Adventures of Robin Hood, The, 285
Adventures of the Flying Cadets, 38
Adventures of Tom Sawyer, The, 312
Advice to the Lovelorn, 512
Advise and Consent, 391
Affairs of Annabel, 434
Affairs of Cellini, The, 544
Affectionately Yours, 81
Afraid to Talk, 354, 358
After the Thin Man, 341, 483
After Tonight, 462
Age of Consent, The, 151, 320, 354
Age of Innocence, The, 99
Aggie Appleby—Maker of Men, 243
Ah, Wilderness!, 254, 355-7
Air Mail, 78
Airport, 430
Alaskan, The, 532
Albert, Eddie, 18–25, 39, 56
Albright, Hardie, 26–33
Alex the Great, 236
Alias Jimmy Valentine, 34
Alias Mary Dow, 199
Alibi, 410
Alice in Wonderland, 123, 237
All-American, The, 229, 358, 497
Allegheny Uprising, 173

All Men Are Enemies, 520
All Quiet on the Western Front, 152
All the Fine Young Candidates, 73
All the Way Home, 47
Aloha, 402
Along Came Youth, 164
Always Goodbye, 42, 338
Amateur Gentleman, The, 341
Amateur Orphan, An, 408
Amazing Grace, 224
Ambassador's Daughter, The, 349
American Madness, 156, 298
American Romance, An, 174
American Tragedy, An, 164, 274, 277, 318
Among the Living, 207
Among the Missing, 151
Andy Hardy's Private Secretary, 286
Angel from Texas, An, 19
Angel on My Shoulder, 31
Angel's Holiday, 526
Animal Kingdom, The, 242
Annabel Takes a Tour, 434
Anna Christie, 89
Annapolis Farewell, 151
Anne of Green Gables, 328
Annie Oakley, 231
Another Dawn, 285
Another Face, 171
Another Language, 60
Anthony Adverse, 367
Anthony and Cleopatra, 269
Antigone, 62
Arctic Flight, 422
Are These Our Children?, 318, 357
Arizona Mahoney, 142
Arizona Raiders, 143
Arizona to Broadway, 181
Arizonian, The, 231
Arkansas Traveler, The, 62
Armstrong, Robert, 34–41, 129, 151, 156-7
Around the World in 80 Days, 436, 464, 470
Artists and Models, 440

Assigned to Danger, 457
Atlantik, 345
Attack!, 22
Avalanche, 115
Awful Truth, The, 79, 81

Babe Ruth Story, The, 90
Babes in Bagdad, 100
Baby Cyclone, The, 35
Baby Face, 133
Baby Take a Bow, 181
Bachelor Apartment, 318
Bachelor Bait, 237
Bachelor of Arts, 366
Bachelor's Daughter, The, 191
Back Street, 96–7, 99
Bad and the Beautiful, The, 464
Bad Boy, 404
Bad Company, 519
Badge of Honor, 140
Bad Girl, 178, 180, 196
Badlands of Dakota, 207
Bad Men of Missouri, 421
Bailout at 43,000, 333
Ballad of the City, 47
Bandido, 464
Bandit of Sherwood Forest, 369
Bandits of Corsica, The, 272
Bank's Half Million, The, 34
Barbary Coast, 171, 492
Barefoot in the Park, 47
Bari, Lynn, 42–9
Barker, The, 151
Barnes, Binnie, 20, 50–7, 270
Baroness and the Butler, The, 42
Bataan, 428
Batman, 392, 472
Battle of Broadway, 173
Battle of the Sexes, 160
Bat Whispers, The, 411
Beal, John, 58–65
Beau Geste, 88, 102, 173
Beautiful Blonde from Bashful Bend, The, 470
Beautiful Cheat, The, 257
Beauty and the Boss, 383
Beavers, Louise, 66–73
Because of You, 168
Becky Sharpe, 167
Bedelia, 286
Bedtime Story, A, 519
Beg, Borrow, or Steal, 62
Beginning or the End, The, 174
Behind Red Lights, 31
Behind the Mask, 156
Bellamy, Ralph, 76–85, 157
Belle of the Nineties, 449
Beloved, 97, 498
Beloved Bachelor, The, 374
Beloved Brat, The, 255
Beloved Infidel, 23

Beloved Rogue, The, 402
Beloved Traitor, 408
Below the Sea, 78
Belyi Orel (The White Eagle), 488
Beneath the Twelve-Mile Reef, 464
Benson Murder Case, The, 374
Berlin Express, 377
Best Man, The, 458
Best of the Badman, 115
Betrayal, The, 338
Between Us Girls, 99
Be Yourself, 35
B. F.'s Daughter, 362
Bickford, Charles, 86–93, 122, 139, 142, 151, 168
Big Broadcast of 1936, 434
Big Circus, The, 464
Big City Blues, 354
Big Country, The, 88
Big Hand for the Little Lady, A, 91, 130
Big Hello, The, 470
Big House, The, 89, 410–11
Big Jake, 116
Big News, 35
Big Time, 128, 221, 510
Billion Dollar Scandal, The, 36, 156
Bill of Divorcement, A, 60, 366, 383
Billy (Budd), 64
Billy the Kid, 174, 286, 298
Biography, 31
Birthday Blues, 402
Birth of the Blues, 173
Bits of Life, 532
Black Camel, The, 196
Black Castle, The, 272
Black Cat, The, 384
Black Pearl, The, 464
Blessed Event, 104, 510
Blind Adventure, 36
Blind Alley, 81, 190, 413
Blithe Spirit, 159
Blonde Saint, The, 461
Blonde Venus, 403
Blood and Sand, 44
Blood Money, 164
Blood of Fu Manchu, The, 272
Blood on the Sun, 38
Blues in the Night, 428
Blue Skies, 517
Blue, White and Perfect, 428
Body and Soul, 338
Boles, John, 94–101
Bolivar, 338
Bombardier, 20
Bombay Clipper, 245
Bomben Auf Monte Carlo, 489
Bombshell, 69, 512
Bombs over Burma, 536
Boomerang, 552
Border Cafe, 61
Border Flight, 203

Bordertown, 360
Born Reckless, 510
Boston Blackie, 413–4
Bottoms Up, 97
Bounty Killer, The, 143
Bowery, The, 544
Boy and the Eagle, The, 406
Boyfriend, 526
Boy Meets Girl, 79
Boys from Syracuse, The, 18–9, 307
Boys Will Be Boys, 34
Bramble Bush, 184
Brave Tomorrow, 63
Breezing Home, 54
Brian, Mary, 102–9, 128, 275
Bride of Frankenstein, The, 140
Bride of the Colorado, The, 96
Bridge of San Luis Rey, The, 46, 349
Brief Moment, 133, 454
Brigham Young—Frontiersman, 173
Bright Eyes, 181, 524, 526, 530
Bright Lights, 190
British Agent, 243, 467
Broadway Bad, 311
Broadway Hostess, 506
Broadway Serenade, 286
Broadway Thru a Keyhole, 156, 330
Broken Lullaby, 277
Brooklyn Orchid, The, 237
Brother Orchid, 81
Brother Rat, 18–9, 418
Brother Rat and a Baby, 19, 418
Brown of Harvard, 102
Brute Force, 90
Buck Rogers, 142
Buckskin Frontier, 550
Bulldog Drummond at Bay, 312
Bulldog Jack, 544
Bullfighter and the Lady, The, 464
Bungalow, 13, 152
Bureau of Missing Persons, 214
Burnt Offerings, 392
Butter and Egg Man, The, 19
Buy Me That Town, 428
By Candlelight, 341
By Your Leave, 504

Cabaret, 23
Cabin in the Cotton, 28
Cabot, Bruce, 34, 78, 110–17, 143, 165
Caged Fury, 143
Caine Mutiny, 430
Call a Messenger, 142
Called on Account of Darkness, 403
Call Her Savage, 462
Call It a Day, 255, 285, 367
Call of the Wild, 434
Cameo Kirby, 221
Camille, 461
Campus Flirt, The, 461

Candlelight, 374
Candyapple, The, 64
Cape Forlorn (The Love Storm), 284
Captain Barnacle, Diplomat, 326
Captain Carey, U.S.A., 349
Captain Caution, 113
Captain Eddie, 46, 90
Captain from Castile, 470
Captain Hates the Sea, 251
Captain Newman, M.D., 23, 530
Captain of the Guard, 96
Captain Scarlet, 272
Captive Girl, 143
Captured!, 359, 374
Capture of Budapest, 377
Caravan, 278
Cardinal Richelieu, 468
Cardinal, The, 391
Career Woman, 356
Carefree, 79
Carnival, 199, 510
Carolina, 151, 222
Carrie, 22
Carrot and Cub, 62
Casanova Brown, 368
Case of Sergeant Grischa, 410
Case of the Lucky Legs, The, 506
Case of the Stuttering Bishop, The, 190
Casino Murder Case, The, 374
Cass Timberlane, 292, 362
Casta Diva (The Divine Spark), 278
Castle on the Hudson, 389
Cat and the Canary, The, 62, 400
Cat Creeps, The, 518
Cat People, 479
Caught, 164
Cavalcade, 52, 56, 254, 358–9, 363
Celebrity, 35
Central Airport, 199
Chance at Heaven, A, 165
Chandler, Helen, 61, 118–25
Change of Heart, 181
Channel Crossing, 157
Charlie Chan in City of Darkness, 44
Charlie Chan in Rio, 312
Charlot, 52
Charming Deceiver, The, 157
Charter Pilot, 44
Chase, The, 63, 116
Chasing Danger, 44
Chatterbox, 278
Checkers, 34
Chetniks, 494
Cheyenne Autumn, 316, 464
Child of Manhattan, 97
Children of Pleasure, 249
Children's Hour, The, 254
China Clipper, 416
China Girl, 46
Chinatown Charlie, 533
Chinese Parrot, The, 533

Chocolate Soldier, The, 22
Christopher Strong, 122
Chubasco, 232
Chu Chin Chow, 535
Cisco Kid and the Lady, The, 468
City Streets, 250, 374
Clairvoyant, The, 544
Clans across the Seas, 58
Clarke, Mae, 39, 126–31, 278
Claudia and David, 443
Clear All Wives, 512
Clearing in the Woods, A, 47
Clearing the Range, 196
Cleopatra Collins, 72
Clive of India, 468
Close Harmony, 236, 433
Coast Guard, 167
Cock of the Air, 411
Cody of the Pony Express, 406
College Coach, 190
College Humor, 434
College Rhythm, 434
Colorado Sunset, 142
Comancheros, The, 116
Come and Get It, 205
Comeback Trail, The, 144
Come Out of the Pantry, 544
Coming Out Party, 165
Comet over Broadway, 285
Command Decision, 91, 174
Condemned Women, 199
Coney Island, 470
Confession, 285
Confessions, 282
Confessions of a Co-Ed, 110, 277
Confessions of a Nazi Spy, 347, 376
Connecticut Yankee, A, 22
Convention in Cuba, 61
Cook, Donald, 122, 132–7, 168
Coquette, 68, 78
Coroner Creek, 200
Corregidor, 342
Corsair, 411
Counterfeit, 426
Countess of Monte Cristo, The, 544
Count of Monte Cristo, The, 341
County Chairman, The, 223
Court-Martial of Billy Mitchell, The, 83, 91
Cowboy for Chris, A, 143
Crabbe, Larry "Buster," 138–45, 164
Cradle Song, The, 26, 91, 254, 439
Craig's Wife, 99
Crash, The, 28
Crawling Hand, The, 323
Crazy House, 307
Crime Doctor, 362
Crime of Dr. Forbes, The, 500
Crime of the Century, The, 164, 251
Criminal Code, The, 156–7, 277
Criminal Lawyer, 552

Criminals Within, 357
Crimson City, The, 533
Crimson Romance, 28
Cromwell, Richard, 146–53
Crooked Sky, The, 422
Crooner, 189, 383
Cross Channel, 422
Cross Country Romance, 457
Crossfire, 332
Crouching Beast, The, 251
Crowd Roars, The, 188, 245, 354
Cummings, Constance, 79, 154–61
Curly Top, 97
Curse of the Cat People, The, 479

Dance, Fools, Dance, 188
Dance, Girl, Dance, 81
Dance Hall, 470
Dancers in the Dark, 28
Dancers, The, 128
Dance Team, 180, 196
Dancing Lady, 42
Dangerous to Know, 440, 536
Danger Street, 528
Daring Years, The, 235
Dark Hazard, 504
Das Schicksal der Renate Langen, 345
Daughter of Shanghai, 142, 536
Daughter of the Dragon, 534
Day at the Races, A, 304, 340
Daybreak, 122–3, 191, 397
Day of the Locust, The, 392
Days of Wine and Roses, The, 91
Daytime Wife, 55
Death at the Broadcasting House, 284
Death Kiss, The, 383
Death Takes a Holiday, 439
Decameron Nights, 56
Dee, Frances, 162–9, 277
Deep Purple, The, 34
Deep Valley, 422
Der Morder Dimitri Karamosoff, 489
Derumberkanuta Morgen, 372
Desert Gold, 140
Desert Hawk, The, 270, 463
Desert Pursuit, 422
Desert Song, The, 96, 99, 115
Destination Unknown, 78
Destry Rides Again, 173
Devil and Daniel Webster, The (All That Money
   Can Buy), 479
Devil Dancer, The, 533
Devil Dogs of the Air, 360
Devil Is a Sissy, The, 285
Devil Is a Woman, The, 468
Devil Is Driving, The, 403
Devil Is Yellow, The, 360
Devil's Holiday, The, 276
Devil's in Love, 311
Devil's Lottery, The, 338

Devil's Skipper, The, 220
Devil to Pay, The, 156
Dial M for Murder, 143
Diamond Jim, 52, 468
Diamond Lil, 69
Diamonds Are Forever, 116
Diary of a Chambermaid, The, 349, 390
Die Wunderbar Luge der Nina Petrovna, 345
Dinky, 449
Dinner at Eight, 278, 512
Dinner at the Ritz, 376
Dinty, 532
Disgraced, 112, 520
Disorderly Conduct, 78, 196, 402
Disorderly Orderly, The, 217
Dispatch from Reuter's, A, 19
Dive Bomber, 81
Divorce, 115
Divorcee, The, 410
Divorce of Lady X, The, 54
Dr. Jekyll and Mr. Hyde, 63, 286
Dr. Socrates, 190
Doctor Takes a Wife, The, 442
Doctor X, **229**, 510, 543
Dodge City, 113, 312
Dominant Sex, The, 278
Donlevy, Brian, 42, 170–7
Donna Senza Nome, 480
Don't Get Personal, 182, 199
Double Alibi, 360
Double Man, The, 430
Double Wedding, 62
Doubting Thomas, 439
Dough Boys, 196
Dove, The, 461
Downhill, 284
Down to the Sea in Ships, 364
Dracula, 122–3, 383
Dragnet, 108
Dragstrip Riot, 546
Dramatic School, 506
Dream of Kings, A, 286
Dressed to Kill, 428
Drift Fence, 140
Dry Martini, 195
Dude from Montana, The, 272
Dude Goes West, The, 20
Dude Ranch, 263
Duel in the Sun, 90
Duffy of San Quentin, 333
Duke of Chicago, 239
Dumbells in Ermine, 35
Dummy, The, 433
Dunn, James, 129, 178–85
Dvorak, Ann, 61, 151, 164, 186–93
Dynamite, 88, 296, 299
Dynamiters, The (The Gelignite Gang), 422

Each Dawn I Die, 46
Earthbound, 44

East of Java, 89
Easy to Love, 504
Ebb Tide, 205, 426
Edge of Darkness, 62
Edward, My Son, 286
Eight Girls in a Boat, 299, 398
Eight Iron Men, 406
Eilers, Sally, 78, 129, 157, 194–201
Ellery Queen, Master Detective, 81
Ellery Queen's Penthouse Mystery, 536
El Señor y La Cleopatra, 464
Elstree Calling, 534
Emma, 148
Enter Laughing, 47
Enter Madame!, 341
Escape to Danger, 191
Escape to Witch Mountain, 24
Eurydice, 62
Eve of St. Mark, The, 404
Everybody Sing, 306
Every Day's a Holiday, 426
Everyman Today, 63
Everything Is Thunder, 398
Everything's on Ice, 357
Exclusive, 205, 426
Excuse Me, 95
Exile Express, 493
Ex-Lady, 454
Ex-Mrs. Bradford, The, 36
Experiment Perilous, 377
Expert, The, 402
Extra Day, The, 480

Facts of Life, The, 73
Fallen Angel, 90, 115
Fall Guy, The, 128, 249
Family Affair, A, 356
Fanny, 62
Fanny Foley Herself, 122
Fan, The, 270
Farmer, Frances, 202–9
Farmer's Daughter, The, 90
Farmer Takes a Wife, The, 89, 526
Farrell, Glenda, 210–19
Fast Company, 433
Fast Life, 410
Fast Workers, 36, 129
Fazil, 96
Fetchit, Stepin, 66, 220–5
Fifty Fathoms Deep, 148
55 Days at Peking, 378
Fight for Your Lady, 434
Fighting O'Flynn, The, 270
Fighting 69th, The, 81
Final Edition, 129
Finders Keepers, 433
Finishing School, 165, 264
Finn and Hattie, 263
Fireball Forward, 23
Firebird, The, 366

Firefly, The, 306
Fire Over Africa, 56
First Born, The, 532
First Hundred Years, The, 54
First Kiss, The, 542
First Lady, 231, 367
Fit to Fight, 328
Five and Ten, 397
Five Bloody Graves, 458
Five Came Back, 413
Flame of Barbary Coast, 191
Flame of Love, The, 534
Flame of New Orleans, The, 115
Flap, 316
Flash Gordon, 140, 142–4
Flash Gordon Conquers the Universe, 142
Flash Gordon's Trip to Mars, 142
Fleet's In, The, 433
Flight Angels, 81, 421
Florida Special, 199
Flowing Gold, 207
Flying Devils, 78, 320, 355
Flying Down to Rio, 454
Follies, 48
Follow the Leader, 229
Follow Through, 162
Fools for Scandal, 79
Footsteps in the Dark, 81
Forbidden, 78, 401
Forever Amber, 270
Forever and a Day, 286
Forgotten Babies, 402
Forgotten Commandments, 454
Forlorn River, 142
For the Love of Mike, 236
For Those Who Think Young, 39
Forty Carats, 56
Forty-five Fathers, 526
42nd Street, 214
Foster, Preston, 44, 61, 226–33
Four Daughters, 19
Four Devils, 364
Four Faces West, 90, 168
Four Feathers, The, 543
Four Frightened People, 243
Four Horsemen of the Apocalypse, The, 378
Four Men and a Prayer, 269
Four Mothers, 19
Fourposter, The, 63
Four Horseman, The, 358
Four Wives, 19
Fox Movietone Follies of 1929, 221
Francis Joins the WACs, 47
Frankenstein, 96, 129
Free Love, 504
Free Wheeling, 402
French without Tears, 269
Frisco Jenny, 133
From Hell to Heaven, 384, 434
From Here to Eternity, 22
Front Page, The, 81, 104, 128–9

Fugitive Kind, The, 315
Fugitive Lady, 56
Fugitive, The, 39
Full Confession, 199
Fuller Brush Girl, The, 22
Fun in Acapulco, 378
Fury, 113

Gaiety George, 270
Gallagher, Richard "Skeets," 234–9
Gallant Lady, 403
Gallant Sons, 257
Gambling, 251
Gambling on the High Seas, 450
Gang Busters, 38
Gang Buster, The, 249, 434
Gangs of New York, 190
Gargan, William, 81, 112, 165, 240–7
Gaslight, 152
Gasoline Love, 540
Gateway, 54, 462
Gay Adventure, The, 390
Gay Deception, The, 167, 346
Gay Diplomat, The, 504
Gay Paree, 126
General Spanky, 278
Gentleman's Agreement, 552
Gentle Julia, 526
Gentle People, The, 20
George White's 1935 Scandals, 182, 320
Getting Gertie's Garter, 56
Ghetto, The, 242
Ghost of Frankenstein, The, 81
Ghost Talks, The, 221, 517
Giant, 530
Gibson, Wynne, 156, 164, 248–53
Gift of Gab, 52
Ginger, 526
Gingerbread Lady, The, 48
Girl Crazy, 264, 320
Girl Friend, The, 449
Girl from Calgary, The, 330
Girl from God's Country, The, 550
Girl from London, A, 282
Girl from Tenth Avenue, The, 284
Girl in Every Pot, A, 35
Girl in 419, The, 181
Girl in the Hat Box, The, 488
Girl of the Golden West, The, 456
Girl Rush, The, 22
Girls' Dormitory, 474–5, 526
Girls of the Road, 190
Girl with the Moving Eyes, 266
Give Me Yesterday, 58
Glad Rag Doll, The, 68
Glamorous Nights, 312
Glamour, 157
Glass Key, The, 174, 257
G-Men, 36, 190
Goddess, The, 72

Go-Getter, 367
Going Places, 367
Gold Diggers of Broadway, 68
Gold Diggers of 1935, 214, 500
Gold Diggers of 1937, 215
Golden Harvest, 504
Gone with the Wind, 66, 312, 357
Good Bad Girl, The, 128
Goodbye Again, 62, 122, 504
Good-Bye Kiss, The, 194
Goodbye, My Fancy, 47
Good Fairy, The, 467
Good Men and True, 31
Good News, 138
Good Night Ladies, 251
Good Old Soak, 356
Good Sport, 68
Go West, Young Lady, 485
Grand Parade, The, 518
Granville, Bonita, 254–9
Great Adventures, The, 328
Great American Broadcast, The, 436, 470
Great Commandment, The, 62
Great Dictator, 436
Great Expectations, 278, 549
Great Flirtation, The, 341, 384
Great Gatsby, The, 76
Great Guy, 129
Great Impersonation, The, 81
Great McGinty, The, 173
Great Man's Lady, The, 174
Great Victor Herbert, The, 306
Great White Hope, The, 414
Greeks Had a Word for It, The, 28, 383
Green Archer, The, 312
Greene, Richard, 266–73
Green, Mitzi, 260–5
Grumpy, 276
Guadalcanal Diary, 231, 428
Guest in the House, 81
Guilty Generation, The, 156
Guilty of Treason, 91, 257
Guilty, The, 257
Gunfighters of Abilene, 143
Gun for a Coward, 292
Guns of Darkness, 286
Gypsy Colt, 168

Half Angel, 167
Half-Naked Truth, The, 510
Handle with Care, 311, 524
Hands Across the Table, 79
Hangmen Also Die, 174
Happiness Ahead, 290
Happy Landing, 168, 468
Hard to Get, 433
Hard to Handle, 104
Harmony Lane, 398
Harold Lloyd's World of Comedy, 156
Harvey Girls, The, 231

Hatari, 116
Hat Check Girl, 196
Hat, Coat and Glove, 60
Hatful of Rain, A, 430
Haunted Honeymoon, The, 159
Havana Widows, 214
Havoc, 78
Headline Shooter, 165
Heads Up, **229**
Heartbreak, 28
Heartbreak Kid, The, 23
Hearts in Bondage, 129, 182, 384
Hearts in Dixie, 221
Heaven Knows, Mr. Allison, 494
Heaven on Earth, 366
He Knew Women, 381
Helldorado, 79
Hello Frisco, Hello, 436
Hello, Sister!, 180
Hell's Angels, 188
Hell's Heroes, 88
Her Bodyguard, 251
Here Comes the Navy, 498
Here Comes Trouble, 320
Here's to Romance, 366–7, 506
Her First Beau, 292, 526
Her Husband Lies, 440
Her Man, 276–7, 518
Her Wedding Night, 236
He Was Her Man, 312
Hi, Nellie!, 212
His Girl Friday, 81
His House in Order, 284
His Woman, 242
Hitler's Children, 257
Hit the Deck, 63, 457
Hold Back the Dawn, 173
Hold 'em Yale, 140
Hold Me Tight, 199
Hold that Girl!, 181
Hold that Woman, 182
Holiday, 54, 78
Holiday Inn, 72
Holiday in Spain, 378
Hollywood Round-Up, 521
Hollywood Speaks, 504
Holmes, Phillips, 104, 128–9, 156, 274–81
Honey, 235, 260–1, 264
Honey Girl, 34
Honeymoon in Bali, 306
Honeymoon, The, 542
Hoopla, 151, **229**
Hooray for Love, 454
Hostess with the Mostess, The, 72
Hotel for Women, 44
Hotel Imperial, 112
Hound of the Baskervilles, The, 269
House Across the Street, The, 422
House by the River, 552
House Divided, A, 122, 397
Housemaster, The, 279

House of a Thousand Candles, The, 278
House of Seven Gables, The, 360
Housewife, 190
Huckleberry Finn, 264
Humaine, 479
Human Beginnings, 23
Human Growth, 23
Hunted Men, 426
Hunter, Ian, 269, 282–7
Hurry Sundown, 392
Hush Money, 26
Hustle, 24
Hutchinson, Josephine, 288–93

I Am a Fugitive from a Chain Gang, 212, **229**
I Am a Widow, 340
I Am Suzanne!, 454
I Am the Law, 62
I Believed in You, 97
Ice Station Zebra, 430
Idiot's Delight, 237, 388
I'd Rather Be Rich, 458
If I Had a Million, 164, 251, 439, 454
If I Were King, 167
I Found Stella Parish, 284
If This Be Sin, 270
I Give My Love, 355
Ihre Majestat Die Liebe, 345
I Knew 3,000 Lunatics, 31
I Know What I Like, 62
I Like It That Way, 447
I'll Cry Tomorrow, 22
I'll Tell the World, 513
Illusion, 276
I Loved a Woman, 504
I Loved You Wednesday, 311, 340
I Married a Doctor, 291
I Married an Angel, 55
Imitation of Life, 66, 69, 70, 72
Impact, 174, 536
Impatient Maiden, 129
Indiscreet, 489
Infernal Machine, 504
Informer, The, 231
In Harm's Way, 116, 392
Inheritors, The, 58
In His Steps, 356
In Old Arizona, 410
In Old Chicago, 173
Inseparables, The, 338
Inside Story, The, 443
Inspiration, 188
Instant of Truth, 333
Interlude, 554
Internes Can't Take Money, 426
In the Matter of J. Robert Oppenheimer, 64
Intimate Stranger, The, (Finger of Guilt), 160
Into the Blue, 160
Invisible Man, The, 498
Iron Man, 35

Island of Lost Men, 536
Isle of Fury, 360
Is My Face Red?, 320, 519
I Spy, 199
Is Zat So?, 35, 38, 440
It Comes Up Love, 286
It Had to Happen, 320
It Happened in Flatbush, 428
It Happened One Night, 513
It Pays to Advertise, 237
It's a Bet, 124
It's All Yours, 347
It's in the Bag, 56
Ivanov, 62
I've Got Your Number, 214
I Wake Up Screaming, 245
I Walked with a Zombie, 168
I Wanted Wings, 173, 421
I Was an Adventuress, 269
I Was an American Spy, 192
I Was a Prisoner on Devil's Island, 200

Jackie Robinson Story, The, 72
Jack London, 72
Jalna, 284, 299, 384
Jarr Family Discovers Harlem, The, 326
Java Head, 536
Jennie Gerhardt, 133
Jessie James, 173
Jewel Robbery, 28
Jezebel, 152, 360
Jigsaw, 390
Jimmy and Sally, 181
Joe and Ethel Turp Call on the President, 245
Joe Butterfly, 391
John and Julia, 160
John Gabriel Borkman, 26
John Loves Mary, 422
Johnny Belinda, 62, 90
Johnny Eager, 216
John Paul Jones, 115
Johnny in the Clouds (The Way to the Stars), 400
Johnson, Kay, 82, 88–9, 275, 294–301
Joker Is Wild, The, 22
Jollyanna, 62
Jones, Allan, 133, 302–9
Jory, Victor, 310–17
Josette, 476
Journey's End, 266, 381
Joy Girl, The, 121
Juarez, 462
Judge, Arline, 78, 151, 318–25
Judge Priest, 222, 366
Judy, 35
Julia Misbehaves, 470
Julius Caesar, 266
June Moon, 164, 250, 434
Jungle Jim, 143
Jungle Man, 142

Jungle Siren, 142
Just Like Heaven, 366
Just Off Broadway, 428

Kansan, The, 550
Kansas City Princess, 214
Kate Plus Ten (The Queen of Crime), 506
Kathleen, 442
Keep 'Em Rolling, 165
Keep Smiling, 526
Kelly, Paul, 156, 326–35
Kentucky, 269
Kick-In, 250
Kid Comes Back, The, 418
Kid from Kokomo, The, 418
Kid Galahad, 19, 416, 418
Kid's Clever, The, 220
Kiki, 476
Killer McCoy, 174, 184
Killer Shark, 406
Kim, 377
King for a Night, 520
King Kong, 34, 36, 39, 112, 540, 543–4, 546
King of Alcatraz, 426, 440
King of Burlesque, 320, 434
King of Chinatown, 536
King of Gamblers, 142
King of Jazz, The, 96
King of the Bandits, The, 463
King of the Congo, 143
King of the Jungle, 139, 164
King of the Rocket Men, 130
King Steps Out, The, 312
Kismet, 381
Kiss and Make Up, 504
Kiss before the Mirror, The, 133, 374, 498
Kisses for Breakfast, 550
Kissin' Cousins, 217
Kiss in the Dark, A, 422
Kiss of Death, 174
Kit Carson, 44
Knockout Reilly, 102
Knowing Men, 338
Koenigsmark, 341

Lad An' a Lamp, A, 402
Laddie, 500
Ladies Day, 20
Ladies Must Live, 421
Ladies of the Big House, 250, 454
Lady and Gent, 251
Lady, Be Careful, 142
Lady Behave, 199
Lady Bodyguard, 20
Lady by Choice, 449
Lady for a Day, 214
Lady from Chungking, 536
Lady in a Jam, 81
Lady in the Lake, 428

Lady Killer, 129, 360
Lady on a Train, The, 81
Lady Surrenders, A, 504
Lady Tubbs, 398
Lady Who Lied, The, 460
Lady with a Past, 383
Lady with Red Hair, 312
Lady X, 55
La Femme en Bleu, 480
Landi, Elissa, 78, 336–43
Larceny with Music, 307
La Ronde, 480
Last Days of Pompeii, The, 231
Last Flight, The, 122, 383, 542
Last Hunt, The, 430
Last Mile, The, 229
Last of the Mohicans, The, 54, 113, 142
Last of the Redmen, The, 143
Last Parade, The, 156
Last Train from Madrid, 462
Last Warning, The, 96
Las Vegas Nights, 307
Laughter in Hell, 497
La Vida Bohemia, 462
Lawless Eighties, The, 143
Lazy Lightning, 540
Leatherneck, The, 35
Lederer, Frances,.20, 46, 60, 167, 344–51
Legion of the Condemned, The, 542
Lemon Drop Kid, The, 428, 513
Lend an Ear, 62
Lend Me Your Husband, 364
Leopard Lady, The, 35
Le Petit Cafe, 164
Les Beaux Jours, 474
Les Miserables, 60
Let 'em Have It, 113
Let's Go Native, 236
Let's Live a Little, 494
Let Us Be Gay, 196
Liberty Jones, 62
Life Begins, 229, 354, 357
Life Begins at Forty, 151
Life Begins in College, 500
Life of Emile Zola, The, 79, 404
Life of Her Own, A, 192
Life of Vergie Winters, The, 99, 254
Light of Western Stars, The, 312
Light Up the Sky, 47
Lillian Russell, 44
Liliom, 58, 510
Limehouse Blues, 536
Linden, Eric, 78, 112, 151, 165, 278, 352–7
Lindsay, Margaret, 81, 358–63
Lisbon, 349
Little Caesar, 212
Little Foxes, The, 64
Little Man, What Now?, 398
Little Men, 403, 436
Little Minister, The, 60
Little Miss Marker, 115

Little Old New York, 269
Little Orphan Annie, 264
Little Princess, The, 269, 286, 288, 367, 468
Little Shepherd of Kingdom Come, The, 152
Littlest Rebel, The, 89, 99
Little Tommy Tucker, 52
Little Women, 165, 355, 398
Lives of a Bengal Lancer, The, 151
Living on Love, 182
Locket, The, 457
London, 338
Lone Ranger, The, 258
Lone Wolf in Paris, The, 347
Lone Wolf Meets a Lady, The, 312
Lone Wolf Returns, The, 440
Long Day's Journey into Night, 64, 160
Longest Yard, The, 23
Long, Long Trail, The, 195
Long Lost Father, 122
Long Night, The, 191
Long Way Home, The, 63
Looking for Trouble, 157, 320
Lorna Doone, 271
Lost Horizon, 549–50, 552
Lost in Alaska, 265
Louise, Anita, 269, 364–71
Love Among the Millionaires, 236, 261
Love and Hisses, 476
Love before Breakfast, 231
Love Crazy, 442
Love, Honor and Behave, 418
Love in the Rough, 483
Love Is a Racket, 164, 189
Love Is Better than Ever, 292
Love Laughs at Andy Hardy, 257
Love Letters, 368
Love Mart, The, 461
Love of Sunya, The, 95, 99
Love on a Bet, 454
Lover Come Back, 156, 436
Loves of an Actress, 374
Love Starved, 320
Love that Brute, 470
Loyal Lives, 410
Luckiest Girl in the World, The, 549
Lucky Boy, 212, 242
Lucky Devils, 112
Lucky Stiff, The, 39, 176
Lukas, Paul, 96, 157, 164, 372–9
Lulu Belle, 216

MacKenna's Gold, 316
McLintock!, 116
McQ, 23
Madame Butterfly, 99
Madame Du Barry, 312, 366
Madame Satan, 298
Madame Spy, 544
Madame X, 62
Made for Each Other, 72

Made on Broadway, 199
Mad Genius, The, 133
Mad Holiday, 341
Mad Miss Manton, The, 485
Madonna's Secret, The, 349, 443
Mad Wednesday, 323
Magic Box, The, 266
Magnificent Brute, The, 54
Magnificent Doll, The, 390
Magnificent Dope, The, 46
Magnificent Fraud, The, 428
Magnificent Lie, The, 78
Maid of Salem, 255
Main Event, 35
Maisie, 286
Make Me a Star, 277
Maltese Falcon, The, 89, 442
Man Betrayed, A, 168
Man for All Seasons, A, 64
Man from Toronto, The, 284
Manhattan Merry-Go-Round, 190
Man I Killed, The, 277
Man I Married, The, 348, 493
Man in the Mirror, The, 506
Man in the Saddle, The, 540
Man-Made Woman, 96
Manners, David, 28, 122, 278, 380–5
Man of Quality, A, 170
Man of the Forest, 139
Man of the World, 250
Man of Two Worlds, 341, 346
Man on the Eiffel Tower, The, 390
Man Power, 102
Man's Castle, 403
Manslaughter, 68
Man to Man, 277
Man Wanted, 383
Man Who Came Back, The, 34
Man Who Cheated Himself, The, 552
Man Who Found Himself, The, 61
Man Who Lived Twice, The, 79
Man Who Played God, The, 133
Man Who Wouldn't Die, The, 428
Man Who Wouldn't Talk, 428
Man with Two Faces, The, 129
Many Rivers to Cross, 292
Maracaibo, 349
Margie, 46
Marie Antoinette, 367
Marriage Playground, The, 104, 260
Marry Me, 284
Mars Attacks the World, 142
Mary Burns, Fugitive, 171
Masquerade in Mexico, 191
Massacre, 190
Match King, The, 28
Matriarch, 47
Maybe It's Love, 500
Meanest Gal in Town, The, 237
Meet Me After the Show, 22
Meet the Girls, 42

568

Meet the Stewarts, 168
Melody for Three, 546
Melody Lingers On, The, 290
Member of the Wedding, The, 406
Men Are Such Fools, 418
Men Must Fight, 278
Men of the North, 462
Men on Call, 128
Merchant of Venice, The, 26, 31
Mercy Plane, 182
Meredith, Burgess, 60–1, 386–93
Merrily We Live, 190, 255
Message to Garcia, A, 99
Metropolitan, 468
Michael O'Halloran, 251
Michael Shayne, Private Detective, 428
Midas Run, 472
Middle of the Night, 217
Midnight, 347
Midnight Alibi, 122
Midnight Court, 190
Midnight Story, The, 464
Midshipman, The, 461
Midsummer Night's Dream, A, 284, 312
Mighty Joe Young, 39
Milky Way, The, 245
Millie, 366, 518–9
Millionaire, The, 383
Million Dollar Baby, 320
Million Dollar Legs, 142, 434
Million Dollar Weekend, 457
Mind Reader, The, 156
Mine Own Executioner, 390
Miracle in Harlem, 223
Miracle in the Rain, 246
Miracle Man, The, 411
Miracle of Morgan's Creek, The, 174
Miracle of Our Lady of Fatima, The, 464
Miracle on 34th Street, 90
Miracle Woman, The, 383
Miracle Worker, The, 316
Misleading Lady, 242
Miss Annie Rooney, 245, 404
Mississippi, 439
Miss Liberty, 20
Miss Swan Expects, 62
Mr. and Mrs. Smith, 457
Mr. Blandings Builds His Dream House, 66, 72
Mr. Boggs Steps Out, 124
Mr. Lucky, 299
Mr. Moto's Gamble, 42
Mr. Pim Passes By, 58
Mister Roberts, 63
Mr. Satan, 237
Mr. Scoutmaster, 168
Mr. Wu, 532
M'Liss, 61
Modern Cinderella, A, 171
Mom and Dad, 32
Monte Carlo, 162
Montgomery, Douglass, 122, 278, 394–401

Moonlight and Pretzels, 107, 447
Moonstone, The, 384
Moon over Burma, 231
Moore, Dickie, 402–7
Morals of Marcus, The, 284
More Pay—Less Work, 102
More the Merrier, The, 89
Morning After, The, 199
Morris, Chester, 408–15
Morris, Wayne, 20, 416–23
Mortal Storm, The, 257
Moskva V Oktjabre (Moscow Laughs and Cries/
    When Moscow Laughs), 488
Most Dangerous Game, The, 36, 138, 544
Most Precious Thing in Life, 133, 151
Mother's Boy, 121, 171
Mother's Cry, 383
Mountain Justice, 290
Move Over, Darling, 442
Movie Crazy, 156
Mummy, The, 140, 383
Murder Goes to College, 142
Murder in the Zoo, 439
Murder with Pictures, 440
Music in the Air, 97, 398
Music Man, The, 23
Music Master, The, 121, 364
Mutiny in the Big House, 89
My American Wife, 347
My Bill, 255, 404
My Blue Heaven, 552
My Daughter Joy (Operation X), 270
My Favorite Spy, 38
My Favorite Wife, 440, 442
My Friend Flicka, 231
My Lips Betray, 97
My Love Come Back, 19
My Lucky Star, 269, 468
My Man Godfrey, 190, 440
My Six Convicts, 62, 464
My Son, My Son, 168, 292
Mystery Broadcast, 251
Mystery of Edwin Drood, 384, 398
Mystery of the Wax Museum, 543–4
My Woman, 520

Nameless Men, 220
Name the Woman, 151
Nana, 31, 129, 278, 490
Nancy Drew, Detective, 257
Navy Blues, 20, 436
Ned McCobb's Daughter, 35
Nevada, 140
Never Too Late, 554
New Klondike, The, 328
New Moon, The, 122
News Is Made at Night, 44
New York, 235
New York Nights, 461
Nice Women, 164

Night after Night, 156, 251
Night at the Opera, A, 304
Night before the Divorce, The, 46
Night Court, 277
Night in Montmartre, A, 52
Nightmare, 174
Night Mayor, The, 510
Night of June 13th, 164
Night of the Party, The, 284
Night World, 129
Nine-Fifteen Revue, 318
Nine Girls, 368
Ninth Guest, The, 28
Nocturne, 47
No Hard Feelings, 23
Nolan, Lloyd, 44, 424–31
No More Frontiers, 60
No More Ladies, 437
No Mother to Guide Her, 503
None But the Lonely Heart, 550
No Other Woman, 354
No Questions Asked, 171
No Ransom, 278
North Star, The, 528
Northwest Frontier (Flame over India), 286
North West Mounted Police, 231
Not As a Stranger, 91
Not for Sale, 282
Nothing But the Truth, 226, 249
No Time for Comedy, 62, 506
Now Barabbas Was a Robber, 270
Now I'll Tell, 520
Now, Voyager, 257
Nuisance, The, 512
Nun and the Sergeant, The, 494

Oakie, Jack, 104, 164, 432–7
Obey the Law, 403
O, Evening Star, 18
Of Human Bondage, 165, 299
Of Mice and Men, 89, 389
Oh, Yeah!, 35
Oil for the Lamps of China, 290
Oil Raider, The, 140
Okay, America!, 358
Oklahoma, 22
Old Arizona, 468
Old Dark House, The, 358, 497
Old Hutch, 356
Old Kentucky, 220
Old San Francisco, 533
Oliver Twist, 403
Olivia (Pit of Loneliness), 480
Once in a Lifetime, 434
Once to Every Woman, 544
One Heavenly Night, 96
One Hour Late, 320, 520
One Hour with You, 504
One in a Million, 320

One Is Guilty, 79
One Man's Journey, 165
One More River, 549
One Night in the Tropics, 307
One Rainy Afternoon, 346
One Sunday Afternoon, 542
One Touch of Venus, 99
Only the Brave, 104, 276
Only Yesterday, 97
On Our Merry Way, 390
On Trial, 360
On Your Toes, 19
Orchestra Wives, 46, 470
Orders Is Orders, 284
Orders to Kill, 23
Oscar, The, 184
Our Betters, 366, 462
Our Fighting Navy (Torpedoed!), 153
Our Hearts Were Growing Up, 174
Our Neighbors, the Carters, 506
Our Town, 64
Our Very Own, 135, 192, 552
Out of the Blue, 191
Out of the Fog, 20
Outward Bound, 121
Over the Hill, 180, 196

Pace that Kills, The, 39
Pack Up Your Troubles, 44, 526
Paddy O'Day, 526
Paddy, the Next Best Thing, 360
Paid, 35, 397
Painted Desert, The, 518
Painted Hills, The, 333
Pals to the End, 39
Pandora's Box, 345
Paramount on Parade, 236, 261, 276, 542
Paris at Midnight, 102
Parisian, The, 338
Parlor, Bedroom and Bath, 196
Parole Girl, 78
Party Husband, 133
Passion Flower, 89, 298, 402
Passport to Hell, A, 338, 374
Past of Mary Holmes, The, 237, 354
Paths of Glory, 422
Patrick, Gail, 20, 438–45
Payment on Demand, 168
Penguin Pool Murder, The, 36
Pepper, 526
Perfect Marriage, 20
Perfect Understanding, 504
Perfumed Lady, The, 171
Personal Maid, 454
Persons in Hiding, 521
Peter Pan, 102, 107, 532
Petrified Forest, The, 62, 506
Petrus, 480
Peyton Place, 430

Physician, The, 284
Piccadilly, 534
Picture of Dorian Gray, The, 152
Picture Snatcher, 78
Pier, 13, 44
Pierre of the Plains, 115
Pirates of the High Seas, 143
Pit Stop, 176
Place in the Sun, A, 277
Plain and Fancy, 47
Plainsman and the Lady, The, 443
Plainsman, The, 88
Planet Outlaws, 142
Plastic Age, The, 460–1
Playboy of Paris, 164
Play, Genius, Play!, 31
Playing Around, 410
Pleasure Cruise, 504
Plough and the Stars, The, 231, 255
Plunder Road, 422
Pointed Heels, 236, 276
Poor Little Rich Girl, The, 500
Poppy, 151
Poppy Is Also a Flower, 464
Port of the Seven Seas, 62
Portrait in Black, 430, 538
Possessed, 237
Potomok Chingis—Khana (Storm over Asia),
  488
Potters, The, 235
Power and the Glory, The, **229**
Praise House, 72
President Vanishes, The, 330
Pretty Little Parlor, 81
Price of Things, The, 338
Pride of the Legion, The, 310
Pride of the Yankees, The, 20
Prince of Tempters, The, 102
Prisoner of Shark Island, The, 500
Private Affairs of Bel Ami, 168, 191
Private Jones, 497, 510
Private Life of Don Juan, The, 52
Private Life of Henry VIII, 52, 54
Private Scandal, 278
Private Wives, 237
Professional Soldier, 500
· Professionals, The, 83
Pryor, Roger, 446–51
Public Enemy, The, 126, 129, 131, 133, 188
Puddin'head, 349
Purchase Price, The, 28
Pursuit of Happiness, 346
Pursuit of the Graf Spee, 286

Quarterback, The, 421
Queen of the Mob, 81
Quicker 'n a Wink, 368
Quick Millions, 196
Quiet American, The, 115

Racketeer, The, 35
Racket, The, 236
Rain, 76, 242
Rainbow on the River, 72
Ramona, 186
Rascals, 526
Rat Race, The, 436
Rawhide Years, The, 246
Raymond, Gene, 26, 164–5, 452–9
Real Glory, The, 299
Reap the Wild Wind, 66, 89
Rebecca, 304
Reckless, 304
Red Barry, 142
Red Dancer, The, 78
Red Dust, 454
Red-Headed Woman, 411, 413
Red Lantern, The, 532
Red Mill, The, 194
Red Peppers, 55
Red Salute, 31
Reducing, 196
Remarkable Andrew, The, 174
Remember Last Night?, 157, 199
Rendezvous, 54
Rendezvous with Annie, 20
Renegades, 310
Resurrection, 96, 462
Retire In, 179
Return of Dracula, The, 349
Return of Doctor X, 421
Return of Sherlock Holmes, The, 276
Return of Jesse James, The, 192
Return of the Cisco Kid, 44, 468
Reuben, Reuben, 22
Reunion in Reno, 168
Rhythm of the Islands, 307
Rhythm on the Range, 205
Riches and Romance, 107
Rich Man's Folly, 164
Ride a Crooked Mile, 206
Ride On, Vaquero, 468–9
Riders of Death Valley, 89
Right Approach, The, 530
Right to Live, The, 290
Right to Love, The, 383
Rio Rita, 96
Riptide, 237
Rip Van Winkle, 76
River's End, 312
Road Back, The, 152
Road House, 433
Roadhouse Murder, The, 354
Roadside, 78
Road to Reno, 237
Road to Yesterday, 410
Roaming Lady, 544
Roaring Ranch, 196
Roar of the Dragon, 320
Robin Hood of Eldorado, 113, 356

Rocket Ship, 140
Rogue's March, 272
Roland, Gilbert, 20, 460–5
Romance in Manhattan, 346
Romance in the Rain, 447
Romance of the Underworld, 34, 96
Romance in the Dark, 99
Roman Holiday, 22
Roman Scandals, 384, 498
Romero, Cesar, 466–73
Room Service, 18, 31
Roots of Heaven, The, 22, 378
Rose Bowl, 142
Rosemary's Baby, 83
Rose of the Golden West, 461
Rose of the Rancho, 99
Rose-Marie, 304
Royal Family of Broadway, The, 104
Royal Mounted Rides Again, The, 39
Ruby Gentry, 292
Ruggles of Red Gap, 115
Running Wild, 102
Russet Mantle, 31, 61

Sacred Flame, The, 290
Sadie McKee, 454
Sailor Be Good, 434
Sailor's Lady, 142
Sailor's Luck, 181, 199, 311
St. Louis Blues, 426
Sally, 112
Sally in Our Alley, 284
Salomy Jane, 78
Salto Mortale (Trapeze), 489
Salty O'Rourke, 115
Salute, 121, 221
Salute to France, 390
Salvation Nell, 122
San Antonio, 332
San Francisco Docks, 389
Santa Fe Trail, The, 263
Sap from Syracuse, The, 433
Saturday Night, 26, 68
Say, Darling, 23
Scandal, 96
Scarface, 188
Scarlet Letter, The, 31
Scarlet Pimpernel, The, 243
Scent of Mystery, 378
School for Wives, 170
Sea Bat, The, 89
Sea Hawk, The, 462
Sea Hound, The, 143
Sea Legs, 433
Search for Beauty, 36, 140
Second Choice, 410
Second Chorus, 389
Second Hand Wife, 78
Second Little Show, The, 318
Secret Agent of Japan, 46

Secret Code, The, 330
Secret of Convict Lake, The, 192
Secret of Madame Blanche, The, 278
Secret Six, The, 78
Secrets of an Actress, 285
Secrets of the Lone Wolf, 312
Seed, 96, 99, 402, 504
See the Man Run, 23
Sensation Hunters, 320
Sergeant Ryker, 430
Servants in the House, The, 76
Seven Sinners (The Wrecker), 159
Seventh Heaven, 476
70,000 Witnesses, 277
Shadow Laughs, The, 467
Shadow of the Eagle, 270
Shadow, The, 312
Shady Lady, 35
Shame, 532
Shanghai Bound, 102
Shanghaied Love, 148
Shanghai Express, 535
Sharpshooters, 42
She Couldn't Say No, 410, 450
She Couldn't Take It, 426
She Done Him Wrong, 69, 462
She Got What She Wanted, 510
She Had to Choose, 140
She Loves Me Not, 60, 62
Shepherd of the Hills, The, 76
Sheriff of Fractured Jaw, 115
She's Got Everything, 456
She's No Lady, 190
She Was a Lady, 520
She Wrote the Book, 501
Ship from Shanghai, The, 296
Shock, 46
Shooting High, 526
Shoot the Works, 320, 434
Show Boat, 99, 133, 221, 304
Show Folks, 35
Show of Shows, The, 410
Show Them No Mercy, 113
Sign of the Cross, The, 336, 338–9
Silk Harry, 251
Silk Hat Kid, The, 129
Silver Cord, The, 165, 354
Silver Queen, 115
Silver Spoon, The, 284
Silver Tassie, The, 52
Silver Whittle, The, 23
Simon, Simone, 474–81, 526
Sin, 338
Sinfonia Fatale (When in Rome), 401
Sing As You Go, 266
Sing, Boy, Sing, 292
Single Sin, The, 298
Singleton, Penny, 482–7
Sinners in the Sun, 411
Sinner Take All, 360
Sin Town, 433

Sisters, The, 284, 367
Sisters Under the Skin, 340
Sitting Pretty, 126, 434
Sixth Commandment, The, 364
Skidoo, 392, 472
Skippy, 264
Sky Devils, 188
Sky Hawk, The, 121
Skylark, 55
Skyline, 28
Sky Raiders, 38
Sleepers East, 251
Sleepers West, 428
Sleep No More, 38
Slide, Kelly, Slide, 328
Small Town Deb, 526
Small Town Girl, 54
Smart Blonde, 215
Smartest Girl in Town, The, 454, 456
Smash-up—The Story of a Woman, 20
Smiling Ghost, The, 421
Smilin' Through, 286, 457
Smoky, 115, 311
Snowed Under, 506
So Big, 28, 402
Sob Sister, 180
Social Lion, The, 236
Society Girl, 180
So Ends Our Night, 168, 493
Sofia, 457
Soldier of Fortune, 494
Soliloquy, 62
Sol Madrid, 378
Somewhere in France, 159
Somewhere in the Night, 292, 428
Song, 534
Song and Dance Man, The, 330
Song of Bernadette, The, 89
Song of Songs, 28
Song of the City, 360
Song of the Islands, 436
Song of the West, 96
Son of Frankenstein, 291
Son of Fury, 207, 299
Son of Kong, The, 36
Sophie Lang Goes West, 142
Sophie's Place, 472
Sorrowful Jones, 115
So This Is Marriage?, 95
Souls at Sea, 167
Sound and the Fury, The, 63
Southern Yankee, A, 174
South of Pago Pago, 207
South Sea Rose, 88
Spanish Cape Mystery, 520
Special Delivery, 328
Spendthrift, 107
Spiral Staircase, The, 23
Spirit of Youth, The, 366
Spitfire, 79
Split Second, 333

Spoilers, The, 298, 362
Sporting Blood, 245
Sport Parade, The, 242
Springfield Rifle, 333
Spring Madness, 388
Springtime in the Rockies, 470
Spy, The, 298
Squadron Leader X, 191
Square Crooks, 35
Square Jungle, The, 333
Squaw Man, The, 88, 402
Stagecoach, 173
Stage Door, 31, 440
Stage Door Canteen, 81
Stage to Tucson, 200, 422
Stairs of Sand, 276
Stand by for Action, 174
Stand Up and Cheer, 97, 181, 222
Stanley and Livingstone, 269
Star for a Night, 320
Star Is Born, A, 91, 107
Star Witness, 402
State Fair, 196, 311
State of the Union, 82
State's Attorney, 519
Stay Away, Joe, 392
Steamboat 'round the Bend, 223
Sten, Anna, 79, 278, 285, 488–95
Step Down to Terror, 292
Stepping Along, 102
Stocks and Blondes, 236
Stolen Harmony, 426
Stolen Heaven, 277, 456
Stolen Holiday, 285
Stolen Identity, 349
Storm Center, 333
Story of G.I. Joe, The, 390
Story of Louis Pasteur, The, 291, 367, 404
Story of Temple Drake, 243
Strange Cargo, 286, 376
Strange Case of Clara Deane, The, 164, 250
Strange Interlude, 284
Strange Love of Molly Louvain, The, 148, 189, 510
Stranger in Town, 189, 383
Strangers on a Honeymoon, 159
Street Girl, 433–4
Street of Chance, 389, 440
Street of Women, 497
Streets of San Francisco, The, 39
Strictly Dishonorable, 96, 374, 467
Strike It Rich, 257
Strike Me Pink, 171, 199
Stronger than Desire, 190
Strongest Man in the World, 472
Stuart, Gloria, 60, 97, 496–501
Study in Scarlet, A, 535
Sturme Der Leidenschaft
   (Storms of Passion/The Tempest), 489
Submarine D-1, 418
Submarine Patrol, 269
Successful Calamity, A, 28

Such Good Friends, 392
Sudden Fear, 223
Suicide Fleet, The, 35
Sullivan's Travels, 81
Sun Also Rises, The, 22
Sundown, 115
Sunrise at Campobello, 83
Sunshine and Shadows, 68
Sun Shines Bright, The, 223
Sun Valley Serenade, 44
Suppressed Desires, 76
Sure Fire, 35
Surrender, 78, 349
Susan and God, 113
Susannah of the Mounties, 312
Susan Slade, 430
Suspense, 257
Sutter's Gold, 52, 513
Swamp Fire, 142
Sweepings, 354, 498
Sweet and Lowdown, 46
Sweetheart of Sigma Chi, 140
Sweetie, 433
Sweet Mama, 381
Sweet Music, 190
Swell Head, 403
Swing High, 518
Swing Your Lady, 487
Sword of Sherwood Forest, 272
Sympathy, 249
Syncopation, 284

Take a Chance, 181
Take, The, 23
Talent for Loving, A, 472
Tales from the Crypt, 272
Tales of Manhattan, 442, 470
Talk of the Devil, 199
Talk of the Town, 216
Tall, Dark and Handsome, 470
Tammy and the Doctor, 363
Tampico, 46
Tarzan the Fearless, 139
Task Force, 422, 552
Teahouse of the August Moon, The, 22, 63
Temptation Harbour, 480
Tender Is the Night, 378
Ten-Minute Alibi, 278
Ten Nights in a Bar Room, 58
Ten Who Dared, 64
Terror Is a Man, 349
Texan, The, 542
Texas, Brooklyn and Heaven, 184
Texas Rangers, The, 426
Thanks a Million, 190
That Certain Woman, 285, 367
That Girl from Paris, 434, 456
That Lady, 464
That Lady in Ermine, 470
That Night!, 63

That's Gratitude, 58
That's My Boy, 138, 148
That Uncertain Feeling, 389
Their Big Moment, 299
There Goes My Girl, 456
There Goes the Groom, 388
There's a Future in It, 191
There's Always Tomorrow, 52
There's Magic in Music, 307
These Three, 254
They Call It Sin, 383
They Came to Blow Up America, 494
They Knew What They Wanted, 245
They Made Her a Spy, 199
Thief of Bagdad, The, 532
Things Are Looking Up, 243
Thin Man, The, 467, 483
Third Alarm, The, 366
Thirteenth Chair, 341
Thirteen Women, 299
This Day and Age, 88, 151
This England, 159
This Is My Affair, 173
This Is the Life, 526
This Mad World, 298
This Man Is Mine, 79, 157, 299
This Modern Age, 188
This Reckless Age, 164
This Thing Called Love, 55
This Was Paris, 190
This Way Out!, 58
Thoroughbred, 520
Thousands Cheer, 99
Three-Cornered Moon, 28
Three for Bedroom C, 239
Three Godfathers, The, 413
365 Nights in Hollywood, 181
Three Musketeers, The, 55, 376, 500
Three on a Match, 189–90
Three on a Honeymoon, 199
Three-Ring Marriage, 236
Three Russian Girls, 494
Three Sinners, 374
Three Sisters, The, 26
Three Smart Girls, 54
Three Sons, 245
Three Wise Girls, 129
Thru Different Eyes, 221
Thunder Below, 189, 374
Thunderhead, Son of Flicka, 231
Thundering Herd, The, 140
Thunder Trail, 462
Tiger Bay, 535
'Til We Meet Again, 55
Time of Your Life, The, 422
Time to Kill, 428
Tin Pan Alley, 436
Tip-Off, 35
Toast of New York, 205
Tobin, Genevieve, 122, 502–7
Tol'able David, 148

Toll of the Sea, The, 532
To Mary, with Love, 285
Tom Brown of Culver, 151
Tom Brown's School Days, 292
Tom, Dick and Harry, 389
Tomorrow and Tomorrow, 374
Tomorrow the World, 81
Tom Sawyer, 263–4
Tonight at 8:30, 55
Too Many Parents, 203
Too Much Harmony, 237, 434
Torchy Gets Her Man, 215
Torture Garden, The, 392
To the Last Man, 139
Tower of London, The, 286
Town Boy, 78
Tracy, Lee, 104, 128–9, 156, 508–15
Trader Horn, 122
Trade Winds, 81
Tragedy of Youth, The, 220
Traitor Spy, 113
Transatlantic Merry-Go-Round, 264
Traveling Husbands, 156
Traveling Saleslady, 214
Treasure of Matecumbe, 555
Treasure of the Sierra Madre, The, 91
Tree Grows in Brooklyn, A, 178, 183, 428
Trial Marriage, 195
Trial of Vivienne Ware, The, 133, 237
Trigger Tricks, 196
Trip to Bountiful, The, 63
Tropical Trouble, 398
Trouble with Angels, The, 56
True to the Army, 307
Truth about Youth, The, 383
Tuna Clipper, 404
Turn Back the Clock, 129, 512
Twelfth Night, 26
12 Angry Men, 63
Twelvetrees, Helen, 112, 142, 276, 516–23
Twentieth Century, 56, 122
20,000 Leagues under the Sea, 378
Twice Blessed, 442
Twin Beds, 216
Two Kinds of Women, 250, 277
Two Little Bears, The, 23
Two Lovers, 374
Two Seconds, **229**
Two Who Dared, 493
Two Years Before the Mast, 174

Unashamed, 519
Uncertain Glory, 377
Uncle Sam of Freedom Ridge, 328
Uncle Tom's Cabin, 68
Undercover Doctor, 428
Underground, 338
Under Two Flags, 475
Unfaithful, 133
Unfinished Symphony, 123

Unforgiven, The, 92
Unmarried, 142
Unpublished Story, 270
Up in Mabel's Room, 56
Upper World, 403
Up Pops the Devil, 237

Valient Is the Word for Carrie, 320
Valley of Decision, 231
Valley of the Giants, 418
Vampire Bat, The, 544
Vampire, The, 63
Vanity Street, 122
Varsity, 275
Vice Squad, The, 374
Village Tale, 299
Virginian, The, 104, 174
Virgin Lips, 96
Viva Villa!, 512–3, 544
Vogues of 1938, 483
Voice in the Wind, 349
Voice of Bugle Ann, The, 355
Voice of the Turtle, The, 62, 422

Wagons Roll at Night, The, 19, 20
Wake Island, 174
Wake Up and Dream, 447
Walking Down Broadway, 180
Walking on Air, 454
Walls of Jericho, The, 192
Wanderer of the Wasteland, The, 140, 440
Warrior's Husband, The, 340, 384
War Song, 242
War Wagon, The, 116
Washington Merry-Go-Round, 156, 510
Water Hole, The, 96
Waterloo Bridge, 129, 397
Watermelon Man, 131
Way to Love, The, 190
We Americans, 95
Wedding March, The, 540, 542
Wedding Night, The, 79, 492–3
Week-End in Havana, 470
Week-end Millionaire, 107
Wee Willie Winkle, 468
We Have Our Memories, 182
We Have Our Moments, 199
Welcome to Britain, 390
We Live Again, 492
Wells Fargo, 167, 426
We're Going to Be Rich, 173
We're Only Human, 549
We're Rich Again, 141
Western Bend of the River, 223
West of Singapore, 358
Westward Passage, 254
We Were Dancing, 442
We Were Strangers, 463
We Who Are about to Die, 61, 231

When Johnny Comes Marching Home, 307
When Knights Were Bold, 544
When Strangers Meet, 151
When the Daltons Rode, 173
When Were You Born?, 360, 536
Where Angels Go—Trouble Follows, 56
Whiffs, 24
Whirlpool, 133
Whistler, The, 501
White Angel, The, 284
White Banners, 231, 255, 257, 299
White Cradle Inn (High Fury), 286
White Hunter, 475
White Unicorn, The, 286
Wicked, 338
Wife, Husband and Friend, 55
Wild and Woolly, 526
Wild Bill Hickok Rides, 115
Wildcat, 142
Wild Girl, 78
Wild Harvest, 428
Wild Horse Stampede, The, 540
Wild Party, The, 276, 433
Wild Waves, 60
Wing and a Prayer, 90
Wings of the Navy, 312
Winner Take All, 403
Winterset, 61, 386–7, 389
Wintertime, 470
Withers, Jane, 292, 524–31
Without Children, 404
Without Regret, 341
Wolf Man, The, 81
Woman, 440
Woman and the Puppet, The, 468
Woman Disputed, The, 461
Woman in Red, The, 504
Woman in Room 13, The, 78, 338
Woman of Distinction, A, 349
Woman of Experience, A, 519
Woman on the Beach, The, 90
Woman Rebels, A, 384
Woman to Woman, 401
Woman Trap, 410
Woman Unafraid, 237
Women Love Once, 374
Women in War, 130

Women of Pitcairn Island, The, 47
Wonderful Country, The, 436
Wonder of Women, 366
Wong, Anna May, 532–9
Won Ton Ton, the Dog Who Saved Hollywood, 224
Words and Music, 162, 517
Working Girls, 164
Working Man, The, 28
World Accuses, The, 403
World Changes, The, 360
World Premiere, 207
Wray, Fay, 34, 36, 112, 136, 276, 540–7
Wrecker, The, 504
Wren, The, 61
Wrong Road, The, 152
WUSA, 116
Wyatt, Jane, 23, 83, 548–55

Yank at Eton, A, 286
Yank Comes Back, A, 390
Yellow Canary, The, 270
Yellow Ticket, The, 338
Yes, My Darling Daughter, 286, 506
You Belong to Me, 513
You Can't Beat Love, 231
You Gotta Stay Happy, 20
You Live and Learn, 215
Young America, 78
Young Bride, 354, 519
Young Doctors, The, 23
Young Eagles, 374
Younger Brothers, The, 422
Young Mr. Lincoln, 152
Young Sinners, 26
Young Widow, 485
You're in the Navy Now, 22
Youre Telling Me, 140
Yours for the Asking, 237
You Said a Mouthful, **229**
Youth Runs Wild, 404

Zaza, 506
Zenobia, 223
Zluta Knizka (The Yellow Ticket), 488
Zoo in Budapest, 454